Nonconformist Art

Frontispiece
Vladimir Yankilevsky
Details of *Pentaptych, No. 2:*
Adam and Eve, 1980
Mixed media
(See pp. 290–91 for complete work)

Nonconformist Art

The Soviet experience
1956–1986

The Norton and Nancy Dodge Collection
The Jane Voorhees Zimmerli Art Museum
Rutgers, The State University of New Jersey

General Editors: Alla Rosenfeld and Norton T. Dodge

With over 500 illustrations, 326 in color

THAMES AND HUDSON
In association with the Jane Voorhees Zimmerli Art Museum

This book is published in conjunction with the
inaugural opening of the exhibition "From Gulag to
Glasnost: Nonconformist Art from the Soviet Union"
at the Jane Voorhees Zimmerli Art Museum,
October 1995. It is supported in part by a grant from the
National Endowment for the Arts, a Federal agency
in Washington, D.C., and the Avenir Foundation.

Designed by Lawrence Edwards
Produced by Thames and Hudson and copublished with
the Jane Voorhees Zimmerli Art Museum

First published in hardcover in the United States of
America in 1995 by Thames and Hudson Inc., 500 Fifth
Avenue, New York, New York 10110

Library of Congress Catalog Card Number 95-60469
ISBN 0-500-23709-3

Printed and bound in Singapore

Contents

Note on transliteration

Whenever Russian names or words appear in a publication that is not printed in Cyrillic, some system of transliteration has to be utilized. For this catalogue we have generally adopted the system of transliteration employed by the Library of Congress. However, for the names of artists, we have combined two methods. For artists who were or are active chiefly in Russia, we have transliterated their names according to the Library of Congress system even when more conventional English versions exist: e.g., Aleksandr Rodchenko, *not* Alexander Rodchenko; Vasilii Kandinsky, *not* Wassily Kandinsky. But in the case of artists who emigrated to the West, we have used the spelling that the artist adopted or that has gained common usage: e.g., Vitaly Komar, Alexander Melamid, Dmitri Plavinsky.

Ukrainian names, words, and geographical terms are transliterated according to the system developed for the Ukrainian Encyclopedia and utilized by the Slavic Department of the New York Public Library. In this catalogue, the former Russian version of a name or place is sometimes given in parentheses for clarification: e.g., Odesa (Odessa), Volodymyr (Vladimir) Naumets.

The Armenian artists discussed in this catalogue are from the Independent Republic of Armenia (formerly Soviet Armenia) where the eastern Armenian dialect is the national language. However, all diaspora Armenians, except those from Iran, use the western dialect. The English spelling used for artists' names in this publication, therefore, is based on their spelling and pronunciation in eastern Armenian. But, in the case of artists who emigrated to the West, we have used the spelling that the artist adopted or that has gained common usage: e.g., Vagrich Bakhchanyan.

Names and other words in Estonian, Latvian, and Lithuanian are given in the original language.

Note on titles of works used in this catalogue

Untitled - an artist's designation of a title
(Untitled) - title of the work could not be located or confirmed
(   ) - descriptive or working title assigned to the work

Every effort has been made to provide lifedates for all artists mentioned in this catalogue; however, in some cases it has proved impossible to locate this information.

Introduction

It is rare that a single collection is able to corner the market, so to speak. How often does one collection document in great depth virtually every aspect of an important avant-garde movement? Or canvass the culture of an entire, globally significant geopolitical area through its most vital period of artistic activity? Finally, what are the chances of that same collection of art, representing the work of hundreds of artists and intellectuals, serving as a succinct symbol of the worldwide struggle for freedom of expression and human rights? Nonetheless, these are the distinctive attributes of the Norton and Nancy Dodge Collection of Nonconformist Art from the Soviet Union.

No serious evaluation of the twentieth century can ignore the global impact of the Soviet Union in the field of politics or in the field of art. In this sense, the Dodge Collection, consisting of works by more than nine hundred unofficial and dissident artists, constitutes an unprecedented tool for understanding Soviet culture. Here is a unique record of the development of key aspects of Soviet life throughout the Cold War, in particular, the thirty years between Khrushchev's criticism of Stalinism in 1956 and the introduction of *glasnost* by Gorbachev in 1986. The Dodge Collection offers a rare and comprehensive opportunity to understand, through art, those aspects of Soviet society that have substantially affected world history.

The generous donation of the Dodge Collection to the Jane Voorhees Zimmerli Art Museum not only makes an enormously informative collection accessible to the public, but it also lays the groundwork for future scholarly investigations into the world once cloistered behind the Iron Curtain. When he accepted the Dodge Collection, Rutgers President Francis L. Lawrence emphasized the university's commitment to establishing an aggressive multidisciplinary program of research and instruction in the forefront of Soviet studies. With the assistance of the Federal government, Rutgers University has made major strides toward this goal. The acquisition of the Dodge Collection immediately establishes the Zimmerli Art Museum as an important center for research on the culture of the former Soviet Union.

The purpose of this initial publication is to introduce the general parameters of Soviet nonconformist art as it is charted in the Dodge Collection. Included in this volume is a representative selection of the ten thousand and more artworks in the Dodge Collection. These works demonstrate the greatly varied styles, subjects, and media employed by hundreds of dissident artists, working not only in Russia but also in eleven former Soviet republics. Fifteen leading scholars of Soviet unofficial art have contributed essays to this volume that make significant inroads into this relatively new field of art-historical study.

Soviet underground or nonconformist art is not what many "freedom-loving" Americans might expect. In the United States, in the heyday of the Cold War, such concepts as "democracy" and "America" were often represented idealistically. For many Americans, including political leaders and government officials, these ideological concepts were best encapsulated by the illustrative art of Norman Rockwell or Andrew Wyeth. Ironically, this was precisely the sort of sentimentalized realism that the Soviet bureaucracy used to promote and glorify their own political system. But Socialist Realism, the substance of official Soviet art, was rejected by unofficial artists in the Soviet Union. In its place, nonconformist artists looked to their historical, philosophical, religious, and national roots, as well as to radical Western art: Surrealism, Abstract Expressionism, Pop Art, and other avant-garde movements, all of which were frowned upon just as often in conservative America as they were in Communist Russia.

For Soviet nonconformist artists, the creation of art meant risking harassment, repression, imprisonment, or loss of employment. Instead of the opportunities for success and material gain afforded Western artists, Soviet dissidents faced isolation and almost certain financial sacrifice. Thus, we can say that the works in the Dodge Collection embody the purest rationale for the creation of art: the struggle for freedom of self-expression in spite of—and in defiance of—a repressive government. No museum director could ask for a collection that aspires to a more worthy artistic ideal.

For more than thirty years, Norton Dodge accumulated this massive collection, cared for it, promoted it, and documented it through exhibitions, catalogues, and conferences. Dr. Dodge's choice of its ultimate institutional home is a source of great pride for all of us at Rutgers University, and especially here at the Zimmerli Art Museum. I owe a great debt to the vision of George Riabov, who first donated his own considerable collection of Russian art to the museum and, then, with the conviction that the two collections would complement each other, introduced me to Norton Dodge.

The dedication and farsightedness demonstrated by Norton Dodge in preserving the work of the many artists in the Soviet Union who risked their earthly comforts and their lives for art's sake is reinforced by the same qualities in his wife Nancy Dodge. Together, the Dodges have shown extraordinary generosity toward Rutgers and the Zimmerli Art Museum. I am certain their faith in our endeavors will be justified. Already, Zimmerli curators Jeffrey

Wechsler and Alla Rosenfeld have exemplified the university's commitment by their skillful organization of this publication and of the collection's permanent installation.

The incredibly complex and physically demanding process of integrating the Dodge Collection into the Zimmerli was made possible by generous grants from the National Endowment for the Arts and the National Endowment for the Humanities, as well as from various private sources. And, of course, this tremendous task could not have been achieved without the masterful talents of the Zimmerli's small but highly professional staff.

I am profoundly grateful to Nancy and Norton Dodge, to President Francis L. Lawrence, and to the members of the Zimmerli Board of Overseers, who wisely judged the efficacy and the appropriateness of bringing the Dodge Collection and the Zimmerli together. Their decision will certainly stand as a landmark in the history of Rutgers University and will set the course of the Zimmerli Art Museum for generations to come.

Phillip Dennis Cate
Director
The Jane Voorhees Zimmerli Art Museum

1 | Notes on collecting nonconformist Soviet art

Norton T. Dodge

Stalin's death in 1953, followed by Khrushchev's denunciation of Stalin's excesses in a secret speech to the Party leadership three years later, initiated a process of change in the Soviet system that was clearly expressed in the arts. Under Stalin, all the arts had been closely controlled so that they would support and advance the Communist Party's policies and programs. During the political and cultural thaw that Khrushchev initiated in 1956, a number of artists courageously began to test the new limits being established by Party censors and the KGB. In literature, the thaw was expressed by the greater latitude permitted in official publications and by the emergence of uncensored *samizdat* (or self-published) publications. Copies of these dissident publications began to be spirited to the West, broadcast back to the Soviet Union by Radio Liberty at dictation speed, and often republished in Russian, English, and other languages. A number of works by writers such as Boris Pasternak, Alexander Solzhenitsyn, and Andrei Voznesensky were reviewed favorably in the West and became bestsellers.

In contrast to the literary stars, leading nonconformist painters and sculptors, such as Eli Beliutin (b. 1925), Ilya Kabakov (b. 1933), Ernst Neizvestny (b. 1925), Vladimir Nemukhin (b. 1925), Oscar Rabin (b. 1928), and Evgenii Rukhin (1943–1976), were largely unknown in the West, except to a small number of specialists such as John Berger, John Bowlt, Franco Miele, and Paul Sjeklocha. Several factors contributed to this disproportionate neglect of the visual arts. First, printed texts could be carried across borders and disseminated more easily and cheaply than could works of art. Traveling exhibitions of art would have required advance planning and the expense of catalogue production, a near-impossibility given the uncertainties and obstacles inherent in the Soviet situation at that time.

Second, while many Western art historians had long been aware of the remarkable outburst of artistic creativity in Russia during the dozen years before and after Lenin's seizure of power in 1917, few were aware of the post-Stalin emergence of Soviet nonconformist artists. This gap in knowledge was initially filled by specialists in the fields of Russian literature and history, who also had an interest in the exciting developments in Soviet art (notably John Bowlt and Frederic Starr in the United States and Karl Eimermacher in Germany).

Third, assurance of a reliable and sufficient supply of nonconformist art to the West was not possible because of the Soviet government's repressive policies and restrictions on the export of nonconformist art. Consequently, the interdependent network of collectors, dealers, auction houses, galleries, and museums could not readily organize the exhibitions or produce the catalogues necessary to stimulate critical interest in nonconformist Soviet art. Two active supporters of this art in the 1960s were Dina Vierny in Paris and Eric Estorick in London.

Fourth, when exhibitions of nonconformist art did begin to take place in the late 1970s, Western critics often linked the work to familiar European or American artists or art movements of which the Soviet artists generally had little or no knowledge. Such criticism often suggested that nonconformist art was derivative and dated, and, therefore, unlike dissident literature, of little interest or significance.

It has been said that collectors are born, not made. This is certainly true in my case. My mother came from a long line of accumulators of family memorabilia and genealogical data. My father, a professor of physics at the University of Oklahoma when I was young, was an even more obsessive collector who never discarded anything. His many filing cabinets, boxes, and chests contained everything connected with his work and hobbies. The desks and tables in his offices both at home and at the university overflowed with papers, correspondence, reports, journals, books, maps, and hundreds of charts of the river systems we canoed in the 1950s and 1960s. His collection of photographs and colored slides numbered in the thousands and recorded his own travels as well as the family's adventures.

My own collecting instincts were manifested early. In the usual way small boys have, I accumulated rocks, stamps, coins, and a multitude of odds and ends. At the age of nine or ten, however, my best friend and I began a "nonconformist" collection of thousands of discarded whiskey, rum, and gin bottles of all sizes, shapes, and brands—all in the very "dry" state of Oklahoma. The main sources for this illegal contraband were the university's sorority and fraternity houses, the stadium bleachers after a big football game, and the trashcans of various respected citizens of Norman, Oklahoma.

My interest in art also began early. As an asthmatic child, I was often bedridden and had to stay home from school. During those long days, I would make drawing after drawing of cowboys, Indians, horses, and cattle. I also created elaborate plans and layouts for farmsteads, ranches, and sundry structures, and made detailed designs for automobiles, boats, airplanes, spaceships, and other real or futuristic machines. When I was about ten, I became the protégé of Professor Joe Taylor at the university's art department and spent many hours in his studio/classroom, working on whatever interested me at the time. By my early teens, however, I had too many competing interests to undertake a career as an industrial designer or artist. Therefore, my persistent interest in art was later sublimated in my pursuit of art collecting, photography, and art-historical writing.

My interest in Soviet nonconformist art emerged in stages, beginning with Russian language studies at Cornell University. I later received a master's degree in Russian Regional Studies at Harvard University. In 1953, while I was working on my Ph.D. in economics at Harvard's Russian Research Center, Stalin died. Recognizing this as an opportunity, I encouraged my father, then a retired college president, to apply for visas for us both to visit the Soviet Union to study their educational system. Repeated requests to the Soviet Embassy in Washington and some subtle persuasion finally brought results, and we arrived in Leningrad in April 1955.

At the Hermitage Museum, one of the first stops on our obligatory tour of the city, we found marvelous early works of Picasso, Matisse, Gauguin, and other French Postimpressionists. These works had just been brought out and placed on view after years in deep storage. But Soviet underground artists were nowhere to be seen at that time. It was still too early. Furthermore, our daily activities were controlled by Intourist, and any deviations from our itinerary would have been reported to the KGB. Hence we did not find or visit any underground artists on that trip. But the times were changing.

My first contacts with nonconformist artists came on my second visit to the Soviet Union in 1962. The initial contact was with a young philology student who had shared a room at Moscow State University (MGU) with a friend of mine from Harvard. The philologist had initially begun to study art at a leading Moscow art institute, but became rapidly disaffected because of the restrictions imposed there on his artistic freedom. He showed me his own work and then introduced me to a number of his artist friends. More importantly, near the end of my stay, he took me to a private apartment exhibition, reputed to be the first in Moscow since the 1920s devoted entirely to abstract art. This exhibition featured the forbidden abstract works of Lev Kropivnitsky (1922–1994), one of a distinguished family of nonconformist artists. The artist's mother, Olga Potapova (1892–1971), had begun painting abstract works early in the century, and his father, Evgenii Kropivnitsky (1893–1979), was one of the earliest artists to deviate from Socialist Realism. Lev's sister, Valentina Kropivnitskaia (b. 1924), and her husband, Oscar Rabin (b. 1928), were both leading Moscow nonconformists. In addition to the Kropivnitsky exhibition, paintings by other artists could be seen elsewhere in the apartment. A small abstract work on paper by the nearly blind nonconformist Vladimir Yakovlev (b. 1934) attracted my attention. Before leaving, I was able to acquire this uncharacteristic work (Fig. 1:1), plus a suitcase-sized work by Kropivnitsky, titled *Outer Galactic Logic* (Fig. 1:2).

On that same trip, I also met the then-obscure collector of Russian avant-garde art, George Costakis. Pete MacDonald, who had been a Deep Springs College classmate, was stationed at the U.S. Embassy in Moscow, and his wife, Allen, who tutored Costakis's children in English, arranged a meeting with Costakis at the Canadian Embassy where he worked. I then went to his apartment to see his incredible collection of avant-garde and nonconformist art, which was crammed into a few rooms, under beds and sofas and covering every wall and even part of the ceiling. The nonconformist part of his collection included works by Anatolii Zverev (1931–1986), Dmitrii Krasnopevtsev (1925–1995), Dmitri Plavinsky (b. 1937), Vladimir Nemukhin, Lydia Masterkova (b. 1929), Oscar Rabin, Evgenii Rukhin, and others.

Staff members at other embassies led me to artists willing to accept the risk of informal contact with Western diplomats and their friends. Connections such as these opened vital windows to the West for these isolated artists and provided them with access to Western art journals, catalogues, and other publications. Art sales and access to Western goods were another benefit. Because of such embassy connections, the artists Oscar Rabin, Dmitri Plavinsky, and Sergei Bordachev (b. 1948) led me to other like-minded artists such as Vladimir Nemukhin, Viacheslav Kalinin (b. 1939), Joseph Kiblitsky (b. 1946), and

Fig. 1:1
Vladimir Yakovlev
(Untitled), 1962
Watercolor on paper
40.8 × 28.9 cm

Fig. 1:2
Lev Kropivnitsky
Outer Galactic Logic, 1960
Oil on canvas
69 × 44.5 cm

then on to others in ever-expanding circles. I also learned of the work of important forerunners of these new nonconformists, artists like Robert Falk (1886–1958), Aleksandr Tyshler (1898–1980) (Pl. 1:5), Anatolii Shugrin (1919–1950) (Pl. 1:4), and Vladimir Sterligov (1904–1973).

Nina Stevens, a Russian woman who was married to an American correspondent in Moscow, opened many other doors. Following in Costakis's footsteps, she began collecting nonconformist art in the 1960s, when she and her husband lived in a picturesque rambling log cabin in central Moscow. At one of their Saturday afternoon receptions, where guests from the diplomatic and media communities could mingle and meet one or two artists, I was able to see their extensive collection and enjoy a varied and unlimited supply of delicious Russian *zakuski*, mountains of caviar, and much vodka. Later, with the assistance of George Riabov, Stevens brought a part of her collection to the United States for exhibition. Fortunately, I was able to acquire some fifty of these early works, which filled crucial gaps in my own collection.

Sophia Shiller (b. 1940), a Soviet artist who emigrated to the U.S., arranged for me to visit her charismatic former teacher, Eli Beliutin, who was also a collector. His apartment, shared with his art-historian wife, Nina Moleva, was filled with *objets d'art*, antique furniture, classical sculpture, museum-quality icons, and many doleful Renaissance paintings. In contrast, in his nearby cellar studio, I found hundreds of his own colorful, dramatic works. One of these, a huge Postimpressionist canvas covering an entire wall, depicted Lenin encased in an ice coffin that was being carried by members of the politburo, cast as the Apostles, with Stalin in the role of Judas (Pl. 1:2). This painting was an extremely dangerous statement for its time. Beliutin was one of the early leaders of the nonconformist movement, organizing provocative exhibits as early as the mid-1950s. As a mentor and teacher he opened the doors of artistic creativity to hundreds of his students. Several of these were key participants with him in the fateful Manezh showdown with Khrushchev in 1962.

My visit to the apartment/studio of Vasilii Sitnikov (1915–1987), whom I also first met at the Stevens home, illustrates the excitement of tracking down an artist at that time. Ironically, Sitnikov's apartment was located close to the headquarters of the KGB on Dzerzhinsky Square. As was often the case with nonconformist artists, his rooms were in a crowded communal apartment shared with several other families. In order to be alerted to arriving visitors, particularly foreigners, he dangled a string out of his second-story window with a colorful tab on the end so

Fig. 1:3
Vasilii Sitnikov
Portrait of an Inmate, 1942
Graphite on paper
27 × 17 cm

that a bell in his room could be rung. He would then meet the visitors at the door and guide them through the apartment, past his fellow tenants, to his own rooms. I came away with a particularly prized drawing that Sitnikov had made of a fellow patient in a mental hospital. The image showed the man confined in a strait-jacket, but, significantly, Sitnikov could never complete the mouth of his fellow sufferer, who had, in effect, been muted by his forced incarceration (Fig. 1:3).

Few artists' apartments were as centrally located or as easy to find as Sitnikov's. Usually, I would have to use inadequate prerevolutionary maps and scribbled instructions, poorly heard in Russian over the telephone, to figure out how best to get to a given address. I never used hotel telephones because they were often tapped. Instead, I would seek out a working payphone on the street and use one of the scarce two-kopeck pieces required to operate it.

To get to an artist's address, I would sometimes take a bus or the metro, but, more often, I would opt for a cab if

I could find one. They were often scarce. Sometimes, I would find the driver of an official vehicle hanging out in front of the hotel, willing to moonlight for a price. The drawback, of course, was that one could never be sure if the driver was harmless or if he was reporting to the KGB. My preference was to take a regular cab, but even this choice offered no guarantee that my destination would not be reported. Consequently, I would typically ask to be dropped off at a point just beyond my real destination so that it could not be clearly identified.

Most buildings under five stories high had no elevator, so I would have to climb the stairs. Timed light switches would often switch off before I could reach the right floor and locate the desired apartment, leaving me groping around the hallways in total darkness, sometimes having to feel my way back to the stairs or to an elevator so I could get back to the main floor and begin all over again. I quickly learned to carry a small flashlight or book of matches with me at all times.

Soviet nonconformist art expresses the power of the human spirit in the struggle to overcome the suffocating constraints of a totalitarian system. Since the fate of such art was uncertain during the tense time of missile crises and the Berlin Wall, I felt that the preservation of some record of it outside the Soviet Union was very important. While Western art historians were the people who should logically undertake such a record, few of them had access to this material. Therefore, I made it my mission to preserve—through photography or collecting—a sample of the best of this art, until others, better equipped and prepared, could assume the responsibility.

As I gained knowledge and experience, and as opportunities to see and acquire nonconformist art multiplied, my goals in this area changed. Initially, my purpose was to seek out all art created after Stalin's death that deviated markedly from the official Party line. This broad category included art that was: critical of the Soviet leadership and its policies (Pls. 1:3, 1:9); abstract, Surrealist, or Hyperrealist, or, in Soviet jargon, "formalistic" (Figs. 1:4, 1:5; Pls. 1:6, 1:7, 1:8, 14:9); Conceptual or Sots Art (Fig. 1:6; Pls. 1:10, 1:13, 1:14); religious (Fig. 1:7; Pl. 1:1); erotic or pornographic (Fig. 2:7); or some combination of these (Fig. 1:8).

I also sought realistic art if it showed the harsh realities of Soviet life, as opposed to Socialist Realist art, which was more surreal than real in its overpositive portrayal of Soviet life. For example, the multitalented Sergei Volokhov (b. 1937) created a whole rhapsody on the wonders of Soviet waste disposal (Pl. 1:11), just as Mikhail Romadin (b. 1940) created a satirical version of a Soviet traffic jam (Pl. 1:18). Krasnopevtsev depicted a fish and

Fig. 1:4 (*above*)
Andrei Grositsky
Tea Kettle, 1984
Oil on canvas
90.6 × 110.7 cm

Fig. 1:5 (*top right*)
Sergei Bordachev
(Untitled), 1973
Ink and watercolor on paper
47.7 × 36 cm

Fig. 1:6
Gennadii Garnisov
Izvestiia, 1963
Oil on canvas
61 × 83.9 cm

Fig. 1:7
Gendelev
Star of David with Thorns, n.d.
Pen and ink on paper
30.5 × 21.5 cm

Fig. 1:9
Dmitrii Krasnopevtsev
(Untitled), 1973
Oil on fiberboard
60.5 × 46 cm

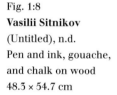

Fig. 1:8
Vasilii Sitnikov
(Untitled), n.d.
Pen and ink, gouache,
and chalk on wood
48.3 × 54.7 cm

two bottles hanging lugubriously like corpses (Fig. 1:9), while Hagop Hagopian (b. 1923) chose to show a basket of fertile but fragile Armenian eggs threatened by sharp, dangerous-looking Russian tools and dark ominous gloves (Pl. 1:16).

My initial focus was on art produced in Moscow and Leningrad, but this was later enlarged to include the art of the Baltic republics and the Transcaucasus (Pl. 1:19). Because of the limited foreign presence in these areas, special attention and effort was required. There was no consular representation in Leningrad in the 1950s and 1960s, and the foreign media, centered in Moscow, scarcely noticed art events in Leningrad or lesser cities. Fortunately, I came to know two American exchange students, Janet Kennedy and Alison Hilton, who each spent a year in Leningrad in the early 1970s doing research on the history of Russian art. Sarah Burke, who directed a Russian language program in Leningrad for several summers, was also very interested in contemporary art. These three young scholars acquainted me with a number of important nonconformist artists, who then led me to others.

Making contact with artists in areas where I had no leads at all, such as the Transcaucasus or the Ukraine, was especially difficult. Serious collecting of Ukrainian non-conformist art had to wait until much later, when I could find help from collectors such as Polina Gluzman or artist intermediaries such as Noi Volkov (b. 1947) and Dmitrii Dymshits (b. 1951). Fortunately, in Yerevan, I met an artist by chance at the Museum of Modern Art, who then led me to several other nonconformist artists during a whirlwind evening. In Georgia, I had a few names to start with. In Estonia, a tour guide and fellow academic, Stephen Feinstein, helped me make crucial initial contacts. But I was never able to collect art in person in Latvia or Lithuania. I had to fill in many important gaps in the Baltic area with the advice and help of Elena Kornetchuk, Eda Sepp, Mark Svede, and Visvaldas Nenishkis.

A major breakthrough in Moscow collecting came in the mid-1970s, when the artist Borukh (Boris Shteinberg) (b. 1938), brother of Eduard Shteinberg (b. 1937), led me to Tatiana Kolodzei, an art historian and the former wife of the collector-archivist Leonid Talochkin. A pattern soon developed that was repeated each time I came to Moscow.

Whenever possible, I would meet Tatiana in the early afternoon after she finished work. We would then visit two, three, and, sometimes, four artists before late-night exhaustion set in. She herself had already become a major Moscow collector. With her help, I met nearly two dozen key Moscow nonconformists who had previously been either unknown to me or outside my reach.[1]

One of the most interesting meetings Tatiana arranged was with Ilya Kabakov. To reach his studio one had to climb many flights of stairs to the attic of his building, and then walk along planks laid end to end across the heavy ceiling beams of the floor below. These led to a large, heavy door opening into a spectacular studio space under the building's peaked roof. In this spacious, well-lit environment, Kabakov did his bread-and-butter illustrations for children's books as well as his own challenging Conceptual art, ranging from small-scale albums to huge works on pressboard. My heart fell when I saw that these large artworks could not be rolled up and spirited across the border. Exporting such works with official approval at that time would have been out of the question. But in the early 1980s Garig Basmadjian, one of my main art suppliers, succeeded in getting permission to export a number of these large works, as well as some by Vladimir Yankilevsky (b. 1938), Viktor Pivovarov (b. 1937), and others. Kabakov's large paintings had to be lowered carefully by ropes from the window of his attic studio to a waiting truck which took them to the Export Salon for shipment. Only then did Basmadjian learn that his hard-won arrangements had gone awry. Someone further up in the hierarchy had rescinded the required export permits. As a result, all the artworks had to be returned by the route they had come.

This failure was a major blow because I was sure Kabakov would emerge as a critically praised artist as soon as his work was shown in the West. This had happened to Vitaly Komar (b. 1943) and Alexander Melamid (b. 1945), the brilliant pair of collaborative artists whose imaginative Conceptual work was featured along with a number of Kabakov's small pieces at the exhibition organized by me in Washington, D.C. in 1977. Komar and Melamid's show in New York at Ronald Feldman's gallery in that year was a major critical success. Feldman, who became a Kabakov enthusiast as soon as he saw his works at the Washington exhibition, finally succeeded in organizing an exhibition of his major pieces and installations in New York in 1988. This widely reviewed exhibition, along with several simultaneous ones in Europe, helped launch Kabakov as a world-renowned artist.

Rimma and Valerii Gerlovin (b. 1951 and 1945) were another pair of Conceptual artists whom I met through Tatiana. Unlike Komar and Melamid, whose efforts were always collaborative, the Gerlovins worked both separately and together, as in their *Zoo* happening. In another provocative performance at a picnic, they wore jumpsuits with a nude female figure painted on Rimma's costume and a nude male figure on Valerii's (Fig. 2:9). These painted costumes had an immediate shock value and raised questions about the relation of painting to reality, our concept of gender, and our notion of the erotic and the pornographic.

Another revelation was my visit with Tatiana to the cellar studio of Yankilevsky in an unprepossessing area of Moscow. His works were unlike any others I had seen in the Soviet Union or elsewhere. Yankilevsky had shown in the famous Manezh exhibition, where he and his work had been excoriated by Khrushchev. The works in his studio ranged from small prints with grotesque, Surrealistic mutant figures to huge bas-relief triptychs featuring figurative side panels connected by a horizontal abstraction. The most important of these was a five-part work titled *Adam and Eve*, which included two weary, work-worn life-sized figures—male and female—entering two adjacent communal apartments (Fig. 13:11). The doorways included actual doors that Yankilevsky had salvaged from demolition sites. This artwork (like Kabakov's large installation of communal apartment living at Feldman's exhibition in New York in 1988) reflected the drab reality of Soviet communal life. Unfortunately, in order to acquire any of these large works by Yankilevsky, I had to wait for help from Garig Basmadjian and Eduard Nakhamkin in the mid-1980s.

Another memorable visit was to Oleg Tselkov's apartment on the outskirts of Moscow. I had already acquired some of his prints and two medium-sized oils from photographer-dealer Vladimir Sychev, so I was anxious to meet Tselkov and see his larger paintings. These powerful works stretched from floor to ceiling in the small apartment, creating an overwhelming impact on the viewer. Works on such a large scale only became available after Tselkov emigrated to Paris, where he somehow managed to take them.

My visit to Kinetic artist Francisco Infante (b. 1943) was another major delight. His varied works included ingeniously constructed mechanical works, employing simple motors and various scavenged components. These rotated in the darkness with multiple flashing lights, producing beautifully evolving color combinations and patterns on the walls, all of this being accompanied by modern third-stream music.

Apartment exhibits by groups of nonconformists began to be coordinated fairly systematically in Moscow in the mid-1970s. These were held simultaneously in a half-dozen private apartments or studios each spring. If one were in Moscow at the right time and knew where to go, one could get acquainted easily and quickly with a great variety of work by dozens of artists. Catching major nonconformist exhibitions, such as the one at the Beekeeping Pavilion in 1975 or those held periodically at the Union of Moscow Graphic Artists' gallery, also depended on one's luck. Fortunately, I was able to attend a number of these large exhibitions. They were almost always attended by huge crowds of viewers, who waited patiently for many hours for admission. To the chagrin of the Party leadership, the public thirst for new and challenging cultural experiences was unquenchable.

My growing collection of Soviet nonconformist art had a quite different exhibition history in the United States. After an initial exhibition of fifty works on paper at the American Association for the Advancement of Slavic Studies (AAASS) convention in St. Louis in 1976, a much larger and more comprehensive exhibition was presented at the AAASS Convention in Washington, D.C., in 1977. The second show was accompanied by a 120–page catalogue, *New Art from the Soviet Union: The Known and the Unknown*, and a two-part symposium at the Kennan Institute. A few months later, a smaller version of the exhibition and a similar symposium were repeated with great success at Cornell University. At that time, the collection consisted of approximately fifteen hundred works by some two hundred artists.

After these two exhibitions, it seemed clear that the Soviet authorities would finally be aware, if they had not already been aware, of what I had been up to during the previous fifteen years. New ways needed to be found to acquire the art and to spirit it out of the country. More and more, I depended on the help of others—Western friends and artists and collectors who emigrated from the Soviet Union, bringing art with them. For example, Josef Yakerson (b. 1936), a Leningrad artist who emigrated to Israel, shipped a number of huge and provocative canvases carefully rolled up and concealed in Oriental rugs. I acquired a number of these from him in Beersheba during a month-long visit to Israel. On that same trip, I also saw the striking naive paintings made by Yefim Ladyzhensky (1911–1982) before his tragic suicide, and the artwork and major collection of Mikhail Grobman (b. 1939). Another source was Western diplomats leaving the Soviet Union. At the end of their tours of duty, they sometimes brought interesting art out along with their household goods.

Eduard Nakhamkin and his son-in-law, Nathan Berman, who established a number of Russian art galleries in New York and California beginning in 1975, have long been important sources for me. My former student and colleague, Elena Kornetchuk, who heads the International Images Gallery in Sewickley, near Pittsburgh, became another major supplier with official rights for U.S. sales. Fortunately, the Soviets' need for dollars, combined with Elena's knowledge and persistence, resulted in her having many questionable or unapproved works released for export.

Garig Basmadjian also became a major source, first of Armenian art and then of nonconformist art from other parts of the Soviet Union. In the summer of 1988, Basmadjian exhibited the best of his Paris gallery's extensive collection at the Tretyakov Gallery in Moscow and then at the Hermitage Museum in Leningrad. A year later, during a visit to Moscow, he left his hotel one morning, accompanied by two young men, never to be seen again. It is suspected that the Russian mafia or the KGB or even some combination of the two were responsible for his disappearance. The case is still unsolved. The loss of this dear friend cast a long shadow over my collecting, although his sister Vartoug bravely continues to operate the Galerie Basmadjian in Paris. Occurrences such as this have prohibited my wife and me from visiting the Soviet Union in recent years.

In addition to the art dealers already mentioned as major sources, others who became interested in nonconformist art in the late 1970s or 1980s and who have been helpful include Phyllis Kind, Gregory Vinitsky, Diane Beal, Richard Fraumeni, Alexander Levin, and Vladimir Umansky. I have also received a great deal of wonderful help and sound advice for many years from Margarita and Victor Tupitsyn. Konstantin Kuzminsky and Alexander Glezer have each contributed greatly in special ways. Galina Main in Germany played a pivotal role in obtaining major works by Eric Bulatov (b. 1933) (Pl. 1:17), Eduard Gorokhovsky (b. 1929), Semyon Faibisovich (b. 1949), Vadim Zakharov (b. 1959), and other major artists.

Since first becoming acquainted with my collecting activities in the mid-1970s, my wife, Nancy Ruyle Dodge, has respected the magnitude of this project and my need to explore it in depth. Fortunately, we have similarly broad and historically oriented tastes in art and the same goal of achieving a comprehensive collection of Soviet art from the Cold War period. Prior to the 1977 exhibition in Washington, we attended the extensive exhibition of nonconformist art at the Institute of Contemporary Art in London. We then visited émigré artists in Paris including

Pl. 1:1 (*opposite*)
Anatolii Putilin
Angel, 1978
Tempera on canvas
122.5 × 92.3 cm

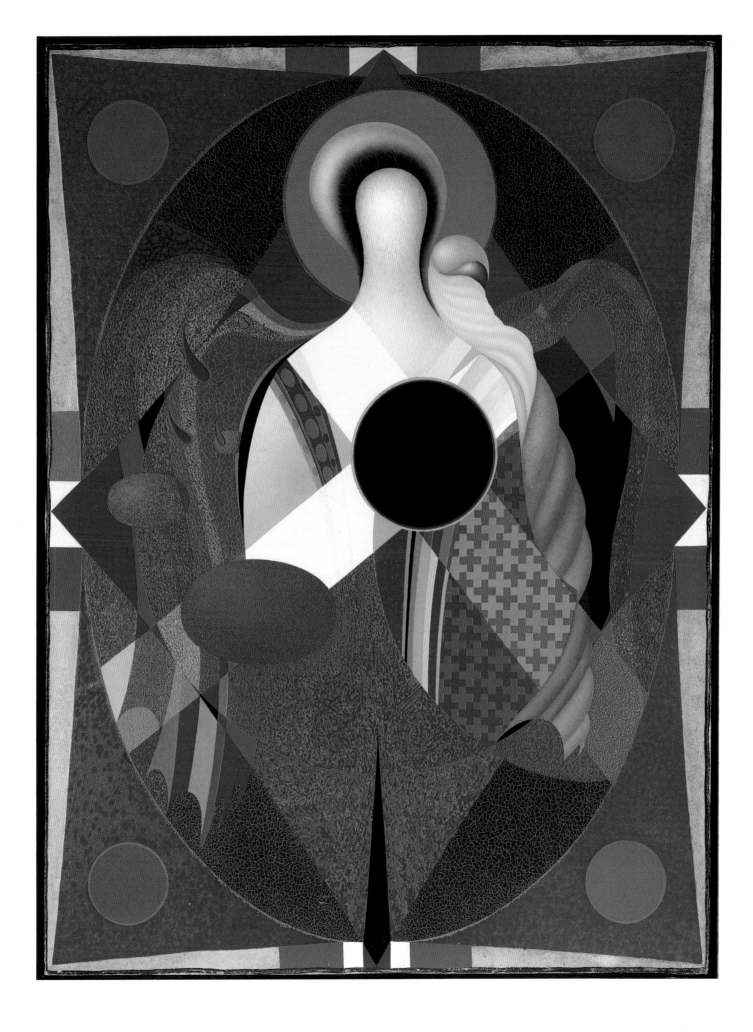

Pl. 1:2
Eli Beliutin
(Lenin in His Ice Coffin),
1962
Oil on canvas
198 × 303 cm

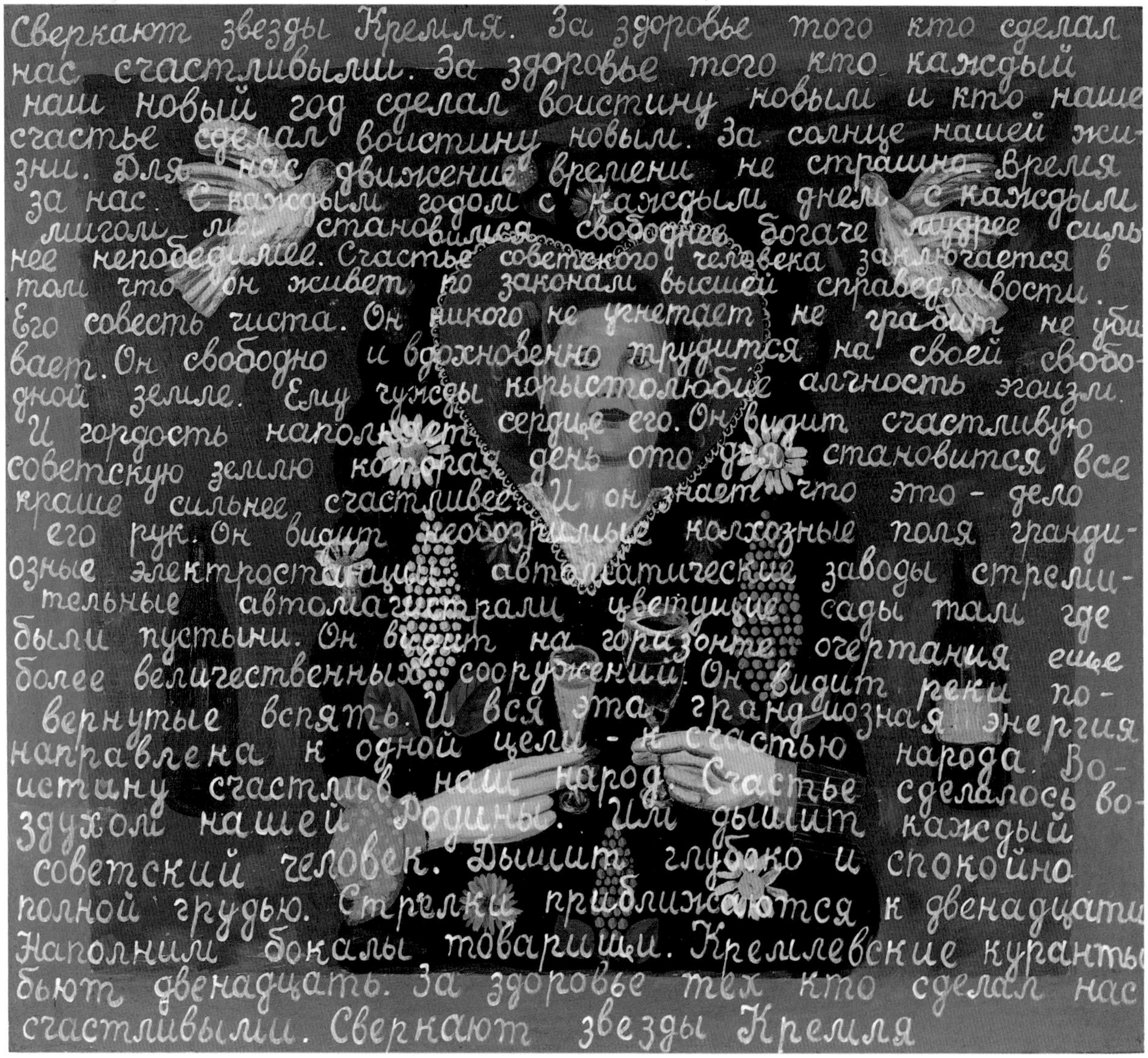

Pl. 1:3
Arkadii Petrov
Aunt Niusia, 1981
Oil on fiberboard
74.5 × 85 cm

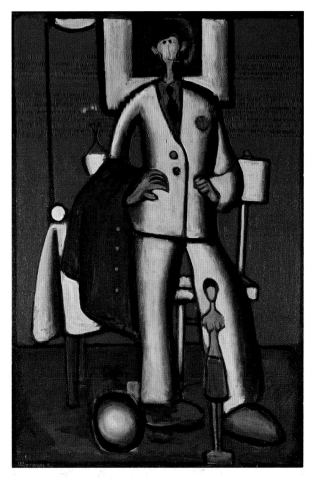

Pl. 1:4
Anatolii Shugrin
(Untitled), n.d.
Oil on canvas
109.6 × 73.5 cm

Pl. 1:5 (*above right*)
Aleksandr Tyshler
The Girl with a Cat, 1976
Oil on canvas
57.7 × 47.5 cm

Pl. 1:6
Anatolii Zverev
Summer, 1965
Oil on paper
59.8 × 42.6cm

Pl. 1:7
Genia Chef
St. Sebastian, 1973
Collage and oil on panel
63 × 49.2 cm

Pl. 1:8
Sergei Shablavin
Sky over the City, 1978
Oil on canvas
84 cm in diameter

Pl. 1:9
Rostislav Lebedev
Belomorcanal, 1988
Oil on fiberboard
100.6 × 22.7 cm

Pl. 1:11
Sergei Volokhov
From the series *Myths
and Legends*, 1976
Oil and collage on canvas
119.5 × 78.6 cm

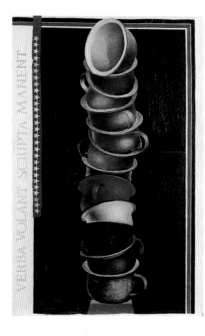

Pl. 1:12
Grisha Bruskin
From the series *The Birth
of the Hero*, 1985
*Official with the Kremlin
Tower*
Plaster, cardboard, and oil
41.5 × 18 × 13.5 cm
*Marshal with the Slogan
"Socialism Is Invincible"*
Plaster, cardboard, and oil
33.5 × 17.5 × 11 cm
*Male Demon (Ketub
Mariri)*
Copper
38 × 21.5 × 27 cm
Pioneer with Little Flag
Copper, cardboard, and
oil
30.5 × 18 × 11 cm
Soldier with Frontier Post
Plaster, cardboard, and oil
40 × 20 × 15.5 cm
Angel with Six Wings
Plaster
50 × 22.5 × 12 cm

Pl. 1:13
Aleksei Tiapushkin
"Problematism!", 1976
Tempera on canvas
67 × 117.2 cm

Pl. 1:14
Rostislav Lebedev
*Superpowers and
Supernations*, 1981
Pen and ink and collage
on paper
55 × 107.2 cm

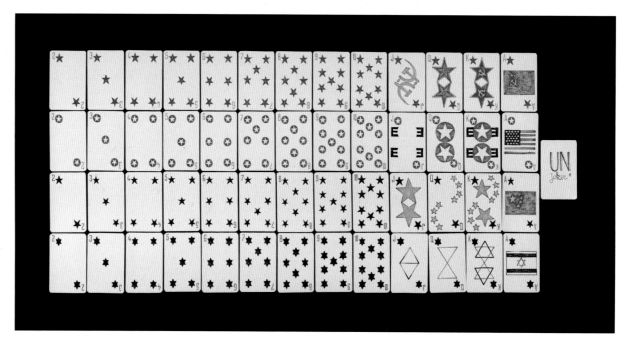

Pl. 1:15
Grisha Bruskin
Fragment from Part III
of the *Fundamental
Lexicon*, 1986
Oil on linen
112 × 76.5 cm

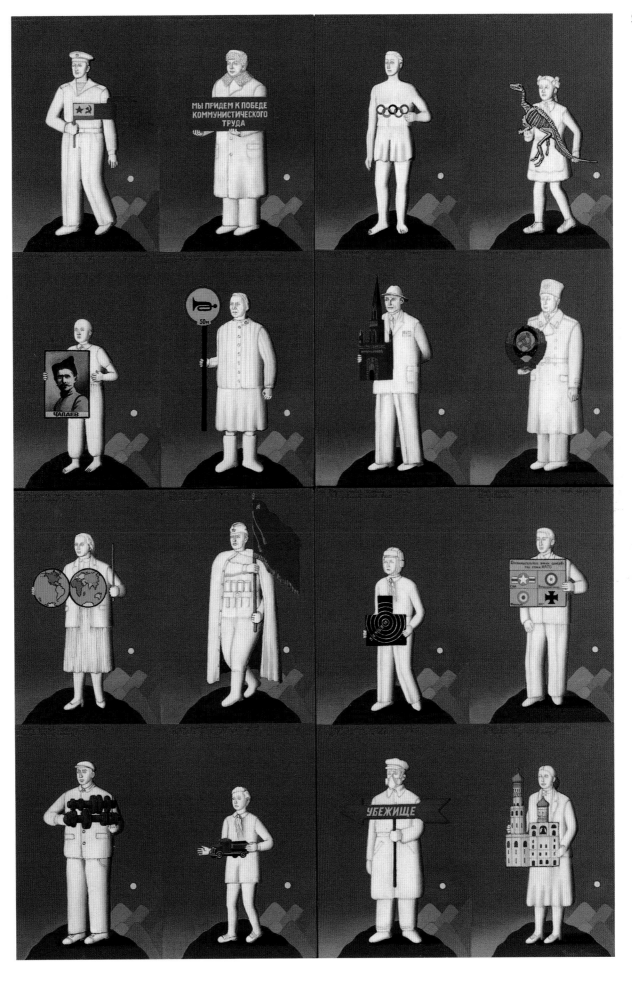

Pl. 1:16 (*right*)
Hagop Hagopian
*Still Life with Tools,
Gloves, and Eggs*, 1975
Oil on canvas
60.3 × 81 cm

Pl. 1:17 (*below*)
Eric Bulatov
Krasikov Street, 1977
Oil on canvas
150 × 198.5 cm

Pl. 1:18
Mikhail Romadin
Traffic Jam, 1985
Oil on canvas
100.5 × 131 cm

Pl. 1:19
M.M. Mirdzhavadov
Bull, 1983
Oil on canvas
78 × 98 cm

Pl. 1:20
Grisha Bruskin
Alephbet #14, 1985
Oil on linen
116.2 × 97.2 cm

Pl. 2:1
Dmitrii Tegin
Asphalt Workers, 1959–60
Oil on canvas
149.5 × 298 cm

Pl. 2:2
Georgii Tsereteli
*Into the Future with
V.I. Lenin*, n.d.
Oil on canvas
160 × 120 cm

Pl. 2:3
Klever
Papa, 1969
Oil on canvas
99.3 × 74.2 cm

Pl. 2:4
Aleksandr Arefiev
(Untitled), 1953
Gouache and watercolor
on paper
31.2 × 43 cm

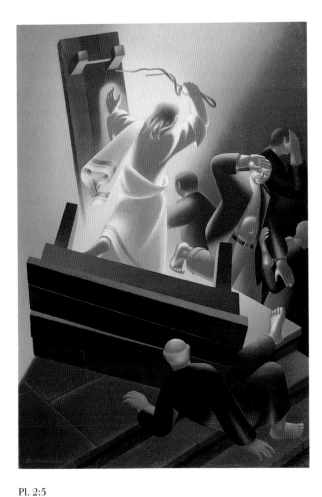

Pl. 2:6
Oscar Rabin
*Went to the Store. Back
Soon. Oskar*, 1976
Oil on canvas
99.5 × 79 cm

Pl. 2:7
Aleksandr Sitnikov
The Composer, 1986
Oil on canvas
113.5 × 72.5 cm

Pl. 2:5
Vladimir Ovchinnikov
*Banishment of the Money
Changers from the
Temple*, 1982
Oil on canvas
119 × 80 cm

Pl. 2:8
Joseph Kiblitsky
Man of 1956, from the
series *Madhouse*, 1974
Oil on canvas
80 × 65 cm

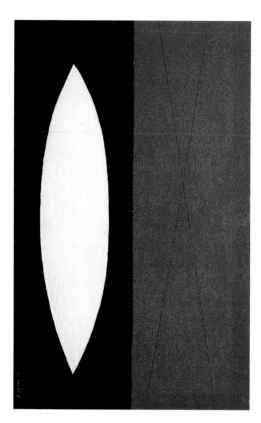

Pl. 2:9
Valerii Yurlov
Counter-form, 1959
Oil on canvas
120.5 × 75.2 cm

Pl. 2:11
Olga Bulgakova
At the Table in Moonlight,
1982
Oil on canvas
103.4 × 113.5 cm

Pl. 2:10
Mikhail Taratuta
Russian Roulette, 1985
Gouache, ink, and
printed image on
cardboard
71.3 × 49.5 cm

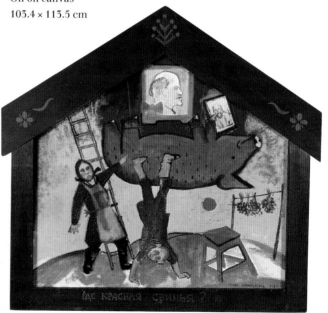

Pl. 2:12
Vladimir Samsonov
Where Is the Red Pig?,
1984
Oil and tempera on panel
103.5 × 111.5 cm

Pl. 2:14
Boris Orlov
(Untitled), 1979
Painted wood
86 × 52 × 9.5 cm

Pl. 2:13
Eli Beliutin
Landscape, 1952
Oil on canvas
107 × 70 cm

Pl. 3:1 (*left*)
Vladimir Veisberg
*Composition with
Pyramids and Sphere*, 1979
Oil on canvas
49 × 59 cm

Pl. 3:2
Vladimir Nemukhin
Poker on the Beach, 1974
Oil and playing cards on
canvas
69 × 79.7 cm

Pl. 3:3 (*right*)
Lydia Masterkova
(Untitled), 1971
Oil on canvas
153 × 108 cm

Pl. 3:4 (*opposite*)
Oscar Rabin
(Untitled), n.d.
Oil on canvas
105.6 × 85.5 cm

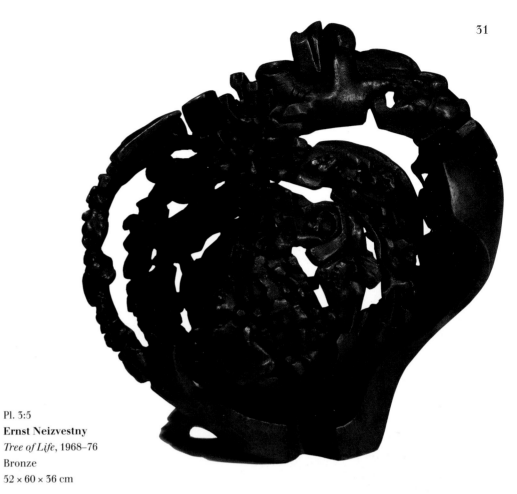

Pl. 3:5
Ernst Neizvestny
Tree of Life, 1968–76
Bronze
52 × 60 × 36 cm

Pl. 3:6
Oscar Rabin
Still Life, 1975
Oil on canvas
98 × 90.2 cm

Pl. 3:7
Leonid Lamm
Assembly Hall, Butyrka Prison, 1976
Watercolor on paper
49.8 × 49.8 cm

Pl. 3:8
Oleg Tselkov
Falling Mask, 1976
Oil on canvas
120.2 × 80.3 cm

Pl. 3:9
Samuil Rubashkin
*Passover—Why Is This
Night Different from All
Other Nights?*, 1973
Oil on canvas
100 × 80.2 cm

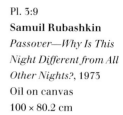

Pl. 3:10
Dmitri Plavinsky
The Tortoise, 1967
Oil on canvas
100.5 × 150.5 cm

Pl. 3:11
Aleksandr Kharitonov
Landscape with Shrine, 1972
Oil on illustration board
26.4 × 36.6 cm

William Brui (b. 1946), Mikhail Chemiakin (b. 1943), Aleksandr Leonov (b. 1937), Lev Nusberg (b. 1937), and Anatolii Putilin (b. 1946). These experiences encouraged us to continue to expand the collection and to fill in gaps both in terms of types of art and the geographical regions represented, with the ultimate aim of making it a more comprehensive reflection of Soviet reality.

The pioneering nonconformists of the 1950s, 1960s, and the early 1970s were and probably will remain central to the collection, but many works by younger and some older artists have been added. It was mutually agreed that the collection should seek to demonstrate what could be achieved creatively despite the adverse Soviet conditions. This meant that émigré art created in the freedom of the West, no matter how interesting, would not be included in the collection. The collection has remained focused on nonconformist art produced in the Soviet Union during the post-Stalinist years of repression. This meant that the collection could not end with Brezhnev's demise, as was originally expected, since there was no real change in the system under his successors Andropov and Chernenko. Fortunately, a dramatic change for the better came with Gorbachev's introduction of *glasnost* and *perestroika*. Political control of the arts evaporated almost overnight and the difference between unofficial and official art lost much of its significance. As fear of KGB reprisals faded in 1987 and 1988, market influences increased. It seemed to us, therefore, that 1986 should be the terminal year for the collection.

Nancy and I also decided that while the collection was being rapidly increased in size and scope in the 1980s and early 1990s, the task of exhibiting and publicizing the art should not be neglected. We had already found that exhibitions were not easily arranged at major museums because of the long lead-time required. Also, no museums we approached were ready to exhibit art that was not already widely accepted by art critics and art historians. As a consequence, over the next fifteen years, exhibitions similar to that shown in Washington and later at Cornell University in 1977 were held at a dozen colleges and universities, where arrangements were much easier and interest was much greater.[2] Students and faculty who saw these exhibitions invariably reported them to be among the most interesting their institutions had presented. Jonathan Ingersoll, director of the gallery at St. Mary's College of Maryland, was tremendously helpful not only in exhibiting the work at St. Mary's but also in assisting with exhibitions elsewhere.

One of the most satisfying exhibitions was "Nonconformists," shown at the University of Maryland gallery in 1980, with a satellite exhibition at the Jewish Community Center of Greater Washington in Rockville, Maryland. Margarita Tupitsyn, who contributed to that show's catalogue, soon moved to New York City with her husband Victor, a mathematician, visual poet, and art critic. There they helped to organize and supervise the Contemporary Russian Art Center of America, for which Margarita served as curator. For two years, the Center occupied a vast space generously provided by Eduard Nakhamkin at the corner of Houston and Broadway in SoHo. Our first exhibition, "Russian New Wave," included the work of twenty artists and opened in December 1981. Over the next two years, before Nakhamkin was forced to sell the building, eight more exhibitions were organized, five of which were accompanied by catalogues.[3]

When the SoHo space was closed, new locations for exhibitions had to be found. Among the more distinctive or unusual exhibits were a month-long exhibition in 1984 of forty works with a religious or spiritual theme at the Washington National Cathedral, seen by an estimated fifteen thousand visitors; a one-day exhibition of Conceptual art at the Kennedy Center in 1986, featuring Vitalii Rakhman (b. 1945) and Aleksandr Shnurov (b. 1955), and an exhibition at the Washington Project for the Arts (WPA) in 1985, when the AAASS held another major convention in Washington, D.C.[4] The WPA exhibition led to a later two-part exhibition at the New Museum in New York of Sots Art and AptArt for which Margarita and Victor Tupitsyn were responsible. More recently, several exhibitions were held at the Fondo del Sol Visual Art and Media Center in Washington, D.C., and an exhibition of Baltic art, curated by Eda Sepp with my assistance, was held at a Canadian government gallery in Toronto, in conjunction with the biennial convention of the American Baltic Association.[5]

Artworks from the collection also made up a significant proportion of the exhibition "The Quest for Self-Expression," held at the Columbus Museum of Art in 1990 (it later traveled to the University of North Carolina in Greensboro and the Arkansas Art Center in Little Rock). Some works from the collection were shown in exhibitions organized by Alexander Glezer in the Senate and House office buildings. Many works have also been loaned to exhibitions at major museums, such as the Centre Georges Pompidou in Paris and the Jewish Museum in New York.

The Firebird Gallery in Alexandria, Virginia presented a series of exhibitions between 1984 and 1988 under the supervision of the director Dennis Roach.[6] He helped generously in the preparation of the catalogues for these exhibitions as well as for a half-dozen exhibitions at the

C.A.S.E. Museum of Contemporary Russian Art in Jersey City.[7] This small pioneering museum, established by Arthur Goldberg and directed by Alexander Glezer, had an active program of exhibitions featuring the works of non-conformist artists in the Soviet Union as well as of artists who had emigrated to the West. Glezer had also headed a similar museum established earlier in Montgeron, outside Paris. He had somehow managed to negotiate permission to bring his very considerable collection with him to the West when he was expelled from the Soviet Union in 1975. It formed the core of exhibitions he organized throughout Europe. One of his major exhibitions, coordinated by Michael Scammell, was at the Institute of Contemporary Art in London in 1977.

As Glezer's commitments in the Soviet Union increased after *glasnost*, when he could safely return to the Soviet Union, I became the acting director of the C.A.S.E. Museum for a number of years. It was at the opening of the Sergei Sherstiuk (b. 1951) exhibition at C.A.S.E. in 1990 that I met Dennis Cate, director of the Zimmerli Art Museum at Rutgers University. George Riabov had brought Cate there to explore the possibility of the Dodge Collection being entrusted to the Zimmerli, where his own historically oriented collection already resided.

Now that the Dodge Collection is established at Rutgers, my wife and I are delighted and much relieved. The collection at last has a permanent home at a major educational institution with a fine museum, an excellent art history department, and several other departments with significant involvement in the study of the former Soviet Union. An interdisciplinary approach to all aspects of the collection is thus assured. Furthermore, the collection is now safe from both fire and theft, and will be preserved "in perpetuity" with proper climate control. It is also important that New Brunswick is only an hour from New York City, where there is great interest in all aspects of Russian and Soviet art. And it is also relatively close to our home at Cremona Farm in Maryland.

It was of particular concern to Nancy that the collection be maintained as a single body of works and not dispersed. It is a unique and irreplaceable record of a significant period in art history, as well as of the sociopolitical and cultural history of the former Soviet Union during a critical period of change. Preserving the collection intact at one well-located institution, she felt, would greatly facilitate its use as a research resource for students, scholars, and critics.

The task of cataloguing and photographing the collection over the past several years was begun at Cremona with the help of Charles Fick, John Kopp,

Cindy Schartman, and others. This work has continued at the Zimmerli Museum, coupled with the preparation of this catalogue. Preparing it has also highlighted a number of gaps in the collection. While these cannot all be filled, a number of significant additions to the collection have been made in recent years. Some of the artists we have not been able to treat adequately in the following chapters are Andrei Grositsky (Fig. 1:4), Genia Chef (b. 1954) (Fig. 1:10; Pl. 1:7), and Grisha Bruskin (b. 1945).

I had missed Bruskin on my visits to Moscow in the 1970s, so it was eye-opening to see his large multipaneled painting *Fundamental Lexicon* at Sotheby's New York preview for the Moscow auction in the summer of 1988. At the sale, that work drew the record price of $415,756. We have only recently been able to acquire for the collection several older paintings and sculptural figures, featuring Bruskin's cast of mythic archetypes drawn from Judaism and Soviet Socialism (Pls. 1:12, 1:15, 1:20). These archetypes form Bruskin's own personal mythology, which has a Sots Art dimension.

I also missed Vadim Sidur (1924–1986), a sculptor of

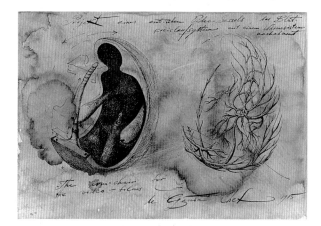

Fig. 1:10
Genia Chef
The Armchair for Video Films, 1985
Pen and ink on paper
20.8 × 29.7 cm

Fig. 1:11
Vadim Sidur
Invalid, 1962
The Wounded, 1963
The Sacrifice, 1965
War and Peace, 1965
Aluminum

powerful works related to the human condition reacting to various forms of stress. Recently, a number of his sculptural pieces have been added to the collection (Fig. 1:11). There are, of course, many other artists and artworks we would have liked to include in the collection and in this book, but those must wait for the future.

Despite its considerable size, the Dodge Collection cannot adequately reflect the full story of the developments in nonconformist art across the whole expanse of the Soviet Union during the critical thirty-year period from gulag to *glasnost*. Nevertheless, we hope the collection has sufficient breadth and depth to provide the basis for extensive research, evaluation, and exhibiting by staff, art historians and other faculty, students, and visiting scholars for years to come. One question that might be examined is the effect on a Soviet artist's work of being shifted by emigration or by the collapse of the Communist system from the oppressive, politically controlled environment of the Soviet system to a much freer sink-or-swim system where market influences are in control. The recent Soviet experience has provided conditions not unlike those available to a biologist who can change at will the environmental parameters in his experiments in order to observe the effects of these changes on the behavior of his research subjects. The art historian now has a unique opportunity for much the same kind of analysis in the arts.

We also feel there are important insights and lessons to be drawn from the collection, both for the future of the former Soviet Union and for our own. Renee and Matthew Baigell, in preparing their book of interviews with nonconformist artists, asked what these lessons might be.[8] Here are some of the responses:

* We can learn that well-crafted, powerful, compelling, and even beautiful art can emerge from the cruelty, fear, and stultifying effects of political oppression and deprivation.

* We can learn that man's striving for freedom of self-expression through art cannot long be suppressed by even the most offensive and intrusive of totalitarian systems.

* We can learn to appreciate the importance to us all of the courageous artists who dared, with their colleagues in the other arts, to lead the struggle for freedom of expression in the Soviet Union. Like the little boy in the Hans Christian Andersen fairy tale who spoke out when he saw that the emperor was wearing no clothes, Soviet nonconformists helped create and enlarge the cracks in the Soviet totalitarian edifice that finally brought the system crashing down.

* We can also learn that we must keep constant guard against those forces and persons who seek to suppress freedom of expression in our own society. This freedom is a precious heritage with which we have long been blessed and which we must never take for granted but always cherish and defend.

Notes

1. These included Rimma Gerlovina and Valerii Gerlovin, Eduard Gorokhovsky, Francisco Infante, Ilya Kabakov, Viacheslav Koleichuk, Vitaly Komar and Alexander Melamid, Dmitrii Krasnopevtsev, Viktor Pivovarov, Eduard Shteinberg, Mikhail Shvartsman (b. 1926), Anatolii Slepyshev (b. 1932), Boris Sveshnikov (b. 1927), Aleksei Tiapushkin (1919–1988), and Vladimir Yankilevsky. I also met the widows of the painters Samuil Rubashkin (1906–1975) and Ullo Sooster (1924–1970).

2. Exhibitions were at St. Mary's College of Maryland (1977–1991); Antioch College (1978); Columbia University, with the Pratt Institute (1978); Montgomery Junior College (1979); Dickinson College (1979); University of Minnesota (1982); University of Wisconsin, River Falls (1982); Phillips Academy (1986); University of North Carolina (1986); Kennesaw College (1987); and Charles County Community College (1991). Individual works have also been lent to other college exhibitions.

3. These exhibitions were "Russian New Wave" (1981–82); "Vagrich Bakhchanyan: Visual Diary— 1/1/80–12/31/80" (1982); "New Art from the Soviet Union: Selections" (1982); "Henry Khudyakov: Visionary Nonwearables" (1982); "Baltic Images I—Raul Meel: Line, Shape, and Form" (1982), "Baltic Images II—Latvia, Lithuania, and Estonia: Selected Contemporary Works" (1983); "Lydia Masterkova: Striving Upward to the Real & Russian Women Artists" (1983); "Gennady Zubkov and the Sterligov Group" (1983); and "Come Yesterday and You'll Be First" (1983; originated at City Without Walls in Newark, N.J., with Margarita Tupitsyn as curator).

4. The exhibition included a mock-up of an AptArt show, and was accompanied by the catalogue *AptArt: Moscow Vanguard in the 80s*, with an introduction by Margarita and Victor Tupitsyn and designed by Leonid Lamm.

5. This exhibition, "Baltic Art during the Brezhnev Era: Nonconformist Art in Estonia, Latvia, and Lithuania," was held at the John B. Aird Gallery in Toronto in 1992.

6. Among the exhibitions organized by the Firebird Gallery were "Soviet Artists in Exile at Home and Abroad: Leningrad" (1984), "Soviet Artists in Exile at Home and Abroad: Moscow" (1984), "Leonid Lamm: Recollections from the Twilight Zone, 1973–1985" (1985), "Back to Back: Rakhman-Shnurov" (1986), "Post Socialist Realism: The New Soviet Reality" (1987–88).

7. This museum of the Committee for the Absorption of Soviet Emigrés (C.A.S.E.) was initially known as the Museum of Russian Artists in Exile. The exhibitions shown there included "Evgeny Mikhnov-Voitenko: Abstract Visions" (1988), "Eduard Gorokhovsky" (1989–90), "Dmitri Krasnopevtsev: A Retrospective Exhibition" (1990), "Sergei Sherstiuk: Soviet Post Socialist Realism" (1990–91), "Alexander Shnurov: Twelve Year Perspective, 1978–1989" (1990), and "Alexander Kharitonov" (1991).

8. Renee Baigell and Matthew Baigell, eds., *Soviet Dissident Artists: Interviews after Perestroika* (New Brunswick, N.J.: Rutgers University Press, 1995).

2 | Soviet art under government control

From the 1917 Revolution to Khrushchev's thaw

Elena Kornetchuk

Control is established In the decade and a half following the 1917 October Revolution in Russia, the Communist Party achieved direct control of the arts, a crucial step in the process of reshaping the cultural life of the country and using art to advance the goals of the Party. Of course, this was not a new phenomenon for Russia. Political control of art dates back to Russian antiquity. For centuries, Russian art primarily served the Church, the Imperial Court, or the gentry. This relationship between rulers and artists did not change significantly until 1863, when a group of Russian artists, known as the *Peredvizhniki* (Itinerants), broke with the conservative traditions of the Imperial Academy of Fine Arts in St. Petersburg.

The Itinerants initially believed that art was a vehicle for social exposure and criticism. To practice their credo, they formed the Association for Itinerant Art Exhibitions in 1870. By breaking away from the stifling rule of the St. Petersburg Academy of Fine Arts, the Itinerants became the first Russian artists to free themselves to pursue their own sociocultural beliefs. By the turn of the century, the Russian art world had evolved to the point of producing one of the most experimental art movements of the period. This path-breaking movement, which lasted from about 1910 until the early 1930s and encompassed multiple stylistic tendencies, came to be known as the Russian avant-garde. Marc Chagall (1887–1985), Vasilii Kandinsky (1866–1944), El Lissitzky (1890–1941), Kazimir Malevich (1878–1935), and Liubov Popova (1889–1924) are among the better known artists of this period.

Though the Bolsheviks were to change profoundly the artistic values prevalent in Russia at the time of their takeover, Lenin, like Marx and Engels, paid little attention to the question of aesthetics. Nevertheless, Lenin made it clear that he supported the principle of *narodnost* and therefore preferred representational to nonobjective art.[1] Though he shared a dislike for modern art movements with G.V. Plekhanov, Russia's first Marxist theorist and art critic, Lenin must also have agreed with Plekhanov that turning the "muse" of an artist into a "state muse" would inevitably lead to a decline in art.[2] Whatever his artistic influences, Lenin confined himself to ordering the destruction of old tsarist monuments and replacing them with monuments to the Revolution.[3] This was the first Soviet act dictating the subject matter of art.[4]

First steps in initiating control Both traditional and avant-garde artists were affected by the Revolution. Under the leadership of A.V. Lunacharsky, head of Narkompros (People's Committee for Enlightenment) and first Soviet Commissar for Education, many artists of the avant-garde accepted administrative and pedagogical posts in the new government. Indeed, they competed in their efforts to establish a new cultural world order: Proletkult (The Proletarian Cultural Educational Organization) was the first to formulate the concept of a separate proletarian culture.[5] Though many artists' groups claimed that they had developed the only correct approach to such a culture, the Communist Party made little effort to establish an official aesthetic theory of art.[6] Only when Proletkult attempted to dominate the Soviet art scene did Lenin order its submission to Narkompros. He declared: "Proletarian culture must be a legitimate development of those reserves of knowledge which mankind has cultivated under the suppression of capitalist society, of landlord society and of bureaucratic society."[7] Clearly, Lenin felt that a claim by one school of art to the title of the official representative of proletarian art was both ideologically and practically harmful.

Nevertheless, artists were encouraged to relate their activities to the development of the new Communist state. As Proletkult was rendered ineffectual, other organizations sprang up to replace it. Ultimately, one organization, AKhRR (The Association of Artists of Revolutionary Russia), can be held responsible for greatly curtailing the aesthetic freedom of Soviet artists and for leading to state control of the arts. AKhRR accomplished this by placing itself at the disposal of the Revolution and asking the Communist Party to advise it how artists should work.[8] In advocating a return to representationalism, AKhRR declared:

Our civic duty to mankind is to make an artistic
documentary record of the greatest moment in
history, with all its revolutionary urgency. We shall

depict the present day: the daily life of the Red Army, the workers, the peasantry, the revolutionaries, and the heroes of labor. We shall provide a real picture of events and not abstract concoctions that discredit our revolution in the eyes of the international proletariat.[9]

The Party made no effort to curb the new group's activities. By 1926, Narkompros was helping to finance AKhRR's VI Exhibit,[10] and by 1925, the Soviet government was openly supporting AKhRR's activities.[11] Thus, though AKhRR had to compete with other artistic organizations, it came to dominate Soviet art. In wanting to make art comprehensible to the common man, AKhRR adopted the slogan "Art to the Masses." To this end, the association rejected abstract art and advocated "heroic realism."[12]

As a result of this push for realism, avant-garde art began to disappear and the avant-garde artists gradually abandoned the world of painting for what they felt to be more publicly oriented fields: film, set design, utilitarian design, political posters, and, especially, architecture. Artists who were not assimilated in this process or were later disillusioned by it, were either eased out of their positions or emigrated from the Soviet Union. The life of Kandinsky, the founder of abstract art, presents such an example. In 1918, he was appointed a member of the visual arts' section of Narkompros. Between 1918 and 1921, he taught in Vkhutemas (Higher State Art Technical Studios) in Moscow, instructed at Moscow University, and founded the Museums of Painterly Culture. Yet, by the end of 1921, when the euphoria of the Revolution had subsided, he felt that his creativity could no longer grow in the sociopolitical context of Russia. So Kandinsky departed for Berlin. Similar fates befell Marc Chagall, Naum Gabo (1890–1977), and Anton Pevsner (1844–1962).

Control under Stalin As Stalin gained full control of the Communist Party in the late 1920s, less and less experimentation in art was tolerated. In 1929, Stalin ousted the relatively liberal Lunacharsky as Commissar of Education. One year later, at the Sixteenth Communist Party Congress, Stalin called for an art that was "national in form and socialist in content."[13] In his efforts to prove that he was Lenin's true heir, Stalin republished Lenin's remarks about art that showed a clear distaste for avant-garde styles.[14]

As Stalin tightened his grip, government control of the arts became increasingly direct and oppressive. The official end to the exciting developments in Russian avant-garde art came on April 23, 1932, in the form of a Party decree titled "On the Reconstruction of Literary-Artistic Organizations." This proclamation called for the establishment of specific unions under the effective control of the Communist Party for each separate art form.[15] Though this resulted in the end of AKhRR's artistic domination, there was no immediate move to establish a U.S.S.R. union of artists. While realism was clearly the preferred style in art, the Party had yet to enforce any one particular style.

Stalin's first Five Year Plan, an aggressive assault on the country's economic and social problems, came to be known as the "Second Revolution." It led to new attacks on the avant-garde.[16] One of Stalin's aims was to include art in the first Five Year Plan. The new doctrine of Soviet art, known as Socialist Realism, was proclaimed at the First Congress of Soviet Writers in 1934. The job of formulating this doctrine, which was applicable to the visual arts (Pls. 2:1, 2:2) as well as to literature, was assigned to Maxim Gorky, the dean of Soviet literature and the most viable bridge between the prerevolutionary and contemporary styles of writing. The doctrine was officially supported by Andrei Zhdanov, head of the Leningrad Communist Party Organization and the Secretary of the Central Committee, who was in charge of ideological affairs.

The formal endorsement of Socialist Realism did not result in the immediate pronouncement of a single approach to painting, use of a certain style, or adherence to a single theme. At first, all works inspired by Communist ideology were proclaimed representative of Socialist Realism. Before long, however, the government began to rid itself of anyone who deviated from the approved style.

Interestingly, unacceptable art was much more clearly defined by the authorities than Socialist Realism. Three main categories were defined. Such works were to be excluded from exhibitions or official acquisition and might lead to difficulties with the authorities for the artist. A variety of punishments were developed for infractions, some based on content, others concerned with form. These categories of unacceptable art were:

1. Political art: Art that was not supportive of Party policies and programs such as collectivization, industrialization, or the development of military might was unacceptable (Pl. 2:3). Also disapproved of was art that mocked the clichés of Socialism or that did not show the leaders of the Party or government positively. Art showing the sordid side of Soviet life was also unacceptable (Figs. 2:1, 2:2, 2:3, 2:4, 2:5, 3:10; Pls. 2:4, 2:8, 3:4).

2. Religious art: Art critical of religion was, of course, encouraged, but art that was in any way supportive of religion was unacceptable (Pl. 2:5). Even paintings of churches or objects of veneration were disapproved of (Figs. 1:7, 2:6, 12:5; see Hilton's essay generally).

3. Erotic art: Pornography was very broadly defined by the authorities and even nudity was borderline (Figs. 2:7, 2:8, 2:9; Pl. 2:6).

4. "Formalistic art": Styles that were considered beyond the pale included abstraction, Cubism, Surrealism, Pop Art, Conceptual Art, and unconventional art of almost any kind (Figs. 2:10, 2:11; Pls. 2:9, 2:10, 2:11). Even Impressionism was condemned until the Khrushchev-era thaw.

Such strictures on art by the authorities guaranteed that official art was usually cliché-ridden, vapid, and uninteresting. Nonconformist art, in contrast, was often very interesting and relevant to the realities of life. Sometimes an artwork represented a combination of several of the prohibited categories, making it particularly offensive to the authorities and of great interest to the public (Figs. 2:12, 2:13; Pls. 2:10, 2:12, 2:14). One of the strategies of the nonconformist or unofficial artists after Khrushchev's thaw was to challenge the limits set by the authorities, to see how far they could go without having their works removed from an exhibition or without having the entire exhibition closed down. Earlier, during Stalin's reign, few artists would have dared to test the waters in this way because the consequences were far more devastating.

In 1936, the All-Union Committee for Artistic Affairs was formed to take over the direction of all Soviet art. That year also marked the beginning of the great purges, which many artists did not survive unscathed. The purge of "formalists" in the arts began with attacks on the composer Dmitrii Shostakovich (1906–1975) and other "slovenly artists."[17] By 1939, "formalist" artists had become virtually nonexistent in the Soviet Union. While insisting that Soviet artists must participate in the political guidance of the country, Stalin gained even more effective control over the arts when he became chairman of the Council of People's Commissars in 1941.[18] At this point, Socialist Realism became the only accepted method in art and the Soviet avant-garde was finally forced completely underground.

For a time, the exigencies of World War II postponed a thorough implementation of artistic control. Though artists were mobilized to paint national and historical subjects or war scenes, a general relaxation in the cultural sphere marked the war years when other concerns were of paramount importance. Once World War II was over and increasing international tension degenerated into the Cold War, however, an ideological alert occurred in the Soviet Union.[19] The disciplining of all forms of art under

Fig. 2:1 (*top*)
Leonid Lamm
Labor Camp near Rostov-on-Don, 1976
Watercolor and gouache on paper
37 × 56.3 cm

Fig. 2:2 (*above right*)
Vladimir Ivanov
Friday (*The Quarrel*), 1973
Pen and ink on paper
58.3 × 34.9 cm

Fig. 2:3 (*above*)
Vladimir Nekrasov
Checking Papers, 1975
Pen and ink, watercolor, and gouache on paper
31.7 × 43.7 cm

Fig. 2:4 (*right*)
Valerii Titov
(Untitled), n.d.
Oil and cloth on canvas
195.4 × 113.5 cm

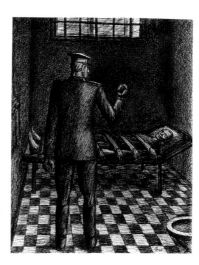

Fig. 2:5
Leonid Lamm
Punishment (Leonid Lamm with Warden in Butyrka Prison), 1975
Pen and ink and watercolor on paper
45 × 35.9 cm

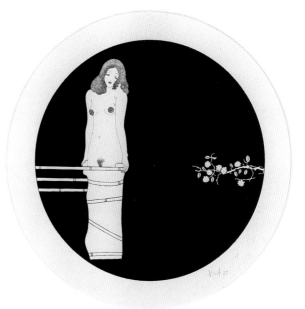

Fig. 2:6
Dmitri Plavinsky
*Church of the
Annunciation in the
Village near Zagorsk,*
1975
Etching
64.5 × 145.8 cm

Fig. 2:9 (*below*)
**Valerii Gerlovin and Rimma
Gerlovina**
Zoo, 1977
Performance, March 1977
Gelatin silver print
37.3 × 26.5 cm

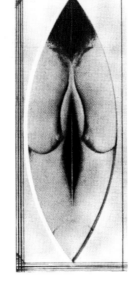

Fig. 2:7 (*left*)
Aili Vint
(Untitled), 1987
Photo etching
14.9 × 6.3 cm

Fig. 2:8
Tõnis Vint
(Untitled), 1975
Lithograph
20.4 cm in diameter

Fig. 2:10
Sergei Volokhov
Thinker, 1975
Oil and cloth on canvas
118.5 × 79 cm

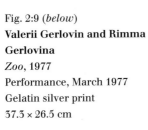

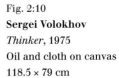

Fig. 2:11
Viacheslav Koleichuk
Möbius, 1975 (executed 1985)
Brass on wooden base
64.5 × 50 × 22 cm

страна наша была окружена тогда со
всех сторон врагами - как и сейчас...

кулаки не хотели коллективизи-
роваться...
- Не отдам !!!

рис. вверху. - Марфа! Ты замечательная
кулацкая вдова, да!
- ааа... ещё ... ооо... ещё !
- Да! настоящая кулацкая вдова!
рис. внизу. - Вместо тово, чтоб научить
мине пысать, щитать и чытать...

- Товарищ, Сталин уделяет большое внимание вам, Крестья-
нам - кулакам!
- Я ...
- Скажи им, скажи сукиным сынам!...

-Павлик вас заложил, тятя!
- Мать вашу, суки, твари!

позднее...
- Выездная сессия приговаривает
троцкистского Вредителя, кулака
Прохора Морозова к 25 годам
заключения!...

лозунг: "Беречь зерно! Это наше об-
щенародное богатство!
- юный герои Павлик...
- Мы устроим тебе свою выездную
сессию, стукач!
- Два брата Прохора - сенька и матвей
и его дядя Абрам оставались на свобо-
де...

- Это слишком постно для меня!
- по питательности это мясо уступает нашим
кулацким коровам...
- ...и даже Грибам...

Это преступление скоро раскрыли...
- ... и приговаривает семена морозова и абрама-
дядю Прохора Морозова - к высшей мере наказа-
ния - расстрелу ... и матвея морозова - к 25 годам
заключения...
лозунги: "бдительность - наше оружие!"
"все на борьбу с кулаком!"

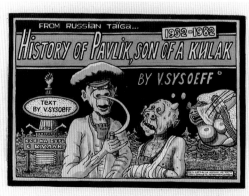

после войны матвея морозова повесили
как предателя...

- вот такая история случилась в дикой таёжной дере-
вушке 50 лет назад, сынок
- А быть павликом - это хорошо, или плохо, дедушка ?!

эту "History" прошу передать в пользование коллекционеру
людмиле Кузнецовой.
В. Сысо___ (см. на обороте) →

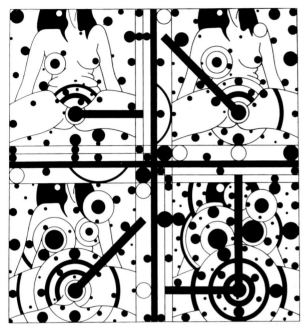

Fig. 2:13
Leonhard Lapin
Woman—Machine X, 1975
Stereotype
42.5 × 40.5 cm

the secretary of the Central Committee. His official invitation to artists to create artworks critical of Soviet society launched a lively debate which resulted in greater freedom of expression under Khrushchev.

How control was exercised How was control over art achieved and exercised? Several organizations were created by Stalin to oversee the Soviet art world and to ensure that the goals laid out by the Communist Party were achieved. A brief review of some of the institutions that were established by the government to oversee the Soviet art world reveals an impressive network for control.

1. The Ministry of Culture of the U.S.S.R.: Though the ideological committee of the Communist Party exercised ultimate control over art policy, the main operating decisions were left to the Soviet Ministry of Culture and two special sections within the Ministry: the section for fine arts and the section for the protection of monuments. The Ministry's committees on art matters included members of the two other major organizations of Soviet art: the Soviet Academy of Arts and the U.S.S.R. Union of Artists. However, major decisions of all these bodies had to be approved by the minister or his deputies.

The Ministry directly supervised some of the most important art institutions in the country, overseeing such well-known museums as the Tretyakov Art Gallery in Moscow and the Hermitage Museum in Leningrad. It managed three art publishing houses and operated the Central Scientific Research Laboratory for the Conservation and Restoration of Works of Art. Through its Administration of Art Exhibits, the Ministry organized major exhibitions at home and abroad, and at the same time controlled the exportation of art.

The Ministry of Culture had its own committee for purchasing and commissioning art. Thus, many Soviet artists, regardless of Union affiliation, worked directly for the Ministry. After the Ministry acquired a work of art, it was often included in traveling exhibitions or given to a museum. Artists who distinguished themselves by exceptional achievements or services were given cherished awards, medals, and honorary titles. The title "People's Artist of the U.S.S.R." was the highest honor given for contributions to the Soviet fine arts. The highest medal of recognition was the Lenin Prize, awarded for the creation of exceptional works of art.

Ultimately, the Ministry functioned as the supervisory body for the entire organization of Soviet art. It therefore worked closely with the ministries of culture in various republics and the hierarchies of institutions under them,

the direction of Zhdanov and an attack on modern Western art resulted in increased cultural rigidity and isolationism.[20] The collection of the Moscow State Museum of Modern Art was dispersed and Aleksandr Gerasimov (1881–1963), president of the Soviet Academy of Arts, attacked "cosmopolitanism" in the arts, accusing numerous Soviet art critics of "lacking a healthy love of country."[21] The Communist Party stressed again that the avowed mission of Soviet art, which was to be simple and obvious enough to be understood by everyone, was to advance Communism.

In summary, under Stalin's rule, the Party used art to reinforce the Socialist system's efforts to transform society. Many artists acquiesced in the curtailment of aesthetic freedom and became tools of the Party. Under Stalin, Russian art had come full circle since the Itinerants broke away from the St. Petersburg Academy of Fine Arts in 1863: from officially controlled art to a large measure of aesthetic freedom to officially controlled art, now with heavy costs for deviation.

Dramatic changes were to occur in the post-Stalin era which would affect the official doctrine of Socialist Realism as it applied to the visual arts. Stalin's series of letters about "Marxism and Questions of Linguistics" anticipated changes in the interpretation of Socialist Realism.[22] The letters demanded that art express more criticism from the people. In soliciting criticism, Stalin clearly intended that art should be more than "pretty pictures." This position was reiterated at the Nineteenth Communist Party Congress in 1952 by Georgi Malenkov,

Fig. 2:12 (*opposite*)
Viacheslav Sysoev
The cover and nos. 2, 11, 13, 15, and 17 from the series
History of Pavlik, Son of a Kulak, 1980
Ink and gouache on paper
24.3 × 37 cm (each)

the local academies of art, and the local branches of the U.S.S.R. Union of Artists.

2. The Academy of Arts of the U.S.S.R.: Whereas the Ministry of Culture was responsible for the whole arena of Soviet art, the Soviet Academy of Arts served as the educator of Soviet artists and of society as a whole. Established by the Council of Ministers in 1947, the Academy was considered the highest creative and scientific center in the area of fine arts. It was responsible for putting into practice the Party line. In this endeavor, it was helped by the Scientific Research Institute of the Theory and History of Fine Arts. Of course, the Communist Party exercised close control over all aspects of the Academy's work.

The Academy was run by a presidium, which was elected for a period of three years by a general meeting of members and associate members. The presidium was responsible for defining and implementing the general plan of work at the Academy. It was also responsible for liaison with all government institutions of the Soviet Union.

The Academy was comprised of members (academicians), honorary members (foreign artists), and associate members. All were divided into three sections: painting, sculpture, and graphic arts. To become a member of the Academy, one had to be prominent in the fine arts. Only individuals with substantial qualifications and the approval of the Party could be nominated to Academy institutions or public organizations. Nominees were then elected to the Academy by a general meeting of members and honorary members.

During its periodic sessions and conferences, the Academy held discussions of the aesthetic problems that concerned the Party and the Soviet art community. One of the early goals of the Academy was "to combat formalism, naturalism, and other features of contemporary bourgeois decadent art."[23] But its rigid outlook weakened as official enforcement of Socialist Realism became more relaxed after Stalin's death. Nevertheless, the organization was criticized for being overly conservative in its work, promoting exclusivity, and remaining isolated from the mass of Soviet artists.

3. The Union of Artists of the U.S.S.R.: In comparison with the Ministry of Culture and the Academy of Arts, the Union of Artists had the greatest day-to-day impact on professional Soviet artists since it was their major employer. Its predecessor, Vsekokhudozhnik (The All-Russian Cooperative of Artists), was founded in 1929, under the leadership of Y.M. Slavinsky. This organization included painters, graphic and applied artists, sculptors, and architects. It dispensed commissions, recommended pur-

chases, lent money to artists, and contributed to setting up exhibitions. Vsekokhudozhnik's goal was to create unity and creative uniformity in the arts by subordinating Soviet art to the discipline of the Party during the industrialization and collectivization drive of the late 1920s and 1930s.[24]

A union of artists for the city of Moscow was established by a 1932 Central Committee resolution called "On the Reorganization of Literary-Artistic Organizations."[25] This prompted the formation in the following years of similar local organizations throughout the Soviet Union designed to strengthen Party control further.

Enforcement of the prescribed art style of Socialist Realism in the various Soviet republics led to an attempt to establish a national artists' union in 1939, when the Soviet of People's Commissars of the U.S.S.R. passed a resolution "On the Formation of a Union of Artists of the U.S.S.R."[26] An organizational bureau, later known as the Organizational Committee, was created, but because of the interference of World War II and the trials of postwar recovery, the First All-Union Congress was convened only in 1957. At that time, the Union of Artists of the U.S.S.R. was finally formed and a board of administration elected. The latter was responsible for enforcing ideological-aesthetic policies within the Union as well as carrying out the decisions of the All-Union Congress and reporting to the Congress on its progress.

For conducting everyday business, the board of administration elected a secretariat from within its own group. Numerous commissions served as consulting bodies to the secretariat. Together, they organized artistic and social activities for the Union members. Thus, there were commissions for monumental art, for the decorative and applied arts, for poster art, and for work with young artists and art historians. These sections served the diverse needs of the Union.

The U.S.S.R. Union of Artists established branches in all fifteen Soviet republics, as well as in various regions, districts, and cities. Through the Art Fund, which was founded in 1940 and then placed under the direction of the secretariat, Union members (and nonmembers) received monetary support. The Fund provided artists with commissions similar to those given by the Ministry of Culture. Sections within the Fund handled the manufacture of materials for art use, legal assistance to Union members and their families, construction and maintenance of studios, and other benefits.

Like the Ministry, the Union of Artists had a publishing house that produced books, albums, catalogues, and reproductions of Soviet art. The Union sponsored its own publications, such as the magazine *Ikusstvo* [Art] and the *Information Bulletin* of the board of administration of the Union of Artists.

Toward the end of its existence, the Union counted approximately twenty-five thousand members.[27] To apply for admission, an artist had to submit a written application, works of art or (for art historians) pieces of art criticism, and obtain three recommendations from Union members. Participation in special entrance exhibitions and in republic and All-Union exhibitions was also required. Though most applicants were graduates of art institutes, an art diploma was not required. More important was political conformity. Elections were held by secret ballot not more than three times yearly. Upon acceptance into the Union, artists had to follow its regulations. Failure to comply with regulations could result in dismissal and loss of all privileges. An artist could be dismissed for political reasons as well as for such seemingly minor reasons as failure to pay membership dues for two consecutive years.

Like the Academy, the Artists' Union organized and directed the artistic activities of its members. One of its basic concerns was the organization of national and international art exhibitions, often with the help of the Ministry. Thus, all three major Soviet art organizations offered Soviet artists an opportunity to display their work. The opposite side of the coin was the power to exclude artists from any and all opportunities for public exhibition.

The Union of Artists was held in high esteem by Party and government officials in the 1960s and 1970s, but it lacked the inclination to initiate and promote change and innovation. It was openly criticized in the Gorbachev era for its inability to encourage and stimulate artistic work and to respond to the real needs of the artists. The Union's rigidity as well as the broader political events of the time were ultimately causes of its demise.

4. Other art groups: A small number of artists were not members of the artists' unions. Some worked according to the criteria established by the government for art and were known as "nonprofessional" artists. They worked independently at home or in studios at local clubs. In some republics and regions, the Soviet Union set up special museums of "national and nonprofessional art." Some nonprofessional artists eventually graduated from art institutes and pursued careers in art. Other artists, not members of an artists' union, worked for publishing houses or for such organizations as the Moscow Joint Committee of Graphic Artists (also known as the Gorkom Grafikov or the Graphics Union). Generally, organizations like that of the graphic artists were less rigid than the Artists' Union and more experimentation was evident in the work of their artist members.

Nonconformist and unofficial artists This panoply of institutions with their array of regulations and controls and carrots and sticks were able to reshape the nature and form of art in the U.S.S.R. But they were unable to give it much vitality or life. Beyond these establishment groups, a comparatively small number of opposition artists, at first several dozen and then several hundred, emerged in the 1950s and 1960s. They came to be known by a variety of names, such as dissident, underground, unofficial, left-wing, or nonconformist artists.[28] It is evident that these nonconformist artists began to surface during the "thaw," the cultural relaxation which took place under Khrushchev. Until the advent of *glasnost* and *perestroika* in 1986, these artists were perceived by the government as constituting a challenge to the official system since they did not subscribe to the doctrine of Socialist Realism. Instead, like the avant-garde of the 1910s and 1920s, they were searching for new or better artistic ways of expressing themselves and communicating with the public.

In their efforts to be independent and free of ideological control, many dissident artists refused to join the official arts organizations, although in most cases they would not have been welcome if they had wished to join. This forced them to support themselves by holding jobs unrelated to their art or to depend on the largesse of spouses, relatives, and friends. A few were fortunate enough to sell their art through official organizations and to go abroad to mount their own commercial exhibitions.[29] Others during this early period, primarily in Moscow, were able to sell some to diplomats or to representatives of the news media assigned to the Soviet Union.

The unofficial exhibitions of nonconformist artists that were aimed at increasing their visibility were usually shut down by the hostile official art bureaucracy since these nonconformist artists did not serve the goals of the Communist Party. The government also tried to minimize and suppress their activities with a variety of obstacles.

Foreshadowing Stalin's demise At the Nineteenth Communist Party Congress, held in October 1952, only four months before Stalin's death, a turning point in policy toward contemporary Soviet art became evident. At this Congress, Georgi Malenkov, secretary of the Central Committee and deliverer of the main report, called for a new freedom in criticism. Furthermore, Mikhail Suslov, the Party's chief ideologist and arch-conservative, attacked the theory of *beskonfliktnost* (nonconflict), saying that

Soviet art had become both "sweet and empty."[30] As artists had become fearful of developing anything that contradicted official dogma, he argued, the lack of conflict depicted in art had created a stagnant art form. He neglected to explain that it was the Party's harsh treatment of anyone deviating from Socialist Realism that had caused this fear in the first place.

Given these circumstances, the impact of this new principle in art was not immediate. At the 1952 All-Union Art Exhibition, an exhibition held annually in Moscow to review the artistic events of the year, conventional scenes from workers' lives and busts of Stalin predominated. But in contrast to the positive review of the 1951 All-Union Exhibition, which had featured similar artworks, the 1952 version was heavily criticized, thereby showing the beginning—although very halting—of a policy change in art. Among the terms used to describe the exhibition were such phrases as "superficial decorativeness"[31] and "soulless workmanship."[32] Soviet artists were said to lack the deep knowledge of expressing life. A common complaint was that neither the artist nor his work showed any creativity.[33]

The new direction in art favored abandoning old patriotic themes. While it was safe to paint such famous defenders of Russia as Emilian Pugachev and Mikhail Kutuzov, it was no longer considered socially useful. Having emerged victorious from World War II, the Party must have concluded that reinforcing Soviet Russia's past should no longer be the primary concern of art. Depicting the positive role of people in developing society and solving its problems—even through conflict—was now deemed more important.

Though this new direction was encouraged in Soviet art after 1952, it was by no means an invitation to broad experimentation. Thus, Anatolii Zverev (1931–1986), who in the 1960s became known as an important artist in Moscow unofficial art circles, was dismissed from art college for "formalism." Elsewhere, other artists were considered to have gone beyond acceptable bounds as they united in an effort to overcome the strictures of Socialist Realism. In Leningrad, the first known group of underground artists was formed around Pavel Filonov (1883–1941).[34] These Leningrad artists were interested in experimentation, as were other nonconformist artists, such as the Arefiev Group[35] in Lenigrad and Eli Beliutin (b. 1925), who was active in Moscow.

From Stalin's demise to Khrushchev's rise When Stalin died in March 1953, there was no abrupt change in the attitudes and institutions supporting Socialist Realism. In death, Stalin continued to be depicted in major Soviet paintings just as he had been in life. The first posthumous issue of *Iskusstvo* featured on its cover a painting of Stalin standing at his desk.[36] In the background of this portrait is a sketch of a Kremlin tower, symbolizing the focus of Soviet power. Inside was another painting of Stalin, this time in his famous Napoleonic pose, a different representation of power. These visual reminders of the continuing authority of Stalin and the Party were reinforced by a government directive exhorting people to rally around the Party.[37] Thus, art continued to serve the Party's interests.

The discussion of problems in art policy and practice introduced at the Nineteenth Communist Party Congress continued after Stalin's death. The thematic and formal dimensions of Socialist Realism also began to be openly debated. In an effort to understand the new Party directive in art better, the Organizational Committee of the Artists' Union and the Academy of Arts formed discussion groups focusing on the apathy prevalent in all aspects of Soviet art. Art critics were accused of a lack of original thought. The Ministry of Culture and the Union of Artists were both criticized for mishandling exhibitions. No art organization was above reproach. Clearly all feared coming into conflict with Stalinist doctrine.

The official goal in 1953 was to persuade Soviet artists to avoid trite subject matter, to make art seem less dull and more lively. The new role of the artist was "to see life in its continuing development—in the conflict of opposites, in the conflict of the new with the old, to be able to show fundamental contradictions."[58] Despite this appearance of relaxation, the many schools of the Russian avant-garde referred to as formalism and abstract art remained anathema to the Party. Although various artists argued in defense of Impressionism and abstract art at the 1952 All-Union Art Exhibition, the Party's official policy was to continue "to struggle with the vestiges of formalism [and] impressionism in the art of certain painters, sculptors, and printmakers; to struggle with the attempts by some artists and critics who under the guise of opposing naturalism are trying to remove impressionism and formalism from attacks and trying to discredit realism."[59]

In 1953, Malenkov attempted to consolidate his power by appealing to many different groups and initiating some relaxation in the arts. The spirit of criticism that resulted from this relaxation was felt in all cultural areas. Thus, the short story writer, Konstantin Paustovsky (1892–1968), declared war on philistinism in literature at the All-Union Conference of Young Critics.[40] Another prominent writer, Ilya Ehrenburg (1891–1967), who reportedly owned the largest private collection of French Impressionist paintings in the U.S.S.R., openly discussed the decline of all Soviet arts since World War II.[41] The critiques of Paustovsky and Ehrenburg were reiterated in the field of music by the noted composers Dmitrii Shostakovich and Aram Khachaturian.[42] Both musicians supported the artist's right to independence and originality.[43]

Art forms were permitted to vary, but still within limits. Some abstract art was tolerated as long as it served to give merit and understanding to the subject matter. However, if the technical skills of the artist were seen to play a role simply as "an example of pointless abstract workmanship and in no way serve the content, then they only destroy the artistic form and are not constructive."[44]

As it became more common to criticize the status of Soviet art in the immediate post-Stalin period, the mode of functioning of the artists' unions was also attacked. Artists and art historians felt that the "theory of nonconflict" had distorted art and had led to an embellishment of reality. Unnamed artists, writers, and critics were accused of ignoring real life in their works and of fearing to depict contradictions and human shortcomings. In fact, due to the "theory of nonconflict," paintings depicting any type of problem or conflict were censored as pessimistic and withheld from exhibitions.[45]

The widespread criticism of Soviet art by members of the artistic elite showed that the pronouncements on art at the Nineteenth Communist Party Congress had been taken seriously. Although Aleksandr Gerasimov, the conservative president of the Academy of Arts of the U.S.S.R., concentrated his attacks on the pernicious influence of formalism, other artistic leaders continued their constructive critique of Soviet art. Thus, Boris Ioganson (1893–1973), chairman of the Organizational Committee of the U.S.S.R. Union of Artists, shifting the blame from the artists to the art apparatus, criticized the art organizations and their leaders for the absence of creative artworks.[46]

In 1954, a major breakthrough in literature occurred with the publication of Ehrenburg's novel *The Thaw*. This event inaugurated a new era of artistic freedom. Interestingly, the novel's protagonists are artists—Volodya Pukhov, a successful Party-line painter, and Saburov, an artist who struggles to produce original works. At the time, it was widely believed that Saburov opposed the Party line. He was called "abnormal" and "schizophrenic," terms often applied to nonconformist artists in the U.S.S.R., even in the 1980s.

After the appearance of *The Thaw*, Saburov types began to surface more frequently in Soviet art. Thus, Eli Beliutin, then a young professor of painting at the Textile Institute in Moscow, who was already doing nonconformist work

privately (Pl. 2:13), founded the Free Studio of Art. Beliutin encouraged his students to experiment in free-form techniques. He developed a considerable following in Moscow where his students came to be known as the *Beliutintsy*.

A review of the literature of post-Stalin art provides insight into changes in the classification for the accepted subject matter of official Soviet art. For the most part, these subject classifications remained similar to those used in the Stalin era: *kolkhoz* (collective farm), industry, history, sports, everyday life, the struggle for peace, and wars of liberation. However, the classification of "the leader and his companion-in-arms" disappeared. Hero-worship of a single leader was superseded by glorification of collective leadership. The other most visible new trend in art was the call for simplicity. Instead of the pathos of struggle and the unbending will of men fighting for the fatherland, paintings for the first time showed a cheerless gloom and mute incomprehension before suffering and death. Eventually, this thematic change developed into the Severe Style, a movement whose chief proponents were Pavel Nikonov (b. 1930) and Nikolai Andronov (b. 1926) (Fig. 2:14).

The authorities had finally realized that the dynamic qualities of revolutionary romanticism had turned into bombast and exaggeration. The rift between Communist propaganda and Soviet reality had become too large even for artistic expression to bridge. Art had to be brought closer to life for public involvement. Such recognition expanded the confines under which artists had been working. An especially noteworthy example of this expansion is the fact that nudes once again became approved subject matter.[47]

By 1955, Socialist Realism was no longer confined to its original definition. A good indicator of the change in official interpretations of art was that Impressionism again became acceptable. The rehabilitation of Impressionism was formally marked by the exhibition "Fourteenth to Twentieth Century French Art," held at the Pushkin Museum in Moscow in November 1955. The paintings came from the collections of Soviet museums, which, up to this time, had not been allowed to exhibit these works.[48]

Meanwhile, the goal of the All-Union Art Exhibition planned for 1957 in Moscow was to celebrate the achievements of forty years of strict adherence to Stalinist interpretations of Socialist Realism. Indeed, artists were encouraged to go beyond the old strictures:

In preparation for the exhibit one must totally overcome the still existing narrow, one-sided understanding of the method of Socialist Realism, to put an end to the calm on the monopoly to

Fig. 2:14
Nikolai Andronov
Monday in Ferapontovo,
1963–64
Oil on canvas
140 × 173 cm

represent the art of Socialist Realism by artists only in one manner, one style.[49]

Some young Soviet artists responded to the perceived thaw in official policy with activities that anticipated the unofficial art movement of the 1960s. Thus, young Moscow sculptors Vadim Sidur (1924–1986), Vladimir Lemport (b. 1922), and Herbert Silins (b. 1926) organized a group of artists interested in modernist trends. Another group, calling itself The Icon, was founded at the Orlov Art Institute in Yeletz. And painters Anatolii Zverev (Pl. 4:7) and Vladimir Veisberg (1924–1985) (Fig. 2:15)—the former an unofficial artist, the latter an official "left-winger" highly criticized for his continuation of the traditions of the old avant-garde—began to sell their works directly to the Moscow intelligentsia and a few Western collectors.[50]

The liberalization of art policy continued despite occasional and possibly perfunctory warnings from some art leaders. Although the editors of *Literaturnaia gazeta* claimed that 1955 was the year that inaugurated a "general amnesty of all ideas,"[51] Boris Ioganson reminded artists to maintain the "Party spirit":

> We well know that recently some artists and art historians taking refuge in words about the necessity to encourage the development of diverse artistic personalities, have strived to revive non-ideological, pure aesthetic art. [But we must continue] . . . the struggle for Party spirit and nationality . . . [and for the] ideological purity of our art, the struggle with all kinds of deviation from the principles of Socialist Realism, be it aestheticism, formalism, naturalism, or the cult of pure form.[52]

This meant that one no longer had to paint according to one firm prescribed formula. Yet, one had to be careful and not push too far in one's experimentation, as officials were still grappling with how to delineate the precise parameters of Socialist Realism and were far from letting go.

Malenkov's resignation in 1955, promptly followed by the disgrace of his chief supporter, Minister of Culture Alexandrov, had no negative effect on this liberalizing trend. In fact, the calls for a break with the narrow and anti-historical approach to the representational arts continued to be heard.[53]

The Khrushchev thaw The upheaval in the arts, as in so many aspects of Soviet life, reached its climax with Khrushchev's Secret Speech at the Twentieth Communist Party Congress in 1956 which criticized Stalin's crimes against the Party and the people of the U.S.S.R. For the first time, Stalin's reputation as well as his policies were attacked from the highest podium in the nation. Khrushchev announced that there were "many roads to Socialism" and that "peaceful coexistence" with other countries was possible.

Immediately after Khrushchev's speech, on February 25, 1956, Suslov attacked the "cult of personality" as it pertained to the arts. In its place, he upheld the principle of collective leadership. He declared that under one-man rule, i.e., Stalin, "creative initiative had been inevitably stifled and crushed."[54] By this pronouncement, Suslov seemed to intimate that no individual could impose his artistic dogma on others under collective leadership.

Shortly after Khrushchev's Secret Speech, large paintings and busts of Stalin were removed from the Tretyakov Gallery in Moscow. Widespread attacks began against former artistic supporters of Stalin's dictums. Art historian Arkadii Ginevsky led some of the attacks, claiming that the "cult of personality had done considerable harm . . . [and had led to the creation of] pompous pictures bearing the imprint of machine production."[55] Reversing his stance of previous years, Gerasimov came out in favor of greater freedom of style and subject matter. Despite his earlier opposition to Impressionism, he now admitted its "technical" contributions to the history of painting. However, Gerasimov had become an embarrassment to the new policymakers. By the end of 1956, he was forced to resign from the presidency of the U.S.S.R. Academy of Arts.

On the organizational level, many other changes were taking place in Soviet art. The Philosophical Institute of the Soviet Academy of Sciences created a special section devoted to aesthetics, presumably to develop a new Party line on the arts. At the same time, the Ministry of Culture instituted a commission system to improve the economic status of the artists and to encourage them to create more new artworks. It further decreed that specialized stores be opened for the sale of paintings, prints, and sculpture. This decree established what were, in effect, art galleries, and Soviet art was sold publicly for the first time since the Stalin era had begun. Art was no longer to be treated only

as a form of propaganda, it was also a consumer item. In addition, spacious artists' studios were to be constructed in Moscow, Leningrad, and Kiev. Every effort was being made to improve the well-being of the Soviet artist.

Khrushchev's policy of "peaceful coexistence" and of "many roads to Socialism" created momentous changes in the arts. Because of the separation of technology from ideology, some technical developments utilized in Western art had become acceptable for use in creating Soviet art. Artists were hoping that similar liberalizing considerations would be applied to content, but the uprisings in Poland and the Hungarian Revolution put such tendencies on hold.[56] Nevertheless, the momentum created by the Secret Speech and its effects in all areas of the arts were irreversible. Artists knew they still had to be careful about violating the Party line, but they were not about to relinquish their newly gained freedom.

An assessment of the first four post-Stalin years shows an attempt to define a new Party line in art. The art establishment and its officials were clearly reevaluating Socialist Realism. They seemed to have agreed with philosopher Georg Lukács, who said: "Socialist Realism has turned into something that I call government-issue naturalism."[57] And it had become evident that such prominent Soviet artists as Arkadii Plastov (1893–1972), Martiros Sarian (1880–1972), Aleksandr Deineka (1899–1969), and Pavel Korin (1892–1972), who had all been attacked in the 1940s, could no longer be criticized as formalists and their works withheld from exhibitions. Thus, the general thrust was toward broadening the interpretation of Socialist Realism in art. It was agreed that experimentation in art could originate from new, though officially dictated, content, and that innovation in form was necessary when it augmented the approved content. At all times it was clearly stressed that the artist must remain the Party's helper in educating society. An artist could never lose sight of Marxist-Leninist theory, which he had to apply creatively to his artworks. However, a new liberalism would sweep Soviet art as Khrushchev gained increasing control of the Communist Party in the second half of the 1950s.

Fig. 2:15
Vladimir Veisberg
(Untitled), 1968
Oil on canvas
70 × 77 cm

Notes

1. A.V. Lunacharsky, *Lenin i iskusstvo: Vospominaniia*, vol. 2 of *Ob izobrazitel'nom iskusstve*, ed. T. Gureva (Moscow: Sovetskii Khudozhnik, 1967), p. 10.

2. G.V. Plekhanov, *Iskusstvo i obshchestvennaia zhizn'*, vol. 14 of *Sochineniia*, ed. D. Ryazanova (Moscow: Gosudarstvennoye Izdatel'stvo, 1924), p. 136.

3. A. Pavliuchenkov, "V.I. Lenin i izobrazitel'noe iskusstvo," *Iskusstvo* 4 (1975): 9–18. This article lists all decrees and activities concerning art that involved Lenin from 1918 to 1923. Examples of some decrees promulgated by Lenin are the 1918 decrees: (1) "Concerning the Removal of Monuments Erected in

Honor of the Tsars and Their Servants and the Planning of Monuments to the Russian Socialist Revolution," and (2) "Concerning the Allocation of One Million Rubles for the Erection of a Monument to Karl Marx."

4. Lunacharsky, *Lenin i iskusstvo*, p. 9.

5. Many organizations placed themselves at the service of the Communist regime. Such groups included the Futurists under the leadership of Vladimir Mayakovsky and literary groups like The Smithy and October.

6. Lunacharsky, *Lenin i iskusstvo*, p. 12.

7. V.I. Lenin, *Polnoe sobranie sochinenii* (5th ed.; Moscow: Gospolitizdat, 1959), vol. 41, pp. 304–5.

8. Evgenii Katzman, "Kak sozdavalsia i razvivalsia AKhRR," in *Zapiski khudozhnika* (Moscow: Akademiia Khudozhestv SSSR, 1962), p. 19.

9. "Deklaratsiia Assotsiatsii Khudozhnikov Revoliutsionnoi Rossii," in I.M. Gronsky and V.N. Perelman, comps., *Assotsiatsiia Khudozhnikov Revoliutsionnoi Rossii: Sbornik vospominanii, statei, dokumentov* (Moscow: Izobrazitel'noe Iskusstvo, 1973), p. 289.

10. Katzman, "Kak sozdavalsia i razvivalsia AKhRR," p. 32.

11. Ibid., p. 44.

12. "Deklaratsiia Assotsiatsii Khudozhnikov Revoliutsionnoi Rossii," p. 289.

13. Joseph Stalin, "XVI S'ezd Kommunisticheskoi Partii Sovetskogo Soiuza," *Pravda*, June 27, 1930.

14. Donald D. Egbert, "Communism and the Arts in Russia" (Princeton University, 1964, mimeographed), p. 181.

15. "O perestroike literaturno-khudozhestvennykh organizatsii," in Gronsky and Perelman, comps., *Assotsiasiia Khudozhnikov Revoliutsionnoi Rossii*, pp. 329–30.

16. For an overview of the artworks of this period, see A.G. Fedotova, *Zhivopis' Pervoi Piatiletki* (Leningrad: Khudozhnik RSFSR, 1981).

17. "Putanitsa vmesto musyki," *Pravda*, Jan. 28, 1936.

18. Joseph Stalin, "XVIII S'ezd Kommunisticheskoi Partii Sovetskogo Soiuza," *Pravda*, Mar. 11, 1939.

19. Following the takeover of the Baltic states, Estonia, Latvia, and Lithuania, there was an ideological "cleansing" of the arts and many "noncompliant" artists were sent to prison, to Siberia, or worse.

20. Egbert, "Communism and the Arts in Russia," p. 311.

21. Aleksandr Gerasimov, "Za Sovetskii patriotizm v iskusstve," *Pravda*, Feb. 10, 1949.

22. Joseph Stalin, "Marksizm i voprosy lingvistiki," *Pravda*, June–Aug. 1950.

23. "Piataia sessiia Akademii Khudozhestv SSSR," *Iskusstvo* 3 (1953): 3.

24. B.V. Veimarn and O.I. Sopotzinsky, eds., *Sovetskoe izobrazitel'noe iskusstvo: 1917–1941* (Moscow: Iskusstvo, 1977), p. 13.

25. "O perestroike literaturno-khudozhestvennykh organizatsii," pp. 329–30.

26. "Novye formy organizatsii tvorcheskoi zhizni," *Iskusstvo* 9 (1967): 2.

27. Vitalii S. Manin, Secretary, U.S.S.R. Union of Artists, interview with the author, Moscow, Dec. 15, 1989; additional interview material provided by Aleksandr Sitnikov, member, Russian Union of Artists, March 1993.

28. Another term now employed to refer to such work is the "other art." The recent two-part catalogue *Drugoe Iskusstvo: Moscow, 1956–76* includes one hundred recognized "other" artists in Moscow. When other parts of the Soviet Union are included, the number significantly increases.

29. For additional information about the Soviet art bureaucracy, see Elena Kornetchuk, "The Organizational Dimension of Soviet Art," in *The Politics of Soviet Arts* (Ann Arbor, Mich.: UMI Press, 1982), pp. 54–69.

30. G.M. Malenkov, *Otchetnyi doklad XIX S'ezda Partii o rabote TsK VKP(b)* (Moscow: Gospolitizdat, 1952), p. 73.

31. G. Nedoshivin, "O probleme tipicheskogo v zhivopisi," *Iskusstvo* 1 (1953): 20.

32. Ibid.

33. "Sovetskoe izobrazitel'noe iskusstvo v 1952 godu: O vsesoiuznoi khudozhestvennoi vystavke," *Iskusstvo* 1 (1953): 3.

34. Camilla Gray, *The Russian Experiment in Art, 1863–1922* (New York: Harry N. Abrams, 1962), p. 190.

35. Artists included in the Arefiev Group: Rikhard Vasmi, Aleksandr Arefiev, Valentin Gramov, Vladimir Shagin, and Sholom Shvarts.

36. *Iskusstvo* 1 (1953): cover.

37. "Ot Tsentral'nogo Komiteta Kommunisticheskoi Partii Sovetskogo Soiuza, Soveta Ministrov Soiuznykh SSR i Presidiuma Verkhovnogo Soveta SSSR," *Iskusstvo* 1 (1953).

38. "Otvetstvennost' khudozhnika pered narodom," *Iskusstvo* 4 (1953): 4.

39. M. Kurilko, "Na uroven' trebovanii naroda. Zametki o Vsesoiuznoi khudozhestvennoi vystavke," *Komsomol'skaia Pravda*, Jan. 31, 1953.

40. Konstantin Paustovsky, "Mysli, spornye i besspornye," *Literaturnaia gazeta* (May 20, 1953).

41. Ilya Erenburg, "O rabote pisatelia," *Znamia* 10 (1953): 165–66.

42. Aram Khachaturian, "O tvorcheskoi smelosti i vdokhnovenii," *Sovetskaia muzyka* 11 (1953): 7–13.

43. Dmitrii Shostakovich, "'Radost' tvorcheskikh iskanii," *Sovetskaia muzyka* 1 (1954): 40–42.

44. N. Dmitrieva, "Nekotorye voprosy estetiki," *Iskusstvo* 3 (1953): 67.

45. E. Polishchuk, "Problema konflikta v sovetskoi siuzhetnoi kartine," *Iskusstvo* 1 (1954): 29.

46. Boris Ioganson, "Temam sovremennosti—dostoinoe reshenie," *Iskusstvo* 3 (1954): 5.

47. S. Donskoi, "Trends in Contemporary Soviet Sculpture," *Bulletin of the Institute for the Study of the History and Culture of the USSR* 7 (1954): 37.

48. "Po Sovetskomu Soiuzu," *Iskusstvo* 3 (1956): 79.

49. "Podgotovka k Vsesoiuznoi Khudozhestvennoi vystavke-vazhneishaia zadacha tvorcheskikh soiuzov," *Iskusstvo* 5 (1955): 4.

50. "Za posledovatel'noe provedenie printsipov sotsialisticheskogo realizma," *Iskusstvo* 4 (1954): 3–4.

51. *Literaturnaia gazeta* (Apr. 23, 1955).

52. Boris Ioganson, "Vsesoiuznaia khudozhestvennaia vystavka 1954 goda: Vsenarodnyi smotr," *Iskusstvo* 2 (1955): 10.

53. "On the Question of the Literary and the Artistic Treatment of the Typical," *Kommunist* (Dec. 1955): 12–24.

54. Mikhail Suslov, "Rech' tovarishcha M.A. Suslova," *Pravda*, Feb. 17, 1956, pp. 8–9.

55. Arkadii Ginevsky, "Na kanune s'ezda," *Iskusstvo* 3 (1956): 21.

56. V.M. Molotov, "Vystuplenie V.M. Molotova, protiv anarkhii v intellektual'nom proizvodstve," *Sovestkaia kul'tura*, Nov. 20, 1956.

57. "Gyorgy Lucacs on Stalinism and Art," *East Europe* (May 13, 1964): 23.

3 | Art as politics and politics in art

Michael Scammell

Introduction The era of unofficial or nonconformist art in the Soviet Union is generally agreed to run from about 1956 (the year of Khrushchev's Secret Speech) to about 1986 (when Gorbachev introduced his policies of *glasnost* and *perestroika*). It thus spanned a period of thirty years, during which the Soviet Union rose to unprecedented heights of power and self-confidence, extending its ideas and influence into every corner of the globe, and then with dizzying speed imploded and collapsed in a welter of self-doubt and recrimination, its empire gone and even its viability as a state called into question.

Clearly, the causes of this dramatic collapse have to be sought in a variety of factors: economic weakness, military overextension, a backward social and industrial structure, and the pressure of competition with the capitalist world. But an equally important element in the state's disintegration was the draining of meaning from the ruling Marxist-Leninist ideology, which sapped the confidence of the country's leaders and led in the long run to the total loss of the state's legitimacy. In this process of ideological erosion, the arts played an important role. Literature, the traditional keystone of Russian culture, was the arena in which most of the important battles were first fought and was also the leading instrument of change, but a significant part in this transformation was also played by the visual arts.

The problem faced by painters, sculptors, graphic designers, and their colleagues was that Soviet culture, as it had developed under Stalin, no longer offered the means for the development of their personal talents or for them to engage with the world in a meaningful way. Though they were lavishly provided with the social and material prerequisites for creating art, these artists were deprived of any autonomy in their choice of subject matter, artistic strategy, or interpretation of meaning. They were hemmed in and tied down by a rigid application of the sterile doctrine of Socialist Realism.[1] The dogmatic application of this style blocked any creative encounters with their nation's past or present, with religion or spiritual values, with contemporary artistic developments elsewhere in the world, or even with their own subjective psychologies.

It was the search for a way out of this dead end that led to the emergence of the "unofficial" or "nonconformist" artists. This was never a unified movement or group, but the artists were bound by common problems and shared goals. Inevitably, as the very name given to them implies, their aspirations and activities bore a pronounced political coloration (despite their sincere protestations to the contrary). Indeed, the terms "unofficial" and "nonconformist" could not help but carry a political dimension, since the "un" and the "non" depended for their definition on the existence of a politically sanctioned official and conformist art to which this alternative art was opposed.[2]

The Khrushchev "thaw," 1956–66 In the context of the stagnation of all intellectual and cultural life under Stalin, his death in 1953 and the rapid rise to power of Nikita Khrushchev brought about a minor revolution in the lives of visual artists. In particular, Khrushchev's Secret Speech of 1956, in which he launched his campaign of modernization and de-Stalinization, marked a major break with the past. This also initiated a period of liberalization and relaxation that looked as if it would lead, and sooner rather than later, to an era of vastly increased freedom of expression.

At first, this optimism seemed justified. Khrushchev understood the perniciousness of the Iron Curtain, and one of his first acts was to open up channels through which Soviet intellectuals could begin to receive information about Western intellectual and cultural life. A potent symbol of this new development was the Sixth World Festival of Youth and Students, held in Moscow in the summer of 1957. Three pavilions at the exhibition site in Sokolniki Park were stocked with over 4,500 works of art by young artists from fifty-two countries. The quality of these works was uneven, but for the first time in over twenty-five years Soviet artists were able to learn about the latest developments in the West. The profusion of styles, the vitality of imagination, the variety of experimentation, and the sheer freedom and exuberance of Western artists was overwhelming to the Soviet artists.

Equally significant was the fact that they were able to watch young foreign painters working in specially built studios, and even to paint alongside them for a few hours. Vladimir Nemukhin, who was to become an influential figure in the unofficial art movement, later commented that the Soviet spectators were able "to recognize in foreign artists their own selves and their own strivings."[3] Anatolii Zverev (1931–1986), a young art student who also later became an unofficial artist, was inspired by watching American Abstract Expressionist Garry Colman at work. As a consequence, Zverev introduced abstract elements into his portraits along with a greater degree of spontaneity and emotionalism. The results were not all like Socialist Realism, and this disturbed his professors.[4]

Another important influence on Soviet painters was the exhibition of works by Pablo Picasso that opened in Moscow in October 1956 and moved to Leningrad the following year. Picasso seemed "safe" to the authorities, first because he was a renowned member of the Communist Party in France, and second because the works in question had lain for decades in the vaults of Soviet museums, unexhibited and unappreciated. In addition, they already "belonged" to the U.S.S.R., in the formal sense of the word. The impact of these hitherto proscribed works was colossal, however. As with the youth festival, huge lines of visitors formed each day to view the paintings. Meetings and discussions were organized throughout the city to debate the meaning of Picasso's work. The idea that abstract and nonfigurative art was not only possible but perhaps even acceptable was beginning to take root.

This led to demands that the works of Russia's own modern masters (Malevich, Kandinsky, Chagall, Tatlin, Rodchenko, and so on) be put on display. For a variety of reasons these demands were not met, but they reminded everyone—particularly young Soviet artists—of the glorious achievements of the Russian avant-garde. This was a national heritage to be proud of, and perhaps to build on. Closer investigation revealed that not all the prominent artists of the revolutionary period had died, emigrated, or been incarcerated in labor camps. A few continued, practicing what the writer Isaac Babel once called "the genre of silence."[5] With surprising freedom and boldness, they painted, drew, and designed in private.[6] Painters like Malevich, Rodchenko, and Pavel Filonov had created works in the late 1930s and early 1940s that provided a vital bridge to that most glorious era of Russian art, and some of their colleagues were still alive in the 1950s.[7] Meanwhile, a small number of modernist painters, not directly connected with the revolutionary avant-garde

(e.g., Robert Falk and Aleksandr Tyshler), were also rediscovered and studied by younger artists.[8]

Much of this ferment occurred within the confines of the official art establishment of the time, though it was never a mainstream movement. In Leningrad, Vladimir Sterligov (1905–1973), a former student of Malevich, and his wife Tatiana Glebova (1900–1985), a student of Filonov, gathered a group of young painters around them at the Herzen Pedagogical Institute, and began to introduce them to concepts of organic form and geometrical abstraction. In Moscow, some of the more adventurous members of the Moscow Section of the Artists' Union formed their own Group of Eight, in which they also experimented with abstraction (e.g., Eduard Shteinberg, Vladimir Veisberg, and Pavel Nikonov), or painted Impressionist portraits that emphasized light and color at the expense of realistic form (e.g., Boris Birger). Sculptors Ernst Neizvestny (b. 1925) and Vadim Sidur (1924–1986) began to push their monumental designs in a more Expressionistic direction, and art teacher Eli Beliutin (b. 1925) established a semi-official school where Abstract Expressionism gradually became the most favored style. At a higher level, the First Congress of Soviet Artists elected a decidedly liberal board of directors to the Artists' Union in 1957, forcing out a number of hardliners who had been enforcing fidelity to Socialist Realism.

Despite certain setbacks, such as the attack on Boris Pasternak in 1958 for publishing *Doctor Zhivago* abroad, the liberalization of the arts continued under Khrushchev, and reached a high point during the years 1959–62. Two young poets, Evgenii Yevtushenko and Andrei Voznesensky, became practically "matinee idols" through the force of their controversial verse and their power as inspired public readers. The annual Poetry Day drew hundreds of thousands of young people to concert halls to listen to their favorite poets. Young novelists like Vasilii Aksyonov became bestsellers with Salinger-like stories that gave vent to the angst and discontent of the younger generation. Issues like anti-Semitism, the devastation of the countryside, the destruction of churches, and the ravages of industrialization began to be discussed in print. In the fall of 1962, permission was given to publish Alexander Solzhenitsyn's *One Day in the Life of Ivan Denisovich*, which was to cause a sensation with its revelations about the labor camps.

There was excited talk among intellectuals of an end to censorship and the abandonment of Socialist Realism as the only permitted style. In the art world, the climax came in December 1962, just before the publication of Solzhenitsyn, with the opening of a huge exhibition at the Manezh of work by members of the Moscow Section of the Artists' Union, called "Thirty Years of Moscow Art." Although the vast majority of the works exhibited were still painted in standard Socialist Realist style, there were a surprising number that showed signs of independence and innovation. The exhibition also included a selection of paintings by some of the experimental artists of the 1930s and 1940s (including Falk, Tyshler, David Shterenberg, and Nikolai Drevin), and several works by members of the Group of Eight (like Birger, Nikonov, and Veisberg). More daringly, after the exhibition had already opened, sculptor Neizvestny and members of Eli Beliutin's studio, including Sophia Shiller (b. 1940) and several other experimental artists, were invited to display their work in three small rooms on the second floor. It seemed as if experiment and innovation were being cautiously welcomed at last, and that even the more daring painters and sculptors would find a niche in the official Soviet art world.

A day or two after the Beliutin works were hung, Khrushchev himself made an official visit to the exhibition, accompanied by several high Party officials. As he toured the main halls he seemed visibly annoyed by a number of the semi-abstract paintings by Falk, Shterenberg, and members of the Group of Eight. But nothing unusual occurred until he was ushered into the three rooms upstairs. Almost immediately his manner changed. After only a cursory glance at the walls, he exploded with righteous wrath:

> As long as I am Chairman of the Council of Ministers we are going to support a genuine art. Are you pederasts or normal people? I'll be perfectly honest with you. We aren't going to give a *kopeck* for pictures painted by jackasses. History can be our judge. For the time being history has put us at the head of this state, and we have to answer for everything that goes on in it. Therefore we are going to maintain a strict policy in art. . . . Just give me a list of those of you who want to go abroad, to the so-called "free world." We'll give you foreign passports tomorrow, and you can get out. Your prospects here are zero. What's hung here is simply anti-Soviet. It's amoral. Art should ennoble the individual and arouse him to action. And what have you set out here? Who painted this picture? I want to talk to him. What's the good of a picture like this? To cover urinals with? The people and government have taken a lot of trouble with you, and you pay them back with this crap.[9]

Opinions differ as to whether the last-minute invitation to exhibit Beliutin's work had represented a genuine desire to bring the experimentalists into the main fold of the art establishment or whether it was simply a provocation planned by reactionaries who knew of Khrushchev's impending visit. Whatever the case, the government's reaction was swift and negative. Three days after Khrushchev's visit, the Moscow Section of the Artists' Union was officially censured for permitting "formalism" and, during the following months, a thorough purge of liberals in the artistic establishment was carried out. Several of the nonconformist artists were officially reprimanded (including Birger, Veisberg, and Sidur), and some who were still students were expelled from school. Those who escaped public censure retired to their studios in silence, hoping to wait out the storm.

Throughout 1963, liberals in the arts were on the defensive; censorship was tightened again and it looked as if the advances made during the thaw would be reversed. This seemed even more likely when Khrushchev himself got into trouble as a result of Soviet humiliation over the Cuban Missile Crisis, and was replaced in 1964 by Leonid Brezhnev. One of the reasons given for ousting Khrushchev was the ferment and instability provoked by de-Stalinization, and hardliners pointed specifically to the arts as a center of disaffection. A struggle ensued between defenders of the liberal opening and advocates of greater discipline, and for two to three years the outcome seemed uncertain. The writings of Solzhenitsyn became a symbolic battleground in this fight, and repeated attempts were made by liberals to publish his two big novels, *The First Circle* and *Cancer Ward*. In the end, they were not published, and in the fall of 1965 a typescript of *The First Circle* and other unpublished works by Solzhenitsyn were confiscated during a raid by the KGB. That same week, two relatively unknown young writers, Andrei Siniavsky and Yulii Daniel, were arrested and accused of smuggling out stories and publishing them pseudonymously in the West.

The Brezhnev reaction, 1966–76 The public trial of Siniavsky and Daniel in January 1966 resulted in their being sentenced to terms in the labor camps. This was clearly intended as a demonstration to all intellectuals that there would be severe consequences for those who did not toe the official line. And, indeed, this trial heralded a much harsher government line on nonconformity in the arts. It served notice that all possible measures would be employed to maintain discipline and obedience. On the official level, this policy succeeded. Remaining liberals and liberal sympathizers were gradually weeded out of all the official unions, committees, schools, and journals. Ideological purity was restored. But on another level, and in a quite unforeseen fashion, this policy backfired spectacularly.

The problems for the authorities began when the courageous behavior of Siniavsky and Daniel in court inspired vigorous anticensorship protests nationally and internationally. In the Soviet Union, this spontaneous response led directly to the formation of a highly vocal dissident movement. Further arrests and trials only fanned the flames of protest. Thus, even though the authorities succeeded in imposing discipline and conformity on public life by the end of the decade, an underground culture had come into being that was self-sustaining and even expanding, despite the often cruel acts of repression.

Independent-minded writers gradually stopped submitting their works for publication in official Soviet outlets and started circulating them in *samizdat* or sending them abroad (the very thing the Siniavsky-Daniel trial had been intended to stop). Underground newspapers and journals came into existence to publish this unofficial literature, and to chronicle the repression of intellectuals, religious groups, national minorities, and nonconformists of every stripe. Discussion groups met regularly in private to discuss subjects that were forbidden in public, and a whole alternative world of artistic, intellectual and political exploration opened up in opposition to official culture.

Many painters, sculptors, and graphic artists participated in this alternative culture. Very soon, an unofficial art movement came into being that paralleled and intersected with the larger dissident movement. The initiative shifted from quasi-respectable groups like the Group of Eight and the Beliutin circle to unofficial artists who had never been a proper part of official culture at all. Of these, the Lianozovo Group (including Lydia Masterkova, Vladimir Nemukhin, Dmitri Plavinsky, and Oscar Rabin), named for the small village outside Moscow where most of them lived and worked, proved to be the most active and influential. Most members of this group earned their living as illustrators and graphic artists and did their serious easel work at home in their spare time. They did not participate in the painting section of the Artists' Union at all, and consequently could not exhibit in official galleries. Instead, they got their exposure to the public mainly through small exhibitions in private apartments that began to be held in the early 1960s. A Moscow art historian and critic, Ilya Tsirlin, who gave informal lectures and led discussions on contemporary art in the West, was the first to show work by members of this group. Sviatoslav Richter, the celebrated pianist, showed works by another unofficial artist, Dmitrii Krasnopevtsev

Fig. 3:1
Evgenii Kropivnitsky
(Portrait of a Young Girl)
variant from the 1959
watercolor, 1973
Pen and ink and colored
pencil on paper
25.5 × 20 cm

(1925–1995), and the composer Andrei Volkonsky held an exhibition of paintings by the older painter and poet Evgenii Kropivnitsky, the intellectual guru of the Lianozovites (Fig. 3:1).

Unofficial exhibitions were the visual equivalent of *samizdat*, but were physically cumbersome and required much greater effort and resources than the typing of manuscripts. Hence, the role played in collecting and exhibiting unofficial art by prominent figures in the cultural establishment acquired a special significance: only successful writers and performers had the money or time to buy art and put it on display. This fashion also spread to some of the more adventurous scientists, who became influential patrons not only by virtue of their relative wealth, but also because of their privileged position in Soviet society. They were also able to find unconventional premises for art exhibitions. As early as 1960, it seems, a way was found to exhibit unofficial art in scientific research institutes and their club premises. In 1962, the year of the Manezh exhibition, at least two exhibitions of unofficial art were held on academic premises in Moscow (including one by the Beliutin Studio Group). By 1965, other exhibitions in Moscow had been held at the prestigious Kurchatov Institute of Atomic Physics, the Physics Institute, the Institute of Biochemistry, and the Institute of Hygiene and Occupational Health.

In Leningrad, the situation was similar. The thaw generally had a weaker impact there than in Moscow, mainly because the ideological vigilance of the Party was greater, but the Moscow Beliutin group had its counterpart in a similar group of young artists gathered around Vladimir Sterligov.[10]

As the ideological net tightened after 1966, the unofficial artists grew increasingly dissatisfied. Their ranks were now being swelled by those who formally remained members of the Artists' Union but were excluded from exhibitions, including most of the Group of Eight and the Beliutin Studio Group. Small informal exhibitions were certainly a defense against complete anonymity, but they were invariably improvised, were usually held at short notice without publicity, and were always subject to sudden cancellation at the whim of the authorities. Members of the Lianozovo Group were particularly restive, since none of them had ever participated in any Artists' Union activities and they had paid a high price by staying outside it in order to emphasize their independence. Their informal leader, Oscar Rabin (b. 1928), had in fact achieved a breakthrough by becoming the first ever unofficial artist to have his work shown abroad, first as a participant in an otherwise fully official show in London in 1964, and more significantly with a one-man show at the Arleigh Gallery in San Francisco in 1965.[11] Yet in Moscow his work could not be seen at all.[12] Consequently, in the increasingly activist climate of the mid-1960s, Rabin and his colleagues decided to challenge the authorities by adopting a higher profile and pressing harder to get their paintings exhibited.

Their first attempt came in January 1967, when a young admirer and collector, Alexander Glezer, organized a group show of twelve artists at the Druzhba Workers' Club in an outlying district of Moscow. With a mixture of luck and *chutzpah*, Glezer succeeded in hoodwinking the censors into letting him print tickets, and he invited several foreign diplomats and journalists to see the show. This was in recognition of the fact that a few of the more enterprising foreigners in Moscow had already begun to visit apartment exhibitions and even to buy some of the work on display, thus creating a small market that encouraged and helped to support the unofficial artists. The presence of journalists also ensured that the show would be publicized abroad, if not in Moscow itself. In any event, the show was closed down by the local Party committee after only two days, and four months later was harshly attacked in the art press. A Party decree was passed, specifying that in the future all art exhibitions in the capital would have to be approved by the Moscow Artists' Union.

In March 1969, the Lianozovites tried again with a smaller group show at the Institute of World Economics and International Relations, but the Party secretary closed it down after only forty-five minutes. Oleg Tselkov, who had moved from Leningrad to Moscow, tried a one-man show at the Architects' Center in 1971; this lasted a mere fifteen minutes before being banned. Increasingly, it began to look as if the unofficial artists had reached a dead end. As with most factions of the dissident movement, they were subjected to regular surveillance by KGB operatives, infiltrated by informers, and harassed whenever they threatened to step out of line. In the aftermath of the invasion of Czechoslovakia and suppression of the movement to establish "Socialism with a human face" (which had made a deep impression on Soviet artists and intellectuals),[13] Soviet society seemed headed for a new ice age. This was confirmed by the sensational deportation of Alexander Solzhenitsyn in 1974 for publishing volume one of his labor-camp history, *The Gulag Archipelago*.

Solzhenitsyn's expulsion unleashed a new, even more extreme campaign of harassment against dissidents. One of the leading unofficial painters in Leningrad, Evgenii Rukhin (1943–1976), who had made a point of joining forces with the Lianozovites, twice had his windows smashed while away on visits to Moscow, and was warned by the police not to "leave home so often." Another Leningrad painter, Yurii Zharkikh (b. 1938), was detained on the street by the KGB and threatened with a trial if he did not denounce his friends. Two young artists in Moscow, Vitaly Komar and Alexander Melamid, were showing their work to a group of friends at home when the police burst in and hauled everyone present to the police station for questioning. Oscar Rabin was temporarily arrested and falsely accused of stealing a watch. For several months he was hounded by anonymous telephone callers asking to borrow copies of *The Gulag Archipelago*. It was all as Rabin had predicted after Solzhenitsyn's arrest: "Now he's off their hands they'll be free to turn against us."

It was Rabin who proposed what turned out to be a momentous breakthrough. As early as 1969, he had suggested that the best way for the unofficial artists to get round restrictions on their exhibitions was to hold an open-air show. His colleagues had rejected the idea, fearing that it would provoke an even worse confrontation with the authorities. However, the new sanctions against them suggested that they now had nothing to lose. Accordingly, on September 2, 1974, the artists sent a letter to the Moscow City Council informing them of their intention to hold an exhibition on a vacant lot in the Moscow suburb

Fig. 3:2
"First Fall Open-Air Show of
Paintings" ("The Bulldozer
Exhibition"), Moscow,
September 15, 1974
Photo courtesy of Sarah
Burke, San Antonio

Fig. 3:2
"First Fall Open-Air Show of
Paintings" ("The Bulldozer
Exhibition"), Moscow,
September 15, 1974
Photo courtesy of Sarah
Burke, San Antonio

Fig. 3:3
"First Fall Open-Air Show of
Paintings" ("The Bulldozer
Exhibition"), Moscow,
September 15, 1974
Photo by Vladimir Sychev,
courtesy of the photographer

of Cheryomushki. Their choice of such an obscure site was guided by a desire to avoid the all-encompassing regulation against "disturbing public order," a law that had been used repeatedly by the authorities to ban dissident demonstrations. Three days after the letter was dispatched, the artists were summoned by a Council official. He told them that, although there was no regulation specifically prohibiting such an exhibition, they would be well-advised to call the whole thing off.

The artists declined. The original Lianozovo Group had now convinced dozens of other artists to join them, and their mood was determined. After returning home from the meeting, they sent out invitations to friends and selected Western journalists. On the appointed day, Sunday, September 15, 1974, the artists arrived at the site with their canvases and easels, only to be met by a bunch of "volunteer workers," who pretended to be cleaning up the lot that very day (Fig. 3:2). Suddenly, the "workers" jumped on some of the artists, wrestled them to the ground, snatched their pictures away, and threw them into dumptrucks, which made off at high speed. When some of the artists resisted, bulldozers were brought up and ran over many of the pictures, including two by Rabin. Water cannons were used to control the crowd and to clear the site, drenching artists and spectators alike. Rukhin, Rabin, Rabin's son Aleksandr, and Nadezhda Elskaia were arrested. Fifteen pictures were mutilated (Fig. 3:3) and another three were burnt in an impromptu fire started by the "workers."[14]

It was a harsh encounter, but by inviting Western journalists to witness the scene and thus ensuring that pictures and accounts of it would be flashed around the world, the artists had clearly outwitted the authorities. They followed it up with an ultimatum, threatening to return to the site in two weeks unless they were allowed to exhibit elsewhere. After ten days of hard bargaining,

the Moscow City Council conceded permission for them to hold a show in Izmailovsky Park, in another suburb of Moscow. On September 29, the "Second Fall Open-Air Show of Paintings," as it was called on the typewritten invitations, opened triumphantly. This time, over seventy artists took part and thousands of visitors turned up in festive mood to gape at the forbidden fruit (Fig. 3:4).

Buoyed by their victory, the unofficial artists applied for, and were granted, permission to stage exhibitions of their work in official galleries in both Moscow and Leningrad. The Leningrad exhibition opened as planned on December 22, when fifty-three painters exhibited 206 works at a four-day show at the Gaz Palace of Culture. But in Moscow the artists refused to proceed. Three young painters from the Izmailovo exhibition had been committed to insane asylums, and two well-known unofficial artists had been threatened with similar treatment. Two other artists were abruptly called up for military service, and Glezer, a principal organizer of the show, was detained and threatened by the KGB and then beaten up in the street on his way home.

The Moscow artists called on their Leningrad colleagues to join them again in a single, large joint exhibition, and a public announcement was made. The authorities responded by promising separate exhibitions in Moscow and Leningrad, containing only the best of the unofficial artists, and excluding the unknowns. The artists reluctantly agreed to this plan, though the option of a later joint exhibition was retained. The Moscow exhibition opened in February at the Beekeeping Pavilion of the Exhibition of Economic Achievements, but the Leningrad show never materialized. In response, the Moscow and Leningrad groups announced again that they would hold a big open-air show in Leningrad on May 25 to match the earlier one in Izmailovsky Park. A few days later, Rabin was expelled from the Moscow Illustrators' and Draftsmen's Union (his only guarantee of freelance work and

Fig. 3:4
"Second Fall Open-Air Show
of Paintings," Izmailovsky
Park, Moscow,
September 29, 1974
Photo by Grigorii Verkhovsky

Fig. 3:5 (*far right*)
Interior view of the Palace of
Culture Pavilion at the
Exhibition of Economic
Achievements, Moscow,
September 1975
Photo by Grigorii Verkhovsky

welfare benefits) and his son Aleksandr was suddenly pronounced fit for military service (despite an earlier exemption on medical grounds). In Leningrad, three prominent members of the artists' action group were called in for questioning by the KGB and threatened with arrest if the exhibition went ahead. The organizers bowed to pressure and the show was cancelled.

It looked as if the unofficial artists had been defeated, but in the fall of 1975 two separate exhibitions were again allowed, one in Moscow in September, for ten days, at the Exhibition of Economic Achievements (Fig. 3:5), and one in Leningrad in October, also for ten days, at the Nevsky District Palace of Culture. Both shows were heavily attended. But in February 1976, the Leningrad artists were informed that there would be no more independent exhibitions and that, in the future, they would have to go through the Artists' Union. Their cause suffered a further setback when one of their two leaders, Evgenii Rukhin, died in a mysterious fire in his studio. Police investigations took the form of an inquisition of unofficial artists, and an attempt to stage an exhibition in his memory was crushed.

In Moscow, the attempt to coopt the unofficial artists took a different and more benign form. Several unofficial artists, including even some practitioners of Pop Art, were allowed to participate in an unconventional exhibition organized by the Moscow branch of the Artists' Union in 1976. That same year, the Union of Moscow Graphic Artists established a painting section specially designed to accommodate the unofficial artists, and even sanctioned an exhibition of their work called "Seven Artists." Three of the seven artists were also included in an officially sponsored exhibition of Soviet art at the Metropolitan Museum in New York in the spring of 1977.

The era of stagnation, 1976–86 If it looked by 1977 as if official channels were opening up for the unofficial artists,

the opposite was in fact true. In the first place, the opening was very small and selective: the majority of the unofficial artists were still not admitted to any union, were not permitted to exhibit in official galleries, and continued to be restricted to apartment exhibitions. Secondly, the point of the "opening" was not to embrace the unofficial artists and allow them to widen the horizons of the art world, but rather to absorb and stifle them, and to ensure that they no longer stimulated unrest and dissent in others. The exhibitions of the mid-1970s, therefore, were not the harbingers of better things to come, but a swan song, a last empty gesture before the unofficial artists were relegated once again to limbo.

The result—on the surface at least—was a decade of stifling conservatism, reaction, and conformity. The larger dissident movement was to all intents and purposes crushed. Many of its leaders had been arrested and incarcerated in labor camps or, as in the notorious case of Andrei Sakharov, sent into internal exile. In addition, an ingenious new tactic by the government allowed an increasing number of dissidents to emigrate to the West. By the mid-1980s, over one hundred leading Russian writers had moved to the West, including the Nobel-Prize winning Solzhenitsyn, the future Nobel Prize winner Joseph Brodsky, and such outstanding authors as Andrei Siniavsky, Vladimir Voinovich, and Vasilii Aksyonov. Also in the West were ballet dancers Rudolf Nureyev, Mikhail Baryshnikov, and Natalia Makarova; musicians Vladimir Ashkenazy, Mstislav Rostropovich, and Maxim Shostakovich; the film director Andrei Tarkovsky, the theatre director Yuri Liubimov, and chess grandmaster Viktor Korchnoi. For every one of these famous artists, there were scores who were less well known but who had also fled to the West.

Among painters and sculptors the situation was similar. By the late 1970s, Mikhail Chemiakin (b. 1943) had established an enviable reputation for himself in Paris and New York. Ernst Neizvestny had acquired studios in New York and Stockholm. Oscar Rabin, Aleksandr Rabin (b. 1951), Valentina Kropivnitskaia, Eduard Zelenin (b. 1938), Oleg Tselkov, and a host of others were in Paris. Lydia Masterkova, Igor Kholin (b. 1923), and Oleg Prokofiev (b. 1928) were in London. And in the following years, Komar and Melamid, Leonid Lamm (b. 1928), Rimma Gerlovina (b. 1951) and Valerii Gerlovin (b. 1945), Leonid Sokov (b. 1941), and Vagrich Bakhchanyan (b. 1938) moved to New York. Others went to France, Israel, Austria, Scandinavia, or other parts of the United States.

These departures did not end the unofficial art movement in the Soviet Union. On the contrary, the places of the émigrés were taken by colleagues or younger people, and the artists who did go acted as a living bridge between those who stayed and Western culture. Many of the artists who remained behind were also fortified by the fact that their paintings were being exhibited in the West in ever-increasing numbers. This was partly because of the activities of collectors like George Costakis, Nina Stevens, Alexander Glezer (who emigrated with his collection in 1976), and Norton Dodge, who not only went to great lengths to acquaint themselves with the unofficial artists and buy their work, but also organized exhibitions of non-conformist artists. Western diplomats and journalists who had visited the studios of the unofficial artists, attended exhibitions and purchased paintings while serving in Moscow (and later Leningrad), also began to lend works for these exhibitions in the West; and, last but not least, those artists who had emigrated demonstrated their solidarity by helping their friends to get shown in the West as well.

Meanwhile, younger artists in the Soviet Union were exploring avenues that made them less dependent on official art organizations for their activities. A flourishing Conceptual Art movement came into existence with its own practitioners and its own self-selected audience. Happenings and performances were staged either in private apartments or at open-air sites in woods and fields, beyond the vigilant eyes of the authorities. Art photography attracted many artists. Albums and small-scale works that could be passed from hand to hand, and depended on visual puns for their impact, became a popular vehicle of expression. And the youngest generation of all, many of whom belonged to the loosely associated group of the *semidesiatniki* ("seventies artists"), began to subvert Socialist Realism from the inside by subtly distorting its canons, ironizing its subjects, and satirizing its political message, while taking advantage of their relatively privileged position as "youth artists." They were the breakthrough generation, who succeeded in eroding the official art establishment by joining and deconstructing it, thus converging with the unofficial artists and preparing the way for the explosion of freedom that came with *perestroika*.

Art as politics As this brief history makes clear, the development of the unofficial art movement was unavoidably involved with politics from its very inception, whether its members wished it or not. Indeed, it could not be otherwise in a society where every kind of artistic activity was strictly controlled and prescribed from the very outset. As has frequently been noted, in a system where everything is defined as political, it is impossible to escape politics, since the very attempt to do so is itself a political act. And it was true on the everyday practical level: to operate as an artist in the Soviet Union, receive studio space, purchase materials, and have the right to defer another job, one had to undergo the appropriate academic training and belong to the appropriate union. This was equally true in the realm of creativity: in order to pursue such a career one was obliged to submit one's work to ideological controls in terms of style, content, and meaning.

Not surprisingly, the logic of this equation was not immediately apparent to painters and sculptors at the beginning of this period. In the aftermath of Stalin's death, as we have seen, creative artists of all kinds were seduced by Khrushchev's liberalization into thinking that the official ideology, and therefore official practice, could be stretched and modified to accommodate their creative needs. Initially, these needs were appropriately modest, since everyone realized that a certain gradualism was inevitable. Moreover, artists of all descriptions had been traumatized by the terror that accompanied Stalin's rule. But as the situation eased and as artists began to explore the new avenues opening up to them, they became bolder and more demanding, especially when pressure on them was reintroduced. In a certain sense, the artists were "educated" by the authorities into realizing that their work was more political than they had thought. Once this idea had sunk in, many of them followed the logic of this realization and became truly political, concluding that they were damned if they did, and damned if they did not.

But, in the beginning, this was not the rule. When the Group of Eight started exhibiting their works, for instance, their experiments were entirely formal. Their paintings were not violently at odds with Socialist Realism, even when they turned out, on close inspection, to have elements of abstraction, Expressionism, or ornamental-ism in them. When Boris Birger took the hackneyed motif of Don Quixote for his subject, for instance, the work was dominated by a glittering, light-filled sky, with the figures of Quixote and Sancho Panza relegated to tiny blobs in the foreground, while his nude figures tended to melt into the background. Vladimir Veisberg, an influential figure among other artists, tended to specialize in still lifes that were also dissolved in light and gestured only tentatively toward abstract compositions (Pl. 3:1). It was true that their subjects and their treatment veered toward the inti-mate and the private, rather than toward the heroic and the monumental preferred by the establishment, and the same was true of the work produced by artists studying under Beliutin in Moscow and Sterligov in Leningrad. But their aims were overridingly aesthetic, not political, and their inspiration depended in equal parts on Russia's own artistic tradition and on contemporary developments in Western art.

In the early days of the thaw both tendencies seemed respectable. Khrushchev himself had opened the way for more contacts with the West and, unlike Stalin, he had traveled there personally. Also, Khrushchev's political slogan about a "return to Leninist norms" seemed to form a neat parallel to the artists' fascination with the art of the 1920s. Meanwhile, being largely apolitical, the artists argued only for diversity within the framework of official culture, even conceding that Socialist Realism should remain the guiding principle of that culture. Unfortu-nately for them, however, Socialist Realism was not just about aesthetics and artistic methods, it was a control mechanism, and that mechanism lay in the hands of the Party (and, through the Party, in the hands of the Party-appointed art establishment). Up until the Manezh exhibition, most artists had managed to forget or lose sight of that uncomfortable reality, but Khrushchev's outburst and the ideological purge that followed it made the situa-tion crystal clear.

Within days of Khrushchev's diatribe, Vladimir Serov (1910–1968), the head of the Academy of Arts and a promi-nent Socialist Realist painter himself, had gone out of his way to attack "those renegades who betray the principles of popular art and grovel before modern, decadent, bour-geois, abstract art."[15] Aleksandr Deineka, another laure-ate of Socialist Realism, declared: "There once existed Kandinsky and Falk. They are artists we can live and work quite well without, and create our own art."[16] Thus the leadership explicitly blocked exploration of Western aesthetics and Russia's own artistic past.[17]

The Party leaders, it seems, were genuinely shocked by the Pandora's box they had opened in encouraging writers and artists to pursue their creative interests more freely, and were determined to force it shut again. But the writers and artists were even more shocked, and even those who considered themselves loyal (the vast majority) felt that they were being branded renegades and turned into polit-ical activists against their will. What they had not realized until that moment was that, as Igor Golomshtok has noted, in the context of a totalitarian society, fidelity to culture and cultural traditions, even "painting still lifes with bottles," is a form of protest.[18] They simply needed to be educated.

When the initiative passed from members of the Union of Artists to the Lianozovo Group (which, as we have seen, was joined or supported by many from both the Group of Eight and Beliutin's group), the political confrontation between the artists and the authorities grew sharper. At least three members of the Lianozovo Group—Lev Kropivnitsky (1922–1994), Vladimir Nemukhin (b. 1925), and Lydia Masterkova (b. 1929)—were uncompromising exponents of Abstract Expressionism, albeit with fig-urative elements (Fig. 1:2; Pls. 3:2, 3:3). All three had long since concluded that there was no place for them in offi-cial exhibitions and they no longer even submitted their work. They understood that whatever their own inten-tions, their paintings would be regarded as a threat by the establishment.

It was their friend Oscar Rabin (b. 1928), the most self-consciously political and the most militant of the Lianozovites, who became their unofficial leader. Rabin had started out as a more or less conventional painter in the Socialist Realist manner, but like Nemukhin and Mas-terkova he was influenced by some of the Western exhibi-tions he saw between 1957 and 1962. He was also greatly affected by the work of Oleg Tselkov, another unofficial artist. Dissatisfied with his conventional productions, Rabin stumbled across the idea of imitating a child's manner of painting, and soon his work was filled with Expressionist visions of his environment.[19] These paint-ings made a strong impact with their crude, vivid colors and their bold imagery. At the same time, Rabin remained a realist, producing innumerable paintings of the modest cottage in which he and his wife (artist Valentina Kropivnitskaia) lived in Lianozovo. In the same style, he also painted the higgledy-piggledy log cabins and crum-bling apartment buildings that surrounded their house, the local railroad station, and other homely details of the urban scene.

But if the works of most abstractionists presented an indirect threat to the authorities, Rabin's challenge was much more obvious and immediate. Instead of idealized images of Soviet prosperity, lyrical landscapes, or portraits of Soviet notables, Rabin painted the opposite: pictures of suburban slums, desolate streets, abandoned cemeteries, scrawny cats, smoking chimneys, and dilapidated hovels (Pl. 3:4). He was a natural polemicist. His objects in his still lifes were not selected at random for their lines or colors; rather, his still lifes showed things like a smoked herring and a tumbler of vodka placed atop a torn copy of *Pravda* featuring bombastic headlines. This was Rabin's comment not only on the daily meal of an average working man, but also on the use he had for the Party newspaper. In his landscapes, Rabin might show the view of Moscow from this same worker's room, looking out of the crooked window of the barracks toward the city glowing a lurid red; on a table before the window rests a ten-ruble note and a pornographic picture, comments on the occupant's lifestyle and interests (Pl. 3:6).

Rabin's pictures of the dreary everyday reality of working-class life had their parallels in the stories of young writers like Vladimir Voinovich and Georgi Vladimov, both of whom became dissidents. Rabin's confrontational style also fueled the activism of the Lianozovites. It was no accident that it was Rabin who proposed the open-air exhibitions that produced a breakthrough for the unofficial artists. But he was by no means alone, for there were other forms of political comment just as unwelcome to the authorities. On the most basic level, it was a question of subject matter. Boris Sveshnikov (b. 1927), who had been sentenced to eight years in the gulag while still an art student, quite naturally turned to portraying his surroundings, even while still in a prison camp. "That was absolutely free art," he later recollected. "I received my bread ration and painted what I wanted. Nobody directed me. Nobody took any interest in me."[20]

Sveshnikov found in the gulag precisely what Solzhenitsyn had discovered—that in Stalin's Russia, the freest place of all (if you survived) was prison. Of course, none of the labor-camp overseers dreamed that they would end up immortalized by the prisoners in their charge, or that the spiritual freedom enjoyed by those prisoners would be what energized their stories and pictures when they were finally released. During the 1950s, shortly before his release, Sveshnikov completed a series of unique pen-and-ink drawings of scenes from camp life. Ten to fifteen years later, reproductions of these drawings circulated widely throughout the dissident world. These were not standard realist works, even though their subjects were easily recognizable. They had a hallucinatory, dream-like quality that recalled the stories of another ex-gulag inmate, Varlam Shalamov. Not surprisingly, the subject matter of Sveshnikov's sketches and Shalamov's writings was itself enough to ensure their total ban in the Soviet Union. As late as 1991, Sveshnikov (who had abandoned the camp theme by the mid-1960s) had still never had an exhibition in Russia.

Another painter of prison life whose works had a hallucinatory quality was Leonid Lamm (b. 1928), who was jailed in 1973 for daring to apply for emigration. His watercolors of Butyrka Prison (Pl. 3:7) present images that are instantly recognizable to readers of Anatolii Marchenko, Vladimir Bukovsky, or other political dissidents who were jailed for their activities and later wrote about them. Lamm's pictures were so accurate and evocative that they even earned the admiration of his guards. But the guards, as fellow denizens of the gulag, also possessed a kind of freedom denied their fellow citizens, for those outside the prison were not allowed to see such works at all.

Depictions of the seamy side of Soviet life or "difficult" subjects like prisons and prison camps were acknowledged as controversial, of course, by both artists and officials alike. But completely different kinds of works were also perceived as politically charged based on their formal qualities rather than their subject matter. For example, the two most prominent unofficial sculptors of the period, Ernst Neizvestny and Vadim Sidur, were overwhelmingly preoccupied with the human figure, as were most official sculptors. Furthermore, as veterans of World War II, both took as a subject wartime combat, a politically "safe" topic if ever there was one. Yet their treatment of this subject was perceived by the authorities as being at odds with official practice, for what they tried to express was the individual pain and suffering of war, rather than the abstract glory. They also departed from a strict realism and used Expressionist exaggeration and distortion to underline the intensity of the emotion they were trying to convey.

Sidur remained an Abstract Expressionist throughout his career, extending his studies of suffering to include political prisoners, the downtrodden and bereaved, and all outcasts from society. As a consequence, he was never granted an official exhibition; only a handful of grave monuments and an occasional open-air piece could be seen by the public at large. Even Sidur's lighter side proved to be too controversial for acceptance by the establishment. His explicit variations on male and female anatomy, suggestive sexual positions, and endless works on the theme of physical love were too outspoken to be redeemed by their playful distortions and fantastic manipulations of the human form (Fig. 3:6). Similarly, his

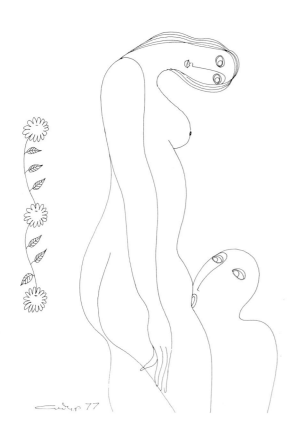

with the optimism and realism of official art, was very pronounced among many other unofficial artists as well. Vladimir Yankilevsky (b. 1938), a friend of Neizvestny and pupil of Beliutin, is hard to classify; he has been described variously as a Conceptualist, a Surrealist, and an Abstract Expressionist. Like Neizvestny, he distorted his images in order to express their essence better, and abandoned conventional realism in order to create a fantastic world that conformed to a set of laws of his own devising. In an extensive series of etchings called *Anatomy of the Senses*, Yankilevsky portrayed the human body in an incredible variety of grotesque poses. He then deconstructed the body into its component parts, reconstituted the parts in fantastic combinations, and finally dissected them, in order to transform the parts into individual homunculi. Like Sidur, Yankilevsky did not flinch from displaying and exaggerating the sexual characteristics of his figures, and it is striking that both artists called their grotesque variations on human anatomy "mutants" (or "mutations," in the case of Sidur). These works referred, of course, to the dangers of nuclear war, though in terms that were at variance with Soviet propaganda.

Yankilevsky also created an album of etchings called *City—Masks* (Fig. 13:10), devoted to "the destruction of the human personality as it ceases to live a conscious life and becomes a part of some mechanism."[21] Interestingly enough, this description could be applied just as aptly to the work of Oleg Tselkov (b. 1934), who is best known for an immensely powerful set of paintings of just such masks. Tselkov had stumbled across the idea of painting faces as masks (or masks as faces) in 1960, and continued this practice for about ten years before turning them around and painting their backs (in the form of backs of heads). The idea sounds banal in the telling, but Tselkov

Fig. 3:7 (*above*)
Ernst Neizvestny
Cry, from the series
Monarchy, 1974
Etching
32.2 × 63.5 cm

Fig. 3:6 (*left*)
Vadim Sidur
(Untitled), 1977
Pen and ink on paper
29 × 20.2 cm

ingenuity in turning "found" objects (pipes, tools, utensils, old bits of machinery, and so on) into clever and provocative sculptures was insufficiently respectable to soften the outrageousness of the concept and the unconventional character of Sidur's subjects.

Neizvestny also maintained his deep interest in human form and the dimensions of suffering, but moved stylistically in the direction of Surrealism. In his graphic work especially, he sought to express complex emotions through Surrealist composite images (Fig. 3:7), and it is not surprising that, like several of his peers (most notably Chemiakin), he was drawn to illustrating the works of Feodor Dostoevsky, whose novels of suffering and spiritual redemption, though banned under Stalin, held a powerful attraction for artists and intellectuals during the Khrushchev era. Even in the extensive sketches for his optimistically titled and monumentally conceived sculpture *Tree of Life* (Pl. 3:5) (still, after many years, in the planning stage), it was images of pain and distress that tended to predominate in Neizvestny's work.

The desire to seek a deeper reality through manipulation or distortion of the human form, while clearly at odds

Fig. 3:8
Valentina Kropivnitskaia
Russian Motif, 1976
Graphite on paper
42.8 × 61.2 cm

was able to wring a wealth of variations from this simple discovery. His pictures were simultaneously simple and complex, beautiful and sinister, abstract and realistic (Pl. 3:8). He denied that these works had any political intent: "I never tried to make any specifically social comment, in the way Rabin does, for instance. I tried to make my social attitudes 'universal,' to create works that would have the same impact everywhere, whether in my own country, in America, or somewhere like Guinea."[22] Yet the concept of dehumanized faces reflecting people who had been reduced to parts of some mechanism had an undeniable resonance in the Soviet context that made them recognizably political and therefore unacceptable. Rabin himself spotted the power and relevance of Tselkov's imagery right away and derived much of his own inspiration from it.

Important though it was, this rediscovery of the more painful sides of the Soviet Union's past and present was not the only political dimension to the work of the unofficial artists. Equally powerful was the search for viable alternatives to the grim reality they saw around them. This often led them to turn to Russia's national roots and traditions, a past that preceded the era of Communism, or to parts of the world where Communism held no sway, namely Western Europe and the United States.

A good example of the turn to tradition is the work of Valentina Kropivnitskaia (b. 1924), the daughter of Evgenii Kropivnitsky and the wife of Oscar Rabin. In her paintings, she created a unique visionary world inhabited

by gentle, rabbit-like creatures in pastoral settings (Fig. 3:8). Such images contrasted sharply with her husband's pictorial universe, not to mention the brutal realities of Soviet society. A kindred spirit, Aleksandr Kharitonov (1931–1993), spent the 1950s and 1960s creating a series of miniature paintings that explored the riches of Russian folklore. His pointillist technique was inspired by Byzantine and Russian iconography and old Russian church embroidery, with its intricate use of beads and gemstones (Pl. 3:11).[23]

Such an exploration of the past ("reactionary and escapist," according to the official view) inevitably led to the forbidden subject of religion, which is inescapably intertwined with Russian history and the Russian national character. In the same way that writers of the "village prose" school explored the place of the Christian religion in the lives and beliefs of their peasant characters, so Kharitonov, and to a lesser extent Kropivnitskaia, populated their works with religious objects and symbols: old churches and church cupolas, bells, crosses, graveyards, holy men, and motifs from Russian icons and frescoes. Sidur and Rabin, among others, also introduced religious subjects and motifs into their work, as did a young Surrealist, Eduard Zelenin from Vladimir, a city famous for its churches, icons and frescoes. Two other painters who explored texture and architectonics in the context of medieval religious art were Dmitri Plavinsky (b. 1937) and Viacheslav Kalinin (b. 1939). Plavinsky, in particular, developed a thickly encrusted impasto surface (Pl. 3:10) and rich patina in his oil paintings that seemed to mimic the effects of aging on the religious objects (Bibles, crosses, chalices, etc.) that he portrayed (Pl. 12:4).

The Orthodox Church and its rituals naturally stood at the center of this trend, but just as vital and rewarding, and considerably more controversial and politically dangerous (in light of Soviet anti-Semitism), were the attempts by Soviet Jews to explore and recover their religious heritage. Like Christian artists, many Jewish artists were attracted to the textures and forms of surviving religious artifacts, like ruined synagogues, tombstones, ancient scrolls, and Hebrew manuscripts. They also depicted rabbis or holy men, painted portraits of Jews with pronounced Semitic features, and showed celebrations of Jewish rituals that were still banned in the Soviet Union in the early 1970s (Pl. 3:9). Jewish art also possessed an inescapably international dimension, given that it paralleled a rise in Jewish emigration supported by Jews from Israel and the West.

Once the immensely popular modernist exhibitions of the late 1950s and early 1960s had opened the eyes of

Soviet artists to the sheer richness and variety of art in Western Europe and America, there was no going back. Its influence was seen almost everywhere, from the vivid colors and primitivist perspective of Rabin, through the abstract experiments of Veisberg, Nemukhin, Masterkova, and Shteinberg, to the Surrealist fantasies of Yankilevsky, Tselkov, and Kalinin. The sculptors Neizvestny and Sidur were likewise deeply indebted to the work of such Western precursors as Picasso, Henry Moore, and Barbara Hepworth.

This process of influence and assimilation continued for three decades and was particularly noticeable during the late 1970s and early 1980s, when various forms of Conceptual Art became popular with the younger and more adventurous unofficial artists. Conceptualism was not new to the Soviet scene. Ilya Kabakov (b. 1933), a member of the Beliutin group, had been experimenting with forms of both Conceptual and Pop Art since the early 1960s, as had his friend and colleague Eric Bulatov (b. 1933). Francisco Infante (b. 1943), the son of a Spanish Civil War veteran (hence the unusual name), had come to Conceptualism by way of Kinetic Art, which also had Western

connections, though it was equally influenced by Russian Constructivist art of the 1920s.

In those early days, Conceptual Art concerned itself for the most part with politically neutral subject matter. But this did not stop the authorities from proclaiming its very practice a politically hostile act. (Kabakov and Bulatov had been among those attacked at the Manezh show after Khrushchev's visit.) In the late 1970s, proponents of happenings and performance art (under the leadership of the Collective Actions Group) and the leaders of the Conceptualist AptArt movement insisted on remaining apolitical as a point of principle. But in Sots Art, Russian Conceptualists found a way of combining the ironically self-conscious methods of commentary devised by Western artists with a renewed form of ideological content. The key to this development was the Russian artists' skillful assimilation of the devices of Western Pop Art, the difference being that the "pop" iconography satirized was that of Socialist politics (hence the abbreviation "sots") rather than commercial advertising.

The acknowledged masters and leaders of Sots Art were Vitaly Komar (b. 1943) and Alexander Melamid (b. 1945), who worked in a bewildering variety of media, ranging from academic easel painting to performances. They also explored a tremendous variety of themes, by no means limited to political subjects. Their political commentaries, however, were what first attracted international attention to them, not least for the wit with which they were executed. In their paintings, Komar and Melamid often included parodies of political posters and Party slogans or playful manipulations of the ubiquitous images of the father-figures of Soviet ideology: Marx, Engels, Lenin, and Stalin. They exploded the clichés and pieties of Soviet ideology by lampooning them, and made fun of the ideology's hypocrisies (Fig. 15:2).

Another favorite target for Komar and Melamid was Socialist Realism itself, in all its forms. In *Plan for a Blue Smoke Producing Factory* (1975), they painted an industrial building in the sanitized neoclassical style beloved of Socialist Realists, but showed it belching clear blue air into an atmosphere thick with smog. This was a comment both on industrial pollution and on the cosmetic function of a Socialist Realist art itself, employed to conceal the truth rather than reveal it. Not surprisingly, Komar and Melamid ended by voting with their feet and emigrating to New York.

Komar and Melamid, the AptArt artists, the Collective Actions Group, and the other early Russian Conceptualists created a space in which new kinds of political commentary—less earnest and less aggressive, but in the long

Fig. 3:9
Boris Orlov
(A Russian Thinks About Himself First ...), 1982
Pen and ink on paper
34.7 × 24.2 cm

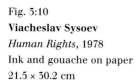

Fig. 3:10
Viacheslav Sysoev
Human Rights, 1978
Ink and gouache on paper
21.5 × 30.2 cm

run no less destructive—could take place. But this was just one element in an increasingly sophisticated and diverse art scene. Leonid Lamm created stylized but realistic paintings of Butyrka Prison, while Boris Orlov (b. 1941) commented on the problem of alcoholism in the Soviet Union. Instead of portraying a vodka bottle in the realist manner of Rabin, Orlov imagined it on an Olympic dais with the other winners, bottles of beer and port and beer (Fig. 3:9).

Viacheslav Sysoev (b. 1937), who had been painting realistic allegories of imprisonment in the late 1970s, turned first to Russian folk art and then to the traditional *lubok* (popular print) to find a form for his social and political commentary (Fig. 3:10). Still later, he made parodies of cheap comic books, in which he related the saga of his own persecution, arrest, and interrogation by the KGB. These tales were accompanied by grotesque illustrations in imitation of contemporary pulp literature (Fig. 3:11). Sysoev was also interested in pornography, but not in the "innocent" sense of producing a commodity or as part of some preoccupation with human anatomy (as with Sidur and Yankilevsky, who were literally accused of being pornographers), but as a form of political protest.

In all these manifestations, the essential difference between the political art of the 1980s and that of the preceding decades was the existence of an ironic distance. Even realists in the 1980s were self-conscious and ironic. "Messages" still came in the form of allegorical or symbolic content, but these were no longer the result of a serious need to evade or outwit the censors. Instead, they were the product of deliberate choice, invariably implying a nod and a wink on the part of the artist. On the other hand, political content freely infiltrated other types of art, so that even a semi-abstract series of screenprints by Raul Meel (b. 1940), such as his *Windows and Landscapes*, would metamorphose to show not just any windows, but windows with bars (Figs. 7:16–7:19). Viewers could supply their own commentaries.

This last period of unofficial art coincided, of course, with the last years of Soviet rule, and its productions were not simply a result, but also a symptom, of the regime's demise. It is too soon to determine exactly when the decline began or to define the role that the visual arts may have played in hastening that process. Looking back, however, it is easy to see that the thaw of the late 1950s

Fig. 3:11 (*left*)
Viacheslav Sysoev
Adam & Eve [Life is
Wonderful], 1982
Gouache and watercolor
on paper
68.8 × 48 cm

was a crucial turning point. We will never know if the system would have succeeded in saving itself as a form of "Socialism with a human face" by continuing and broadening Khrushchev's reforms. Perhaps the system might have metamorphosed into something resembling a social democratic regime. In the event, the attempt to turn back the clock and reimpose Party discipline led only to an empty, Pyrrhic victory.

It is clear, too, that the decline of Communism as an ideological and intellectual force, which became obvious after the reversal of the thaw, left a spiritual vacuum that had to be filled somehow. It was the natural role of creative artists of all kinds to try to fill that vacuum. At the same time, the artists' task was also educational: to show a small but growing audience the possibilities for renewed spiritual growth, to reacquaint them with their interrupted (but by no means dead) heritage, and to reconnect them with the mainstream of world culture. Together with other creative elements in Soviet society, they accomplished this task, though it is too soon to determine how much of the art they produced will have lasting value. But that is clearly not the most important point. The stifling fetters of Socialist Realism have been broken, and the system that forged them is gone. In that struggle, the unofficial artists played a noble part, and for the future they left a fascinating legacy to build on.

Notes

1. See Elena Kornetchuk, "Soviet Art under Government Control," in this volume.

2. It is not clear when or how the terms "unofficial" and "nonconformist" came into being to describe Soviet artists. The first public use of the word "unofficial" in this context seems to have occurred in Paul Sjeklocha and Igor Mead, *Unofficial Art in the Soviet Union* (Berkeley and Los Angeles: University of California Press, 1967). The authors were two young Americans who worked on the American Graphic Arts Exhibit and toured the Soviet Union in 1963–64, meeting several "unofficial" artists who had come to view the exhibition. "Nonconformist" appears to have come into use later, and was the term preferred by many of the artists themselves, especially after the open-air exhibitions of 1974 and 1975. A later designation, preferred by some Conceptual artists, was "alternative."

3. From the archive of Alexander Glezer. Quoted by Igor Golomshtok in Igor Golomshtok and Alexander Glezer, *Unofficial Art from the Soviet Union* (London: Secker and Warburg, 1977), p. 89.

4. Ibid., pp. 89–90.

5. At the First Congress of Soviet Writers in 1934, Babel spoke about the difficulties he was experiencing in writing according to the tenets of the newly proclaimed doctrine of "Socialist Realism."

6. This is becoming clearer from recent exhibitions devoted to the achievements of Russian modernism, e.g., "The Avant-Garde in Russia, 1910–1930" at the Los Angeles County Museum of Art, July–September 1980; "Rodchenko-Stepanova: The Future Is Our Only Goal" at the Österreichisches Museum für angewandte Kunst, Vienna, May–July 1991; "The Great Utopia: The Russian and Soviet Avant-Garde, 1915–1932" at the Guggenheim Museum, New York, September–December 1992.

7. Natan Altman, for instance, did not die until 1970, having lived to see a retrospective of his work in 1969. Nadezhda Udaltsova died in 1961; Aleksandr Vesnin in 1959; Varvara Stepanova in 1958; and Aleksandr Rodchenko in 1956. Vladimir Tatlin had died in 1953, while Pavel Filonov, Ivan Kliun, and Gustav Klucis had died in the early 1940s.

8. Falk died in 1958 and Tyshler in 1980.

9. Accounts differ as to what exactly Khrushchev said, but there is considerable agreement on most of his remarks. This quotation is based on the versions given in Sjeklocha and Mead, *Unofficial Art in the Soviet Union*, p. 94, and Priscilla Johnson and L. Labedz, eds., *Khrushchev and the Arts: The Politics of Soviet Culture* (Cambridge, Mass.: MIT Press, 1965), pp. 102–3.

10. For the purposes of this brief survey, I am limiting my discussion to Moscow and Leningrad. Unofficial artists were also active in Pskov, Vladimir, and other cities, as well as in the Baltic republics and in the Transcaucasus. Many of these artists also participated in exhibitions in Moscow and Leningrad. Developments in these areas are discussed elsewhere in this volume.

11. These breakthroughs were due in large measure to the efforts of the London-based art dealer Eric Estorick, who managed to establish a special relationship with the Soviet art authorities in the early 1960s and was an admirer of Rabin's work.

12. The availability of certain works of art abroad that could not (officially) be seen by Soviet citizens was another parallel with *samizdat*, although the phenomenon was far rarer (for obvious reasons) in the case of paintings and sculpture.

13. Links between Czech writers and artists and their Soviet colleagues, especially those active in the dissident movement, were especially close between about 1964 and 1968. Soviet intellectuals followed developments in Czech political and cultural life with great intensity, and concluded (correctly) that the suppression of the Czechs would have immediate negative consequences for their own attempts at achieving greater autonomy.

14. For more detailed accounts of this exhibition, see Oscar Rabin, *L'Artiste et les bulldozers: Être peintre en URSS* (Paris: Editions Robert Laffont, 1981), and Alexander Glezer, *Chelovek s dvoinym dnom* (Montgeron, 1979).

15. Sjeklocha and Mead, *Unofficial Art in the Soviet Union*, p. 98.

16. Golomshtok and Glezer, *Unofficial Art from the Soviet Union*, p. 108.

17. Leonid Ilyichev, the Party's Secretary for Propaganda, knocked down the Leninist norms argument in his meeting with writers and artists on December 17, 1962: "It is one thing to combat the consequences of the cult of personality in order to assert the Leninist standards of life . . . and another to deal blows, under the guise of the struggle against these consequences, to our society and our ideology. . . . The question of creative freedom must be fully clarified. . . . We have full freedom to fight for communism. We do not have and cannot have freedom to fight against communism." Quoted in Sjeklocha and Mead, *Unofficial Art in the Soviet Union*, p. 100.

18. Golomshtok and Glezer, *Unofficial Art from the Soviet Union*, p. 87.

19. Ibid., pp. 154–55.

20. Ibid., p. 93.

21. Artist's statement, quoted in ibid., p. 163.

22. Ibid., p. 159.

23. Quoted by Tatiana Sokolova in *Kharitonov*, exh. cat. (Jersey City, N.J.: C.A.S.E. Museum of Contemporary Russian Art, 1991), p. 6.

4 | "Nonidentity within identity"

Moscow communal modernism, 1950s–1980s

Victor Tupitsyn

Nonidentity is the secret telos of identification.

—THEODOR W. ADORNO

Introduction When characterizing any alternative, it is logical to begin with that which it is opposing. In speaking of alternative art in the Soviet Union, then, one must consider the vast culture of Socialist Realism, which, over the course of almost sixty years, undertook the mythologization of Soviet power. In considering this culture, we should not accept the widespread myth that Socialist Realism was a collective artistic practice. This is correct only in the very narrow sense that Socialist Realism was a manifestation of what were, in fact, the extremely individualistic thought-forms (*Gedankenformen*) of certain Party leaders and theoreticians.

In the former Soviet Union, those ideological leaders formed a sort of "superstructure," while the actual workers on the cultural front served as the corresponding "base." In addition to artists and other cultural workers, this base included art critics, who described Socialist Realism in the spirit of its own mythological traditions. The relationship was that of the mythographer to mythology, a cathartic adhesion. This situation radically contradicted the conventional Marxist version of the critical function as defined by Brecht and the Frankfurt School. In fact, the only time Soviet critics experienced Brecht's "alienation effect" was in relation to bourgeois art. In the case of Socialist Realism, any potentially productive alienation these critics might have experienced was replaced by an undistanced (and, consequently, uncritical) relationship to the work.

This cozy connection between the institutional superstructure and the uncritical base of cultural laborers was the chief product of what might be called "the affirmative culture of Socialist Realism" (to paraphrase Max Horkheimer). On the one hand, official artists experienced a degree of freedom in their profession. They did not have to worry about the caprices of the art market, since their works were bought by their colleagues on the purchasing committees with money allotted by the government (either through the Ministry of Culture or the Artists' Union). On the other hand, this system bound those artists to the autocratic structure by a form of legalized blackmail. The purchase prices paid by these committees bore little relation to artistic value: money was given for loyalty, for position in the hierarchy, for attention to the rules of the game. In fact, the "prices" were more like rewards to official artists for the fulfillment of responsibilities that had been assigned by their political superiors. Understandably, the rigid institutionalization of such relations and practices left no space for alternative creative forms. Thus, any oppositional cultural tendencies in Stalin's time, if they existed at all, were rare exceptions to the rules and were fraught with the possibility of severe repercussions.[1]

To discuss the conditions under which alternative art emerged as a sociocultural phenomenon, we must first recall the way Soviet society took shape in the post-revolutionary period. One bellwether of the changes taking place was the shifting Socialist policy toward public housing. Immediately following the Revolution, Lenin issued a decree requisitioning all city apartments so that they could be divided among the poor: the standard of decency was set at one room per person. By 1924, this norm had been reduced to eight square meters per person. Following the death of Lenin in 1924, and the curtailing of the NEP (New Economic Policy), a new attitude toward collectivization emerged, which, in retrospect, seems to mark the beginning of the so-called Stalinist revolution. Under Stalin's plan, rural peasants were recruited, often forcibly, to work on collective farms. Other peasants were wiped out, banished to Siberia, or forced to migrate to urban areas, a massive relocation that initiated many of the housing problems that persist to this day.

Stalin exploited this situation in order to further his project of collectivizing, or "de-individualizing," the consciousness and the daily life of the Soviet people. By law, city apartments became as populous as anthills and beehives. Such *uplotnenie* reached its climax when two or three different tenants had to live in one room. Families of every variety, belonging to various social, national, and cultural-ethnic groups, were forced to live together in a single communal body. Toilets, showers, and kitchens became the laboratories of this "great experiment" in

Pl. 4:2
Vladimir Nemukhin
Composition, 1961
Oil on canvas
157 × 107.5 cm

Pl. 4:1
Eli Beliutin
Suffering, 1973
Oil on canvas
131 × 69 cm

Pl. 4:3
Dmitrii Krasnopevtsev
Pipes, 1963
Oil on fiberboard
55.5 × 66 cm

Pl. 4:4
Nikolai Vechtomov
Requiem, 1960
Oil on canvas
88.5 × 113 cm

Pl. 4:5
Vladimir Nemukhin
Black Card Table
(Dedicated to Anatolii
Zverev), 1986–87
Oil, playing cards, and
wood on canvas
100.1 × 100.7 cm

Pl. 4:6
Vladimir Piatnitsky
(Untitled), *c.* 1969
Watercolor on
illustration board
48 × 31.5 cm

Pl. 4:7
Anatolii Zverev
Self-Portrait, 1974
Oil and tempera on
canvas
108.3 × 70.2 cm

Pl. 4:8
Mikhail Shvartsman
(Untitled), 1982
Oil on panel
99 × 75 cm

Pl. 4:9
Vagrich Bakhchanyan
(Untitled), 1969
Mixed media
35.5 × 44.4 cm

Pl. 4:10
Mikhail Roginsky
(Fuck You), 1966
Oil on canvas
65 × 74.5 cm

Pl. 4:11
Ilya Kabakov
*I Told Him If You Want to
Live with Me, Behave
Yourself . . .*, 1981
Oil on fiberboard
113 × 203.6 cm

Pl. 4:12
Mikhail Roginsky
Red Door, 1965
Mixed media on
fiberboard
175.5 × 80.2 cm

Pl. 4:13
Eduard Shteinberg
Composition, March 1979,
1979
Oil on canvas
120 × 85 cm

Pl. 4:14
Oleg Vassiliev
Figure in Space, 1977
Oil on canvas
123 × 246 cm

Pl. 4:15 (*below*)
**Vitaly Komar and
Alexander Melamid**
(Quotation), n.d.
Tempera on cloth
76.5 × 372 cm

Pl. 4:16 (*above*)
Rostislav Lebedev
Situation No. 2, 1979
Painted wood
134 × 148.5 × 85 cm

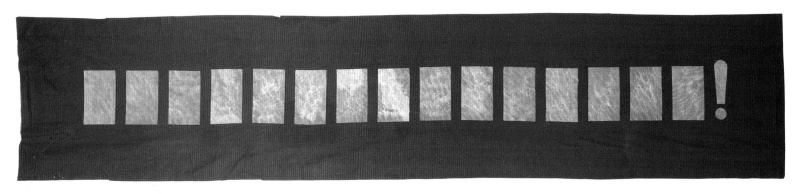

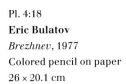

Pl. 4:17
Eric Bulatov
Glory to CPSU
(Communist Party of the
Soviet Union), 1975
Colored pencil on paper
22 × 22 cm

Pl. 4:18
Eric Bulatov
Brezhnev, 1977
Colored pencil on paper
26 × 20.1 cm

Pl. 4:20
Dmitrii Prigov
(Perestroika), 1986–87
Pen and ink on paper
20.3 × 14.5 cm

Pl. 4:19
Ivan Chuikov
(Untitled), 1977
Oil on fiberboard
113.5 × 106 cm

ОГОНЁК

ИЗДАТЕЛЬСТВО „ПРАВДА", МОСКВА № 25 ИЮНЬ 1975

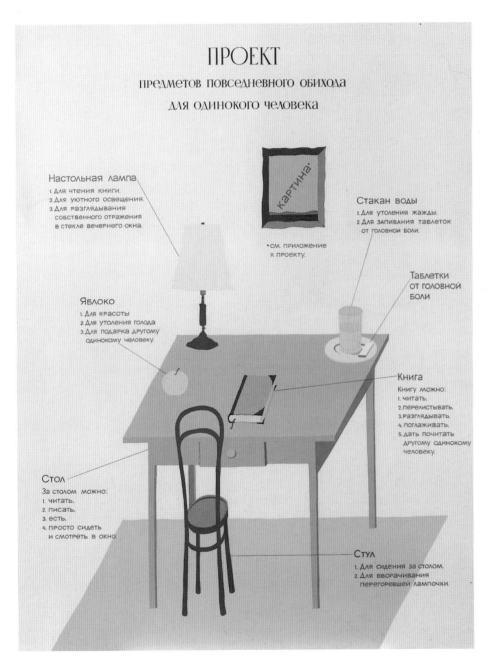

Pl. 4:21 (*opposite*)
Oleg Vassiliev
Ogonyok, No. 25, 1980
Oil on canvas
122 × 91.7 cm

Pl. 4:22
Viktor Pivovarov
From the series *Plan for the Everyday Objects of a Lonely Man*, 1975
Oil on fiberboard
170.8 × 130.3 cm

Pl. 4:23
Andrei Abramov
Frame, 1979
Pen and ink on paper
29.8 × 21.2 cm

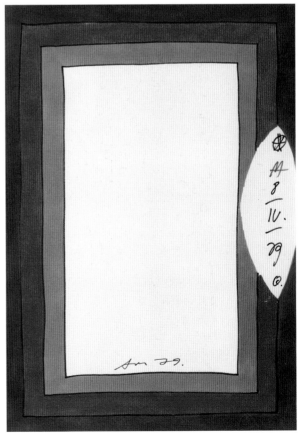

Pl. 4:24
Aleksandr Kosolapov
(Untitled), n.d.
Layered fabrics on
canvas over panel
20.5 × 30.8 × 12.5 cm

Pl. 4:25
Aleksandr Kosolapov
*The Finale of World
History*, 1975
Pastel and pen and ink on
illustration board
30.5 × 36.8 cm

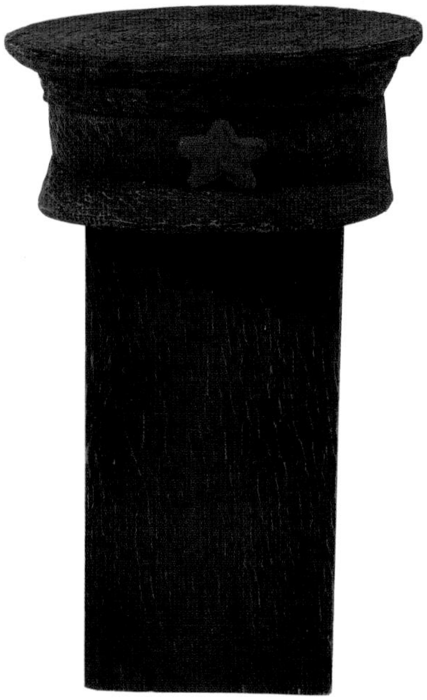

Pl. 4:26
Boris Orlov
(Untitled), 1984
Painted wood
41 × 27 × 31 cm

Pl. 4:27
Leonid Sokov
*Project to Construct
Glasses for Every Soviet
Person*, 1976
Painted wood
11.3 × 33.3 × 31 cm

Pl. 4:29
Eduard Gorokhovsky
Untitled, 1980
Oil on canvas
110.4 × 90.5 cm

Pl. 4:28
Leonid Sokov
Threatening Finger, 1975
Painted metal
31.5 × 21 × 7.5 cm

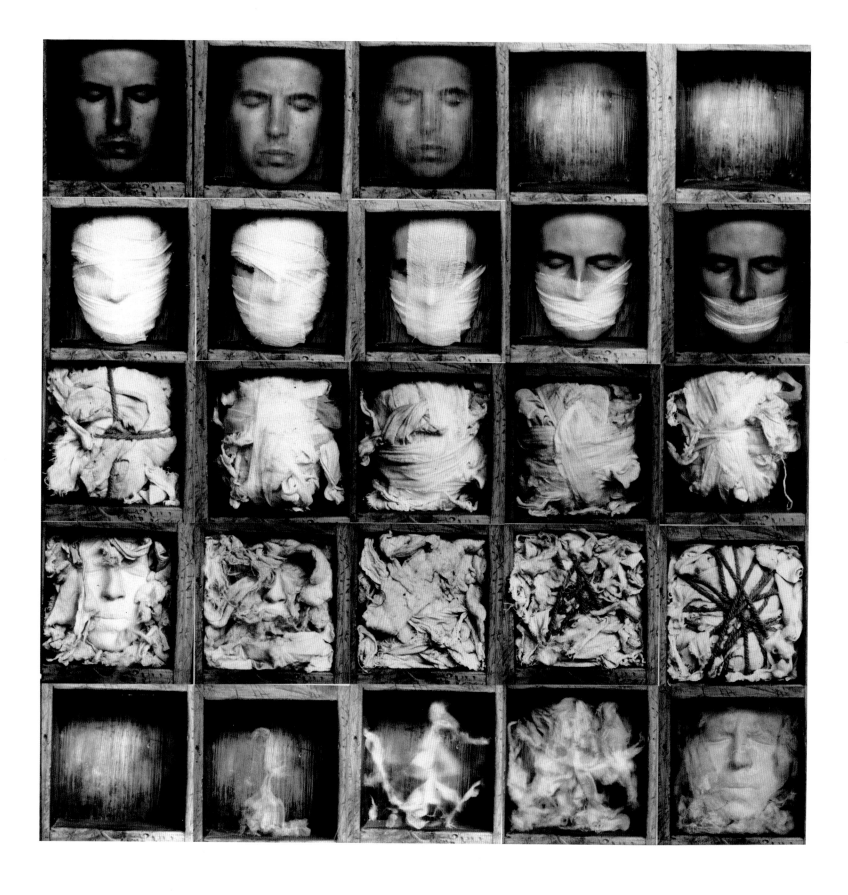

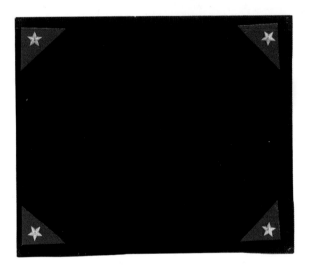

Pl. 4:31
**Andrei Monastyrsky
(Collective Actions Group)**
*Series of Velvet
Paperworks with
Railroad Emblems:*
Fragments of the
installation following the
performance titled *Audio-
Perspectives of Journeys
to the Countryside,* 1983
Mixed media
33 × 39.5 cm (each)

Pl. 4:30 (*opposite*)
Igor Makarevich
Stratigraphic Structures,
1976
Photomontage
101 × 101 cm

Pl. 4:32
Rimma Gerlovina
Cube-Poems, 1974
Fabric, paperboard, and
paper
8.5 × 8.5 × 8.5 cm (each)
Each cube contains its
own statement or poetic
line:
*I think someone is
looking at us from behind;
The black square; A grave.
I am already dead.
One square kilometer of
Mongolia; A soul. Don't
open it or it will fly away;
Little Miss Fogelson
running round the
garden.
Don't disturb me; Over
me; Imagine this white
cube in a red sphere.*

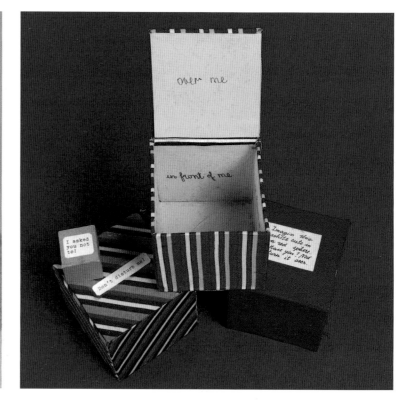

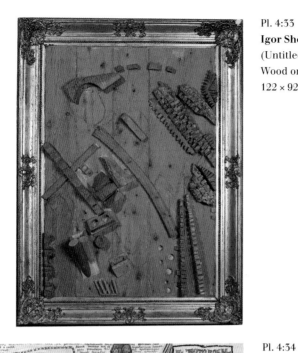

Pl. 4:33
Igor Shelkovsky
(Untitled), 1971–76
Wood on wooden panel
122 × 92 × 13 cm

Pl. 4:34
**Konstantin
Zvezdochetov
(Mukhomor [Toadstool]
Group)**
Theater of War, 1982
Pen and ink and crayon
on paper
61.8 × 86.4 cm

Pl. 4:35
Aleksei Tiapushkin
Pictorial Experiment,
1964
Oil on canvas
121 × 91 cm

Pl. 4:37
Aleksandr Drewchin
Provincial Dogs, 1976
Oil on panel
124.7 × 139 cm

Pl. 4:36
Sergei Anufriev
No. 3 in the series
Children's Playground, 1986

Watercolor and gouache
on paper
29.7 × 42 cm

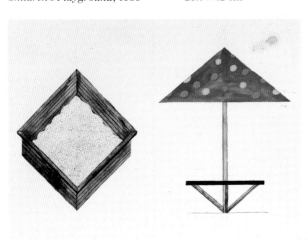

Pls. 4:38 and 4:39
Irina Nakhova
Scaffolding, 1984
Diptych
Oil on canvas
149.5 × 150 cm (each)

Pl. 4:40
Pavel Peppershtein
Grandfather, Why?, 1986
Colored pencil and ink on
paper
37.2 × 24.5 cm

mass communalization. Thin walls and partitions afforded no guarantee of what Westerners call "privacy." The inhabitants of the communal *thermae* were at once "prison guards" and "inmates" in their relations with one another. Neighbors, from whose "love" there was nowhere to hide, denounced each other to the secret police in mutual surveillance.

The frustration inherent in such an Orwellian living arrangement was exacerbated by a binary opposition between the overcrowded apartment and the myths of the extracommunal space: "triumphal feats of construction," trials of "enemies of the people," and so on. The scale of the psychoideological pressure resulting from the state's imposition on its subjects, the signs and codes of status and authority, were, in a word, unprecedented. The paradox, however, lies in the fact that despite the aforementioned contrasts and dichotomies, officialdom always managed to convince its communal counterpart that the source of the latter's troubles and miseries resided abroad.

In communal life there were no actions other than speech acts: everyone was drawn into a process of "serial" talking (ranging from harmless gossiping to extreme cases of verbal abuse). As a result, "with the passage of time, the monstrous dough of spoken kitsch rose,"[2] leavened with the yeast of a Dionysian sensibility characteristic of relations within peasant families, collectives, and agrarian sects. Thus, the urban peasantry of Stalin's epoch not only swallowed and assimilated other forms of class identity (such as the proletariat and intelligentsia), but also "built" for themselves their own "house of being," known as communal speech. The very notion of difference had gradually dissolved into the swamp of the Same, and the wizardry of a political language game had triumphed over the rhetorics of class consciousness.[3]

The language of the Soviet *kommunalka* (i.e., communal dwelling) is unique. In the West, a communal dwelling means a ghetto, but in the U.S.S.R. almost everyone lived in the same sort of ghetto. And if, in Europe and America, communal living is a phenomenon of a minority, that fact at least ensures that communal speech has not fallen prey to elitist theories that focus on discourses of power or resistance but not on the lexicon of what has been defeated, broken, or reduced to the level of verbal garbage. *Kommunalka* has always been an autonomous linguistic organism, with its own textual laws. But alongside that communal speech, *homo communalis* also knew another (Apollonian) tongue, i.e., the voice of power blaring from the Soviet radio.

A recognition of the complex relations between the *kommunalka* and the extracommunal, mythical machine is reflected, for example, in the memoirs of poet Vsevolod Nekrasov. Characterizing the poems of his colleague Genrikh Sapgir, Nekrasov (whose style absorbed the entire range of communal intonations) insists that: "The real Sapgir is nonetheless the old (communally oriented) poems; no sort of mythology . . . outweighs them."[4] For entirely understandable reasons, Nekrasov incriminates the mythology (which, moreover, is not necessarily of a Soviet blend) and its alliance with the authoritarian tongue. As a result, this mythology is seen as negative, while communal speech is endowed with positive characteristics.

It is no secret that total communality and total power are essentially forms of social perversion. Both are sadomasochistic utopias and, as such, they sometimes substitute quantity for quality (this was the case in the U.S.S.R.). Therefore, any given "retreat" from communalism or individualism offers no guarantee against the possibility of the overwhelming resumption ("eternal" return) of the other. In nontotalitarian societies, communalism and individualism balance each other out, forming odd combinations, including "neutral" and "complex" terms (an example of the latter would be the postindustrial corporate structure). But, in countries where fragmentation and individualism have reached their limits, the need for the "Other" is most sharply felt. In such cases, a nostalgia for collective corporality bears witness to what the German philosopher Theodor W. Adorno, in his *Negative Dialectics*, calls "nonidentity within identity."

In the United States, for example, such "nonidentity within identity" is manifested in television talk shows, which make up the bulk of the daytime programming. Such shows are a school for confessional-cathartic communality. They also remind us that, in addition to being speech-oriented, communal artistic vision is primarily cathartic—and therefore noncritical. Still, within its own rules of usage, communal speech practices have been primarily dialogic, if not toward "issues," then at least toward styles and appearances. That is why the artistic language of alternative Russian culture, rooted in its communal heritage, seems so ambiguous to foreign eyes.

The end of the 1950s, the beginning of the 1960s After the death of Stalin in 1953, a few more years were needed for the fresh air of the Khrushchev thaw to become perceptible in the art world. In the spring of 1956, immediately following the Twentieth Congress of the Soviet Communist Party, the artists Ullo Sooster, Boris Sveshnikov, and Lev

Kropivnitsky returned from confinement. As a result of the Central Committee's resolution "On Overcoming the Cult of Personality and Its Consequences" (passed that same year on June 30), the exclusive right to the status of individuality, which had be usurped by the Party's upper echelons, lost its earlier "infallibility." Now, for the first time, the creative intelligentsia had a chance to decommunalize, to cease being solely the "ancient choir" in a typically Soviet "optimistic tragedy."

In 1958, the Studio School at the Institute of Improvement of Qualifications of Graphic Arts Workers, which had existed since 1954 under the direction of Eli Beliutin (b. 1925), passed to the protection of the Committee of Graphic Designers. In his speech at the opening of the Studio, Beliutin had criticized the "wingless realism" of official art. Instead, he called for a "passage through the entire worldwide history of human culture, including modernity, so as to analyze the most diverse methods, the principles of decorativity and expression—Egypt, the Renaissance, the prehistoric epochs, the present day—to pick out the very best with the aim of taking all of it as arms." As this quotation makes clear, even though Beliutin was at odds with Socialist Realism as a system of representation, he nonetheless remained faithful to the politics of holism that lay behind the rhetoric of official art and defined it as the sum total of humanity's creative darings. Beginning in the summer of 1957, Beliutin's students went on collective trips for practice in the area around Moscow (Krasnyi Stan). At the end of 1959, having become the first private educational institution in the history of Soviet art, the Studio School found a home on Taganskaia Street. Among those who taught or were educated there were Vladimir Yankilevsky (b. 1938), Viktor Pivovarov (b. 1937) (Pl. 4:22), Boris Zhutovsky (b. 1932), Ernst Neizvestny (b. 1925), Lev Zbarsky, and Sophia Shiller (b. 1940).

At about the same time, the Lianozovo Group emerged, consisting of the artist/poet Evgenii Kropivnitsky (1893–1979) and the artists Olga Potapova (1892–1971), Valentina Kropivnitskaia (b. 1924), Oscar Rabin (b. 1928), Lev Kropivnitsky (1922–1994), Lydia Masterkova (b. 1929), Vladimir Nemukhin (b. 1925), and Nikolai Vechtomov (b. 1923), as well as the poets Nekrasov, Sapgir, and Igor Kholin. These people, like the Studio School group, did not manifest any particular unanimity on the plane of aesthetic purpose: their coherence as a group was based on their shared search for a new sociocultural identity. In other words, they sought to create a neocommunal body, but in a voluntary and noncoercive way.

While the interests of Beliutin and many of his charges

clearly gravitated toward Expressionist abstraction (Pl. 4:1), no aesthetic consensus could be observed among the members of the Lianozovo Group. The pictorial works and sketches of Rabin constituted an exception, as they shared much—in a narrative sense—with the poetry of Kropivnitsky, Kholin, Sapgir, and Nekrasov. Rabin was linked to these poets by a taste for the socially grotesque, becoming almost a medical examination of the plagues and blemishes of the surrounding reality. It would be an exaggeration to regard the art of this "barrack" wing of the Lianozovo Group as being in any way an example of critical discourse. The reaction to reality characteristic of Rabin's subjects and his compatriots bears the mark of a communal vision of the world. That is to say, they share the cathartic vision of those condemned to stick together with the object of love and the object of hate.

The aestheticization of misery is precisely what distinguishes the representatives of the de-classed communal intelligentsia of the thaw era from their predecessors (the Socialist Realists), who created a paradisiac image of history. Moreover, the Expressionist palette of Rabin's pictures of the late 1950s and early 1960s corresponds neatly to the hysterogenic atmosphere of barrack existence. Stamped upon his works are crooked Moscow streets with ramshackle homes and barracks, hungry cats on roofs and beneath gates, and the claustrophobia-filled "living" spaces of communal apartments. Blame for these miserable living circumstances is laid on the absurdity of existence or on some anonymous character, who—in Ilya Kabakov's opinion—appears before communal consciousness simply as "it." This faceless, formless androgynous "it" is chief among the *dramatis personae* of the ghetto-centric narrativity associated with the creative experience of the forefathers of "nonconformism"—from Rabin and Oleg Tselkov to the artists of the Leningrad "Barracks School" (Shvarts, Vasmi, Shagin, and Arefiev).[5]

Masterkova and Nemukhin, who formed another faction of the Lianozovo Group, were associated stylistically with Abstract Expressionism. They became particularly interested in that movement in 1958, after an exhibition of American art was shown in Moscow. At the same time as Nemukhin turned increasingly from nonfigurative to semi-abstract compositions (Pl. 4:2), Masterkova changed these proportions in the opposite manner. Nemukhin, whose first experiments with modernist visual vocabulary can be traced to the late 1940s (Fig. 4:1), is best known for his still lifes with playing cards, fighting cocks, and fragments of card tables (Pl. 4:5). This entire iconography, borrowed from the sphere of heated games, corresponds well with the vitality of his

Fig. 4:1
Vladimir Nemukhin
Still Life with Fish, 1946–47
Graphite on paper
20.2 × 14.2 cm

artistic character. In the majority of cases, these props were semantic conventions designed to heighten the effect of accident, intrigue, and indeterminacy (i.e., everything that would contrast with the doctrine of predetermination of social processes professed by the Soviet establishment). Later, Nemukhin added "cuts" to his canvases in the manner of Lucio Fontana; in most cases, they were illusory, but occasionally (as, for example, in those things created together with Anatolii Zverev) they were real.

In one of his poems Nekrasov writes: "Lydia Masterkova paints orchestrally." And it is true. The mention of this name brings to mind painterly forms with circles ("planets") and ciphers on them, subordinated to musical rhythms. For the most part, these ciphers are either zeros and ones or nines. Such a significant spacing bears witness to an extreme maximalism and an uncompromising quality that exclude any chance of reconciliation with the idea of an "arithmetic mean." As far as Masterkova's early works are concerned, her first abstractions were distinguished by the passion of the organic forms and colorful surfaces that collide with one another. Subsequently,

she began to glue old bits of lace and fragments of ecclesiastical attire (chasubles and the like) to the surfaces of her canvases. The use of lace (which in the context of those years may be considered the antithesis of a "masculine" relation to *faktura* [texture] and to the "politics" of material selection) placed the artist in an isolated position in the patriarchal world of Muscovite alternative art. Brocade fabrics, reminiscent of the vestments of Orthodox priests, fulfilled a different role in Masterkova's pictures: their aim was to identify socially nonengaged creation with religious asceticism.

Generally speaking, the notion of being one of the "chosen" and of having a spiritual mission (ideas that were common in Masterkova's texts of this period) were not alien to other representatives of "dissident modernism."[6] Thus, for example, Oleg Tselkov considered (as indeed he does to this day) that he does not paint, but simply "executes" his own works.[7] Here, supernatural forces supplant the historical giver of orders: the Party and government. Another candidate for the post of chief inspirer is "I myself," i.e., the artist as Zarathustra. At the end of the 1950s, this kind of heroic individualism was associated with the sculptors Vadim Sidur (1924–1986) and Ernst Neizvestny.

A few words must be said about Vechtomov, the author of surreal, uninhabitable landscapes characterized by the toxicity of their painterly palette. According to their creator's own words, the typically low horizon of these compositions resulted from a psychological trauma he experienced during World War II (Pl. 4:4). While fleeing from German captivity, Vechtomov crawled for several successive days along the steppe, seeing before himself day after day only the low line intervening between the earth and sky from the point of view of a crawling man. In a certain sense, the metaphor of flight, rooted in Vechtomov's psyche, extends as well to the dispositions of his colleagues Nemukhin and Masterkova. All these artists, to equal degrees, ignored the languages of communalism and power. They made these topics taboo and consequently displaced them, not only from the zone of consciousness but also (for the time being) from the sphere of the unconscious. The vacuum that was formed as a result was filled in, in Kabakov's words, "by the sweet visions, magical sights, and original worlds that had unfolded before one's eyes."[8]

However, as we have already seen, the artists at this time knew no vision other than a cathartic one. Therefore, anything that envisaged a Brechtian "alienation effect" or might lead to the realization of the "critical function" was immediately crossed off the list of phenomena worthy of attention. This response was linked not only to the experience of communality, but also to memories of the Stalinization of culture. That is why in the late 1950s the very notion of a "critical function" was still identified with the "verdictive" language of Zhdanovism (in the 1930s, "criticism" of writers or artists often landed them in prison or labor camps). Muscovite alternative art, alas, would frequently be overrun with such "criticism," with some modifications, in the course of its thirty-year history.

Reflecting on the first steps of Russian dissident—or, in my terminology, "communal"—modernism, one must necessarily look at such early representatives as Boris Sveshnikov (b. 1927), Vladimir Veisberg (1924–1985), Dmitrii Krasnopevtsev (1925–1995), Mikhail Shvartsman (b. 1926), Dmitri Plavinsky (b. 1937), Aleksandr Kharitonov (1931–1993), and Vladimir Yakovlev (b. 1934). After his return from the labor camps in 1954, Sveshnikov settled in Tarusa (130 kilometers from Moscow), and at the very beginning of the 1960s moved to Moscow. He brought with him from confinement a large number of sketches executed in the manner of the Old Masters (from Botticelli to Dürer) and in the spirit of Goya's *Los Caprichos*.

In these works, the theme of prison life acquires a certain atemporality; some of them might be confused with illustrations for Dante's *Inferno*. This type of apprehension of time and space was termed by literary theorist Mikhail Bakhtin the "Dantesque chronotope" or "the chronotope of vertical time." Within such a framework, the temporal distinction between narration and what is narrated vanishes and—in exchange—they are endowed with the status of simultaneity. And Sveshnikov's temporal response to the Stalin years was not isolated. In one of his poems, Boris Pasternak even refers to them as "the years of timelessness." Many dissident modernists applied precisely this interpretation to the period that succeeded the era of the Russian avant-garde, considering that Russia seemed to have "fallen out of culture" during that time.

A similar eschatologism, which occurs in the work of many of Sveshnikov's contemporaries, is "the death of time." Veisberg, having attempted—like Pushkin's Salieri—"to verify harmony with algebra," composed his meditative works (including his *White on White* series) from the most minuscule units of color. For the most part, he painted still lifes and portraits, reaching an ecstatic frenzy by cutting himself on his arms and chest. Veisberg admitted frequently that he selected as models only those whom he had seen in his nightmares lying in their coffins. In time, both the objects and characters in Veisberg's

pictures were reduced to the level of "eidoi." In 1962, his address "The Classification of the Basic Forms of Coloristic Apprehension," presented at a symposium on the structural study of sign systems (under the aegis of the Soviet Academy of Sciences), summed up his investigations into the principles of colorism in world painting from El Greco and Titian to Cézanne and Matisse.

Krasnopevtsev's metaphysical compositions (Pl. 4:3) diverge from those of his forerunners—Morandi, de Chirico, and Cornell—in that his *natures mortes* with fragments of elegantly deceased civilizations stamped on them may, as artist Sergei Essayan says, be called "supra-mortes." As Krasnopevtsev himself notes, they "speak to us of the god of an all-destroying age."[9] With regard to the so-called "hieratures" (or "divine hierarchies") of Shvartsman (Pl. 4:8), it may be said that their reductionism is of a clearly expressed Jungian type. Admirers of the French philosopher Gaston Bachelard might be said to be close in spirit to the ecstatic quest for "archetypes" taken up by Shvartsman. Commenting on this aspect of his work, the artist claims that they "concern man's relation to his experiences in life and in death, before whose face he leaves an iconic trace of himself in the grave."[10] In the light of this grim pronouncement it seems far from coincidental that, in 1973, the sculptor Vadim Sidur began to execute a series of works with the title *Coffin Art*.

Unlike Krasnopevtsev, Dmitri Plavinsky's artistic routes run not only through the demesnes of *poesis*, but also through the churchyard of *physis*. In his compositions, full of an eschatological syncretism, one discovers old scripts, ossified fish and amphibians, and fragments of things and meanings that have irretrievably lost their contexts, their temporal and spatial coordinates. Interestingly, discourse and corporality are not separated in Plavinsky's works (as they are, for instance, in Michel Foucault's "archive") but, on the contrary, coexist symbiotically. The allegory is transparent: death is just as pluralistic as the *kommunalka* insofar as they are both devoid of discriminatory ambitions.

Kharitonov's path is the combination of orthodox ethics (and, in a number of cases, iconography as well) with the painterly aesthetic of modernism. Like Mikhail Larionov (1881–1964) and Natalia Goncharova (1881–1962), he turns to the primitive and to kitsch, but without any trace of irony, without succumbing to the temptation to mock. His pointillist paintings advocate the ideas of wonder and spiritual harmony, that is, everything which was missing in communality and the officialdom, which were, from the viewpoint of the nonconformist, "submerged in sin."

Fig. 4.2
Vladimir Yakovlev
White Flower, 1974
Gouache on paper
58.7 × 40.8 cm

The case of Yakovlev, a painter valued extraordinarily by his compatriots for his still lifes with flowers and fish (Fig. 4:2), as well as for his abstractions and portraits, is yet another facet in the paradigm of the "myth of originality" (to use Rosalind Krauss's apt phrase). From Goya and Van Gogh to Egon Schiele and Antonin Artaud, the tradition of modernism not only legitimized but canonized the image of the madman-genius. In accordance with this tradition, insanity is considered a necessary correlate of artistic talent. In this sense, the clinically ill Yakovlev, who was almost deprived of his eyesight but "compensated" for this defect with creative vision, was and remains a legendary figure to his admirers. When, in the 1980s, his relatives had Yakovlev institutionalized, the artist's colleagues (Nemukhin and others) visited him regularly. His release from the hospital could not be arranged until the early 1990s.

I would like to close this section by recalling several exhibitions of Western modernist art which took place at the end of the 1950s and left an ineradicable trace on the collective psyche of Muscovite visual culture. The list of these exhibitions includes an exhibition of Picasso's works at the Pushkin Museum in 1956 (organized with the cooperation of Ilya Ehrenburg, a friend of Picasso's); the international open-air exhibition in Gorky Park under the aegis of the Sixth World Festival of Youth and Students (in July and August 1957); the 1959 Sokolniki Park exhibition of American art in which the paintings of Rothko, Pollock, Motherwell, Gorky, de Kooning, and others were displayed; and finally, in that same building two years later, the French national exhibition.

If, until this point, alternative artists had oscillated between the Scylla of communality and the Charybdis of Socialist Realism, denying to each the "presumption of authenticity," then from the end of the 1950s the myth of Western modernism came to incarnate authentic reality. In the U.S.S.R., which lacked the sociocultural context necessary to understand its contradictions, this mythic modernism was never able to go beyond the romanticized biographies of its heroes or the limits of pure aesthetics. But a positive side of the exchange between East and West was that Soviet artists were able, finally, to become acquainted with paradigms of individual authorship apart from the communal setting, paradigms devoid for the most part of the authoritarian individualism of the Party elite.

The 1960s The 1960s mark the decommunalization of a remarkably broad mass of alternative artists. At this time, many of them quit their communal abodes and began to work in studios, which became the incubators for developing new forms of relations in the art world. In the studios, shows were arranged, poems and theoretical texts were read, and opinions and literature—including books on Western art—were exchanged. For the most part, these artists earned their keep making children's books (for example, Sooster, Kabakov, Pivovarov, Eric Bulatov, Oleg Vassiliev, and Eduard Gorokhovsky) or by collaborating with popular-science publishers or journals (as did Sobolev and Nemukhin). Such a minimal form of participation in the Soviet artistic industry at least gave the alternative painters and sculptors the right to studios.

In the framework of these studios all sorts of groupings took shape, held together if not by a unity of artistic purpose then by their common fate and by their shared opposition to the establishment. These fellowships were laboratories for the re-creation and rediscovery of the paradigms of individual authorship usurped (in the "years of timelessness") by the authoritarian "I" of state power. Decommunalization took place also at the level of the everyday. This was expressed in the sweep of Khrushchev's building programs, which were charged with the resettling of people from the communal apartments of Stalin's time. The "new lands" program (in Siberia and Kazakhstan), which provided for the migration of "productive forces" to rural localities, also helped to lessen the population density in the nation's cities. A few years later Khrushchev, already removed from power, admitted to a journalist that his chief service to the nation had been to improve housing conditions in order to "let people live."[11]

Alongside this contact in studios there arose other, previously unheard-of phenomena: the arrangement of shows of non-Socialist Realist art in clubs, scientific research institutes, youth cafés (such as the Aelita and the Blue Bird), and in private apartments (such as those of the composer Andrei Volkonsky, the art critic Ilya Tsirlin, the pianist Sviatoslav Richter, and the dissident Aleksandr Ginzburg). There arose jazz clubs and literary artistic salons connected with the names Ullo and Lydia Sooster, Sobolev, Yurii Mamleev, Aleona Basilova, and Mikhail Grobman. All of the musical performances, theatrical productions, and literary publications that helped to counter Socialist Realism's "symbol of faith" deserve their own investigations, as do other cultural phenomena from the early 1960s.

In the visual arts, however, from 1960 to 1968, there was a remarkable series of exhibitions and evening programs at Moscow's Mayakovsky Museum dedicated to the artistic heritage of El Lissitzky, Mikhail Matiushin, Elena Guro, Gustav Klucis, Pavel Filonov, Kazimir Malevich, Vladimir Tatlin, Vasilii Chekrygin, Larionov, Goncharova, George Yakulov, Olga Rozanova, and Marc Chagall. The artists who visited these exhibitions were able to familiarize themselves with the history of the Russian avant-garde, which—to the surprise of many—could not be reduced to the three F's: Robert Falk, Vladimir Favorsky, and Artur Fonvizin.[12]

In December 1962, there was an exhibition at the Manezh, which displayed the works of Sooster, Sobolev, Neizvestny, Beliutin, Zhutovsky, Yankilevsky, and others. The leaders of official culture invited Khrushchev and the upper echelons of the Party to the opening with the aim of stirring them up against their enemies, the unofficial artists. The scandal that erupted at the opening and the subsequent persecution of "deviant" art marked a watershed in the history of unofficial art. Like a mollusk extricating itself from its shell, the communal body of Muscovite dissident modernism worked itself free of the ghetto's limits for the first time. The infantile phase or, in Lacan's terms, the "mirror stage" of alternative art drew to a close. The artists recognized the utopianism of their hopes for linearity and continuity in the process of the convalescence of cultural life.

The events at the Manezh are treated in greater detail elsewhere in this book. For the purposes of our approach to the history of Muscovite alternative art, we are interested in the changing balance in the interrelations of communality and that which Nietzsche termed "the art of will to power." At the meeting of Party and government representatives and the artistic intelligentsia which took place in January 1963 in the House of Receptions in the Lenin Hills, Khrushchev summarized the arguments of the "nonconformists," saying, in effect: "They needn't be put in jail, but rather into the madhouse."

Later, under Brezhnev, Khrushchev's words were made literal: madhouses became laboratories for the forcible "re-education" and re-formation of aesthetic views. As had once been the case in Stalin's camps, in the asylums communal experiences were reinscribed: along with doses of insulin, patients received injections of communal psychology. In 1993, the Petersburg artist Afrika (Sergei Bugaev), having passed a month in a psychiatric hospital in the course of executing an artistic action, informed me that he had "nowhere before experienced such a degree of imperativity to merge with the communal body."

To the list of the characteristics that constitute the image of the communal modernist, I would like to add four more types: the hobo, the "holy fool," the hippie, and the schizoid. The first type, which was taking shape already at the end of the 1950s, is identified first and foremost with Anatolii Zverev (1931–1986), who became the talk of the town thanks to his spontaneity and knack for improvisation. These skills were demonstrated in many genres, styles, and tendencies from animalism and impromptu portraits (Pl. 4:7) to abstract and figurative compositions. Leaving aside the unconditional significance of his legacy, the chief novelty he introduced to the Moscow art world was his abolition of distinctions between life and the artistic act. Once, for instance, while working on a series of portraits in the home of Aida Khmeleva, Zverev painted using, along with paint squeezed from tubes, toothpaste and cigarette butts, and accompanied his Action Painting with medleys on the piano and improvisations in verse. A fragment of one of these verses went, as I recall: "A Tartar boy shoots from a bow. Fu-u-u-ck sings the bowstring after the arrow flies off." Drunkenness and vagrancy (which brought about his premature death in 1986), together with his enviable gift for improvisation, won Zverev the reputation of the muse's beloved, and added a number of supplementary features to the Muscovite paradigm of the "myth of originality."

The role of the holy fool, like that of the hobo, is inseparable from the Russian tradition of opposition to the establishment. An intolerance of power, characteristic of all periods of Russian history, developed to the point that alternative individuality was forced to resort to camouflage. The drunkard and the holy fool were forms of social (or, to be precise, asocial) expression forbidden to ordinary members of society. Like Zverev, Vasilii Sitnikov (1915–1987) had a virtuous command of methods of "playing the fool." His bag of holy fool's tricks included both jocular manners and a passion for folkloric articulations. Sitnikov wore an untucked shirt and workboots, collected icons, and gave painting lessons to numerous pupils, who were hypnotized by their teacher's Rasputinesque charm and the intensity of his heavy-handed artist-like pose. Shocking his charges, he painted with a bootbrush, attaining precise enough visual effects nonetheless. Sitnikov's subjects varied from kitschy representations of Russian churches powdered with New Year's snow to nudes and genre scenes of a caricatural or grotesque sort. In 1980, having emigrated to New York, Sitnikov made the acquaintance of two or three gallery dealers (with my help), promising that "for prison fare and accommodation in barracks" he would paint for them a number of epochal pictures over several years. It goes without saying that no contracts were concluded. Not long before his death, I ran into him in the East Village. In his hands he held a huge brush for washing the floors of corporate lobbies. "Finally I have obtained a brush suitable for the scale of my painterly grandeur," he said in parting.

The artist Vladimir Piatnitsky (1938–1978), who died of a drug overdose, can be considered the Russian incarnation of self-destructive tendencies in the mold of Jack Kerouac. The swarms of communal freaks (Pl. 4:6) populating his surreal-absurdist fantasies are subordinated to a psychedelic logic, which is also not alien to the heroes of the underground writer Yurii Mamleev's stories. It is no accident, for example, that in one of Piatnitsky's paintings a character, drawn with a portrait-like resemblance to the artist himself, holds in his hands a then-unpublished volume of Mamleev's texts. With regard to this writer, it should be said that, in the 1960s, his salon on Yuzhinsky Lane was a crucial factor in the formation of yet another paradigm of artistic and bohemian behavior, the "schizoid."[15] Interestingly, this concept arose and became popular in Moscow more than a decade before Deleuze and Guattari's *Anti-Oedipus*, in which "schizoidness" and "schizoanalysis" are developed into a means of critical analysis. Finally, in speaking of Piatnitsky and Mamleev, we should mention Viacheslav Kalinin (b. 1939), who was distinct from them in that his communalist works move from madness and frustration to orgiastic carnivality. The absence of psychedelic horizons in Kalinin (Fig. 13:2) is made up for by the Rabelaisian riotousness of nature and what Bakhtin called the "lower bodily strata."

As we have already noted, the 1960s were associated not only with artistic alternatives, but with social experimentation as well. This was often connected with the search for new forms of intellectual and creative fellowship. Like the Lianozovo Group, Sretensky Boulevard cannot be linked with any sort of creative programs or characteristics of a professional persuasion. Instead, it was another link in the reinterpretation and redefinition of communal language games and their rules. After all, every citizen of the U.S.S.R. who has studied in a Soviet school, graduated from an institute, or served in the army, even if he or she was lucky enough to have his or her own apartment or studio, is nonetheless a product of this communal environment. Kabakov was correct in stating that "he knows himself insofar as he is a communal dweller" and that "to transcend the boundaries of the Communal is to become an angel."[14]

What took place in the unofficial art world in the 1960s was linked to a changeover from institutional forms of communality to contractual ones. It was contractual communality, or neocommunality, based on the principle of optional communalization, that became the ecological niche for Muscovite alternative art over the course of three decades—right up to *perestroika*. Among the artists generally borne in mind when the words "Sretensky Boulevard" are pronounced, one may list: Sooster, Sobolev, Neizvestny, Yankilevsky, Shteinberg, Pivorarov, Bulatov, and Kabakov (Pl. 4:11).

Yankilevsky's sketches, paintings, and triptychs are remarkable by dint of their texture and the phantasmagoric quality of the anthropomorphic and mechanistic elements found in them. These may be considered incarnations of the communal unconscious, not in a Jungian sense, but rather as that which has been conditioned by the extraordinary scale of the mass of stereotypes characteristic of the communal ghetto. (To make Lacan concrete, we may assert that the communal unconscious is structured like communal speech. And, on the strength of the clichéd nature of communal speech, almost everything which is displaced into the unconscious—save for the prelingual [the infantile period of life]—coincides to a significant degree for the majority of communal dwellers.) When gazing at Yankilevsky's compositions, in which foreshortenings of a deformed anthropomorphism are laid atop a rigid structure of communications nets and aggregates in the spirit of Francis Picabia and Max Ernst, Nietzsche's words concerning "Dionysus the crucified" spring to mind.

In the case of Eduard Shteinberg (b. 1937), the "communal unconscious" revealed itself during his search for a symbolic father. This quest was preceded by the unmasking of the cult of personality at the Twentieth Communist Party Congress and the removal of Stalin's mummy from Lenin's Mausoleum in 1961; these were dramatic, nationalized examples of what psychoanalysis defines as "the death of the father." (Incidentally, the very fact of the "dispersal" of the Mausoleum's inhabitants cannot be regarded as anything other than the "master-plot" of decommunalization.) With Shteinberg, the lost paternal icon was supplanted by the patriarch of the Russian avant-garde: Kazimir Malevich. Shteinberg not only appropriated Malevich's visual language, but also to some extent "corrected" his legacy, developing the religious potential of Malevich's abstractions to their extreme and truncating their secular signification (Pl. 4:13). In the 1980s, Shteinberg wrote a letter to "the beloved Kazimir Severinovich" (Malevich), which became a manifestation of the "supplantation" and resurrection in the Fiodorovian sense of the deceased "parent." (Nikolai Fiodorov [1828–1903] was an influential Russian philosopher who advocated the symbolic resurrection of the deceased "fathers.")

Curiously, a few years before Shteinberg's letter, Lev Nusberg (b. 1937), founder of the Movement Group, staged a similar correspondence with Malevich. The Movement Group was formed in 1962, and included, besides Nusberg, Francesco Infante (b. 1943), Rimma Zanevskaia, Viacheslav Shcherbakov (b. 1941), Viktor Stepanov (b. 1943), Galina Bitt (b. 1946), and others. The group focused on the propagation and development of Kinetic Art, the design of artificial environments, and on the staging of outdoor theatrical spectacles with elements of happenings and body art. Independent of Nusberg and colleagues, Kineticism was practiced by Viacheslav Koleichuk (b. 1941), who exhibited with the Movement Group at the Kurchatov Institute of Atomic Energy in 1966.

For Nusberg, the task of art boiled down to the symbiosis of the natural and the artificial (Fig. 4:3); in the era of Sputniks and cosmic euphoria he was able to convince Soviet officialdom of the actuality of his pop-science fantasies, which gravitated—at the level of design and architectural forms—toward the aesthetics of the 1920s (from Malevich and Lissitzky to Tatlin and Pevsner). Like many of his compatriots (for example, Ernst Neizvestny in *The Tree of Life* [Pl. 3:5]), Nusberg's megalomania was based

on a belief that the world's progress could be assured under the aegis of a single artistic project. Nusberg, incidentally, enriched the Muscovite variant of the "myth of originality" with yet another Zarathustrian facet—the "will" to leadership and tutorship.

In 1970, Infante broke off from the Movement Group, having created, along with Nonna Goriunova (b. 1944), his own collective under the name ARGO. The aim of the group was, in Infante's words, "to bring to fruition planned projects for artificed spaces." For many, Infante's "artifacts" are identified with fragments of nature reflected in mirrors. This doubling, like the installations with mirrors themselves, is somewhat reminiscent of the earlier works of Robert Smithson.

Among those who, along with Shteinberg, Nusberg, Infante, and Koleichuk, maintained the traditions of the 1920s, we should mention the students of Vladimir Sterligov (1905–1973) in Leningrad and those of Mikhail Chernyshov (b. 1945) in Moscow. In 1963–64, Chernyshov, having studied the legacy of geometric abstractionism in Western periodicals, laid these forms atop the visual kitsch of communal life—from wallpaper to clippings from magazines with representations of tanks and airplanes. A peculiar Pop Art resulted that anticipated the American Neo-Geo of the 1980s.

Chernyshov frequently socialized with and exhibited works alongside Mikhail Roginsky (b. 1931), who had previously been a stage designer. About 1963, Roginsky introduced into his visual lexicon representations of everyday objects—Primus stoves, irons, matchboxes, and the like

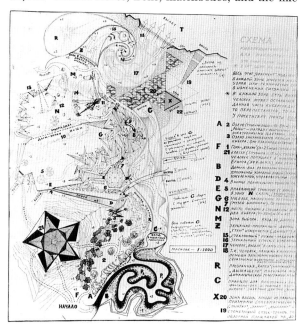

Fig. 4:3
Lev Nusberg and the Movement Group
Plan of Cybertheater: Art-World, 1966
Gelatin silver print
38.9 × 37.9 cm

(Pl. 4:10). Of those things he brought into the repertoire of alternative art production, a few pieces merit special consideration: *Red Door*, a readymade from 1965 (Pl. 4:12), the façades of Moscow buildings (1965), a stove on the floor (1965), and streetcars and scenes in the Moscow subway. Like Van Gogh in his time immortalizing worn-out boots, Roginsky painted eminently unprepossessing pants hung off a chair.

It might seem that this entourage of objects is similar to those employed by Rabin in his "barracks" motifs. In fact, however, Roginsky's works herald another apprehension of the same iconography. If Rabin's objects serve as witnesses for the prosecution, wailing about the crimes of an extracommunal "it," then with Roginsky their self-sufficiency is returned to them. In their unsightly everydayness the artist found his own theme, amortized to no one else: the theme of coexistence with things, or—and this is just the same—the ability of the ghetto residents to relinquish their hostility toward things and to accept their objecthood and texture. The argument that Roginsky created a Russian Pop Art is mistaken: in contrast to the West, where the fetishization of consumer culture could not fail to be reflected in art, in the U.S.S.R. this remained utopian.

In the 1960s, the first art collectors and art collections appeared. At the beginning, the collectors were Alek Rusanov, Evgenii Nutovich, Nina Stevens, and Leonid Talochkin. Later came Alexander Glezer and Tatiana Kolodzei. George Costakis filled an important role by collecting works of the earlier Russian avant-garde alongside works by contemporary artists. In the same decade, the American economics professor Norton Dodge took up collecting. His collection of alternative art, assembled over the past thirty years, exceeds all the collections mentioned above in terms of both volume and level of representation. Overall, the sale of works to foreigners in the 1960s became an economic factor that played an increasingly important role in the infrastructure of communal modernism. However, as this was considered illegal, the purchasers—accredited journalists and diplomats in Moscow—for the most part acquired works of small dimensions so as to export them in their suitcases. From this practice the term "suitcase style" arose to denote modestly scaled artworks destined for export.

As far as the "enlightening" mission of foreigners in Moscow is concerned, the fact is that, alas, with rare exceptions, these people had only vague notions of the actual artistic and sociocultural issues and problematics of vanguard art in their own countries. The entirety of the critical consensus of the time did not fall within their purview. All they could offer their Russian friends in the guise of *Kulturträger* were books or catalogues of museum shows promoting art that had already become synonymous with money and capital investment. Contemporary trends in American and European art proved to be beyond the reach of these types of catalogues and publications. Thus, the nonconformists accidentally identified themselves not with the marginal activities or iconoclastic gestures of their Western contemporaries, but with "ascendant" culture, that which had already been tamed, assimilated, and, in the final analysis, endorsed by the institutions of power. As a result, Soviet alternative artists, while remaining in opposition to domestic officialdom, served unwittingly as apologists for the Western cultural establishment. This latter circumstance to a certain extent explains the unfavorable reactions of the leftist critics to exhibitions of the nonconformists' work abroad.

After Brezhnev came to power in 1964, the organization of alternative exhibitions in Moscow turned into its own sort of Russian roulette. Thus, for example, the exhibition of Lianozovo painting (with the addition of several works by Plavinsky, Shteinberg, and Valentin Vorobiev) at the Friendship Club on the Enthusiasts' Highway in 1967 was closed down by the authorities two hours after it opened. This event, which was officially accused of "ideological sabotage," provoked an irate reaction in the Soviet press. Meanwhile, other important shows of paintings and graphics passed without any particular action by the authorities. Among these were a show of Kulakov's abstract works at the U.S.S.R. Academy of Sciences Institute of Physics (1967) and a whole sequence of short-running expositions in the Blue Bird café, among them Komar and Melamid's collaborative show "Retrospectivism" (1967) and individual shows by Kabakov, Bulatov, and Vassiliev in 1968, and by Anatolii Brussilovsky, Vagrich Bakhchanyan (Pl. 4:9), and Petr Belenok in 1969.

By 1968, Vassiliev (b. 1931) had already turned out a number of key devices (pass keys) and "ramming" contrivances permitting a passage through the walls of planar "fortifications" (Fig. 4:4). Having reinterpreted the legacy of his teachers, Favorsky and Falk, Vassiliev conceptualized painterly space by embedding rectilinear surfaces in it and by supercharging the pressure of light (Pl. 4:14). Vassiliev's methods of creating so-called "high and deep spaces" give rise to effects reminiscent simultaneously of X-rays and visual aids on spectral analysis. Despite the fact that some story is always told in Vassiliev's pictures, narrative always remains optional. The true subject of these works is going through the purgatory of visuality.

Fig. 4:4
Oleg Vassiliev
Spatial Composition, 1986
Oil on illustration board
93.5 × 70.2 cm

This approach is summed up in his painting *Ogonyok, No. 25*, 1980 (Pl. 4:21), in which streams of pure visuality issuing from the painting's corners incinerate a source of speech, in this case an orator located in the painting's center.[15] Among Vassiliev's landmark works, which are part of the Dodge Collection, are five paintings under the general title of *Space—Surface* (1968) and the triptych *Stroll* (1975).

Understandably, the accenting of problems of visuality in a country enthralled by speech practices, whether communal speech or the language of power, is a classic example of Don Quixotism. Nonetheless, a few other artists were able to realize the cost-price of this problematic, including Bulatov, Sergei Essayan (b. 1939), Aleksandr Yulikov (b. 1943), and Ivan Chuikov (b. 1935). More than the others, Chuikov is concerned with the epistemological examination of the visual. For him, visuality is an antinomy arising from the "collision of reality and fiction." In his words, it is "the result of the operation of turning the relations of the subject and object of apprehension inside out." Chuikov is famed for his cycle of "window frames" with images drawn on them (Pl. 4:19) that carries the conflict between the presumption of spatial reality (behind the window) and flat representation (on its surface) to its

limit. Chuikov's conception of representation as "a fine pellicle" has something in common with Nietzsche's concept, in *The Birth of Tragedy*, of "the veil of Maia"; with this veil, Apollo, the god of illusions, camouflages the ugliness of the reality, identified with Dionysus. In other words, Chuikov's window is an attribute of communal (i.e., Dionysian) reality, while the image laid on it like sediment is a salutary (i.e., Apollonian) illusion, protecting abstraction from everyday associations.

The 1970s Curiously, every communal modernist of the 1960s or 1970s would always choose a famous artist from the past to identify with. For Kabakov, it was Vermeer; for Bulatov and Vassiliev, it was Velázquez; for Masterkova, it was El Greco; and for Nemukhin, it was Zurbarán. Perhaps the experience of being socially displaced (discharged from the "here-and-now") prompted them to seek spiritual identification with past lives, thoughts, and things. The vacancy of their own situation was filled by a Western European past "displaced" (or deferred) by "natural causes," i.e., chronologically, territorially, historically. Allegorically speaking, the nonconformists trapped themselves in the double-bind of Milton's *Paradise Lost* (space) and Proust's *Temps perdu* (time). They viewed art history as if it were a sort of paradise in which one could establish tenancy. This is understandable, considering that any museum of fine arts is—in a way—a *kommunalka*, where artists from different epochs end up "living" together.[16]

In the 1970s, finally, the infantile play of the "it"—which the Muscovites had for so long avoided examining—came to a close. Despite all its respectable moral groundings, this persistent disinclination to analyze "it" was not without a certain psychopathological element. In fact, it was similar to the Soviet tradition in the 1960s of pulverizing the "rudiments" of individualism between the millstones of communality and power. By focusing on the languages of communality and power and denying or disavowing their relation to those terms, any communal (or neocommunal) modernist was hindering his or her rebirth from a *homo communalis* into a socially responsible personality. In short, without a case-study analysis and description of these languages, any attempt to overcome them would be extremely problematic.

Although Kabakov (b. 1933) is the chief chronicler and deconstructor of the communal world order, it would be rash to suppose that his art is a punitive expedition or crusade against communality. There is a paradox in the fact that, being the destroyer of the Bastille of speech, he nevertheless did not cease to be its captive. The artist has on several occasions pointed out that "creativity comes from fear and anguish." His confession that repression and fear "are part of my life and my mind" echoes both Manfredo Tafuri's *Architecture and Utopia* and Harold Bloom's *Poetry and Repression*. After he began to exhibit in the West at the age of fifty-four, Kabakov displayed a rare talent for the art of installation. In the opinion of his New York dealer Ronald Feldman: "Only two artists known to me commanded comparable capabilities: Joseph Beuys and Edward Kienholz." Kabakov, who shares responsibility with Komar and Melamid for the initiation of Soviet ("communal") Postmodernism, was for a long time famous primarily as an illustrator of children's books.

In the second half of the 1960s, he came to understand that this genre corresponded entirely with infantilism and the illustrational nature of the communal vision of the world. The devices and skills of illustrative drawing probed and selected over ten years by Kabakov proved acceptable for re-reading in the context of a "grown-up" thematic. This discovery inspired Kabakov and gave a powerful stimulus to his evolution as a Conceptual artist. Of course, to the informed reader this should appear as nothing other than a regular instance of the literariness peculiar to the Russian artistic tradition. However, one should not submit to the temptation of referring the communal-speech vision to the *Peredvizhniki* tradition or Socialist Realism, the imagery of which corresponds either to the slogans of prerevolutionary egalitarianism or to the "mythical speech" of Stalinist culture. In contrast to both of these, the language of the communal apartment is based on a different kind of psycholinguistics.

Beginning in 1971, Kabakov set about creating a series of albums with the title *Ten Characters*; these related the lives of various dwellers in a multi-apartment residence. All ten heroes, taken together, make up a complete spectrum of relational clichés, speech acts, and behavioral stereotypes, sketching out an existential profile of communal ecology. It is interesting that the camouflaging of the authorial "I" behind a veil of characters (Pl. 4:11) became, thanks to Kabakov, a phenomenon rather typical for Muscovite communal Conceptualism. An example of this is Viktor Pivovarov's album *Don't You Recognize Me?* (1981), in which identification of the individual represented as the author is made difficult by the fact that on each page the human form is hidden behind everyday objects.

Vitaly Komar (b. 1943) and Alexander Melamid (b. 1945) are also artists with an audioclastic orientation. However, in contradistinction to Kabakov, they subject not communal, but authoritarian discourse to a deconstructive reading. The target of their hunterly instincts turns out to be the "mythical" (extracommunal) speech that functioned in explicit or implicit forms in the visual clichés of the Socialist Realist tradition. Their experiments in the early 1970s addressed without mediation the problem of logocentrism as manifested in the framework of the Soviet painterly canon. Some examples of this approach are the easel painting in the style of a poster, *Don't Babble* (1974), or the "anonymous" slogans of mass propaganda from 1972, signed by Komar and Melamid, *Our Goal Is Communism* or *We Were Born to Make Our Dreams Come True* (Pls. 15:13, 15:14).

For all its parodic quality, Komar and Melamid's gesture in signing these works was a phenomenon unique to alternative art. For the first time, the communal "I" encroached on the authorial rights reserved for the extracommunal "it." In the work known as "Quotation" (Pl. 4:15), we discover even rows of white quadrangles sketched on a red background and placed within quotation marks. In all, these empty places, suitable for the insertion of pearls of authoritarian speech, form a semblance of a Minimalist painting. Nonetheless, its speech structure (a speech "eidetics"), even without a specific concretized message, is perceived as an incarnation of the will to power and terror.

In Komar and Melamid's Conceptual project *A Circle, a Square, a Triangle—for Every Home, for Every Family* (1975), in the Dodge Collection, the artists construct a parallel between the Platonic eternal ideas "linked *a priori* to nothing" and the ideology of Socialist Realism, operating—as in the case of *Quotation*—with "NOTHING." And this latter, according to "the famous artists of the beginning of the 1970s,"[17] is always vacant for communication (home delivery) of codes of status and authority, whose speech character is also commented upon in the work entitled *The Essence of Truth*, 1975 (Fig. 15:2).

In 1976, at Ronald Feldman's gallery, American art lovers were able to familiarize themselves with the first exhibition of Komar and Melamid's Sots Art works; this marked the beginning of their intensive career of exhibitions in the West. Several years after their emigration from the U.S.S.R., these artists (now living and working in New York) were able to announce their new version of Sots Art, which they termed "nostalgic Socialist Realism" (1981). Alongside a deconstruction of the holism and teleological ambition of Stalinist art, "nostalgic Socialist Realism" renewed (on a Postmodern level, of course) the search for "lost fatherhood" undertaken by Shteinberg and Nusberg in the 1960s.

Although the use of phrases attributable to an extracommunal "it" is characteristic of the work of Eric Bulatov

(b. 1933), his approach differs from Komar and Melamid's Sots Art in that, from his point of view, the extracommunal "it" is not exhausted by "mythical speech" alone, but entails the presence of an ontological horizon. The specific character of his reading of the Socialist Realist representational canon lies in the discrediting of the ontological ambitions of authoritarian speech (Pls. 4:17, 4:18). This takes place not in a fit of destructive fervor, as is sometimes the case with Komar and Melamid, but rather with the aim of sweeping away obstacles on the path to truth. In Husserl's philosophy, this sort of "sweeping away" is identified with the procedure of "bracketing" (the phenomenological epoché). In this connection, Bulatov's method may be termed phenomenological Sots Art.

Thus, for example, in his painting *Danger*, 1972–73 (Pl. 15:1),[18] inscriptions in the painting's four corners caution against a cathartic cohesion with the Socialist Realist representation; danger remains in the fact that such a representation might (by mistake) be taken for a final truth and totality. "Social space is not all of reality," warns Bulatov. The very same message, and the very same demand for the preservation of phenomenological vigilance when faced with "it," can be read in the painting *Krasikov Street* (1972). At present, the artist lives in France. A solo exhibition at the Centre Georges Pompidou in Paris (1989) crowns the long list of his museum shows.

Apparently, all the aforementioned deconstructive paradigms, from Sots Art to the Kabakovian examination of the communal body, have suffered from one-sidedness. Sots Art aimed at the subversion of the state's "mythical speech," but took a rather tolerant position toward the "speech-vision" of the communal with its Dionysian features. The latter can be seen in Komar and Melamid's paintings, as well as in the works of such artists as Leonid Sokov (b. 1941), Aleksandr Kosolapov (b. 1943), Boris Orlov, Dmitrii Prigov (b. 1940) (Pl. 4:20), Rostislav Lebedev (Pl. 4:16), and the Kazimir Passion Group. Likewise, Kabakovianism, in its attempt to place the heritage of the communal utopia under erasure, that is, to deconstruct it, has never directly challenged the Apollonian ambitions of the extracommunal superego (i.e., the state).

Sots Art is sometimes spoken of as a variety of Pop Art, adapted to the specifics of Socialist Realism, which propagandized with illustrations for utopian narratives of a Soviet type. If one accepts this interpretation, it would seem to apply to the work of Kosolapov (Pls. 4:24, 4:25), Sokov, and Orlov (Pl. 4:26), but by no means to Komar and Melamid or Bulatov. In fact, when he showed his first experiments with ideological material to Komar and Melamid in 1973, Kosolapov was surprised to hear them respond: "This is no sort of Sots Art, but American consumer stuff."

In Kosolapov's work *Study, Sonny* (1975), an assiduous schoolboy and a policeman who encourages him are reduced to the level of comic-book heroes or advertisement panels. From 1972 to 1975 Kosolapov produced, along with appropriations of political iconography, pop objects in the spirit of Claes Oldenburg: padlocks sewn together from rags; a hand pressing a doorbell button; yogurt being poured into a glass, and so on. His contribution to Sots Art lies in the discovery of points of resemblance between the mechanisms of depersonalization that Soviet power applied with regard to communality and those that are still used by capitalists with the aim of controlling the mass of consumers.

Sokov's sculptural baggage from the 1970s includes *Threatening Finger* (1975), a mobile which moves as if giving a warning (Pl. 4:28), and *Project to Construct Glasses for Every Soviet Person* (1976), a painted wood sculpture which makes fun of viewing the world through red stars (Pl. 4:27). Sokov wants to connect Sots Art with folkloric thematics. In his sculptural compositions, executed in the "political *skazka*" (fairy tale) genre, the protagonists of Socialist Realist myth become crude toys, characters in medieval marketplace dramas, or heroes in a pulp novel bestiary. In one work, Stalin has a bear's paw and beastly claws, Khrushchev turns into a "weeble,"[19] and Andropov's ears start to move. Like many of Sokov's works, this one takes up a tradition of popular humor and suggests that the version of Sots Art he favors derives from the heart of the "urban peasantry," from the depths of communality.

Sots Art culminated in an exhibition in New York at the New Museum of Contemporary Art, organized by Margarita Tupitsyn in 1986. The show included works by Komar and Melamid, Sokov, Bulatov, Kosolapov, Lamm, and the Kazimir Passion Group (Aleksandr Drewchin, Kosolapov, Vladimir Urban, and Victor Tupitsyn). That this movement continued to agonize until the end of the 1980s is evidenced by Prigov's newspaper installations or the sculptures of Grisha Bruskin (b. 1945), which "caught and outpaced" the Socialist Realists with regard to Socialist "realistic-ness." From 1986 to 1988, Eduard Gorokhovsky (b. 1929), who had earlier been known for his semi-Conceptual silk-screens (Pl. 4:29), created a series of post-Sots Art paintings, including a Divisionist portrait of Stalin in which each of the 1,488 elements of color ("strokes") prove to be, upon closer examination, a stenciled image of Lenin.

Fig. 4:5
Igor Makarevich
(Surgical Instruments),
1978–79
Oil on canvas
131 × 315 cm

Andrei Monastyrsky (b. 1949) and the Collective Actions Group ("CA"), which formed in 1976, are linked with the conception of the *Journeys to the Countryside*. Over the course of fifteen years, many representatives of the alternative art world participated in these actions, some as viewers, some as participants. Among the key participants, along with Monastyrsky, were artists Nikita Alekseev, Nikolai Panitkov, Georgii Kizevalter, Igor Makarevich (b. 1943) (Fig. 4:5; Pl. 4:30), and Elena Elagina, and philologists Sergei Romashko and Sabina Hansgen. These artists' search for a common alternative to the language of communality and the language of power resulted in their escape from the urban environment.

By staging their performances outside Moscow, they revisited that agrarian space from which the expansion of the "Law of the Commune"[20] toward the city had begun in the 1920s. Having rejected iconoclastic gestures and attitudes, Monastyrsky and the Collective Actions Group aimed at curing the visual (which was infected with speech practices). In a certain sense, the discourse of the group is reminiscent of the strategies of the Art and Language Group, whose discovery boiled down to the fact that a literary sequence, exhibited in a gallery context "with the rights of a painting," automatically loses the property of legibility and obtains a visual dimensionality. This dovetails nicely with Monastyrsky's assertion that "in the actions of 'CA' language manifests itself in an utterly unexpected place."

I am reminded of an installation by Kabakov called *The Man Who Flew into Space from His Apartment*. In one of the rooms of the communal *thermae* that he reconstructed for his first show at Ronald Feldman Fine Arts in 1988, there was an enormous hole in the ceiling through which a man had catapulted himself, that is, had escaped from the prison of communal language. It would seem that Monastyrsky is exactly this Kabakovian character. The

Collective Actions Group's oeuvre consists of an enormous amount of factographic materials and accessories (Pl. 4:31). These texts, diagrams, and photographs are now compiled in a six-volume collection called *Journeys to the Countryside*.

Emigration from the U.S.S.R. began in the 1970s. Within ten years, the list of Muscovite artists who had emigrated included Grobman, Yurii Kuper, Mikhail Kulakov, Genzikh Khudiakov, Bakhchanyan, Kosolapov, Masterkova, Vorobiev, Vladimir Grigorovich, Vitalii Dlugi, Oleg Kudriashov, Oleg Prokofiev, Sitnikov, Nusberg, Grigorii Perkel, Essayan, Aleksei Khvostenko, Roginsky, Komar, Melamid, Tselkov, Igor Shelkovsky, Neizvestny, Rimma and Valerii Gerlovin, Sokov, Drewchin, Mikhail Odnoralov, Lamm, Vitalii Rakhman, Aleksandr Shnurov, and many, many others. Rabin's 1978 trip outside the country resulted in his expulsion: a decree from the President of the Supreme Soviet of the U.S.S.R. deprived him of his Soviet citizenship.[21] As a result, he and his wife, artist Valentina Kropivnitskaia, received political asylum in France.

After ending up in the West, many of these artists experienced the shock of dual "orphanhood" prompted by the simultaneous loss of both their parental languages: the "paternal" (authoritarian speech) and the "maternal" (communal speech).[22] This psycholinguistic drama was also sharply experienced by those who remained in the homeland. Correspondence and information exchanges reached an incredible incandescence in the 1970s, which to a significant degree updated the image of the West in the eyes of the Soviet intelligentsia. A performance by the Gnezdo (Nest) group (Gennadii Donskoi, Mikhail Roshal, Viktor Skersis) titled *Race toward Jerusalem* (1978) may be considered a reaction to these circumstances, as might Makarevich's Conceptual project *Traveling Gallery of Russian Artists*, in which the author asked emigrating artists to leave their fingerprints, which were then blown up and put on display, becoming a symbol of a sociocultural identity in the process of being lost.

Several important exhibitions took place at the beginning of the 1970s. The following shows are worth mentioning: a show at the Exhibition Hall of MOSKh of works by Vladimir Veisberg, Nikolai Andronov, Natalia Egorshchina, and Pavel Nikonov (1973); the Kineticists' exhibition in the Artists' House on Kuznetskii Bridge Street (1973); Komar and Melamid's installation entitled *Heaven* in a private apartment in Kolomenskoe; and the exhibition by Vladimir Piatnitsky, Valerii Gerlovin, Andrei Demykin, Natalia Shibanova, Aleksei Paustovsky, and Sergei Bordachev in the latter's apartment.

Certainly, however, the culmination of the exhibition activity of the 1960s and 1970s was the so-called Bulldozer Show, which took place on September 15, 1974. In the two weeks prior to the show, my wife Margarita and I were visited by Nemukhin, Masterkova, Rukhin, and Rabin, who let us in on their plan to organize an outdoor exhibition. In their opinion, the empty space alongside our house seemed the most suitable place for this type of event. In accordance with their plans, our apartment on Ostrovitianov Street (in Beliaevo) would become a repository for works to be exhibited, and also a place to sleep for the artists the day before the show so that they might avoid arrest on the way to the lot. Naturally, we had no objections, and everything went forward as planned, with one important exception.

In contrast to the primarily oral confrontations of the Manezh era, the show in the empty field on September 15, 1974, resulted in a serious physical reprisal by the authorities with the help of bulldozers, fire trucks, and policemen in civilian clothes. Many of the works on display were destroyed, and their creators were beaten, arrested, or subjected to administrative sanctions (that is, they lost their jobs, were "laid up" in hospital for forced cures, etc.). The bulldozer event, fraught with human rights violations, seriously damaged the already dubious reputation of the Soviet government in the West.

A desire on the part of the Party bureaucracy to improve its image in the eyes of "world society" led to the organization of a second outdoor exhibition. This one took place two weeks after the first one in Moscow's Izmailovsky Park. Although this exhibition was, in essence, foisted upon the artists by the government, the intensity of the negotiations and compromises connected with it had no precedent in the history of relations between nonconformists and the officialdom. In the fourteen-day period following the exhibition in Beliaevo, during which time its participants were subjected to incessant pressure from the authorities, Rabin's organizational talents manifested themselves. He not only demonstrated an enviable sang-froid, but also a thorough knowledge of the Soviet system. However, his authoritarian inclinations were no less in evidence. Thus, for example, when negotiations with the KGB became bogged down, Rabin called on his cohorts to go out into the same vacant lot where the bulldozer carnage had taken place on September 15. Nipping in the bud any manifestations of indecision amongst the artists, he declared: "If such great people as Mandelshtam, Tsvetaeva and Pasternak were delivered in sacrifice to their epoch, then God has ordered for us the same." Rabin's strategy was completely vindicated: the strong of this world made concessions, and an officially sanctioned "unofficial" exhibition took place on September 29 in Izmailovsky Park. No provisions were

Fig. 4:6
Moscow artists at the Beekeeping Pavilion, February 1975
First row, left to right: Nikolai Vechtomov, Oscar Rabin, Lydia Masterkova, Aleksandr Kharitonov, Dmitri Plavinsky, Vladimir Yakovlev, Eduard Shteinberg, Aleksei Tiapushkin, Petr Belenok, Otari Kandaurov. Second row: Oleg Tselkov, Vladimir Yankilevsky, Vladimir Nemukhin, Eduard Drobitsky, Aleksandr Yulikov, Igor Snegur, Viacheslav Kalinin. Photo by Igor Palmin, courtesy of the photographer

made for censorship, and no limitations on the number of participants were imposed. As far as numbers of viewers are concerned, the four-hour exhibition broke all attendance records.

The events described above forced the Party leadership to reconsider its relations with the artistic intelligentsia. A decision was reached to do away with unsolicited and uncensored art, but by peaceful means, without bloodshed. To this end, the artists were quite literally "shoved" into official creative organizations, one of which turned out to be the unknown Gorkom Grafikov, otherwise known as MOKKhG (the Moscow Joint Committee of Graphic Artists). An alternative to this type of job placement was the law on parasitism, and therefore few of the "venerable" nonconformists were able to avoid recruitment into MOKKhG.

The authorities envisaged not only the liquidation of unofficial art as a social phenomenon, but also the establishment of control over alternative artists by means of the Gorkom and other similar institutions. In brief, the extracommunal "it" in due time set about institutionalizing contractual corporality. The next "permitted" exhibition under the aegis of the Gorkom took place at the VDNKh (Exhibition of Economic Achievements) in the Beekeeping Pavilion in February 1975. Twenty painters, each of whom had close ties with foreign diplomats and journalists, took part in the show (Fig. 4:6). In September of the same year, an exhibition at the VDNKh House of Culture included 522 works by 145 artists. In addition to the better-known artists, this show included Aleksei Tiapushkin (Pl. 4:35), Anatolii Slepyshev, Andrei Abramov (Pl. 4:23), Nikita Andrievich, Katia Arnold, Soren Arutiunian, Lev Bruni, Sergei Volokhov, Igor Voroshilov, Aleksandr Kalugin, Samuil Rubashkin, Evgenii Izmailov, Nata Konysheva, Nikolai Kuk, Evgenii Bachurin, Nadezhda Elskaia, Vitalii Rakhman, Viacheslav Sysoev, Boris Turetsky, and Aleksandr Shnurov.

A Gorkom seven-artist exhibition in May 1976, and a group show in the MOSKh Exhibition Hall (in which twelve artists participated, including Drewchin with his "Provincial Pop Art" [Pl. 4:37]), can be listed along with other examples of the successful assimilation of communal modernism within the framework of Socialist Realist institutions. One should not, however, consider the cultural politics of the Soviet authorities one hundred percent effective. As Foucault has written: "There exists no concrete, fixed place which is the seat of rebellions, just as there is not a single formula of revolution. There are various points where all this arises, and various forms of resistance."[23]

Fig. 4:7
Sven Gundlakh
(Untitled), 1982
Pen and ink, collage,
and lithograph
61.5 × 86.5 cm

The validity of this observation is supported by the continuing apartment exhibitions and studio shows at the end of the 1970s. These were given in the workplaces of Mikhail Odnoralov and Volodymyr (Vladimir) Naumets and in the apartments of Liudmila Kuznetsova, E. Renova, Aida Khmeleva, and Mikhail Chernyshov. Chernyshov combined exhibitions of works in his lodgings with performances in parks, in which he and his colleagues in the Star Group approved the principles of visual geometry, which were then used in abstract painting. In 1976, an exhibition in Sokov's studio became a noteworthy event. Along with Sokov, the following artists took part in the show: Chuikov, Sergei Shablavin, Igor Shelkovsky, Yulikov, and the Gerlovins.

Rimma Gerlovina (b. 1951) was represented there by her "cubelets" (Pl. 4:32).[24] Externally reminiscent of Malevich's "Architectons," these cubes, upon closer inspection, turned out to be agents of speech: on their faces (both from the outside and inside) could be read fragments of communal conversations in the spirit of Kabakov or the poet Lev Rubinshtein. Rephrasing an old definition of Socialist Realism, we may say that these art objects are modernist in form and communal in content. Valerii Gerlovin's metallic structures (like, for example, his *Spermatozoid*) were put together from modules used by children in edifying play. The painted reliefs of Igor Shelkovsky (b. 1937) also made a strong impression; they skillfully managed to transfer Divisionist principles from painting to sculpture (Pl. 4:33). After emigrating to Paris, Shelkovsky put out—between the end of 1979 and the mid-1980s—seven issues of the art magazine *A-Ya*, which played a significant role in the history of alternative art.

The first half of the 1980s In the 1980s, contractual communality ceased to be merely a means of "subcultural survival" and became an object of aesthetic reflection as

Fig. 4:8
Sergei Mironenko
(Sergei Was Here,
19–21.05.82), 1982
Pen and ink and collage over
district map of Moscow
61.9 × 86.4 cm

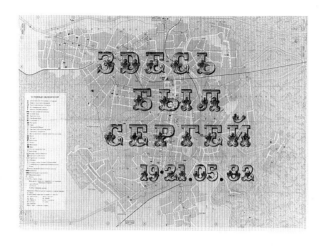

Fig. 4:9 (*top right*)
Gia Abramishvili
Incidents on the
Boulevard, 1985
Oil on canvas
119.7 × 79.4 cm

Fig. 4:10
Andrei Yakhnin
(Shick), 1986
Oil on canvas
120 × 150 cm

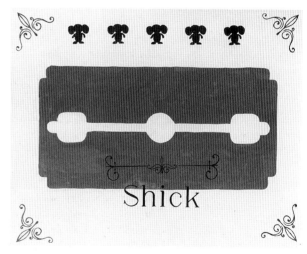

well. On this plane, AptArt may be considered the most precise copy of its era. AptArt (a series of apartment exhibitions in Moscow in 1982–84) happened to be the next Postmodernist strain that it makes sense to speak of as a "movement." Despite the fact that there had been apartment and studio shows earlier, to exhibit under the aegis of AptArt became a style, and not simply a "grudging necessity," as it had been in the 1960s and 1970s.[25] It also manifested a desire to reenact the *kommunalka*, but only as a playground instead of as stageboards for "philosophical investigation."

Graffiti and "Santa Claus aesthetics" together with a subversive appropriation of the accessories of the Soviet communal objecthood and an immeasurable carnival energy were the baggage of this Soviet variety of the New Wave. As an elemental protest against the semi-religious and eschatological concerns of the communal modernists, the new movement declared its "nonidentity within identity" (that is, within the communal milieu as a whole), thereby establishing their own neocommunal image by means of a generational conflict. The best example is the photo series by Vadim Zakharov (b. 1959) titled *I Acquired Enemies*, in which the artist subjects the "patriarchy" of Moscow nonconformist art to what one may refer to as *kommunalnaia razborka* (a phrase designating the malicious dressing-down of one's neighbors in conversation). For instance, to Shteinberg he quips: "Shteinberg, you are powdered Malevich."

Among the major exhibitions of AptArt was the one that was organized in the apartment of Nikita Alekseev in October 1982, with the participation of the Mukhomor or Toadstool Group, including Sven Gundlakh (Fig. 4:7), Alexander Kamensky, Sergei and Vladimir Mironenko (Fig. 4:8), and Konstantin Zvezdochetov (Pl. 4:34), plus Alekseev, Natalia Abalakova and Anatolii Zhigalov,

Zakharov and Skersis, Roshal, the Peppers, and others. In 1983, after the formation of the AptArt gallery, the artists organized two open-air exhibitions: "AptArt in Plein Air" in May, and "AptArt beyond the Fence" in September. In addition to the first show's participants, these two included Yurii Albert, Andrei Filippov, and Georgii Kizevalter. At the same time that Sots Art was demythologizing the mythical speech of Socialist Realism, AptArt was able to do the same thing in relation to the communal modernism of the 1960s and 1970s.[26] Moreover, the carnivalesque aspects of AptArt hint at the ability of its participants to acknowledge their communal heritage: unlike their predecessors—who lived and worked in denial of their communal psyche (i.e., in conflict with their communal

Fig. 4:11
Konstantin Latyshev
Gorbachev's Brothers, 1988
Oil on fiberboard
123.5 × 156 cm

Fig. 4:12
Yurii Leiderman
(Untitled), 1983
Crayon and pen and ink on
paperboard
20.9 × 14 cm

sensibility)—the AptArt artists have finally come to terms with what (or who) they really are.

The death of AptArt in 1984 was violent: the authorities accused the artists of participation in pornographic activities. However, the movement was able to escape disintegration and was reborn under *glasnost*. The so-called Kindergarten Group, which included Garik Vinogradov, Nikolai Filatov, and Andrei Roiter, together with the residents of the Furmanny Lane studios, constituted a new paradigm of AptArt and should be interpreted as a formula for cooperation and mutual sympathy between young alternative artists. The youngest representatives of this coterie are the Champions of the World (Gia [Guram] Abramishvili [Fig. 4:9], Boris Matrosov, Andrei Yakhnin [Fig. 4:10], and Konstantin Latyshev [Fig. 4:11]) and the Medhermeneutics (Sergei Anufriev [Pl. 4:36], Pavel Peppershtein [Pl. 4:40], and Yurii Leiderman [Fig. 4:12]), who, in their texts, performances, and installations, explore what they call "the Unknown."

As an epistemological instrumentation indispensable for the detection of the Unknown, the Medical Hermeneutics proposed a strategy of "inspection." From 1985 to 1986, the Kindergarten Group put together exhibitions of works by Igor Kopystiansky and Svetlana Kopystianskaia, Sergei Shutov, Sergei Volkov, Naumets, and Alekseev, while the Champions of the World, initially under the influence of Zvezdochetov, enticed such residents of Furmanny Lane as Igor Zaidel and Vadim Fishkin into their orbit. It is worth noting that the studios on Furmanny Lane were situated in an abandoned building where there had earlier been a school for the blind, while the Kindergarten was housed on premises where there had once been a kindergarten. These two facts, by some strange confluence of circumstances, bring together the psycholinguistic characteristics of communal corporality, its "blindness" (that is, the speech, rather than the visual character, of its "vision") and its infantility.

Until fairly recently, feminist intellectual *praxis* had not been welcomed by Moscow's alternative artists. In 1987, Natalia Nesterova (b. 1944) and several other Muscovite female artists ardently denied any chance for viewing their artistic oeuvre within the framework of a feminist agenda. One can perhaps relate this denial to their lack of awareness of the importance of such issues as gender, body politics, male dominance, and sexism, and of the artist's responsibility to reflect critically upon these themes. But this sort of attitude is now rapidly changing thanks to the steady stream of Western literature that now flows into Moscow. One specific manifestation of such a change was the organization of the first feminist art exhibition in Moscow at the Oktiabrskaia Exhibition Hall in September 1990. In the absence of Larisa Zvezdochetova, Maria Serebriakova, and Svetlana Kopystianskaia, who at that time were traveling or working abroad, the list of participants consisted of Anna Alchuk, Elena Elagina, Maria Konstantinova, Vera Miturich-Khlebnikova, Irina Nakhova, Sabina Hansgen, and Elena Shakhovskaia. In this group show, titled "Rabotnitsa" [Working Woman], the artists engaged in a subversive reexamination of the ways women are represented in official and private signs, codes, and visual stereotypes throughout the culture.

Nakhova (b. 1955) is represented in the Dodge Collection by several works from the mid-1980s (Pls. 4:38, 4:39). Prior to that, her art was influenced by the drawings and paintings of Pivovarov. At the decade's end, Nakhova became involved in the combination of the architectural background of residential space with painterly, graphic, and sculptural elements. This installation genre, known by the name "Room as a Medium," is associated in the West with the names of Imi Knabel, Günther Förg, Gerhard Merz, and Reinhard Mucha. At the same time, Nakhova began to paint dramatic images reflecting the features of a post-catastrophic consciousness: ruins, fragments of bygone cultures, and uninhabited spaces. Unsuitable for ecologists, it is nonetheless endowed with a sense of peace and harmony.

I would also like to draw attention to the fates of some of those artists who emigrated from the U.S.S.R. As I have already noted, they were forced to experience a shock of dual orphanhood connected with the loss of that which structured their lives in their homeland, namely, the will to communality and the will to authoritarian power. Having turned up abroad, many tried at first to reproduce one or the other structure, cohering into communal bodies and simultaneously attempting to control totally (in the spirit of Soviet leaders) the process of the West's familiarization with the alternative "image" of Soviet culture. At the end of the 1970s, the Russian diaspora in Paris found itself smashed into several quasicommunal factions competing with one another, such as Vladimir Maximov's group versus Andrei Siniavsky's group (in literature) and Mikhail Chemiakin's group versus Lev Nusberg's group (in art).

In contrast to the Soviet *kommunalka* of the post-Stalin era, with its characteristic Platonism with regard to both sympathies and phobias, the Parisian communal bodies, to one degree or another, were driven by mercantile considerations. Maximov and his journal *Kontinent* were subsidized by Germany's far-right financial circles, and

Chemiakin, in the course of securing the status of leader of the artistic emigration, spent large sums of money—made by selling paintings—on the publication of such items as the journal *Apollon* (1977).

In the context of the approach to the history of Russian contemporary art being developed here, the disputes in Paris are relevant in that the extracommunal "it," identified in the U.S.S.R. with the Party ideocracy, assumes a different form for the Russian émigré in the West: financial power. The activities of Igor Shelkovsky constitute an exception to this rule. The publication of the journal *A-Ya*, which he edited, was made possible for the most part by the resources of Moscow communal Conceptualism: for instance, Bulatov's painting *Danger*, conveyed to the United States by *A-Ya* coeditor Alek Sidorov, was bought by Norton Dodge in 1984; the profit covered the publication of four issues of the journal.

The activities of Russian émigrés in New York reached their peak in 1981, when Dodge opened the Contemporary Russian Art Center of America at 599 Broadway in SoHo. Margarita Tupitsyn was the museum's curator. In the two-and-a-half years of its existence, the Center organized a number of important group exhibitions with titles such as "Russian New Wave"; "Women Artists: 1934–1983"; "Baltic Art"; "Gennady Zubkov and the Sterligov Group"; and "Selections from the Norton Dodge Collection." These exhibitions, like the catalogues the Center published, attracted swarms of viewers and generated a significant number of reviews in the New York art press. Prior to that, such attention was reserved for the shows of Komar and Melamid, with whose names alternative Russian art was associated in the late 1970s and early 1980s.

The chronicle of this art, alas, did not escape relapses of Parisian ghettocentrism with all its side effects, even leading to a physical confrontation between artists of a Sots Art orientation (the Kazimir Passion Group) and the apologists of the so-called "Russian Samizdat" (the Gerlovins, Bakhchanyan, Anatolii Ur, Nusberg, and others). As a result of the Center's activities, the American public was able to receive a fuller conception not only of the Muscovite communal modernism of the 1960s and 1970s, but of the Russian Postmodernism of the 1980s as well. Following the loss of its home in SoHo at the end of 1983, the Center's activities were reoriented. Tupitsyn began to organize Russian shows in other exhibition spaces, while Dodge continued to support these projects by publishing and editing catalogues.

Of particular note are the Sots Art exhibitions at the Semaphore Gallery in New York (1984) and the New Museum of Contemporary Art in New York (1986), where

AptArt was displayed alongside Sots Art. Each of the exhibitions organized by the Center traveled to museums in the United States and Canada. In the 1980s, through the efforts of Margarita Tupitsyn and myself in the United States and Boris Groys in Germany, a solid groundwork was laid for a theoretical discourse focusing on Russian art using Western critical methodologies, including the French poststructuralism of the 1960s and 1970s.

Alongside these exterior forms of reflection, there existed another, internal form of the apocryphal description of Soviet cultural ecology. This language was developed in the late 1970s and mid-1980s by Kabakov, Monastyrsky, Joseph Bakshtein, Vladimir Sorokin, and others, and at the end of the last decade by a later group that included Peppershtein, Anufriev, Leiderman, and Mikhail Rykhlin. In Leningrad, the same role was and continues to be played by the theoreticians Victor Mazin, Olesya Turkina, and Alla Mitrofanova, and the artists Timur Novikov, Afrika, Andrei Khlobystin, and Monroe (Vladislav Mamyshev). The texts of all of these authors are still awaiting translation into and publication in foreign languages.

The hubbub concerning Gorbachev's Russia, which reached its zenith in 1988, may be termed an instance of Orientalism.[27] In the 1920s and 1930s, Western intellectuals like Walter Benjamin, René Etiemble, Louis Aragon, and André Gide invested their Orientalist aspirations in the Russian revolutionary (read: communal) experiment, for they perceived it as the model of the universal future. A diametrically opposite ideological construct emerged in the late 1980s, when it became clear that the promise of the communal future was not going to be fulfilled. Instead, contemporary Russia is beginning to resemble the historic past of Western Europe and America, in particular the moment of "wild" capitalism at the turn of the century.

This new image of Russia has led to a dramatic reversal of the previous Orientalist paradigm: the utopian worldview has given way to a nostalgic one in which the communal is identified with "yesterday" rather than with "tomorrow." At the end of the 1980s, Russia became for the West what the Orient had been for it in Victorian times: a target and object of sublimated desires, fantasies, intrigues, and self-deceptions. Now that the "new wave" of Orientalism and the Russian art boom that accompanied it have subsided, it may be said that in the interrelations of the pairing "the West/Russia" (or, more precisely, "the West/Russian artists") one can observe a mutual parasitism and an absence of authentic interest.

While abroad, visitors from Moscow, Leningrad, or Odesa (Odessa) demonstrated the full range of qualities and shortcomings[28] proper to the communal world-order, from warmth and generosity to infantility and political incorrectness. In turn, they were able to discover that, with rare exceptions, Western intellectuals are incapable of equitable contact with their colleagues from Russia: it is always sugared with paternalism together with Orientalist or neocolonialist "manners." For the American or European cultural establishment, its Russian counterpart is cannon fodder for narrativity, an aboriginal pantry of experimental raw material, the discursive processing of which (refining) is licensed by the West. Russian authors publishing in the West must spend no small amount of time battling for the right to theorize. Moreover, as a result of this, kind academic protectors turn into rivals on guard.

Finally, I would like to say a few words about an event that took place in the heat of *perestroika* and which, to a significant degree, drew the odyssey of Muscovite underground visual culture to a close. I have in mind the Sotheby's auction in Moscow, which was a spectacular incarnation of all the accumulated Orientalist reveries and which brought to realization a successful sale of the works of Soviet alternative artists on their own territory in 1988. The triumph of hard (Western) currency over local ideology heralded not only an end to the two-world condition between the (neo)communal body of Moscow bohemia and the art of power, but also the beginning of the disintegration of both.[29]

Notes

1. I have in mind the artists Aleksandr Tyshler, Ivan Kudriashov, Antonina Sofronova, Eurosinya Plastova, Maria Siniakova, Vladimir Sterligov, Tatiana Glebova, Petr Sokolov, and others.

2. Ilya Kabakov, from a conversation with Victor Tupitsyn, "From the Communal Kitchen: A Conversation with Ilya Kabakov," *Arts Magazine* (Oct. 1991): 50.

3. Thus, the thesis of Stalin's book, *Questions of Linguistics*, that language is politically predetermined and class-free, literalizes the ultimate "ends" of Stalinist "means." Since the post-revolutionary avant-garde had initially associated itself with the proletariat, the dissolution of the latter is what among other reasons prompted the former to commit suicide by becoming a vehicle for the glorification of Stalinism. Evidently, the phenomenon of the dissolution of class consciousness in the "lower depth" of urban peasantry and the retreat of the proletariat "beneath its bar" (as Lacanians would put it) appears to be in agreement with the Benjaminian notion of "unconscious proletariat" or, for that matter, the "political unconscious."

4. *Drugoe iskusstvo: Moskva, 1956–76*, exh. cat. (Moscow: Moskovskaia Kollektsiia/SP Interbuk, 1991), vol. 1, p. 261.

5. It took no less than fifteen years for this extracommunal "it" to find, at last, the recognizable features of

Fig. 4.13
Armen Bugayan
Untitled, 1986
Pen and ink on paper
60.8 × 42.8 cm

government Party power. The de-conspiratizing of which we are speaking found a place in the art of the Sots artists, who considered Rabin their precursor (this concerns his 1964 work *Passport* in particular, as well as his still lifes with *Pravda*). In the interest of fairness it must be said that Rabin's dissidence was wholly reflected in his organizational activity that was aimed at consolidating the unofficial artists in their opposition to the authorities.

6. The idea of being chosen can be found in Masterkova's autobiography and in her early poems. Archive of Victor and Margarita Tupitsyn.

7. *Drugoe iskusstvo*, p. 83.

8. V. Tupitsyn, "From the Communal Kitchen," p. 53.

9. *Drugoe iskusstvo*, p. 139.

10. Ibid., p. 59.

11. Ibid., p. 9.

12. Falk, Favorsky, and Fonvizin were masters for many of Moscow's alternative artists, including Bulatov, Vassiliev, and Kabakov.

13. Among others, the artist Armen Bugayan (Apis) (Fig. 4:13) was a frequent visitor to the Yuzhinsky Lane salon.

14. From an unpublished conversation with Victor and Margarita Tupitsyn, 1992.

15. This orator is a Party leader giving a speech in a Kremlin assembly hall. The image was printed on the cover of the magazine *Ogonyok*, which served as the point of departure for Vassiliev's painting.

16. This is presumably the case with the Dodge Collection at the Jane Voorhees Zimmerli Art Museum in New Brunswick, N.J.

17. Here, we cite Komar and Melamid's own ironic self-definition that was inscribed on their *Double Portrait* (1972).

18. According to Bulatov, Vassiliev, and Kabakov, all three of them were fond of railroad posters in the early 1970s. In this context, the railroad crossing sign "Danger," which warned against the approach of trains, became one intertext for Bulatov's painting *Danger*. Kabakov even has an essay on the subject, titled "Two Railwaymen."

19. A toy that had its American heyday in the 1970s, as in "weebles wobble but they won't fall down."

20. The "Law of the Commune" is phrase coined by Leopold von Sacher-Masoch.

21. A similar decree was later issued to deprive Igor Shelkovsky, editor of the journal *A-Ya*, of his Soviet citizenship.

22. The use of a term such as "maternal" in the case of communal speech is not accidental here. Likewise, Gilles Deleuze, in his *Masochism, Coldness, and Cruelty* (New York: Zone Books, 1991), identifies hegemony of speech immanent to agrarian sects and collectives (the "Law of the Commune") with the so-called "Oral Mother."

23. Michel Foucault, *Histoire de la Sexualité*, vol. 1, *La Volonté du Savoir* (Paris: Gallimard, 1976), p. 126.

24. These cubelets resemble Petr Miturich's *Graphic Dictionary* (1919), a visual interpretation of Khlebnikov's "Starry Alphabet."

25. This thought is borrowed from Margarita Tupitsyn's book *Margins of Soviet Art: Socialist Realism to the Present* (Milan: Giancarlo Politi Editore, 1989), p. 100.

26. AptArt exhibitions were reconstructed in America by the present author in several exhibition spaces between 1983 and 1986. The last one was organized by Victor and Margarita Tupitsyn at the New Museum of Contemporary Art in New York in 1986. Norton Dodge published a catalogue of this show.

27. The Orientalist subtext of the West's exaltation concerning the *perestroika* era is analyzed in many texts by the present author. See, for example, Victor Tupitsyn, "East-West Exchange: The Ecstasy of (Mis)Communication," in David Ross, ed., *Between Spring and Summer: Soviet Conceptual Art in the Era of Late Communism* (Cambridge, Mass.: MIT Press, 1990); and Margarita and Victor Tupitsyn, "Green Dream in a Red Chamber," in *Khudozhestvennaia volia* (Moscow: Nauka Publishing House, 1993).

28. A sharp criticism of the current Moscow art situation can be found in Victor Tupitsyn, "On (z)Ontico-(z)Ontological Difference," *Kabinet* (Summer 1994). Also, see Victor Tupitsyn, "L'arte russa in esilio dall'essere al non essere," *D'Ars* 141 (Fall 1993): 42–45.

29. The outstanding question is, what will happen to the communal space while authoritarian power is being replaced by the power of money? Everyone who regularly visits Russia has noticed a process of intensive growth in the real estate market, particularly for those willing to pay in hard currency. The reason for this lies not only in the desire of foreigners to buy apartments there but also in the fact that in Russia there are only two "prestigious" cities, Moscow and St. Petersburg. Everyone who becomes rich in Siberia, the northern regions, or anywhere else buys apartments in the best areas of these two cities. Here is an example of how it happens. Let us say that somewhere in the center of Moscow three different families live in one big communal apartment. A wealthy investor buys (through an agent) three small private apartments in peripheral areas and offers to let these three families move into them. As a rule, they accept such deals. Meanwhile, the family of the wealthy investor moves to the large, now vacant communal apartment. As a result, the rich gradually settle in the center of the city and the poor are pushed to the outskirts. Thus, the Soviet dichotomy power/communal is turning into a Western type of dichotomy, namely center/periphery. Inhabitants of the Soviet urban ghettos, who were hitherto not aware of the difference between the center and the periphery, now face the new reality of it.

5 | "A great city with a provincial fate"

Nonconformist art in Leningrad from Khrushchev's thaw to Gorbachev's *perestroika*

Alla Rosenfeld

For centuries, the city of St. Petersburg (Petrograd, Leningrad) was synonymous with Russian culture. Even in the West, most people had heard of the Hermitage Museum and the Kirov Theater of Opera and Ballet. But in such a relatively short period, this beautiful city experienced three revolutions, a civil war, Stalin's purges, and a devastating nine-hundred-day seige by the Nazis during World War II. It was also in this city that thousands of poets, writers, and artists were arrested, exiled, or executed by the Soviet government from the late 1920s through to the 1970s.

Founded by Peter I (Peter the Great) in 1703 as a stronghold and trade port on the Baltic Sea, St. Petersburg quickly became one of Russia's largest cultural, industrial, and scientific centers, and the second city in size after Moscow. In 1712, Peter I transferred the capital of the Russian state from Moscow to St. Petersburg. The new capital was one of the first cities in the world to be developed following a deliberate plan; it was built rapidly according to designs executed by eminent Russian and foreign architects. In 1918, however, Vladimir Lenin and other leaders of the Soviet government moved the capital from Petrograd (as St. Petersburg had been renamed in 1914) back to Moscow.

After that, Petrograd (which was renamed Leningrad after the death of Lenin in 1924) lost its position as a leading political and cultural center and became an isolated place, called by one Russian writer a "great city with a provincial fate." More recently, the concentration of Western diplomats and media representatives in Moscow has further contributed to Leningrad's relative isolation. Since foreign consulates were opened in Leningrad only in 1973, before that date most diplomats and tourists entered the U.S.S.R. through Moscow and spent the bulk of their time there.

As a result of Leningrad's status, when Soviet nonconformist art began to gain international attention in the 1970s, it was the Moscow artists who achieved the greatest notoriety. Nonconformist artists in Leningrad were less well known in the West, a fact that contributed to the opinion that new developments in Leningrad art were "insignificant" or "secondary." To many observers, Leningrad nonconformists were more traditional and less experimental. Leningrad did not, for example, develop Sots Art, as Moscow did, and Conceptual Art appeared in Leningrad much later than in Moscow. In fact, many developments in Leningrad were parallel with those in Moscow but were significantly different. Events in Moscow simply attracted more worldwide attention.

The Dodge Collection illustrates the major developments in Leningrad nonconformist art, reflecting its range and diversity. Although it is difficult to offer a complete survey of all the names, works, and concerns of Leningrad artists, this essay will outline the chronological development of Leningrad nonconformist art, focusing on the several periods of development and the key groups or artists who gave this art its distinctive character.

The influence of Russian avant-garde art of the 1920s on the unofficial subculture in Leningrad in the 1930s and 1940s Between 1910 and 1930, St. Petersburg was one of the major artistic centers of the world, a place where many innovative ideas in the visual arts were born. In the 1920s, there were four major avant-garde art movements in Leningrad, centered around Pavel Filonov, Mikhail Matiushin, Kuzma Petrov-Vodkin, and Kazimir Malevich. Students of these four artists continued to influence the artistic underground well into the 1940s and 1950s, creating living links between the old avant-garde and the new, post-Stalin generation of nonconformist artists.

One of the leading figures of the Leningrad avant-garde in the 1920s and early 1930s was Pavel Filonov (1883–1941). In 1925, he established the Filonov School, also known as the Collective of Masters of Analytical Art. Among the forty or so artists associated with this group were Tatiana Glebova (1900–1985), Pavel Kondratiev (1902–1985), Alisa Poret (1902–1984), and Mikhail Tsybasov (1904–1967). Filonov's school held several major exhibitions in the late 1920s and early 1930s, but during the Stalin era the nearly abstract art of Filonov and his students could not be tolerated. Many members of Filonov's group were declared "enemies of the people"; some were arrested and one even committed suicide after a long period in prison. In spite of this repression, a number of artists associated with Filonov's group continued to paint, using his analytical method, well after their master's death in 1941.

Another important source of artistic inspiration for many later artists was the movement headed by two key figures of the Russian avant-garde, Mikhail Matiushin (1861–1934) and Elena Guro (1877–1913). While other artists were interested in Cubo-Futurism, Matiushin and Guro sought a return to nature, carrying out extensive research not only in physics and biology, but also in Eastern religion. Matiushin conducted a studio in Spatial Realism for his group, which was known as Zorved (*Zorkoe vedanie*, or "See-Know"). He was also one of the founders of Ginkhuk (Institute of Artistic Culture) in Leningrad, where Malevich was at one time director and the teaching staff included such famous avant-garde artists as Filonov and Vladimir Tatlin.

Between 1923 and 1926 Ginkhuk was the first art research center in the world devoted to the theory of contemporary art, especially such movements as Futurism and Suprematism. While head of the department of Organic Culture at Ginkhuk, Matiushin developed his concept of "expanded seeing," which allowed for the possibility of transposing sounds into visual form. He conducted extensive research into problems of color, form, and perception, focusing mainly on two areas: the relationship between colors and their environments and the effect of motion on colors. The main goal of Matiushin's research was to formulate what he called "the sensation of the Fourth Dimension."

Ginkhuk suffered a tragic fate. In 1926, the major Leningrad newspaper published an article that was critical of it. Titled "Monastery on State Support," the piece accused Ginkhuk teachers of producing anti-Soviet propaganda. Shortly thereafter, Ginkhuk was shut down. However, Matiushin's disbanded department at Ginkhuk became the basis for the Matiushin School, which included the Ender family, Nikolai Kostrov (b. 1901), Evgenia Magaril (b. 1902), Olga Vaulina, and Irina Valter (1903–1993), among others.

Kuzma Petrov-Vodkin (1878–1939), who taught at the Academy of Arts in the 1920s, also created his own school and greatly influenced Leningrad artistic culture, especially with his idea of "spherical perspective." From his studio came such Leningrad masters as Leonid Chupiatov (1890–1941), Petr Sokolov (1892–1938), Evgenia Evenbakh (1889–1981), and Benita Essen, who influenced the later nonconformists.[1]

Fig. 5:1
Sholom Shvarts
Boxers, 1954
Tempera on fiberboard
46.3 × 40 cm

The 1950s and 1960s: Appearance of the first groups of nonconformist artists After World War II, one of the first groups of nonconformist artists to emerge was the Arefiev Group, or ONZh (Association of Impoverished Artists). This group included artists Aleksandr Arefiev (1931–1978), Rikhard Vasmi (b. 1929), Valentin Gromov (b. 1930), Vladimir Shagin (b. 1932), Sholom Shvarts (b. 1929) (Fig. 5:1), sculptor Valery Titov, and the poet Roald Mandelshtam. Arefiev, Gromov, Shagin, and Shvarts studied at the end of the 1940s at the Secondary Art School affiliated to the Academy of Fine Arts. All were later accused of painting "formalist" works and expelled.[2]

This circle of intelligent and talented people were forced to live in extreme poverty, and they often depicted in their paintings the depressing nature of everyday existence in the Soviet Union: the streets, the crowded apartments, the cafés, and the social clubs. Poet Konstantin Kuzminsky, an important figure in Leningrad nonconformist culture, called these artists "Neorealists."[3] Every member of the Arefiev Group was influenced by the work of the Circle of Artists, an earlier avant-garde faction that from about 1926 to 1932 synthesized many of the leading European art trends, from Cézannism to Cubism.

Aleksandr Arefiev, the acknowledged leader of the group, was sentenced to the labor camps twice for a drug addiction stemming from his military service. During the

1950s and 1960s, Arefiev's work focused on the brutal reality and poor conditions of life in the lower depths of Soviet society: police brutality, scandals, executions, and street fights (Pl. 5:4). The highly emotional, Expressionistic style of Arefiev's paintings is also reflected in the titles of his various series: *Murderers*, *Hanged Men*, *Violent Acts*, and *Toilets*. But he also dealt with the mundane dreariness of everyday Soviet life. "I had a policy," Arefiev once stated, "of depicting only the most banal subjects, those which were previously treated by many other artists . . . and to compare what I achieved with the versions of the other artists."[4] The scandalous and antiheroic stance of Arefiev's work was diametrically opposed to the official Socialist Realist style, which glorified the accomplishments of Socialism. In 1978, one year after emigrating to Paris, a despondent Arefiev died of a drug overdose.

Vladimir Shagin, another leading artist of the group, was also expelled from the Secondary Art School for "formalism" (the rumor was that he glued a real feather onto his realistic still-life assignment). Nonetheless, he was able to continue his studies at the Tavricheskaia Art School (presently known as Serov Art College). Alexander Rapoport (b. 1933), a fellow student at the time, recalls that when Shagin was required to paint a nude model, he used such a bright yellow for modeling the body that the teachers were shocked. After a year and a half, Shagin was expelled from this school, too. For a while, he earned a living playing guitar and contrabass in a small jazz ensemble. Then, during the 1960s, Shagin worked as a laborer, painting solely on weekends. It was only in 1974, after he began receiving disability compensation, that Shagin was able to devote himself entirely to painting.

While in art school, Shagin married his fellow student Natalia (Neizel) Zhilina (b. 1933). She later participated in most of the unofficial art exhibitions of the 1970s and 1980s. For these activities, she was fired from the Artistic Fund, where she had worked as a graphic artist for twenty years. Zhilina's work is closely connected with St. Petersburg. In her colorful, kaleidoscopic views of cities, she frequently depicts bridges, canals, parks, buildings, and trolley cars (Pl. 5:1).

Like many unofficial artists, Rikhard Vasmi (Pl. 5:2) chose to do low-paid, politically undemanding jobs, such as those of furnace stoker, housepainter, and manual laborer. "The fact that I was never allowed to call myself officially an artist had a very positive influence on my personal development," Vasmi says. "The less official a person's life is, the more personal freedom this person has."[5]

While members of the Arefiev Group often depicted the

hardships of daily existence, Lenina Nikitina (b. 1931) (Fig. 5:2) dedicated many of her works to the horrors of the nine-hundred-day siege of Leningrad during World War II. Dark childhood reminiscences are reflected in Nikitina's work: only ten years old when the war began, she was compelled to endure the death by starvation of both her mother and her sister.

Josef Yakerson (b. 1936), who avoided joining any of the nonconformist groups, also turned to disturbing themes in his work. He frequently depicted suicides, the sufferings of Christ, and scenes at the morgue (Pl. 5:5). Even after his emigration to the West in 1973, his utterly unorthodox approach to the subject of the Crucifixion—

Fig. 5:2

Natalia Tsekhomskaia

The Artist Lenina Nikitina, 1984

Gelatin silver print with watercolor and ink additions

59.4 × 49.1 cm

the expressiveness of the face of Christ, the unprettified portrayal of the mutilated body, the clearly expressed deformation—often brought angry reactions from religious groups. As Yakerson recalls: "When my religious series *The Crucifixion* and *Judas' Suicide* were exhibited in Israel, fanatically inclined Jews threatened to stone me for painting Christian subjects. In America, Christians told me I ought to be burned together with my paintings for such a portrayal of Christ."[6] Yakerson's works became symbolic of what suffering a man can bear, in any country and in any century.

During the period of the thaw following the death of Stalin, French Impressionist and Postimpressionist paintings, many of which had been in storage for years, were again put on view at the Hermitage Museum. In the late 1950s and early 1960s the Hermitage also showed several exhibitions that included modern art, such as "French Art of the Nineteenth and Twentieth Centuries from the Louvre and Other French Museums" and exhibitions of British, Belgian, Italian, and Scandinavian art.[7] These exhibitions gave Leningrad artists their first opportunity, in many cases, to see works by such artists as Cézanne and Picasso (in 1956), not to mention young American artists like Jasper Johns, Robert Rauschenberg, and James Rosenquist (who were included in exhibitions organized by the U.S. State Department and shown in Moscow and Leningrad in 1963).

These exhibitions evoked an extraordinary range of feelings, from enthusiasm for the new to curiosity, disgust, and rage.[8] The works of some Russian avant-garde artists were also shown in the 1960s, including an exhibition of works by Vladimir Sterligov and Tatiana Glebova in LOSKh (Leningrad Section of the Artists' Union) in 1965. However, an exhibition of works by Pavel Filonov in 1966 was closed by the authorities after only one day. Even so, Konstantin Kuzminsky recalls, more than three thousand people packed the hall on that one day to see the Filonov exhibition, their coats overflowing the checkroom and spilling out onto the stairs.

A series of innovative exhibitions of works by young Leningrad artists was also initiated at various locations. Among the first was the exhibition of works by Oleg Tselkov (b. 1934) and Ilya Glazunov (b. 1930) at the Leningrad Electro-Technical Institute in 1956. Other attempts were made to show nonconformist works in the lobbies of various research institutes, clubs, and cafés, but these frequently resulted in the exhibition being closed before it opened. When an exhibition was allowed to remain open, there would usually be negative reviews in the local newspapers.

Often those involved in organizing such exhibitions,

including the artists, would suffer. Offenders could lose their jobs or their memberships in the Artists' Union. Some were even arrested and imprisoned. In 1964, for example, several young artists and poets who worked at the Hermitage—including Mikhail Chemiakin (b. 1943), Valerii Kravchenko, Oleg Liagachev (b. 1939), Vladimir Ovchinnikov (b. 1941), and Vladimir Ufliand (b. 1937)—organized an "Exhibition of Workmen Artists" in the staff area of the museum. After just three days the exhibition was closed by the KGB, all the works were confiscated, and all the participants, as well as the museum director M.I. Artamonov, who had supported the show, were fired. In addition, the KGB tracked down viewers who had written favorable comments in the visitors' book, and many of those people lost their jobs as well.

Because of the difficulties of exhibiting in museums or other public places, nonconformist artists began to show their work in private apartments. One such exhibition was organized in an apartment on Liteinyi Prospect in downtown Leningrad as early as December 1963. That small show included works by Andrei Gennadiev (b. 1947), Henry Elinson (b. 1935) (Fig. 5:3), Boris Nikolashchenko, and Aleksandr Tovbin. Another important exhibition of ten artists took place in 1971 in the studio of Vladimir

Fig. 5:3
Henry Elinson
(Untitled), 1974
Pen and ink on paper
30.2 × 22.1 cm

Ovchinnikov on Kustarny Pereulok. The day after it opened, this exhibition was destroyed by the KGB and all the works were confiscated. Ovchinnikov also had his studio taken away. Despite their limited space, poor lighting, and other drawbacks, apartment exhibitions became a regular feature of the Leningrad art scene in the 1970s, just as they did in Moscow.

Another early group of Leningrad painters, started in the 1960s, included Anatolii Basin (b. 1936), Igor Ivanov (b. 1934), Evgenii Goriunov (b. 1944), and others. These artists studied with Osip Sidlin (1909–1972), a noted teacher at the Kapranov Palace of Culture. Sidlin, who had studied under Aleksandr Osmerkin (1892–1953) at Vkhutein and also took lessons from Kazimir Malevich and Kuzma Petrov-Vodkin, encouraged the artists of this group to develop the artistic traditions of the Russian Cézannists, active in the early 1900s, known as the Jack of Diamonds. Sidlin's pupils also studied the eighteenth-century still lifes of the French artist Jean-Baptiste Chardin. They spent much of their time working outdoors, but the main aim of Sidlin's teaching was to create a symbolic generalization rather than to convey an immediate impression of nature.

One of Sidlin's students, Igor Ivanov, whose work once seemed "too traditional for avant-gardists and too avant-garde for traditionalists,"[9] later became an organizer and long-term contributor to the TEV (Association for Experimental Exhibitions). His studio on Vladimirskaia Square became an important meeting place for discussions among unofficial artists in the mid-1970s. Under the influence of Cézanne, Ivanov sought to capture in his paintings solid tangible reality, the textures of materials, and the volume of things.

Ivanov's favorite motif was the doll (Pl. 5:3). This was inspired by the artist's play with his daughter, Larisa; he told her stories about the different dolls in her collection as if they were real people. Soon he began painting still lifes of these increasingly anthropomorphic dolls, giving each one different personal characteristics. For Ivanov, the doll was a symbol of both "people as marionettes" and "dolls as people," concepts that have a strong tradition in the history of Russian art, appearing, for example, in Petr Tchaikovsky's ballet *The Nutcracker* and Igor Stravinsky's *Petrouchka*. Similar motifs can also be found in the work of the turn-of-the-century St. Petersburg World of Art group. Ivanov's series of people-like toys ends with the image of a broken doll discarded with the garbage.

Groups and exhibitions in the late 1960s and 1970s
During the 1960s, a large group of artists gathered around

Vladimir Sterligov, a former student at Ginkhuk. The group initially included artists Sergei Spitsyn (b. 1923), Elisaveta Aleksandrova (b. 1930), Gennadii Zubkov (b. 1948), and art historians Alla Povelikhina and Evgenii Kovtun. Later, this group also included Aleksandr Nosov (b. 1950), Aleksei Gostintsev (b. 1950), Aleksandr Kozhin (b. 1950), Elena Gritsenko (b. 1947) (Pl. 5:8), Valentina Solovieva (b. 1946), Mikhail Tserush (b. 1948), Yurii Gobanov (b. 1941), and Vladimir Smirnov. Sterligov, who developed the Suprematist ideas of Malevich and organic forms of Matiushin in his work, was arrested at the end of 1954, along with two pupils, and sentenced to five years in a labor camp.

Returning to Leningrad, he developed his new ideas of spatial structure in art, which he called the "chalice-cupola curve." After Sterligov's death in 1973, his students continued to gather and exchange ideas at the studio of Tatiana Glebova, Sterligov's widow and herself an accomplished artist. Every artist in the group was well trained in Sterligov's system yet had an individual manner of painting. This was perhaps the most isolated and monastic artistic circle in Leningrad.

Gennadii Zubkov, who became the new leader of the Sterligov group, said of his teacher: "He was a living thread, a little bridge connecting the culture of the 1920s and 1930s and the lack of culture in the '50s and '60s."[10] Zubkov studied first at the Department of Graphic Arts at the Herzen Pedagogical Institute and then began to work regularly with Sterligov in 1964. Zubkov's own work lies in a range between representation and abstraction, combining formal and philosophical problems. His paintings are often flat, without volumetric modeling (Pl. 5:13). Avoiding one-point perspective and illusionism, Zubkov is attracted to Petrov-Vodkin's spherical treatment of space and to Malevich's theory of the "additional element."[11]

One of the major figures in the evolution of nonconformist art in Leningrad was Nikolai Akimov (1901–1968), the famous graphic artist of the 1920s and 1930s and a producer and artistic director at the Theater of Comedy. After Stalin's death in 1953, a department of stage design was established in the Leningrad Institute of Theater, Music, and Cinematography and Akimov was named the head. To enrich his teaching, Akimov brought back from his theatrical tours to the West books, catalogues, and slides of contemporary Western art. With these materials, he gave his students a broad view of contemporary art, and, importantly, full freedom to experiment. Thus, instead of founding an "Akimov School," he helped launch the careers of a diverse range of nonconformist artists, including Evgenii Mikhnov-Voitenko

(1932–1988), Vitalii Kubasov (b. 1937), Igor Tiulpanov (b. 1939), Mikhail Kulakov (b. 1933), Yurii Dyshlenko (1936–1995), Alek Rapoport, and Oleg Tselkov (whose later artistic career was in Moscow and Paris).

Akimov's student Igor Tiulpanov, for example, employs Surrealist imagery in his meticulous illusionistic paintings, incorporating stylistic elements from Leonardo da Vinci, Hieronymus Bosch, and Jan van Eyck (Pl. 5:7). These paintings are pictorial retracings of the artist's subconscious and show characteristics of what Freud called "dream work," including the existence of contrary elements side by side, the condensation of two or more objects or images, and the use of objects that have symbolic value.

Yurii Dyshlenko's style, on the other hand, was radically different (Pl. 5:6). After graduating from Akimov's department at the Institute, Dyshlenko worked at the Saransk Theater and as a book illustrator. Returning to Leningrad, he began to paint abstract or semi-abstract works, which often made reference to spiritual imagery, popular culture, and mechanical reproduction. As Victor Krivulin noted regarding Dyshlenko's painting: "the concept underlying his work is bound up with the idea of time, with the use of a particular psychological phenomenon in the perception of temporal relationships translated into spatial relationships."[12] To achieve his goal, Dyshlenko treated his paintings as logical systems. Believing that there was a correspondence between the spectrum of colors and a musical scale, he developed special color combinations equivalent to musical chords.

Evgenii Mikhnov-Voitenko's early artistic training was in the academic nineteenth-century tradition, but with the stimulus of Akimov he became actively interested in abstract art, soon becoming totally committed to abstraction (Pl. 5:9). Remaining unentangled in cultural politics, he devoted himself entirely to perfecting and elaborating his artistic vision by creating thousands of abstract works on paper. These works, largely in gouache, reflect his love and appreciation of music.[13] Mikhnov-Voitenko participated in a number of group shows of nonconformists in Leningrad, but during his lifetime his only solo exhibitions were in the United States.

Mikhail Kulakov, also a student of Akimov who graduated from the Institute in 1962, worked as an illustrator for the Lenizdat publishing house and as a stage designer for various theaters in Moscow and Leningrad. Kulakov's interest in Russian icon painting, which was a major influence during his formative period in the second half of the 1950s, was later enriched by his acquaintance with the

work of Chinese and Japanese painters influenced by Zen. In fact, many of Kulakov's abstractions, which contain symbolic signs of spirituality, undoubtedly relate to his deep interest in Far Eastern thought. After he had discovered the work of Mark Tobey, Jackson Pollock, and Georges Mathieu in the mid-1960s, Kulakov began to experiment with gestural abstraction. This work culminated in a series in which the overall painting becomes increasingly spontaneous while the individual gesture-splashes become increasingly precise (Pl. 5:11). During his "Leningrad period" (1959–76), his canvases became very textural through the use of such materials as nitroenamels, plaster, sand, and bitumen.[14] In 1975, Kulakov had his first one-man show—in Rome (where he moved the following year); he has never had an exhibition in the Soviet Union.

Other early Leningrad nonconformists who devoted themselves primarily to abstract art were Gleb Bogomolov (b. 1933), Leonid Borisov (b. 1943), William Brui (b. 1946), Aleksandr Leonov (b. 1927), Oleg Liagachev (b. 1939) (Fig. 5:4), Anatolii Putilin (b. 1946), Yakov Vinkovetsky (1938–1984), and Boris Zeldin (b. 1944).

Bogomolov gradually moved from painting figurative works to symbolic representation to complete abstraction by the mid-1970s. He is interested in the evolution of culture, which he visualizes as a generalized "cultural space" consisting of a conglomeration of cultural objects, religious and philosophical ideas, and mystical experience. His abstract paintings express the mutual influence of these elements (Pl. 5:10).

While still in his teens, Brui developed a distinctive abstract style (Fig. 5:5). His informal teachers had been members of the Russian avant-garde. Therefore, it was Malevich, Lissitzky, Tatlin, and Kandinsky who influenced Brui, rather than modernist developments in the West. Also important for Brui's development was his work after hours at an experimental printshop in the 1960s. The experimental abstract works Brui was printing there were considered too extreme by the censors, so he was denied further access to the printshop. One of Brui's most ingenious early works is the book *Ex Adverso*, which reflects the ideas he gained from studying Leningrad Suprematists and Constructivists. The book consists of abstract etchings and poems, and can be read from front to back or from back to front.[15]

Boris Zeldin, who earned a degree in Russian literature from Leningrad University, began to paint abstractions in late 1970. His works consist of freely flowing poured shapes achieved by the combination of a special chemical process and emotive gestural brushstrokes. In spirit, they

Fig. 5:4
Oleg Liagachev
Summer Garden Walk, 1972
Handcolored drypoint
27.2 × 30.2 cm

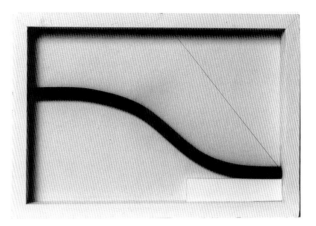

Fig. 5:6 (*right*)
Leonid Borisov
Composition, 1977
Mixed media on
fiberboard
41.3 × 60.3 cm

Fig. 5:5
William Brui
(Untitled), 1967
Etching
60 × 44.5 cm

show a connection with the Russian Constructivist tradition as well as with American Abstract Expressionism.

Leonid Borisov (b. 1943) is also primarily an abstract artist, but his work occasionally has Sots Art overtones (Fig. 5:6). He participated in many of the unofficial art exhibitions in Leningrad, beginning in the early 1970s. Borisov explains that his imagery "comes from ideas which arise in this way: I wake up in the morning and look at the ceiling. On the ceiling images of new pictures appear."[16] The work which results is reminiscent of that of Muscovite Eduard Shteinberg (b. 1937). Like Shteinberg, Borisov is a direct spiritual descendant of the Russian avant-garde artists of the 1920s. He expresses the same elegant simplicity and subtle combinations of colors that characterized the earlier movement.

Since the early 1960s Aleksandr Leonov has produced

dynamic abstract canvases (Pl. 5:14). According to the artist, in these works "the chief antinomies such as white and black, plus and minus, top and bottom, the heavens and the earth . . . interacting with the colorful ground, call for [a] dimensional sculptural solution."[18] Leonov often incorporates elements of Op Art in his paintings, and he also has a marked preference for black and white, which are for him "the main source of energy, the clash of two notions."[18]

Before emigrating to the West in 1972, Alexander Ney (b. 1939) had already begun creating abstract paintings and Surrealistic sculptures (Pl. 5:19). He is best known for his unusual sculptural technique that involves perforation. Ney's vibrant, intricate, and imaginative terracotta sculptures in the Dodge Collection are comprised of a multitude of minuscule geometric shapes resembling calcified sea urchins. The textured coral-like surfaces of animals, human heads, and figures are achieved by inserting tiny tools of varying shapes into the soft clay.

Although abstract painting emerged in Leningrad in the 1960s and 1970s, figurative art predominated. A major painter who used distorted or simplified figurative forms was Mikhail Chemiakin. He played an important role in the unofficial art world of Leningrad in the mid- to late 1960s, and was a founder and leader of the St. Petersburg Group of painters. As a boy of fourteen, Chemiakin was very impressed by an exhibition catalogue of Filonov's work. Chemiakin was also influenced by the turn-of-the-century World of Art group and developed a strong interest in eighteenth-century Russian culture. He found further inspiration in Western art, especially in the work of Velázquez, Rembrandt, and Vermeer. Expressing his view of art, Chemiakin commented: "Art which rejects beauty is as a shadow of a person rejecting its owner."[19]

To create artistically congenial surroundings, Chemiakin assembled a large collection of antiques in his communal apartment on Zagorodny Prospect and often depicted the old vases, bronzes, and artifacts in his early still lifes (Pl. 5:12). These works were based on his own philosophy, which he called "metaphysical synthetism." But the emphatic Christian tone of metaphysical synthetism made it completely unacceptable to the Soviet authorities. Chemiakin was incarcerated for a time in a mental institution and eventually, in 1971, he was expelled from the Soviet Union, with only his dog and two dried apples, which he used for a still life.

Members of Chemiakin's group, who followed the principles of metaphysical synthetism, were Vladimir Ivanov, Volodymyr (Vladimir) Makarenko (b. 1943), Anatolii Vasiliev, Oleg Liagachev, Evgenii Esaulenko (b. 1944), and Vladimir Petrov. After Chemiakin's emigration to France, this group disintegrated. But his work continued to influence many younger artists, including, for example, Andrei Gennadiev (Pl. 5:16), whose paintings and graphics are reminiscent of Russian icons, an art form that Gennadiev considers "the most complete and perfect form of the revelation of Beauty in the World." Gennadiev frequently combines in his work a variety of symbols from different cultures and periods, such as esoteric Christian symbols, ancient Egyptian iconography, the signs of the zodiac, and even Chinese ideograms. Yurii Liukshin (b. 1949) is another artist whose work reflects Chemiakin's influence. Liukshin works mainly as an illustrator, using the media of watercolor, lithography, and hand-colored etching, all in the spirit of the St. Petersburg Group.

Vladimir Ovchinnikov, one of the most prominent early unofficial figurative artists, exhibited in 1964 with Chemiakin and others at the ill-fated "Exhibition of Workmen Artists" at the Hermitage Museum.[20] Ovchinnikov, who followed academic traditions in his painting, nevertheless was as much a *persona non grata* with the authorities as abstract or Surrealist artists because of the ironic, sociocritical, and often religious nature of his work (Fig. 12:3; Pl. 5:15). His distinctive, simplified, flat, naive style employs heavy-bodied, tubular figures reminiscent of the peasants and workers painted by Malevich or Botero. But more importantly, Ovchinnikov vividly portrays the atmosphere of spiritual bankruptcy, moral decline, and emptiness typical of daily life in Soviet Russia. Fusing Russian subject matter with myth and religion, he presents personages from ancient mythology and the Old and New Testaments, in combination with figures from contemporary Soviet society in the setting of modern-day Russia—a Russia still primitively rural and backward yet embraced by a modern military-industrial state.

Vladlen Gavrilchik (b. 1944), a former naval officer as well as a poet and artist, became an important figure in the Leningrad underground. Gavrilchik considers the artists of the Arefiev Group to be his predecessors. His first works, executed in the mode of naïve or primitive art, were characterized by simple stylized forms, meticulousness, and pedantic attention to detail (Pl. 5:17). However, from the mid-1970s onward, irony, parody, and the grotesque predominate in his increasingly politicized works. Gavrilchik often uses primitivist stylistic elements to portray the gloomy reality of Soviet life. With a great deal of sarcasm, he represents the stereotypical images of the Soviet people and their rituals (*Choir of the Old Bolsheviks*, *The Communist Party*, and *Holiday Parades*).

Anatolii Belkin (b. 1953), who participated in the first major apartment exhibit in Leningrad as well as in the Gaz and Nevsky Palace of Culture exhibitions, synthesizes many diverse artistic traditions in his work. Among the artists who have influenced his artistic style, Belkin says, are Klee, Miró, Mondrian, and Chagall. In his early drawings and prints, he depicted the realities of Leningrad life in the streets and in crowded communal apartments (Fig. 5:7). His later compositions include fantastic insects, birds, and animals combined with the artist's handwritten words and numerals. Sometimes Belkin uses collage, incorporating pieces of manuscripts, photography, and real objects into the vibrating surfaces of his paintings.

Fig. 5:7
Anatolii Belkin
Apartment, 1976
Etching
Collection of the artist

Although denying that there are separate Moscow or Leningrad schools, he states: "my work belongs to Leningrad."[22] He says he feels that he is "a part of [the] bridges, courtyards, and roofs" of the city.[22]

Vladislav Afonichev (b. 1946), also an early participant in the unofficial movement, works in an expressive and always obviously figurative style. He depicts the horrors of war, violence, poverty, and invalids with brutally distorted figures. Afonichev's disturbing works often carry anti-Soviet messages. Similarly, the grotesque figures of Kiril Miller (b. 1959) often reflect the gloomy realities of Soviet Russia leavened with ordinary people enjoying simple pleasures (Pl. 5:18).

During the 1970s the disparate groups and circles of unofficial artists in Leningrad became more unified in the face of official opposition.[23] By the mid-1970s, almost all nonconformist artistic activities began to be viewed by the authorities as anti-Soviet political action. In response to these pressures, the first leaders of a broad-based Leningrad underground movement emerged—Yurii Zharkikh (b. 1938) and Evgenii Rukhin (1943–1976). Both were well connected with the Moscow nonconformists, especially Oscar Rabin.

Zharkikh was responsible for compiling a proposed charter for the TEV (Association for Experimental Exhibitions) in Leningrad. The art authorities in Leningrad said that only the Union of Soviet Artists in Moscow could give permission for the establishment of such an association. Zharkikh did not give up, however, and traveled to the Ministry of Culture in Moscow to press his case. While returning to Leningrad by train, a powder, like mustard gas, was placed in his shoes while he slept. The poison crippled him and kept him in hospital for three months. This provocation by the KGB was designed to intimidate the nonconformist artists and to stifle and abort their efforts to have exhibitions free of official control. In his own paintings, Zharkikh sought to find a symbol of moral purification through the image of the Crucifixion, and to depict "an intermediary state . . . the state when you no longer live your former life, but haven't yet begun your next life."[24] As he stated in 1971: "Eternal abstract life against the backdrop of death was the threshold of my new art."[25]

Rukhin, an active leader of the nonconformist artists in Leningrad as well as in Moscow, worked in a style reminiscent of the early paintings of Johns, Rauschenberg, and Antonio Tàpies. He incorporated into his paintings actual objects, such as old newspapers, paint tubes, locks and keys, pieces of old furniture, antique objects, and impressions made in the paint of actual icons. He transformed these familiar objects into elements of an abstract design and juxtaposed them with ironic warnings from contemporary material life (for example, packing case stencils saying "Dangerous to life") (Pl. 5:23). Rukhin employed nearly square canvases for his abstract compositions, explaining that "this shape is most independent of the proportions of a portrait (vertical) or of a landscape (horizontal)."[26] Rukhin was one of the organizers of the landmark "Bulldozer Exhibition" in Moscow in 1974, and was one of four artists arrested. In May of 1976, Rukhin died in a studio fire that was believed by many to have been started by the KGB.

With the international approbation generated by the "Bulldozer Exhibition," the artists were able to win permission to hold a second open-air exhibition two weeks later (on September 29, 1974 in Izmailovsky Park). Rukhin, Zharkikh, Ovchinnikov, and Igor Siniavin (b. 1937) represented the Leningrad nonconformists in that exhibition. Returning to Leningrad, Rukhin and Zharkikh contacted LOSKh (Leningrad Section of the Artists' Union), requesting permission to have a comparable exhibition of Leningrad nonconformist artists. After several frustrating meetings between the nonconformist artists' committee (consisting of Leonov, Zharkikh, Ovchinnikov, Siniavin, and Rukhin) and the LOSKh representatives, special permission was finally received, but with the condition that the artists exhibiting follow "the rule of three No's: No anti-Soviet propaganda, No erotic subjects, and No works with religious imagery." The decision as to whether to include a particular work in the exhibition was to be made by a LOSKh committee and thus depended entirely on the judgment of the committee members. Seven works with very subtle religious images were not approved for exhibition and had to be removed. In protest, several artists refused to take part.

This first "officially" sanctioned exhibition of nonconformist Leningrad art opened, nonetheless, in the Gaz Palace of Culture in December 1974 (Fig. 5:8). Some two hundred works by fifty-two artists were shown, and public interest in the exhibition was high. Over four days, as many as fifteen thousand people visited the exhibition. In spite of bad weather, a line formed long before opening time. On the first day, in order to get into the exhibition hall before it closed at 6:00 p.m., visitors had to be in line before the doors opened at 11:00 a.m. On the second day visitors had to line up before 9:00 a.m., and on the third and fourth days they had to be there before 6:00 a.m. Viewers could only enter the exhibition in very small groups and for a maximum of fifteen minutes. Despite the complete lack of publicity in the official media, news

Fig. 5:8
Group of artists before the
opening of the exhibition
at the Gaz Palace of Culture,
Leningrad, December 1974
Photo by Gennadii Prikhodko

Fig. 5:9
View of the exhibition in the
Nevsky Palace of Culture,
Leningrad, September 1975
Photo by Gennadii Prikhodko

about the nonconformist exhibition spread quickly throughout the city, bringing an astonishing response. In notebooks at the entrance there were 900 positive responses by attendees of the show, 400 neutral, and 150 highly negative (written primarily by workers brought in by the militia specifically for this purpose). These four December days were very important in unifying the rather scattered Leningrad artistic avant-garde and can be seen to have ushered in a new chapter in the history of Leningrad nonconformist art.

Another landmark exhibition took place at the Nevsky Palace of Culture between September 10 and September 21, 1975 (Fig. 5:9). That show included eighty-eight artists from Leningrad and a few from Moscow. The artists all wore special pins made for them in one night by Yurii

Petrochenkov (b. 1942). Among the participants were Leonov, Rukhin, Dyshlenko, Zakharov-Ross, Tiulpanov, Gennadiev, Zharkikh, Galetsky, Borisov, Esaulenko, Putilin, Bogomolov, Nekrasov, and the artists of the Sterligov group.

In October 1976, a nonconformist exhibition of mostly abstract works was held at the Ordzhonikidze Palace of Culture; it included works by Mikhnov-Voitenko, Vasiliev, Zakharov-Ross (Pl. 5:27), Dyshlenko, Putilin, and Borisov. The display of works had been carefully planned. Many people were impressed by the mixed media assemblage of Igor Zakharov-Ross (b. 1943) titled *System of Coordinates*, a double-sided construction that integrated various sound, electrical, and holographic effects. In other works, Zakharov-Ross used some electrical parts smuggled from

Fig. 5:10 (*right*)
Konstantin Kuzminsky
(wearing a wreath on his
head) during the exhibition
in his Leningrad apartment,
September 1974
Photo by Gennadii
Prikhodko, courtesy of the
Collection of the Institute of
Modern Russian Culture,
Los Angeles

the Institute of Nuclear Energy. His first performance was called *I Want to Go to America* (1975) and featured the artist dressed in a jacket depicting an American flag, burning an object resembling a Soviet passport. Zakharov-Ross later organized a number of happenings and performances with many participants.

Exhibitions as large as those held at the Gaz and Nevsky were rare, but from 1975 to 1979 many smaller exhibitions of nonconformist Leningrad artists continued to be organized in private apartments. Very close ties existed between nonconformist Leningrad artists and such writers and poets as Joseph Brodsky, Evgenii Rein, and Konstantin Kuzminsky. Even before the exile of Brodsky and Chemiakin, Kuzminsky's apartment on Krasnaia Street was a permanent salon of the arts and one of the major gathering places for nonconformists (Fig. 5:10). In September 1974, eight hundred people attended an exhibition at Kuzminsky's small apartment, where twenty-three artists showed 128 works.[27] The exhibition featured works by Anatolii Belkin, Yurii Galetsky, Vladlen Gavrilchik, Andrei Gennadiev, Oleg Liagachev, Evgenii Mikhnov-Voitenko, Yurii Petrochenkov, and Yakov Vinkovetsky.[28]

Also active in the 1960s and 1970s were a few talented loners, such as Aleksei Khvostenko (b. 1940), Solomon Rossin (b. 1937), Gennadii Ustiugov (b. 1937), Valentin Levitin (b. 1931), and Vadim Rokhlin (1937–1985).

Fig. 5:11
Vadim Rokhlin
Drawing for the painting
Stripping Off His Clothes,
1976–77
Graphite on paper
60.5 × 82.1 cm

Rokhlin, who was just forty-eight when he died of a heart attack in 1985, was practically unknown to the public. Like many other unofficial artists, he was trained not as a painter but as an architect. Having participated in the exhibitions in the Gaz and Nevsky Palaces of Culture in 1974 and 1975, he gave up architecture in 1980 and devoted himself entirely to painting for the remainder of his life. The main theme of Rokhlin's work is the most fundamental human struggle between good and evil (Fig. 5:11). Rokhlin often turned to the Gospels for subjects, freely interpreting them and creating surreal scenes with grotesque, tormented figures. He was severely criticized for his Surrealistic works in the major Leningrad newspaper *Leningradskaia Pravda*, and was unable to arrange any personal exhibitions during his lifetime. As a result, the bulk of the work of this talented master was known only to his close friends.

Leningrad Surrealist Ilya Murin (b. 1943) has a strong interest in the turn-of-the-century World of Art group. In his drawings and etchings, Murin uses unexpected juxtapositions of objects, often giving familiar images magical qualities.

During the 1970s, there was some initial interaction between official and unofficial artists. Several nonconformist artists became members of the official Union of Artists, while some members of the left wing of this Union—for example, Nikolai Sazhin (b. 1948) and Konstantin Simun (b. 1934)—began to exhibit their work with unofficial artists. At the group exhibition of eleven official artists in 1971, featuring works by such artists as Zaven Arshakuni, Marina Azizian, German Egoshin, Yaroslav Krestovsky, Valerii Vatentin, and Simun, many of the official paintings were characterized by innovative styles or

themes. Some official artists started to create non-conformist works.

Nikolai Sazhin's early artistic career was typical for an official artist. After graduating from the Ilya Repin Institute of Painting, Sculpture, and Architecture, he taught at the Serov Art College and became a member of the Union of Artists, working as an illustrator (a very common occupation for nonconformist artists). In 1974, he started exhibiting with unofficial artists. Sazhin's work has a very wide thematic range: from ancient myths to biblical legend, from Russian folklore to Eastern philosophy. He has also absorbed various St. Petersburg artistic traditions, taking his inspiration from the refinement of the World of Art artists, the naiveté of primitivism, and the experimentalism of the Russian avant-garde artists of the 1920s.

Viacheslav Mikhailov (b. 1945) also began as an official artist. His diploma work required for graduation from the Ilya Repin Institute was deemed worthy of inclusion in the permanent collection of the Museum of the Academy of Fine Arts. Mikhailov also achieved the high honor of receiving Lenin's Komsomol Prize. However, in his free time Mikhailov painted quite different cycles of pictures with associative and allegorical subjects often in violent and bloody conflict, reminiscent of some of Francis Bacon's work. His *Rembrandt's Lessons I* (Pl. 5:21) directly appropriates Rembrandt's *Anatomy Lesson of Dr. Tulp* (1632), but depicts ghost-like semihuman figures gathered around the corpse being dissected. The light in the painting, as in Rembrandt's work, seems to be generated by the subjects themselves, an aspect that heightens the sculptural quality of the work. The highly expressive relief texture of Mikhailov's work is achieved by using gypsum padding and heavy impasto.[29]

Like unofficial art, the pursuit of religious belief—Christianity, Judaism, and Islam—was another form of nonconformism in Soviet society.[30] In postwar Leningrad, Jewish life and religion, like Christianity, had to go underground, and many meetings and seminars devoted to the Jewish religion, traditions, and culture were secretly held in private apartments. The last officially approved exhibition devoted to Jewish culture was "Jews in Tsarist Russia and the USSR," held at the State Museum of Ethnography in Leningrad in 1939. From that time, even the depiction of a Torah or typical Jewish characters was considered religious propaganda and was cause for severe punishment. In spite of this, many Leningrad artists with Jewish backgrounds based their art on forbidden national and religious themes.

Anatolii Kaplan (1902–1980), one of the few Jewish artists tolerated by Stalin, preserved the world of his childhood in his paintings, ceramics, etchings, and lithographs, which were often illustrations of Sholom Aleikhem's stories (Fig. 5:12). Showing the traditions of Jewish people, Kaplan portrayed a bygone era—the hard but colorful everyday life in prerevolutionary Jewish *shtetlach* in a style closely connected with old traditions of folk-art culture. Kaplan did not search for new themes, and the range of his motifs changed very little from those of the 1930s. Ironically, in spite of his talent and the public admiration for his work, he never lived to see even a single one-man show of his work in his own country. Nonetheless, Kaplan's book illustrations and prints influenced many Jewish artists of the younger generation.

Mark Klionsky (b. 1927) was initially a very successful official artist who participated in many state-sponsored exhibitions and received many government commissions. However, in 1958 he began a series of etchings and lithographs expressing the suffering of the Jewish victims of the Holocaust. Since this was not an official theme, Klionsky could not work openly on this series. He worked only at night, hiding the etchings during the day under a

Fig. 5.12
Anatolii Kaplan
Matchmaker, 1967
Lithograph
57.5 × 40.5 cm

5 "A great city with a provincial fate":
Nonconformist art in Leningrad from the Khrushchev thaw to Gorbachev's "perestroika"

113

Pl. 5:1
Natalia Zhilina
Walks around Tsaritsino,
1984
Oil on canvas
119 × 99 cm

Pl. 5:2
Rikhard Vasmi
(Standing Nude), 1960
Tempera on canvas
51 × 40.7 cm

Pl. 5:5 (*opposite*)
Josef Yakerson
In the Midst of the Dead,
1966
Oil on canvas
247 × 250 cm

Pl. 5:3
Igor Ivanov
Two Dolls, 1979
Oil on canvas
66.5 × 84.2 cm

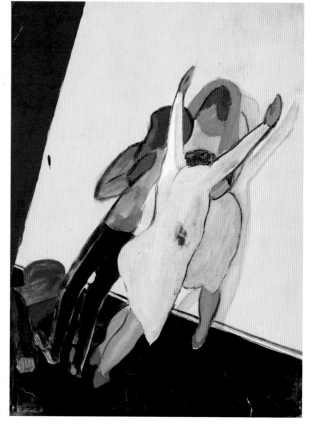

Pl. 5:4
Aleksandr Arefiev
(Untitled), n.d.
Gouache and graphite on
paper
42.2 × 31.2 cm

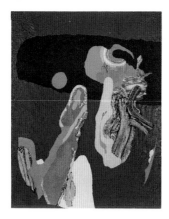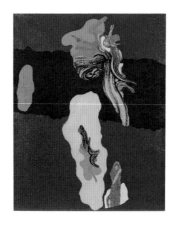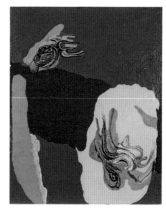

Pl. 5:6
Yurii Dyshlenko
Fable, 1975
Oil on canvas
74.5 × 59.5 cm (each)

Pl. 5:8
Elena Gritsenko
Portrait, 1976
Oil on canvas
42 × 38.5 cm

Pl. 5:7
Igor Tiulpanov
Memory Chest, 1973
Oil on canvas
116.7 × 158.5 cm

Pl. 5:9
Evgenii Mikhnov-Voitenko
(Untitled), 1976
Gouache on paper
37 × 24.2 cm (each panel)

Pl. 5:10
Gleb Bogomolov
Composition in Red, 1984
Oil on canvas
52.5 × 111 cm

Pl. 5:11
Mikhail Kulakov
The Sword, 1975
Oil on canvas
88.6 × 63.7 cm

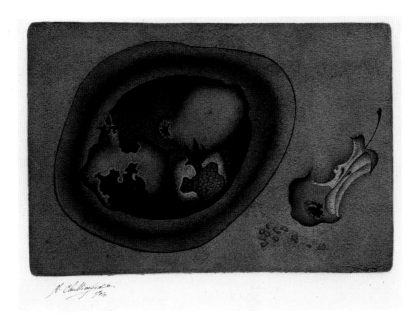

Pl. 5:12
Mikhail Chemiakin
(Still Life), 1971
Etching
15 × 22 cm

Pl. 5:13
Gennadii Zubkov
Fragment of Golgotha,
1979–81
Gouache and collage on
paper
58.8 × 50.1 cm

Pl. 5:14
Aleksandr Leonov
The Game, 1977
Oil on canvas
100.4 × 228.4 cm

Pl. 5:16
Andrei Gennadiev
(Untitled), *c.* 1989
Oil pastel and watercolor
on paper
101.5 × 72.9 cm

Pl. 5:17
Vladlen Gavrilchik
(Untitled), 1974
Oil and tempera on
illustration board
31.4 × 37.3 cm

Pl. 5:18
Kiril Miller
Winter Swimmers, n.d.
Oil on canvas
70.8 × 101 cm

Pl. 5:15 (*opposite*)
Vladimir Ovchinnikov
Shuvalovo Station, 1978
Oil on canvas
107.8 × 138.3 cm

Pl. 5:19
Alexander Ney
Villager, 1971
Ceramic
41 × 42 × 33 cm

Pl. 5:23 (*opposite*)
Evgenii Rukhin
(Untitled), 1975
Mixed media on canvas
96.5 × 100 cm

Pl. 5:20
Mikhail Taratuta
Composition [. . . Toward the High Effectiveness of Collective Labor], 1979
Watercolor and pen and ink on paper
29.5 × 42 cm

Pl. 5:21
Viacheslav Mikhailov
Rembrandt's Lessons I, 1985
Mixed media on fiberboard
104.2 × 128 cm

Pl. 5:22
Alexander Rapoport
Supper, 1975
Oil on canvas
133.1 × 133.4 cm

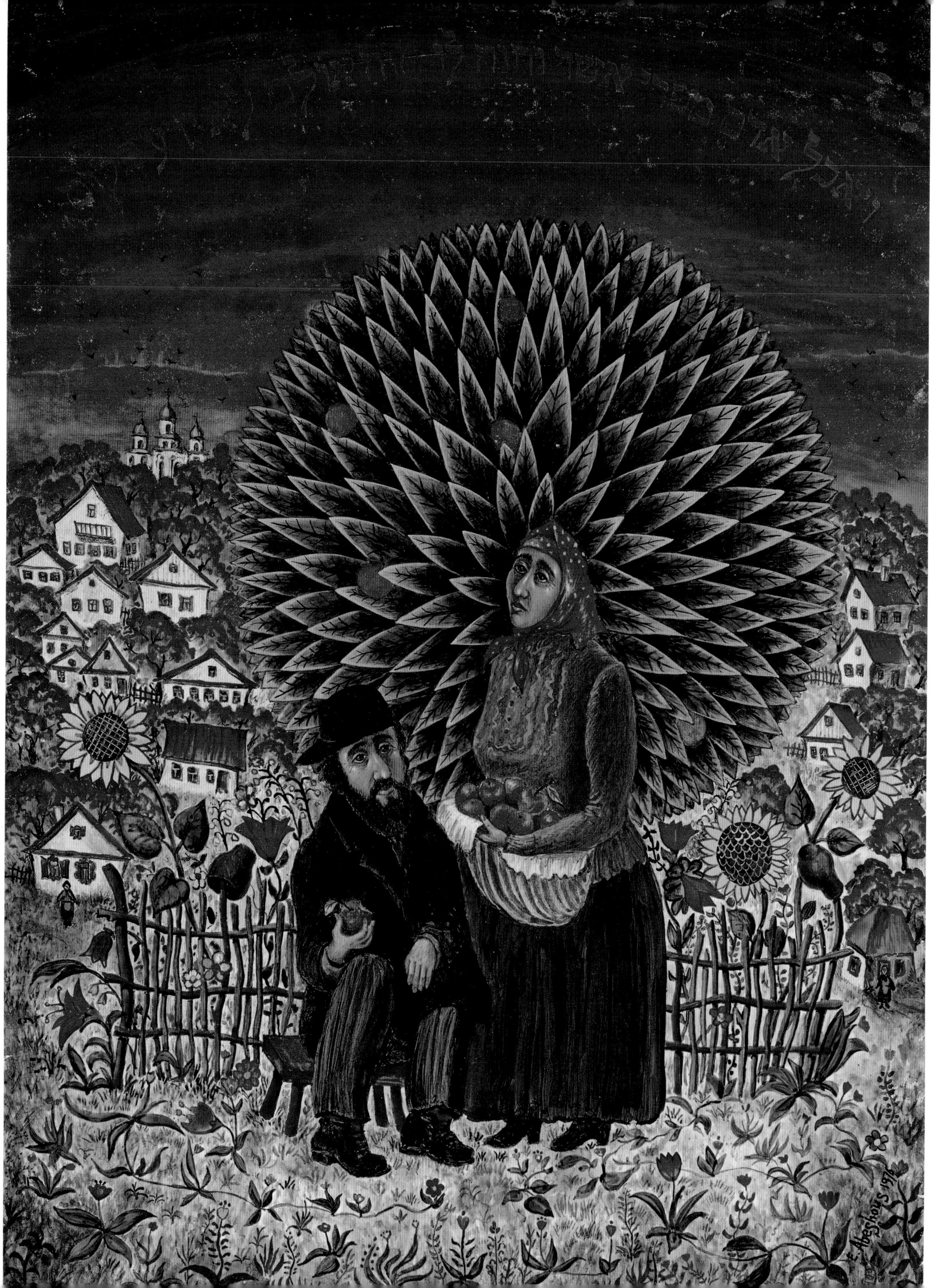
E. Abeshaus 1976

Pl. 5:24 (*opposite*)
Evgenii Abezgauz
Adam Ate and Ate of the
Fruit That Eve Gave Him
But Knew Nothing, 1975
Fluorescent tempera on
paper mounted on wood
56 × 40 cm

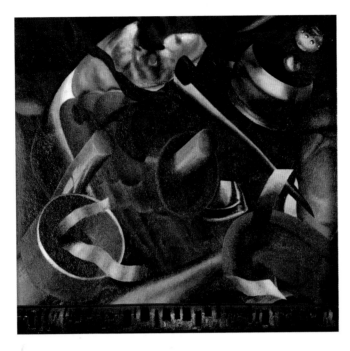

Pl. 5:25
Sergei Kovalsky
Concerto Grosso, 1982
Panel from triptych
Oil and wood on panel
95 × 103.2 cm

Pl. 5:26
Aleksandr Manusov
Sunset, 1986
Oil on canvas
70.5 × 100.5 cm

Pl. 5:27
Igor Zakharov-Ross
(Untitled), 1974–75
Oil on canvas
119.5 × 59.6 cm

Pl. 5:28
Valentin Gerasimenko
Car Parts, 1970
Etching and
carborundum
35 × 28.1 cm

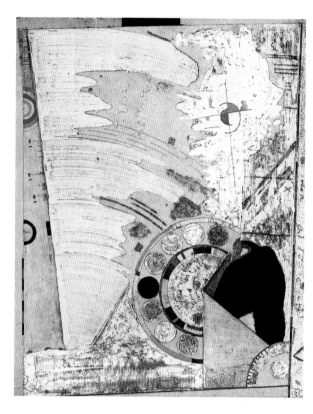

Pl. 5:31 (*opposite*)
Elena Figurina
*Return of the Prodigal
Son*, 1986
Oil on canvas
129.8 × 105.2 cm

Pl. 5:30
Vadim Voinov
The Manifesto, 1982–83
Mixed media on panel
62.5 × 44.5 × 10 cm

Pl. 5:29
Evgenii Orlov
The House, 1984
Oil on canvas
60.2 × 80.4 cm

Pl. 5:32
Timur Novikov
(Untitled), 1984
Oil on canvas
99.5 × 154 cm

Pl. 5:33
Inal Savchenkov
(Untitled), 1986
Oil on canvas
200 × 160 cm

Pl. 5:34
Dmitrii Shagin
University Yard, 1982
Gouache on paper
24 × 31.9 cm

Fig. 5:13
First Exhibition of Jewish
Artists (ALEF Group),
Leningrad, November 1975
Photo by Gennadii Prikhodko

painting depicting Lenin. Realization of his true artistic talents came only after his emigration to the West.

Evgenii Abezgauz (b. 1939) saw the need for collective action by Jewish artists in Leningrad and in 1975 became one of the key founders of an unofficial organization of Jewish artists, ALEF, named after the first letter in the Hebrew alphabet (Fig. 5:13). ALEF began by organizing a daring apartment exhibition of twelve artists at Evgenii Abezgauz's small apartment in November 1975. Included in the exhibition were Abezgauz himself, Anatolii Basin (b. 1936), Aleksandr Okun (b. 1949), Aleksandr Gurevich (b. 1929), Aleksandr Manusov, Osip Sidlin (1909–1972), Alexander Rapoport (b. 1933), and Mikhail Taratuta (b. 1961), among others. This was the first exhibition of Jewish art in Leningrad in more than thirty-five years. To have enough space for the paintings, furniture had to be piled in the bathroom. Israeli tunes were played as participating artists explained their works to the visitors. Amazingly, more than four thousand people attended this crammed exhibition during a single week. On the last day, some two hundred people were waiting in line to see the exhibition when it opened. The artists now recall an ordinary-looking man who attracted little attention when he viewed the show. As he was leaving he asked if there was a book in which he could write his comments. After he had left, one of the artists happened to look in the book and read "See you, KGB."[31]

Although ALEF was initially organized as a group of Jewish artists, it was not based "on a similarity of styles or even themes, but on a sense of shared concerns for threatened values." Some of its members were interested in Christian as well as Jewish themes. Therefore, the group displayed neither philosophical nor stylistic unity. The first ALEF exhibition initially sought to show works somehow connected with Jewish life and traditions, or which revealed something of the Jewish "soul and mentality." A manifesto compiled by Alexander Rapoport stated that ALEF artists wanted to overcome the influence of the *shtetl* culture and to find the sources of art in a more

ancient Jewish culture. Their goal was to build a bridge from that past to the present and on again into the future. As it turned out, even the main idea of the show, how Jewish themes should be reflected, was understood differently by each ALEF artist.

Abezgauz was a successful engineer before giving up engineering at age thirty and enrolling in the Mukhina School of Industrial Arts. He created genre scenes from traditional Jewish life represented by such witty works as *Adam Ate and Ate of the Fruit That Eve Gave Him But Knew Nothing* (Pl. 5:24). His works reflect the influence of folklore, popular prints (*lubki*), and Russian lacquered miniatures. As in folk art, all elements of landscape, people, and animals are painted with equal attention, and inscriptions in Hebrew are incorporated into his compositions. While still in Russia, Abezgauz became a member of a union of artists, though ironically not the Russian one but that of Israel, where he later emigrated.

Taratuta, the youngest member of ALEF, studied informally with Abezgauz and began exhibiting with the group when only fourteen years old. Although his art was politically provocative (Pl. 5:20), he was hassled by the authorities on different grounds. He was arrested while demonstrating with his parents, the well-known "refuseniks" Aba and Ida Taratuta. After emigrating to Israel in 1987, he then settled in New Jersey.

Another more senior member of the group, Alexander (Alek) Rapoport, took an active part in the creation of TEV and ALEF and also participated at the Gaz and Nevsky Palaces of Culture exhibitions. Rapoport's family suffered during Stalin's purges. By the time Alek was four, both of his parents had been arrested. His father was shot in 1939, and his mother was sentenced to ten years in a labor camp. Alek was expelled twice from the Serov Art College, first as a student and later as a teacher. When he protested against the rigidity of the system of teaching there, he was accused of "ideological sabotage." In addition to his training at the Serov Art College, Rapoport studied stage design under Akimov. According to Rapoport, his art of the 1970s is based on three sources: Byzantine art, Rembrandt, and Rouault. His images have expressively distorted faces, stylized elongated figures (Pl. 5:22), and often deal with Jewish religious themes and the problems of hate and violence.

The late Aleksandr Manusov became a member of ALEF after taking part in the Gaz Palace of Culture exhibition in 1974. After graduating from the Mukhina School of Industrial Arts, Manusov worked as a designer at a Leningrad factory and painted in his spare time (Pl. 5:26). His works from the series *Bathers*, *Still Lifes*, and *Promenades* combine different artistic aspirations and the experience of the diverse plastic techniques, including those of Cézanne, the German Expressionists, and such Russian artists as Robert Falk (1886–1958) and Victor Borisov-Musatov (1870–1905). Manusov's cycle of works on biblical subjects communicates eternal, timeless, philosophical messages rather than illustrating specific events.

Aleksandr Gurevich, another ALEF member, participated in almost all of the unofficial exhibits in Leningrad. Like many other nonconformists, he began his career as an engineer and later attended the Mukhina School. His favorite subjects are taken from the Gospel, although he tends to interpret them in a present-day context, evaluating contemporary events through the prism of theology and legend. His works have a theatrical quality about them; even the spatial organization of his compositions is reminiscent of a theatrical stage.

The major concluding event of the so-called Gaz-Nevsky period (1973–76) was the founding of the TEV (Association for Experimental Exhibitions). The goal of this association was the unification of all Leningrad nonconformist artists to help organize mutual exhibitions and to coordinate all types of exhibition-related activities. Nonetheless, given the unrelenting pressure of the government and the KGB, the emigration of artists continued through the 1970s and, by the early 1980s, almost half of the major participants of the nonconformist movement in Leningrad had either been forced to emigrate or had left Russia voluntarily.

The 1980s: Developments under "perestroika" In late 1981, in an effort to break through the official obstruction of free exhibitions, sixty-one Leningrad nonconformists united to prepare the largest apartment exhibition in Leningrad's history. The artists misled the KGB by spreading contradictory rumors about the time and place of the exhibition, which actually opened on November 14 in N. Kononenko's apartment on Bronnitskaia Street. A few

Fig. 5:14
Valerii Lukka
Remembrance of the Army, 1975
Mixed media on fiberboard
96.5 × 68 cm

days later, the KGB learned its exact location and turned off the electricity. But this did not stop viewers from using candles to see the artworks. During the four days of the exhibition, about two thousand people found their way to it, never knowing if attendance might lead to arrest. The participating artists became the first members of a new artistic association called TEII (Association of Experimental Visual Art), which carried on the TEV aim of providing support for nonconformist artists of all tendencies, irrespective of their formal training.

In the 1980s, many TEII exhibitions were held at the Kirov Palace of Culture and in the Leningrad Palace of Youth. During this time, TEII membership increased more than threefold and about five hundred artists exhibited under its auspices in the period before *perestroika*. We have already mentioned artists who were well known before joining TEII. Some of the other most interesting artists who gained recognition in the late 1970s and early 1980s were VIK (Viacheslav Zabelin) (b. 1953), Sergei Sergeev (b. 1953), Elena Figurina (b. 1955), Sergei Kovalsky (b. 1948) (Pl. 5:25), Evgenii Orlov (b. 1952) (Pl. 5:29), Igor Orlov (b. 1959), Konstantin Troitsky (b. 1953), Aleksandr Lotsman (b. 1947), Valerii Lukka (b. 1945) (Fig. 5:14), Felix Volosenkov (b. 1944), Vadim Voinov (b. 1940), and Evgenii Tykotsky (b. 1941).

The work of the TEII members differs widely in style, content, and quality. Sergei Kovalsky, one of the founders of TEII and its archivist, creates sociopolitical Conceptual works often based on language clichés, whereas Elena Figurina, the only woman on the council of the TEII, works in a brightly colored primitivist mode. Neither had formal art training. Kovalsky's background was in typography, art history, and music; Figurina, who graduated from the Aircraft Industry Institute in 1979, worked as an engineer, but joined TEII in 1977. Since then, her striking works, influenced by the Russian icon tradition and German Expressionism, have been included in all the unofficial exhibitions, as well as many exhibitions abroad. Her colorful works combine a pastoral innocence in the form of children, birds, and animals with forebodings of violence and evil (Pl. 5:31). She explains: "I want to discover throughout my paintings that proportion of good and evil, of beauty to ugliness, which is in people."[32]

Valentin Gerasimenko (b. 1935), a close friend of Figurina, initially studied geography, but took up painting in the mid-1950s, developing his style under the influence of the Arefiev Group. He became increasingly active in the nonconformist movement in the mid-1970s. Etching became his favorite medium in the early 1980s, allowing him to pursue his interest in the texture of different organic structures, mimicking striation, blisters, and holes (Pl. 5:28).[33]

Vadim Voinov (b. 1940) began creating collages and assemblages in 1979, using objects that had been previously issued in large editions and that had little if any material value, such as old photos and postcards, used tickets and receipts, medals, clocks, prison locks, household utensils, and various other discarded items (Pl. 5:30). By combining these objects in different ways or reinterpreting their meaning by including them in a special context, Voinov gives them new life, creating a kind of special symbolism which reflects people's lives and thoughts during the epoch of Stalinism. This focus reflects Voinov's study of history at Leningrad University and his present work as a curator at the Museum of the History of Leningrad. The fact that the artist's family was directly affected by Stalin's purges (his father was arrested in 1949) has had a great influence on him.

Sergei Sergeev (b. 1953) began his artistic career working as a stage designer for the Kirov Ballet Theater, but he was always interested in painting. He joined the TEII, working in his favorite genres of still life and portraiture. His imaginary portraits, such as those of the nonconformist artists Gleb Bogomolov and Timur Novikov (Fig. 5:15), are not made in the traditional way, with the subject sitting before the painter. Rather, these portraits are based on Sergeev's subjective "idea" of each person. He was very influenced by New Wave music and believes that the furious pace of modern life, based on new technological equipment, affects the psychology of his subjects.

In the mid-1980s, many different informal groupings and subgroupings were formed in Leningrad which supplemented the larger TEII.[34] In 1984, Dmitrii Shagin (b. 1957) (Pl. 5:34), a son of artists Vladimir Shagin and Natalia Zhilina, together with Vladimir Shinkarev (b. 1954), put together the MITKI group from among the circle of their closest friends. The group included Victor Tikhomirov (b. 1951), Aleksandr Florensky (b. 1960), Olga Florenskaia (b. 1960), Aleksei Semichev (b. 1959), Igor Churilov (b. 1959), and Andrei Medvedev (b. 1959). Some artists of the older generation, such as Shagin and Zhilina, also often exhibited with MITKI.

MITKI is not only a group; it is a way of life, a philosophy, and a specific style of behavior. The group's credo is based on the formula: "Orthodoxy, Autocracy, Nationality." The members exemplify a new type of Slavophile, who proclaims a return to traditional Russian values and gives their preference to "non-Western drawing and Russian bread."[35] MITKI try to accept the terrible conditions of Soviet life, and even find a way to enjoy it: "Do not think that a MITEK [singular of MITKI] does not taste the really bad quality of Russian wine, but since there is nothing else available, he enjoys that one."[36] The sources of MITKI's inspiration are varied: primitivism, northern Renaissance painting, and the subcultures of children, criminals, and the military. Their work is representational but usually with distortions in form and perspective. If artists of Arefiev's group had the poetry of Roald Mandelshtam, MITKI have the poetic prose of Vladimir Shinkarev.

Timur Novikov (b. 1958) (Pl. 5:32), who became a major force in the Leningrad artistic community in the late 1970s, began to work almost exclusively with fabrics in the mid-1980s, creating collages of varying patterns, sometimes using glittering fabrics and adding photo-

Fig. 5:15
Timur Novikov (left) and Gleb Bogomolov (right) pose beneath their portraits by fellow artist Sergei Sergeev (center), who is standing below his self-portrait

collage to the fabric surface. Art critic Victor Mazin referred to Novikov's work as "textural Minimalism." In an interview with Victor and Margarita Tupitsyn, Novikov explained that he used fabric for "purely utilitarian purposes."[37] He said: "Everything is from Larionov, who in many ways took his start from folk arts in which you don't find painting on canvas. Folk art is generally textiles."[38] For Novikov, his work on fabric could "be both a tablecloth and the highest form of art."[39] This use of textiles enabled the artist to exhibit in unconventional spaces as well as to take his works out of the country easily.

Novikov was a member of The Chronicle (Lepotis'), a group organized by Boris Koshelokhov (b. 1942) in 1976 and consisting of ten members, including Figurina and Leonid Fedorov. Koshelokhov, who worked as an electrician, plumber, and construction worker, was influenced by the Arefiev Group, and took up painting in 1976. After his trip to Italy, he began using graphite-like color fields on a scratched base layer with black contours under the influence of the Arte Cifra group. Since the end of the 1980s, he has used a three-color scheme of yellow, blue, and red, often employing technological waste materials.

In 1982, Novikov, together with Oleg Kotelnikov (b. 1958), Ivan Sotnikov (b. 1961), and Evgenii Kozlov, founded the group The New Wilds, later renamed The New Artists group, and, subsequently, the Friends of Mayakovsky Club.[40] The New Artists expanded to include Sergei Bugaev (Afrika) (b. 1966), Vadim Ovchinnikov (b.

1941), Vlad Gusevich (b. 1949), Andrei Krisanov (b. 1966), Oleg Maslov (b. 1965), and Inal Savchenkov (b. 1966) (Pl. 5:33). These artists do not limit themselves to the visual arts, but create handmade books, invent unconventional musical instruments, and produce "avant-garde" clothing and even "artistic" cuisine.[41] Many of The New Artists' members participated in the activities of the experimental performance group Pop Mechanics, organized in 1981 by jazz pianist and composer Sergei Kuryokhin. They are also writers, film directors, and actors. Their motto is "Everybody can be a painter."

Kotelnikov is one of the founders of The New Artists and, in addition to his work as a painter, he has taken part in many films, founded the punk group NCh/VCh, and helped organize performances of the Pop Mechanics. Kotelnikov's large-scale "savage" paintings are often executed on polythene, glass, and walls, and resemble the art of the Neue Wilden in Germany and that of Figuration Libre in France. Another member of The New Artists, Savchenkov, was once a cartoonist, a fact which is reflected in the way his paintings combine abstract and figurative elements in highly stylized and simplified ways.

Evgenii Yufit (b. 1961) was an initiator of the Necrorealist Group, which included Andrei Mertvy (b. 1959), Vladimir Kustov (b. 1959), and Aleksei Trupyr (b. 1965). At the beginning of the 1980s, Yufit made photographs of acts of rape and decomposition, and then, inspired by Edward von Hoffman's steel engravings, he produced the first necropictures. Art critic Victor Mazin describes Necrorealism as an appeal "to the inhuman in the human being, to what is alien in him, to his oppressed body, which is always only a communicative surface linking that which is his and that which is not."[42] Necrorealism focuses on overcoming the fear of death and celebrates the necrophiliac pleasure experienced in this process. As Jork Rothamel has noted, the Necrorealists are concerned "not merely with the process of dying and decomposition in nature, but also with the phenomenon of the spiritual mortification of the living image (and not merely the visual image, but acoustic, tactual, olfactory images as well) through reproductions."[43] Although it is also involved with photography, painting, installation, and lectures, the medium in which Necrorealism is most expressive is film.

Formerly an actor and musician, artist Sergei Bugaev (known in Russia by his nickname Afrika) emerged on the Leningrad art scene just before *perestroika*. In his work, Afrika combines images drawn from the Russian avant-garde culture of the 1920s, Soviet mass media of the

Fig. 5:16
Valerii Mishin
Dance, 1985
Lithograph
49.3 × 44.2 cm

Stalin period, and Western Postmodernism, using found materials, posters, and photographic images. His *Green Stalin*, created by painting a small plaster bust of Stalin green, is an example of his ironic approach.

The thaw in state control and the collapse of state support for the arts has not made the lives of Leningrad artists easy. The internal market for contemporary art in St. Petersburg is in its infancy. To date there are only about a dozen art galleries, and just a few collectors other than visiting foreigners. In these hard economic times, art is an unnecessary luxury for most Russians. Therefore, it is easier today to find work by former leading nonconformists in galleries in New York, London, Berlin, and Paris than in St. Petersburg.

Perestroika has confronted nonconformist Leningrad artists with a spiritual crisis, since dissident art has suddenly been converted from something very personal, important, and lofty into a commodity. The underground has gone, and the differences between the categories of "official" and "unofficial" art (which were defined during the Khrushchev-Brezhnev era) have all but vanished. Now you can find works of former official and nonconformist artists together at the same exhibitions. Moreover, there are now many former official artists who have started working in abstract, Expressionist, or Surrealist modes. But often these works, driven by market imperatives rather than politics, are full of clichés and are no more than secondhand versions of the Western models of the last decade. Such works have lost the heart and soul of those made in the post-Stalin, pre-Gorbachev decades in which the struggle for freedom of artistic expression was a unifying and motivating force.

Notes

1. In 1932, a resolution of the Central Committee of the Communist Party "On the Reorganization of Literary and Artistic Organizations" abolished all artistic groups, and in 1934 Socialist Realism was proclaimed to be the only accepted artistic method. A Party-controlled Union of Artists of the U.S.S.R., finally established in 1957, united various artists of completely different artistic styles and groups. Membership of this Union was necessary to practice as a professional artist. The ideas of Russian Cubo-Futurists and Constructivists were stamped as "formalistic" and their works were transferred from museum displays into storage. At the same time, interest in modern Western art, which by the end of 1920s was qualified by the authorities as "bourgeois" and "reactionary," came to be viewed as almost a criminal matter. In the course of Stalin's purges, many Leningrad artists faced loss of employment, confinement in mental institutions, or imprisonment in labor camps.

2. "Formalism" was defined in the *Kratkii slovar' terminov izobrazitel'nogo iskusstva* [Dictionary of art terms], published in Moscow in 1965, as "reactionary trends in art and aesthetics, connected with the ideology of decaying capitalism." According to this dictionary, "reactionary formalist art includes such styles and movements as Cubism, Futurism, Constructivism, Surrealism, and Dadaism. . . . All these different formalistic trends are based on the separation of form from content and on the superiority of form over content." In the same dictionary, there is a statement that the "fight against formalist art is the primary goal of Soviet art" (*Kratkii slovar' terminov izobrazitel'nogo iskusstva* [Moscow: Sovetskii Khudozhnik, 1965], pp. 177–78).

3. These artists were strongly influenced by Italian Neorealist cinema. Such important films as *The Nights of Kabiria*, *The Road*, *The Roof*, *Rocco and His Brothers* were shown at international film festivals in Russia in the 1950s and 1960s.

4. Quoted in A. Basin, ed., *Gazanevskaia kultura o sebe* (Leningrad and Jerusalem: Abudalo, 1974–89), p. 23.

5. Selma Holo, ed., *Keepers of the Flame: Unofficial Artists in Leningrad* (Los Angeles: University of Southern California, Fisher Gallery, 1990), p. 82.

6. Mikhail Chemiakin, "Joseph Jackerson," *Art of Russia and the West* 1 (Mar. 1989): 60.

7. During the 1950s and early 1960s the following exhibitions of modern and contemporary Western art were held at the Hermitage: "Art of Belgium and Holland, 18th–20th Centuries" (1954); "Finnish Art of the 19th and 20th Centuries" (1955); "French Art, 17th–20th Centuries" (1956); "Art of Scandinavia" (1956); "British Art, 16th–20th Centuries" (1956); "Paul Cézanne" (1956); "Contemporary Italian Drawing" (1956); "Art of Belgium, 19th–20th Centuries" (1956); "Pablo Picasso" (1956; Hermitage Museum Archive, Report of the Department of Western Art, File 1, list 11, #760); "Contemporary Graphic Arts of Argentina" (1958; Hermitage Museum Archive, File 1, list 11, #1053); "Rockwell Kent" (1958; Hermitage Museum Archive, #1055); "Albert Marke" (1958; Hermitage Museum Archive, #1165); "Max Lingner" (1959; Hermitage Museum Archive, #1335); "Contemporary Art of Yugoslavia" (1961; Hermitage Museum Archive, #1137).

M.I. Artamonov, director of the Hermitage, in response to an article published in *Look* magazine in 1955, noted that at that time one could see on display at his museum six works by Monet, two by Degas, five by Renoir, two by Pissarro, three by Sisley, eight by Cézanne, six by Gauguin, one by Derain, two by Bonnard, thirteen by Matisse, and five by Picasso. However, many works by Impressionists and Postimpressionists were still being kept in the museum's storage area. (All information from the Hermitage Museum Archive was provided for this essay by Elena Solomakha, Curator, Hermitage Museum Archive.)

8. For example, very positive as well as extremely negative comments were written about Picasso's exhibition at the Hermitage. Among positive remarks were the following: "Exhibitions such as this open our eyes to real 'free' art and help us to realize how crippled Soviet art is"; "You should give all the artists of our country the full freedom of creativity"; "For a long time our people were guarded from the bad influence of the West and that's why we cannot fully appreciate this type of art. In order to understand it, you should learn more about it. I can hardly believe that this art, which is so popular in the other part of the globe, is a phenomenon that might be neglected." Negative comments included these: "Picasso's art is a nightmare, nonsense, filth, abomination! Even cave-man drawings cannot be compared with this filthy disgusting daub!"; "There should be no place for this type of art in our Socialist society!" (Hermitage Museum Archive, Fund 1, list 11, #815).

9. Aleksandr Borovsky and Vladimir Butakov, "Parallel'no zhizni," *Iskusstvo Leningrada* 2 (1990): 77.

10. *The Leningrad Show: The Fellowship for Experimental Art*, exh. cat. (Point Reyes Station, CA: Gallery Route One, 1988), p. 50.

11. On Gennadii Zubkov, see "Evidence of Things Not Seen: Gennady Zubkov and the Leningrad Sterligov Group," in Charlotte Douglas and Margarita Tupitsyn, *Gennady Zubkov and the Leningrad "Sterligov" Group,*

exh. cat. (New York: Contemporary Russian Art Center of America, 1983), p. 6. See also Kazimir Malevich, "An Introduction to the Theory of the Additional Element in Painting," in K.S. Malevich, *The World as Non-Objectivity: Unpublished Writings, 1922–1925*, ed. Troels Anderson (Copenhagen: Borgens-Forlag, 1976).

12. V. Krivulin, "Yuri Dyshlenko," *A-Ya* (1982).

13. On Evgenii Mikhnov-Voitenko, see Norton T. Dodge and Alexander Glezer, eds., *Evgeny Mikhnov-Voitenko: Abstract Visions*, exh. cat. (Jersey City, N.J.: C.A.S.E. Museum of Russian Contemporary Art, 1988).

14. See Enrico Crispolti, *Mikhail Koulakov: Un itinerario segnico spiritualistico dal Surrealismo astratto all'oggettualita spaziale*, exh. cat. (Milan: Nuove Edizioni Gabriele Mazzotta, 1988), pp. 37–38. In this catalogue, Kulakov divides his thirty years of artistic activity into three periods: the Moscow period (1956–59); the Leningrad period (1959–76); and the Roman period (1976–88).

15. On Brui and Zelding, see Dodge, ed., *Two Artists in Two Worlds: William Brui and Boris Zeldin*, exh. cat. (Mechanicsville, Md.: Cremona Foundation, 1979).

16. Quoted in Holo, ed., *Keepers of the Flame*, p. 48.

17. Quoted in Alexander Glezer, *Contemporary Russian Art* (Paris, New York, and Moscow: Third Wave Publishers, 1993), p. 436.

18. Ibid.

19. Quoted in Tatiana Yurieva, "Sintetism dara," *Iskusstvo Leningrada* 3 (1989): 81.

20. On Ovchinnikov's works, see Marie-Thérèse de Foras, Alexander Glezer, Jemma Kvatchevskaya, and Dwight Roesch, *Vladimir Ovchinnikov*, exh. cat. (Jersey City, N.J.: Museum of Russian Contemporary Art in Exile, 1986).

21. Quoted in Holo, ed., *Keepers of the Flame*, p. 44.

22. *Anatoli Belkin*, exh. cat. (New York: Eduard Nakhamkin Fine Arts, 1989), p. 5.

23. During the 1960s and 1970s another group of Leningrad artists, including B.F. Golovachev, Y.A. Gusev, V.K. Kagarlitsky, A.M. Daniel, and S.M. Daniel, united around their teacher Grigorii Dlugach. These artists formed an association known as Ermitage. Dlugach had previously studied at the Academy of Fine Arts, where he was greatly influenced by Petrov-Vodkin. Artists of this group studied the art of the Old Masters at the Hermitage.

24. Glezer, *Contemporary Russian Art*, p. 458.

25. Ibid.

26. See "Artist's Statement," in *Rukhin*, exh. cat. (Jersey City, N.J.: Museum of Russian Contemporary Art in Exile, 1989), p. 17.

27. The positive public response to nonconformist exhibitions convinced the artists to seek governmental approval of such efforts. In 1976, a group of twenty activist Leningrad artists sent an open letter to the Twenty-Fifth Congress of the Communist Party of the Soviet Union, in which they stated: "Exhibitions at the Gaz Palace of Culture in 1974 and at the Nevsky Palace of Culture in 1975 showed the tremendous response of the general public to this kind of art. . . . However, the Leningrad Department of Culture ignores the existence of independent artists who are not in the system of the Artists' Union or the Academy of Arts. We would like to ask you to support the founding of the Leningrad Association of Experimental Exhibitions . . . and to give us an opportunity to exhibit regularly by renting us available exhibition spaces." This and further letters from the TEII never received a response from Moscow.

28. Among other early important participants in the nonconformist movement were Vitalii Kubasov and Vladimir Nekrasov. There exist no full-scale studies of Leningrad nonconformist art in English, although some recent exhibition catalogues as well as articles published in American and Russian periodicals deal with its different aspects. See, for example, Yurii Novikov, "Chetyre dnia v dekabre," *Iskusstvo Leningrada* 1 (1990): 97–102; and Aleksandr Borovsky, "Neformaly: mezhdu proshlym i budushchim," *Iskusstvo Leningrada* 3 (1989): 39–47.

29. There were many other members of the left wing of the official Artists' Union in Leningrad who produced innovative works, freely experimenting with themes, form, and color. Included in this group of artists were Valerii Mishin (Fig. 5:16), Natalia Mokina, Viktor Pakhomkin, Tatiana Shirikova, and Vladimir Umansky. Each of these artists and many others deserve fuller treatment, but unfortunately space is not available to do them justice here.

30. For a thorough discussion of religious expression in Soviet nonconformist art, see Alison Hilton, "Icons of the Inner World: The Spiritual Tradition in the New Russian Art," in this volume. See also Alla Rosenfeld and Jeffrey Wechsler, *Struggle for the Spirit*, exh. cat. (New Brunswick, N.J.: Jane Voorhees Zimmerli Art Museum, 1992).

31. This story is recalled in Basin, ed., *Gazanevskaia kultura o sebe*, p. 238. This book also contains some other interesting information about ALEF exhibitions (Ibid, Archive No. 2 by V. Nechaev and M. Nedrobova, pp. 191–261).

32. Quoted in *The Leningrad Show*, p. 16. On Figurina's work, see also Tamara Chudinovskaia, *Elena Figurina*, exh. cat. (1990).

33. On Gerasimenko's work, see Tatyana Schekhter, *Valentin Gerasimenko*, exh. cat. (1990).

34. One of these groups, Ostrov (Island), was founded in 1985 and consisted of only six artists, five of whom were members of TEII. This was later expanded to thirty artists. They considered their group "an island, which is very different from the ocean of visual arts surrounding it." Nikolai Bogomolov, Yurii Brusovani, Aleksandr Volkov, Aleksei Isakov, Liudmila Karsavina, and other members of this group declared "contemporary realism" as their artistic credo.

35. Isa Ibragimov, "Vozvraschennaia devstvennost," *Iskusstvo Leningrada* 1 (1990): 61.

36. *Mitki, opisannye Vladimirom Shinkarevym e narisovannye Aleksandrom Florenskim* (Leningrad: Smart, 1990), p. 18.

37. Margarita Tupitsyn and Victor Tupitsyn, "Timur and Afrika," *Flash Art* 151 (Mar.-Apr. 1989): 124.

38. Ibid.

39. Ibid.

40. In "Timur and Afrika," Timur Novikov notes that Larionov was "the first avant-gardist who (among other things) occupied himself with fashion as well as—in the 1910s—artistic cooking." He was doing "soup from wine, little bread figures of animals and birds, ornamental plants, and so on. He even had a manifesto called 'Rayonnist Cooking.'" Ibid.

41. Quoted in Jork Rothamel, "The Dimension of Conservatism: Aspects of St. Petersburg Art Today," in *Contemporary St. Petersburg Art*, auction catalogue (St. Petersburg, 1992), p. 14.

42. Ibid., p. 15.

6 | Lost in the widening cracks and now resurfaced

Dissidence in Ukrainian painting

Myroslava M. Mudrak

The history of Ukrainian painting in the period from the relaxation of the enforcement of Socialist Realism in the late 1950s through the more repressive Brezhnev regime and up to *perestroika* (which is called *perebudova* in Ukrainian) is a story of many unknown artists, several distinct geographical centers, and a variety of aesthetic directions. The groupings of artists during this period were loose and without theoretical formulations. The paintings in the Dodge Collection illustrate some of the issues involved in Ukrainian dissident art and, together with a few representative works from neighboring republics (Belarus and Moldova), serve as a reminder of the extremely complex sociopolitical and cultural circumstances in which artists had to try to establish an aesthetic direction for themselves.[1]

Despite the pervasive atmosphere of repression that persisted in the Soviet Union even after Stalin's death, there was a broadening demand for greater artistic freedom on the part of the Ukrainian intelligentsia in the late 1950s and early 1960s. One of the leaders of this drive toward a new wave of artistic production was the avant-garde filmmaker Oleksander Dovzhenko (1894–1956), who much earlier had created such classic films as *Zvenihora* (1928), *Arsenal* (1929), and *Earth* (1930). Dovzhenko became the spokesman for a younger generation of artists who were bent on a revitalized artistic life for the Ukraine. In 1955, on the occasion of the All-Union Exhibition of Visual Arts in Moscow, Dovzhenko stated:

> Art cannot evolve according to predetermined precepts. There is in the creative nature, both invention and experiment, and even sometimes courageous extremes in the artistic search. . . . I do not exhort artists to take up abstraction, nor to pursue some sort of individualistic aestheticism, but I am deeply convinced that it is necessary to expand the parameters of Socialist Realism.[2]

Dovzhenko's beckoning call to artists, the first in the Ukraine since the 1920s, paved the way for a virtual renaissance of Ukrainian culture. This project was energetically undertaken by a rejuvenated generation of the cultural elite who brought about a fundamental revolution in all forms of art. At the same time, this movement opened a Pandora's box,

prompting an unrelenting drive by artists toward all new forms of expression.

The pivotal year in this rapid shift in the direction of new art in the Ukraine was 1961. In that year, a group of dissident poets led by Lina Kostenko and Vasyl' Symonenko established themselves under the collective name "Sixtiers" (*shestidesiatniki*). Their poems were filled with a sense of urgency and intent, as well as personal integrity, steadfast humanism, and sincere patriotism. Through such poetry, notions of the personal were rehabilitated, and the poets were able to counter the "cult of personality" which had by then cast such a pall over artistic expression in the Soviet Union. As the "Sixtiers" grew in strength, they encouraged art that was unfettered by external pressures and imposed directions, and they opened the way for a burst of creative endeavors and experimentation.

By the beginning of 1963, Khrushchev had started to show a more intrusive interest in contemporary art and poetry, and had begun to take a more critical public stand on the subject. He vigorously opposed any and all new directions in the arts that did not draw on naturalistic content and depiction. Thus began a wave of repression that initially whittled down the numbers of nonconformists and sent signals of warning to those who continued to pursue these activities. As a result of Khrushchev's opposition, all experimental artists and writers experienced severe critical attacks. Such catch-all terms as "abstractionism" or "formalism" were used to brand their work "inferior" and part of the negative "bourgeois nationalist" subculture.[3] Ironically, however, later artists were inspired by these early manifestations of independence and they continued the efforts of the Sixtiers, even if it meant going underground.

To deal with Ukrainian art of the 1960s and 1970s, particularly in such key centers as Kiev, L'viv (L'vov), or Odesa (Odessa), therefore, is to talk about repression and, today, rehabilitation. A tragic case in point is that of the Kiev artists Viktor Zaretsky (1925–1990) and his wife Alla Horska (1929–1970). During the first half of the 1960s, they chose to work on monumental projects, mainly mosaic murals that represented unusual subjects from Ukrainian folklore and history. Although Zaretsky had trained under the rigorous academic Serhii Hryhoriev and appeared to be an unimpeachable disciple of realism, like many of his contemporaries he simultaneously worked in the forbidden Impressionist mode.[4] He practiced the aesthetics of *le style moderne*, alongside an appliqué art that utilized Ukrainian folk motifs. Meanwhile, Horska's studio, like that of Liudmyla Semykina, was a meeting place for young artists and writers after the disbanding of the Creative Youth Club.

In addition, Zaretsky and Horska were actively involved in the political organization of dissident artists. In 1968, they and a host of other artists, including Opanas Zalyvakha (b. 1925), signed an open letter addressed to the leaders of the Communist Party demanding a loosening of the strictures that had been imposed on artists since 1965. The reprisals for this action were fierce. In November 1970, Alla Horska was brutally murdered in mysterious circumstances at her father's home. Her body was discovered by Zaretsky, who had been called to the house anonymously. He was immediately placed under arrest and charged with the murder of his wife. Without a hearing, he was found guilty and sent to a labor camp for over a decade. These events demonstrated the extreme lengths that the KGB was willing to go to in order to curtail the activities of the Ukraine's cultural elite. The fear of similar reprisals spread throughout the artistic community and sent shock waves among human rights groups then forming in the Ukraine. Horska's death was followed by a series of arrests in Kiev that put an end to all gatherings. External pressure intensified during the mid-1970s, preventing meetings and private showings of artists' works.[5]

Although these moves against Ukrainian artists coincided with a wide offensive by the authorities against the creative intelligentsia in Leningrad and Moscow, the case of Horska and Zaretsky was particularly extreme. In a tragic and poignant way, it mirrored equally repressive tendencies experienced by artists in the western Ukraine in the 1970s. With L'viv and Ivano-Frankivs'k (Ivano-Frankovsk) as key cultural centers, the western Ukraine had erupted with artistic fervor during the 1960s. Because of its position between Poland and Russia, the western Ukraine (especially the region known as Galicia) had always been caught in a struggle to maintain its own national identity against the alien forces that encroached on either side. For artists such as Opanas Zalyvakha, this struggle brought forth an interest in primitivism, paganism, Byzantinism, and other elements of the region's past. Zalyvakha turned to his nation's rarely tapped mythological and art-historical heritage for his subject matter, and dedicated himself to the study of the Ukraine's unique visual symbolism. The price Zalyvakha paid for his revivalist interest in Ukrainian folk traditions

was a long sentence in a labor camp.[6]

Whether the work of Ukrainian artists was focused on the indigenous artistic heritage or on Western art history depended on the individual artist and the circles with which he or she maintained contact (Fig. 6:1).[7] Often these two sources were blended in such a way that even in seeking to rediscover his or her national roots, the artist used design patterns found in local fiber works, ceramics, and painted crafts as a formalist convention in his or her work. Foremost among the goals of the independents was the quest to infuse art with the individualistic world-view that had been suppressed for so long in Soviet art. In addition, they sought to reinstate and protect artistic freedom; this would allow for a level of experimentation with materials, techniques, subjects, and styles that had been denied since the 1930s and seemed lost forever. But, above all, in these diverse nonconformist and, therefore, unofficial circles in the Ukraine and elsewhere, the artists sought to reanimate their own artistic integrity. In most cases, such practices resulted in exclusion from the Artists' Union and loss of the privileges, such as they were, afforded by membership.[8]

The struggle endured by the Ukraine's nonconformist artists was symptomatic of larger issues that beset the republic during the 1960s and 1970s. Many historians have noted that from the time of the artificial famine instigated in the Ukraine in 1933, there was a systematic destruction of Ukrainian culture by the Soviets. Meanwhile, the natural resources of the vast territories occupied by the Soviet Union were being consolidated. A unified culture, dominated by the influence of Russia, was being adopted as the approved expression of all the Soviet peoples, despite official declarations of friendship and equality among the republics.[9] The Ukraine, Belarus, and Moldova were often berated as "the provinces," regions of little concern to Muscovites and even less to Western observers outside the émigré diaspora. But, as early as 1962, Western scholar Robert Sullivant noted that Moscow watched the cultural evolution of the Ukraine far more closely than that of the other republics. In addition, he observed that the restrictions placed upon the Ukraine by the central government were far more rigorous. In the literary and visual art worlds, for instance, strident censorship was implemented against any creative works that might distinguish the Ukraine from the other republics. Any cultural philosophies championed in individual works that depicted Ukrainian culture as developing in opposition to, or separately from, the culture of Russia or that of any other republic were quickly eradicated.[10]

Most innovative artists in the Ukraine tended to be drawn to the monumental art section of the official Art Fund; there, they found fewer restrictions on their creative endeavors

and greater possibilities for the public display of their work.[11] According to Ivan Simchich, head of the art department of the L'viv Cultural Association: "Despite the strong influence of a state patronage that rewarded a certain conformity, many artists retained a portion of their creative energy for art that was more private and which explored realms of the imagination in less conventional ways." During the postwar Russian domination, Socialist Realism, the Communist-sanctioned art style, was the curse of Ukrainian artists. "They painted secretly, for themselves," Simchich has said, "or if they wanted to be exhibited, they painted in allegories the Russian censors could not understand."[12]

In the late 1960s and early 1970s, clever maneuverings within the canons of Socialist Realism in Kiev were made by established artists such as Mykola Hlushchenko (1905–1977) and Tatiana Yablonskaia (b. 1917). But their respectable status also meant a duplicitous existence. Although Yablonskaia was a member of the Art Academy of the Ukraine—her renowned composition *Bread* (1948) was virtually the model for successful Socialist Realist painting—she had no trouble showing paintings that went beyond the officially sanctioned themes and terms of Socialist Realism. For instance, she was one of the first artists allowed to depict such humanistic subjects as old age and loneliness, even though she drew her inspiration from the dire existence experienced by so many under the Soviet system. In her *Odynoka* [Alone] (1970), an old woman, "dark as the earth,"[13] is portrayed bent over some household chore beside a window in her cottage, darkened with age and years of neglect. This portrayal is a far cry from the heroic depictions of athletic-looking, smiling workers, but is instead an actual depiction of life as observed by the artist.

Such departures from Socialist Realism did not become prevalent until the 1970s, and were sometimes, as in the case of Vladimir Bakhtov (b. 1954), drawn from the illustra-

tional automatism of Surrealism. Bakhtov's sinewy figures have the same psychological edge as Yablonskaia's monumental forms, while evoking the unusual dream world of Surrealism. With almost medieval resolve, Bakhtov draws on paganistic, ritualistic components that suggest moral and ethical codes, sharp divisions between good and bad, and dichotomies between old and new (Fig. 6:2). Oscillating between two styles—one earthy and robust, the other lithe and wistful—Bakhtov creates in his works elaborate metaphors in which the forces of nature symbolize an existence of perpetual uncertainties and irresolution.

As more artists produced work that went beyond the limits of Socialist Realism, many found themselves frustrated in their attempts to exhibit. Artists in all three major centers of Ukrainian art in the 1960s—Kiev, L'viv, and Odesa—faced the dilemma of having no channels open for the display of their work. Consequently, they began holding exhibitions in places other than those controlled by the Artists' Union. Some scientific institutions, like the Institute of Cybernetics in Kiev, offered their premises to nonconformist artists. But most of the nonconformist exhibitions were held in artists' studios or apartments under very difficult conditions (Fig. 6:3). Such "apartment exhibitions" became the lifeline for artists in these cities.

The artists of Odesa were aware of the historical significance of the apartment exhibitions, and in 1976 they sought to record the sense of the moment by distributing a questionnaire to all participating artists. This questionnaire asked three basic questions: 1) what is your view of apartment exhibitions?; 2) what artists shown are of most interest to you?; and 3) what characterizes your own work? In response to the first question, the artists indicated overwhelmingly that they had no alternative venues for showing their work. The reason, as indicated in the majority reaction to the third question, was that official art exhibitions made no room for artworks that resulted from a strong inner drive to explore the language of art for its own sake.

The forms of artistic self-expression practiced in the Ukraine were various, to say the least. Pure abstraction was not widespread; figuration and representational art predominated, bolstered by narrative content and proliferated through graphics and graphic illustration. Illustration of the classics, whether it was the works of Ivan Franko, Taras Shevchenko, Lesya Ukrainka, or contemporary poet-laureates, became standard fare for almost all Ukrainian artists of the 1970s. Illustrations derived from Shevchenko's romantic poetry by Yurii Kovalenko, for example, communicate the poet's sentimental attachment to the land and the soul of the people, as well as the links he stressed between the generations. Kovalenko's work employs a

Fig. 6:2
Vladimir Bakhtov
River of Dreams, 1985
Etching and aquatint
50 × 71.3 cm

Fig. 6:3
Exhibition of Odesa artists in
the apartment of Vladimir
Sychev, Moscow
Photo courtesy of Myroslava
Mudrak

and 1970s by way of contraband literature entering the western Ukraine through Poland. L'viv, the cultural-artistic center of the western Ukraine, has always had a "Western European" face.[14] More often than not, these two directions—the local and the international—were integrated.

The work of Anatolii Brussilovsky (b. 1932) and Mikhail Brussilovsky (b. 1931) demonstrates quite clearly this blending of universal stylistic pursuits with local artistic concerns. Both Brussilovskys reveal a predilection for baroque form, a tendency catalyzed in the work of both artists by a distinct Rubenesque handling. Additionally, Anatolii Brussilovsky's works from the *Japanese Zodiac* series, 1984 (Pl. 6:4), offer the viewer yet another sensual experience, with a "Far Eastern" orientation. This comes through in the sinewy curvaceousness of the voluptuous figures and the lucid, epicurean flavor of the forms. The pastel colors add to some of the lurid overtones suggested by the image.

In striking contrast to this manner, Mikhail Brussilovsky often employs conventional methods of Orthodox icon painting in his work. In *Homo Sapiens*, 1974 (Pl. 6:8), the surrounding frame, with its "stories in miniature" connected to the main image, recalls the icons of St. Nicholas. This frame of episodic scenes (called *zhytiia* in true icons)

rugged style that recalls the vulgar expressivity of artists of the 1910s, such as the Burliuks, who worked in the Ukraine. Quite opposite in feeling are the illustrations by Valentina Melnychenko (b. 1946) to Ukrainka's classic *Lisova pisnia* [Forest song]. These works show Melnychenko's typically intricate and involved drawing style (Fig. 6:4). Intertwining lines begin to form figure and nature motifs, and languorous, fluid forms interweave with subtle changes of light and dark. Lithography fosters such linearity and, in this case, it allows Melnychenko's succulent, vibrant forms to emerge as rich as when encountered in nature.

Some Ukrainian artists discovered creative freedom in the recovery of the artistic vitality of their own national art, especially the folk traditions that embodied their historical spirit. Others sought to stretch the confines of their acquired experiences and explored Western artistic sources, which they quickly assimilated. Because of the proximity of the western Ukraine to Western Europe, some limited access to Western art was possible during the 1960s

Fig. 6:4
Valentina Melnychenko
(Untitled), n.d.
Lithograph
32 × 23.7 cm

expounds upon the details of the life of the topical figure presented in the central area. The main theme or subject is thus made richer and clearer. In Brussilovsky's case, the theme concerns the creation of man and his evolutionary development. Clearly, the style of both Brussilovskys varies from work to work, in some cases even evoking a direct indebtedness to influences of the avant-garde of the 1920s, especially the work of Pavel Filonov (1883–1941).

David Miretsky (b. 1939) studied at the Kiev Art Institute from 1965 to 1969, and then exhibited in several non-conformist exhibitions in Kiev and Moscow before emigrating to the U.S. in 1975. His down-to-earth Bruegelesque paintings of ordinary men and women engaged in after-hours activities led to his arrest and the seizure of some of his paintings in Moscow. By coincidence, President Nixon visited the U.S.S.R. in 1974, and the Soviets were compelled to release Miretsky and his paintings in order to avoid unfavorable coverage in the international press (Pl. 6:2).

But the experiences of Kiev artists suggest only one side of the complex story of Ukrainian art during this time, and focus too narrowly on one geographical area. As previously mentioned, a very strong seat of artistic modernism had also been established in the city of L'viv. As the most Western-looking Ukrainian city, L'viv had actively participated in Western modern art movements with its own dominant secessionist style, a strong Cubo-Expressionist tendency, and Surrealist manifestations.[15] But in the 1970s, L'viv also nourished the art of several well-known contemporary artists, including Igor Kopystiansky (b. 1954) and Svetlana Kopystianskaia (b. 1950).

Despite Igor Kopystiansky's subsequent success in Moscow and elsewhere, his art is deeply rooted in his native city of L'viv. The city's architectural monuments and the work in its museums fed his imagination and became the source for his appropriation of artistic images and styles. Many of his works, like *Construction I*, 1985–86 (Pl. 6:1), draw on images readily available in the L'viv Art Gallery. By abstracting them from their context in the gallery, copying them as his own, and then subjecting them to a process of ruination and decay, Kopystiansky seeks to deconstruct their historical meanings. What is surprising to many Western-ers is that, by the early 1980s, such Postmodernist strate-gies were already available to Soviet unofficial artists. Like the American Postmodernists Mike Bidlo and Sherrie Levine, to whose work his own is often compared, Kopystiansky was influenced by the repeated motifs of Minimalism (Fig. 6:5). In addition, his later works not only give credit to his borrowings from the classics, but also endow his works with layerings of artistic experience. There is a general pre-occupation with time-wornness, a certain aged quality that

Fig. 6:5
Igor Kopystiansky
Untitled, 1974
Oil on canvas
45.2 × 60 cm

is concerned with experience, wisdom, and the dialectic between permanence and impermanence. As one Western critic has noted:

> Kopystiansky paints nearly perfect paintings and then sets about destroying them; in some instances, the unflawed work is left to stand for some time before being destroyed, and though this painting was done before Kopystiansky came to New York, it was destroyed after he arrived. Untar-nished it was not dangerous; it is by undermining his own craft that Kopystiansky gives these works their ominous or tragic aspect.[16]

Svetlana Kopystianskaia, who received her education in the Ukraine and later moved to Moscow, has said that her art is directly linked to literature. "This is not a chance deci-sion," she stated, "for literature in Russia has traditionally been assigned a leading role in culture as a whole.... The book was regarded as a sacred object and the writer as a prophet and the conscience of society."[17] Many of her paint-ings have used line after line of the written word to convey the shapes and shadings of the objects in a painting—much as halftone dots do in offset printing (Pl. 15:26). Some of her text-lined canvases are bunched, compressed, folded, or even bundled for artistic effect (Pl. 6:20).

Her preoccupation with page layout and typeset text is linked to the deeply rooted tradition of painting with which L'viv is associated, dating back to the sixteenth century, when in the L'viv shops of Ivan Fedorov (d. 1583) the first books, adorned with extravagant woodcuts, were born, the most noteworthy of which was the world-famous Ostrog Bible of 1581. The achievements of Fedorov and his followers pro-vided the historical background for a renaissance of book design in the early twentieth century and for which L'viv became a key center.

Other regions of the Ukraine beyond L'viv also made impressive strides toward artistic individuality. In many ways, Odesa's distance from key administrative centers (and also from the international diplomatic and news networks of Moscow and Leningrad) allowed its artists to develop independently. The predominantly multicultural constituency in Odesa also encouraged a cosmopolitan flair in artistic expression, and a freer atmosphere at the end of the 1960s and in the early 1970s was supported to some degree by the Odesa Artists' Union itself. This is documented by the fact that in 1971, with the support of Artists' Union members Yurii Yegorov (Egorov) (b. 1926) and Oleksander Atsmanchuk (1923–1974), a five-man exhibition was organized at the Artists' Union building. Included were the works of Lucien Dulfan (b. 1942), Viktor Maryniuk (b. 1939), Volodymyr Strelnikov (b. 1939), and Stanislav Sychov (b. 1937), artists whose works contained none of the prerequisites of official Soviet paintings. However, when a similar exhibition was staged in 1972, this time with eight artists participating, the official artists sponsoring the show retreated to the more sobering, hard-line position of the Union, attacking the exhibition for its deviations from Socialist Realism. So ended the support of unofficial art by official circles in Odesa.

What remains clear is the history of artistic defiance and staunch independence in this area. In 1967, Odesa artists Stanislav Sychov and Valentyn Khrushch (b. 1943) organized an outdoor exhibition in front of the opera house, the old Palais Royal building, in central Odesa. The authorities, who could not fathom abstraction as a means of expressing the artist's deepest spiritual or philosophical thoughts, attacked the exhibition as formalist, and after only three hours the local militia forcibly closed it down. Even though the actual coup was short-lived and its effect limited, the Odesa show was an important event for Ukrainian dissident art. From that date forward, important contemporary art in the Ukraine went underground. Despite brief appearances in 1971–72 and again in 1976, it remained clandestine until 1986. Nonetheless, within that period a number of artists surfaced whose names will always be associated with the Odesa school of contemporary art.

Dulfan's works, like his 1978 painting *Reflection of the City* (Pl. 6:3), dramatically summarize the two key features of Odesa painting, namely texture and color. But it was the dynamic activities of Sychov and Khrushch that formed the core of Odesa art. Valentyn Khrushch had no formal artistic training but learned his craft by studying works in museums and absorbing the painting techniques of late nineteenth and early twentieth-century Odesa painters, such as Kyriiak Kostandi (1852–1921). One of the most daring

Fig. 6:6
Valentyn Khrushch
(Untitled), 1980
Mixed media on panel
74.5 × 31.8 cm

and innovative members of the Odesa group, Khrushch quickly assimilated the avant-garde trends of the West such as Pop Art and Conceptual Art and adapted them to his own working method. During the 1970s, he worked in a rapid manner, mostly *alla prima*, as he sought to straddle the aesthetic problems of realism and abstract art (Fig. 6:6). He was a prolific artist, producing many thematic series and concentrating heavily on textural variations in individual compositions. For instance, he created an entire series of monochromatic paintings which were variations on the theme of whiteness, but which also carried subtle erotic connotations. More generally, however, he dealt with the Odesa environs, the port and the Black Sea beaches.

Almost without exception, the Odesa artists were painters of representational images who quickly abandoned such work to respond to their growing passion for the abstract or the surreal. Sychov, a case in point, is a master of the silhouetted form and the dark, mysterious passages of night. His works are different from those of his colleagues by virtue of his preoccupation with the subterranean, psychological aspects of the back streets and with the night moods of Odesa's environs. Generally, Odesa's art contrasts strongly with other centers of underground art in the Ukraine in that the artists seem to take most of their pleasure in aesthetic delight, as in Sychov's *Dance* (1977). Absent are the inexorable statements disparaging the Soviet state often seen in work from Moscow. But also absent (though not completely) are the demonstrations of struggle for political liberation that characterize the art of L'viv and Kiev. Although activism could be observed in all three cities simultaneously, differences in degree nonetheless distinguished the centers from one another.

It was, in fact, in Odesa, far from the hotbeds of national feeling and fervor, that a more worldly air and a new aesthetic practice were cultivated. From the early 1970s, the artists of Odesa were actively engaged in contemporary art movements that ranged from figuration to total abstraction and even to assemblage. The topography of Odesa and its environs, suffused with a warm, moist, and dense atmospheric light, inspired different sensibilities. The craggy rock formations along the Black Sea and the flat planes of the expansive shoreline give a sense of space and textural breadth that, consciously or not, was constantly reiterated in the work of its artists. And, even amid the sun-drenched pan-Mediterranean landscape, Odesa artists could not ignore the vestiges of ancient cultures that emanated from the Black Sea. Thus, depictions of the local stone-goddess (*kamiana baba*) energize the works of Volodymyr Strelnikov and Valerii Basanets (b. 1941). Equally common in Odesa are references to a modern cult, the cult of Kostandi. The Kostandi Association thrived in the southern Ukraine during the 1920s and celebrated Kyriiak Kostandi, the instigator of modern art trends in Odesa at the turn of the century. The Kostandi Association encouraged all sorts of artistic experimentation without attempting to perpetuate any single style.[18] But what dominated this group was a rugged attachment to the environment. Artists such as Evgenii Rakhmanin (b. 1947) and Viktor Risovich (Pl. 6:19) perpetuate this legacy.

As a consequence of its complex history, Odesa was more ethnically diverse and less committed to promoting national identity than any other part of the Ukraine. Even to speak of Odesa artists as being strictly Ukrainian is beside the point, since the city's longstanding multiculturalism meant that nonconformist art was practiced there not only by Ukrainians, but also by Russians, Jews, Ossetians, and representatives of many other ethnic minorities. The Jewish contingent in modern and contemporary art was especially strong in Odesa, and it is this group of artists whose work was marketed best in the West and is thus most familiar to Western audiences. The Dodge Collection is especially rich in examples from the Jewish artistic community in Odesa.

Although many of these Jewish artists spent much of their professional lives outside the Ukraine, their roots were firmly planted in Odesa. For example, even in Israel, Yefim Ladyzhensky (1911–1982) continued to create compelling works in a primitive mode that dealt expressly with his childhood and youth in Odesa.[19] His series concerning the Jewish experience (e.g., *The Wandering Jew*) and his series of paintings titled *Growing Up in Odesa* draw heavily on literary and dramatic works by authors such as Isaac Babel (Pl. 6:14). His art is therefore filled with messages about the pathos of the human condition (Pl. 6:22). Yet, surprisingly, his work also includes wit, humor, and a jocular tone, especially in its treatment of the day-to-day affairs of the ordinary population (Pls. 6:5, 6:6).

These qualities, with their distinct overtones of primitivism, are shared by a younger Jewish artist from Odesa, Noi Volkov (b. 1947). Volkov grew up in Odesa, but received his advanced art training at the Mukhina School in Leningrad. He has made the theme of his coming to maturity in Odesa a key focus of his art. Around 1976, when he was accepted into the Artists' Union, Volkov began to distance himself from the whimsical, colorful, miniaturistic renderings of peasants he had begun making while visiting Armenia. His newly somber style was increasingly political in content and led to trouble with the KGB (Fig. 12:4). As a consequence Volkov emigrated to the United States in 1989.

More closely linked in spirit with the Ukrainian artists of Odesa was Lev Mezhberg (b. 1933), who was born in Odesa and graduated with high honors from the Odesa College of Fine Art in 1958. He became well known in collectors' circles after being named one of the "Six Best Painters in Russia" in 1967.[20] Along with Lucien Dulfan and Akim Levich (b. 1933), Mezhberg was a progenitor of the nonconformist art movement in Odesa; he was one of the first artists to begin to reveal the complexity of contemporary Soviet art in the late 1960s. His paintings are evocative of a constant struggle by civilized mankind against the ominous suggestion of uncivilized demise. Devoid of people but rich with memory, Mezhberg's works (Pl. 6:18) strongly suggest an abundant, if rarefied and totally abstract, version of the symbolic worlds of nineteenth-century Russian painter Vasilii Vereshchagin (e.g., *Apotheosis of War*, 1871) and the Armenian painter Martiros Sarian. The works by Mezhberg in the

Dodge Collection demonstrate his stylistic consistency over the fifteen years immediately preceding his emigration to the United States in 1973.

Yurii Yegorov was another artist in Odesa circles who had a strong influence on both Ukrainian and Jewish artists. He entered the art world as a true Sixtier; his debut in Socialist Realism in 1957 established him as an official artist in good standing.[21] His portraits and landscapes depict the surroundings and people around him. He does not analyze, and no extraneous paraphernalia appears in his compositions; he wants the portrait to represent the whole person. The very source of his art is the secret that each person holds within himself. His works are like parables or pictures of premonitions. He frequently uses the motif of the ship, often shown with a raised flag, and his intimate ties to the Black Sea have also since been taken up by his protégés (Pl. 6:17).

Yegorov's influence on Ukrainian painters, particularly Volodymyr Strelnikov, is evident in the use of thick impasto and a tendency to go repeatedly over every element. Strelnikov, an Odesa-born artist (Pl. 6:16) who began his artistic training at the Odesa Art School before undertaking independent studies in 1960, is a courageous artist. His works range from the primitivistic treatment of simple, everyday themes via a fundamental study of color values to a clean and crisp treatment of the cosmopolitan city. He began to show with the Odesa Artists' Guild, and later took part in exhibitions sponsored by the Union of Artists. Eventually, he was accepted into official exhibitions in Odesa, Kiev, Moscow, Latvia, and Bulgaria. But after 1972, his works were displayed only in unofficial exhibitions which he helped to organize in Moscow, Odesa, Kiev, and Leningrad. Following his participation in two exhibitions of Ukrainian artists in Moscow in the 1970s, Strelnikov began to be harassed by the KGB and so chose to emigrate to the West.

As with Strelnikov, many of the reprisals against Ukrainian artists in the 1970s had less to do with aesthetic transgressions than with their demonstrations of Ukrainian nationalism. So long as artists did not voice Ukrainian concerns, the administration generally allowed them to pursue outlawed formalist styles without serious repercussions. Other important Odesa artists of this period include Alexander Freidin (1926–1987), Israel Kligman (b. 1927), Emmanuel Snitkovsky (b. 1933), Zhanna Snitkovskaïa (b. 1934), Vadim Grinberg (b. 1947), Nina Volkova (b. 1946), and Shimon Okshteyn (b. 1951). Freidin is one of the older artists who has had a significant influence on younger Odesa nonconformists. His elegant, simplified paintings and drawings on textured paper—often sensitive and perceptive portraits—set a standard for serene excellence (Fig. 6:7).

Fig. 6:7
Alexander Freidin
Portrait, 1982
Oil on fiberboard
37 × 36.3 cm

Kligman depicts Odesa life in the raw—horse traders, wheeler-dealers, lechers, and the like—in thickly layered brushstrokes. Emmanuel Snitkovsky produced officially commissioned monumental sculptures as well as nonconformist paintings and drawings on the side. His wife, Zhanna, had an important solo exhibition in 1974 featuring abstract painting and works with Jewish themes that was closed down by the authorities. (Emmanuel's prolonged difficulties with a commission for a Babii Yar memorial sculpture prompted the couple to emigrate to the United States in 1978.) Grinberg was trained in graphic design in Odesa, but his extracurricular nonconformist work included a large iconostasis in metal, a miniature winged piano, and oversized sculptures of fruit and vegetables made of molded leather. His work, while avant-garde, assimilates and reflects many different cultural traditions. Vadim's wife, Nina Volkova, also grew up in Odesa but received her art training at the Mukhina School of Industrial Arts in Leningrad. Her art in Odesa was more traditional than her husband's, and included a Pop Art-inspired series depicting Soviet cigarette packs and portraits in styles appropriated from Old Masters and well-known avant-garde artists. The couple moved to Moscow in 1986 and more recently to Los Angeles. The youngest of this group is Okshteyn, who studied in Chernivtsi before completing his studies at the Odesa Art College. Prior to his emigration in 1979, he began to develop a Lindner-like style which he has elaborated more fully in the United States.

Odesa, Kiev, and L'viv, strong centers of artistic culture

Fig. 6:8 (*left*)
Semyon Katsevich
Road of Death, 1961
Oil on illustration board
49.9 × 69.7 cm

Fig. 6:10 (*right*)
Valerii Pogorelov
Continent, 1985
Oil on canvas
80.1 × 80.4 cm

Fig. 6:11 (*right*)
Vachegan Narazian
Absurd Travel, 1983
Tempera and gouache on
fiberboard
74.8 × 85 cm

Fig. 6:9
Pavel Brozgol
*Still Life with White
Coffee Pot*, 1973
Oil on canvas
85 × 60.2 cm

since ancient times, are only a few of the communities in the Ukraine that were caught up in the search for new national artistic directions during the 1960s and 1970s. Add to these cities the newer industrial hubs formed early in this century, such as Kharkiv (Kharkov) in the eastern Ukraine or Dnipropetrovs'k (Dniepropetrovsk, formerly Ekaterinoslav) on the Dnipro (Dnieper) river, and one will recognize the great range of artistic influences on contemporary Ukrainian painting. These distinct centers offered very different interpretations of the country's artistic heritage, particularly in relation to Constructivism.[22] Ironically, however, these outlying artistic enclaves were closed off and isolated, without the opportunities for contact with the West that one could find in Kiev, L'viv, or Odesa.

Kharkiv, one-time capital of the Ukraine and second only to Kiev in size, is a major cultural, educational, and research center. Its prominence in art is more in the area of printmaking than painting. Among the many noted printmakers from Kharkiv are Vladimir Nenado (1935–1981), Evgenii Solovlev (b. 1943), and Vitalii Kulikov (b. 1935). A younger master printer trained in Kharkiv is Sergei Tsetkov (b. 1958), whose works were recently added to the Dodge

Collection. The most significant nonconformist painter is Semyon Katsevich (b. 1926), who has eschewed protest in order to concentrate his energies on creating Expressionistic improvisations. His subjects are often drawn from world history, as in the case of his *Road of Death* (Fig. 6:8), which depicts victims of the Holocaust.

The influence of French Cubism can be seen in the widely exhibited still lifes of Pavel Brozgol (b. 1933) (Fig. 6:9). Vitalii Kulikov was also influenced by French Cubism and Russian Constructivism. The work of Evgenii Bykov (b. 1941) shows the influence of Cézanne, Bonnard, and Vlaminck. Petro Mos (b. 1948), who was refused membership of the Kharkiv Artists' Union, draws on ancient Ukrainian legends, tales, and folk motifs with a sharp sense of humor. The work of Victor Gontarov (b. 1944), a member of the Artists' Union from the mid-1970s, differs radically from Socialist Realism. His one-man show in Kharkiv in 1980 attracted much attention in cultural circles as well as sharp criticism from the leadership of the Artists' Union.

Dmitrii Dymshits (b. 1951), who trained at the Kharkiv Institute of Art, began as a realist but then turned to a form of Expressionism (Pl. 6:13) which evolved into what Halyna

(Galina) Sklyarenko has called "symbolic romanticism." Other important Kharkiv nonconformists include: Valerii Pogorelov (b. 1954), whose range of styles includes abstract earth-toned compositions (Fig. 6:10); Vachegan Narazian (b. 1957), who creates a fantasy world in his prints and oils (Fig. 6:11); and Gennadii Lesnichy (b. 1957) and his wife Lena Lesnichaia (b. 1957), whose paintings were initially dark, foreboding, and dramatic, not unlike those of the German Expressionists. All of these nonconformist artists, even those who were members of the Artists' Union, had difficulties with the authorities. However, their isolation in Kharkiv made them more cautious than artists in Moscow or Leningrad. By being less aggressive and remaining "underground," they did not provoke dramatic confrontations with the authorities.

Other key figures of the nonconformist movement in the Ukrainian visual arts of the 1970s hailed from remote regions. Volodymyr (Vladimir) Makarenko (b. 1943) and Feodosii Humeniuk (Gumeniuk) (b. 1941) both trained in the Dnipropetrovs'k Art School, where they were steeped in Socialist Realism before coming under the influence of Yakiv Kalashnyk (1927–1967). Kalashnyk, who had been trained at the Art Academy in Riga, introduced his students to the modern trends in Western European art. In later years, Humeniuk openly acknowledged that Kalashnyk was the first teacher to show his charges that copying nature was not the sole way of making art. Also, prior to their official training, in their own self-styled search for artistic roots, Humeniuk and Makarenko were frequent visitors to the Yavornytsky Museum in Dnipropetrovs'k, which housed not only archaeological finds from the region but also artifacts from the Kozak or Cossack period of the seventeenth and eighteenth centuries. Their fascination with the Cossacks, who personified nationhood and nation-building, became the focus of many of their works (e.g., Humeniuk's *Day*, 1973 [Pl. 6:7]) and was an example of traditional symbolic content translated into modern-day terms.

Of similar interest to them was the image of the Kozak Mamai, a legendary hero personifying the democratic spirit of the Cossacks, who is often crudely rendered in folk paintings on plain wooden boards.[23] A classic folkish character, the Kozak Mamai has been drawn upon repeatedly as a source by contemporary artists who gain inspiration from its lively formal qualities: flat space, stark contrasts of color, and a fluid organization of simple shapes. How widespread this image has been is demonstrated by the paintings of Anatolii Schopin (b. 1941) an Odesa artist whose works easily maneuver between two very different modes, the academic and the folk.[24]

A similar process can be found in the work of Humeniuk,

who sought to synthesize the academic precepts of Ukrainian Baroque painting, the formal and spiritual qualities of old Ukrainian icons, and some aspects of modernity, such as the independent compartmentalizing of color. Other symbolic motifs drawn from folk art are also called into action. These include the rooster, the historical symbol of national awakening and Christian faith and resurrection, and the female body, an embodiment of nation, fecundity, and rebirth.[25] Meanwhile, references to the Mother of God, the Holy Wisdom (Hagia Sophia and Mother Protectress), also recur in the work of Humeniuk and Makarenko. But their work surpasses the bounds of local ethnography. What surfaces in their art, especially that of Humeniuk, is a reverence for lost tradition, for suppressed religion, and for usurped dignity.

When both Humeniuk and Makarenko decided to pursue advanced art training in Leningrad, they were uninhibited in their experiments with technique. Makarenko's close association with Mikhail Chemiakin at this time influenced his choice of colors and the calligraphic unity of his images. He also adopted Chemiakin's characteristic technique of repainting a surface that had already been worked over texturally. Moreover, just as Chemiakin presented a whole range of symbolic imagery, so too Makarenko retained a very personal vocabulary of signs and symbols stemming from tender childhood memories in his own art. Their fragility is enhanced by the tenuous and transparent qualities of the watercolor medium he used. Makarenko's art also calls to mind, more by suggestion than by plan or direct influ-

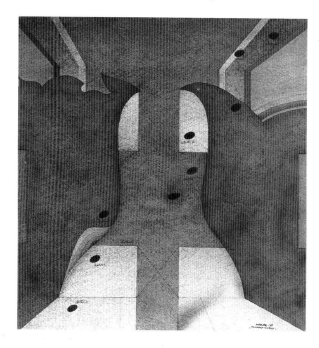

Fig. 6:12
Volodymyr (Vladimir) Makarenko
Metaphysical Form, 1975
Watercolor and pen
and ink on paper
33.7 × 32.1 cm

Pl. 6:1
Igor Kopystiansky
Construction I, 1985–86
Oil on canvas
167.5 × 152.5 × 160.5 cm

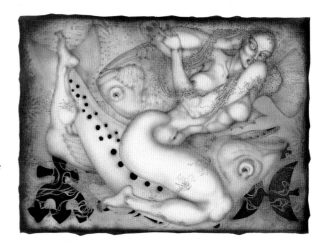

Pl. 6:3
Lucien Dulfan
Reflection of the City, 1978
Oil on fiberboard
45 × 63 cm

Pl. 6:2
David Miretsky
Russian Trinity, 1976
Oil on canvas
123.8 cm in diameter

Pl. 6:4
Anatolii Brussilovsky
Pisces, from the series *The Japanese Zodiac*, 1984
Watercolor and pen and ink on paper
65 × 89 cm

Pl. 6:5
Yefim Ladyzhensky
A Good Bra, 1967
Oil on canvas
89 × 99.5 cm

Pl. 6:6
Yefim Ladyzhensky
Bootblack, 1974
Oil on canvas
90 × 98.5 cm

Pl. 6:7
**Feodosii Humeniuk
(Gumeniuk)**
Day, 1973
Oil on canvas
75 × 86.6 cm

Pl. 6:9
**Volodymyr (Vladimir)
Naumets**
(Untitled), 1984
Oil on canvas
300.5 × 203 cm

Pl. 6:8
Mikhail Brussilovsky
Homo Sapiens, 1974
Oil on canvas
152 × 173 cm

Pl. 6:10
Sergei Sherstiuk
*The Men of One Family,
1941*, 1985
Oil on canvas
All these Sherstiuk men
are uncles of the artist
except as noted. Seated:
Dmitri (died 1943), Sergei
(died winter of 1942–43—
artist's grandfather).
Standing: Aleksei (died
1942), Vasilii (died 1944),
Grigorii, Viktor, Daniil.
182 × 221.5 cm

Pl. 6:11
Sergei Sherstiuk
The Men of One Family,
1945, 1985
Oil on canvas
Seated: Daniil (now
dead). Standing: Viktor
(still living), Grigorii
(now dead).
182 × 221.5 cm

Pl. 6:12
Sergei Sherstiuk
The Cosmonaut's Dream,
1986
Oil on canvas
148 × 198.5 cm

Pl. 6:13
Dmitrii Dymshits
The Prophet, 1983
Oil on canvas
81.7 × 65.2 cm

Pl. 6:14
Yefim Ladyzhensky
Red Cavalry, 1965
Oil on illustration board
87 × 62.5 cm

Pl. 6:15
Vitalii Sazonov
(Untitled), 1979
Mixed media on canvas
100 × 75.2 cm

Pl. 6:16
Volodymyr Strelnikov
(Untitled), 1976
Colored pencil and pen
and ink on paper
29.4 × 21.1 cm

Pl. 6:17
Yurii Yegorov (Egorov)
(Seascape, Odessa), 1986
Oil on illustration board
42.8 × 50.4 cm

Pl. 6:18
Lev Mezhberg
Old City, 1965
Oil on canvas
95 × 115 cm

Pl. 6:19
Viktor Risovich
Moonlit Night, 1974
Oil on illustration board
21.7 × 42.2 cm

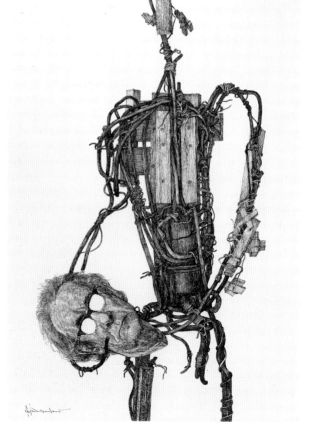

Pl. 6:20
Svetlana Kopystianskaia
(Untitled), n.d.
Mixed media
84 × 84 × 5 cm

Pl. 6:21 (*above right*)
Yevhen Petrenko
Bioengineering, 1984
Oil on canvas
79 × 89 cm

Pl. 6:22
Yefim Ladyzhensky
From the series
Carcasses, 1971
Pen and ink on paper
90.3 × 62 cm

ence, the mystical aura of certain Symbolist painters, particularly Jan Zrzavy, a Czech painter of the 1920s. This indirect influence is evident not only in Makarenko's titles (which refer to meditative moods and introspection), but also in the elegant linearity overlaid with intense, deep colors and the internalized moments of individual experience in his works (Fig. 6:12).

Despite the highly personal and politically innocuous nature of such imagery, by the mid-1970s Makarenko's work was being interpreted by the authorities as potentially subversive. Because Makarenko made frequent references to the Ukraine's history—if only in an inventive, phantasmagoric fashion—that message, hidden in symbolism, was sought out, exposed, and castigated. In this way, it was suggested that the erotica that pervades Makarenko's work was less a reflection of his own sensual fantasies than a critique of all that was forbidden in Soviet life. For these reasons, and because of Makarenko's involvement with the St. Petersburg group of dissidents (known in the West as the Leningrad Group), his work came under ever-greater scrutiny. Eventually, he was denied residency in Leningrad and moved to Tallinn, Estonia, where the freer and more "Western" artistic climate typical of the Baltics proved more conducive to his creative efforts.

It was in Tallinn that Makarenko pursued what he called "metaphysical synthetism," the blending of native symbolic and mystical traditions with the formal developments in Western art since Impressionism.[26] The lithe and attenuated female form, rendered neither realistically nor idealistically but with elliptical plasticity, is a trademark of Makarenko's art, as it was for the Ukrainian-born painter and sculptor Alexander Archipenko. Since he is extremely sensitive to color, Makarenko's paintings in oil, watercolors, gouache, or acrylic (materials with which he works easily and interchangeably) are suffused with a warm elegance, ideally harmonized, so that no single hue dominates. The impression created by Makarenko's art is best described by Kiev art historian Dmytro Horbachov, who wrote: "The mystique of his works carry the viewer from beyond an erotic wave into a world of the immaculate, and then what comes over you is a cloudy sensation about that which will never be again."[27] Because of the melancholic tone of his works and his subtle incorporation of script, both characteristics of the popular Kozak Mamai image, Makarenko has been nicknamed by his peers "Kozak Makar." Many critics have also noted the influence of traditional fresco painting on Makarenko's art. This is apparent in his use of flattened forms, shallow spaces, and a linear composition creating in the whole a polyphonic rhythm. The French critic Hélian Bernard has said: "The art of Kozak Makar is filled with

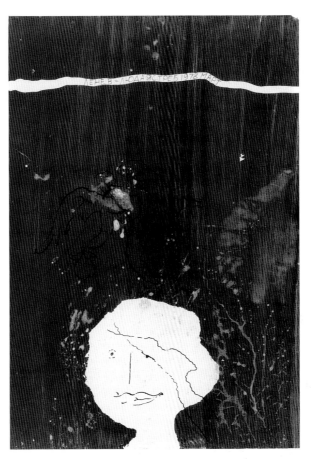

Fig. 6:13
Liudmyla Yastreb
(Untitled), 1978
Tempera and pen and ink
on paper
28.9 × 20.3 cm

the creativity of the great Italians—Fra Angelico, Botticelli; they [his works] emulate the quests of the Symbolist, Gustave Moreau, within the realm of the subconscious."[28]

The echoes of historical, folkloric, and traditional sacred art that weave themselves through Makarenko's painting and are also apparent in the work of Humeniuk, comprise an important aspect of the work of other Ukrainian artists, including Liudmyla Yastreb (1945–1980), Volodymyr (Vladimir) Naumets (b. 1945), and Vitalii Sazonov (1947–1986). Yastreb's early paintings from the 1960s consisted of genre scenes, initially rendered in a realistic manner. Like Strelnikov, Yastreb is a courageous woman of Amazon-like artistic prowess and prolific output. Even in such elemental works as drawings or watercolors, her work is typified by a buoyancy and a *joie de vivre* that stems from the lightness and airiness of her compositions. Her characteristic flatness and linearity, and the collage techniques that she uses, result in unpredictable combinations of form and color (Fig. 6:13). At one time, she painted architectural landscapes that brought together a geometric and orderly arrangement of planes of color. But these gave way to figural compositions, mostly of women. Even though female imagery has always been a mainstay of the Odesa School, Yastreb's iconographic focus on women is unique. Issues around the representation of women have had a special significance in her life, both artistically and personally, representing a kind of spiritual bridge over the intractable ideological surge.

Just as Strelnikov and Yastreb sought to introduce a spiritual element into their paintings through diaphanous pastels and the symbolic image of the virginal woman, Naumets sought to explore spirituality through a rugged tooling of the painted surface. Naumets's chief visual source was the *Theotokos*, the Byzantine treatment of the Mother and Child in icons. He borrowed generously from the figural and color elements of the icon and rearranged them into abstract compositions (Pl. 6:9). The foundation of his compositions, however, is the Greek cross, against which are arranged silhouettes of the Hodigitria and cocoon-like references to the embryonic child. As in a true icon, the spiritual combines with the material in Naumets's art and is carried through by the reference to the *oklad* (the protective metal covering on the face of icons, leaving exposed only the parts indicating flesh). Inspired by the precious quality of icons and reinforced by the application of gems to the surface of the *oklad*, Naumets would include textural features in the surface of the work while also laying bare the features on a human face.

Another artist of this group, Vitalii Sazonov, came to painting without a formal art education, but with a strong passion for archaeology, history, and sacred art.[29] Sazonov's interest in art began when he discovered Vasilii Kandinsky's 1912 essay *On the Spiritual in Art*, a pedagogical tract on enhancing spiritual components in painting through a deliberate and conscious exploitation of abstract form. Unlike the work of Makarenko and Humeniuk, which was tethered to the figurative and remained firmly rooted in the human form, Sazonov's paintings are mostly nonobjective. Sazonov approached art from the twin vantage points of modern art theory and abstract concepts of Orthodoxy as explored in the texture, color, and composition of old icons (Pl. 6:15). After spending a year in Estonia near Makarenko, Sazonov moved to Moscow and began to take part in unofficial exhibitions and demonstrations for artistic freedom. Because of his political activism, he was ultimately forced to leave the Soviet Union.

A new wave of artistic restrictions in the 1970s brought many festering dissatisfactions to the fore, along with a rising and increasingly open opposition to officially sanctioned art. Ukrainian nonconformist artists working in Moscow and Leningrad drew the attention of artists and diplomats to the Ukrainian cause and voiced their own desires for cre-

ative freedom by participating in nonconformist art exhibitions. Moscow was still one of the few places in the Soviet Union where unofficial art shows were tolerated by the authorities, if only temporarily. But more importantly, Moscow was where the foreign press reported on unofficial exhibitions, providing rare exposure and news coverage for struggling and politically engaged artists from the hinterlands. Of the Ukrainian enclave in Moscow, Humeniuk and Makarenko were the most active in exhibiting their works and, for that reason, they were soon better known in the West than in the Soviet Union.

Humeniuk not only participated in exhibitions of nonconformist art in Leningrad but was also the primary organizer of the "First Exhibition of Ukrainian Nonconformist Art" in Moscow. This exhibition took place at the apartment of Slava and Aiida Sychov from November 28 to December 8, 1975. In addition to works by Humeniuk and Makarenko, the show included paintings, prints, and drawings by four other artists: the Odesa artists Sazonov, Strelnikov, and Yastreb, and Oksana Pavlenko (1895–1991), who had belonged to the Ukrainian avant-garde as a Boichukist painter in the 1920s and had taught in the Moscow Vkhutein.[30] The mere fact that these artists were assembled as a group to manifest their artistic dissent was historically significant. But what lent even more weight to the occasion was the fact that an exhibition statement was drawn up that outlined the need on the part of these artists to give credibility to their Ukrainian identity.[31] This statement stressed the common national bond among these artists even though they were forced to pursue their art outside their homeland.

Due to the success of the first exhibition, a second was planned. For this occasion, the original six artists were joined by seven others, mostly from Odesa. In all, the thirteen artists were represented by about two hundred paintings, prints, and drawings, shown again in the Sychovs' apartment from March 12 to March 23, 1976. A second manifesto was issued and displayed during this exhibition; it once again emphasized the common heritage shared by the artists, rather than proclaiming some stylistic or aesthetic kinship. These two apartment exhibitions prompted a third exhibition in the freshly whitewashed studio belonging to Naumets. This show included four artists: Naumets, Sazonov, Strelnikov, and Aleksandr Anufriev (b. 1940), an Odesa artist whose work (Fig. 6:14) should not be confused with that of his son, Moscow artist Sergei Anufriev.

The daring gesture of singling out Ukrainian art for public exhibition in Moscow was met with heavy-handed repercussions by the authorities. Since Humeniuk was widely recognized as the instigator of the actions and the inspira-

Fig. 6:14
Aleksandr Anufriev
(Archangel), n.d.
Painted wooden relief
36 × 27.9 cm

tion for many Ukrainian artists, he was punished with ever-increasing obstacles in his daily life, the most devastating of which was the withdrawal of his residence permit for Leningrad. As a result, he had to return to Dnipropetrovs'k. He lived there as if in exile, but he never relinquished the pace and passion of his artistic practice. Despite the isolation, Humeniuk's art continued to flourish. Today he once again finds himself in St. Petersburg as a ringleader and inspiration to a still younger generation of Ukrainian artists working outside their homeland.

The quandary of whether to stay in the Ukraine or go to Moscow or abroad was faced by most Ukrainian nonconformist artists. In fact, their fate often pivoted around this question. Those who decided to stay took on a survivalist mentality. Among the more dramatic examples of this were Kiev painters Sergei Sherstiuk (b. 1951) and Serhii (Sergei) Geta (b. 1951). Unlike the work previously discussed, Sherstiuk's is large in scale and suffused with deep irony. He takes the heroic, monumentalized character of Socialist Realism and flips it on its back, but without the cynicism and sarcasm of Sots Art. This approach was Sherstiuk's way of dealing with the ostentation and grandness that the Soviets used to face the world. Every official Soviet action, no matter how mundane, was meant to be majes-

tic, as well as ponderously monumental. Sherstiuk's paintings can be read as a crafty reflection of this falsely heroic attitude, even though the subjects are mostly friends and family shown in everyday domestic occupations. These same subjects are also shown in the classic roles of Socialist Realist art, namely as workers, soldiers, students, and field laborers. The sitters' surroundings are filled with attributes that identify their social roles, their assigned places within a society depersonalized by the atmosphere of Soviet life. But, unlike typical Socialist Realist art, Sherstiuk's paintings are not centered on the act of labor. What occupies his interest is the quiet, personal moments that underscore the individual natures of his sitters. As a result, although these works are large in scale, they represent private rather than public moments.

Sherstiuk's art can be labeled Photorealist, Superrealist, or Hyperrealist (the Soviet term), insofar as it uses the techniques of artists like Richard Estes to depict life-size couples sharing apartment life, a private vacation, or high jinks in the artist's studio. Photography obviously played a critical role in producing both the snapshot effect of the scenes and its simulation in painting. One of the main differences between Sherstiuk's method and that of the Photorealists is that he aggressively demonstrates that his works are paintings and not just large photographs. For example, he deliberately allows spurts of paint from the spray-can to remain on the surface—they retain their integrity as paint and so remind the viewer of the artistic process. Among the most powerful of Sherstiuk's works are two in the Dodge Collection: *The Cosmonaut's Dream*, 1986 (Pl. 6:12), which shows a dead or dreaming astronaut in his space gear near a collective farm with nineteenth-century overtones; and *The Men of One Family, 1941 and 1945*, 1985 (Pls. 6:10, 6:11), a diptych that shows, first, the seven males of the extended family at the start of World War II, and then the three wounded uniformed men who survived.

Like Sherstiuk, Serhii Geta never knows what moments his camera will capture. He shoots his photographs from waist level without even looking through the viewfinder. Such uses of chance as the arbiter of artistic process became popular among Kiev artists during the late 1970s. The reliance on karma or destiny led to the willful integration of unexpected moments into their art. This attitude was not rooted in negativism but its opposite. The ability to accept things as they were in Soviet life was merely one manifestation of an earnest desire for change and spiritual renewal. Not knowing for sure in what direction or into what untried realms of thought their paths might lead them, these artists abandoned themselves to all chance encounters. Highly imaginative in their approach, they succeeded in circumventing dictatorial dogma to create sly, comic-style anatomies of their culture. Thus, the artist became a sort of medium through which daily occurrences were captured, the camera ensuring that an objective stance was preserved and maintained. But their paintings are not merely the image shot by the camera transferred onto canvas. Rather, like a Dadaist gesture, that snapshot moment is just the beginning of a string of associations that are not ultimately flippant but rather constitute a deep response to the human condition (Fig. 6:15). Using the photograph as a starting point, the artists employ montage and airbrush to fuse the disparate, often contradictory moments of a single Soviet experience by concretizing the true and the real. The artist is able to purge himself of that reality and thereby escape from it.

Escapism of a more fictive, technological sort is explored by Yevhen Petrenko (b. 1946). Petrenko is another Kiev artist who normally specializes in graphic art, yet proves himself a master of painterly abstraction. His paintings seem to explode with vertiginous clashes of broad, sweeping tracts of color; within the frame of futuristic forces and a medieval, almost mystical, treatment of a tumultuous, swirling environment, Petrenko's paintings are dramatically provocative in their cosmic sensibilities. Forms flying through the air recall the lofty surges of spiritual movement as depicted in the frescoes on the spandrels of Ukrainian churches, which cross into an illusory realm of spatial depth and a sense of the beyond. In works like *Bioengineering*, 1984 (Pl. 6:21), Petrenko seems obsessed by some apocalyptically transformed world, while flirting with the psychology of technology. This merging of the here-and-now with a futuristic ambience recalls the work of Klyment Red'ko (1897–1956), an avant-garde Kiev painter of the 1920s who created the concept of the "electro-organism."[52]

Arsen Savadov (b. 1962) and Georgii Senchenko (b. 1962) graduated from the Kiev Institute of Fine Arts in 1987 and in the same year burst upon the art scene in both Moscow and Paris with the huge collaborative painting *The Sorrow of Cleopatra*, which shows Cleopatra riding a giant tiger. This work was widely reproduced in the press in both cities. There was nothing to compare it to in Moscow, and Paris found it equally puzzling. The term "trans avantgarde" was employed by one Parisian critic to describe it, but this term hardly did justice to the broad learning and complex philosophical perceptions that underlay this and their other joint artworks in both larger and smaller formats. The works in the Dodge Collection, which are illuminated from behind, were initially created in 1985–86, but reconstructed in 1989 in a more refined, high-tech format (Fig. 6:16).

The quest to form a homogeneous society by assimilat-

Fig. 6:15
Serhii (Sergei) Geta
Talk, 1981
Graphite on paper
61.5 × 70.2 cm

ing and mixing different nations together and blurring the territorial differences between them was always an integral part of the Soviet Communist vision. What has resulted is a situation that, for the time being, still makes it difficult to talk about national schools of contemporary art in the regions of the former Soviet Union. What is more, the task of identifying specific traits as part of an independent cultural evolution is made more complex by the ponderousness of official Soviet histories that have tried to create a common historical root for the rise of Russia, Belarus, and the Ukraine, as well as Moldova. Unlike the Baltic states, which were forcibly incorporated by the secret agreement with Ribbentrop, or the Transcaucasus, which does not share the same European cultural core as other parts of the U.S.S.R., the Ukraine, Belarus, and Moldova are discrete cultural regions. During the Soviet period, they were mercilessly drawn into a contrived history which perpetuated the point of view of imperialist Russia. Thus, until now, the work of artists from Moldova, Belarus, and the Ukraine has only benefited Russian culture. When these regions struggled to maintain their own identities, their artists were seen as weakening Russian culture and were suppressed or allowed to fall into obscurity.

This perspective was perpetuated by the hegemonic rule of Socialist-Communist ideology and has permeated the attitudes of Russian society over the past seventy years. During that period, Russia maintained a dominant role not only in political matters, but in cultural issues as well. As a result, the study of any aspect of culture in the post-Stalin, pre-Gorbachev period necessarily reflected a point of view centered on and emanating mainly from Moscow. The political leadership rarely thought of regional autonomy, so it comes as a shock to us today even to think of the separate artistic cultures that flourished in these separate republics. For the most part, their histories have gone unnoticed and unrecorded.

It is important, then, that the Dodge Collection also contains a modest sample of the kind of art produced during these years in Belarus and Moldova. As in the Ukraine, in those republics one could sense an emphatic tendency toward an artistic development focused on aesthetic issues. Drawing heavily on the avant-garde of the 1910s and 1920s that emerged in such centers as Vitebsk and Minsk, contemporary Belarus artists offered the Western world a glimpse of the kind of art that had been flourishing all along outside the rarefied artistic environments of Moscow and Leningrad. The work of artists like Valerii Martynchyk (b. 1948), Genia Khaskevitch, and Valerii Bobrov (b. 1945) vibrantly recalls the legacy of Chagall's floating worlds, Filonov's layering of paint surfaces, and Kandinsky's geometrical ordering of the most minute shapes. Like Lissitzky's

Prouns, many of the works of these younger artists are focused on abstract forms that manipulate, through optic play, and activate, through subtle color choices, the spaces they occupy. Evoking the balanced measures of Malevich's paintings, the shapes in Martynchyk's works are at once centered and weighted while projecting beyond the parameters of the painting's frame. What is most striking about these paintings is their monumental scale, a particularly bold direction for the late 1970s, when works had to be transported covertly and displayed in clandestine quarters. Martynchyk, in particular, played a leading role in organizing the Belarus underground in Minsk. This group emerged in 1987 under the name "Forma," which has now allowed us to recognize the existence of an organized nonconformist movement in Belarus.[33] Valerii Slauk, a nonconformist printmaker, adds another dimension to the art of Belarus. His Surrealist depictions of the vicissitudes of rural life are both comic and tragic.

Leonid Pinchevsky (b. 1942) grew up in the small provincial town of Beltsy in Moldova, the small republic to the southwest of the Ukraine. During World War II, some seventy percent of Moldovian Jews were killed by the Germans. But Pinchevsky's mother managed to escape to the Urals, where Leonid was born. They were only reunited with his father in Beltsy after the war in 1947. Pinchevsky studied art in Kishinev before returning to Beltsy in 1963 to try to develop a distinctive style and to find himself as an artist. In 1967, he met the artist Viktor Pivovarov while visiting Moscow and, through him, he came into contact with Kabakov, Yankilevsky, and others in the Sretensky Boulevard group. These Moscow influences affected him deeply and triggered a series of paintings called *Living Houses*, which he continued even after his emigration to the United States in 1982. These fanciful paintings depict anthropomorphic houses with various personalities.

Censorship was severe and the threat of reprisal omnipresent until the mid-1980s, but the number and influence of nonconformist artists in the Ukraine, Belarus, and Moldova only increased and spread. Today, with the tumultuous changes that have occurred in the whole of the Eastern Bloc, there is still very little reporting on political or cultural activities in any of the republics other than Russia. The artworks preserved in the Dodge Collection are an important first step in attempting to remedy this neglect. They serve as a reminder of the nuanced variations in dissident artistic expression from region to region; as such, they allow the prevalent diversity to be better understood and appreciated.

Fig. 6:16
Arsen Savadov and
Georgii Senchenko
(Untitled), n.d.
Mixed media on canvas
100.5 × 101.5 × 10 cm

Do you prefer the seaside or the mountains? You are stretched out on a meadow in the mountains. Everything around you is quiet. The blue sky is above you, and the sun shining brightly. You are stretched out on a meadow in the mountains. Everything around you is quiet, the blue sky is above you, and the sun is shining brightly. You are looking at the sky, your glimpse catches a light cloud, ease and tranquillity envelopes everything. You feel very peaceful. You smell the scent of the pine trees. You are relaxed. You are not preoccupied by the idea of the imminent war.

Notes

1. The pathos of these circumstances could only be heightened by the abusive misruling of the republics by her so-called native sons. During the Brezhnev era, the Ukraine had two Communist Party leaders, Petro Shelest and Volodymyr Shcherbytsky. Shelest's tenure as the First Secretary of the Ukrainian Communist Party lasted from 1963 to 1972 and it featured a limited resurgence of Ukrainian self-assertiveness that, within a short period of time, turned into a quiet cynicism. In May 1972 Shelest was removed from his post in Kiev for being "soft" toward his Ukrainian compatriots and was replaced by Shcherbytsky, a fierce rival and long-time member of Brezhnev's "Dnipro" clan, who denounced Shelest to his Moscow cohorts for his "local patriotism." Shcherbytsky's rule was characterized by a complete submission to Moscow. He was a proponent of harsh, uncompromising treatment when dealing with dissent. He remained in power, supported as he was by the anti-reformists in the Kremlin, until Gorbachev's ascendancy.

2. From Oleksander Dovzhenko, *Works* (1960), vol. 3, p. 113; quoted in *Knyzhkovyi znak shestydesiatnykiv* [Bookplate of those of the sixties] (South Bound Brook, N.J.: V-vo Sv. Sofii, 1972), p. 9.

3. See Bohdan Krawciw, ed., *Sixty Poets of the Sixties* (New York: Prolog, Inc., 1967), p. v.

4. Viktor Zaretsky began serious study of painting during the crucial late Stalin years (1947–53) in the Kiev Art Institute. Recognized for his talent as a realist painter, he was named a Stalin Fellow and became a member of the Union of Artists. Nevertheless, Zaretsky was troubled by the imperative to paint realistic portraits of Communist leaders rather than to be true to the art of painting. To survive, Zaretsky turned to graphic art. Still dissatisfied with his decision to turn his back on painting, he left Kiev and returned to the regions of his youth along the Don river, where the bright southern sun and the sight of the people's honest labor provided creative inspiration for the artist. He painted the mineworkers at the day's end honestly and truthfully. He later turned to the theme of the farmer, the agricultural laborer in the Chernobyl region, and spent several years painting in that area, working side by side with herders, milkmaids, and husbandmen as a means of restoring and protecting his artistic dignity.

5. Alla Horska's only solo exhibition was organized by her friends and took place in her studio on the day of her funeral, December 7, 1970. Since Zaretsky spent most of the 1970s in a labor camp, his impact on the younger generation came about surreptitiously and only after his release in the early 1980s. Official rehabilitation of his artistic standing has only taken place in the last two years.

6. Opanas Zalyvakha has only recently been rehabilitated, but since then he has had a tremendous impact on contemporary Ukrainian art. L'viv artists, in particular, stress their indebtedness to Zalyvakha. His work came to attention in the West in 1967 with the publication of *Lykho z rozumu* [The misfortune of intellect] (Paris: First Ukrainian Printers in France, 1967) by the Ukrainian journalist and dissident writer Viacheslav Chornovil. This book was later published in the U.S. as *The Chornovil Papers* (New York: McGraw Hill, 1968). Chornovil wrote: "Zalyvakha refused to take the well-trodden path and to follow in the hundred-year-old footsteps of the *peredvizhniki*. He searched for other, more creative means of self-expression." See Chornovil, *The Chornovil Papers*, pp. 17, 117–30.

7. Besides Zalyvakha, other artists of his generation who ignored the dictates of Socialist Realism included Halyna Sevruk and Bohdan Soroka (b. 1940). But neither of these "artists of the sixties" had as extensive an impact on the future art of the western Ukraine as Zalyvakha.

8. The distinction between official and unofficial artists is ill-defined, even though it is based on membership of the Artists' Union. Nonetheless, those artists who worked for the Art Fund, for instance, or were teachers at schools of art, but were not members of the Artists' Union, were also regarded as "official." Essentially employed by the state, they did not, however, enjoy the privileges of the Artists' Union members. Many of these artists belonged to dissident circles and, even while they carried out all sorts of official commissions (e.g., decorating bus shelters, designing public murals, and producing an endless array of official portraits of Party leaders), privately they delved into every kind of experimental art from pure abstraction to outdoor installations.

9. Chornovil, *The Chornovil Papers*, p. 121.

10. Robert Sullivant, *Soviet Politics and the Ukraine, 1917–1957* (New York: Columbia University Press, 1962), pp. 226–30; see also James E. Mace, *Communism and the Dilemmas of National Liberation: National Communism in Soviet Ukraine, 1918–1933* (Cambridge, Mass.: Harvard Ukrainian Research Institute, 1983), pp. 267–301.

11. The Art Fund was the official organ for official art commissions, a Soviet agency that also oversaw all sales and purchases of art in the Soviet Union. It had separate administrative units in all the republics and chapters in most major cities. Many of the artists, who in private produced nonconformist art, were registered members of the monumental art sections of the Art Fund and carried out all sorts of commissions for public projects aimed at the ideological edification of the population at large.

12. Ivan Simchich, quoted in Richard Lytle, *Contemporary Art from Ukraine: An American Perspective* (New Haven: Yale University School of Art, 1992), p. 8.

13. Tatiana Yablonskaia, interview with Daria Darewych (Oct. 7, 1988), cited in Daria Darewych, "Soviet Ukrainian Painting, ca. 1955–1979: New Currents and Undercurrents" (Ph.D. diss., University College, London, 1990), p. 153, n. 91.

14. During the early modernist period of the 1920s and 1930s, many L'viv artists traveled widely and exhibited their works in Paris, Berlin, and Prague. Many also studied abroad, especially in the academies of Poland. Locally, publications on the modern art of the West abounded, while the School of Paris and the particular influence of Fernand Léger pervaded the stylistic directions of artists such as Pavlo Kovzhun (1896–1939), Sviatoslav Hordyns'ky (1906–1992), and Roman Selsky (1903–1991).

15. By 1960, L'viv artists had taken up a variety of twentieth-century art movements, especially Surrealism. While Roman Selsky pursued these formal concerns openly through the organization of ARTES (the Artists' Union), his wife, Margit Selska (1903–1980), liked to incorporate collage and photomontage into her textural compositions. Older artists in L'viv formed a group around Roman and Margit Selsky; younger ones met regularly with Karlo Zvirynsky (b. 1923) or Volodymyr Urishchenko (b. 1932). Yet another group of writers, poets, and artists met in Odesa at the home and studio of Liudmyla Yastreb and her husband Viktor Maryniuk. These support groups helped the artists establish a context for their ideas. However, they did not give the artists access to the public at large. For instance, a little known artist, Karlo Zvirynsky, who had totally abandoned figuration by 1960, kept all of his abstract work in his studio—a fact only recently revealed. Surrealist influences can also be detected in the work of some of the younger L'viv artists like Bohdan Soika (b. 1938), Liubomyr Medvid (b. 1941), Petro Markovych (b. 1937), and Ivan Zavadovsky (1937–1983), whose paintings were also not exhibited.

16. Andrew Solomon, "Igor Kopystiansky," in *Novostroika (New Structures): Culture in the Soviet Union Today* (London: Institute of Contemporary Arts, 1989), p. 48.

17. Igor and Svetlana Kopystiansky, interview with Elena Leontova, "Igor and Svetlana Kopystiansky: Through the Glass Darkly," *Flash Art* (Oct. 1993): 112.

18. See V. Afanasiiev, *Stanovlennia sotsiialistychnoho realizmu v ukrainskomu obrazotvorchomu mystetstvi* [The establishment of Socialist Realism in the Ukrainian visual arts] (Kiev: Mystetstvo, 1967), pp. 69ff.

19. Ladyzhensky was born in Odesa but began his art studies in 1924 at the Academy of Fine Arts in Leningrad. Much of his creative life was spent designing sets for the theater and later for films. His suicide in 1982 resulted, in part, from his disappointment with the poor reception his art received in the West following his emigration to Israel in 1978.

20. *Contemporary Ukrainian Art*, exh. brochure (London: Red Square Gallery, 1990), n.p.

21. V.P. Zeltner, *Yurii Nikolaevich Egorov: Zhivopis', risunok. Katalog vystavki* (Moscow: Sovetskii Khudozhnik, 1989), n.p.

22. The city of Kharkiv is associated most closely with the Ukrainian Constructivist artist Vasilii Ermilov (1894–1968). Ermilov's paintings of the 1910s and 1920s reveal a predilection not for painterliness but for cerebral plastic organization of the elements of composition.

23. Kozak Mamai was generally depicted as a stock character resting cross-legged with his horse tethered nearby. He is recognizable by his accouterments: a flask and a *bandura*, the stringed national instrument of the Ukraine, used by itinerant blind bards to warn the

1911111111111111111

population of impending danger or to hail, through song, the victories of the Cossack warriors.

24. Anatolii Schopin was born in the Ukrainian village of Anatolyevka. He studied first at the Odesa College of Fine Art under Yegorov and then at the Mukhina Art Institute in Leningrad where he graduated in 1970. He was a member of the U.S.S.R. Union of Artists and had been painting since 1958. The Odesa Art Museum held a one-man show of Schopin's works in 1984. See also the brochure for the exhibition "Contemporary Ukrainian Art," presented at the Red Square Gallery in London, June 12–July 15, 1990.

25. Feodosii Humeniuk, "My Rediscovery of Ukraine through Visual Art," in *Echoes of Glasnost in Soviet Ukraine* (Toronto: Captus University Publications, 1989), p. 219.

26. R.S., "Volodymyr Makarenko," *Journal of Ukrainian Studies* 2 (Spring 1977): 56–57.

27. Dmytro Horbachov, "Kozak-Paryzhanyn" [Parisian Kozak], *Vsesvit* [Universe] 6 (1992): 193.

28. Hélian Bernard, *Volodymyr Makarenko*, exh. cat. (Lyons: L'Association Champs des Arts, 1985), n.p.

29. Although Sazonov was born in Siberia, he lived in the western Ukraine and Crimea from 1952 to 1964, and then moved to Odesa where he stayed until 1974. He studied history at Odesa University before turning his attention to art. In 1975, he moved to Tartu, and thereafter lived in Paris.

30. Boichukism, the neo-Byzantine style of painting, was formulated by the Ukrainian painter Mykhailo Boichuk (1882–1937[?]). He traveled to Paris in 1907 and attracted a small group of painters to his style of panel painting in tempera that fused the qualities of early Renaissance frescoes with the Byzantine tenets of medieval art. When, in 1918, the Ukraine declared her independence and the first Ukrainian Academy of Arts was founded in Kiev, Boichuk returned to become part of the core teaching faculty. The idea of the guild or workshop lay at the heart of Boichukism and provided the basis for establishing various brigades of monumental painters who, throughout the 1920s, painted murals for the Ukrainian government in various public places. While depicting agricultural themes and ennobling the good qualities of the peasant, the murals also educated the population about the new ideology.

Vkhutein (Higher State Art Technical Institute) replaced, in name only, Vkhutemas (Higher State Art Technical Studios), the specialized educational institution founded in 1920 for the advanced artistic and technical training of artists in the Soviet Union after the Revolution. They also served to prepare highly qualified master artists for industry as well as instructors and directors of professional and technical education. Pavlenko's teaching was in the realm of ceramics.

Under attacks of "bourgeois nationalism," the Boichukist school of muralists was decimated, yet another casualty of the widespread liquidation of cultural organizations that swept over the Ukraine during the 1930s. Boichuk was arrested in the autumn of 1936 and perished in prison in 1937. (See S. Bilokin', "Vidome-nevidome?" [The known and the unknown], *Kul'tura i zhyttia* [Culture and life], Mar. 5, 1989, p. 4.) The circumstances surrounding Boichuk's death, even a firm death date, are still unclear. Soviet sources still cite "1939(?)" as the end of his life. Even though Boichuk was technically rehabilitated in the 1960s, only in the Gorbachev era did it become possible to explore his life and the activities of the *Boichukisty*. Such inquiry was initiated through a series of lectures organized in Kiev in 1984.

31. See Appendix B in Darewych, "Soviet Ukrainian Painting," p. 420.

32. Klyment Red'ko, "Declaration of Electro-organism" (Dec. 25, 1922), translated in *Ukrajinska avangarda, 1910–1930* (Zagreb: Muzej suvremene umjetnosti, 1990), pp. 208–9.

33. See "Conversation with Valerii Martynchyk," *Dekorativnoe iskusstvo* (1989); "Sketches of a Portrait of Valerii Martynchyk," *Spring Magazine* 10 (1988); "Minsk Avant-Garde," *Iunost'* 3 (1990); and "What to Do?" *Belarus Art* 10 (1990).

7 | Estonian art under Communism

Olga Berendsen

Before World War II, the city of Tartu (Dorpat) had been the cultural and educational center of Estonia, just as the capital city of Tallinn was the political and financial center. Tartu had been the site of the only Estonian art academy, the Art School "Pallas," established in 1919. Teaching at the school was based on the individual studio principle and represented almost all contemporary trends, with the exception of Surrealism. By the 1930s, however, most of the modern "isms" had faded and the predominant approach was that of the School of Paris. By this time, "Pallas" had developed its own style characterized by loose brushwork, tightly knit compositions, and a strong interest in color/light relationships.

The intense creative activity during the years of Estonian independence (1918–40) was called to a sudden halt by the Soviet invasion in the summer of 1940 resulting from the Molotov-Ribbentrop pact. Estonia became incorporated as one of the "republics" of the U.S.S.R., with the consequent loss of all essential liberties. Sovietization of the country had started. From that point forward, artistic activity was directed toward the service of the Communist Party, the main task being the promotion and embellishment of Party festivals and parades with paintings, posters, and slogans. A severe blow to the visual arts was the closing of "Pallas," which was then reorganized into a state institution with the new name "The Art School of Konrad Mägi," after the school's first director. The new curriculum stressed the teaching of Communist subjects, such as Marxist philosophy and the history of the Communist Party.

The first stage of the Soviet occupation ended with the outbreak of war between Germany and the U.S.S.R. in the summer of 1941. The Baltic states were quickly overrun and occupied by the Germans from 1941 to 1944. Since the German military forces were not particularly interested in changing the cultural or educational life of Estonia, the Estonians themselves sought to eliminate Communist influences and every effort was made to re-create the prewar conditions. The former Art School "Pallas" was reestablished, although its main activity during the war was to offer short-term courses.

The artistic community suffered greatly during this period. Already by 1941 many of the left-wing artists (e.g., Aino Bach, Eric Adamson) had fled to the U.S.S.R. During the German occupation, many right-wing artists escaped to the West if they could (e.g., Eduard Wiiralt, Agaate Veber, Eduard Rüga, Harry Haamer). Thus, by the end of the war, a once-vital artistic community had shrunk considerably and was gravely weakened.

The Soviet reoccupation of Estonia, beginnning in 1944 and lasting almost fifty years, brought about further significant changes. For instance, the Art School "Pallas" was yet again closed and subsequently reorganized into the State Art Institute of Tartu. Then, in 1951, the school was moved to Tallinn since Soviet policy was to establish a strong central government in the capital city. The removal of the art school was only the first blow to Tartu, as various restrictions were soon imposed on the city and its venerable university. Gradually the independent spirit of Tartu was broken and the war-ravaged city sank into provincial obscurity.

When the former art school of Tartu was relocated to Tallinn, it was united with the State School of Applied Art to form the Estonian State Art Institute. This new institution had two faculties or divisions: first, the faculty of studio and applied arts, with departments of painting (including set design), sculpture, printmaking (subdivided into graphic art, commercial art, poster art, and book design), ceramics, and design (in glass, metal, leather, textiles, and fashion); and, second, the faculty of architecture (with subdivisions in furniture and interior design) and industrial art. Also in Tallinn was the Experimental Graphic Studio, which had been established in 1947 as a practical necessity to assist graphic artists faced with a shortage of materials and printing presses.[1] The studio provided its members with presses, materials, studio space, and the assistance of a technician. The development of this program was slow in the beginning, but by the end of the 1950s the Studio had become a first-rate institution and a place for creative work and discussion.

The period of Soviet domination following World War II

brought with it the introduction of Socialist Realism and a complete change in local approaches to art. Socialist Realism had as its primary task the glorification of the Communist Party and its governing apparatus and the depiction of the happy life of the people under Socialism in the U.S.S.R. This subject matter was controlled and often dictated by the Party. The most important formal quality of a work of art, especially in painting and graphics, was exemplified in the linear character of Russian icon painting and nineteenth-century Russian Realism. Color was important only insofar as it defined the local color, with preferences for browns and grays.

The Estonian Communist Party was the controller of all the arts, and immediate supervision was the task of the local artists' union. The Soviet Estonian Artists' Union was established in 1943 in Yaroslavl, in the U.S.S.R., by artists who had retreated east with the Red Army in 1941.[2] This organization was transferred to Tallinn in 1945, together with the artists who had returned with the army. They brought with them the Socialist Realist style learned in the U.S.S.R. Estonian artists who had remained in their homeland during the war were reluctant to follow the new approach, and two of the more important ones, A. Vabbe (1892–1961) and J. Greenberg (1887–1951), seemed to stop painting altogether (although, as was learned after their deaths, they continued painting in seclusion, each in his own style).

After Stalin's death in 1953, there was a period of relative relaxation of Party strictures; this mood dominated the Khrushchev era, from 1954 until 1964.[3] In the arts, this period is often referred to as the "thaw" because some aspects of personal liberty were restored. Some sense of this relaxed mood can be gleaned from the directives of the Artists' Union. In 1957, for example, the Ninth Congress of the Artists' Union found the existing definition of Socialist Realism too dogmatic and agreed that personal style and ethnic characteristics were indeed important aspects of art.[4]

With official pressures subsiding, many older Estonian artists returned to their prewar "Pallas" style, which they later modified under the influence of modernism. Some young printmakers at the Art Institute had already begun to ignore the prescribed path of Socialist Realism. For models they had turned to the work of the older generation, such as Estonian graphic artist Eduard Wiiralt (1898–1954), whose richness of expression and facility in all graphic techniques were widely admired. Wiiralt was the only Estonian to work in the Surrealist idiom (even if it was only for a few years) (Figs. 7:1, 7:2). The younger artists were also inspired by another master, Kristjan Raud

Fig. 7:1
Eduard Wiiralt
The Preacher, 1932
Lithograph
Collection of the Estonian
National Museum

Fig. 7:2
Eduard Wiiralt
Hell, 1930–32
Copper engraving and
etching
Collection of the Estonian
National Museum

(1865–1943), whose subjects were taken mostly from Estonian folklore, and who had created a very individual expressive style with angular, heavy forms (Fig. 7:3).

The first of the young graduates to break away from the official style was Vive Tolli (b. 1928), who graduated from the Art Institute in 1953.[5] Her favorite subjects were derived from Estonian folklore and poetry. Her style retains some of the angularity of Raud's work, but her figures are slender and lyrical instead of heavy and heroic. Her work is distinguished by a fine, almost filigree-like surface ornamentation that is restricted to specific areas within the composition. By the 1970s, she had begun to focus on mainly universal themes and symbols. A good example is her *Wind Shelter*, 1972 (Fig. 7:4), which alludes to the storm of life. Her prints also included nearly abstract urban scenes and structures.

Peeter Ulas (b. 1934), who graduated in 1959, used in his early works strong simplified forms with a tendency toward flat surface representation.[6] Later, however, following a trip to Italy in the 1970s, he directed his attention to the possibilities of deep space created through architectural forms. His *Evening*, 1974 (Pl. 7:1) is a modernization of Baroque illusionism as seen in the ceiling paintings of the Church of St. Ignatius in Rome. In Ulas's version, the soaring figure of St. Ignatius has been replaced by an orchid.

In his early works, Herald Eelma (b. 1934),[7] a 1959 graduate of the Art Institute, preferred a strong rhythmic composition of compact expressive shapes against a contrasting background. Since the 1970s, he has concentrated on single three-dimensional forms on a white ground, stressing the symbolic nature of the representation. His *Dance*, 1980 (Fig. 7:5) depicts a contemporary young man

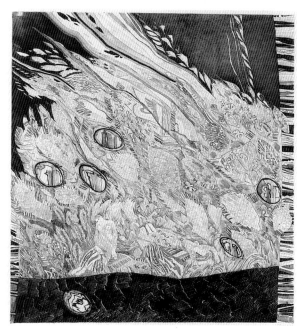

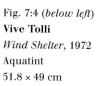

Fig. 7:3 (*left*)
Kristjan Raud
Death of Kalevipoeg, 1935
Charcoal on paper
Collection of the Estonian
National Museum

Fig. 7:4 (*below left*)
Vive Tolli
Wind Shelter, 1972
Aquatint
51.8 × 49 cm

Fig. 7:5
Herald Eelma
Dance, 1980
Lithograph
61.5 × 49 cm

in jeans (the most fashionable clothing in Estonia at that time), holding a row of small dancing figures dressed in Estonian national costumes. According to Eelma, a man cannot separate himself from his country or its history, for he carries the past within himself.

Like an explosion, the abrupt and brief awakening for contemporary art in Estonia occurred in the early 1960s. This period, now often referred to as the "golden age," preceded Khrushchev's fall from power in 1964, and the reinstitution of cultural repression under Brezhnev. The Estonian artists who came of age in the 1960s could not recall the Stalin years and behaved almost without fear. It was an exceptionally gifted and courageous generation, and interest in the West continued to grow. By this time contacts had been established with Poland, Hungary, and Czechoslovakia, and news about the West was easily obtained from Finnish television (Tallinn is only sixty miles from Helsinki and the Finnish language is easily understood by Estonians). Information was also received from the BBC, the Voice of America, and Radio Liberty. Contacts were established with relatives and friends who

had emigrated or escaped to Sweden, Canada, and the U.S. Information about artistic trends in the West came by means of books and magazines (*Art News* was a favorite source), and, as permission for travel to the West became easier to obtain, trends in the U.S. could be followed more closely. Jazz festivals were organized in Estonia and comic strips were published (the first was Donald Duck).

But at the same time cultural Russification was becoming ever more intense, and the accompanying influx of Russians into Estonia started to reach dangerous proportions.[8] The greater the pressure from Russia, the greater was the determination among the young artists to preserve Estonian culture and the characteristic Estonian view of the world. They sought to assert that Estonians were not Slavs and that their language and ethnic heritage, belonging to the Finno-Ugric group, were more Western and markedly different from those of the other ethnic groups in the U.S.S.R.

Another important source of information about contemporary art was the Moscow artistic underground, although contacts with them were forbidden, as were exhibitions of their works in Estonia. For Estonians, the main conduit was the painter Ullo Sooster (1924–1970).[9] Already in his days as an art student in Tartu, Sooster had been predominantly interested in Picasso, Surrealism, and modernism. In 1957, after being released from a Siberian prison camp, he settled in Moscow, where he felt he could have more contact with Western art. His early works are Surrealistic, but in his later years he turned increasingly toward abstraction (Pl. 7:2).

This growing awareness of cultural movements outside Estonia contributed to the student unrest that rocked the university in Tartu during the 1960s. There, the slogan chanted by the students was "Yanks, go behind the Lake of Peipus." (In order to go behind Peipus—i.e., to Russia— one had to pass through Estonia.) At the Art Institute in Tallinn, where studies in art history ended with Impressionism, the students demanded greater access to contemporary developments in Western art. In 1964, students at Tallinn formed themselves into an organization called ANK '64.[10] Meeting at the coffeehouse called Pegasus, they sought to inform and instruct each other in the development of modern art, and aspired to free themselves from the constraints of Socialist Realism—or at least enlarge the meaning of "realism." The art students were soon joined by music and theater students, as well as by young poets and writers. Their collaborative efforts led to art exhibitions, happenings, and performances in the manner of the theater of the absurd—anything that involved spontaneity, the subconscious, and the creative process.

A prominent representative of this trend was Tõnis Vint (b. 1942), a leader of ANK '64, who held regular gatherings of the group in his apartment and was the major theorist of the group. Vint later became one of the provocative editors of *Kunst*, the leading contemporary journal in Estonia, and a major intellectual leader in the effort to free art from Party dogma. Vint was interested in Oriental philosophy, astrology, and, most of all, divination. His aim was to discover the hidden message in the signs and symbols of many different nations and cultures and establish their correspondence to one another. His early works are

Fig. 7:6
Tõnis Vint
Room I, 1973
Lithograph
45 cm in diameter

sometimes semi-abstract and Minimalist. In his lithograph *Room I*, 1973 (Fig. 7:6), a room has been reduced to a few basic white shapes on a black background. To enliven the work, he has introduced an erotic half-nude female figure, whose form contrasts with the sharp angularity of the room's architecture. The stylized figure recalls those of the English artist Aubrey Beardsley, whom Vint greatly admired. Vint's abstract geometric prints often consist of elegant and delicate arrangements of simple geometrical forms in white or red on a uniform black or white ground. These are the signs of divination, and the black ground symbolizes for Vint the night of the universe. "Tonis Vint's preoccupation with Jungian archetypal theories, Eastern symbolism, the semiotic meaning of I Ching, and psychogeometry has influenced a whole younger generation of Estonian artists," critic Eda Sepp notes. "This preoccupation with hidden meaning is an artist's response to totalitarian pressure, an activity which alarmed the Soviet authorities."[11]

A second explosion of nonconformist student activity occurred in 1969 with the establishment of a new art group called SOUP '69.[12] These students were advocates of Pop Art, as suggested by the allusion to Andy Warhol's paintings of Campbell's Soup cans in their name. They excited by both the use of the intense enamel colors of Pop and the artistic liberty implied by their selection of subjects from the banal, everyday environment.

An important leader of this group was Leonhard Lapin (b. 1947), a close friend of Tõnis Vint. By profession Lapin was an architect, and some of his graphic works of the 1960s and 1970s reflect the influence of Russian Constructivism. Others that deal with machines in motion seem to borrow from Léger. In one series of prints, Lapin explores the machine-like aspects in the eroticism of the female figure, using this as a metaphor for the conflict in modern society between technology and humanism. In his purely abstract works, he prefers a single, universally known geometrical form-symbol, such as a red cross. Lapin often gives these signs a political meaning, as, for instance, in *Red Square*, 1980 (Pl. 7:6; see also Pls. 7:4, 7:5, 7:7, 7:8), which alludes to Red Square at the Kremlin. Lapin's square is not perfect, but has an eroded corner—a witty political critique. In the 1980s, Lapin was particularly interested in the work of Malevich and the Suprematists. He continues to work with Malevich's square, bringing it to its utmost limits in his series *Process*.

Emphasizing the importance of fantasy over literary content in art, the ANK '64 movement released young artists from the confines of Socialist Realism. SOUP '69 furthered this process but also initiated a more intellectual, unemotional, and detached approach, justifying the free choice of themes. SOUP '69 also introduced into painting and graphics intense colors and sleek finishes, a style that was in direct opposition to the gray-brown tones and turgid brushwork of official art. By the mid-1970s, this Estonian avant-garde movement had reached its maturity, having acquired considerable influence nationally and among certain nonconformist artists in Leningrad, including Rukhin.

Many of these Estonian nonconformists were interested in the local landscape. Toomas Vint (b. 1945), for example, is best known for his paintings of the lush Estonian fields and forests under an expansive sky.[13] The human presence is only occasionally referred to by an object, as in his *Forgotten Doll Carriage*, 1979 (Pl. 7:3). A similarly idyllic character is seen in the seascapes of Aili Vint (b. 1945), who is also known for her erotic subjects (Fig. 2:7; Pl. 7:10). Stillness and isolation from the rest of the world is felt even more strongly in the prints of Mare Vint (b. 1942).[14] In a lithograph from 1978 (Fig. 7:7), she shows a corner of a dreamy park with huge deciduous trees. This work expresses a longing for the peace and calm of a timeless arcadian place. Curiously, while this representation of an empty landscape might very well have portrayed an idealized vision of isolation, it also reflected the actual situation in rural Estonia. During this period, in order to prevent escape to the West, much of the seacoast was closed to civilians. The closing of rural schools and libraries in the 1970s, and the continuing collectivization of farms, emptied many of the old villages. As empty farmhouses fell into ruin and farmsteads became overgrown, an eerie silence pervaded the once-lively countryside.

A more complicated and ambiguous approach was taken by another group of artists who introduced Pop Art elements into their works. One of the best known is

Fig. 7:7
Mare Vint
Underground Passage, 1978
Lithograph
35.6 × 35.4 cm

Andres Tolts (b. 1949), a leader of SOUP '69.[15] In a painting from 1983 (Pl. 7:13), a bowl of apples on a table is placed in front of a deep north Estonian landscape, while two more apples hang mysteriously from a cord above the bowl. This is a work of great order and harmony, differentiating clearly between space and objects. At first, the representation appears perfectly rational, but the ambiguous placing of the table in front of the empty landscape, as well as the dangling fruit, tends to contradict the ostensible logic. Here, Surrealism enables the artist to incorporate several layers of meaning into his work. A similar use of Surrealist devices, such as combining still life and landscape elements or interior and exterior views, is evident in the work of several other young artists of this period (including Ando Keskküla [Pl. 7:9] and Tiit Pääsuke). Marje Üksine (b. 1945) is also ambiguous in some of her works, as in her drypoint *Portrait*, 1976 (Fig. 7:8), in which the demarcation between interior and exterior, landscape and seascape is made deliberately vague.[16] It is even hard to say whether this is actually a portrait or just a still life. The work is suffused with a mysterious calm that unites its parts.[17]

Instead of idealizing the urban scene according to Socialist Realism, one group of artists was not afraid to portray the ugly aspects of the contemporary city. Allex Kütt (1921–1991), for example, liked to depict motorcycles and urban youth gangs in a Photorealist style, as in his 1981 aquatint *Street I* (Fig. 7:9).[18] Similarly, Jüri Palm (b. 1937) frequently paints scenes of urban violence, crime, and congestion.[19] Characteristic is *The Mystery of the*

Fig. 7:11 (*right*)
Kaisa Puustak
The Depot, 1977
Etching and aquatint
42.1 × 46.5 cm

Fig. 7:8
Marje Üksine
Portrait, 1976
Aquatint
39.8 × 43 cm

Fig. 7:9
Allex Kütt
Street I, 1981
Aquatint
44.3 × 40.2 cm

Fig. 7:10
Jaan Elken
Untitled, 1978
Oil and collage on
canvas
130 × 97.4 cm

Fig. 7:12 (*right*)
Urmas Ploomipuu
A Sunday on Lake Peipus,
1975
Etching
42 × 41.5 cm

House, 1979 (Pl. 7:11), with its Surrealistic cramped space, faceless bursting bodies, and clashing colors. Jaan Elken (b. 1954) also portrays the destructive nature of the modern city-dweller; in his paintings graffiti and broken street signs abound (Fig. 7:10).[20] Heitti Polli (b. 1951), another artist working with such themes, combines anonymous concrete housing and portraiture (Pl. 7:12).

Kaisa Puustak (b. 1945) re-creates the city in entirely different terms.[21] She sometimes depicts sunlight glinting off glass skyscrapers in a matter-of-fact manner or she shows a railroad station, as in her etching *The Depot*, 1977 (Fig. 7:11). Her interest obviously lies with the great engines and not with the human figures who seem to disappear in the shadows. By the 1980s, Puustak had turned primarily to still life, using only a few everyday items, like a basket of potatoes or a loaf of bread surrounded by the empty, tranquil space.

Urmas Ploomipuu (1942–1990) found his subject matter in the common people, preferably in happy holiday situations.[22] Using Photorealism, he tried to capture the effect of a snapshot or a halftone illustration. In his etching *A Sunday on Lake Peipus*, 1975 (Fig. 7:12), he creates a round area like the opening of the camera lens and places within it two figures in a boat. The entire surface of the etching is then covered with a meticulous crisscross pattern in imitation of a grainy photographic or printed surface—an idea with roots in Pop Art.

The paintings, multilayered serigraphs, and watercolors of Malle Leis (b. 1940) are uniquely her own.[23] Her primary subjects are flowers, vegetables, and portraiture.

Fig. 7:13
Concordia Klar
Outside the Snowstorm, 1978
Etching and aquatint
48.8 × 61 cm

Fig. 7:15 (*far right*)
Vello Vinn
Exchange, 1977
Etching
48 × 63.5 cm

Fig. 7:14
Silvi Liiva
Game I, 1978
Etching
49.4 × 43.8 cm

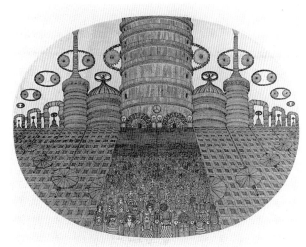

work of Jüri Arrak (b. 1936), a leading member of ANK '64, probably displays the greatest thematic richness and fantasy of all.[24] He was first trained as an engineer but, soon after graduating in metal design from the Art Institute, chose painting and printmaking as his media. His fantastic primitive world is often inhabited by naive, comical, short-haired, stocky men. They are uniformly painted with a flat color and seem sometimes like metal cutouts. In *Backyard*, 1972 (Pl. 7:17), Arrak creates primordial figures whose behavior recalls characters from Estonian folk tales. Other works by Arrak, such as *Medieval Plague*, 1981 (Pl. 7:16), develop subjects from the Middle Ages or from Estonian legends in order to keep alive the national tradition. Not surprisingly, Arrak had more than the usual troubles exhibiting and selling his work, both in Estonia and abroad.

In the etchings of Concordia Klar (b. 1938), we escape into a dream world of slender and elegant musicians dressed in fancy turn-of-the-century ballgowns. The musical instruments they play are complicated inventions of the artist, sometimes incorporating household utensils or fixtures. The mood is dreamy and lyrical. There is little background, though occasionally the figures are surrounded by vegetation like the huge, stylized, tulip-like flowers in *Outside the Snowstorm*, 1978 (Fig. 7:13). These big flowers are related to the floral patterns of Estonian folk costumes. In Klar's work, they symbolize the way in which fleeting sensations may embody the enduring character of ethnicity and nationality. In sharp contrast to the elegant works of Klar are the prints of Silvi Liiva (b. 1941).[25] Her works are inhabited by ugly, primitive women who are often shown as frightened, as in *Game I*, 1978 (Fig. 7:14). This threatening world clearly derives from

The objects she depicts are divorced from their realistic settings and made to float inexplicably across the surface of a uniformly colored background (usually black). Leis uses intense enamel colors and defines her forms carefully by modeling with various tonalities. Only occasionally does a partially depicted human figure accompany the flowers, as in her painting *The Longest Day*, 1977 (Pl. 7:14).

Other artists working on the edge of acceptability took their themes from the past, from folklore, history, or mythology. These subjects sometimes irritated the Party watchdogs because of their nationalistic implications. The

the work of her favorite artists: Hieronymus Bosch, Paul Delvaux, and Salvador Dalí.

Entirely different is the rich fantastic land conjured up in the work of Vello Vinn (b. 1939).[26] Using symmetry, deep perspective, stylization, a fine etching line, and modern photolith techniques, Vinn creates big open spaces defined by fantastic architectural settings where curious goings-on take place. His critical commentaries on the contemporary scene often use photolithography to depict the contemporary conflict between technology and humanity (Fig. 7:15).

In Estonia, abstract art is generally known by the common term "geometric art." The most prominent representatives of this genre are Tõnis Vint[27] and Leonhard Lapin.[28] But if these two artists are quite well known at home and abroad, internationally the best-known Estonian abstract artist is Raul Meel (b. 1941). Trained as an engineer, Meel is an autodidact in art.[29] His aesthetic vocabulary is comprised almost entirely of lines, which he sometimes draws by unconventional means. He uses these lines to create simple compositions that explore the fundamental relationships between sky, earth, man, and time. He usually works in series and one of his earliest and best known is a group of serigraphs called *Under the Estonian Sky*, 1973–77. The vast series consists of more than a thousand prints. Here, he shows the effect of slight variations in curving lines, which subsequently create new tensions and rhythms. His more politically charged works came later. In another extended series, consisting of thirty-five parts, Meel transformed four identically shaped maps of Estonia by using differently colored grids or lines (Pl. 7:15). In another group, called *Windows and Landscapes* (Figs. 7:16–7:19), first presented at the Baltic Graphics Triennale in 1986, repeated black silhouettes of the map of Estonia form a frame around a central barred window for the lower two of a four-work grouping and around circular forms for the upper two. Critic Eda Sepp has pointed out that "Meel's window is framed by Estonian contours and provides a reference for his place, his language, his condition, and outlook, and determines his world view from which there is no escape, hence the barlike windows which limit his freedom and scope. It is not only a political barrier, but also a general human condition."[30]

Artists of several different generations turned to abstraction in the 1970s, often continuing that work into the 1980s. Evi Tihemets (b. 1932), for example, created lithographs of wavy bands of color floating toward each other (Pl. 7:18). In the series *Games*, she introduced overlapping round and square shapes of contrasting colors to create images that resemble dart boards. Sirje Runge (b. 1950) is a young designer and abstract painter. In works such as *Geometry VIII*, 1976 (Pl. 7:19), she manipulates form and color fields to create the illusion of movement reminiscent of Op Art.

The 1980s were a transitional period that moved from totalitarianism to democratic freedom. As living conditions worsened and Russification intensified, Estonians resolved to save their language and cultural identity from annihilation. In this period, the study of the Russian language actually declined and the number of dissidents increased. High school students in Tallinn and university students in Tartu demonstrated. In 1980, forty prominent intellectuals, including writers, artists, and poets, signed an open letter in defense of Estonian language and culture.[31]

This Estonian opposition was always nonviolent, resulting mainly in peaceful gatherings at historically significant sites on the occasion of former national holidays. Brezhnev's death in 1982, and the subsequent deaths of Andropov and Chernenko, did not appreciably change the situation in Estonia. Even in the early Gorbachev years, beginning in 1985, little changed. But during the period of *glasnost* and *perestroika*, Estonian opposition grew in strength and concessions were gradually made.

In Estonia, this period under Gorbachev is known as the "Second Awakening," the first national awakening having occurred in the latter half of the nineteenth century. The popular singing festivals which originated in the First Awakening were revived in Tallinn in the summer of 1988 as a new form of nonviolent opposition; this was the so-called Singing Revolution, a dramatic expression of national unity and hope for freedom. During the summer nights, thousands of Estonians, young people especially, would gather on the song-festival grounds to sing forbidden national songs, wave the blue, black, and white flag of independent Estonia, and listen to political speeches. The largest of these festivals occurred on September 11, 1988, when over three hundred thousand people joined together publicly to demand freedom for Estonia.

How were all these events and changes reflected in the art of Estonia, especially in graphics and painting? In general, the 1980s followed the course set by the 1970s. Maybe this seems placid and uneventful, especially when compared with the active artistic culture of Latvia and Lithuania. Indeed, some Estonian critics have called the art of the 1980s conservative and stale, and referred to the decade as a period of artistic stagnation. But this criticism does not seem fully justified when one takes into account the fact that the nonviolent Estonian opposition was as

Figs. 7:16–7:19
Raul Meel
*Windows and Landscapes
I–IV*, 1986
Screenprint
100 × 88 cm (each)

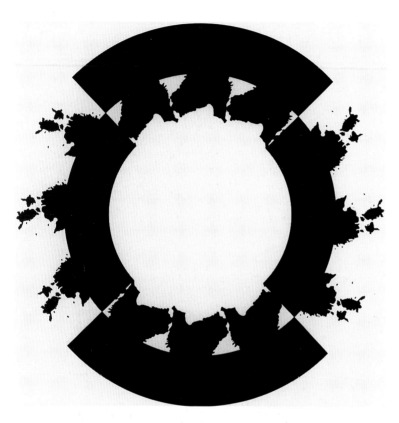

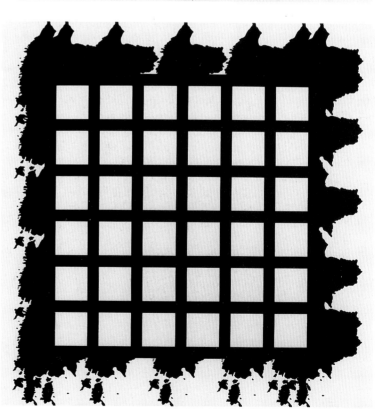

Pl. 7:1
Peeter Ulas
Evening, 1974
Etching
90.1 × 63.8 cm

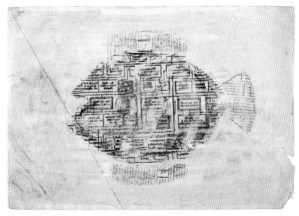

Pl. 7:2
Ullo Sooster
(Untitled), n.d.
Watercolor and
monotype
20.5 × 29.5 cm

Pl. 7:3
Toomas Vint
Forgotten Doll Carriage,
1979
Oil on canvas
92 × 70.2 cm

Pls. 7:4–7:8
Leonhard Lapin
Signed Space, 1978
Self-Portrait, 1979
Red Square, 1978
The Corner Problem, 1980
The Black Triangle III,
1978
Oil on canvas
100.5 × 90.5 cm (each)

Ando Keskküla
The Beach, 1976
Oil on canvas
71 × 90 cm

Aili Vint
(Untitled), 1986
Photo etching
10.6 × 13.8 cm

Pl. 7:11
Jüri Palm
The Mystery of the House,
1979
Oil on canvas
111 × 191 cm

Pl. 7:12
Heitti Polli
In the City, 1982
Oil on canvas
110.5 × 194 cm

Pl. 7:13
Andres Tolts
(Dangling Apples), 1983
Oil on canvas
127.5 × 148.5 cm

Pl. 7:14 (*opposite*)
Malle Leis
The Longest Day, 1977
Oil on canvas
100 × 100 cm

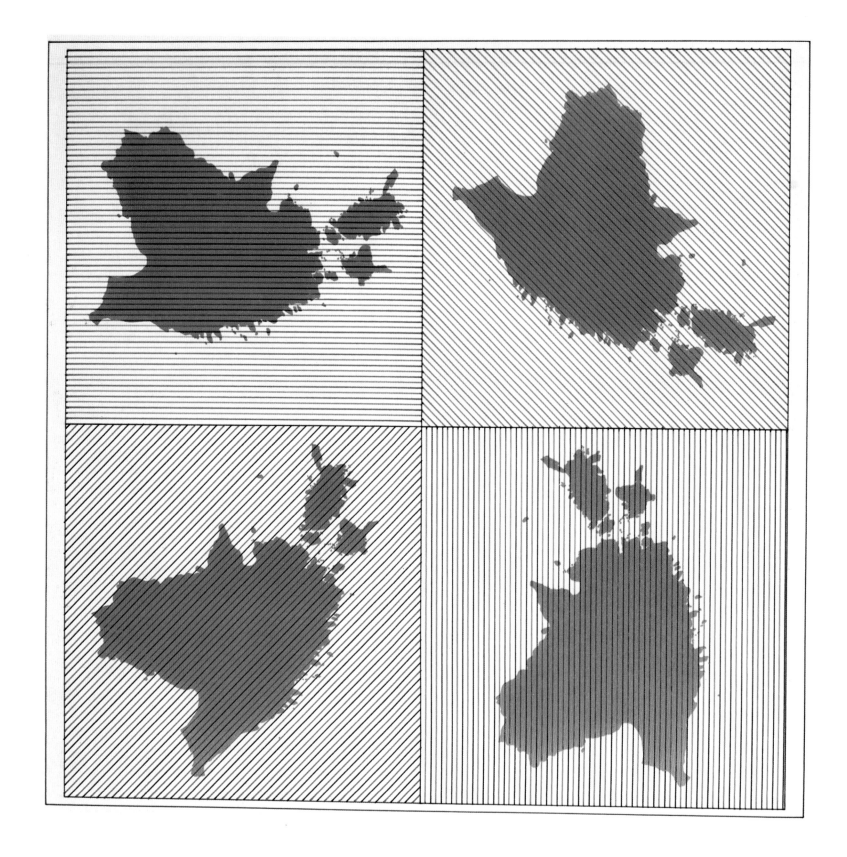

Pl. 7:16
Jüri Arrak
Medieval Plague, 1981
Oil on canvas
114 × 146 cm

Pl. 7:17
Jüri Arrak
Backyard, 1972
Lithograph
47 × 61.1 cm

Pl. 7:15 (*opposite*)
Raul Meel
Estonia #15, 1980
Screenprint
42.3 × 41 cm

Pl. 7:18
Evi Tihemets
(Untitled), 1974
Lithograph
88 × 90 cm

Pl. 7:20
Illimar Paul
Flying, 1980
Screenprint
50.2 × 50.3 cm

Pl. 7:19
Sirje Runge
Geometry VIII, 1976
Oil on canvas
89.8 × 100 cm

Pl. 8:1
Miervaldis Polis
Raphael and Polis, n.d.
Photolithograph
29.3 × 21.6 cm

Pl. 8:2
Rūdolfs Pinnis
Remembrance of Spain,
1983
Oil on canvas
100.2 × 100.5 cm

Pl. 8:3
Jānis Pauļuks
Nude, n.d.
Oil on canvas
80.3 × 120.5 cm

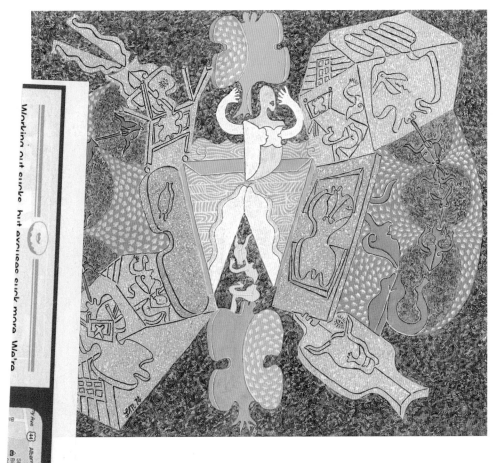

Pl. 8:4
Leonīds Mauriņš
Mummery—Folk Motif,
1974
Oil on canvas
81 × 91.2 cm

Pl. 8:5
Auseklis Baušķenieks
The Bus Has Gone, 1974
Oil on illustration board
48.4 × 68 cm

Pl. 8:6
Oļģerts Jaunarājs
Silence, 1965
Tempera on paper
38.5 × 54.3 cm

Pl. 8:7
Malda Muižule
*The Old Scarecrow of My
Childhood*, 1977
Etching and aquatint
49.3 × 65 cm

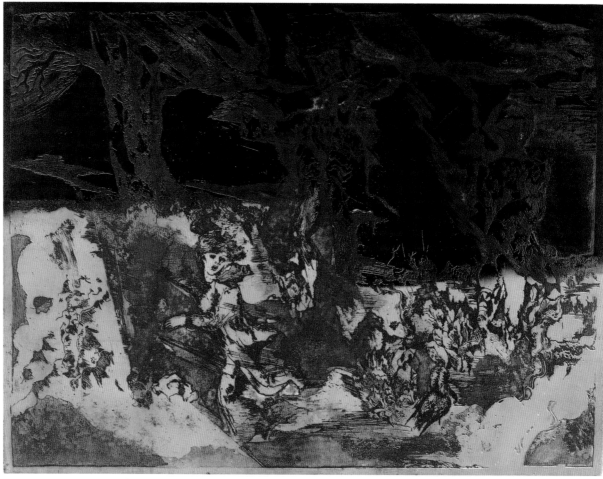

Pl. 8:8
Džemma Skulme
Caryatids, 1986
Oil with ink and graphite
on canvas
99.8 × 120.5 cm

Pl. 8:9
Juris Dimiters
Still Life, 1980
Oil on fiberboard
61 × 42.2 cm

Pl. 8:10
Līga Purmale
Reflection, 1975
Oil on fiberboard
81 × 74 cm

Pl. 8:11
Ojārs Ābols
From the series *Processes
on Earth*, 1978
Mixed media on canvas
100.5 × 100 cm

successful as the more dramatic events elsewhere in helping to deconstruct the Communist world.

One must also remember that, in the 1970s, the non-conformist Estonian avant-garde had achieved a leading position within the Soviet art world. Estonian artists were widely admired for their technical proficiency, creative power, and distinctive ethnic and national characteristics. Thus, when the repression increased in the 1980s, many Estonian visual artists expressed their opposition by calmly continuing in their 1970s manner. These artists had already demonstrated their opposition to the rule of the Kremlin through their earlier rejection of Socialist Realism.

Symbols and strategies developed in the 1970s gained new meaning in the independence struggles of the 1980s. Jüri Arrak, for example, had used the colors of the national flag in his earlier works. And Illimar Paul (b. 1945) had produced serigraphs with forms suggesting colored paper cutouts, as in his *Flying*, 1980 (Pl. 7:20).[32] In that work, a carefully knotted figure in the sky is colored with the blue, black, and white stripes that obviously refer to the Estonian flag, making a clear allusion to the artist's hope for renewed national independence. Abstractionist Raul Meel also participated in this symbolizing tendency of the 1980s. His serigraph *Embrace* (1987) represents a map of Estonia as seen from four different positions, a motif he had used before. But in this instance the maps were superimposed with red hands and arms. His series *Windows and Landscapes*, with its barred windows, also symbolizes imprisoned Estonia and its yearning for liberty.

The younger nonconformist artists, those who graduated from art schools in the 1980s, generally followed in the footsteps of their masters. Many of them had been students at Tõnis Vint's Studio 22, and at the beginning of the decade were working in the style of geometric abstraction. Siim-Tanel Annus (b. 1960), a graphic and performance artist, is the most original and best known of these younger artists.[33] In his early drawings, like the untitled one he made in 1976 (Fig. 7:20) when he was only sixteen, Annus used a very fine structural line to achieve a compositional balance. In the 1980s, his works became far more symbolic and representational. In the relief print *Towers in the Sky* (1983), the church towers reaching toward the heavens are surrounded by rays of light that impart a strong religious feeling to the image. According to the artist, his works are momentary visions from the depths of his subconscious, on the borderline between life and death.

Ene Kull (b. 1953) fuses black and white circles, ovals,

Fig. 7:20
Siim-Tanel Annus
(Untitled), 1976
Pen and ink on paper
61.4 × 38 cm

Fig. 7:21
Mari Kurismaa
In the Town, 1986
Oil on canvas
110.1 × 101 cm

squares, and parallelograms into rich, continuously transforming patterns, as in her lithograph *DY3* (1982).[34] Mari Kurismaa (b. 1956), who sometimes exhibits metaphysical tendencies, also manipulates basic geometrical forms, though in paintings like *In the Town*, 1986 (Fig. 7:21) she generally preserves their autonomy. The imagery of Raini Johanson (b. 1961), on the other hand, is conceived as a

Fig. 7:22
Ado Lill
The Axe, 1984
Aquatint
17.3 × 13.2 cm

Fig. 7:22
Ado Lill
The Axe, 1984
Aquatint
17.3 × 13.2 cm

Fig. 7:23 (*far right*)
Avo Keerend
Still Life with Olives, 1984
Lithograph
48.8 × 45 cm

right-angled gridwork pattern recalling scientific diagrams. In contrast to these Vint students, René Kari (b. 1950) creates complicated, almost three-dimensional abstract forms from curving facet-like planes of various colors. Ado Lill (Fig. 7:22), a law-school graduate who later studied for two years at the Art Institute, started out as an Action Painter but subsequently became a Minimalist with a strong interest in the color theories of Josef Albers.[35]

Many established artists made dramatic changes in their oeuvres during this decade, but quite often these alterations were designed to emphasize the Estonian roots of their art. Avo Keerend (b. 1920) moved toward abstraction in the 1980s, creating prints like *Still Life with Olives*, 1984 (Fig. 7:23), but in doing so he deliberately paid homage to the Estonian geometric abstractionists of the 1920s. At the same time, he also started to use intense colors, a clear reflection of the influence of Konrad Mägi (1878–1925), the foremost colorist in Estonia and the first director of the Art School "Pallas." Mägi's Impressionist and Fauve-inspired approach was originally designated unacceptable by the Communist Party, but in 1968 a commemorative exhibition of his work was organized and, by the 1980s, intense colors as well as other forms of color

exploration had begun to appear in the work of Keerend and other artists. Sirje Runge, for example, also started to explore subtle color tonalities at this time. Her paintings from the early 1980s, like *Landscape 23* (1982), consist of dreamy, dematerialized fields of color with slight tonal variations intersected by rectangular color areas of related but darker tonalities. These works remain mysterious and without any evident message. In contrast, Jüri Arrak started to use charcoal as his medium in this decade, following the historic example of Kristjan Raud. In these works, Arrak explores the relationship between men and animals (Fig. 7:24).

International stimuli and influences became increasingly evident in Estonian art as wider foreign travel became possible. Vello Vinn's prints sometimes represent monsters that appear to be constructed of readymade parts, as in his photo etching *Wednesday I*, 1983 (Fig. 7:25). In such works, Vinn reminds the viewer of Arcimboldo, the sixteenth-century Italian artist who created men of vegetables and other recognizable objects. Peeter Ulas divides his prints into three horizontal registers reminiscent of the paintings of Mark Rothko. Within these tiers, Ulas then examines natural atmospheric and geological forms (Fig. 7:26).

There were other general stylistic tendencies among Estonian artists in the 1980s, including a movement toward more compact compositions and more generalized form. The narrative background of earlier decades was

often abandoned in favor of a uniform blank ground. There was, in addition, a noticeable interest in preserving the autonomy of the two-dimensional surface plane behind which opens a narrow ledge-like space (this is notable in the work of Vive Tolli, Tõnis Vint, and Evi Tihemets). The hard-edge painting style of Hyperrealism often gave way in the 1980s to a soft painterly brushstroke reminiscent of the "Pallas" style (as in the work of Jaan Elken). The popularity of Hyperrealism declined, and Symbolism and Surrealism become dominant. In 1989, the Worldwide Association of Surrealism, which includes artists, writers, and poets, was established in Tallinn.

What has developed slowly, but is apparent today, is the revival of artistic life in Tartu, a city which for many years was deprived of its cultural heritage. This restoration began in 1957, when, as in the nineteenth century, the University of Tartu established a studio-art program, now known as the Art Cabinet (*Kunstikabinett*) in the Education and Methodology Department.[36] By 1967, the art students had organized an association, called Visarid (i.e., someone in opposition, not satisfied), which was comparable to the ANK '64 movement in Tallinn. The new program offered studio training in drawing, watercolor, oil, ceramics, and metalwork to all university students and, in particular, to the future elementary teachers of history and languages as a secondary field of teaching. As in the nineteenth century, the program has been successful. Furthermore, in 1988 a division of the State Art

Fig. 7:24
Jüri Arrak
Company at the Table, 1982
Charcoal
70 × 100 cm

Fig. 7:25 (*above right*)
Vello Vinn
Wednesday I, 1983
Photo etching
47.2 × 31.8 cm

Fig. 7:26 (*right*)
Peeter Ulas
Earth, Earth, 1982
Etching and aquatint
88.9 × 63.5 cm

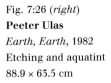

Institute of Tallinn was established at the University of Tartu with a five-year curriculum. At present, however, the university is considering integrating it as a university department.

In 1988, local artists, writers, and poets established the Art Association of Tartu, modeling it after the Art Association of "Pallas," which existed from 1918 to 1940. The earlier association was responsible for the creation of the Art School "Pallas" in 1919. And while the reborn organization has not yet reached that high level of development, it has opened a small studio and an art gallery for the exhibition of contemporary art, the first of its kind in Tartu. Until now, artists in Tartu have valiantly tried to keep alive the style of "Pallas."[37] With these new developments in Tartu, only one question remains: Will there be a School of Tartu that will return the artistic life of the city to its former level of distinction?

The same question may be asked with regard to Estonian art in general now that there exists a new democratic situation, where art is free from censorship, where artists have the right to organize their own exhibitions, and where a free exchange of ideas is a regular possibility.

Notes

1. There there has long been a strong interest in, and enjoyment of, the graphic arts in Estonia. The origin of printmaking goes back to the early nineteenth century: a drawing and graphic arts program was instituted at the University of Tartu in 1803. Its principal purpose was to train medical and botany students so they could record their discoveries. They were also trained in printmaking to be able to translate their drawings into prints for publication. The program proved equally beneficial for students interested in art, however, and by the second half of the century there were Baltic-German and Estonian graphic artists working in Estonia and St. Petersburg. The university discontinued the printmaking program in 1892 when photography superseded lithography as the primary medium of illustration. But by then the graphic tradition was well established at Tartu and, when "Pallas" was created in 1919, the graphic arts played a significant part in its curriculum. By the end of the 1930s there was a small but important group of young printmakers among the school's graduates.

2. R. Loodus and E. Lamp, *Nõukogude Eesti kunstide kroonika, 1940–1965* (Tallinn, 1970), p. 6.

3. Walter C. Clemens, Jr., *Baltic Independence and Russian Empire* (New York: St. Martin's Press, 1991), pp. 61ff; Mart Laar, Lauri Vahtra, and Heiki Valk, *Kodu lugu II* (Tallinn: Perioodika, 1989), pp. 78ff; Toivo U. Raun, *Estonia and the Estonians* (Stanford: Stanford University Press, 1987), pp. 189ff.

4. Loodus and Lamp, *Nõukogude Eesti kunstide kroonika*, p. 35.

5. B. Bernstein, "Vive Tolli," in *Ringi sees ja ringist välja* (Tallinn: Kunst, 1979), pp. 76–114.

6. Martti Soosaar, *Ateljee-etüüde 2* (Tallinn: Kunst, 1990), pp. 35–42.

7. Irina Solomõkova, ed., *Nõukogude Eesti kunst, 1940–1965* (Tallinn: Kunst, 1970), pp. 168–69.

8. Tõnu Parming and Elva Järvesoo, eds., *A Case Study of a Soviet Republic: The Estonian SSR* (Boulder, Colo.: Westview Press, 1978), pp. 21ff; Raun, *Estonia and the Estonians*, pp. 228ff.

9. Mari Pill, "Ülo Sooster—novaator ja traditsioonide kandja," *Kunst* 68 (1986): 24–31.

10. Leonhard Lapin, "Startinud kuuekümnendatel," *Kunst* 68 (1986): 16–23.

11. Eda Sepp, "Estonia: Art as Metaphor of Its Time," in Norton Dodge, ed., *Baltic Art during the Brezhnev Era: Nonconformist Art in Estonia, Latvia, and Lithuania*, exh. cat. (Toronto: John B. Aird Gallery, 1992), p. 14.

12. Ibid. In the contemporary Estonian literature, including newspapers and magazines, there is no mention of the ANK '64 or SOUP '69 movements.

13. *Myth and Abstraction: Actual Art from Estonia*, exh. cat. (Karlsruhe: Badischer Kunstverein, 1992), pp. 110–11.

14. Soosaar, *Ateljee-etüüde 2*, pp. 98–103.

15. Evi Pihlak, "Andres Tolts," in *Uued põlvkonnad 1* (Tallinn: Bit Rotaprint, 1988), pp. 58–67.

16. J. Hain, "Marju Üksine," in *Uued põlvkonnad 2* (Tallinn: Bit Rotaprint, 1988), pp. 54–64.

17. The artist's indebtedness to de Chirico is particularly apparent in his 1983 drypoint and aquatint titled *Hommage au Giorgio de Chirico*.

18. Lehti Viiroja, "Allex Küti ateljees," *Kunst* 41 (1972): 12–17.

19. Evi Pihlak, "Maailm läbi kontrastide," *Sirp and Vasar* 14 (Apr. 8, 1977): 8.

20. Evi Pihlak, "Jaan Elken," in *Uued põlvkonnad 1*, pp. 62–64.

21. Vappu Vabar, "Kaisa Puustak," in *Uued põlvkonnad 2*, pp. 65–69.

22. Mai Levin, "Urmas Ploomipu korrastatud maailm," *Sirp* 7 (Feb. 14, 1992).

23. Evi Pihlak, *Malle Leis* (Tallinn: Kunst, 1988).

24. Soosaar, *Ateljee-etüüde 2*, pp. 104–11; *The Supernatural World of Jüri Arrak* (Sewickley, Penn.: International Images Ltd., 1987).

25. Soosaar, *Ateljee-etüüde 2*, pp. 15–21.

26. Ibid., pp. 58–65.

27. Tamara Luuk, "Eesti moodsa kunstiloo lühikonspekte. Hommage à Tõnis Vint," in *Uued põlvkonnad 2*, pp. 70–80; Stephen E. Feinstein, "The Avant Garde in Soviet Estonia," in Norton Dodge, ed., *New Art from the Soviet Union*, exh. cat. (Washington, D.C.: Acropolis Books, 1977), pp. 31–34.

28. Harry Liivrand, "Leonhard Lapin Kadriorus," *Kunst* 73 (1989): 7–17; Sepp, "Estonia: Art as Metaphor," pp. 9–21.

29. Harry Liivrand, *Raul Meel*, exh. cat. (Tallinn: State Art Museum, 1989).

30. Evi Pihlak, "Sirje Runge," in *Uued põlvkonnad 1*, pp. 65–68; and J. Klimov, "Geomeetriast maastikuni," *Kunst* 64 (1984): 36–39.

31. Charles F. Furtado, Jr., and Andrea Chandler, *Perestroika in the Soviet Republics* (Boulder, Colo.: Westview Press, 1992), pp. 65ff.

32. Ibid.

33. L. Viiroja, "Illimar Pauli vabagraafika," in *Uued põlvkonnad 2*, pp. 29–53.

34. E. Pihlak, "Siim-Tanel Annus," in *Uued põlvkonnad 2*, pp. 85–87.

35. *Myth and Abstraction*, pp. 163–67.

36. H. Liivrand, "Vestlus Ado Lillega," *Kunst* 70 (1987): 34–35.

37. Jaak Olep, Introduction, *TRO Kunstikabinet: The Art Studio of Tartu State University*, ed. K. Põllu, exh. cat. (Tartu: Trü Rotaprint, 1970), n.p.

8 | Nonconformist art in Latvia

Smaller measures, to equal effect

Mark Allen Svede

In discussing Soviet nonconformist art, many commentators instinctively set up dramatic oppositions between official and unofficial culture. These often come complete with aesthetic or moral equivalencies, and, as we all know from our good Cold War-era upbringing, nothing clarifies right and wrong better than rigid categories of behavior. Eclipsed by this tidy story of heroic struggle are these facts: that some of the artistic outlaws were, in other areas of their professional lives, very much part of the restrictive establishment; that their unorthodox production was at times supported by less ideologically fixated government agencies; and that official art was not invariably sterile and unofficial art was not always interesting. Such deviations are notably frequent in the history of Soviet Latvian art. Although aesthetic oppositions certainly existed in Latvia, an understanding of them is not to be gained by relying on the historical scenario often posited for Russia.

The advent of official Soviet art in Latvia was itself something of an anomaly. When the Baltic states were annexed by the Soviet Union in 1945, the doctrine of Socialist Realism was already more than a decade old. Its tenets arrived fully formed, so rather than experiencing a gradual constriction of creative freedom, Baltic artists were called to judgment at the height of Stalin's power with little chance to ameliorate their political or stylistic accountability.[1] On the other hand, whatever leniency any advance notice of the new aesthetic policy might have afforded the local intelligentsia was dubious, given the liquidation of some of the most devoutly Communist Latvian émigré artists working in Russia prior to the annexation.[2] By the same token, expectations that cultural autonomy would be ensured by Stalin's high-sounding nationalities policy were destroyed by the brutalization of the art community during the first Soviet occupation of Latvia in 1940–41 with its mass deportations. Even sympathetic leftist artists who fled eastward to avoid the subsequent Nazi invasion fell to the Stalinist terror.

Such violence against the small Latvian art circles, first in Moscow and then in Riga, aggravated the scarcity of reputable prewar figures that could be construed as Socialist models. The finest existing Latvian paradigms of Socialist Realism, those by Gustav Klucis (1895–1944), Voldemārs Andersons (1891–1942), and Kārlis Veidemanis (1897–1944), were rendered unavailable by the death and disgrace of those artists.[3] Because there was no true ascendancy of an indigenous Communist faction and, because of this, no gradual development of the mechanisms for state control of artistic education and production, an obvious foreign authority was imposed and Party-dominated institutional structures (artist unions, revisionist museums, a reorganized Academy curriculum, etc.) were abruptly installed.[4]

Despite the enormous human tragedy of the annexation, the stylistic shift in Latvian art in the late 1940s was not exactly cataclysmic. While the strictures of Socialist Realism were being refined and enforced to the east, artists in interbellum Latvia had been experiencing a similar stylistic retrenchment, albeit voluntarily. Innovations of the native avant-garde, whose members had synthesized aspects of Expressionism, Cubism, Futurism, Verism, Constructivism, and Purism during the early 1920s, were largely abandoned later in the decade in favor of a romantic pictorialism. Moreover, the notion of an officially sanctioned style of art was already familiar. With the rise of an authoritarian government in 1934, Latvian artists were encouraged to depict an ethnically pure, politically stable society and, on occasion, even the iconographic trappings of a personality cult for leader Kārlis Ulmanis.[5]

Morphologically, post-annexation art remained relatively constant while an ideological veneer was applied to its winsome views of farmers and laborers. Often Socialist content was discernible only in the paintings' titles. In order to circumvent despised political themes, most painters favored landscape and still-life subjects—staples of pre-Soviet art as well. There was, however, one change: of the works touted and exhibited by Soviet cultural authorities, a conspicuous number had maritime subjects, as if belying Russia's strategic interest in Latvian territory. To look at All-Union publications from the late 1940s and early 1950s, one might surmise that only two paintings of note were produced in Latvia: *New Sails* by Eduard

Kalniņš (b. 1904) and *Latvian Fishermen* by Jānis Osis (b. 1926).[6]

Illustration of the official, fictionalized history of Latvia was eventually mandated by 1948, in the wake of Zhdanov's crusade against formalism. The selection of Oto Skulme (1889–1967) as the premier historical painter was a rather bathetic one, given his past accomplishments as a Cubist and leader of Riga's modernists. This divided allegiance would not be the last within his family. Yet, tellingly, Skulme's initial choice of a revolutionary subject was the 1802 Kauguri peasant uprising, an event revered by nationalists—which may account for the subject's popularity with other painters of this period. Again, such revisionist interpretations had precursors in the anachronistic mythologizing of Latvia's past by certain artists in the years before the war.

Creative control was further tightened during the winter of 1949–50 with the expulsion of fifty noncompliant members from the Artists' Union and demotion to candidate status of twenty-one others. These reprisals did little to brighten the complexion of Latvian Socialist Realism. Of genre paintings from this time, a conspicuous number are populated with faceless staffage, and when facial expressions can be discerned, they are mostly circumspect, with eyes averted and mouths tightly drawn. There were, of course, exceptions: the grinning welder or carpenter whose ebullience was all the more implausible in the midst of so much anonymous, dehumanized subject matter.

Overall, as artist Jānis Borgs has described it, the onset of Socialist Realism was the beginning of an ice age for Latvian avant-garde culture—sometimes quite literally, as in the case of Latvians forced to paint *en plein air* in Siberia.[7] Jēkabs Strazdiņš (1905–1958) was one such exile. A beloved official artist of the Ulmanis regime, Strazdiņš glorified the healthy rural life in his realist canvases, all eminently palatable to Stalinist taste. Had he not fought against the Red Army, his tenure at the Academy would surely have continued.[8] Another instance of "good" work in bad standing was that by Indriķis Zeberiņš (1882–1969). In 1906–7, Zeberiņš drew antitsarist caricatures that would later find their way into Soviet books on revolutionary art.[9] His satirical bent proved foolhardy in 1951, however, when the NKVD (former name of the KGB) confiscated his caricature *Kolkhoz Cow*, which mocked the exaggerated claims of collectivization's benefits by depicting a cow with two udders. His trial followed, with testimony by painter Jānis Pauļuks (an artistic renegade himself) to the effect that God may rule the sky, but Stalin rules the earth[10]—which is probably the only paraphrase

of Luke 20:25 in Soviet legal transcriptions. Zeberiņš was the first of several notable figures in Latvian art for whom the term "dissident" would not be synonymous with "nonconformist."

One artist who could lay claim to both offenses was Kurts Fridrihsons (1911–1991). Before the war, Fridrihsons had traveled to Paris, where he made the acquaintance of André Derain and André Gide, initiated a wide-ranging correspondence with Edvard Munch, and cultivated a strong dislike for the dull realism prevalent in his homeland. His own work aspired to great expressivity. In 1950, Fridrihsons was arrested along with a poet, an actor, and two translators who had been holding weekly meetings in an apartment to discuss new French literature, such as essays by Camus, Gide, and Sartre.[11] Known as the French Group, they were denounced as anti-Communist plotters and were subjected to nearly a year of interrogation and torture by the NKVD. Afterward, Fridrihsons and his colleagues were dispatched to prison camps in Kazakhstan.

Khrushchev's denunciation of Stalin in 1956 gave Latvian artists, like their counterparts elsewhere in the empire, renewed hope for artistic freedom. Indeed, to artists like Fridrihsons, it meant physical emancipation. After his return to Latvia in 1956, Fridrihsons began exploring an idiosyncratic style whose coarse, attenuated forms and mannerist color sense had as little to do with the national tradition as they did with Socialist Realism. Accordingly, he had little to do with the official circuit of exhibitions, publications, and commissions.

Jānis Pauļuks (1906–1984) was another painter who flouted convention starting in the 1950s, thereby earning both a reputation as an eccentric, and, ultimately, his ouster from the Artists' Union. In his earliest work, Pauļuks drew steady inspiration from pre-Renaissance Italian art, but his oeuvre soon evolved into a protean amalgam of modern styles, evident in *Nude*, a portrait of his wife Felicita Pauļuka (Pl. 8:3). His portraiture alternately flirted with fussy Parisian decorative modes and plumbed psychological darkness; his landscapes could be pantheistic or utterly deadpan; and even the occasional depiction of social phenomena, like public work projects, inevitably revealed his foremost private concerns: exhilarating color and expansive brushwork. By the late 1950s, Pauļuks was daring to use the tachiste technique of dripping and splashing paint over otherwise soberly representational work. In doing so, Pauļuks became an oasis of the ecstatic within reticent Latvian painting.

Other overt signs of the so-called thaw came belatedly to Latvia. Prospects for liberalization had been compromised the year before when a ten-year retrospective of Latvian painting in Moscow had been lauded by critics unaware that the works they deemed especially praiseworthy were, in fact, pre-Soviet exemplars added to the exhibit at the last moment in order to rectify weaknesses of the selection. The ensuing debate, particularly at the stormy Third Congress of Latvian Artists, threw into doubt any possibility of immediate positive change.[12]

Even so, Latvian art of the late 1950s and 1960s entered a phase analogous to—and, it is claimed, anticipatory of—the Severe Style in Soviet art. Prettified, pedantic sociopolitical themes were further eschewed in favor of quieter monumental figure compositions. Perhaps because forced idealism never gained much currency with them, Latvian artists did not, as a rule, resort to the visual harshness of the Russian variety. One exception was Edgars Iltners (1925–1983), whose angular draftsmanship is credited with inspiring the Severe Style. In paintings by Boriss Bērziņš (b. 1930), on the other hand, restricted color schemes and simplified forms began to recall earlier, more poetic Latvian painting and its stated goal of portraying a peasant's strength in the face of adversity.[13] Other artists instrumental in the trend toward stylization include Biruta Baumane (b. 1922), Rita Valnere (b. 1929), and Indulis Zariņš (b. 1929). As with Pauļuks's applied Action Painting, these artists tested the limits of painterly technique within large, discrete areas of their compositions; the patina on an iron beam on a construction site, the refractive sheen of glass in a tramway car, the shimmer of water over beach rock, the polychrome pattern of wood planks on a raft[14]—each provided the excuse for abstract, Expressionistic manipulation of pigment, often upstaging the figural passages nearby.

By most accounts, the first chance for public display of innovative work was in 1959. Indeed, several remarkable exhibitions were mounted that year. Rehabilitation of the purged avant-gardists occasioned the first display of works by Aleksandrs Drēviņš (1889–1938) since his death almost twenty-two years before, as well as the first local appearance of Klucis's paintings, both in the state museum's show "Art of the Latvian Red Riflemen."[15] Also emerging from disfavor was the painter Hilda Vīka (1897–1963), whose psychomythical fantasies from the 1930s, executed in a hybrid of naive and veristic styles, had been particularly objectionable to the authorities. Vīka was permitted a large solo exhibition, an opportunity given to only three artists in Riga before 1959.[16] Moreover, a posthumous exhibition of key modernist Voldemārs Tone (1892–1956) was the first official recognition granted any Latvian who had fled the Soviet invasion.

Fig. 8:1
Pēteris Smagiņš
Listen to Me, 1958
Pen and ink and
colored pencil
24.2 × 20.1 cm

This unprecedented reckoning with Stalinist history was perhaps most striking in the exhibition of a cycle of graphic work by Pēteris Smagiņš (1901–1970) that illustrated the life of an average twentieth-century Latvian. This included an image of the deportations of June 1941, a topic broached only the year before in the poem "The Unfinished Song" by Harijs Heislers. Ironically, Smagiņš's work has the laconic demeanor and coarseness of propaganda broadsides generated by the Communist underground graphic collective Aktīvo during the Ulmanis years. Aesthetic considerations were subsidiary to political content. This is obvious, for example, in his drawing *Listen to Me* (Fig. 8:1), which shows a *Pravda* reader's attention summoned by a higher source of truth. Despite—or perhaps because of—his role as witness to these times, Smagiņš remains relatively unknown in Latvian art history. His reputation as a dissident, however, was secured in 1966 when he presented 420 of his works to the American Embassy in Moscow, a gift to the John F. Kennedy Presidential Library.[17]

This permissive climate was not to last. In the summer of 1959, Khrushchev visited Riga in response to a marked nationalist trend in the republic's Party leadership, and beginning with the dismissal of Latvia's top officials in July, reprisals continued for several years, with entire government ministries abolished.[18] The cultural backlash commenced in November, culminating in the 1962 ouster of the Minister of Culture, who had futilely opposed Russification policies. Although literature and theater were most debilitated, the visual arts were also affected.[19]

The search for new modes of expression had largely become a retrospective exercise by this time. Because Riga was relatively inaccessible for foreign visitors and its size did not merit local display of the significant exhibitions of contemporary Western art seen in Moscow or Leningrad, most Latvian artists were not exposed to the same cosmopolitan influences that propelled progressive Russian culture. This was hardly perceived as a liability.[20] Rather, in the coming years, Riga's distance from Moscow would serve to mitigate criticism issued from the center and even shield artists from the effects of the Kremlin's more short-lived repressions.

In addition, distance enabled the preservation and study of cultural monuments dating from the independence period that might well have been destroyed in a situation of closer surveillance. Storerooms of the state museum protected a national artistic treasury, including some of Latvia's most radical modernist experiments, while the center of Riga was, quite inexplicably, graced by the towering Freedom Monument, its back intentionally turned toward Russia during its construction in the mid-1930s.[21] Art history students at the Academy wrote theses on officially discouraged topics and, even more riskily, were permitted to draw unpopular conclusions.[22] And it is widely understood that Riga's artistic community grew more democratic in nature than those elsewhere in the Soviet Union, obviating an underground movement and, indeed, some of the intensity that clandestine activity engenders. This relatively benign atmosphere is attributed to the consolidation of control within the Academy and Artists' Union by venerable Latvian artists who paid lip-service to Marxist-Leninist theory but tolerated deviation in practice.[23]

Consequently, the early 1960s saw a modest expansion of formalism. A small number of artists, working independently, widened the range of experiments initiated by Fridrihsons and Pauļuks. Among them, Rūdolfs Pinnis (b. 1902) (Pl. 8:2) gained notoriety for incorporating Fauvist outbursts of color within temperately composed landscapes, still lifes, and portraits.[24] His revival of an overtly ornamental syntax, learned during a decade of study in Paris before the war, erupted in the wake of his brief Siberian internment and finally earned Pinnis his reputation as Latvia's dean of pure painting. By the late 1960s, he was immersed in the mature abstract style of Matisse, which, despite its bold appearance vis-à-vis official art, seemed to stem his creative prerogative.

Elsewhere, the landscapes of Lidija Auza (b. 1914) evinced more structural interests. In her compositions, Auza began to juxtapose thick layers of paint with collaged elements of metal, plastic, etc., a tectonic enterprise unexplored in Latvia since the modernist era. She gradually reduced representational content to the point where works appear essentially nonobjective.

The painting career of Georgs Šēnbergs (1915–1989) existed not only apart from this incremental process of liberalization, but it was a sequestered endeavor that remains unmentioned or misunderstood in Latvian art histories. From the late 1930s until his death in 1989, Šēnbergs painted and sketched portraits, floral still lifes, genre subjects, and grander works of metaphysical content, many of which he reworked incessantly in search of an essential description of the subject. These dense palimpsests defy facile stylistic categorization, incorporating draftsman-like attributes of Leonardo here, the Expressionistic traces of Latvian modernist Jānis Tīdemanis (1897–1964) there, and elsewhere any number of other pictorial affinities. His layered, obliterated, reworked imagery enjoys—or endures—parity with the tactile properties of paint, crayon, or pencil to a degree rarely seen before in Latvian art. Šēnbergs's lapidary manner of brushwork and saturated colors also recall particulars of Redon or Vrubel', and indeed he achieved some of their sensuous, hallucinatory impact.[25]

Careful readers of official Latvian art publications in the 1960s might well have suspected themselves of hallucination when they began to see mild heresies printed on the page. In 1962, doctrinaire historian Rasma Lāce noted a continuance of bourgeois Latvian art's "healthy realist tradition" within Socialist Realism[26]—not untrue, and not an unusual tactic of legitimization, but a bold *a posteriori* linkage so soon after the dismissal of the editors of nearly all major newspapers in 1959 for alleged nationalist sympathies. As early as 1963, the journal *Māksla* [Art], the mouthpiece of the Artists' Union, reproduced nonobjective works by Mondrian and Kandinsky in an article about abstraction versus naturalism. On that occasion, naturalism was illustrated not by Gerasimov, Yablonskaia, or some other titan of Socialist Realism, but by Grant Wood's *American Gothic*.[27] This article, along with occasional reviews of Western European exhibitions and the reprinting of a seminal avant-garde tract by Voldemārs Matvejs (1877–1914), who had in fact unleashed modernist theory on an unsuspecting Riga in 1910 with a related text,[28] signaled growing tolerance for unofficial discourse. As part of this slow recovery, Cubist and Constructivist works were exhumed from the museum storerooms and reproduced within otherwise bland and biased articles.[29]

The Constructivist legacy was partially recovered, appropriately, in the applied arts of the mid-1960s, when geometric abstraction and the idea of the primacy of materials were first officially tolerated in tapestry and object design. The high status accorded to the applied arts in Latvia deems this development more auspicious than we might suppose. Equivocally termed "artistic constructions"—and ostensibly differentiated from art—small sculptures of wire and geometric solids were exhibited by designers, some reminiscent of the work of Naum Gabo.[30] Zenta Logina (1908–1980), one of the first Latvian painters to be shown in Moscow after the annexation, created tapestries and colored plaster sculptures based on cosmological themes.[31] Made and kept in the privacy of her home, these works remain mostly unknown even today.[32] Logina's use of geometric abstraction to express cosmological ideas recalls the work of an earlier Balt, Lithuanian Symbolist Mikalojus Čiurlionis (1875–1911). By the end of the decade, another debt to Čiurlionis would be incurred when painter Leonīds Mauriņš (b. 1943) decorated the ceilings of Rīga's Café Allégro with dizzying visual analogies of music, creating a synaesthesia that would have a formative impact on several key contemporary artists.[33] His love of vibrant composition, biomorphic forms, and intense color can be seen in another work, *Mummery—Folk Motif* (Pl. 8:4), wherein Mauriņš alludes to Latvian motifs, and also, quite possibly, to those of Picasso. Meanwhile, ceramicist Pēteris Martinsons (b. 1931) employed a Cubist vocabulary in his sculptures, both in surface ornamentation and in structure.

Abstraction in easel painting also began in the mid-1960s, initially in the work of watercolorists. Oļģerts Jaunarājs (b. 1907) could be considered Soviet Latvia's first truly abstract artist (Pl. 8:6), having transformed his studies of the structure of ice, mud, and leaves into bona fide compositions.[34] Organic sources for abstraction, and the regenerative, pastoral connotations of such choices, recur throughout the history of Latvian art. Moreover, a work like *Sorrow* proves Jaunarājs to be a consummate colorist, respectful of the traditional subdued Latvian palette. Also seeking the elemental, but looking instead to modern civilization, Kurts Fridrihsons summoned the idiom, if not the transcendental spirit, of Neoplasticism in his *Composition X* (Fig. 8:2). Malda Muižule (b. 1937) worked through the tectonic lessons of Cézanne, Braque, and Delaunay in her early figurative watercolors to arrive at a decidedly unstructured, even frenzied nonobjective style in her prints and paintings of the 1970s (Pl. 8:5).

Fig. 8:2
Kurts Fridrihsons
Composition X, 1967
Brush and ink on paper
64.1 × 48.5 cm

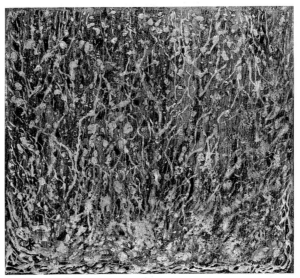

Fig. 8:3
Miķelis Golts
The Forest in Winter, 1979
Mixed media on canvas
over board
100.5 × 111.6 cm

Later, Miķelis Golts (b. 1922) ventured abstraction in mixed media. Clearly an Action painting in technique, *The Forest in Winter* (Fig. 8:3) by Golts concedes figuration in title, like most abstract works of this time. The critical climate during the Brezhnev era once again encouraged ambiguity as a safeguard against censure. Renewed official hostility had closed a 1969 sculpture exhibit of three recent Academy graduates, Aivars Gulbis (b. 1933), Jānis Karlovs (b. 1939), and Juris Mauriņš (b. 1928). Deemed most offensive were their Expressionistic forms, the Kineticism of Gulbis, and the nationalistic subtexts in Karlovs's works *Land* and *Rhythms of an Epoch*.[35]

Oddly, the most sustained, erudite exploration of abstract painting in Latvia was to be made by a paragon among official artists, Ojārs Ābols (1922–1983). In the

Fig. 8:4
**Andris Grīnbergs and
Inta Grīnberga**
The Wedding of Jesus Christ,
August 24, 1972
Performance
Photo courtesy of
Mara Brasmane

Fig. 8:5
Andris Grīnbergs
Creation, 1973
Performance
Photo courtesy of the artist

1950s, as an aspiring Socialist Realist, Ābols pursued his education in Leningrad, where he met Džemma Skulme (b. 1925), daughter of Latvian Academy rector Oto Skulme. Of course, she too was committed to the official style. Eventually, they married and became first couple of the local cultural establishment, but from the start their privileged status provided opportunities to see new art from the West, meet leading Russian intellectuals (some of whom later became dissidents), and realize their professional ambitions. For Ābols, this culminated in his series *Processes on Earth* (Pl. 8:11), which combined pictographs, alphanumeric elements, and map notations into sensuous ecological and pacifist statements. In addition to testing stylistic limits, Ābols was respected by several gifted younger artists for his determination to inform them of developments abroad. On one occasion in 1976, Ābols hid three of them in a sidechamber of a hall where he was required to debrief fifty apparatchiks about the latest trends he had observed during a trip to the Venice Biennale.[36] Ābols's untimely death interrupted this apostasy within the highest ranks.

For her part, Skulme matured into a painter—archaeologist, really—of the eternal feminine principle as found within world art. Latvian peasant mothers as Hellenic caryatids tooled upon icon panels (Pl. 8:8), quotations of Velázquez's *meninas* (Pl. 8:12) and Goya's *majas* (awash on color-field canvases), even *homo sovieticus* cast as a medieval saint (done in the champlevé manner): the breadth of Skulme's sources anticipates the growing pluralism in Latvian art of the 1970s. As significant as her elegant pastiches was Skulme's role as president of the Artists' Union and delegate to the All-Union body, which provided other artists with an intercessor in moments of conflict with the central authorities.[37]

Speaking on a subject of grave concern to such central authorities in the late 1960s and early 1970s, Estonian composer Uno Naissoo said: "If a hippie, naked above the waist and with a cross around his neck, plays a violin . . . this does not mean that the music is bound to be bad."[38] He may well have been referring to the founder of performance and body art in Latvia, Andris Grīnbergs (b. 1946). Youth culture struck Riga in 1965, and soon hippies gathered in medieval Dome Square to play music, paint their faces with flower-power signs, promenade in long hair and jeans, and do other things discouraged by Komsomol. Grīnbergs and his wife Inta Grīnberga (b. 1955), who performed jazz improvisations on the violin, became central figures in this milieu.

Trained in clothing design, Grīnbergs was inspired by the fashion of Mary Quant and the spectacle of Twiggy and Jean Shrimpton, as gleaned from the pages of prized copies of *Vogue* and its Polish approximation *Prze-krój*. The music of Dylan and Melanie, the Woodstock event, and films by Antonioni, Bertolucci, Fellini, and Godard were also influential.[39] In 1968, Grīnbergs began his twenty-five-year self-documentation project *Intimate Provocation*, incorporating staged photography, film, audio recordings, costume, and autobiographical text. Among his documented episodes was the first Latvian happening, *The Wedding of Jesus Christ*, which Inta and Andris Grīnbergs staged in late August 1972 (Fig. 8:4). The shock of a new genre aside, here the provocation occurred on two levels: religion made public and, moreover, religion made apocryphal through its eroticization. In coopting the Incarnation, Grīnbergs could not have made a more symbolic claim to the power of body art, which he began exploring within a four-film series of 1972–73, titled *Self-Portrait*. At about the same time, state security closed a photo exhibition/jam session that Grīnbergs staged in his apartment. This visit prompted Grīnbergs to cut the single print of *Self-Portrait* into tiny, concealable fragments that are only currently being spliced and restored. Unacceptable as open sexuality, modishness, nudity, and anarchy were to Soviet censors, these hallmarks of Grīnbergs's art posed as great an affront to staid Latvian mores. Nevertheless, his spiritual connection to the natural environment (Fig. 8:5) and his attempt to recover suppressed native mythologies could be seen as a continuation of atavistic impulses in earlier twentieth-century Latvian culture.

Biruta Delle (b. 1944) was another significant figure to emerge from the hippie subculture. Expelled from the Art Academy in 1967 and banned from exhibitions, Delle went on to paint Expressionistic works with titles like *Composition on a Baudelairian Theme, Who's Unwanted in the Olive Garden?*, and *Joan Baez Sings for Peace*.[40] With her husband Pēteris Kampars (d. 1993), whose career was one casualty of the 1959 anti-Latvian repression, Delle went on to champion unconventional art, both in exhibitions organized at Kampars's school in rural Kurzeme and within classes held in her suburban studio. The studio's name, Submarine, not only recalls the Beatles' anthem to individuality, but it also conjures the image of undetected maneuvering beneath a heavily patrolled surface.

Coming as further aftershocks of this youthquake, Pop Art and Hyperrealism found fewer adherents in Latvia than elsewhere in the Baltics, and the manifestations were often far stranger. The Pop-influenced work *Cry* by Jānis Osis (b. 1943) glamorized Vietnam-era America, despite exegeses to the contrary in official literature. Jane Fonda, at a microphone, is framed by a street tableau: a topless go-go dancer in a green afro, another woman in hot pants and platform shoes, and a policeman in full riot gear—all too adoringly detailed to make a convincing indictment of corrupt America.[41] Likewise, in his work *Street Musician* (Fig. 8:6), Juris Zvirbulis (b. 1944) shows a Vietnam veteran playing curbside, a fond memory from the artist's trip to San Francisco in 1977. Certain Hyperrealist works communicated, on the other hand, the political banality and moral ambivalence in Soviet society. Lenin, as painted by Guntis Strupulis (1933–1974) in 1970, is a menacing bureaucrat.[42] The painting *The Year 1919* by Aleksandrs Stankēvičs (b. 1932) is similarly disjunctive, its ill-fated Bolsheviks dwarfed by rusticated masonry and enervated by the billows of a red flag overhead, rather like the mock heroes in Sots Art panels by Komar and Melamid.

By comparison, Līga Purmale (b. 1948) and Miervaldis Polis (b. 1948) maintained the impassive gaze of Photorealism, depleting their quotidian subjects of metaphorical substance while accruing literary detail. Purmale chose potentially romantic scenes—tranquil domestic interiors, cattle in misty meadows—but, by radically cropping the image or suppressing perspective, enforced such a uniformity of compositional weight that her paintings seem mostly about inertia, however sublime. In *Reflection* (Pl. 8:10), the extreme close-up of a cow's eye becomes a watery *Weltanschauung*. Polis, despite training as a monumental painter, was often drawn to colloquial subjects and a highly compressed technique.[43] In *Workday on a City Street*, for example, the marginalia of vehicles and passers-by at a building site trivialize the industry beyond them; the manner of depiction is commensurately disengaged. Another painting from his early period, *Brass Band*, was initially assailed by government censors, who mistook the central figure, a slide trombone player, for Lenin. As disturbing as *Reflection* and *Brass Band* were to the censors, Polis and Purmale also agitated artist colleagues by flouting professional protocol when they organized an exhibit of these and similar works in 1975, prior to their graduation from the Academy. Before this, no artist had mounted his or her own solo exhibition without an official invitation—an invitation that would have been withheld before graduation in any case. Their initiative and self-confidence were extremely unusual.

Missing from Latvian Hyperrealism was the ecological dissent couched in many Estonian exemplars. Likewise, the critique of consumerism endemic in Western Photorealism had no imperative in a place where luxury could still be defined as owning a washing machine. As the Latvian standard of living decreased in the later years of

Fig. 8:6
Juris Zvirbulis
Street Musician, 1978
Oil on canvas
105 × 119.5 cm

Fig. 8:7
Lolita Zikmane
Spring: White Locomotive,
1977
Etching and aquatint
42.6 × 49.9 cm

the Brezhnev era, Daina Riņķe and Juris Zvirbulis painted absurd scenes of traffic-clogged superhighways, *kolkhoz* vehicles buried by produce, and worker housing-block idylls constituting nothing less than Socialist Surrealism.

A Surrealist disposition *per se* rarely manifested itself in Latvia before the 1970s. The earliest and most surprising exception to this was Ilze Zemzare (b. 1940), a textile artist who, for a short period in the late 1960s, created a number of paintings and an assemblage in a naive Surrealist style, issuing from a proto-feminist viewpoint. The perilous status of modern woman is rendered concrete in *A Woman's Life*, her odalisque form menaced from below by monstrous elements that could represent anything from negative social forces to her own fears. Shortly thereafter, in the early 1970s, Zemzare's husband Uldis Zemzaris (b. 1928) produced an exceptional series of Surrealist paintings that recall the legendary work of Estonian Ullo Sooster (1924–1970), a patriarch in the Moscow underground art community of the 1960s. Zemzaris was not only inspired by Sooster, but he maintained close ties with like-minded Olaf Maran, who was quietly working as a Surrealist in Tallinn. After these remarkable brief experiments, Zemzare returned to decorative textile

design, Zemzaris began working in his well-known realist fashion, and the mantle was passed to Auseklis Bauškenieks (b. 1910), Juris Dimiters (b. 1947), Lolita Zikmane (b. 1941), and Maija Tabaka (b. 1939), who developed their highly idiosyncratic oeuvres.

A genuine outsider to the establishment, Bauškenieks began painting in his hallmark Divisionist style in the 1950s, then disappeared from view until an exhibition in 1975, when his fantastic imagery and satirical visions of high culture and modernity (Pl. 8:5) amused the public and were held in suspicion by the authorities, who sometimes prevented their display. Dimiters is another artist of unusual humor—although, as a third-generation member of the Skulme dynasty, his critical wit was hardly the result of exclusion from the inner circles. After a sophisticated Hyperrealist phase, he painted a series of enigmatic still lifes (Pl. 8:9) whose bright palette and playful forms belie the sinister connotations of certain recurrent motifs: cages, containers, and contradictory elements *à la* Magritte. Cryptic in quite another way, Lolita Zikmane's graphic work most resembles the variant of Surrealism common throughout the U.S.S.R. in the 1970s: a density of mundane objects whose verisimilitude and juxtaposition encourage a narrative reading but whose blatant incongruities thwart rational assembly. For example, her etching *Spring: White Locomotive* (Fig. 8:7) has a phantom train violating a glade filled with turkeys.

Surrealism's legacy of alienation and disturbance most informed the work of Maija Tabaka, which accounted for her early difficulties with officialdom. Her conflation of psychosexual angst and visual dissonance in paintings like *Narcotic Jungle* (Pl. 8:15) is without precedent in Latvian art. Tabaka created this work in 1977 during a year-long residency in West Berlin, where the liberal environment no doubt amplified its histrionic effects. The painting, claimed by her biographer to be an emblem of Soviet culture,[44] is in fact part of the so-called *West Berlin Cycle*, whose other components chart the social terrain in cosmopolitan Europe and contain portraits of newfound German colleagues.

Tabaka was among the first to take advantage of greater access to the outside world. In 1973, she was one of twenty artists represented in the first exhibition of contemporary Latvian art to be shown beyond the Socialist sphere in almost forty years. This was organized in Düsseldorf by émigré Valdis Āboliņš (1939–1984), whose own participation in the Fluxus movement was inspiring to many Latvians, mostly by virtue of their collective inexperience with flamboyant irreverence and international celebrity. Moreover, his role as executive secretary of Berlin's Neue

Gesellschaft für bildende Kunst (NGBK) conferred prestige on the objects of his attention, and thus, when Āboliņš sponsored Tabaka's year abroad, the hostility she had endured in Riga suddenly dissipated.[45] Indeed, her solo exhibition upon her return drew record attendances and appreciative reviews.[46] With her newly elevated status, Tabaka popularized, in turn, the work of significant artists of the diaspora, like Edvīns Strautmanis (1933–1993) of the Hell's Kitchen group of Abstract Expressionists.

It is no small irony that the distinctly leftist politics of NGBK made possible the cultural exchanges that helped alleviate the predicament of Latvian artists isolated by decades of Communism. Extending that irony, Āboliņš arranged an NGBK exhibition of Soviet revolutionary art in 1977, including works by Drēviņš and Klucis that further validated their radical ideas back in a homeland they never cared to visit.[47] One year later, in Riga, Valdis Celms (b. 1943), Andulis Krūmiņš (b. 1943), and Artūrs Riņķis (b. 1942) exhibited Constructivist-inspired Kinetic sculptures in the show "Form, Color, Dynamic," while Māris Ārgaļis (b. 1954), Ānda Ārgaļi (b. 1943), and Jānis Borgs (b. 1946) created sculpto-architectural works for the city's public spaces, paying homage to the early avant-garde and at the same time extrapolating qualities from Minimalist installations in the West. Veiled threats from officials may have resulted in Māris and Ānda Ārgaļi's lamentable decision to leave the art profession altogether.

Some of these projects were realized within the context of the public festival "Mākslas dienas"—"Days of Art"— which lasted for ten to fourteen days every April, centered in Riga. From its inception in 1978, "Days of Art" became a venue for experimentation because of its temporary, improvisational format. In 1982, for instance, three emergent talents, Aija Zariņa (b. 1954), Ieva Iltnere (b. 1957), and Jānis Mitrēvics (b. 1957), covered tramway cars with bold graphics, not unlike the contemporary graffiti artists of New York. In Riga, however, there was the unwanted onus of comparison with Bolshevik progenitors: namely the agit-trains of the Revolution. Today, the work of these three painters, while consistently addressing the historical parameters of Latvian cultural expression, shows no evidence of political didacticism.

Joint Baltic exhibitions of the late 1970s also expanded artistic discourse and underscored national singularities within the homogenizing Soviet culture. In 1979, Jānis Borgs organized an exhibition of Estonian and Lithuanian graphics in Riga that introduced Latvians to the Estonian hybrid of abstraction, Conceptualism, and Minimalism founded by Tõnis Vint (b. 1942). Yet, contrary to the often-heard comment that Estonians inspired such tendencies in the other Balts,[48] it was Vint's superior knowledge of *raksti*, Latvian folk ornament, as revealed in a Riga lecture, that made a far deeper impression on local artists, stunned that a neighbor knew more than they did about their ancient history.[49] In fact, some Latvian critics today take issue with the notion that Estonian art was more progressive in the 1970s, noting that it was derivative of Finnish models that were themselves collateral.

When most reform-minded artists in the Baltic, regardless of ethnicity, were finally graduating from stylistic apprenticeship at the start of the 1980s, scenographer and graphicist Ilmārs Blumbergs (b. 1943) stood apart as having joined the pan-European cultural dialogue some years before. His fluency in the aesthetics of process art and installation was already evident in his designs for a 1973 Riga production of Andrejs Upīts's *Joan of Arc*, the stage metamorphosing from a Minimalist cavity into an assemblage in the Arte Povera style. Blumbergs's graphic work won international acclaim for its uncontrived Expressionism, in which his lyrical use of calligraphic line and exuberant color are piqued and monitored by a countervailing impulse toward obliteration and the grotesque. Blumbergs is rare among his Latvian peers in that he suffers no *horror vacuui*, preferring spare compositions that elegantly bear grand literary allusion (Fig. 8:8). Painter Henrihs Vorkals (b. 1946) was also working in a Minimalist manner at that moment, his watercolors articulating subtle intellectual processes as clearly as they described physical form. His meditative compositions proved to be influential to the next generation of graphic artists.

Latvia's belated and incomplete experience of foreign trends positioned a new generation of artists favorably

Fig. 8:8
Ilmārs Blumbergs
(Untitled), 1978
Lithograph
56.6 × 74.2 cm

(and quite fortuitously) vis-à-vis the contemporary international scene of the 1980s. For Miervaldis Polis, it was a truncated evolution from Hyperrealism to appropriation, under whose auspices Polis reoriented aspects of the Latvian and European cultural canons within a Postmodern, late-Socialist mindset (Pl. 8:1).[50] The formal revolution in Latvian applied arts continued long enough to be concurrent with the Pattern and Decoration movement and its introduction of craft into the Western institutional mainstream. Experimentation with Kinetic sculpture coincided with the widespread recovery of the Constructivist tradition in the West. And contact with the vestiges of Fluxus occurred at a moment when the possibility of oblique but divergent political expression arose within the art and literature of the Soviet Union.

An artists' collective of such a temperament, called Workshop for the Restoration of Unfelt Sensations, was founded by Juris Boiko (b. 1955) and Hardijs Lediņš (b. 1955) in 1982. Boiko, an autodidact painter and writer, and Lediņš, an architect, were joined by fashion designer Dace Šenbergs (b. 1967), and architects Aigars Sparāns (b. 1955) and Imants Žodžiks (b. 1955). Workshop incorporated photography, earth art, video, music, computer imagery, product design, and *couture* into its performances and exhibitions, expanding both the means and semantics of Latvian art. Whereas Andris Grīnbergs first drew inspiration from hippie culture and Twiggy, Workshop members quoted Zandra Rhodes[51] and emulated the raucous presentation manner and eclectic visual style of the East Village scene. However, this was not merely a succession of inspirations. While Grīnbergs's exuberance and sensuality repudiated Soviet puritanism, Workshop, its very name alluding to conditions of stricture and privation, issued broader challenges to a system that was menacing the indigenous culture.

Boiko and Lediņš began staging private, existentialist actions in the countryside with subtle political implications. Their 1983 *Walk to Bolderāja* is reminiscent of the concurrent "country walks" of Moscow's Collective Actions Group, but the Latvians' route was more politically resonant: Bolderāja, the point at which land meets sea (and where Latvia might hope to meet the West), was to be approached via a railroad track that, alas, terminated at a nuclear submarine base. Their journey, resolute but incomplete, was a testing of, then acquiescence to, geopolitical limits, just as it was a cathartic, willed amnesia on the part of Boiko, whose parents had been railroaded to Siberia and whose writings dealt candidly with the Soviet occupation. Other actions plotted arbitrary boundaries within Latvian historical identity, much like the shifting frontier in Žodžiks's work *A Line in Kurzeme* (Kurzeme being a province that has endured more than its share of political division over the ages).

However, it was the boundary separating a global postindustrial ethos from local sensibilities that increasingly interested Lediņš. The foreign referents of a Workshop performance like *The Opening* of 1985 were often irreconcilable with local experience. If its passage subtitled "Old History" was deliberately anachronistic, another passage titled "Postmodern Nightlife" was equally, though unintentionally, so. This disjunctive state, this discrepancy between Latvian aspirations and Soviet reality, was indicated, perhaps inadvertently, by the theory of Approximate Art developed by Lediņš. The phrase "Approximate Art," in spite of its loftier ambitions of examining the nature of art and creative production within a world of evolving technologies, better described the local situation where advanced technology was unavailable. Latvian artists would have to effect computer-generated graphics by drawing pixels by hand, or replicate ordinary color photographic processes by tinting black and white aviation film with home-brewed vegetable dyes.[52] Without even trying—or because they tried so hard—Latvian artists were fully invested in that feature of Postmodern culture, the simulacrum.

The birth of a cohesive, indigenous contemporary milieu has since been traced to 1984 and an exhibition titled "Nature, Environment, Man," held in St. Peter's Church in Riga.[53] True to its implied theme of interrelationships, the show included almost a hundred artists of various generations and diverse stylistic strains, but the impetus of Latvian artistic culture was clearly situated in the work of two dozen younger participants, most in their twenties and thirties. While officials were not quite able to pinpoint a subversive political message in the quixotic action by Indulis Gailāns (b. 1962)—erecting and tearing down a fence—an installation by several artists was clearly iconoclastic. Both a life-size sculptural rendition and a *tableau vivant* version of Leonardo's *Last Supper* were located where the altar once stood in this desecrated church, stationing onlookers (and, best of all, cultural bureaucrats) in the approximate position of Judas. Elsewhere, what was one to make of an organic automobile by Andris Breže (b. 1958), the nude model in a chamber of shattered mirrors by Ojārs Pētersons (b. 1956), or the Postmodern haystack by Juris Putrāms (b. 1956)? These artists, who first exposed the Latvian public to installations, would, in the coming years, extend the genre in international venues.

They, together with Ivars Mailītis (b. 1956), had a group

exhibition in conjunction with "Days of Art 1985" that was closed by the Cultural Ministry during the first month of Gorbachev's ascendancy, and its curator dismissed from her post in the Young Artists' Union.[54] Such official interference continued well into the 1980s. Mailītis, for example, was prevented from producing his poster *C'est la Vie* (Pl. 8:16), which slyly equated Soviet society with a sinking ship, its monumental rats jumping overboard while the populace sits passively in lifeboats. Ivars Poikāns (b. 1952) was continually berated for his pessimistic depictions of local life, showing its pollution, obese citizens, and, as in the paintings *Sauna* and *Bathhouse* (Pls. 8:13, 8:14), pervasive antisocial behavior.

Even so, *glasnost* occasioned a veritable revival of Situationism, that confrontational movement in Western Europe whose art and ideas helped shape the student unrest of May 1968. Mailītis, for example, staged a blasphemous action for the Great Socialist Revolution holiday youth dance in 1987, titled *Aurora and the Worm*, in which the historic battleship Aurora battled a huge black worm, while Tsar Nicholas II and Orchestra and cartoon character Iskra (Spark [of the Revolution]) contributed to the mayhem from the sidelines.[55] Another action was designed to rouse shoppers from the torpor of standing in ever-present queues, resulting in the age-old charge of "hooliganism."[56] Then, during a film festival, a giant serpent made from fabric with an erotic repeat-pattern designed by Sergejs Davidovs (b. 1959) and Krišjānis Šics (b. 1961) encircled the old Orthodox cathedral and embroiled the fabric's manufacturer in controversy.[57] And as late as 1987, installation and performance artist Oļegs Tillbergs (b. 1956) would find himself escorted away from his action *The Accident* by police. It was no accident that the sight of Tillbergs lying partially within a metal cage in a central square of Riga drew a large crowd. The spectacle sparked a rampage through Old Riga by hundreds of disaffected youths, some of whom received international exposure in the acclaimed documentary about the prevailing spiritual malaise, *Is It Easy to Be Young?*, by cinematographer Juris Podnieks (1950–1993).[58] Shouting liberationist slogans, they ran past the quarantined Freedom Monument toward the Intourist hotel that housed foreign visitors to the "Days of Art". It may have been the twilight of an authoritarian society, but the KGB could still correctly identify Tillbergs's metaphor of dissent.

Compared to the situation in Russia, the local benefits of *perestroika* were so belatedly realized in official culture that many Latvians doubted the authenticity of the reforms. Nonetheless, emboldened artists exhumed the nation's traumas under annexation and made these their subjects. Tillbergs commemorated the mass-deportations of 1941 with a performance and installation of coffins in a switching yard. Fiber artisan Inese Mailīte (b. 1959) and husband Ivars Mailītis honored and helped return to public dialogue the mass graves in Siberia with their totemic sculptures, whose anthropomorphic wrapped-textile forms evoke the winding of shrouds and the transformational powers of cocoons. Figures within this series were then used in their performances, such as *People as Flags*, a ritual of displacement, and also a solemn hoisting of the sculptural forms over the rooftops of Riga at a time when the Latvian national flag was rehabilitated and flown for the first time in fifty years. To Mailīte and Mailītis, however, theirs was the antithesis of a victory monument.[59]

Sculptor Ojārs Feldbergs (b. 1947) enacted what might be called a secular Stations of the Cross in his work *Simple Stone*, performed on the 1989 anniversary of the deportations. Feldbergs subjected ten stones to tortures familiar to any able KGB agent, among them burning, drowning, shooting, and solitary confinement. The abused stones were then displayed on sledges (implying exile in the *taiga*) and eulogized in a corresponding series of poems by Uldis Bērziņš.[60] Others, like Andris Breže and Leonards Laganovskis (b. 1955), redressed aspects of Soviet history

Fig. 8:9
Dace Lielā
Still Life with Sunset, 1986
Oil on canvas
79 × 99 cm

with works that mimicked and thus trivialized labor heroes, gulag architecture, and other staples of repression. Still others, like Dace Lielā (b. 1957) (Fig. 8:9) and Kristaps Ģelzis (b. 1962), behaved as though nothing had ever come between Latvia and its westward orientation— as if naming the evil (or its banality) was acquiescence to its persistent effect.

Latvian art's final and most spectacular act of rebellion against Russian imperialism unfolded as the nation wrested itself free from the Soviet Union. In 1988, archi- tects Juris Poga and Aigars Sparāns, with Ivars Mailītis, submitted a proposal to an architectural competition jury convened in Moscow to select the Soviet pavilion to be built at Expo '92 in Seville. Out of 164 entries, their design was chosen and constructed.[61] Unbeknown to key members of the jury, the winning version was based on the form of an ancient Latvian casket. By the time of the exposition, the pavilion had become identified solely with Russia, represented on the world stage by a mausoleum for the Soviet system it had inflicted on the Latvian people.

Notes

Many thanks to Pēteris Bankovskis, former editor of *Literatūra un māksla* [Literature and art], for his valuable input when I was beginning to write this essay. He was generous with his impressions of several artists discussed early in the chapter, and he confirmed interpretations that I might have otherwise considered mere intuition and left unarticulated.

1. An attempt to prove statistically that the repression of Latvian artists was less severe than elsewhere considered neither the high number of artists who fled to the West nor, indeed, the small population of Latvia (as pointed out in Genoveva Tidomane's response to Zigurds Konstants's paper, "Latvijas māksla pēckara gados Staļina totalitārā režīma apstāklos" [Latvia's art in the postwar years, under the conditions of Stalin's totalitarian regime], at the First World Congress of Latvian Sciences, Riga, July 1991). In contemplating the incidents described here, it is helpful to recall that Latvia had 1.4 million inhabitants after World War II, with only slight growth in the ethnic Latvian population thereafter—meaning the dynamics of a national culture in crisis were played out within an artistic milieu similar in size to that of a large American city.

2. Among the fatalities was modernist painter Aleksandrs Drēviņš, followed by Constructivist Gustav Klucis, a former bodyguard of Lenin. Realist painters Voldemārs Andersons and Kārlis Veidemanis also perished. In all, the purges claimed 73,000 Latvians living in settlements in the U.S.S.R., including practically all adult men (Yuri Boyars, "Nationality and Minority Policies in Latvia," *Baltic Observer*, Sept. 24–30, 1992, p. 11). The deaths of Klucis, Andersons, and Veidemanis were particularly ironic, given their instrumental roles in the invention of Socialist Realism.

3. Instead, distinctly minor figures of the interwar period were elevated as pioneers of Socialist art. One genuinely accomplished pioneer was the Bolshevik poster artist Aleksandrs Apsītis (Alexander Petrov).

4. With *glasnost*, assessment of this period by Latvian historians began in earnest. Early articles that addressed the impact of the annexation on the cultural infrastructure include: Skaidrīte Cielava, "Ieskats 40.–50. gadu mākslas dzīvē Latvijā (1944–1956)" [A

view of art life of the forties and fifties in Latvia], pp. 63–77; Māra Markēviča, "Latvijas Padomju Māksli- nieku savienības darbības daži aspekti (1944–1951)" [Several aspects of the activities of the Soviet Latvia Artists' Union], pp. 78–94; and Aija Nodieva, "Staļinisma mākslas politika Latvijā un mākslinieku likteņi" [Stalinism's politics of art in Latvia and the fates of artists], pp. 51–62—all found in *Doma (rakstu krājums)* [Thought (Collected writings)], vol. 1 (Riga: Latvijas Mākslinieku savienība, 1991).

5. Examples of such work, done by Ludolfs Liberts and Oskars Norītis, can be found in Jēkabs Apinis et al., eds., *Latvijas tēlotājas māksla pieci gadi, 1934–1939* [Five years of Latvia's fine arts] (Riga: Latvijas rākstu un mākslas kameras izdevums, 1939).

6. These works also toured the West as part of various Soviet exhibitions in London, New York, etc.

7. Jānis Borgs, "Pretspēku spriegumā diedzēta māksla: Ieskats avangardism attīstībā Latvijā" [Art springs from tension's counterforce: A view of avantgardism's development in Latvia], *Lettische Avantgarde RIGA Latviešu Avangards* (Berlin: Elefanten Press, 1988), p. 77.

8. The Strazdiņš resumé printed in *Latvijas PSR Valsts mākslas akadēmija* [Latvian SSR State Academy of Art] (Riga: Avots, 1989), p. 254, obliquely notes the end of his lectureship in 1949, followed by the citation of a "major work" titled *Taiga* in 1950. Only ten years later, he was profiled in a significant article (Jānis Pujāts, "Zemnieku žanra meistars [Master of the peasant genre] Jēkabs Strazdiņš," *Latviešu tēlotāja māksla III* [Latvian fine art] [Riga: Latvijas valsts izdevniecība, 1960], pp. 129–54), an indication of his work's eminent compatibility with Socialist Realism.

9. See *Revoliutsiia 1905–1907 godov i izobrazitel'noe iskusstvo. Vypusk chetvertyi. Latvia, Estonia* (Moscow: Izobrazitel'noe Iskusstvo, 1989), pp. 12, 42–43.

10. A brief account of this incident and the resulting trial can be found in the memoir of Indriķis Zeberiņš, *Kas vēlas ar mani krampjos vilkties* [Who wants to wrestle with me] (Riga: Māksla, 1992), pp. 75–76, 81.

11. The other "plotters" were actor Miervaldis Ozoliņš, writer Alfreds Sausne, and translators Maija Silmala and Ieva Lase. These and other details of the French Group case were supplied by historian Jānis Kalnačs in

an interview on July 11, 1992.

12. This episode is described by Jānis Siliņš in his chapter on the fine arts in J. Rutkis, ed., *Latvia: Country and People* (Stockholm: Latvian National Foundation, 1967), pp. 534–35. The vituperative atmosphere of the late 1940s and 1950s is evidenced in Aija Nodieva's publication of several public attacks on individual artists' integrity in "Staļinisma mākslas politika Latvijā . . . ," pp. 51–62.

13. Such a goal was articulated in 1919 by Jāzeps Grosvalds, proselytizer of modern art, who nonetheless exhorted his colleagues in Riga to avoid the "mawkishness" of Expressionism and Cubism, and thus tempered the spirit of Latvian modernism from the start. See Jāzeps Grosvalds, "L'Art letton (Les Jeunes)," *La Revue Baltique* 8 (1919): 25–28. Affinities between the early work of Bērziņš and that of modernists Jēkabs Kazaks and Romans Suta can be seen in his painting *Outskirts of Town* and his pastel *Holiday in a Fishermen's Village*, respectively.

14. Examples of this experimentation include *On the Tram* by Valnere, *Amber Seekers* by Iltners, and *Raftsmen* by Bērziņš, all from 1959 and in the Collection of the State Art Museum, Riga.

15. This was Klucis's second reappearance in Soviet exhibitions since his liquidation, the first having happened one year earlier in "Forty Years of Posters and Satire" at the Tretyakov Gallery. Granted, the examples shown were later works by Drēviņš and Klucis, not those from their Rayist, Suprematist, or Constructivist phases.

16. Those honored were Leo Svemps (in 1956), Ansis Artums and Konrads Ubāns (both in 1957). Numerous small, one-day solo shows had been mounted under the auspices of the Artists' Union.

17. All information about Smagiņš was acquired in conversations with Jānis Kalnačs, who has since published the article, "Nomaļš latviešu grafiķis" [A forsaken Latvian graphic artist], *Literatūra un māksla 49* (Dec. 18, 1992). Later in the 1960s, the Academician Jānis Roberts Tillbergs also painted an image of the deportations, but this was discreetly given to a private collector.

18. The sequence of events is detailed in Romuald J.

Pl. 8:12
Džemma Skulme
(Dialogue), n.d.
Oil on canvas
109.4 × 160 cm

Pl. 8:13
Ivars Poikāns
Bathhouse, 1983
Oil on fiberboard
83.5 × 137.5 cm

Pl. 8:14
Ivars Poikāns
Sauna, 1985
Oil on fiberboard
80 × 120.5 cm

Pl. 8:15
Maija Tabaka
Narcotic Jungle, 1977
Oil on canvas
180.7 × 211 cm

Pl. 8:16
Ivars Mailītis
C'est la Vie, 1982
Oil on fiberboard
90.5 × 240 cm

Pl. 9:1
Jonas Mackonis
(To Be or Not to Be), 1981
Oil on canvas
159 × 119 cm

Pl. 9:2
Romanas Vilkauskas
(Untitled), n.d.
Plastic and wood
48 × 20.5 × 19 cm

Pl. 9:3
Algimantas Kuras
Installation, 1976–78
Oil on fiberboard
96.7 × 83.3 cm

Pl. 9:4
Mindaugas Navakas
(Untitled), n.d.
Bronze
46.5 × 23.2 × 27 cm

Pl. 9:5
Vincas Kisarauskas
The Tribe, 1976–77
Oil on canvas
81 × 101 cm

Pl. 9:7
Kazė Zimblytė
Composition, 1970
Mixed media on
fiberboard
122 × 90 cm

Pl. 9:6
**Eugenijus Antanas
Cukermanas**
(Untitled), 1984
Oil on canvas
107.3 × 66 cm

Pl. 9:8 (*opposite*)
Algirdas Griškevičius
Detail of *Leonid's
Portrait*, 1985
Oil on fiberboard
100 × 58.5 cm

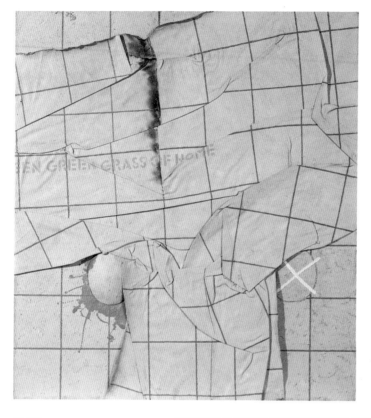

Pl. 9:9
Eugenijus Antanas Cukermanas
Green Green Grass II,
1978
Oil on canvas
83.1 × 76 cm

Pl. 9:10
Linas Katinas
Self-Portrait, 1972
Oil on fiberboard
120.6 × 99.5 cm

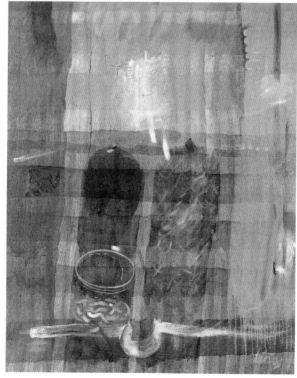

Pl. 9:11
Linas Katinas
Windows, 1979
Oil on canvas
118.5 × 98.5 cm

Pl. 9:12
Antanas Gudaitis
Dramatic Still Life, 1979
Oil on fiberboard
69.3 × 60 cm

Pl. 9:13
Leopoldas Surgailis
Shrovetide Carnival, 1984
Tempera on illustration
board
79.5 × 100.4 cm

Pl. 9:14
Valentinas Antanavičius
Morning, 1979
Mixed media
65 × 57 cm

Pl. 9:15 (*top*)
Jonas Čeponis
Stillness, 1989
Oil on canvas
65.5 × 81.2 cm

Pl. 9:16 (*above*)
Aloyzas Stasiulevičius
Vilnius Sidewalk, 1981
Oil on canvas
80.2 × 100.3 cm

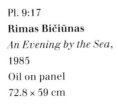

Pl. 9:17
Rimas Bičiūnas
An Evening by the Sea,
1985
Oil on panel
72.8 × 59 cm

Pl. 9:18
Jonas Danilauskas
Full Moon, 1982
Oil on canvas
146 × 114 cm

Pl. 9:19
Raimundas Martinenas
Animal Corps, 1986
Oil on canvas
100.2 × 120.2 cm

Pl. 9:20
Henrikas Natalevičius
From the series *Powerful
People*, n.d.
Oil on canvas
35.2 × 27.3 cm

Pl. 9:21
Leonas Katinas
Composition, 1980
Acrylic on canvas
73.6 × 73.6 cm

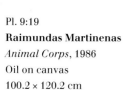

Pl. 9:22
Ričardas Vaitekūnas
Hospital, 1981
Oil on canvas
64 × 91.3 cm

Pl. 9:23
Romanas Vilkauskas
Interior X, 1981
Oil on canvas
90.2 × 110.2 cm

Pl. 9:24
Romanas Vilkauskas
Garage Door, 1982
Oil on canvas
120 × 145 cm

Pl. 9:25
Ričardas Bartkevičius
The Game, 1982
Oil on canvas
89 × 116 cm

Pl. 9:26
Audronė Petrašiūnaitė
(Untitled), 1986
Oil on paper
111 × 100.3 cm

Pl. 9:27
Gintaras Palemonas Janonis
The Statue, 1987
Oil on canvas
116 × 89.5 cm

Pl. 9:28
Algis Skačkauskas
By the Crucifixion, n.d.
Oil on illustration board
88 × 104.5 cm

Pl. 9:29
Henrikas Natalevičius
(Matchboxes), n.d.
Matchboxes, painted with
oil, set in wooden case
31 × 22.8 cm

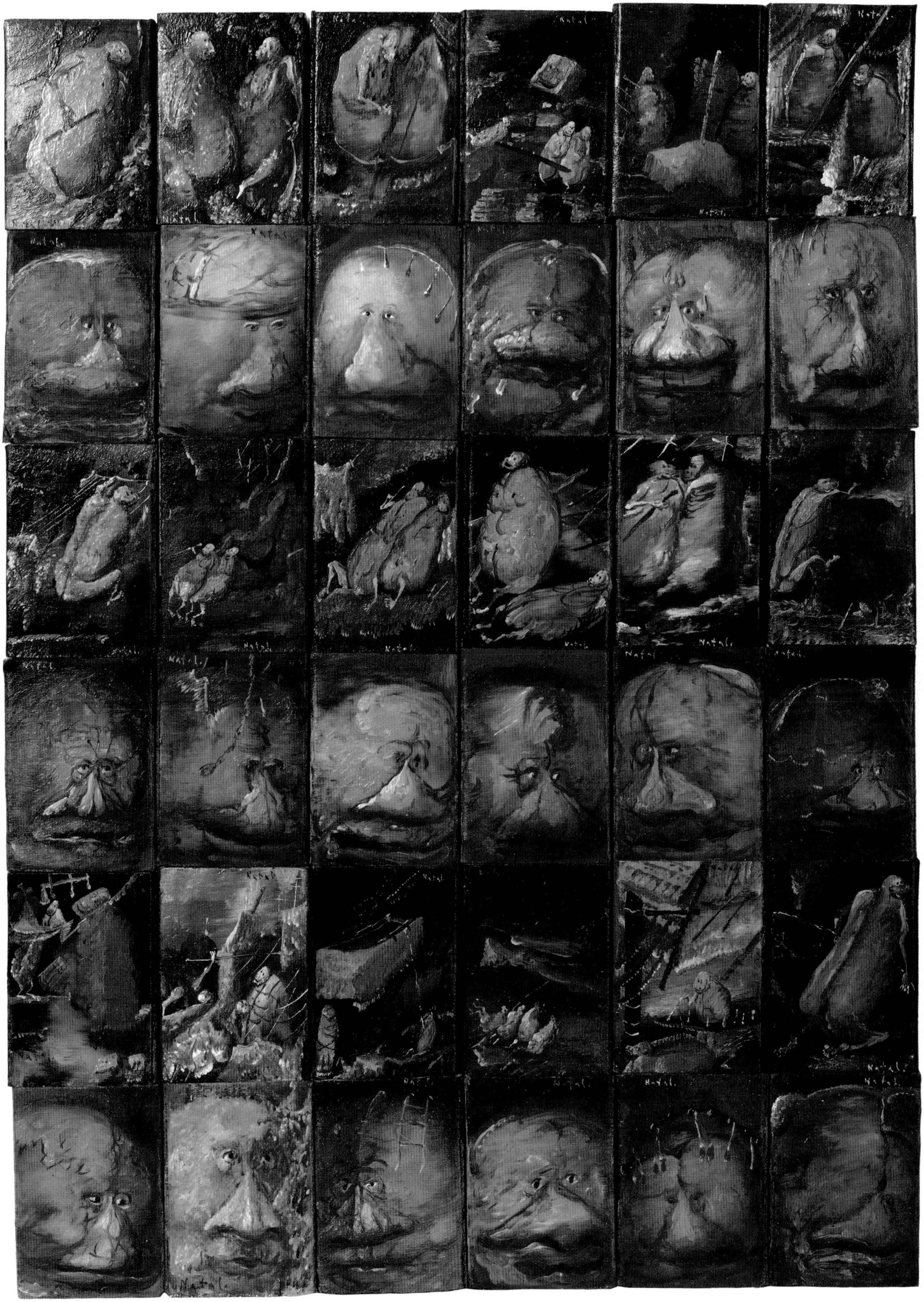

Pl. 10:1
Minas Avetissian
(Untitled), 1961
Oil on canvas
34 × 48.5 cm

Pl. 10:2
Ardashes Hounanian
Cathedral, 1973
Gouache on paper
96.5 × 66.9 cm

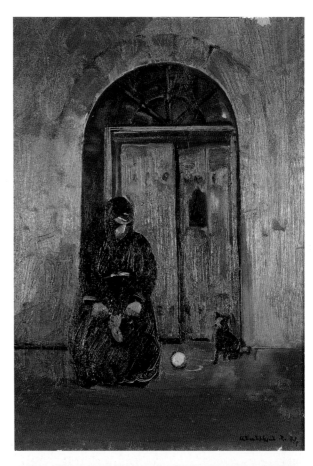

Pl. 10:3 (*above right*)
Hagop Ananikian
Woman at the Door, 1971
Oil on canvas
69.5 × 50 cm

Pl. 10:4
Hagop Hagopian
Outskirts of the Village, 1981
Oil on canvas
73 × 100 cm

Pl. 10:5
Raphael Atoyan
Our Courtyard, 1970
Oil on canvas
90 × 71 cm

Pl. 10:6
Hagop Hagopian
No to the Neutron Bomb!,
1977
Oil on canvas
194 × 298 cm

Misiunas and Rein Taagepera, *The Baltic States: Years of Dependence, 1940–1980* (Berkeley: University of California Press, 1983), pp. 136–41.

19. For a discussion of cultural repression in the Baltic states (and its conclusion that Latvia endured the longest repercussions), see ibid., pp. 155–59.

20. This is stated by Pēteris Bankovskis in his unpublished manuscript, "Some Aspects of Non-Conformist Art in Latvia" (1992), p. 4. Historian Māris Brancis maintains that certain Latvians had the same cosmopolitian influences via frequent trips to Moscow.

21. The preservation of these monuments was nearly miraculous and deserves fuller explanation. Among the most interesting aspects is the Riga curators' decision to preserve secretly works by Klucis ordered to be destroyed by Stalin—work that in its critique of bourgeois Latvian values could hardly appeal to the average nationalist and, conversely, that in its glorification of Stalin could hardly appeal to an anti-Stalinist. Also, an unverified story holds that the Freedom Monument was spared destruction through the intercession of Vera Mukhina, dean of Socialist Realist sculptors, who grew up in its shadow and persuaded the authorities of its inherent aesthetic worth, irrespective of its bourgeois origins and nationalist *raison d'être*.

22. Interview with State Art Academy archivist and academic advisor Genoveve Tidomane, July 2, 1992.

23. This position was recently restated by curator Helēna Demakova in her unpublished essay, "The Fortress 'Painting'/Site: Latvia" (1992).

24. Examples of these can be seen in the reproduction album *Rūdolfs Pinnis. Glezniecība* [Rūdolfs Pinnis: Painting] (Riga: Liesma, 1990).

25. The risk of comparing these lesser-known painters to acknowledged Russian masters is, of course, the diminution of Latvian creativity. A more relevant antecedent for Šēnbergs, for example, would be the Symbolist phase of Jānis Rozentāls, one of Latvia's greatest painters.

26. Rasma Lāce, "Dažas latviešu padomju glezniecības attīstības problēmas" [Several problems of the development of Soviet Latvian painting], *Latviešu tēlotāja māksla IV* (Riga: Latvijas Valsts izdevniecība, 1962), p. 45.

27. See Valerijs Prokofjevs, "Abstrakcionisms un naturālisms," *Māksla*, 17 (1963): 13–14; and 18 (1963): 11–12.

28. The excerpt from Matvejs's treatise *Faktura* (originally published in St. Petersburg in 1914) was titled "Materiālu sakopojums" [Combination of materials], and appeared in *Māksla* 37 (1968): 17, preceded by a reprinted account of his career by his widow Varvara Bubnova. One wonders if the writings of Matvejs had any bearing on Lidija Auza's mixed-media experimentation.

29. For example, Uga Skulme's Cubist landscape *Jēkabmiests* of 1921 was reproduced in *Latviešu tēlotāja māksla V* (Riga: Liesma, 1968), p. 241; the Constructivist photomontages of Klucis had already been seen in Artūrs Eglītis, "Latviešu padomju tēlotājas mākslas pionieri" [Pioneers of Soviet Latvian fine art], *Latviešu tēlotāja māksla III*, pp. 271–78.

30. A photograph of one such object was reproduced in *Māksla* 30 (1966): 17. This design phenomenon, incidentally, was contemporaneous with the work of Lev Nusberg in Moscow.

31. Logina's work was—no surprise—a seascape, as listed in the exhibition catalogue *Vsesoiuznaia khudozhestvennaia vystavka* (Moscow: Gosudarstvennaia Tretyakovskaia Galleria, 1946), p. 40.

32. A 1987 personal exhibition of Logina's cosmos-themed works in Riga's Pēterabaznīca drew the startled approval of actual cosmonauts visiting the show. Information from a conversation with Pēteris Bankovskis (July 1, 1992) and interviews with historian Irēna Bužinska (July 1, 1992, and June 3, 1993).

33. Dialogue between Andris Breže and Ojārs Pētersons, printed in the catalogue *Henrihs Vorkals, Andris Breže, Ojārs Pētersons, Juris Putrāms* (Riga: Latvijas PSR Mākslas Fonds, 1987), n.p. This café is now contained within the Casinos Latvija complex on Kaļķu iela.

34. Information courtesy of historian Māris Brancis, from a letter dated July 31, 1992.

35. Interview with historian Ruta Čaupova, June 10, 1993. In addition, the catalogues, containing an essay by Čaupova, were confiscated and destroyed.

36. Interview with Ivars Mailītis (June 11, 1993), one of the concealed artists; confirmed in subsequent conversations with the other eavesdroppers, Andris Breže and Ojārs Pētersons.

37. There is an uncorroborated account by a former KGB agent of an incident in which Skulme was called to defend an abstract work while she toured an exhibition with an official from the Cultural Ministry. She reportedly invoked the hallowed name of Socialist Realism and proceeded to construct an untenable (yet persuasive) rationale as to why the nonconformist work in question satisfied the conditions of official art.

38. He went on to admit: "Let us remember that in fact we have always sanctioned (tacitly or even officially) everything that has acquired international circulation; only we have been late by up to ten years." Quoted in the cultural weekly *Sirp ja Vasar*, Oct. 29, 1971; cited in *Estonian Events* 29 (1971): 5.

39. Films by these directors were openly screened by the Cinematographers' Union. Information about Grīnbergs and the hippie scene is taken from conversations with Grīnbergs and Māra Brašmane (July 13, 1992) and subsequent correspondence.

40. Biographical information about Delle was supplied by historians Jānis Kalnačs and Edvarda Šmite.

41. This is not the same Jānis Osis who painted the celebrated Socialist Realist work *Latvian Fishermen*.

42. Nonetheless, this figured prominently in Skaidrīte Cielava's fawning article, "Latviešu mākslinieku ļeņiniāna" [Latvian artists' Leniniana], *Latviešu tēlotāja māksla VIII* (Riga: Liesma, 1980), verso p. 16. For the 1991 Riga exhibition "Interferenzen: Kunst aus Westberlin, 1960–1990," it was pressed into service as part of an installation by German Ulrich Baehr parodying cults of personality, a fundamental misreading of the work.

43. The censors' mistaking the trombonist for Lenin was explained by Polis in conversation, June 20, 1994. Polis of late rejects the labeling of his work as Photorealist, favoring the neologism "PhantomArt." See Niels Peter Juel Larsen, "Im Schatten des Gulag," *Zeit Magazin* (Mar. 27, 1992): 34. But his early works give little evidence of his later philosophical concerns.

44. This interpretation was given by Zigurds Konstants in *Maija Tabaka* (Rīga: Liesma, 1983), n.p.

45. The stimulative effect of Āboliņš on Latvian culture (and Tabaka's reputation) is explained by Jānis Borgs in "Ein Neger unter Eskimos im keuschen Riga," *Valdis Āboliņš, Miss Vietnam mit rohem Hering im Mund: Fluxus, Realismus und die Rīga-Konnekschen* (Berlin: Elefanten Press, 1988), pp. 81–94.

46. Noted in an introduction by Inese Riņķe in the catalogue *Contemporary Soviet Painters from Riga, Latvia* (New York: Eduard Nakhamkin Fine Arts, 1989), p. 6.

47. This irony extended into recent times, when the contemporary Latvian artists showcased in NGBK's 1988 exhibition "Lettische Avant-garde RIGA Latviešu avangards"—artists working to liberate Latvian culture—were said to be greeted in Berlin by hosts waving little red flags.

48. Most recently, Estonian curator Ants Juske endeavored to rank the Baltic nationalities in terms of inventiveness, as noted by Marja-Terttu Kivirinta in *Siksi* 1 (1992): 45.

49. Interview with Irēna Bužinska, July 1, 1992. As a direct consequence, Ansis Epners made a film, with Vint's collaboration, about *raksti* titled *Lielvardes josta* [The belt of Lielvarde]. Estonian artist Leonhard Lapin also gave two revelatory lectures about early Estonian modernism.

50. Polis also formulated theories of representation, published as "Dažas hipotēzes par mākslas, zinātnes un tehnikas sakarībām" [Several hypotheses about the interrelationship of art, science and technique], *Māksla* 98: 6–9. His strength as a philosopher emboldened Polis to defend work before a censorship committee with recondite art theory (Larsen, "Im Schatten des Gulag," p. 34).

51. The progressive British fashion designer is quoted in Hardijs Lediņš, "Zeitgeist und geistige Toposphäre," *Lettische Avantgarde RIGA Latviešu avangards*, p. 30.

52. Information on photographic technique from Boris Mangolds's introduction to the catalogue, *Stepping Out of Line: Contemporary Photography from Latvia* (Millersville, Penn.: Millersville University, 1992), n.p.

53. Borgs, "Pretspēku spriegumā diedzēta māksla," p. 77. Compelling images of this exhibition were reproduced in the Hungarian journal *Mozgó Világ* 12 (1984): 18–30. Incidentally, the moment of inspiration for "Nature, Environment, Man" came while the three young artists were hidden in the closet by Ojārs Ābols, listening to his recollections of the previous Venice Biennale.

54. Conversation with Andris Breže, June 30, 1991.

55. Interview with Ivars Mailītis, June 11, 1993.

56. Interview with Irēna Bužinska, July 1, 1992.

57. According to one of its creators, Sergejs Davidovs (interview, July 7, 1992), the factory director was fired. The ensuing trouble with the authorities recalls the predicament of Tonis Vint when he published a folio of erotic images in a 1974 Estonian youth magazine. This is described in Stephen C. Feinstein, "The Avant-Garde in Soviet Estonia," in Norton T. Dodge, ed., *New Art from the Soviet Union: The Known and the Unknown* (Washington, D.C.: Acropolis Books, 1977), p. 32.

58. Podnieks himself is deserving of further discussion in future studies of dissident Latvian culture, having occupied a position in the national psyche analogous to that of, say, Václav Havel in Czechoslovakia.

59. Photodocumentation of these by Michael Lange can be found in Larsen, "Im Schatten des Gulag," pp. 20–21, 24–27.

60. Images of Feldbergs's sculpture series are reproduced, with the Bērziņš poems, in *Parasts Akmens* [Simple stone] (Riga, 1992).

61. Not surprisingly, the covert symbolism is unmentioned in an article published mid-project by Jānis Lejnieks: "Expo-92. Maskava-Sevilja (caur Rigu)" [Expo '92: Moscow-Seville (via Riga)], *Māksla* 4 (1989), pp. 6–9. The true meaning was revealed with great relish by Mailītis and Poga (June 11, 1993).

9 | Semi-nonconformist Lithuanian painting

Alfonsas Andriuškevičius

Lithuanian art has had a long history of involvement with historical, mythological, and folkloristic subjects. Even in the latter half of the nineteenth century, when Lithuania was under tsarist rule, the use of these themes was a form of political resistance and assertion of a national cultural identity. At the beginning of the twentieth century, the painter and musician Mikalojus Konstantinas Čiurlionis (1875–1911) became the founder of modernism in Lithuanian art. He was an important influence on many later painters who would find inspiration and spiritual sustenance in the regional folk tradition, especially as Lithuania's national consciousness grew during its period as an independent state between the two world wars. The expression of a national cultural identity through art survived the difficult Stalin years following World War II and continued into the Khrushchev-Brezhnev period, during which the line between official and unofficial art became less clear.

In the period from Stalin to Gorbachev, it is sometimes difficult to determine which Lithuanian artists should be classified as conformists and which as nonconformists. One can find a few clear-cut conformist artists at one extreme and an even smaller number of radical nonconformists at the other. But what about the majority, who are in-between? These are the gifted Lithuanian painters who were given an opportunity to exhibit their works or to have them reproduced in contemporary art publications, such as *Tapyba* [Painting] and *Lietuvos grafika* [Lithuanian graphic art]. However, since at the same time these artists were also undermining the dogmas of Socialist Realism, they were often reprimanded or even punished by the authorities.

This ongoing conflict reflected strong tensions not only between Lithuanian artists and local Party arts officials, but also between Party officials in Moscow and Vilnius, Lithuania's capital, regarding cultural policy. In spite of its declarations of support for national differences, Moscow was not interested in encouraging an emergent Lithuanian national identity or in reviving the region's historical memory. In fact, Moscow's policy was just the opposite. In 1961, for instance, when the fourteenth-century castle in the old Lithuanian city of Trakai was being restored, Nikita Khrushchev's son-in-law, Aleksei Adjubei, published an article in the Moscow daily *Izvestiia*, clearly criticizing the Lithuanian authorities for maintaining the "feudal past." Khrushchev made similar remarks, which led to a reduction in the scale of the restoration effort. But Antanas Sniečkus, the leader of the Communist Party in Lithuania who had permitted the restoration, refused to punish anyone involved, and it continued without much publicity.

This conflict over the preservation of the Lithuanian cultural identity is well expressed in a painting by Jonas Mackonis (b. 1922) known as *To Be or Not to Be*, 1981 (Pl. 9:1). This work must be read on two levels. On one level, it is a typical Socialist Realist painting, complete with heavy excavation equipment clearing the way for some kind of modern construction. On the other level, it shows the destruction of ancient Lithuanian historical monuments to make way for a Soviet architectural atrocity. Which of the two levels of meaning the artist wants to convey is not lost on Lithuanian viewers.

During the period of independence (1918–40), especially after 1930, the art of Lithuania was strongly oriented toward contemporary Western art. This tendency was still alive under the Soviet occupation and manifested itself at every possible opportunity. The Communist authorities in Lithuania, particularly during the post-Stalinist period, could not ignore this fact. It resulted in a more tolerant attitude toward some phenomena of mid-century Western art, though this toleration was of a very special kind. For instance, in 1967, the Minister of Culture, Lionginas Šepetys, a former head of the department of the Central Committee of the Lithuanian Communist Party and later its Second Secretary, published a substantial, well-illustrated book entitled *A Sketch on Modernism*, the first of its kind in Lithuania or the U.S.S.R. In it, the author severely attacked Expressionism, Surrealism, Op Art, and Pop Art. But the book provided many good reproductions of works from these trends, thus providing information about the artists and revealing the principles of their art. At a time when only Impressionism and Socialist Realism were acceptable, Šepetys's book was a rare source of information.

Communist officials, in forcing artists to conform to the Party's purposes, regulated not only the subject matter of art, but also its means of expression. They demanded portrayals of the glorious deeds of the Red Army, the class struggle, the selfless work of the Soviet people, the advancement of workers, and so forth. Stylistically the regime pushed Lithuanian artists toward academic naturalism, although the means of expression was left alone for a while. One could observe this situation first in 1940, when the Soviets initially occupied the country, and later for about two years from 1944 to 1946 when the Soviets returned. After 1956, however, there was a reversal as Lithuanian artists tried to shake off the yoke of earlier restrictions and attempted to regain their own visual language.

Throughout this period, the subject matter used by many artists in their paintings remained unchanged, despite pressures from the authorities. The works of Jonas Švažas (1925–1976) serve as an example in this case. Švažas was one of the organizers of the coup which led to the restoration of post-Stalinist Lithuanian painting. His works are somehow ambiguous: their forms and bright colors say something essential through their connection with universal human values, but their subject matter is in many cases merely propaganda and completely consistent with the official line. One of the artist's early works, *A Worker* (1958), caused a controversy because of its form, but was innocent from the standpoint of subject matter. In the same way, many other gifted Lithuanian artists were nonconformist in the form of their art, yet more or less conformist in subject matter. As a result, they were allowed to exhibit and to have their works reproduced, and as such were able to influence the development of Lithuanian art.

There were other ways of avoiding official restrictions. As a rule, the subject matter of an artwork is revealed in the title, so artists who were trying to sneak their works into official exhibitions often used double titles: a picture had one title at an exhibition and another in an artist's studio. One well-known painting by Vincas Kisarauskas was called *Three Masks* (1976) publicly, in order to obscure its religious content; in private, it was called *Supper at Emmaus*. The Dodge Collection includes a work by Kisarauskas titled *The Tribe*, 1976–77 (Pl. 9:5).

Art authorities during the post-Stalinist period were often less concerned with an artist's studio life than with his or her public statements. This circumstance gave artists a chance to be active on two fronts: one part of their production was meant for official show, the other for their friends and their intimate circle. Painter Silvestras Džiaukštas, for example, was included in almost every official exhibition of the 1960s and 1970s. In these paintings of the "class struggle," one could see the Soviet activist killed by the hand of the partisan "forest brothers," or the Soviet "people's defenders" returning from a combat mission. Džiaukštas's works, at first criticized for their manner of expression, later gained official recognition and became a symbol of modern Socialist Realism. The press made much of them, and they fetched good prices. Meanwhile, in his studio, Džiaukštas worked on canvases of another kind: grotesque pictures dealing with the theme of war and nudes full of dramatic expression. Other artists were even more radical. Sculptor Vytautas Šerys (b. 1931) once exhibited an officially sanctioned portrait of a priest-turned-atheist, while at the same time making a modern crucifix for an altar in a church in Šakiai.

Three factors determined the classification of art as undesirable by the authorities: subject matter, psychological atmosphere, and means of expression. Of course, the authorities preferred artworks dealing with heroic Soviet workers, but what subjects did they prohibit? First of all, any depiction of religious themes in official art was out of the question. Soviet officials not only opposed art dealing with religious subjects but also the use of religious symbols in art. This rule was sometimes carried to ridiculous extremes. At the group exhibition of young artists in Vilnius in 1979, painter Kostas Dereškevičius showed a landscape with a church. It goes without saying that the church tower was topped with a cross. When attending the exhibition opening, the painter was shocked, as was I, to find that the cross had been scraped out by officials of the Artists' Union!

Themes involving the history of Lithuania as an independent state were also a cause for trouble. Portraits of political figures from the past were unacceptable unless they depicted people connected with the so-called "democratic movement." The authorities also discouraged symbols that might suggest a negative attitude toward Soviet social reality. At a group exhibition held at the National Library in 1983, the authorities showed great concern over three works by Romanas Vilkauskas that depicted large doors painted yellow, green, and red—the colors of the outlawed flag of independent Lithuania— each secured with a huge padlock. Was the artist saying that Soviet society was closed off, isolated, locked up? Vilkauskas was required to explain the meaning of his paintings before a meeting of officials of the Artists' Union.

Although he denied the paintings had any political significance, their real meaning was evident to most viewers.

For the Soviet authorities, "figurative pictures" were most favored; landscape paintings and still lifes were considered less important. Consequently, it is not difficult to understand the remark by the well-known figurative painter Sofija Veiverytė (b. 1926) regarding the nonfigurative works of a young artist, Algimantas Kuras (Pl. 9:3). Veiverytė said disparagingly: "Is this stuff worth depicting? One must tackle serious themes!"

The authorities demanded heroic and optimistic artworks. Dramatic works were not favored unless drama was mixed with optimism. This important principle of Socialist Realism was typified by the title of Vsevolod Vishnevsky's popular 1933 play: *Optimistic Tragedy*. Irony was regarded as the opposite of optimistic tragedy. God forbid irony! Irony in art, an inherent trait of modern art according to the critic Ortega y Gasset, was understood by the Soviets as humiliating to the human being, though irony toward the "people's enemies" was permitted. One could use grotesquerie or a cartoon style to depict Soviet enemies, but such behavior toward loyal citizens was not welcomed. As a result, the paintings of Valentinas Antanavičius and the newer works of Arvydas Šaltenis, in which one could feel a dose of irony, were regarded with great suspicion.

Since the Soviet authorities were so concerned with the regulation of subject matter, theme, and symbol, it goes almost without saying that they were opposed to abstract art. They labeled abstraction apolitical and lacking in a positive ideological position: it was deemed hollow art. For a long time, Vasilii Kandinsky, the father of abstract art, was represented in Soviet reference books as a German rather than a Russian artist. With the rise of nationalistic art after the death of Stalin, yet another of abstractionism's vices was detected. Šepetys summarized this defect in his book, *A Sketch on Modernism*: "Abstractionism destroys the most valuable aspect of art, namely, its national character."

Abstract paintings began to be shown in official exhibitions in Lithuania only at the end of the 1980s. Until then, the works of two gifted Lithuanian artists, Kazė Zimblytė (Pl. 9:7) and Eugenijus Antanas Cukermanas (Pl. 9:6), were prohibited from being shown publicly. Both were, from the very beginning, abstract painters. Leonas Katinas, who belonged to an earlier generation, had faced similar problems.

In paintings with recognizable objects, only a moderate degree of distortion of form and color was allowed by Soviet officials. For decades, there was a tendency in Lithuanian art to avoid academic treatment of the human figure. After the Soviet takeover, it was considered improper to distort a figure significantly. When the tendency toward distortion began to manifest itself again following Stalin's death, the Lithuanian authorities were uneasy. A mild directive to artists said: "If you cannot help distorting, distort moderately, please!" However, in the generation following the "reformers," an immoderate degree of distortion typified the work of Kisarauskas, Antanavičius, Šaltenis, and Ričardas Vaitekūnas. More recently, this tendency toward abstraction has been carried forward in the work of Mindaugas Skudutis, Raimundas Sližys, Algis Skačkauskas, and Ričardas Bartkevičius.

Abstraction was not welcomed in landscape painting either. One group of artists who employed distortion in landscape painting irritated officials by using unnatural forms and colors for recognizable objects. Another group used a high degree of abstraction which made it difficult to identify the objects depicted at all. Landscapes of the first kind were produced by artists such as Antanas Gudaitis, Leonas Katinas, Jonas Švažas, Jonas Čeponis, Aloyzas Stasiulevičius, and of the second kind by Vincas Kisarauskas, Algimantas Kuras, Ričardas Vaitekūnas, Linas Katinas, Rūta Katiliutė, and Dalia Kasčiūnaitė.

The authorities also disapproved of two forms of art that were in widespread use in Western art of the twentieth century: collage and assemblage. Undoubtedly, this stand was due to the officials' fear of novelty. Themes, subject matter, and symbols were easier for the functionaries to decipher. They were not capable of grasping the meaning of space, color, line, and composition. They felt that even if the subject matter of a collage or assemblage were positive, the form was often incomprehensible and undesirable. The official argument was simple: "These means were invented by capitalist artists." Collage was introduced into post-Stalinist Lithuanian painting chiefly by Švažas and Stasiulevičius. Assemblage was introduced by Kisarauskas, but the artist who became most noted for his many assemblages was Antanavičius.

Even if an artist painted in a realistic manner and avoided prohibited subject matter, that artist could still be accused of lacking an appropriately positive political attitude. This became quite clear in Lithuanian art when new forms of realism began to emerge in the 1970s. Like many other artists of the time, Algimantas Švėgžda's early work was strongly influenced by Photorealism. This development was not received enthusiastically by the local authorities or by arts officials in Moscow. At the group exhibition of young artists at the Palace of Exhibitions in

Fig. 9:1
Kazė Zimblytė
Silver Man, 1967
Oil and collage on
canvas
100 × 89.5 cm

Vilnius in 1979, Švėgžda first showed several Photo-realistic works, including one which portrayed a pair of jeans. Based on reproductions of the works in a catalogue, Moscow academician A. Lebedev wrote a stinging critique in the Moscow newspaper *Pravda*, condemning Švėgžda for the meticulous depiction of such "stuff." When Vilkauskas later followed in Švėgžda steps, he was even more of a nuisance to the authorities, for his subject matter from time to time contained specific political references (Pl. 9:2). Another example of Lithuanian Photorealism in the Dodge Collection is the massive array of medals in the painting *Leonid's Portrait* (Pl. 9:8), which is by Algirdas Griškevičius (b. 1954).

To some extent, all artists who violated these taboos could be called "nonconformists" (Pl. 9:4). But, of course, there were different degrees of transgression: some violating more, some violating less; those who sought to redeem their sins and those who made no attempt. As I have suggested, truly radical nonconformists in Lithuania were few in number. First among the nonconformist artists were Zimblytė (Fig. 9:1) and Cukermanas (Pl. 9:9). Unlike the work of other artists, theirs was completely abstract and in no way conformed to the dictates of the Communist Party. Their relations with Party officials and with the Artists' Union were further complicated by the fact that Cukermanas had a diploma in architecture and Zimblytė was certified as a textile master.

To be recognized as a painter in the U.S.S.R. one had to have graduated from an accredited art institution and have been awarded a painter's diploma. Since neither Cukermanas nor Zimblytė met these standards, it created conflict when they tried to participate in painting exhibitions. From 1969 to 1990, they were banned from exhibiting at the Vilnius Triennial of painting, and not a single picture by them was reproduced in six books on Lithuanian painting published in Vilnius between 1961 and 1987. Zimblytė was not allowed to hold a personal show of her works in the main exhibition hall of the State Museum of Art until 1988, and Cukermanas not until 1990. The works of Kisarauskas, Antanavičius, and Linas Katinas were less strictly banned (Pls. 9:10, 9:11).[1] But these five artists were at the extreme end of the spectrum of nonconformity. For the majority of artists whose work violated Soviet taboos yet was more or less acceptable and could be exhibited publicly, the proper name is "semi-nonconformists."[2]

Works by the more radical nonconformists could only be seen in the private apartments of very sophisticated Lithuanian intellectuals. These small exhibitions were often called, with a hint of irony, "salons." In the salon of Judita Šerienė, for example, in the late 1960s and early 1970s the works of Zimblytė, Antanavičius, Linas Katinas, Žilius, and others were exhibited. "Queer" pictures were also shown in the halls or corridors of the Music Academy, the Union of Writers, the Institute of Physics, and the Palace of Artists. It should be noted that the restrictions on exhibiting were not of the same severity in all areas of art. The authorities tended to follow painting and sculpture very closely, but allowed more freedom for those who worked in the field of book design and illustration. Therefore, the art of book design, and graphic design in general, flourished in Lithuania in the 1970s and 1980s. Illustrations were produced not only by graphic masters, but also by painters and sculptors, and were sent by mail to international exhibitions. At home, those who were barred from exhibiting art of another kind were able to take part in book design exhibitions.

The restrictions, taboos, and directives promulgated by Soviet arts authorities during the 1956–86 period were not immutable: they underwent change. Some kinds of art banned during the 1960s were allowed during the 1970s or the 1980s. As a result of these changes, some nonconformist artists, without altering their ways, became semi-nonconformists, and semi-nonconformists became conformists. The easiest way to follow this process and to say something definite about the works of specific artists is to look at the special tribulations, as well as the contributions to the development of

Lithuanian art, of the various generations of artists during these thirty years.

The birth of nonconformist art is due largely to the contribution of the older masters of the pre-Soviet period who influenced the younger post-Stalin generation. In the 1930s, Antanas Gudaitis (1904–1988), a leader of the Ars group, whose members attempted to make Lithuanian art more modern, was an influential representative of pre-Soviet Lithuanian art traditions. His activities as a painter and as a professor at the Institute of Art encouraged a different attitude toward painting from that espoused by Party officials. Gudaitis stressed the importance of art as a specific language and was skeptical of storytelling in painting (Pl. 9:12). He encouraged dramatic painting and the development of new ways in art, but, of course, at the same time was also forced to produce some conformist pictures.

Leonas Katinas (1907–1983) also played an important role, although he, too, contributed to officially approved art. Later, he began to confront the authorities and the unenlightened public as well. The message that his dynamic, vividly colored, semi-abstract landscapes (Pl. 9:21) and still lifes sent to the younger painters was: "This is genuine painting!"

A decisive change took place in the late 1950s and early 1960s with the emergence of a generation of artists born in the late 1920s. Their leader was Jonas Švažas, while other representatives of the generation were Jonas Čeponis (b. 1926), Leopoldas Surgailis (b. 1928), Silvestras Džiaukštas (b. 1928), and Aloyzas Stasiulevičius (b. 1931). They were responsible for two accomplishments. First, they focused on form rather than content. For them, how a painting was made was more important than the subject of the painting. Second, they renewed contacts with Western painting, in particular French, which had been the most important in the prewar period. It must be stressed that other painters, especially artists of the older generation, were also working in this direction, but it was Švažas's generation that gave this phenomenon official status.

At the same time, the leader of this group of artists could not get rid of official demands completely. Like many other artists, Švažas seemed to be caught between expressive freedom (not absolute, of course) and iconographic restrictions (especially concerning subject matter and symbols). Herein lies the reason, I think, for the inability of many of these artists to produce a greater number of important artworks. Their works were not profound enough for the viewers to feel they had made contact with transcendent human values; on the other hand, the paintings failed to represent contemporary social reality either. They were "decorative," in the specific sense of the word used widely by Lithuanian art critics.

Those who compromised their art the least were Čeponis, Stasiulevičius, and Surgailis (Pl. 9:13). This was somewhat easier for Čeponis and Stasiulevičius since they were landscape and still-life painters. Čeponis, painting in the sumptuous and festive tradition of Fauvism, was producing still lifes with flowers and rural and urban landscapes of vivid colors (Pl. 9:15). Stasiulevičius, on the other hand, was influenced by geometric abstraction in his paintings of the roofs of the old town of Vilnius. He was also among the first postwar Lithuanian artists to use collage in his paintings. His thickly impastoed works are distinctive for their original rhythms, contrasts of dimming and flickering surfaces, mysterious light, and unusual choice of color. While these works might be described as "decorative," they are at the same time pregnant with drama (Pl. 9:16).

Nonconformists of the second generation may seem more radical, but in fact they are like a shadow of the first generation. Their works continue the challenge posed by the first generation to the doctrinaire restrictions on subject matter, psychological atmosphere, and means of expression. This second generation includes artists born in or about the early 1930s, including Vincas Kisarauskas (1934–1988), Valentinas Antanavičius (b. 1936), Kazė Zimblytė (b. 1933), and Eugenijus Antanas Cukermanas (b. 1935). Kisarauskas and Antanavičius not only introduced assemblage to Lithuanian painting, they also created a newly dramatic vision of figurative subjects. In his work, Antanavičius often mixes drama with irony (Figs. 9:2, 9:3). To this end, he employs two tactics: the use of a classical compositional scheme and the incorporation of found materials (Pl. 9:14). The various odds and ends and discarded objects Antanavičius uses give his works an effect of "crippled dignity." Even while these paintings demonstrate a subconscious, mythological thinking, they have strong political connotations.

Cukermanas's abstract paintings are unique in several respects. First, one cannot discern in his canvases the gliding movement of the artist's hand; in his more recent works, he dabs at the surface of the canvas with the end of his brush, achieving a specific dynamic effect (Pl. 9:9). This overwhelming dynamism, which often relies on the interaction of large areas of muted color, is unlike that of any other Lithuanian painter. Second, while his colleagues prefer sumptuous, though not necessarily vivid colors, Cukermanas uses meager ones. For this reason, his pictures look ascetic, without any trace of

Fig. 9:2
Valentinas Antanavičius
Washed Up, 1981
Tempera on fiberboard
100.7 × 80 cm

Fig. 9:3
Valentinas Antanavičius
Washed Up II, 1982
Oil on canvas
80 × 62.5 cm

sentimentality. From time to time, he uses letters or other symbols, making it possible to interpret his works in strictly cultural terms. In this way, Cukermanas's work is different from that of most of his colleagues, who employ a culture/nature opposition even when their paintings have no link to natural forms or landscape tradition.

The artists of the third generation, born around 1940, gained visibility at the beginning of the 1970s. The more outstanding among them are Algimantas Kuras (b. 1940), Antanas Martinaitis (1936–1986), Ričardas Vaitekūnas (b. 1940), Kostas Dereškevičius (b. 1937), Arvydas Šaltenis (b. 1944), Algimantas Švėgžda (b. 1941), Linas Katinas (b. 1941), Vladas Žilius (b. 1939), and Rimas Bičiūnas (b. 1945) (Pl. 9:17). They continued to revive and develop the language of art, but were not so constrained by iconographic prescriptions since the political situation had improved somewhat. Some of them, notably Kuras and Šaltenis, produced works that simultaneously expressed universal human values while revealing the bitter truth of contemporary social reality. But the official art functionaries were furious that artists could dare to combine such themes, and I, as a critic, was reprimanded for calling it a "tendency toward deromanticization."

Kuras has exhibited actively since 1963. Although his works do not emphasize subject matter, they can be characterized as dramatic and they have what one critic called "a strong sniff of death" (Fig. 9:4). This mood may reflect the early influence of the English painter Francis Bacon on his work. In addition, Kuras's use of a twilight atmosphere and dark colors, which are both ominous and pleasing, gives his paintings a somber tone. Since the foreground and the far horizon are better lit than the middleground, the viewer must figuratively pass through the dark center; this is a sort of test or trial, like that which might challenge the characters in a mythological story. Finally, the particular type of objects that Kuras depicts also contributes to the special feeling his works engender. He often paints worn-out, abandoned, or ruined artifacts trapped in the dark middleground, unable to reach the horizon and so, by implication, unable to achieve transcendence.

Vaitekūnas bases his paintings on his impressions of the countryside. His beloved motifs are scarecrows, the walls of rural buildings, and the details of peasant interiors. The most distinctive feature of his artistic language is a highly articulated application of color, which he tends to use in its lightest or darkest variations. One can imagine many possibilities hidden in the varying shades. Also, Vaitekūnas uses the so-called double vision of the Symbolists to create a mysterious, polysemous,

Fig. 9:4
Algimantas Kuras
Situation, 1985
Oil on canvas
82.6 × 97.3 cm

Fig. 9:5
Edmundas Saladžius
(Untitled), 1986
Lithograph
32 × 43.5 cm

metamorphosing world, full of danger and the ever-present possibility of death (Pl. 9:22). The work of the graphic master Edmundas Saladžius (b. 1950) is akin to that of Vaitekūnas both in style and spiritual atmosphere (Fig. 9:5). The subject matter of Martinaitis's work derives from fairy tales and legends. But the heroes, with their fantastical anatomical structures and bold coloring, appear threatening. As a result, the atmosphere in Martinaitis's pictures is ambiguous, at once playful and

menacing. His palimpsest-like method of applying paint (many layers are put down, one over another, in short strokes) makes this sense of ambiguity even stronger.

Linas Katinas paints nearly abstract "cosmic landscapes," suggested by his use of space (Pl. 9:10). His paintings resemble the early twentieth-century work of Mikalojus Čiurlionis, perhaps the greatest Lithuanian artist ever. In Katinas's pictures, new worlds are shown in the process of being constructed and deconstructed from elements of culture and nature. There is no peace, only constant change. Compared with Vaitekūnas's paintings, which are "national" in character, Katinas's are "cosmopolitan" and linked to such non-Soviet sources as Eastern philosophy. Katinas's paintings can be called cosmic in another sense: he frequently uses the ovoid form that in mythical thought symbolizes the emerging world. In his works, Katinas combines erudite images with naive form. He is, for instance, one of the first Lithuanian artists to have used bare canvas as a means of expression.

Žilius graduated from the Vilnius Art Institute in 1964, where he specialized in graphic art, a major field of Lithuanian art. His book illustrations and other graphic works were exhibited in officially sponsored group shows throughout Eastern and Western Europe in the late 1960s and 1970s. He also had a number of one-man shows featuring this work in the Soviet Union. In the late 1960s, he made a very powerful series of seven works representing the brutal occupation of Lithuania by the Soviets in 1940 (Fig. 9:6). The authorities objected to this series, as they did to his later turn from graphics to painting. Painting was considered a more ideologically and politically sensitive art form than graphic illustration. But Žilius had been influenced by his growing familiarity with modern Western art. His works from the 1970s include geometric Op Art abstractions and Surrealist images, such as butterflies that suggest flight. These abstract paintings are similar to those of Cukermanas in that they contain little reference to nature or manual labor. However, in their sumptuousness, delicateness, and elegance, Žilius's paintings contrast sharply with Cukermanas's work. When his works were censored in the mid-1970s, Žilius protested by asking for (and receiving) permission to emigrate.

Bičiūnas mixes forms from Lithuanian folk art with the color and style of Fauvism. His pictures are festive and highly decorative. In this respect, he is closer to the spirit of earlier Lithuanian artists, such as Švažas.

At the end of the 1970s, a fourth generation of young nonconformists, collectively nicknamed the "Boschians," began to emerge. Among the most notable artists in this

Fig. 9:6
Vladas Žilius
And Merciless Time, 1967
Ink on paper
23.3 × 16 cm

group were Mindaugas Skudutis (b. 1948), Raimundas Sližys (b. 1952), Henrikas Natalevičius (b. 1953) (Pl. 9:20), Bronius Gražys (b. 1952), Raimundas Martinenas (Pl. 9:19) and Romanas Vilkauskas (b. 1947). The dominant feature of their painting was the depiction of evil. In official Soviet art, evil is generally made banal, but in the work of the Boschians it is represented in a variety of significant ways. As in the historical works of Čiurlionis, evil regains its metaphysical power. However, it is never made literal by direct identification with the Soviet regime or specific social questions. The Boschians also began to employ Surrealist imagery, which was frowned upon by Soviet officials and which until then had only played a very small role in Lithuanian art.

Vilkauskas stands apart from the others of his generation, who were primarily Expressionists or Surrealists. Vilkauskas follows the tradition cultivated by Švėgžda in using Photorealism to depict mailboxes, tools, and garage doors (Pl. 9:24). His Photorealism has evolved to include elements of Symbolism, Conceptualism, and political commentary. Some works by Vilkauskas revive memories of the bad times during the Stalin era, including the deportation of Lithuanians to Siberia after the Soviet occupation. His painting *Interior X*, 1981 (Pl. 9:23) is one of a series of works that depict the use of Soviet newspapers as wallpaper. In this work, the 1940s newspapers have yellowed from exposure to light except where a cross once hung and where, during the German occupation, pictures of saints were placed to hide photos of Stalin. With the Soviet reoccupation of the country at the end of the war, the pictures and the cross were removed, leaving ghostly images of the objects on the wall. Because of their implicitly political content, none of these paintings could be exhibited until 1989.

The primitivist and somewhat Surrealist oils by Jonas Danilauskas (b. 1950), another important artist of this generation, are made dream-like and haunting by his strange use of color and imagery. His *Full Moon*, 1982 (Pl. 9:18), with its framed picture within a picture, is enigmatic and engages the viewer's imagination. While Danilauskas exploits archetypal phenomena and mythical symbols, his works lack the ominous character that pervades the works of Skudutis or Natalevičius (Pl. 9:29).

The fifth and most recent generation of Lithuanian nonconformist artists are those who were born in the late 1950s. These artists, who first gained public attention in the mid-1980s, include Šarūnas Sauka (b. 1958), Vygantas Paukštė (b. 1957), Audronė Petrašiūnaitė (b. 1954) (Pl. 9:26), Algis Skačkauskas (b. 1955), Henrikas Čerapas (b. 1952), Jonas Gasiūnas (b. 1954), Ričardas Bartkevičius (b. 1959), and Gintaras Palemonas Janonis (b. 1959). From the standpoint of style and outlook, this generation is even less unified than previous ones. While Sauka seems to be a sadomasochistic painter under the influence of Surrealism, Paukštė paints a mythical world of harmony expressed in a naive style. The prevailing feature of this generation is an attempt to produce pictures that are "full of hope."[3]

Skačkauskas is a typical representative of Lithuanian Postmodernism. He was influenced by Chagall and the well-established path of Lithuanian Expressionism (Pl. 9:28). Traces of this tradition can be found in every generation, most notably in the work of Gudaitis, Džiaukštas, Antanavičius, Šaltenis, Skudutis, and Skačkauskas. In some respects, Bartkevičius is the artist who is closest in style to Skačkauskas. His works are full of drama and have a strong affinity with those of Francis Bacon and Willem de Kooning (Pl. 9:25). The most interesting aspect of Bartkevičius's work is his mixture of religious and erotic themes. More playful, and therefore closer to Western versions of Postmodernism, is the work of Janonis (Pl. 9:27). He combines elements of figuration, ornamentalism, kitsch, and high art in order to parody classical themes. This is perhaps the clearest signal that a new era of Lithuanian art is coming.

The development of Lithuanian semi-nonconformist art during the years between Stalin's death and the introduction of *glasnost* by Gorbachev was neither linear nor gradual. In terms of subject matter, a great distance was traversed from the depictions of the "class struggle" by official artists and semi-conformists of the first post-Stalinist generation to the Surrealist fantasies and mythical and religious scenes painted by members of the younger generations. On a psychological level, painting moved from shy revelations of subjectivity and drama to cheeky explorations of self-irony and the darkest strata of the subconsciousness. At last, the means of artistic expression in Lithuania had evolved from the morphology of Postimpressionism to the syntax of Postmodernism.

Notes

1. Linas Katinas is the son of Leonas Katinas and signs his works as "Linas" while the father signed his "L. Katinas."

2. The rich body of prints produced by semi-nonconformist Lithuanian artists could not be discussed in this chapter because of space limitations. Therefore, the work of some fine artists who are primarily printmakers have had to be omitted from consideration. Among those of special note are Edmundas Saladžius, Elvyra Kairiukštytė (Fig. 9:7), Mikaloyus Vilutis, Irena Daukšaitė-Gobienė, Algis Jonaitis (Fig. 9:8), Vytautas Šerys, Bronius Rudys (Fig. 9:9), Jūratė Stauskaitė, and Saulius Valius. A number of these artists are represented in the Dodge Collection.

3. In addition to Vygantas Paukštė, of like mind are Audronė Petrašiūnatė, Vaidotas Žukas, Varkulevičius, and Henrikas Čerapas.

Fig. 9:7
Elvyra Kairiukštytė
Youth, 1980
Linocut
65.6 × 86.3 cm

Fig. 9:9 (*right*)
Bronius Rudys
The Second Oratorium, 1986
Graphite and ink on paper
70.3 × 99.9 cm

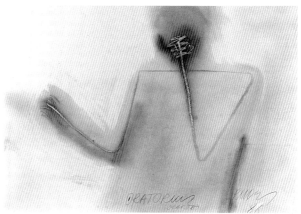

Fig. 9:8
Algis Jonaitis
(Untitled), 1984
Lithograph
47 × 33.6 cm

10 | Light in darkness

The spirit of Armenian nonconformist art

Vartoug Basmadjian

Different cultures unveil different perceptions of light.

—George Yakoulov[1]

Despite being one of the smallest republics of the Soviet Union, the Armenian Soviet Socialist Republic made a significant and distinct contribution to the development of Soviet nonconformist art. Special circumstances and the unique characteristics of Armenian art set it apart from the art produced in Moscow, Leningrad, and other centers of the Soviet Union. Indeed, Armenian art has nurtured its lively independence and national integrity so successfully through the centuries that even when Armenia was incorporated into much larger political entities bent on crushing its spirit and threatening its very existence, its culture survived.

This remarkable resilience and tenacity stems, in part, from the fact that Armenia is one of the oldest cradles of civilization: its art can be traced back almost three thousand years. The capital of present-day Armenia, Yerevan, dates from the seventh century B.C. As Erebouni, it was an active cultural center, and the art of that period developed in the form of sculpture and wall-paintings. In the Hellenistic period, Armenia expanded its borders and, through trade with the West, its culture was influenced by Greco-Roman art.

The adoption of Christianity as the official religion of Armenia in A.D. 301 ushered in a new era. Pagan temples and statues were destroyed and a Christian art prospered. The invention of the Armenian alphabet in the fifth century helped put a national stamp on the native art and literature. The art of medieval Armenia found particularly lively and beautiful expression in illuminated manuscripts (around thirty thousand of which have survived) and in the elaborately carved stone crosses, called *khachkar*, that punctuate the Armenian landscape.

During the subsequent centuries, short periods of Armenian self-rule were generally followed by much longer periods of foreign domination (by the Arabs, Seljuks, Persians, Ottomans, and Russians). The Turkish persecutions of the Armenian people at the end of the nineteenth century culminated in the twentieth century's first genocide: in the 1915 massacres, over a million Armenians were killed. Those who survived this holocaust fled to different parts of the world and formed the Armenian diaspora. The art of the diaspora tended to develop in parallel with the art of the host countries. Of necessity, the art of Soviet Armenia (which became a Socialist republic in 1920) followed the general outlines of Soviet Socialist Realism as it was defined in the late 1920s and later imposed by the Communist political apparatus through the Artists' Union and the Ministry of Culture. Until Stalin's death in 1953, these strictures distorted the natural evolution of Armenia's art and disrupted ties with its national past, especially its religious heritage.

As a form of defiance, a number of nonconformist artists turned for inspiration to the rich Armenian cultural tradition. This strong link with the past helps explain the historical and religious orientation of artists such as Ardashes Hounanian, whose work draws on church architecture and *khachkars*, and Garen Sembatian, whose work depicts fanciful medieval castles, battles, and events of a heroic past in a naive, almost childlike manner. Other artists drew their inspiration from the familiar Armenian landscape—the mountains, deserts, fields, and vineyards—and from the colorful life of the rural villages and markets. The works of such painters as Martiros Sarian, Minas Avetissian, Bagrat Grigorian, and Hagop Hagopian often deal with these themes using styles that range from Postimpressionism to realism.

These historic, religious, landscape, or genre paintings can be recognized as Armenian primarily because of their distinctive Armenian content. But another feature that identifies much of the best contemporary painting as Armenian is the characteristic use of color—bright, warm, natural hues. The artists who use this palette range from Postimpressionists, such as the late Martiros Sarian and his followers, including Minas Avetissian, to abstract painters such as Seyran Khatlamajian and Viguen Tadevossian. While the use of color by these artists may vary slightly from one to another, each uses the bold reds and blues of traditional Armenian art. One finds these same hues in the medieval illuminated manuscripts of Toros Rosslin and Sarkis Bidzag.[2] As Garig Basmadjian has noted:

The eternal source of inspiration for all Armenian art . . . remains in the local colors: the sun, the multicolored tufa stones of pink, red, ochre . . . the blue sky, cloudless for more than three hundred days a year—set against the white majestic background of Mount Ararat.[5]

Martiros Sarian (1880–1972), who dominated Armenian art for almost a century, was born in Nor Nakhichevan, an Armenian trading center near Rostov-on-Don. Beginning in 1897, he studied painting for ten years at the Moscow School of Painting, Sculpture, and Architecture under Konstantin Korovin and Valentin Serov. He then exhibited with a number of groups, including the Blue Rose (1907), and took part in major exhibitions of the Golden Fleece (1907), the World of Art (1910–16), the Union of Russian Artists (1910–11), and the Four Arts Society (1925–29).

During the early years, Sarian's work was influenced by Oriental motifs, but these soon gave way to a major concern with the juxtaposition of light and dark and the use of pure color to delineate form. These qualities later led French critics to dub him "the Blue Fauve" during his retrospective exhibition at the Museum of Modern Art in Paris in 1980. Sarian spent his mature years in Yerevan, painting the Armenian sun and sky, mountains and valleys, farms and villages, markets and people. Little by little, Sarian's paintings became synonymous with Armenia. His colors became the Armenian colors and influenced a whole generation of artists.

Because of its great distance from Moscow, Armenia was able to preserve the identity of its art despite the demand of the Soviet regime that all artists conform to Socialist Realism. This physical and cultural distance attenuated the stultifying effect of dogmatic Party control. The ability and skill of the Armenian leadership in fending off direct interference in Armenia's cultural affairs also played a part in maintaining a degree of cultural independence. Many local Party officials were Armenians first and Party loyalists second. It is also fair to say that the loyalties of cultural officials were seldom challenged, since most postwar Armenian art was largely representational and did not seriously deviate from the strictures of Socialist Realism.

As a consequence, the best Armenian artists—including most of the nonconformist artists—were among the more than five hundred members of the Artists' Union in the Armenian Republic. The Union included artists of all schools: Socialist Realist hacks (the bulk), Postimpressionists (quite a few), Surrealists (some), Photorealists, Abstract Expressionists, and so forth. Similar situations existed in Estonia, Latvia, Lithuania, and Georgia, where artists with proper formal training were almost never excluded from the Artists' Union. Furthermore, the Armenian nonconformist artists generally did not use their art as a political platform for attacking the system; their art was created in spite of the system.

This does not mean that Armenian artists did not face limitations on what they were allowed to represent or that there were no artists who operated outside of what was officially acceptable. The nonconformists were always well aware that if they went beyond established limits they might have their works withdrawn from exhibitions, be disqualified from commissions, lose their jobs, or even worse. Real limits to artistic freedom were recognized, but they were wider, more flexible, and more bearable in Armenia than in Moscow, Leningrad, or Kiev.

In short, because the dominant ethnic group in Armenia had a strong, well-integrated cultural heritage, sustained by its own language and traditions and further reinforced by the physical distance from Moscow, the official artists were able to retain some significant degree of artistic independence. In the Cold War years, what was tolerated and even exhibited in Yerevan would have merited bulldozer treatment in Moscow.[4] In 1972, for example, art critic Henrik Igitian, along with Minas Avetissian and other artists, managed to obtain permission from the authorities to create the Museum of Contemporary Armenian Art, which became the first museum of independent contemporary art in the Soviet Union. Artists donated works to the museum and, since Igitian did not want to fall into an "inverted" suppression of official art, the museum was declared open to all artists. However, almost none of the official artists offered their works. Although many of the works exhibited in the museum would have been considered acceptable for official exhibitions in Moscow or Leningrad, a significant number of the works were in the style or spirit of the unofficial artists of these cities and would have been excluded from officially sanctioned exhibitions there. Surrealism, abstraction, and other art styles that were beyond the pale elsewhere were displayed side by side with the more official paintings. This small museum unquestionably played a unique and important, even a critical, role in furthering the development of modern art in Armenia in the 1970s and 1980s and continues as a tribute to the courage and vision of Igitian and those nonconformist artists who joined him in its creation.

Early development of nonconformist art The breathing space created by the thaw following Khrushchev's denunciation of Stalin's crimes in 1956 provided the necessary conditions for a virtual renaissance of cultural life in Armenia. Books that had long been banned were once again published. Pound, Yeats, and Eliot were translated. Musicians experimented openly. Concerts and poetry readings were organized. The film industry got a wake-up call by the presence of the pathbreaking movie director Sergei Paradjanov.[5] Books on Cézanne, Van Gogh, and Picasso became available on the Art Institute's bookshelves. True, one still needed special permission, but armed with a letter vouching for one's "seriousness" as an art student, one could now borrow these books from the library. It was a time of excitement and enthusiasm for all who were hungry for freedom, self-expression, and artistic creativity.

The Armenian art world was small enough to discourage the development of competing groups or schools of art. Each artist tended to do his or her own thing. The artists' ateliers became the pulse of the capital. It was there that the artists and the poets would meet with visitors and students, scientists and philosophers; it was there that discussions on philosophy and artistic theory would be followed by poetry readings, music, the latest humor from Radio Yerevan, and a bottle of Armenian cognac.

This artistic revival was assisted by a number of factors. Some of these, such as cultural exchange groups and foreign exhibitions and concerts, were common to all the republics in the Soviet Union. Other factors, however, were specifically Armenian. One of the smallest Soviet republics, Armenia was the only one which counted as many of its countrymen in the diaspora as it had within its own borders. Those in the diaspora were not all self-proclaimed exiles; some had been forced to leave western Armenia to escape the 1915 massacres. Beginning in the 1930s and continuing up to the 1950s, some of these forced exiles returned to their homeland, which had become a part of the Soviet Union, with great hopes and dreams, but were met, unfortunately, with a variety of Stalinist repressive measures. The artists among them were no exception. Most artists were not actively persecuted for failing to embrace Socialist Realism; they were simply ignored. Those artists from the diaspora who survived through the difficult Stalinist years proved to be major influences on the generation of artists who emerged after Stalin's death.

Yervand Kotchar (1899–1978) was the most important artist of the Armenian diaspora to return to his homeland. Born in Tbilisi and educated at Vkhutemas (Higher State Art Technical Studios) in Moscow, he settled in Paris in 1923 and had his own personal exhibition there three years later. Kotchar created "Painting in Space," an art form somewhere between painting and sculpture; this art was designed to go beyond the two-dimensional aspect of abstract art, to evolve into space and, as he said, conquer it. Kotchar exhibited with Braque, Chagall, Matisse, and Picasso at the Paris exhibition "Panorama of Contemporary Art" in 1929.

Kotchar emigrated to Armenia in 1936, and became a member of the Artists' Union the following year on the eve of the great purges. Accused of anti-Soviet propaganda in 1941, he was imprisoned and his sculptures were destroyed (including a Surrealist plaster bust of Stalin). Two years later, he was released following the intervention of his childhood friend Anastas Mikoyan, a member of the politburo and Stalin's trusted specialist on foreign trade. In the years that followed, rather than compromise his artistic principles, Kotchar maintained a low profile to keep out of trouble.

In the late 1950s, Kotchar's presence in Yerevan was central to the cultural atmosphere of the capital. For the younger generation of artists, listening to the "maestro" speak about the art scene in Paris in the 1920s was equivalent to having access to a whole library of books on avant-garde art. When Kotchar's monumental work depicting the Armenian hero David of Sassoun was erected in Yerevan in 1959, it became, after Mount Ararat, the most powerful and popular symbol of Armenia.

In contrast, Bedros Konturajian (1905–1956), a one-time student of Fernand Léger in Paris, never managed to come to terms with Soviet life after he moved to Armenia in 1947. Eventually, without a workshop, without artist's materials, and hungry and desperate, he committed suicide in 1956.

Another important diaspora artist who returned to the homeland was Haroutiun Galentz (1910–1967), a survivor of the 1915 Turkish genocide who escaped with other orphans to Syria and then to Lebanon. In 1946 he moved back to Armenia with his family. Since he did not bend to Socialist norms, he too was ignored as an artist until 1962, when he had his first one-man show in Yerevan. His choice of color, his impulsive brushstrokes, and his simplified forms produced an art which was fresh and unashamedly optimistic. His student and wife, Arminé Galentz (b. 1920), still lives in Yerevan and continues to paint in the spirit and style of her late husband.

Alexander Bazhbeuk-Melikian (1891–1966) was also an important influence on the Armenian art of the 1960s and 1970s. He lived in Tbilisi, the colorful capital city of Georgia which has always had a large Armenian population and been a major center for Armenian art.[6] A decade younger than Sarian, Bazhbeuk-Melikian painted in a theatrical, Postimpressionist style, often using subdued, dark backgrounds to set off his figures. His unique source of inspiration was the passionate and sensual female figure. His women, acrobats and dancers, are sure of their beauty, natural in their movements, and comfortable with their nudity. It is surprising that so much *joie de vivre* could be expressed by an artist who lived on the edge of poverty, crowded with his family into a single room and sometimes having to burn his pictures to make space for new ones. At other times, he had to stop painting because he could not afford new art materials. Only after his death did the cultural bureaucracy realize the stature of this great talent. His daughter, Lavinia Bazhbeuk-Melikian (b. 1922), is also an artist, having studied at the Surikov Institute of Art in Moscow before moving to Yerevan. Since 1962, when she participated in a group exhibition with Minas Avetissian, she has been an active member of the artistic scene in Yerevan.

Gevork Grigorian (1898–1976), known as Giotto, was also born in Tbilisi, where he studied at the School of Art and Architecture. He later attended Vkhutemas In Moscow from 1920 to 1921. He lived most of his life in a Tbilisi basement in abject poverty. Whether he painted a still life or a portrait, his subject filled the whole space of the canvas to the very edges, giving us a privileged close-up view and forcing us to imagine the larger reality. Grigorian's palette was limited to browns, yellows, and greenish-blacks; these colors express his pain and suffering without acknowledging the accompanying desperation. With great mastery, he provided the alternative to what has been called the "tyranny of the beautiful" in Tbilisi Armenian art.

The 1970s: The next generation of nonconformist artists

The 1970s were a decade of experimentation and artistic self-discovery in Armenia as elsewhere. As soon as the Soviet system allowed some degree of laxity, the younger generation of artists turned for inspiration to the "masters" who lived among them and whom they loved and respected. This was a major reason why Pop Art, Sots Art, Conceptual Art, and happenings did not find fertile ground in Yerevan in the 1970s, as they did in Moscow. The spirit of Armenian artistic innovation flowered in response to the solid presence of tradition, inspired by the older generation of avant-garde artists. For some artists, this turn to tradition meant a return to the roots of Armenian culture.

The most brilliant talent of this new generation was Minas Avetissian (1928–1975). Born in the north Armenian village of Jajur, he was educated in Yerevan and at the Academy of Fine Arts in Leningrad. It was in Leningrad that he befriended Henrik Igitian, with whom he later created the Museum of Contemporary Art in Yerevan. The prime inspiration for Avetissian's painting is the Armenian land, in particular his native village of Jajur, which figures prominently in a number of his major paintings. It is said that Avetissian gave back to the Armenian village its national identity by expressing its particular rhythm, its traditional values, its down-to-earth concerns, and its infinite wisdom. His canvases burst with color inspired by both the bright Armenian sunlight and the medieval Armenian illuminated manuscripts (Pl. 10:1). Avetissian's mentor, Martiros Sarian, spoke with admiration of him as the artist who "dared to paint the sun."

Avetissian was so beloved that he soon became "Minas" to everyone, including the village folk who, strangely enough, warmed to his modernist rendition of their village. Then tragedy struck. In 1972, Avetissian's studio in Yerevan inexplicably burned to the ground, destroying over a hundred of his best canvases. Despite the profound shock he experienced, Avetissian resumed painting immediately and produced a number of late masterpieces. Then, one fateful day in 1975, a car swerved onto the sidewalk and struck and killed him. After his death, tragedy continued to haunt Avetissian. In 1988, a major earthquake destroyed a building housing seven of his murals, as well as his house in Jajur, which had been made into a museum.

Hagop Ananikian (1919–1977) and Raphael Atoyan (b. 1931) both found artistic inspiration in their hometown of Leninakan (presently known as Gumri). Their canvases are silent reflections of the memories of their childhoods, attempting to bring back to life the everyday people and places recorded by each as a child and expressed with nostalgia. Ananikian's paintings have an unfinished quality that helps evoke a certain atmosphere, character, and moment (Pl. 10:3). In Atoyan's work one feels the desire to return to all that was once specifically Armenian—baking *lavash* (Armenian bread), the village church, the grapevines, even "our door" (Pl. 10:5). Thus nostalgia becomes a subtle political statement.

Ardashes Hounanian (b. 1922) turned to the beginnings of Armenia's religious culture for inspiration. Whether his painting represents a *khachkar* (stone cross) (Fig. 10:1), the interior of a church, or a more abstract composition, the same mystical-religious atmosphere permeates his work (Pl. 10:2). There is an otherworldly quality to his landscapes, places where one would not wish to tread for fear of unwittingly disturbing the past. Alexander Kamensky has this to say about his paintings: "Hounanian's complex rhythms seem to be set to a strange music.

Fig. 10:1
Ardashes Hounanian
Stone Cross, 1971
Gouache on paper
99.1 × 69.3 cm

Armenian tradition is the key to his creations and they certainly have a lot to say to the world. . . . His compositions are visions which speak to us of legendary worlds and constructions which remind us of crystal—sometimes massive and solid and at other times fragile and translucent."[7]

Hagop Hagopian transformed the color of the Armenian landscape, moving from the bright palette of Sarian, which dominated for decades, to a darker palette made up of more desolate shades. Born in Egypt in 1923 and educated in Paris, Hagopian moved to Armenia in 1962. He sees an Armenia in which there are no people in colorful dress; for him, the fields are dry, the trees are desiccated, the vines are barren. Clouds do not bring rain and power pylons outnumber the trees in the rocky landscape. In this silent and almost monochromatic world, there is a sense of sadness and anxiety (Pl. 10:4). Even when human figures are included in his canvases, we cannot see their faces. They are either hidden in semi-darkness, or turning away, or covered by some object. In *No to the Neutron Bomb!*, 1977 (Pl. 10:6), the heads have completely disappeared, taking with them the bodies, and we are left with a horde of overcoats marching in protest, clearly a bit too late.

In Hagopian's still lifes (which are hardly "still"), curious juxtapositions, such as a basket of fragile eggs next to menacing garden tools (Pl. 1:16) or empty gloves reaching toward a fish, communicate the same uneasy feelings and pregnant silences as his barren landscapes. Hagopian, nevertheless, was given the honorary title "People's Artist" and was considered an official painter. Given his somber vision and the hidden messages implicit in his work, this award was testimony to the sometimes arbitrary classification system of Armenia's artistic officialdom. It is also a tribute to Hagopian's artistic talent.

Some Armenian nonconformist artists, such as Gayaneh Khachaturian, turned to painting the realm of the fantastic and surreal. Khachaturian was born in Tbilisi in 1942 and is another of the small number of important Armenian artists who have chosen to live there. In her paintings, she depicts a disquieting world of innocent-looking animals and people engaged in seemingly innocent actions (Pl. 10:7). Each canvas is an episode in a ritual, the exact significance of which remains a mystery to the observer. Nevertheless, one is always enchanted as much by her fantastic world as by her bold use of color.

Edward Kharazian (b. 1939) also turned to painting the fantastic early in his career. Contrary to Khachaturian, however, his world is not at all menacing. The creature who finds the golden egg (Pl. 10:8) is a rather likeable character, the village fool or sage who can at any moment disappear into the background. In Kharazian's later paintings, the background becomes more and more dominant and the figures are transformed into organic forms virtually floating across the surface. Kharazian then further simplifies the forms, dilutes his colors, and produces poetic, almost transparent, abstract compositions.

Martin Petrossian (b. 1936) is another artist who explores the realm of fantasy. His is the world of Armenian folklore and fable, as he has reviewed and edited it. Knights, sages, and mythical animals find themselves in the same compositions as modern women and men. Petrossian's style combines an almost naive approach with a sublime, philosophical one. He uses pastel colors in his paintings and no colors at all in his graphic works so as not to obscure the sensitivity of his line.

Robert Elibekian was born in Tbilisi in 1941. The son of a theater director, he often accompanied his father to work. The wonder of the stage provided a colorful and intense alternative to everyday reality for the budding artist, and he has managed to incorporate this magic into his canvases. The actresses and other models in his paintings perform with subtle elegance and control and express their deepest emotions with understatement and balance (Pl. 10:11). As Russian art historian Dmitri Sarabianov has remarked, Elibekian takes us into a world of pure sentiments where "there is no action, time is at a standstill and motion is suspended. In this world, every detail has an autonomous value."[8]

Varoujan Vardanian (b. 1948) had his first one-man exhibition at the Museum of Modern Art in Yerevan in 1976. In the catalogue, Henrik Igitian calls Vardanian's work "virile lyricism." Vardanian's world combines the allegorical and the dramatic, and his favorite genre is the female portrait or the multiple portrait. His use of color is both subtle and forceful and his texture is refined and original (Pl. 10:10).

Nonconformist Armenian art of the 1970s is also marked by Expressionist tendencies. Ruben Adalian (b. 1929) paints canvases that are expressions of passionate, sometimes violent, sensations. Tortured human forms, headless figures, and hermaphrodites are his symbols of the tragedy of the human condition (Pl. 10:9). While Adalian's debt to Kotchar is unquestionable, there is an added psychological agitation in Adalian's work. Rudolf Khachaturian (b. 1937), another student of Kotchar, experimented with the distorted human form early in his artistic career. At the end of the 1960s, he showed a number of these works to a Moscow art committee, which censured him and threatened him with expulsion from the Artists'

Union. He returned to Armenia with a clearer appreciation of the artistic freedom in his own republic. Later, he succeeded in gaining deserved acclaim in Moscow for his exquisite portraits and still lifes executed in pencil and sepia.

A number of artists adopted an art form on the frontier of realism and Postcubism. Bagrat Grigorian (1939–1992) produced paintings of landscapes and villages in which he reduced these scenes to their simplest forms, superimposing swatches of color as a child would use building blocks to construct the composition (Pl. 10:13). The resulting works have a fresh, childlike quality (Pl. 10:15). Henry Elibekian, the brother of Robert, was born in Tbilisi in 1936, and after living for a while in Moscow and Kiev finally settled in Yerevan in 1972. Painter, sculptor, and stage designer, he has explored in sequence every artistic school and genre. His still lifes are executed with a perfect balance of impulsiveness and control (Pl. 10:16).

Ruben Hovnatanian (b. 1940) depicts a number of different planes in his paintings. He achieves this effect either by actually representing each object with its volume and shadows or by superimposing linear structures where no light source exists. In this latter group of works, only color is used to create the composition of the painting and its transparency. The palette of Raffi Adalian (b. 1941) was restricted to earth colors in his early, finely worked still lifes. These had a characteristic texture, thick in some places and barely painted in others, smoothed out in some areas and coarse in others. His later work is almost white on white. The play of texture that was achieved by the use of paint in his early work is now expressed by other materials stuck onto the canvas.

At his very best, Garen Sembatian (b. 1932) is the most refreshing artist of his generation. He simplifies reality to its elemental forms, thereby transforming and elevating it to a magical and universal plane. His schematic figures, with their black outlines and energetic strokes of color, are reminiscent of children's drawings (Pl. 10:17). The simpler his images get, however, the more we are aware of the legendary symbols of the paintings. Sembatian's simple forms are thus most effective when they awaken the primitive force of our subconscious.

Both Viguen Tadevossian (b. 1944) and Seyran Khatlamajian (1937–1994) show an emotional quality parallel with the art of Arshile Gorky. While Tadevossian is the more lyrical of the two in his finely executed drawings and his abstract canvases (Pl. 10:14), Khatlamajian has the more vibrant line. Freed of the constraints of figurative art, these artists create a visual structure, which, at its best, can be considered a plastic formula for the

Pl. 10:8 (*right*)
Edward Kharazian
I Found the Golden Egg,
1979
Gouache and pen and ink
on paper
35.9 × 48 cm

Pl. 10:7 (*left*)
Gayaneh Khachaturian
*Procession of the White
Court*, 1985
Oil on canvas
81.6 × 87.2 cm

Pl. 10:9 (*left*)
Ruben Adalian
(Untitled), 1981
Oil on canvas
86.5 × 59 cm

Pl. 10:10
Varoujan Vardanian
The Palace of the Angels,
1977
Oil on canvas
81.5 × 100 cm

Pl. 10:11
Robert Elibekian
Nude Models, 1972
Oil on fiberboard
131 × 111.5 cm

Pl. 10:12
Serge Essayan
(Untitled), 1973
Oil on fiberboard
61 × 79.5 cm

Pl. 10:14
Viguen Tadevossian
Refraction, 1977
Oil on canvas
80.2 × 96.5 cm

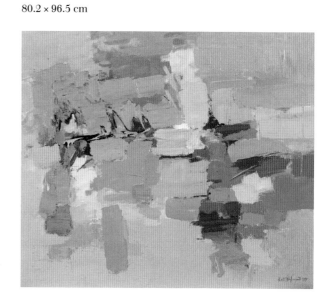

Pl. 10:13
Bagrat Grigorian
(Untitled), 1975
Tempera on paper
51.3 × 73.1 cm

Pl. 10:16
Henry Elibekian
Still Life, Bowl with Fruit,
1976
Oil on fiberboard
47.2 × 58 cm

Pl. 10:15
Bagrat Grigorian
(Untitled), 1982
Acrylic on canvas
48.3 × 58 cm

Pl. 10:17
Garen Sembatian
Castle in the Air, 1974
Oil on canvas
120.5 × 99.7 cm

Pl. 10:18
Nareg Antabian
Agony, 1985
Mixed media on canvas
100 × 100 cm

Pl. 10:19
Yurii Bourjelian
The Beach, 1985
Oil on paper
100.2 × 100.2 cm

Pl. 10:21
Aram Kupetsian
Guitar, 1979
Oil on illustration board
70.3 × 50 cm

Pl. 10:20
Vagrich Bakhchanyan
*Teenager Thinking Over
His Future*, 1975
Collage, graphite, and
colored pencil on paper
43.7 × 30.4 cm

Pl. 10:22
Seyran Khatlamajian
Apricot Tree, 1972
Oil on canvas
54 × 73 cm

Pl. 10:23
Soren Arutiunian
(Untitled), 1977
Gouache on paper
35.4 × 25.1 cm

Pl. 10:24
Kiki (Grikor Mikaelian)
Composition, 1973
Mixed media on canvas
79.5 × 59.5 cm

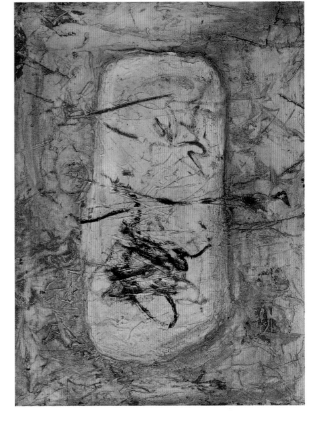

Pl. 11:1
Nikolai Ignatov
(Untitled), 1979
Gouache
47.7 × 35.9 cm

Pl. 11:2
Avto Varazi
(Bleeding Buffalo), n.d.
Wood, wood shavings,
and khaki pants on panel
67.3 × 38 × 10 cm

Pl. 11:3
Alexander Bandzeladze
(Untitled), 1989
Watercolor on paper
73.3 × 102.5 cm

Pl. 11:4
Alexander Bandzeladze
Red and White, 1989
Oil on canvas
90 × 100 cm

Pl. 11:5
**Georgi Aleksi-
Meskhishvili**
Sleeping Body, 1984
Acrylic on canvas
200.5 × 200 cm

Pl. 11:6
Dato Shushanja
(Untitled), n.d.
Mixed media
50.2 × 72.5 cm

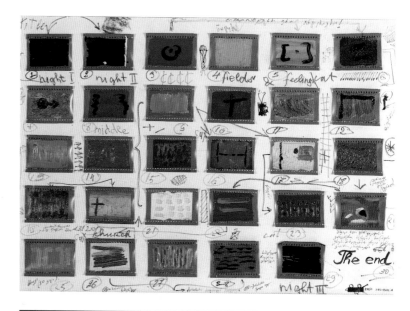

Pl. 11:7
Dato Shushanja
Woman in [Room] #, 1983
Oil on canvas
194 × 293.4 cm

Pl. 11:8
Tina Gomelauri
Yellow Snow, 1990
Oil on canvas
90.5 × 110.5 cm

Pl. 11:9
Nino Morbedadze
Untitled VI, 1982
Gouache, tempera, and
pen and ink on paper
54.8 × 75 cm

Pl. 11:10
Vladimir Kandelaki
Autumn, 1983
Oil on canvas
59.5 × 45.2 cm

Pl. 12:1
Vladimir Arkharov
Novodevichy Cemetery,
1974
Oil on fiberboard
72 × 100.5 cm

Pl. 12:3
Oscar Rabin
Springtime, 1968
Oil on canvas
79.5 × 108.5 cm

Pl. 12:2
Grigorii Perkel
Song of Songs, 1972
Lithograph
51.5 × 41.2 cm

Pl. 12:5
Gennadii Zubkov
Landscape, 1979
Oil on canvas
60 × 67.4 cm

Pl. 12:4
Dmitri Plavinsky
Old Russian Testament,
1965
Mixed media on wood
119 × 183 cm

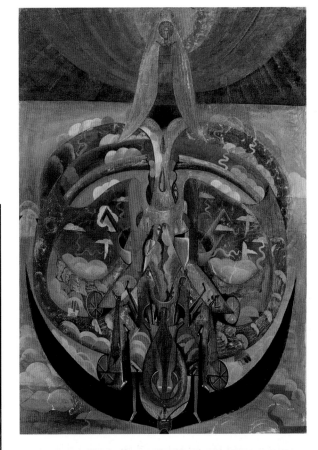

Pl. 12:7
Sergei Potapov
(Gesture), 1985
Tempera and gouache on
tablecloth
112 × 76.5 cm

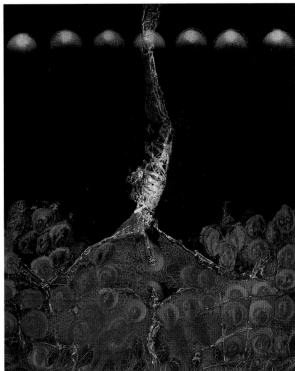

Pl. 12:6
Yurii Zharkikh
Consecration, 1974
Oil on canvas
94.5 × 79.5 cm

Pl. 12:8
Yurii Zharkikh
(Anticipation), 1977
Oil on canvas
51 × 71.8 cm

Pl. 12:10 (*left*)
Tatiana Shirikova
Easter, 1985
Oil on fiberboard
89 × 110.5 cm

Pl. 12:11 (*right*)
Evgenii Rukhin
(Untitled), 1975
Mixed media on canvas
94 × 74.5 cm

Pl. 12:12 (*above*)
**Volodymyr (Vladimir)
Naumets**
(Untitled), 1985
Gouache on paper
105 × 77 cm

Pl. 12:9 (*opposite*)
Aleksandr Kharitonov
*The Approach of a
Mysterious Planet*, 1982
Oil on canvas
40 × 35 cm

Pl. 12:13
Francisco Infante
*Suprematist Games:
Homage to Malevich,*
1969
Cibachrome photograph
51 × 51 cm

Pl. 12:14
**Evgenii Mikhnov-
Voitenko**
Composition, 1975
Gouache and watercolor
on paper
42.4 × 61.5 cm

Armenian spirit: a polyphonic harmony of colors penetrated by sharp and thorn-like lines (Pl. 10:22). This coexistence of peaceful harmony and dramatic disturbance is found in works of many Armenian artists, reflecting the troubled course of Armenian history.

Not all of the Armenian nonconformist artists lived in Yerevan or Tbilisi. Moscow was home to a number of them, including Serge Essayan, who was born there in 1939. His canvases are poetic compositions of human figures in infinite space. He has painted a series of canvases on the theme of the Armenian massacres, reflecting his deep involvement with the Armenian past (Pl. 10:12). Yurii Bourjelian (b. 1921) depicts almost abstract, ethereal landscapes (Pl. 10:19), while his son, Michael Bourjelian (b. 1946), paints Hyperrealistic boxes and perfume bottles. Another Moscow artist of Armenian origin is Aram Kupetsian (b. 1928), who almost exclusively paints still lifes in a Postcubist manner (Pl. 10:21). Both Vagrich Bakhchanyan (b. 1938), whose medium includes phototransfers (Pl. 10:20), mail art, and readymade objects, and Soren Arutiunian (b. 1950), whose art is Surrealistic (Pl. 10:23), now live in New York City. The connection of these artists' work with Armenian themes is less evident.

Artists of the 1980s: The most recent nonconformists

During the 1980s, a new generation of artists emerged in Armenia. These younger artists did not remember the Stalin years and had been brought up in an atmosphere of relative openness. Armenian artists of the older generation, including Sarian, Kotchar, Bazhbeuk-Melikian, and Gevork Grigorian (Giotto), were no longer alive and thus could not exercise a day-to-day influence. Furthermore, the younger artists now had the choice of building on the work of the older generation or rejecting it.

Armen Grigorian (b. 1960) was the founder of the Third Floor Group, so named because during an exhibition at the Artists' Union their works were relegated to an obscure third-floor conference room away from the main exhibition area. Grigorian has managed to free himself from national limits. In an effort to facilitate the communication of his ideas, he incorporates textual material and real objects into the Action Painting on his huge canvases. Even the subject matter of his paintings (metal-studded leather jackets, motorcycles, etc.) is new by Yerevan standards.

Another influential member of the Third Floor is Grigor Mikaelian (b. 1956), known as Kiki. His paintings, by his own admission, are an expression of secret and inexplicable forces within himself, which, once transferred to

canvas, become art. On large canvases, with broad and impatient strokes, using mainly black, Kiki develops the same theme with great mastery (Pl. 10:24).

In the paintings of Armen Hajian (b. 1955) it is not the anatomy of the objects depicted that is important, but their luminous radiation. Color becomes form, and the different layers of superimposed color reflect different intensities of physical, spiritual, and psychic radiation. By contrast, the work of Nareg Antabian (b. 1961) is both explosive and reflective. Texture is such an important ingredient in his abstract compositions (Pl. 10:18) that he does not even shy away from scorching some parts of his paintings to create the necessary controlled accident.

Ashod Bayandour (b. 1947) is the oldest member the Third Floor Group, which has been influenced by American painting and the new wave of Expressionism of the 1980s. "For me, painting is man's way of continuing God's creative process," he says. Known for his graphic work in the 1970s and his innovative approach to painting in the 1980s, Bayandour is now creating installations.

Even before Gorbachev, the Armenian capital was experiencing the first manifestations of change. Gorbachev's *glasnost* validated and accelerated this process. High-ranking officials in the art world were replaced by members of a younger and more tolerant generation. Ara Shiraz, a noted sculptor, became the president of the Armenian Union of Artists. More artists were encouraged and allowed to exhibit, so more artists became members of the Union. Previously, to become a member, an artist not only had to have formal training but also had to have had at least three exhibitions. After *perestroika*, there were no restrictions on exhibiting and, therefore, the requirement of three exhibitions was no longer an effective bar to membership for "undesirables."

Unfortunately, the cultural progress under *glasnost* and *perestroika* was halted by the major earthquake in 1988, which changed all of Armenia's national priorities. Survival took first place; the arts were overshadowed by other pressing needs. As a result, Armenia is now passing through a particularly difficult period of her history. On the road to building a democracy, this newly independent republic is facing a frail economy, a war in Karabakh, the absence of basic necessities, and more. Most of the artists discussed in this chapter still live in their native land. In the absence of canvas and paint and even electricity and fuel, they continue to create an unfettered Armenian art which is more and more universal in expression, the roots of which go back thousands of years.

Notes

1. George Yakoulov, *Autobiography* (Yerevan: Art Gallery of Armenia, 1967), p. 16.

2. Toros Rosslin (active in the mid-thirteenth century) was probably the greatest medieval Armenian artist. He introduced scenes of everyday life into evangelic miniatures. Sarkis Bidzag was active in the first half of the fourteenth century in Cilicia.

3. Garig Basmadjian, Introduction to *Armenian Colors: 12 Contemporary Artists from Soviet Armenia*, exh. cat. (New York: AGBU Gallery, 1978), n.p.

4. On Sept. 15, 1974, an open-air exhibition of nonconformist art was organized on a piece of Moscow wasteland. The authorities arrested the organizers and sent bulldozers and water cannons which destroyed a number of canvases. The exhibition came to be known unofficially as the "Bulldozer Exhibition." It paved the way for a second and successful open-air exhibition two weeks later in Izmailovsky Park.

5. Sergei Paradjanov (1924–1990), artist, set designer, and film director, is best known for his films *Shadows of Our Forgotten Ancestors*, *Horses of Fire*, *The Color of Pomegranates*, *The Legend of Suram Fortress*, *Ashik Kerid*, and a series of documentaries on major artists such as Niko Pirosmani.

6. In the nineteenth century, the two main Armenian cultural centers were Tiflis (now Tbilisi), the Russian administrative center of the Caucasus, and Constantinople (now Istanbul), capital of the Ottoman Empire. Yerevan, then small and provincial, was under Persian rule until 1828. In 1823, the first Armenian printing house in the Caucasus was opened in Tiflis. The Armenian Dramatic Society was founded there in 1901, and the Union of Armenian Artists in 1916. When the Union organized its first exhibition in Tiflis in 1917, forty-five artists participated.

7. Alexander Kamensky, Preface to *Ardashes Hounanian*, exh. cat. (Yerevan: Armenian Artists' Union, 1968).

8. Dmitri Sarabianov, quoted in *Robert Elibekian* (Beirut: Garni, 1992), p. 7.

11 | Nonconformist art of Soviet Georgia

A synthesis of East and West

Elena Kornetchuk

Shortly after the Bolshevik Revolution of 1917, Georgia declared itself an independent state under Menshevik rule. With the official announcement on May 26, 1918, Georgia terminated its 117-year political alliance with Russia, becoming a free democratic state. Unfortunately, this situation lasted less than three years. Soviet Russia annexed Georgia on February 25, 1921. From 1922 to 1936, Georgia was part of a single Transcaucasian republic until it finally became one of the fifteen republics of the U.S.S.R. in 1936.

Despite these political upheavals, the early twentieth century was a period of great cultural ferment in Georgia. During the 1920s, Georgian intellectuals founded the National Art Gallery[1] and the Tiflis Academy of Arts, which supported realistic art and later played a leading role in the development of Soviet Georgian art.[2] The possibility of independence prompted young Georgian artists to accelerate their search for their cultural roots and to establish a national revival of original Georgian art. This traditional Georgian culture, characterized by a blend of local, Byzantine, and Eastern Christian aesthetic styles, continued to flourish.

But many younger Georgian artists were also drawn to the experimental art of the Russian and French avant-garde, and established close ties with those groups. Among the Georgian avant-gardists were Georgy Maisuradze (1817–1885), Romanoz Gvelesiani (1859–1884), Alexander Beridze (1858–1917), David Guramishvili (1857–1926), Grigory Tatishvili (1838–1911), Georgy (Gigo) Gabashvili (1862–1936), Alexander Mrevlishvili (1866–1933), and Moisei Toidze (1871–1953). They are credited with laying the foundation of various genres of representational art.

Some young Georgian modernist painters traveled to Paris to study, and when they returned they greatly influenced the course of Soviet Georgian art. Prominent among these artists were David Kakabadze (1889–1952), Elena Akhvlediani (1901–1979), Ketevan Magalashvili (1894–1973), and Lado Gudiashvili (1896–1980). Niko Pirosmani (1862–1918), Georgia's most renowned self-taught painter, inspired generations of artists with his naive, colorful canvases. Both Kakabadze and Akhvlediani were influenced by modern movements. Kakabadze was especially affected by Cubism and later by abstraction. Though most of them painted landscapes, their imagery was not necessarily figurative or even realist. Instead, the artists created generalized forms with decorative colors. Kakabadze's use of mirrors and strips of metal—later adapted in the 1960s by some Georgian unofficial artists, such as Avto Varazi (1926–1977)—led to his being accused of practicing formalism, a serious offense in the minds of Soviet officials.

Magalashvili and Gudiashvili, on the other hand, were inspired by such ancient Georgian artistic traditions as frescoes and miniatures. Their ornamental art referred back to the Golden Age of Georgia in the eleventh and twelfth centuries. This was the period during which the great cathedrals were built. It was also a cultural high point for carved wood decorations and frescoes, handsome chased work in bas-relief, miniature painting, fine cloisonné enamelling, lavish jewelry, and intricate weaving. During the reign of Queen Tamara (1184–1212), Shota Rustavelli wrote and dedicated to the Queen his epic poem, *The Knight in the Panther's Skin* (*c.* 1200), exemplifying the virtues of chivalry and honor. To this day, Georgian artists reflect Rustavelli's symbolism in their artworks.

With the establishment of the Soviet regime, the development of Georgian art changed. The avant-garde movements of the 1920s were negated. Artists turned to realism as stylistic uniformity was officially imposed. Though Georgian art remained known in the Soviet art world for its hieratic compositions, strong colors, and decorative tendencies, most artists conformed to the new Socialist Realist ideology. Historical and revolutionary themes became popular in the 1930s. Many artists devoted themselves to renditions of the Georgian workers' revolutionary movement. Landscape painting and portraiture continued to develop.

Monumental art reached new heights under Lenin's plan for producing pro-Soviet propaganda. Under the leadership of such artists as Nikolai Kandelaki (1889–1970), the sculpting of heroic images, expansive stone panels, and mosaic reliefs changed the profile of Tbilisi and its environment. As in many other republics of the Soviet Union, some artists escaped into uncontroversial book illustration. Rustavelli's epic, *The Knight in the Panther's Skin*, soon became a common subject.

During World War II, Georgian art was devoted to themes of patriotism. Victory scenes, as well as the iconographic stereotypes of "the leaders" of the Revolution and the Soviet state, frequently appeared in paintings. Georgian poster design was particularly sophisticated, and one of the best-known Soviet war posters, *The Fatherland Calls You*, was by the Georgian artist Irakli Toidze (b. 1902). One positive result of the Soviet victory in World War II was the return of many art treasures to the Georgian Art Museum. Artworks taken by the Georgian Mensheviks when they emigrated in 1921 were returned from France in 1945. Russian and Eastern European paintings were also returned from museums in Moscow and Leningrad.

The cultural thaw initiated by Khrushchev in Russia reverberated in Georgia. In the post-Stalin era, young Georgian artists were officially exposed to Impressionism and Postimpressionism, the newly acceptable modern "isms" in the Soviet Union. A new generation of Georgian artists searched for bold compositional solutions and a freer style of painting. These new talents of the 1950s[3] were particularly interested in appropriating aspects of Renaissance drawing and French modernist painting. They continued their fascination with their own national traditions, especially the art of embossed metalwork and the linearity and frontality characteristic of Georgian painting.

The 1957 World Festival of Youth in Moscow, which for the first time exhibited Abstract Expressionism in the Soviet Union, had repercussions in Georgia. Among the artists most affected was Alexander Bandzeladze (1927–1992), who began to experiment in the late 1950s with early twentieth-century modernism. Unafraid of being ridiculed or dubbed "unofficial," Bandzeladze, like many Moscow artists of his generation, created book illustrations by day and abstract art by night. He had a great impact on other Georgian artists.

Edmund Kalandadze (b. 1923) was another experimental Georgian artist who had trouble with the authorities in the 1950s. He was reprimanded by the Tbilisi Academy of Arts for rejecting naturalism in favor of formal values. To his credit, Kalandadze, who was later Minister of Culture, played a pivotal role in freeing Georgian artists from the dogma of Socialist Realism. Despite his position,

he remained a controversial painter into the 1980s, when he sought an effect of spontaneity and improvisation that contradicted official art.

The 1960s marked a turning point in contemporary Georgian art. Because of Georgia's geographical position on the periphery of the U.S.S.R., official art produced there tended to be less dogmatic. Socialist Realism was never as fully enforced in Tbilisi as it was in Moscow. Unofficial art, as it was beginning to be known in Russia, did not exist. For that matter, there was no Western community, such as foreign press or diplomats, that could be supportive of avant-garde causes. Though Georgian officialdom espoused official Soviet artistic style, it directed its attention more toward aesthetics than the enforcement of Socialist Realist dogma. Most officials seemed to think that "art for art's sake" was more important than the goals of the state. Especially after Brezhnev had emphasized the multicultural aspects of the Soviet Union, lyricism and folklore motifs were deemed acceptable.

Due to the direction in official cultural policy, Georgian artists began to search for new, but permissible, art forms. Some artists were poised to evolve beyond the acceptable patterns of Impressionism. In their pursuit of new artistic directions, they renewed their acquaintance with medieval murals and the Georgian avant-garde. As a result, monumental decorative painting increased dramatically. There was a distinct return to the use of symbols and stylization. Nikolai Ignatov (b. 1937) became known for his frescoes depicting Georgian people and their traditions. His gouaches, such as his untitled shepherd scene (Pl. 11:1), are reminiscent of Mediterranean classicism. Painted in multiple hues of blue, beige, and brown, this artwork captures Old Georgia with its poetic depiction of an ancient church flanked by figures in traditional attire.

Zurab Tsereteli (b. 1934) gained international fame with his monumental mosaic compositions and sculptures. But because he had won the U.S.S.R. State Prize and Lenin Prize, many experimental artists considered him too official and dubbed him the "Leroy Neiman of the Soviet Union." His *Native Land* series certainly confirms his official allegiance. Criticism by fellow artists and art historians did not prevent Tsereteli's monument, *Birth of a New Man*, from becoming the official symbol of the 1996 Olympic Games in Atlanta, Georgia. Bandzeladze, Levan Tsotskiridze (b. 1926), and others tried their hand at religious frescoes, although for these artists it signified a disguised form of protest. This was part of a general attempt by Georgian artists to fuse various influences. This movement resulted in a popular salon style, as well as some esoteric paintings portraying the heroes of the Revolution in an anachronistic Renaissance style.

Several younger artists, who had seen books and magazines about contemporary art in the West, experimented with nonfigurative art. Bandzeladze began to create paintings and watercolors under the influence of Abstract Expressionism. Varazi adapted features of the Paris School and Italian Neorealism. Though he painted such unmistakably stylized Georgian portraits as the untitled female figure, Varazi is best known for the collage-like treatment of his canvases. His application of draped cloth (Pl. 11:2) or chunks of wood to his canvases offended the aesthetic sensibilities of the Georgian Union of Artists. But the innovators in the Soviet art world took note. For example, a similar use of wooden objects would later be seen in the paintings of Leningrad dissident Evgenii Rukhin (1943–1976). Likewise, Varazi's monochromatic still life of a dead fish on a plate with scraps of newspaper glued into the background (Fig. 11:1) is echoed in the art of Armenian Hagop Hagopian (b. 1923) as well as in that of Moscow dissident Oscar Rabin (b. 1928).

Other Georgian artists adopted a variety of new styles. While Dzhibon Khundadze (b. 1927) transformed mountain landscapes into geometric structures, Khita Kutateladze (1924–1979) reflected the late period of Picasso in his art. But what most affected these artists was an unofficial Moscow art exhibition from the collection of Alexander Glezer, held at the Georgian Artists' Union in 1967. Two young Tbilisi artists participated in the exhibition in

a gesture of solidarity. There was even a catalogue, which was unusual for the period. The Georgian cultural elite was astounded, remarking: "We'd never have thought such a thing could happen in Russia! You've actually got some real art!"[4] Despite its distance from Moscow, the KGB closed the exhibition on its fifth day.

On the whole, the 1960s generation of Georgian artists laid the groundwork for future innovations. They helped the younger artists resolve issues of color and form, and their high technical level established professional artistic standards often lacking among Moscow's underground artists, whose main concern was government opposition. On the other hand, the Georgian preoccupation with technical achievements led to their neglect of the subconscious and of spiritual mystery, aspects that made the work of the Muscovite dissidents so intriguing.

The unofficial artists who were most active in Georgia in the 1970s referred to themselves as "the new conscience-builders." The goal of these artists was to resolve all creative problems as well as the issues confronting their Western contemporaries. As a reaction to the thematic demands of Socialist Realism, artists turned to pure genres such as landscape painting and portraiture. Bandzeladze's abstractions were the exception. With most artists, experimentation with painterly techniques, stylistic approaches, and compositions continued. During this time, the artist was a lone seeker, painting for the sake of art alone. He maintained neutrality toward the surrounding world and focused instead only on his artistic searchings. It was within this decade that artists fully assimilated the language of contemporary art.

Several exhibitions during the 1970s signaled changes in official policy. Most important were the one-person exhibitions of Khita Kutateladze and Avto Varazi. Kutateladze, who was only appreciated after this posthumous exhibition, had developed a special affinity for the Georgian landscape. It was his expressive and contrasting use of color patches, often in unlikely hues, that most affected his viewers. Meanwhile, Varazi's monochromatic paintings with collages prompted younger artists to follow his creative lead.

The first unofficial exhibitions of young Tbilisi painters in the capital were held in 1974 and 1975. Some artists like Gia Edzgveradze (b. 1952), a Bandzeladze protégé, began to display in private apartments, similar to the AptArt shows in Moscow. However, most Georgian artists felt that their artistic activism formally began in 1976, when a small group of Moscow and Leningrad dissidents, including Rabin and Rukhin, traveled to Tbilisi to meet with their Georgian counterparts. This summit signaled

...azi
...), n.d.
...edia on wood
....7 × 6 cm

Fig. 11:2
Guram Dolendzhashvili
Eternal Peace, 1979–82
Etching
50 × 75 cm

the formation of an alternative Tbilisi art scene and the beginning of a dialogue with Moscow.

By the end of the 1970s, Georgian artists had found ways to demonstrate openly their various artistic aspirations. They established exhibitions of "one artwork each," allowing artists to select personally how they wished to be represented. The official reappearance of Georgian avant-garde art of the 1920s also encouraged innovative thinking. Stereotypes were renounced, even in attitudes toward tradition.[5] Young artists experimented with multiple stylistic approaches. Figurative art was ignored. Graphic artists, who had once only depicted national subjects and city scenes, now addressed the spiritual condition of man.

Particularly noteworthy were Guram Dolendzhashvili (b. 1943), Nana Churgulia (b. 1951), Sophie Kintsurashvili (b. 1948), Tamaz Varvaridze (b. 1945), and Ian Gigoshvili (b. 1956), who utilized abstractions and metaphors in their work. Dolendzhashvili's finely detailed and filigree-like etchings based on nature frequently combined reality with fantasy. Images like *Eternal Peace* (Fig. 11:2) and *The Beginning of Navigation*, completed between 1979 and 1982, possess macabre qualities, especially in the depiction of the inexplicable skeletal remains in *Eternal Peace* and the grotesque shapes of *The Beginning of Navigation*. Dolendzhashvili's Surrealist approach was widely emulated among Soviet experimental artists in the 1970s.[6]

For young artists, the member of the older generation they most respected was probably Bandzeladze. His

Abstract Expressionist painting, which he had bravely begun in the 1950s in defiance of state regulations, remained a model for the new generation of artists (Pl. 11:3). Gia Edzgveradze, Luka Lazareishvili (b. 1957), and Iliko Zautashvili (b. 1961), students at the Georgian Academy of Arts, regularly visited Bandzeladze at his home for private art lessons. Thus, Bandzeladze became the spiritual father of a tradition of abstract painters, who not only owed him their knowledge but also their impetus to continue their abstract Conceptual experiments. Indeed, his influence may be said to have given birth to the Georgian avant-garde of the 1970s and 1980s.

Bandzeladze earned his title as patriarch of Georgian modern art through his personal quest to develop a means of artistic expression separate from the dictates of Socialist Realism. Like many other Soviet Georgian artists, Bandzeladze first attended the Tbilisi Secondary Art School (1942–47) and then studied at the Tbilisi Academy of Fine Arts (1947–48). In 1949, he participated in his first exhibition, and in 1954 he became a member of the U.S.S.R. Union of Artists. At that point, he became interested in Impressionism, especially the work of Paul Cézanne, Claude Monet, and Auguste Renoir. These interests led him to Pointillism and eventually to Cubism, where he encountered the work of Georges Braque and Pablo Picasso. Within a year, he had broken with the official concepts of painting and the artistic milieu of the Union.

Over the next thirty years, Bandzeladze pursued a career in graphic illustration, receiving numerous prizes and awards. His success in this field won him a nomination for the Lenin Prize in 1958 for his masterful illustration of the nineteenth-century Georgian poem *The Songs of Arsen*. In 1966, Bandzeladze's illustrations for that poem also received the coveted prize for "The Most Beautiful Book in the World" at the Leipzig International Book Fair. Since critical attention focused on his illustrations, Bandzeladze had the freedom to develop simultaneously his abstract style (Pl. 11:4). He was especially influenced by black and white reproductions circulating in the Georgian avant-garde art community, depicting the work of Jackson Pollock (1912–1956), Arshile Gorky (1908–1948), and Willem de Kooning (b. 1904) (Fig. 11:3). No one in any official capacity took his "dabbling" seriously; as Bandzeladze explains in an autobiographical statement: "This was especially so, since I did not taunt anyone, contrary to my colleagues from Moscow."[7] Bandzeladze kept his true work hidden, except from the young artists around him.

In Georgia, Bandzeladze is recognized as the inheritor of

the Russian abstract tradition of Vasilii Kandinsky (1866–1944), who is credited with making the first abstract painting in 1909. Unlike other artists of the nonrepresentational school, however, Bandzeladze never completely severed his links with the human figure. His paintings retained the lyrical quality that characterizes much of Georgian art. On the surface, his images bring to mind the paintings of de Kooning in their intensity of color and form. The works are either full of vibrant saturated color or lacking in color entirely, depending instead on *chiaroscuro*. The brushwork is fluid and gestural, with areas of opaque color flowing through one another. Bandzeladze's paintings are calligraphic with a strong interplay between the varying thickness of line, which in turn creates a dramatic sense of tension and balance. His experiments in modern painting were first officially exhibited in Georgia in 1986. As his students' work began to gain international acclaim in an increasingly free political environment, so, for the first time, did the paintings of Bandzeladze. Despite his untimely death in 1992, he remains an influential force in Georgian art to the present day.

According to Leonid Bazhanov, the Moscow art historian who discovered contemporary Georgian art for Muscovites, Bandzeladze is unique in that he represented the avant-garde in Georgia in the 1970s virtually single-handedly. "Since then, three, and perhaps even four generations of Georgian painters [have been] practically born at the same time—an explosion."[8] This "explosion" became evident in the 1980s, the most important years for Georgian art. During that decade, a variety of eye-opening Georgian art exhibitions rocked not only Georgia, but art centers throughout the U.S.S.R. and in Europe as well.

Georgian art was experiencing a [...] in art were occurring even before *gl[...]* ism, Conceptualism, and all the [...] trans-avant-garde, though conceived y[...] increasingly appeared in Georgian art. Th[...] de marked the change to a new *Weltanschauung* an[...] a new relationship with art. Artists demonstrated a broad range of interests and showed their general disdain for "salon" art. The romanticism of the past was combined with an engagement in the contradictions of contemporary life. Geometric forms were admired and a two-dimensional rendering of space was popular, but the use of metaphors and symbols also became customary.

According to art historians Nana Kipiani and Karlo Kacharava, Georgian artists were adept with the language of contemporary art and did not have to struggle with technique, as younger artists did in some other Soviet republics. As a result, they had the choice of either refuting modernism or reworking it in a new context. Interestingly, many of the artists accepted formalism, yet rejected its aesthetics. They felt that the meaning and mission of art was higher than the simple search for the relationship between depicted objects and figurative planes, higher than the masterful manipulation of specific painterly devices as an end in itself. Instead, they accepted these devices as methods of individual self-expression. Having examined the fundamental issues of art, Georgian artists then saw the creative process as an act of self-knowledge and self-determination in a broader socio-cultural context.[9]

Of course, the Georgian Artists' Union continued to expound the virtues of Socialist Realism. At the 1981 festivities commemorating "Sixty Years of Soviet Georgia and the Georgian Communist Party," Leonid Brezhnev lauded Georgian art for "expressing the versatility of Socialist Realism."[10] And though industrial landscapes and *kolkhoz* scenes still dominated Union art, straightforward renderings upholding the Party line had given way to a newly expressive use of color and to psychological analysis of the subject and its environment.

It was during this "decade of revelations" that the 1983 retrospective of David Kakabadze (1889–1952), a true representative of the European avant-garde of the early twentieth century, took place. His art greatly motivated the abstract work of many younger artists, including Edzgveradze, Zautashvili, Soso Tsereteli (b. 1956), and Dato Mikaberidze (b. 1958). This group of artists were united in their search for personal truth and in their desire to learn about the spiritual world. They gathered information about world religions and immersed themselves in

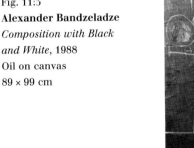

Fig. 11:3
Alexander Bandzeladze
Composition with Black and White, 1988
Oil on canvas
89 × 99 cm

Fig. 11.4
Gia Edzgveradze
Which One Is the Murderer's Knife?, 1985
Oil on canvas
244 × 109 cm

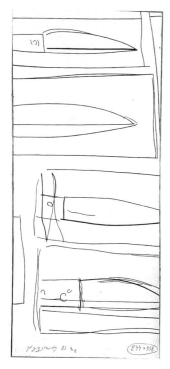

theology and the occult. Much like their mentor Bandzeladze, these artists were influenced by de Kooning, but also by Mark Rothko (1903–1970) and Ad Reinhardt (1913–1967). The searchings of this group, which was led by Edzgveradze but never formally named itself, paved the way to a Postmodernist consciousness in Georgia. This shift resulted in the Conceptual work of Edzgveradze and Zautashvili and the original Minimalist experimentations of Gia Mgaloblishvili (b. 1957).

In 1985, Edzgveradze organized an avant-garde group exhibition in Tbilisi, which turned into a major scandal and was quickly closed. Without question, this was the first official Georgian avant-garde exhibition. A large 1986 group exhibition of the "artists of the 1980s," again in Tbilisi, placed Edzgveradze in a small subgroup that also included Lazareishvili and Zautashvili. The pivotal exhibition for Edzgveradze, however, was one held in Moscow in 1987. Leonid Bazhanov, an active promoter of the Moscow avant-garde and founder of the Ermitage gallery, decided to introduce Moscow to Georgian art.

Bazhanov's "Exhibition of Georgian Non-Figurative Art" featured works by Bandzeladze, Edzgveradze, Lazareishvili, Zautashvili, and Mgaloblishvili. It demonstrated that each artist had his own personal aesthetic approach, even though everyone except Mgaloblishvili showed Abstract Expressionist paintings. Edzgveradze was unique in that he was represented by two different painterly styles. Alongside his lush, colorful, textured abstractions, he mounted his black and white calligraphic paintings which he had developed at the end of the 1970s and in the early 1980s. These controlled-line drawings were in effect Conceptual signs, the duality of spirit denoted by contrasting black and white patches.

In his artist's statement, Edzgveradze explained: "By turning away from color, I carry the principle of convention to its limit. For color, by its nature, is something suspended between life and convention, on the one hand, perceived (and presented to us) as something real, on the other, somehow elusive, ephemeral, flowing. Black and white is a medium of natural duality, of conflict, which is the foundation of the manifestation of existence."[11] This approach is clearly demonstrated in Edzgveradze's 1985 painting *Which One Is the Murderer's Knife?* (Fig. 11:4). The viewer is not only confronted with the concept of murder, but is asked to participate in the act by selecting one of the knives depicted. The artist would elaborate on his philosophy regarding his Conceptual art in future exhibition catalogues, culminating with "The White Manifesto."

It is incorrect, therefore, to assume that Georgian experimental art was directed only toward an Abstract Expressionist style. One group of artists, including Gia Bugadze (b. 1956) and Levan Chogoshvili (b. 1953), focused their artistic endeavors on the rendering of various stages in the history of Georgia.[12] In 1983, depictions of Georgian tsars or the former aristocracy were still forbidden. Despite this taboo, Bugadze concentrated on the romantic history of Georgia, depicting the entire lineage of Georgian kings and queens, often linking them to Christianity by showing their relationship to Adam and Eve as well as to Christ. His battle scenes based on biblical stories contain allegorical references to events in Georgia as well as a running philosophical commentary on national issues.

Chogoshvili, whose grandmother was a member of the prominent Bagration family, founded his artworks on the destruction of the Georgian aristocracy. His elegant family scenes are based on old photographs of his ancestors. Since many Georgians were commissioning such portraits for their families in the 1980s, Chogoshvili believed that Georgia was in a "state of crisis" regarding its own identity.[13] In the mid-1980s, this historical style was still restricted by the government. Indeed, Bugadze and Chogoshvili were officially denounced for their counter-revolutionary acts of painting historical themes and a formal complaint was lodged against them in Moscow.

The largest and most cohesive group of experimental Georgian artists became known in the mid-1980s. Though they had been active individually, the public first gained awareness of them as a group in 1985 when they showed at the Telavi Music Festival. This group, consisting of fellow students at the Tbilisi Academy of Arts, were dubbed "The Artists of the Tenth Floor," since some of them initially worked together on the tenth floor of the Academy, in a room assigned to the graduate student Mamuka Tsetskhladze. In all, there were fifteen members: Gia Dolidze (b. 1959), Mamuka Dzhaparidze (b. 1962), Temur Iakobashvili, Karlo Kacharava (1960–1994), Niko Lomashvili (b. 1959), Gia Loria (b. 1960), Goga Maglakelidze (b. 1962), Koka Ramishvili (b. 1956), Gia Rigvava (b. 1956), Lia Shevlidze (b. 1959), Zurab Sumbadze (b. 1963), Oleg Timchenko (b. 1957), Maia Tsetskhladze (b. 1965), and Niko Tsetskhladze (b. 1959).

Though much of the work was figurative in the early 1980s, by the time of the exhibition, these artists had divested themselves of the strictures of their academic training. Their goal was to unite all styles of late modernism in a Conceptual framework. Since they lacked fine-art materials, they experimented with whatever was available, from shoe polish to house paint to metal and wood. Their first official group exhibit was in 1986 at the Tbilisi

Ethnography Museum, where they showed with Bugadze and Chogoshvili. The works were a mixture of figurative painting, Neoexpressionism, and Neoprimitivism based on Pirosmani and the Russian *lubok*. As the group expanded, the artists moved to a studio belonging to the Marzhanishvili Theater, where they jointly painted the theater walls. They also received encouragement from Georgian-Armenian film producer Sergei Paradjanov to explore beyond the narrow definitions of art. Nevertheless, the group would not permit him to film their exhibition, since they did not want to be connected with someone of official stature.

Though Tsetskhladze and Kacharava were particularly influenced by Georgian cinematography of the 1920s and 1930s, the entire Tenth Floor Group were fascinated by contemporary films, especially those produced by the Germans Rainer Werner Fassbinder and Werner Herzog. They were equally interested in the German art group Cobra, with which they were later often compared. The Tenth Floor Group was also known as "The Free Collegiate of Artists" in Estonia and "The Artists of the New Image" in Russia, and they gave birth to many myths and cinematographic allusions, creating monumental paintings, objects, and albums. They were the first group in Tbilisi to stage performances. In this endeavor, they were greatly influenced by Joseph Beuys (1921–1986), the Neoexpressionism of Georg Baselitz (b. 1938), and the paintings of Francesco Clemente (b. 1952) and Julian Schnabel (b. 1951).

The year 1988 was decisive in the development of contemporary Georgian art. In that year, at the instigation of the Tenth Floor Group, the first retrospective of the Georgian avant-garde was mounted at the Ethnography Museum. The exhibition not only included the Tenth Floor Group, but also such experimental artists as Niko Lomashvili and the well-known poet/critic Dato Chikhladze (b. 1962). That same year, the group participated in a festival of the Soviet avant-garde in Narva, Estonia. At this first important gathering of unofficial artists from the entire U.S.S.R., they were singled out as especially interesting and promising.[14]

During 1988 a number of artists joined together to create an exhibition of "object art." Included were Otar Chkhartishvili (b. 1938), Amir Kakabadze (b. 1941), Georgi Khutsishvili (b. 1941), Levan Magalashvili (b. 1940) (Fig. 11:5), Georgi Aleksi-Meskhishvili (b. 1941) (Fig. 11:6; Pl. 11:5), and Georgii Mikeladze (b. 1946), who condemned "soulless" formalism and pursued human values in their art. They were in search of new plastic means to express the contemporary material world. Their art was based on Georgian stage design, monumental art,

Fig. 11:5
Levan Magalashvili
Adam and Eve, 1983
Mixed media
93.5 × 98 × 33 cm

Fig. 11:6
Georgi Aleksi-Meskhishvili
Letter, 1984
Mixed media
140 × 178 cm

and easel paintings.

Art critic Eteri Shavgulidze praised this group for causing a conflict of opinion, and he said that he hoped that yet more Georgian artists would pursue avant-garde experiments.[15] Magalashvili said: "We used Aesopian language, since we had to speak in hidden terminology under Communist rule. . . . I personally believe that life is a crucifixion. Since art reflects life, art must portray life's horrors and tragedies. An artist's objective should be to destroy established canons and traditions. We had to combat the official requirement to only portray a sunny Georgia."[16]

Gradually, Georgian contemporary art gained increasing amounts of respect throughout the U.S.S.R. Indeed, it even came to be admired internationally in 1988. When Sotheby's opened its auction of primarily Russian underground artists in Moscow, Gia Edzgveradze was the only participating Georgian. That momentous event for the Soviet art world launched Edzgveradze into an international artistic career. He used his new influence to help many other Georgian artists, especially Bandzeladze and his own loose group, to exhibit abroad.

In 1989, there were strong signs that the Tenth Floor Group were about to disband. Disputes between various group members became public during the exhibition "The Georgian Avant-Garde of the 1980s," which was held at the Museum of Ethnography of the Peoples of the U.S.S.R. in Leningrad. One group of artists had abandoned their Postmodernist trans-avant-garde painting and were making object art and installations. They considered these approaches more functional and a better reflection of the progress of contemporary art. By 1990, the rifts in the Tenth Floor Group were even clearer, as Dzhaparidze, Ramishvili, Rigvava, Timchenko, and Tsetskhladze showed separately at the biennial exhibition of avant-garde art in Leningrad.

There, they were joined by fellow Georgian Keti Kapanadze (b. 1962), an erstwhile Edzgveradze student, who in her unusual Conceptual paintings was the first artist in Georgia to deal with feminist issues. Kapanadze began to focus her creative endeavors on Conceptual and Minimal art in 1983, at a time when she also became known as a leader of the Georgian cultural underground. In previous years, she had been absorbed by the "painful problem of the relation between art and the world of consumption," an issue she equated with Western society. Thus, her continuing goal, developed in the early 1980s, was to demonstrate the "pure conventionality of any visual codes and general lack of spirituality in our postindustrial society." The artist considered the relationship between the material and the spiritual world a painful problem and wanted "art to be without nationality."[17] Along with other Georgian artists, Kapanadze continued to participate in group shows at the Gallery of Alternative Art, a coop gallery founded by Dato Chikhladze (b. 1962).[18] Thus a new stage of contemporary Georgian art was born which would develop into the 1990s.

In April 1989, peaceful demonstrations in Tbilisi were forcefully suppressed by the government. Communist rule was discredited and Zviad Gamsakhurdia, the Georgian head of state, was removed in response to the protests due to his dictatorial actions and human rights violations. Despite this political turmoil, Georgian artists remained artistically active. In September 1989, they opened a large retrospective of Georgian alternative art at the Palace of Culture in Tbilisi that included twenty-eight artists representing all facets of Georgian art.

In addition to the well-known artists who had exhibited with Edzgveradze and the Tenth Floor Group, this show included others who had eschewed group assignation. Dato Shushanja (b. 1952), who credits Bandzeladze and Edzgveradze among his influences, showed his large, colorful paintings abstracted from photography. A successful cinematographer in his official life, Shushanja's true dedication was to his painting. As a rule, his small-scale artworks tended to be Conceptual, whereas his large scale works were abstract (Pls. 11:6, 11:7). The influence of the American photographer, Eadweard Muybridge (1830–1904), is evident in Shushanja's preoccupation in many of the Conceptual works with depictions of frozen movements. These stand in stark contrast to the free, almost calligraphic forms of his larger paintings. In both artistic styles, he was influenced by the progressive transition from photography to abstract photography to art as abstraction. Like many of his fellow Georgian artists, Shushanja believes in the underlying goodness of mankind, that which separates man from animals and ultimately makes him noble.[19]

At the same exhibition, Zurab Kurchishvili (b. 1956) presented his naive portraits of the past based on his own memories. His portraiture is in some ways a take-off of the historical style, the difference being that Kurchishvili's ancestors live in his subconscious. Because of his naive style, critics compared him to Pirosmani. Tina Gomelauri (b. 1952) showed Abstract Expressionist paintings (Pl. 11:8), and Iliko Chitadze (b. 1955) was the lone example of Georgian "Sots Art." This 1989 exhibition came to be the most all-encompassing event of the complex and fractured Georgian art scene.

Loners, of course, continued to exist in the Georgian art world. Such fine artists as Nino Morbedadze (b. 1957) (Pl. 11:9) could not find time to be active in groups. Yet, her pen and ink images became known, even during her studies at the Tbilisi Academy of Art (1975–81), for their Surrealistic qualities and concern with the subconscious and with mystical ideas. Her *Untitled IV*, 1993, with a large knife incongruously dominating the sky over an equally strange landscape, was perhaps influenced by Edzgveradze's *Which One Is the Murderer's Knife?* In Morbedadze's case, however, one interprets the knife as a menace to the land of Georgia. Vladimir Kandelaki (b. 1943) felt he was a loner because he had been excluded. As an active member of the Georgian Union of Artists, he was disliked by the experimental few who refused to toe the Party line. However, in private, Kandelaki depicted allegories of Soviet life as well as the suppression of his homeland (Pl. 11:10).

From the earliest beginnings in the pre-Christian era, Georgian artists have demonstrated an uncanny ability to assimilate and reinterpret art. Though Georgian artists have often been isolated from Western concepts, they have always been quick to integrate them with their own national features as their society changed and became freer. Contrary to its Russian counterpart, the Georgian avant-garde avoided conflict with the existing bureaucracy of the state. Their opposition was aimed against the Georgian Union of Artists, against the snobbish, aestheticized milieu of official art.

However, everything changed on April 9, 1991, when Georgia once again became an independent state. Shortly thereafter, the building housing the Artists' Union was gutted by fire, presumably a politically motivated act of arson. Georgian artists increasingly broke with their groups and some moved to the West as bloody cataclysms overtook their newly reborn nation. On the whole, however, common interests and problems still bind today's Georgian artists in their search to unify the past, present, and future, and to develop their own type of "panaestheticism."[20] Their spiritual mentor, Alexander Bandzeladze, summed up the current situation best when he said: "The recent years of democracy have broken the dike and poured forth in a cloudy stream—still reminiscent of anarchy. For the time being, the avant-garde is whirling around its talents in the direction of fame. . . . And again there is the question for me—[and perhaps for the entire Georgian avant-garde] where am I?"[21]

Notes

1. The National Art Gallery was founded on February 1, 1920. It opened as the Central Museum of Fine Arts in August 1932 and was then relocated to the site of the thirteenth-century Metekhi Church in 1933.

2. Among the artists who helped found the Tiflis Academy of Arts in 1922 were Moisei Toidze, Georgy Gabashvili, Yakov Nikoladze, and Yevgeny Lanceray. Its first rector was G.N. Chubinashvili.

3. Among the Georgian artists searching for new artistic freedoms were Bandzeladze, G. Chirinashvili, D. Eristavi, G. Gelovani, E. Kalandadze, D. Khundadze, K. Makharadze, Zh. Medzmariashvili, Z. Nizharadze, G. Totibaidze, and L. Tsutkiridze.

4. Igor Golomshtok and Alexander Glezer, *Soviet Art in Exile* (New York: Random House, 1977), p. 111.

5. Among young 1970s artists who favored experimentation were M. Akhobadze, G. Agapishivili, L. Boyakhchev, A. Chagelishvili, O. Chubinidze, G. Kelesuridz, T. Khutsishvili, A. Parkosadze, I. Patashuri, A. Popiashvili, G. Toidze, and T. Tskhondia.

6. Latvian artist Juris Dimiters (b. 1947) painted Surrealist still lifes severely criticizing Soviet bureaucracy and society. The Surrealist images of Russian painters Olga Bulgakova (b. 1951) and Aleksandr Sitnikov (b. 1949) were often preoccupied with the inner psyche of man. On the other hand, multimedia artist Jüri Arrak (b. 1942) shocked the Soviet art establishment with his bizarre creatures, insinuating the captivity of man's soul in the Soviet system.

7. Alexander Bandzeladze, "Autobiography," unpublished manuscript, 1989.

8. Leonid Bazhanov, untitled, draft for an Amsterdam exhibition catalogue, June 29, 1990, p. 1.

9. Nana Kipiani and Karlo Kacharava, unpublished essay, prepared for the Tbilisi Institute of the History of Georgian Art, 1993, p. 2.

10. Nodar Dzhanbaridze, "K 60-letiyu obrazovaniia SSSR: Poyu moe otechestvo, respubliku moiu! Gruziya," in *Sovetskii khudozhnik* (1982).

11. Gia Edzgveradze, "Artist's Notes on Black and White Canvases," unpublished statement, 1987.

12. Artists in the "historical group" are B. Arbolishvili, G. Bugadze, L. Chogoshvili, G. Gugushvili, T. Kakabadze, D. Kukhalashvili, L. Lagidze, G. Mandjavidze, K. Matabeli, I. Sutidze, and L. Tatishvili. See Nodar Dzhanbaridze, *Quest and Tradition* (Tbilisi, 1989).

13. Levan Chogoshvili, interview with Elena Kornetchuk, Tbilisi, July 12, 1989.

14. *Iskusstvo* 10 (1988): 78.

15. Eteri Shavgulidze, *Predmentnoe iskusstvo*, exh. cat. (Tbilisi: Soyuz Khudozhnikov GSSR, 1988).

16. Levan Magalashvili, telephone interview with Elena Kornetchuk, November 1983.

17. Keti Kapanadze, telephone interview with Elena Kornetchuk, April 25, 1994.

18. For example, in August 1989, Timchenko, Khakhanashvili, N. Tsetskhladze, Keti Kapanadze, Kachavara, Z. Gomelauri, Dzhaparidze, and Chikhladze mounted the exhibition "The New Position," in which each artist presented one work. David Chikhladze, personal communication with Elena Kornetchuk, June 9, 1989.

19. Dato Shushanja, interview with Elena Kornetchuk, 1989.

20. Kipiani and Kachavara, p. 2.

21. "Expressions of Dissidence," exh. brochure (Sewickley, Penn.: International Images, 1991), n.p.

12 | Icons of the inner world

The spiritual tradition in the new Russian art

Alison Hilton

Celebrating Russia's religious heritage today, after seven decades of spiritual and aesthetic impoverishment, crowds of believers and spectators fill the newly resanctified churches, receive the Eucharist, buy icons and liturgical calendars, and flock to street-corner faith healers and occultists. Orthodox Patriarch Aleksei II energetically cultivates alliances with the civil authorities and intelligentsia in Russia and abroad, linking the renewal of the Church with a much needed moral healing for Russia and the world.

Enthusiasm for religion is also evident in Russian museums, galleries, commercial art salons, and street markets. Icons are highlighted at every level, from international exhibitions to kiosks at church portals. Tourists can buy *matreshka* dolls painted with the icons of the *Vladimir Mother of God* and the *Old Testament Trinity*; the great majority of art works recovered from would-be exporters of "contraband" are icons—an ironic sign of the commercial value attached to this art form.[1] While icons, pectoral crosses, embroidered vestments, and impressive church restoration projects have become symbols of a new temporal power for the Russian Church, has their rapid proliferation obscured their essential spiritual value?

Religious and spiritual values are inevitably linked to the moral condition of art. Art has always had a mission in Russia; many Russians who have lived abroad remark that art is taken much more seriously in Russia as an expression of fundamental values than in the West. But do the many depictions of old Russian churches, crosses, icons, and other religious references by such artists as Dmitri Plavinsky (b. 1937), Aleksandr Kalugin (b. 1949), Oscar Rabin (b. 1928), Aleksandr Kharitonov (1931–1993), and Vladimir Arkharov (b. 1937) represent more than a celebration of Russian cultural identity? Do the nonrepresentational, sometimes scarcely physical forms created by Eduard Shteinberg (b. 1937), Gennadii Zubkov (b. 1940), Anatolii Putilin (b. 1946), Siim-Tanel Annus (b. 1960), and Lydia Masterkova (b. 1929) convey a genuine striving for spiritual understanding?

Because the rules of Soviet Socialist Realism prohibited religious imagery, religious references became a means of protest by nonconformists. Similarly, the nonspecific contemplation or emotion that an abstract canvas could elicit denied the validity of a government-imposed aesthetic recipe. Artists who adopted these modes of expression during and after the brief thaw in the 1960s risked a great deal for the sake of artistic freedom. The very process of creating nonconformist art was an ongoing moral commitment. Unquestionably, the restrictions, hardships, and dangers familiar to unofficial artists became part of the content and significance of their art. After the removal of prohibitions against free artistic expression in 1985, the meaning of nonconformist art changed, but such values as integrity and artistic quality remain in place even in the increasingly market-oriented Russian art world.

We cannot fully evaluate the present state or predict the future evolution of the Russian spiritual tradition in art. Many religious images are readily identified, and evocations of spiritual ideas can be sensed in abstract forms. But it is not always easy to understand the aspirations of individual artists or appreciate the artistic influences, interactions, and distinctions within the broad and complex body of work reflecting spiritual values. However, some of these intentions and values can be clarified through historical perspective on the idea of the "spiritual" in Russian art and the development and transformation of the ancient icon tradition in modern times. Surveying the range and variety of art from the 1960s to the mid-1980s based on spiritual concepts, we can identify two major directions. One tendency, numerically dominant, emphasizes the traditional styles of religious art, or the depiction of Russian churches, icon subjects, and images from the Old and New Testaments. The other utilizes abstract forms to convey some manner of religious, spiritual, or metaphysical content. Interestingly, in Russian art, these apparently opposing directions are historically and philosophically related.

The icon, Russia's most characteristic devotional art form, was adopted from Byzantium, center of the Eastern Orthodox Church. The Greek word *eikon* meant "image";

Byzantine worship gave rise to the concept of image veneration. The icon, usually painted on a wood panel, but also embroidered, cast in metal, or printed on paper, has filled the need for private and public devotion from the beginning of the Christian era in tenth-century Russia to the present. Icons depicted the Savior, the Mother of God, saints (including personal patron saints), specific figures and events from the Old and New Testaments, images for contemplation (such as the Cross with symbols of the Passion), and certain miracles connected with Russian saints or with particularly important icons.

The subjects of these paintings and the specific manner in which they were treated were closely regulated by religious authority: the most revered icon types, *The Savior Not Made by Hands* (the mandillion) and the *Vladimir Mother of God*, were required to be direct copies of miraculous images. No painter was permitted to depart from a limited range of facial and figure types, poses, and compositions. Moreover, the icon painter was required to be "pure of spirit," and not tempted to embellish his work with superficial ornament or realistic description. Even the new humanistic climate in fifteenth-century Muscovy after the end of the Mongol occupation, when a few exceptional masters (such as Andrei Rublev) were known by name, did not lessen the importance of precedents and formal archetypes. Originality and individuality were foreign to traditional religious painting.

For nonconformist artists determined to declare their independence from imposed rules, the icon tradition might have seemed a dubious model. But the character of Rublev, as portrayed in Andrei Tarkovsky's film of the same period (1965), offers a peculiarly Russian explanation of the demands of art. Originally entitled *The Passion according to Andrei*, the film showed, in Tarkovsky's words, "that creation demands the sacrifice of one's entire self."[2] A number of films produced in the post-thaw, pre-*glasnost* period by Tarkovsky, Tengiz Abuladze, Sergei Paradjanov, and other directors use religious symbols, above all images of the sacrificed Christ, in ways that confirm the close identification of religious and artistic experience.

A profound tendency toward mysticism, a belief that the artist must fulfill a mission, and a willingness to submerge individuality and external beauty in the quest for moral truth—these are the ideals that characterize Russian art, even after the introduction of Western secular forms in the late seventeenth and eighteenth centuries. Aleksandr Ivanov (1806–1858) spent over twenty years on his work *The Appearance of Christ to the People* (1833–57), attempting to combine the solemnity of icons with the vividness of real observation. He never realized his vision. Meanwhile, the intellectual leader of the mid-nineteenth-century Realist movement, Ivan Kramskoi (1837–1887), considered his pursuit of "artistic freedom" to be a moral choice and portrayed it as such in his painting *Christ in the Wilderness* (1872).[3] At the end of the century, Nikolai Ge (1831–1894) almost obsessively painted agonizing images of Christ's death on the Cross, destroying religious conventions and aesthetic rules to foster his sense of truth.

Less than a decade into the new century, Russian artists were beginning to deny representation itself in order to convey what they conceived as a universal, "nonobjective" or "inner" reality. In quite different ways, the Russian pioneers of abstraction, Vasilii Kandinsky (1866–1944) and Kazimir Malevich (1878–1935), equated art with expressions of spirituality. In his 1911 essay *On the Spiritual in Art*, Kandinsky identified an "inner necessity" in art, based on "moral and spiritual atmosphere." He posited that after "an era of materialist trial and temptation . . . the soul is being reborn again" so that the artist of the future might reject the physical and "serve the *spiritual*."[4] For him, the ultimate form of liberated creativity was abstraction. Kandinsky wrote: "Art is a language whereby we speak to the soul (in a form accessible and peculiar only to this language) of things which are the soul's daily bread and which it can acquire only in this form."[5]

Malevich discovered that "pure form" and "intuitive reason" could transform the material world when he painted his *Black Square* (1914–15; Tretyakov Gallery). At the first exhibition of Suprematist art in 1915, he hung the *Black Square* high in the corner of the gallery, like an icon in the traditional place of honor in a Russian home. Malevich used the square, rectangle, cross, and other geometrical forms as "the basis of a new language" that could express "an entire system of world-building."[6] He told his colleague Mikhail Matiushin: "The keys of Suprematism are leading me to discover things still outside of cognition. My new painting does not belong solely to the earth . . . [but it expresses] a yearning for space, an impulse to break free from the terrestrial globe."[7] He also equated infinite space with "the limit of approaching nothingness," and said that he used the cross form to symbolize the "death of painting."[8]

Philosophically, then, the icon tradition, the pervasive belief in a messianic purpose for art, and the negation of referential subject matter and representation for the sake of pure form are all part of the "spiritual" heritage of Russian art. But another factor—the historical connection between art and ecclesiastical or governmental sponsorship—is also important for understanding the relationship between religious and spiritual themes and the non-conformist rejection of Soviet Socialist Realism and governmental control of art.

A century ago, some of the country's leading painters committed themselves to years of painstaking work designing and executing mosaics and frescoes for the sumptuous Cathedral of St. Vladimir in Kiev. Built in a historicizing, ancient Russian style to commemorate the adoption of Byzantine Christianity by the Kievan Prince Vladimir nine hundred years earlier, the project manifestly supported Tsar Alexander III's conservative, chauvinist policy equating "Orthodoxy, Autocracy, and Nationality." The danger, some artists realized, was that the public responded to an oversimplified notion of cultural orthodoxy, and missed the more subtle, subjective content of the religous imagery and of traditional forms of religious painting.

"A feeling for quiet lyricism and *sincere* mysticism is not accessible to many," Mikhail Nesterov wrote in 1898, shortly after completing his work in Kiev. Deeply religious himself, Nesterov tried to avoid canonical sacred imagery and instead create a sense of meditation, devotion, a unity of the human spirit and nature. He did not expect a wide audience. When Serge Diaghilev invited him to contribute to an exhibition in Munich, he hesitated, thinking: "Perhaps what I wanted to say is too *subjective*, and for the majority of viewers not only incomprehensible but completely unnecessary."[9]

Nesterov's expressive goals, and his uncertainty about realizing them, are strikingly similar to the ambitions and hesitations of many Russian artists in the 1960s and 1970s. The circumstances were obviously quite different: Nesterov and his colleagues were commissioned by the state to create a symbol of Russia's Christian heritage, while Soviet artists were forbidden to recall such prerevolutionary "reactionary" traditions. In both cases, however, the demands of the authorities affected, and limited, the choices open to the artists. Artists worked according to a state-sponsored program or opposed it, but there was little latitude for attention to subtleties and to personal artistic needs.

Soviet artists who tried to transcend or counter official rules had little meaningful outside support: their struggle was interpreted in political, not artistic, terms. All too aware that they were virtually unknown and misunderstood (or worse, unnecessary) in the West, some felt that any attention they gained abroad was due to the exoticism of the Byzantine tradition, the appeal of the "Slavic spirit," a Russian reputation for "profound psychological penetration," and the tragic glamor of spiritual survival behind the Iron Curtain.[10] As one sympathetic American wrote of the pioneering nonconformists Ernst Neizvestny (b. 1925), Eli Beliutin (b. 1925), and their circle:

> Even under the most rigorous of cultural and political dictatorships, here and there tiny pockets of independent intellectual and artistic spirits manage to survive—in the form of "interior immigration" or by "going underground."[11]

It was difficult for the artists themselves, let alone foreign observers, to discover valid visual idioms. While the Soviet authorities denounced abstract styles as "antihumanistic,"[12] some foreign writers lamented that "Russia has not been a nation of painters since their Byzantine school of icons became moribund," and that today's artists have "no immediate tradition on which to draw and this irrevocably results in provincialism, regardless of whether the artist is a realist or a modernist."[13]

Until recently, many artists accepted the view that the only alternative to Soviet Socialist Realism was to be found in the Byzantine icon tradition: the Expressionist and abstractionist works of the early twentieth-century Russian vanguard were unknown; modernism was equated with Western schools, and even the strong, socially critical Realist tendency of the nineteenth century had been swamped by the officially approved "realist" canon. Faced with severe restrictions, and lacking access to actual examples of Russia's rich modernist heritage, some artists developed imaginative mental constructions, defined as "metarealism" and "metaphysical synthetism." The amount and nature of verbal discourse on principles and theories of art is a telling indication of the extreme need they had for communication of a philosophical intent in the absence of possibilities for communicating directly by exhibiting their works.

For example, Otari Kandaurov (b. 1937) defines his system of metarealism according to its "spiritual aspect" (relating to the most deep-seated layers of being, Platonic "realia") and its "plastic aspect" (methods of examining the entirety of experience). The methods themselves are highly spiritual: "revelation in unbelievably concentrated form," and "plastic meditation" in which "the object is irradiated by the light of spiritual bodies."[14] Without discussing religious imagery specifically, he equates his subject matter (ideas) and his painterly language with "In the beginning," the Word of Creation.

The program of metaphysical synthetism, developed by Mikhail Chemiakin (b. 1943) and the St. Petersburg Group in the early 1970s, begins with the declaration "God is the basis of Beauty," and goes on to demonstrate that "Art means the paths of Beauty leading to God." The manifesto

Fig. 12:1
Ernst Neizvestny
The Prophet, 1966
Bronze
93 × 56 × 66 cm

presents several analogies of or metaphors for creation through faith in God, citing the Gospel of St. John, Pythagoras, Greek myth, Goethe, and Russian icons. The final sections of the statement explain various methods of communication through symbols, and conclude:

> The icon is the most complete and perfect form of the revelation of beauty in the world. All the efforts of the metaphysical synthetists are directed towards the creation of a new icon-painting, from pictures to the icon.[15]

One answer to the repression and frustration of the 1960s for many creative artists was to "live within the spirit."[16] Religious imagery and formal or thematic references to Byzantine tradition served essential functions, especially in the early years of unofficial art. They signified concerns and loyalties foreign to official atheism, a search for continuity with the past, and rejection of the material and physical limitations of the present. Most works with religious themes are paintings, drawings, and prints; one exception is Ernst Neizvestny's powerful bronze sculpture *The Prophet*, 1966 (Fig. 12:1). In light of the artist's major works centered about a monumental project encompassing the entirety of human experience, this is less a representation of an Old Testament prophet than a symbol of all human striving and suffering.

Rarely do religious motifs indicate simple escapism. For instance, icons and Gospel books appear in many of Rabin's works (Pl. 12:3), along with street signs, dingy apartments and warehouses, and other details of Rabin's neglected Moscow neighborhood. These juxtapositions show how the contingencies of Soviet life come perilously close to destroying both religion and art. One of Rabin's paintings sets the Crucifixion of an armless Christ against a Russian urban skyline; another places a large truck-route detour sign next to the delicate cupolas of a village church. In Plavinsky's *The Gospel according to St. John* (1966), the imprints of metal icons on a canvas covered with blocks of Old Slavonic text, like precious fragments of ancient manuscripts, are smeared, abraded, or even stamped with the prints of army boots.

Images of this kind expose the mindless destruction of the Russian heritage for the sake of sterile atheism and aesthetic conformity. They are critical, provocative, and powerful statements of a Russian—as opposed to a Soviet—cultural identity. Many Jewish artists also adopted Russian religious imagery: a deliberate choice signifying allegiance to universal cultural values. Some artists, including Anatolii Kaplan (1902–1980), Evgenii Abezgauz (b. 1939), Samuil Rubashkin (1906–1975), and Alexander Rapoport (b. 1933), introduced specific Jewish motifs—

from Old Testament sources, from Jewish cultural traditions, folklore, and life in the provincial *shtetlach* (Pl. 12:2). Several important exhibitions in the Soviet Union and abroad allowed Jewish artists to create a group identity, not necessarily based on similar styles and subjects but on a shared concern for traditional values.

The large, temporary exhibitions of nonconformist art in the mid-1970s, intended to show an encyclopedic range of styles and themes, included a surprising number of works with religious images. One Moscow critic commented that "one can see, whether directly or indirectly, Christian subjects or elements or motifs derived from Christian ritual. Cupolas, crosses, halos, crucifixions, crowns of thorns, little churches, icons, together and separately . . . roam from picture to picture."[17] The range of religious motifs and the stylistic variety in their treatment almost defies categorization. But looking at a body of works by twenty-five to thirty artists of various ages, regions, and religious and educational backgrounds reveals some interesting common ground and some differences. Numerically most important are works based on religious themes and using ancient Russian pictorial styles. The other major means of expressing religious and spiritual themes—through abstract forms—also involves the issue of abstraction as a non-Socialist Realist style, discussed elsewhere. Finally, a few artists consciously seek ways of expressing religious ideas through abstract forms that are derived in part from traditional forms of religious art. These works convey idea without symbol through a unity of form and meaning.

Religious references in nonconformist figurative art range from depictions of scenes, figures, and objects to stylistic reminders of traditional forms. The first group includes: views of Russian churches, monasteries, and shrines by Vladimir Arkharov, Aleksandr Kharitonov, and Aleksandr Kalugin; representations of such religious subjects as the Trinity, the Crucifixion, the Lamentation, and other images of Christ's Passion, in works by Kharitonov, Noi Volkov, Anatolii Zverev (1931–1986), Volodymyr (Vladimir) Naumets, Yurii Zharkikh, and Igor Tiulpanov; the iconic images of the Byzantine Mother of God by Rabin, Eduard Zelenin (b. 1938), and Feodosii Humeniuk (Gumeniuk); angels and seraphim (Volkov, Zharkikh, Kharitonov, Zelenin, Lucien Dulfan [b. 1942], and Sergei Potapov); and scenes of Christian or Jewish celebration by Arkharov and Rubashkin. Evocation of the Byzantine religious tradition through the form of the cross or quotations of icon, mosaic, fresco, or manuscript styles, often involving the incorporation of collage elements or casts made from small metal icons pressed into the gesso surface, is

most fully developed in the work of Plavinsky, Rabin, Evgenii Rukhin, Gleb Bogomolov (b. 1933), and Kharitonov. Finally, a smaller group of works based on abstract forms include subtle references to religious or spiritual traditions, sometimes open to more than one interpretation: Shteinberg, Rukhin, Naumets, Potapov, Gennadii Zubkov, Lydia Masterkova, Anatolii Putilin, and Evgenii Mikhnov-Voitenko all practice this approach.

Religious images are central to Kharitonov's works—delicate, complex pencil drawings and oils on canvas or board, in which tiny, raised brushstrokes resemble mosaics. His *Landscape with Shrine* (1972) and *The Memory of Old Russian Art* (1976–80) suggest bright childhood memories of his grandmother's tales and early visits to churches: they are intimate and harmonious.[18] Other images are more mystical, with flickering hosts of angels creating a counterpoint to the landscape elements in the 1982 works *Golden Russia* and *The Approach of a Mysterious Planet* (Pl. 12:9). Kharitonov's precious and decorative miniaturist style clearly recalls old Russian church embroideries and mosaics. The underlying conception of a pattern gradually growing out of tiny, discrete units, small strokes of the pencil or the tip of the brush merging and solidifying into figures, trees, buildings, and patches of earth or sky reflects Kharitonov's philosophical understanding of the many-layered spiritual history of Russia.[19]

Plavinsky's etching *Church at Night* (1969) and the mixed-media painting *The Walls of a Novgorod Church* (1974) also employ a layered, mosaic-like technique, with a quite different effect of darkness, enigma, and the weight of time. Kalugin's drawings of churches in Kizhi (Fig. 12:2), the Monastery of St. Ferapont, and of Sergiev Posad (1976–79) emphasize a complex but clear linearity, and juxtapose the intricate architectural patterns with the meager, contemplative figures of monks and saints; the style recalls that of topographical metal engravings of the eighteenth and early nineteenth centuries. Also reminiscent of naive descriptive scenes in popular prints (*lubki*), folk paintings, and the borders of provincial icons are Vladimir Arkharov's paintings of religious shrines. Painting in oil on fiberboard, he achieves a brilliant, smooth surface rich in pattern and detail. Though on a larger scale, it is comparable to late icons of the Vladimir-Suzdal region and to the lacquered boxes made in the same area (Palekh, Mstera, and Kholui) in the Soviet period, decorated with scenes from fairy tales as well as contemporary subjects. Like many genuine folk artists, Arkharov cleverly inserts verbal and visual commentary into his work. In *Novodevichy Cemetery*, 1974 (Pl. 12:1), for instance, he punctuates the snowy exterior scene with a cutaway view

Fig. 12:2
Aleksandr Kalugin
Churchyard in Kizhi, 1976
Pen and ink on paper
64.5 × 50.5 cm

Fig. 12:3 (*right*)
Vladimir Ovchinnikov
Cemetery for Dogs, 1978
Oil on fiberboard
96.5 cm in diameter

of the iconostasis of the Cathedral of the Smolensk Mother of God, with two other brightly painted figures of saints, and with the bust sculpted for Khrushchev's memorial by Ernst Neizvestny.

Vladimir Ovchinnikov (b. 1941) and Tatiana Shirikova (b. 1952) also employ a painstakingly descriptive technique, a kind of fantastic realism, to jar the viewer's awareness of unreality. Ovchinnikov's orderly *Cemetery for Dogs*, 1978 (Fig. 12:3), becomes a microcosm; in *Shuvalovo Station*, also 1978 (Pl. 5:15), a small railroad platform has waiting passengers and women workers on the track appearing as angels. Shirikova's corner of an old Russian city, in *Easter*, 1985 (Pl. 12:10), shows various folk-tale types—a prince, a maiden, a village lad, a monk, and a holy fool—all bemused by a band of miniature angels flitting about a decorated Easter egg.

While many artists use historical Russian styles to create a feeling of another world, some artists treat biblical subjects without emphasizing a traditional fresco, mosaic, or icon painting technique; others use traditional styles or formats to bring out a larger array of religious ideas associated with these forms. Noi Volkov (b. 1947) does both. In *Trinity* (1981) and *Black Angel* (1983), he quotes the contours and proportions of icons by followers of Andrei Rublev while applying the paint with broad

strokes of brush and palette knife. In *The Last Supper* (1980), he dismisses icon formulae to present Christ and his followers with Expressionistic, almost claustrophobic intensity. His startling *Christ Appearing to Brezhnev*, 1979 (Fig. 12:4) contrasts the visionary brilliance of the risen Christ with the dark awkwardness of the witnesses.

The Cross and the Crucifixion are among the most frequently employed religious motifs (Fig. 12:5). Laconic, Minimalist presentations in Kharitonov's *The Lamentation*, 1964 (Fig. 12:6), Kandaurov's *Candlestick* (Fig. 12:7), Putilin's untitled drawing, and Siim-Tanel Annus's series of "townscapes" dominated by large crosses contrast with the dense, many-layered cross forms painted by Plavinsky, Bogomolov, and Rukhin. In some of the latter, the crosses are built up out of imprints of metal icons, fabric, and playing cards (Pl. 12:11); in others, such as Plavinsky's *Old Russian Testament* from 1965 (Pl. 12:4), the cross shape becomes part of a closely related image.

Interpretations of the Crucifixion are even more varied in philosophical and emotional content. Igor Tiulpanov (b. 1939) places an Italo-Byzantine crucifixion at the center of his intricate painting *The Mystery* (1975–76) as a fulcrum for his conception of truth and appearance, past and future, "inner" and "outward" vision. Volodymyr (Vladimir) Naumets (b. 1945) continually turns to the

Fig. 12:5
Anatolii Slepyshev
(Morning Procession), 1982
Oil on canvas
100 × 240 cm

Fig. 12:4
Noi Volkov
Christ Appearing to
Brezhnev, 1979
Oil on fiberboard
136 × 71 cm

Fig. 12:6
Aleksandr Kharitonov
The Lamentation, 1964
Oil on canvas
78.4 × 57.8 cm

image of the crucified Christ, showing just a twisted body against a roughly painted background (Pl. 12:12), or sometimes schematized indications of a ladder, spear, and weeping angels. In some works he uses the traditional forms of icons, in others he quotes Italian Renaissance or Baroque sources; but his most powerful renderings convey the Expressionistic intensity of the late nineteenth-century Russian mystic painter Nikolai Ge.[20]

Yurii Zharkikh (b. 1938) surrounds a ghostly white crucified corpus with a grid of staring masks in *Descent into Hell* (1974); in *Consecration*, 1974 (Pl. 12:6), the body hangs disturbingly upside-down above a molten-colored pit from which faces emerge. Zharkikh frequently treats

Fig. 12:7
Otari Kandaurov
Candlestick, 1971
Watercolor and gouache
on paper
51.5 × 35 cm

the theme of regeneration after death. In one painting (Pl. 12:8), the pale, prone bodies of Christ and a pregnant woman stretch across the lower half of the canvas; around them, warm orange and charred grey skull-like faces and tenement buildings with eye-like windows merge to fill the rest of the space. Superimposed on these forms is a faintly rendered Crucifixion, placed horizontally and bisected by the vertical trunk and dark, vein-like branches of a tree.

Using more abstract and geometrical forms, other artists also relate the themes of the Cross and the Tree of Life, the Christian mystery of the Crucifixion and concepts of eternity. Mikhail Shvartsman (b. 1926) explores the structures and motifs of icons, paring down narrative elements and concentrating on smoothly painted, singular forms filling the space of the canvas, as in, for example, *Incarnation of Space* (1970) and *Space of the Trinity* (1986).[21] Sergei Potapov (b. 1947) emphasizes symmetry in his more complex compositions, such as *Tree*

Fig. 12:8
Siim-Tanel Annus
(Untitled), 1976
Gouache on paper
61.5 × 60.2 cm

of Knowledge (1982) and the work known as *Gesture*, 1985 (Pl. 12:7), which combine a central, vertical figure suggesting a risen Christ with radial beams of light or curved mandala-like forms; many have titles evoking the cosmos, eternity, the Trinity, and the apocalypse.[22]

The visual idioms developed by Zharkikh and Naumets and by Shvartsman and Potapov to express both traditional religious themes and more abstract, all-embracing conceptions of the cosmos point to sources beyond traditional Russian iconography. Nevertheless, the goals of all these artists are closely tied to the archetypal ideal of the icon painter, whose images give access to God. In other words, both Christian symbols and abstract forms such as the cross, mandala, circle, and square can serve not only as bearers of values from a traditional, suppressed culture, but also as metaphors for the process of creating art, in itself a spiritual process. Igor Golomshtok points out that in the Soviet Union participation in actual religious worship was so difficult that art was often the only means of "making contact with the spiritual."[23]

The boundary between religious imagery and more general spiritual meaning is sometimes obscure, even deliberately obscured, in works by Naumets and Volkov in which the core image is painted over in heavy, white impasto. Representing a different artistic direction, Shteinberg's crosses and other geometrical shapes appear to float freely on light-colored opaque grounds, while Annus's crosses, rhomboids, and triangles from his 1982–85 print series *Towers to the Heavens* and *Heavenly Cities*, as well as his earlier paintings and drawings, define the centers of pale, Minimalist compositions (Fig. 12:8). The ambiguous relationships between the visual and the material and between the visual and visionary are explored in all these works.

Some of the means of exploration, especially the emphasis on abstract forms rather than figuration, have their sources in philosophical positions and artistic experiments of the early twentieth century. The art of the Russian avant-garde disappeared from Soviet museums in the 1930s, but a few surviving artists continued working in their own personal styles. Robert Falk (1886–1958), an important figure in prerevolutionary avant-garde movements, taught at Vkhutemas (Higher State Art Technical Studios), then spent the difficult years 1928–36 in Paris before returning to Russia; he was one of the few in his generation to survive under Stalin and to maintain a link with the past for younger artists. Aleksandr Rodchenko (1891–1956), who abandoned easel painting in 1921 to work in photography and applied design, resumed figurative painting in the 1930s, and secretly produced

abstractions of rhythmically dripped paint. Aleksandr Tyshler (1898–1980), while working primarily as a designer for the Minsk and Kharkiv (Kharkov) Jewish Theaters in the 1920s, also made purely abstract studies of color and shape and fantastic compositions of interacting figures and architectural structures, in an engaging style of "lyrical Surrealism."[24]

Avant-garde ideas were also preserved and developed by young artists who had studied with Malevich, Matiushin, Filonov, and other colleagues at Ginkhuk (Institute of Artistic Culture) in Leningrad. Most influential was Vladimir Sterligov (1905–1973), who worked in close contact with other former students and developed his own concept of an S-shaped or chalice-shaped curve as a key formative element. Analogous to Malevich's *Black Square*, Sterligov's curved form embodied cosmic properties: reflecting the curvature of space, it contained the world and the "anti-world," color and noncolor, end and beginning. Sterligov said that "if the line is the division of the world . . . the curve [is] its unification."[25] After war service and five years in a Stalinist camp, Sterligov began to work with his wife, artist Tatiana Glebova (1900–1985), and his current and former students to develop the new formulation of space.

In detailed theoretical notes, Sterligov explained his understanding of the visual world as involving a synthesis of the internal and "surrounding geometry" into what he called "spiritual geometry." The idea of synthesis remains important for the Sterligov artists: they do not identify exclusively with either abstract or representational modes, but see art as an overlapping and unification of figurative and nonfigurative elements, a form of "spiritual 'making.'"[26] Gennadii Zubkov, a member of the group since the 1960s, continues to combine abstract and figurative forms in paintings such as *Dunes* (1979–80) and *Countenance of Trees* (1977). They are based on nature but deny representational mass and space in favor of a flattened or suggestively spherical structure, reminiscent of icons and of early twentieth-century abstraction. The curvilinear perspective reveals the unity behind the world of appearances, and offers a spiritual understanding of creation (Pl. 12:5).[27]

Another abstract artist from Leningrad, Evgenii Mikhnov-Voitenko (1932–1988), was not part of the Sterligov group, but his works reflect similar feelings for harmony and unity in nature (Pl. 12:14). He had the good fortune to study with Nikolai Akimov (1901–1968), the founder of the department of stage design at the Leningrad Institute of Theater, Music, and Cinematography.[28] Akimov encouraged his students to try all styles and techniques. Mikhnov-Voitenko began painting abstract compositions in the mid-1960s, mainly in ink wash and gouache on paper. Working rapidly, with a sheet of wet paper placed flat on a table, he controlled the ink and gouache with a palette knife, adjusting for spontaneous blending of colors, producing charged rhythms with thickly pooled paint and light areas scraped with a knife. Many of his works are calligraphic, like subconscious writing; all project and evoke subjective feeling, comparable to emotional responses to music. Mikhnov-Voitenko usually listened to music as he worked, and considered his form of art to be deeply spiritual.

Shteinberg, largely self-taught as an artist, exemplifies the lineage of Malevich's Suprematism. Shteinberg's father had studied in Vkhutemas in the 1920s, and Shteinberg's own works and statements about art often seem to echo Malevich's ideas. His paintings are arrangements of relatively small geometrical forms on opaque, usually light-colored surfaces. For Malevich, the surface, the "face of the new painting," contained infinite potential for expression through form. Shteinberg relies on subjectivity and intuition, declaring that the painting's most important aspects are those that "the corporeal eye cannot see in the painting" because "this cannot be shown on a surface."[29]

Shteinberg articulates the surfaces (or grounds) of his paintings with horizon lines, extending vertically, horizontally, or diagonally across the canvases, providing a framework for the contrasting, freely floating smaller geometrical elements. He sees these zones as equivalent to the traditional hierarchy of the earth, the Church, and the heavens, but he also enforces the unity of the flat surface, the lack of directional movement, the absence of a focus, or a beginning or end. Even a relatively small composition (Pl. 14:10) offers infinite space without dimension—a conception very close to Malevich's freeing of form from "the ring of the horizon and the circle of things."[30] Shteinberg's crosses, rectangles, and triangles are, like Malevich's, extremely pared-down elements of creative force, always reflecting the artist's "yearning for God."[31] Although no contemporary artist has maintained such close stylistic contact with Malevich, several other painters, both abstract and figurative, emphasize the importance of Malevich as a source of inspiration. For instance, Vladimir Nemukhin (b. 1925) credited a pupil of Malevich, Petr Sokolov (1892–1938), with showing him the meaning of creative work, and he compared his own discovery of the formal possibilities of playing cards on a surface to Malevich's invention of the *Black Square*.[32]

The work of Francisco Infante (b. 1943) combines aspects of Malevich's philosophy and structural experiments of both Suprematism and Constructivism. A leading figure in the Moscow Kineticist group Movement (Dvizhenie) in the early 1960s, Infante developed scientific-technological and visionary ideas concurrently. He invented the concept of the "artifact," an "artistic synthesis . . . between a [constructed, geometric] art object and nature."[33] His work takes the form of actions or performances recorded in photographs which, in turn, give rise to whole cycles of analogous formal records. In *Suprematist Games: Homage to Malevich* (Pl. 12:13) he placed geometric shapes made of colored paper on a field of snow; in others, he wrapped tree trunks in reflective foil and arranged mirrors to break up a natural background, creating ambiguity in the meaning of finite and infinite space.[34]

Masterkova, one of the most constant adherents of abstraction, is certainly a spiritual heir of the Russian avant-garde. She was introduced to modernist ideas by her first important teacher at the Moscow Art School, Mikhail Perutsky (1892–1959), a former pupil of Malevich.[35] In the 1950s, Masterkova sought out reproductions of the still-unavailable works of Cézanne, Picasso, and Matisse; and in 1957, Masterkova and other young Russian artists saw the enormous range of stylistic choices at the first exhibition of contemporary painting from abroad at the World Youth Festival in Moscow. By the late 1950s, Masterkova was painting abstract works in brilliant colors, often with fabric, cord, sand, and other textural collage elements; in 1965, she used darker, richer colors and modeled the forms on those of ancient Russian ecclesiastical embroidery and icons, much as Plavinsky did, to emphasize richness and the spirituality of the past. Gradually, Masterkova began to concentrate on the less ornamental, more abstract elements of icons, emphasizing rectangular and circular forms, and reducing her color range to black and brown tones against off-white grounds.

One of Masterkova's key works is *Composition* (1967), a brown square inside a black square covered with a layer of fine black lace that extends beyond the edges. The compositional similarity to icons of the *Savior Not Made by Hands* (the disembodied face of Christ on the mandillion) and to Malevich's seminal *Black Square* is striking, and suggests her awareness of universal, abstract forms of contemplation. But, jarringly, the black and brown square is slit down the center by a narrowing wedge of white paint, leaving only a few uneven threads linking the halves of the center area. The tearing apart of the square might signify Masterkova's realization of the rift between past and present. Her work in the late 1960s and 1970s

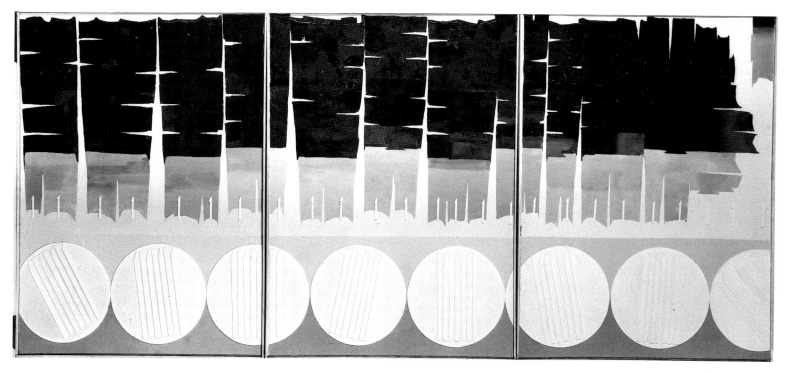

Fig. 12:9
Lydia Masterkova
Triptych No. 3, 1975
Mixed media on canvas
103 × 233.2 cm

grew more gestural and monumental, with a series of large canvases culminating in her 1975 *Triptych No. 3* (Fig. 12:9), a work based formally on the contrast of dark, craggy vertical forms above a row of neatly painted white circles of applied cardboard, each bearing a numeral of kabalistic significance. Like Malevich's abstract shapes, the numerals in Masterkova's works, ranging from zero to the infinite, carry meaning; the balance of gestural and rational, of dark and light, sensuous and spiritual sums up the artist's sense of her world.

Masterkova emigrated in 1976, but a statement she made five years earlier best expresses the nature of the artist's struggle for spiritual truth in Russia:

> To create, at the same time destroying. A feeling of
> the extinction of the planet, moral perfection—does
> this lead the artist to the summits? . . . A constant
> feeling of the great strength of the universe, or, if
> you like, of fate, fills the consciousness and
> becomes an inalienable part of existence. All
> through the inner world.
>
> The essence of a work of art is lofty spirituality.
> . . . Isolation—is the tragedy of the Russian. Outside
> society. There is no feeling of the real world. There
> is only one's own world.[36]

The cultural void perceived by Masterkova and so many of her colleagues in the 1960s and 1970s resulted from the submersion of both the rich aesthetic and spiritual traditions of the Russian Church and the bold philosophical leaps of the early twentieth-century vanguard beneath the monumental banality of Soviet Socialist Realism. Yet, even in the midst of a sensory and intellectual vacuum, some Russian artists could detect a spiritual resonance. Plavinsky, commenting on his images of battered churches, crosses, and manuscripts, wrote that his works were meant to be "the expression of what the object carries through time, that is, a certain degree of spirituality."[37] Perhaps time and experience contributed as much to the spiritual value of forms and images as did any iconographical association. Perhaps the difficulties of participating in religion or spiritual discourse, the efforts needed to discover and make connections with their own estranged past, gave special value to this heritage and encouraged the nonconformist artists to develop their own forms of spiritual expression.

Clearly this need for spiritual expression was a priority, far more so than for any group of artists in any other country. The quantity and variety of spiritual expression in nonconformist Soviet art also shows that the Russian spiritual tradition did not depend only on the rituals and formal models of Byzantine Christianity, although visual forms were always a powerful means of expressing religious ideas in ancient Russia. The spiritual tradition in Russia is not a matter of nostalgia, exoticism, wealth, or poverty. Far less does it have to do with the commercialized religious kitsch or the neo-orthodox fundamentalism that now threaten to dominate the post-*glasnost* era both in Russia and abroad.

In the Soviet nonconformist art made from the 1960s to the mid-1980s, there is an impressive moral commitment and artistic integrity demonstrated by individuals working under what were extremely discouraging conditions. Today, however, there is an uneasy shifting of priorities and perspectives. Many members of the Russian literary intelligentsia have commented on this difference. "The feeling of inner freedom and inner righteousness then was incomparable to what we have now," wrote one Russian novelist. "On the surface, intellectuals can't help but support what is happening today, but the whole intelligentsia shares a feeling of loss, uneasiness and nostalgia." Another writer concluded: "The intelligentsia has ceased to exist in the form it existed for the past 200 years in Russia. There is no longer a historical need for it."[38]

Ultimately, we must consider the implications of easy access to free discourse and to religious expression. For the present, we can conclude that religious and spiritual content has remained important and powerful even when religious art was not available. The Russian religious tradition founded within the aesthetic framework of Byzantine ceremony remained viable even when both the religious basis and the formal vehicles of expression were denied. Under Soviet conditions, creative art offered virtually the only real spiritual tradition.

Notes

1. The exhibition "Return to the Homeland" (1992) at the Tretyakov Gallery in Moscow included among recovered contraband an overwhelming preponderance of icons and religious art.

2. Anna Lawton, "Art and Religion in the Films of Andrei Tarkovsky," in William C. Brumfield and Milos M. Velimirovic, eds., *Christianity and the Arts in Russia* (Cambridge: Cambridge University Press, 1991), p. 154, quoting an interview with the director in A. Frezzato, *Andrej Tarkovskij* (Florence, 1977).

3. Ivan Kramskoi, letters to Vsevolod Garshin (Feb. 16, 1878) and to Fedor Vasiliev (Aug. 20, 1872; Feb. 13, 1875), in S.N. Goldshtein, ed., *I.N. Kramskoi. Pis'ma, stat'i* (Moscow, 1966), vol. 2, pp. 140–41, and vol. 1, pp. 126, 158. Kramskoi led the protest exit of senior students from the St. Petersburg Academy of Fine Arts in 1863 and was a founding member of the Association for Itinerants Art Exhibitions (the *Peredvizhniki*, or Itinerants) in 1871.

4. Vasilii Kandinsky, "O dukhovnom v iskusstve," presented at the All-Russian Congress of Artists in Petrograd, Dec. 1911–Jan. 1912; translated in John E. Bowlt and Rose-Carol Washton Long, eds., *The Life of Vasilii Kandinsky in Russian Art: A Study of "On the Spiritual in Art"* (Newtonville, Mass.: Oriental Research Partners, 1980), pp. 63–65.

5. Ibid., p. 99.

6. Kazimir Malevich, "Suprematism: 34 Drawings" (1920), in Troels Anderson, ed., *K.S. Malevich: Essays on Art*, 4 vols. (Copenhagen: Borgen, 1968–78), vol. 1, p. 123.

7. Dmitri Sarabianov, "Kazimir Malevich and His Art, 1900–1930," in *Kazimir Malevich, 1878–1935* (Los Angeles and Washington, D.C.: Armand Hammer Museum of Art and Cultural Center, Metropolitan Museum of Art, and National Gallery of Art, 1990), p. 167.

8. Kazimir Malevich, "God Is Not Cast Down" (1922), in *K.S. Malevich: Essays on Art*, vol. 1, pp. 213, 215, 221–23; Malevich's statement to Anton Pevsner is quoted in Camilla Gray, *The Russian Experiment in Art, 1863–1922*, edited by Marian Burleigh-Motley (rev. ed., London: Thames and Hudson, 1986), p. 240.

9. Mikhail Nesterov, letter to A. Turygin, Jan. 29, 1898; in Alla Rusakova, ed., *Nesterov. Iz pisem* (Leningrad, 1968), p. 131.

10. Christian Brinton emphasized these qualities in several essays promoting Soviet art, including his introduction to the exhibition of modern Russian art at the Grand Central Galleries, New York, 1924; see Robert Williams, *Russian Art and American Money* (Cambridge, Mass.: Harvard University Press, 1980), p. 95.

11. "How Art Exists under Communism Today," *Art News* (Apr. 1958): 21.

12. D.A. Nalbandian, "Falshivye tsennosti abstraktsionizma" [The false values of abstractionism], *Ogonyok* 32 (Aug. 1975); V. Zvontsov, "Esli tebe khudozhnik imia," *Leningradskaia Pravda*, Oct. 16, 1975.

13. Olga Carlisle, "Moscow 1960: Young Artists and Their World," *Art News* (Sept. 1960): 24.

14. Otari Kandaurov, "Metarealism: Creative Method and Creative Credo (Theses)," in Igor Golomshtok and Alexander Glezer, *Soviet Art in Exile* (New York: Random House, 1977), p. 147.

15. Mikhail Chemiakin and Vladimir Ivanov, "Metaphysical Synthetism," in Golomshtok and Glezer, *Soviet Art in Exile*, pp. 155–57.

16. V. Patsiukov, "Erik Bulatov, Edward Shteinberg," trans. Jamey Gambrell, *A-Ya* 3 (1981): 14.

17. E. Barabanov, "The September Exhibition of Moscow Painters in 1975," in *Vestnik russkogo khristianskogo dvizheniia* [Herald of the Russian Christian movement] (1975), p. 241, quoted in Igor Golomshtok, "Unofficial Art in the Soviet Union," in Golomshtok and Glezer, *Soviet Art in Exile*, p. 98.

18. Tatiana Sokolova, "Alexander Vasilevich Kharitonov: Innovator and Traditionalist," in Norton T. Dodge et al., *Kharitonov* (New York: Museum of Contemporary Russian Art in Exile, 1991–92), pp. 5–6.

19. See M.T. Sokolov, "Fields of Hope: On the Style of Alexander Kharitonov," in Dodge et al., *Kharitonov*, pp. 7–9.

20. For a full range of images, see the catalogue *Vladimir Naumez: Zeichen und Gestalt* (Cologne: Galerie-Forum Lindenthal, 1989).

21. For illustrations and discussion of these works, see Matthew Cullerne Bown, *Contemporary Russian Art* (London: Phaidon, 1989), pp. 66–67, 72.

22. See Elena Viunnik, "Post Symbolism," *Sergei Potapov*, exh. cat. (Moscow, 1992).

23. See Igor Golomshtok's discussion in Golomshtok and Glezer, *Soviet Art in Exile*, p. 98.

24. A documentary film on Tyshler, made by Maria Tavrog in the early 1970s with the artist's cooperation, was only recently released. It is significant that art historians and critics, as well as artists, were beginning to study and write about these little-known successors of the Russian avant-garde in this crucial period. Important articles and documents appeared in *A-Ya*, the unofficial art review published in France by Igor Chelkovsky.

25. Sterligov statement quoted in Evgenii Kovtun, "The Plastic World of Vladimir Sterligov," in Charlotte Douglas and Margarita Tupitsyn, *Gennady Zubkov and the Leningrad "Sterligov" Group: Evidence of Things Not Seen* (New York: Contemporary Russian Art Center of America, 1983), n.p.

26. Terms and ideas from discussion of the Sterligov circle quoted by Kovtun in "The Plastic World of Vladimir Sterligov," and Margarita Tupitsyn in "The Emergence of Man into Spherical Space," in Charlotte Douglas and Margarita Tupitsyn, *Gennady Zubkov and the Leningrad "Sterligov" Group*, n.p.

27. See Charlotte Douglas, in Douglas and Tupitsyn, *Gennady Zubkov and the Leningrad "Sterligov" Group*, n.p.

28. Norton T. Dodge, and Alexander Glezer, eds., *Evgeny Mikhnov-Voitenko: Abstract Visions* (Jersey City, N.J.: C.A.S.E. Museum of Contemporary Russian Art, 1988), p. 4; other former Akimov pupils are Dyshlenko, Kulakov, Rapoport, Tiulpanov, and Tselkov.

29. Patsiukov, "Erik Bulatov, Edward Shteinberg," p. 14.

30. Kazimir Malevich, "From Cubism and Futurism to Suprematism" (1916), in *K.S. Malevich: Essays on Art*, vol. 1, p. 19.

31. Shteinberg's phrase, quoted in Bown, *Contemporary Russian Art*, p. 76.

32. Vladimir Nemukhin, interview (Glezer archive), quoted in Golomshtok and Glezer, *Soviet Art in Exile*, pp. 152–53.

33. Francisco Infante, "On My Concept of the Artifact" (artist's statement, Feb. 9, 1987), quoted in Elena Kornetchuk et al., *Francisco Infante: A Contemporary Moscow Artist*, exh. cat. (Sewickley, Penn.: International Images, Ltd., 1989), p. 16.

34. These and other concepts are discussed by John Bowlt in "Suddenly," in Elena Kornetchuk et al., *Francisco Infante*, pp. 12–15; see also Michel Costantini, "Francisco Infante," *A-Ya* 3 (1981): 38–40.

35. Margaret Betz, "Lydia Masterkova: Striving Upward to the Real," in Norton Dodge, ed., *Lydia Masterkova: Striving Upward to the Real* (New York: Contemporary Russian Art Center of America, 1983), n.p. In 1950, the authorities closed the college for "leftist deviationism" allowed by the faculty and director Nina Kofman.

36. Lydia Masterkova, letter to Ermesto Valentino, Dec. 14, 1969; quoted in Golomshtok and Glezer, *Soviet Art in Exile*, p. 151 (also quoted in slightly different form in Betz, "Lydia Masterkova," n.p.).

37. Plavinsky, statement quoted in Golomshtok and Glezer, *Soviet Art in Exile*, p. 97.

38. Novelist Mikhail Berg and writer and editor Lev Timofeev, quoted by Fred Hiatt, "Russian Intelligentsia Adrift," *International Herald Tribune*, July 20, 1992.

13 | Realism, Surrealism, and Photorealism

The reinvention of reality in Soviet art of the 1970s and 1980s

Janet Kennedy

The concept of realism has been firmly embedded in Soviet art since 1934, when the First Congress of the Union of Soviet Writers endorsed the principle of Socialist Realism. Henceforth, Soviet artists were enjoined to produce "a true, historically concrete depiction of reality in its Revolutionary development." As numerous historians have had occasion to observe, this formula is paradoxical, since it demands that the artist meet the requirements of documentary realism while also depicting contemporary life as bathed in a rosy glow cast by the future victory of Socialism.[1] By its very nature, Socialist Realism directed the artist away from reality into a world of revolutionary fantasy. The gap that opened up between the rhetoric of public speech and the reality of day-to-day life led ultimately to a situation which might be described as "surreal."

Dissident writer Andrei Siniavsky came to the conclusion that only a fantastic realism could capture the contradictions and absurdities of Soviet life. At the end of his essay "What Is Socialist Realism?", Siniavsky called for "a phantasmagoric art . . . in which the grotesque will replace realistic description of ordinary life. Such an art would correspond best to the spirit of our time. May the fantastic imagery of Hoffmann and Dostoevsky, of Goya, Chagall, and Mayakovsky (the most socialist realist of all), and of many other realists and nonrealists teach us how to be truthful with the aid of the absurd and fantastic."[2]

Over the last three decades, Soviet artists have embraced various alternative forms of realism: the fantastic realism advocated by Siniavsky, the consciously contrived Surrealism of unofficial artists working in the 1970s, the Photorealism which emerged at the end of the 1970s, and even a form of "social" (not socialist) realism which appeared in the early days of *perestroika*. Against a backdrop of Socialist Realism, which remained the official doctrine for most of this period, the concept of "reality" underwent some surprising adventures at the hands of those artists whose independent turn of mind prevented them from accepting the official pieties of the Soviet regime.

Indeed, most Soviet unofficial art might be seen as a dialogue with the official notion of Soviet reality. In the earlier stages, the emphasis was on restoring repressed aspects of reality: witness the proliferation of religious motifs and the sometimes violent eroticism of unofficial art in the 1970s. In more recent years, artists have raised questions about the process of representation itself. Photorealism (or *giper* as Soviet critics called it)[3] helped to dismantle the myth that photographs are simply reality once removed. On close inspection, the photograph—for all its appearance of documentary realism—turned out to offer no more secure a grasp on reality than the traditional media of drawing and painting. Additional problems were raised by the typical subject matter of Photorealism: the urban environment. The inherent "unreality" of the cityscape—a manmade creation that often assumes bizarre and unexpected forms—makes it difficult to be certain, in viewing it, where nature ends and art begins. As a consequence, the cityscape has been an inviting subject for artists attempting to expose the artificialities inherent in realistic painting.

The search for an alternative to Socialist Realism began, remarkably enough, in the darkest years of Stalinism. In 1946, Boris Sveshnikov (b. 1927), then a third-year student at the Moscow Institute of Decorative and Applied Arts, was arrested and sentenced to eight years in a Siberian labor camp. Eventually assigned to duty as night watchman in the camp's woodwork shop, he was able to spend much of his time drawing. The camp drawings that Sveshnikov produced between 1946 and 1954 combine precise depictions of the ramshackle camp buildings with a dark fantasy world worthy of Goya.[4] We may be tempted to see traces of Surrealism in some of these drawings, but Igor Golomshtok warns us that such a connection is, at best, in the mind of the beholder. For a camp inmate, reality itself was so fantastic that no outside stimulus was necessary.[5]

Sveshnikov's work in the years following his release defies easy categorization. Although the landscapes and architectural structures that appear in his paintings from the 1950s and 1960s are similar to those in the camp drawings, neither time nor place can be identified with any accuracy. In one painting (Pl. 13:3), for example, we find a group of figures seated on benches outdoors near a construction of wooden poles (a partially built house? an outdoor stage?). The assembled individuals have the weary look of travelers waiting for a train or bus; but otherwise they are an oddly assorted group, some clothed in Soviet-style jackets and caps, others dressed as nineteenth-century travelers. One figure (who could be male or female) is wearing blue drapery like a monk's robe and holding a parasol. The feeling of strangeness and isolation is increased by the pitch-black background and by the faces that peer through the windows of a nearby apartment house. Only the figure in blue is obviously fantastic, but the absence of a clearly defined scenario makes the entire scene disturbing. What are the figures waiting for, and why are they being watched?

In another of Sveshnikov's paintings, *Dance* (1962), the situation is no less ambiguous. Tiny puppet-like figures are dancing in a landscape dotted with Japanese parasols. In the foreground, a fiddler with frog-like feet plays, while in the background an architectural structure with eyes and a mouth seems waiting to swallow up the dancers. This Boschian fantasy bears the imprint of traditional symbolism and, in this respect, is easier to comprehend

than the artist's other works: it is a variant of the medieval dance of death. However, the moralizing tone of a traditional dance of death, which invites the viewer to reflect on the vanity of earthly life, is absent from this painting. Instead, we have an image of fragile beauty, in which the delicate parasols and the fiddler's music remind us of aesthetic pleasures that are no less precious for being transient.

Sveshnikov's paintings have an elegance of line and silhouette—even a kind of beauty—that coexists uneasily with imagery of exhaustion, surveillance, and death. His works from the 1970s, in particular, are full of decorative elements (Fig. 13:1). These paintings invite the viewer to explore an intricate mass of pattern and to discover in it tiny forms and suggestions of forms—birds' heads, human profiles, shapes resembling feathers, and shells. Some are fairly clear, while others barely reach the threshold of recognizability. This indeterminacy places the viewer in a challenging position: she or he must give meaning to the forms rather than simply accept what is given. The uncertainty of this situation is at a considerable remove from the clearly formulated and predigested "messages" that prevail in official Soviet art.

Sveshnikov's work of the 1970s owes a considerable debt to Russian art from the turn of the century, that is to artists like Mikhail Vrubel' (1856–1910), Vasilii Milioti (1875–1943), and Pavel Filonov (1883–1941), who for many years were outlawed from Soviet art history and contemptuously categorized as "decadent." In the 1970s, Sveshnikov adopted a palette of violet and blue tones that is reminiscent of Vrubel's painting, but his debt to turn-of-the-century art goes far beyond color. The feeling of inwardness in Sveshnikov's work, its appeal to the imagination, its dissolving of the human form into a seething mass of organic life are all closely related to Russian Symbolist painting. His decorative fantasy embodies ingredients that are absent from the austerity of "normal" Soviet life—fantasy, color, imagination, and beauty—but, even so, his tightly packed organic imagery is strangely claustrophobic and oppressive. This Symbolist universe, in which nature appears as a dark, fertile, all-powerful force swallowing up everything in its path, is no more comfortable to inhabit than the obviously grotesque fantasies of Sveshnikov's earlier work.

A deep vein of pessimism runs through the unofficial art of the 1960s and 1970s. Oleg Tselkov (b. 1934), for example, proceeded from the assumption that evil is a normal part of life. His paintings and graphic works depict a strange race of humans with low brows and heavy jowls (Pl. 13:1). According to the artist, these creatures are not

Fig. 13:1
Boris Sveshnikov
(Untitled), 1975
Oil on canvas
79.5 × 59.5 cm

Fig. 13:2
Viacheslav Kalinin
Thirsty Man, 1974
Oil on canvas
79.4 × 69.2 cm

to be understood as Soviet man but as universal man. "I am often asked," he says, "what my attitude is to this mankind: do I pity it or do I despise it? My answer is: neither. . . . My attitude is . . . a sort of strange rapture, rather like, say, the traveler who gazes on the mighty eruption of a volcano and exclaims: 'What a wonderful sight!' although he finds it rather terrifying. To me, mankind is just that—a volcano which, although it wreaks destruction on surrounding nature, possesses, in its own way, by virtue of its immensity, something that is not exactly beautiful, but . . . something whose power cannot be denied, and consequently, something which cannot be denied possesses a certain beauty."[6] Evil, Tselkov tells us, is simply a fact of nature, inherent in the human species on both sides of the East-West border (though perhaps with a slightly higher concentration to the east).[7]

For all their brute strength, however, these representatives of Tselkov's humanity appear oddly powerless. Heads take the form of masks that seem to be slipping downward in the picture space; figures have ropes threaded through their mouths, or are bound hand and foot. Except in rare instances, powerlessness is presented as a general condition of humanity. Their only saving attribute is a dumb, amoral endurance. They are "unbending," the artists says, even though their hairless and toothless condition might suggest the aftermath of a nuclear catastrophe.[8]

Another pioneer of unofficial Soviet art was Oscar Rabin (b. 1928), who after his expulsion from the Surikov Art Institute earned a living as a loader on the railways and by working on construction sites. Rabin's paintings introduce us to the grimy suburbs and barracks that constitute the dark underside of the workers' paradise. His realism has elements of fantasy, but it is founded on the very real sights and smells of this barracks environment. Rabin's *Ferris Wheel in the Evening* (Pl. 13:2) is like an inventory of such experiences: we see public toilets, a pair of drinkers, and a copulating couple—arranged as if on a Ferris wheel that hovers over a Moscow suburb. Near the top of the wheel is a corpse laid out on a bier. The corpse is Rabin's friend and fellow artist, Evgenii Rukhin, to whom the painting is dedicated.[9] Rabin also depicts himself, peeping out like a jack-in-the-box, just above the lovemakers.

Each element of this painting represents something that would automatically be repressed by the official guardians of Soviet purity. Sex, drunkenness, and the all-pervasive presence of the KGB have no place in the official version of "Soviet reality." (Rabin's cityscape also includes a militia station and KGB post.) The icon of the Virgin and

Child above Rukhin's body is an obvious violation of taboos against religious observance. Even the sign reading "Repairs" is an unacceptable reminder of the ramshackle condition of much of the urban fabric. Most striking of all is Rabin's refusal to suppress the erotic. In some of his paintings (as in this one), we find images from pornographic postcards; in others, the artist includes reminders of the practice of prostitution.

Another artist who foregrounds imagery of bodily appetites and desires is Viacheslav Kalinin (b. 1939). In his *Leda* (1974), a violent sexual assault is taking place; in *Thirsty Man*, 1974 (Fig. 13:2), a man drinks from a samovar by placing his mouth directly beneath the spout. The urgency of the drinker's gesture would seem to rule out a literal interpretation. This image may be associated with spiritual thirst or with sexual appetite, but it is not a simple tea-drinking scene. Kalinin's work embraces two extremes—the erotic and the sacred—that had been forcibly exiled from official Soviet art. The church towers that appear in the background of this painting and the couple making love in the middle distance are constant presences in Kalinin's paintings. His self-portraits, in particular, are always framed by scenes of drinking, lovemaking, and religious architecture (Pl. 13:5).

Kalinin's *Motifs from "The Tales of Hoffmann,"* 1972 (Fig. 13:3), is a further case in point: it contains church towers, church bells, a crucifix, and a figure in priestly garments holding up a playing card. This card, the queen of spades, is an obvious reference to Pushkin's short story "The Queen of Spades," but it is also an image of sexual temptation (her breasts are exposed). The priest—his head surrounded by a stiff, plate-like collar—plays the role of John the Baptist, his head already on a platter, but

Fig. 13:3 (*opposite*)
Viacheslav Kalinin
*Motifs from "The Tales of
Hoffmann,"* 1972
Etching
65 × 49.2 cm

Fig. 13:4
Juris Dimiters
Music Machine, 1979
Oil on fiberboard
44 × 31.9 cm

unlike St. John, Kalinin's holy man does not appear to be proof against temptation.

Kalinin's deliberate intermingling of the spiritual and the sexual is most vividly apparent in the oil lamp that appears in the foreground of this print. In a work so full of liturgical objects, the lamp retains its traditional religious symbolism, but thanks to the bulging curves at the base of its shade it has acquired a phallic character as well. (Spirituality is further compromised by the presence of flies perching on it.) Kalinin's insistent imaging of the erotic and the spiritual is in sharp opposition to the austere rationality and self-discipline held up by the Soviet authorities as models for human behavior. A similar juxtaposition of spiritual and physical extremes is to be found in the art of Ernst Neizvestny (b. 1925); both Neizvestny and Kalinin envision pain, spirituality, and sexuality in terms of bodily extension and excitement.[10]

When a Western viewer attempts to describe the unofficial Soviet art of the 1970s, the term "Surrealist" inevitably comes to mind. In some cases, the association with Western European art of the 1920s and 1930s has a fairly obvious basis. It would be difficult to deny, for example, that the paintings of Juris Dimiters (b. 1947) have a Surrealist flavor. The limp, organic forms that appear in his still lifes (Fig. 13:4) bring to mind the work of Salvador Dalí and Yves Tanguy. Dimiters's use of a hard-edged "magic realist" technique is also a familiar hallmark of Surrealism. Perhaps most truly in the spirit of Surrealism, however, is the type of situation he creates: the objects in his paintings appear real, concrete, and tangible, but they nevertheless defy definition. What are these limp, yet somehow aggressive forms, which seem constantly to be escaping from boxes and vases? The ambiguity and uncertainty of Dimiters's work transforms the still life from a simple domestic genre into something suggestive and unsettling.

Dimiters is almost alone, however, in offering such a direct imprinting of Surrealism. There are other artists whose work suggests parallels with or even imitation of European Surrealism, but rarely in such a consistent and single-minded way. The painting *Cliff* (1963) by Nikolai Vechtomov (b. 1923) resembles the decalcomania landscapes of Max Ernst; *Bells Are Ringing* by Mark Klionsky (b. 1927) might almost be taken for a lost Dalí; and much of the work of Mikhail Brussilovsky (b. 1931) presents a vision of nature's violence and lawlessness (Pl. 13:4) comparable to that of André Masson. But such examples are relatively rare. Perhaps the most emulated of the Surrealist painters, however, was René Magritte. Reminiscences of Magritte's imagery may be found in prints by

Fig. 13:5
Viktor Pivovarov
The Fly on the Apple, 1972
Lithograph
31.6 × 24.7 cm

Valerii Mishin (b. 1939) and also in the paintings of Brussilovsky.[11] Oversized apples—presumably in homage to Magritte—appear in the work of Eduard Zelenin (b. 1938) (Pl. 13:6) and Viktor Pivovarov (b. 1937).[12] More generally, the mismatched objects of Pivovarov's *The Fly on the Apple*, 1972 (Fig. 13:5) obey the Surrealist principle of displacement perfected by Magritte. Objects appear out of context, altered in scale, and unexpectedly juxtaposed: the white of the page is suddenly interrupted by a landscape; a hand appears in the sky; a large pencil supports a small figure. Overall, however, perhaps because of Pivovarov's deliberately naive style of drawing, the effect is more playful than dreamlike or hallucinatory.

There are other artists whose work has something in common with Surrealism (the principle of displacement, for example), but who remain so peculiarly themselves that comparisons scarcely seem profitable. Petr Belenok (1938–1991), for example, takes fragments of so-called "reality"—usually figures—from photographic sources and sets them adrift in space (Fig. 13:6). Belenok refers to his paintings simply as "panic realism" and claims that his closest affinities are literary rather than artistic.[13] Nino Morbedadze (b. 1957) makes theatrically constructed landscapes (Fig. 13:7; Pl. 11:9) that demonstrate the persistent attraction of Soviet artists to the Surrealist

Fig. 13:6
Petr Belenok
The Source, 1979
Mixed media on
fiberboard
123.2 × 141.8 cm

Fig. 13:7
Nino Morbedadze
(Untitled), n.d.
Pen and ink and gouache on
paper
55 × 75.2 cm

principle of displacement, but there is nothing precisely like them in the original Surrealist movement. Thus, though some comparisons can be made, a search for exact correspondences between Soviet artists and their Western European predecessors is for the most part unrewarding. Even after information about Surrealism became widely available, direct copying was the exception rather than the rule.[14]

In fact, the importance of Surrealism as a category for understanding unofficial Soviet art has less to do with stylistic borrowings or direct imitation than with broad parallels of attitudes and ideas. It is the thematic content of unofficial Soviet art that runs parallel to the central preoccupations of Surrealism. We have already seen that the first generation of unofficial artists, like their Surrealist colleagues, attempted to reintroduce into art a feeling for the sacred and the erotic—instincts that had been repressed, the Surrealists believed, by the utilitarian imperatives of twentieth-century progress. In Soviet art of the 1970s, there was also a response to the more cerebral side of Surrealism; this manifested itself particularly in the work of Leningrad artists and was reflected in the adoption of two images—the eye and the mirror—in the work of Ilya Murin (b. 1942) and Igor Tiulpanov (b. 1939). The eye, understood not as a passive receiver of information

but as the chief organ of the imagination, was a key Surrealist image.[15] Mirrors, too, when they appear in Surrealist paintings tend to defy the laws of physics by reflecting things that should not logically appear. Metaphorically, of course, the transformations of the eye and the mirror in Surrealist art allude to the new possibilities available to painting. Painting, too, was to abandon its mimetic role and become an agent of the imagination.

In Ilya Murin's prints, the Surrealist notion of vision as an active agent of desire acquires quite a literal form. In

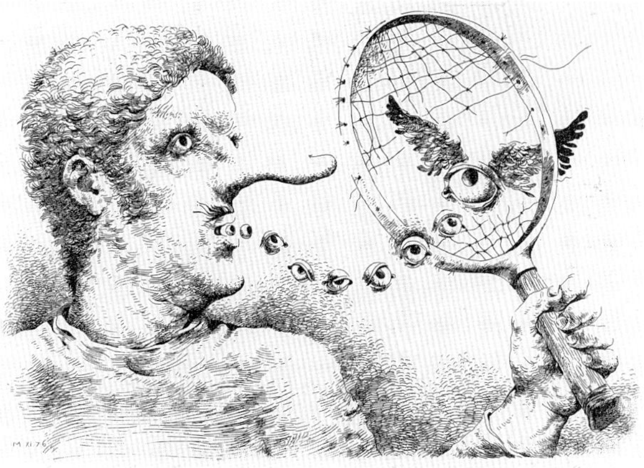

Fig. 13:8
Ilya Murin
Player I, 1976
Etching
19.9 × 29.6 cm

Fig. 13:9
Ilya Murin
(Untitled), 1976
Etching
35 × 40 cm

Pl. 13:1 (*opposite*)
Oleg Tselkov
Golgotha, 1977
Oil on canvas
245 × 190 cm

Player I, 1976 (Fig. 13:8), a mobile eye escapes from a tennis player's mouth, multiplies itself, and bursts through the cage-like grid of his racket. The eye appears here in association with lower sensory organs (the mouth) and with sexual energy (the extended nose of the tennis player has an obvious phallic significance). In another of Murin's etchings (Fig. 13:9), vision again plays a prominent role. Eyes are the most prominent feature of the man at the left (he is a holdover from one of Murin's favorite biblical themes, Susanna and the Elders). This man's bulging eyeballs proclaim him as a voyeur; in fact, since his head lacks a body, he is little more than a roving phallic eyeball. Elsewhere in the print we find another male creature, a rooster; dotted lines emerge from his eye and almost make contact with the nude woman below. The woman's eyes remain in shadow, by contrast with those of her male companions. Aggressive looking is evidently a male prerogative—a sexualized way of grasping the world.

Our understanding of this print is not complete, however, until we consider the mirror located at its center. Since the mirror sits parallel to the picture plane, it is difficult to imagine where the objects reflected in it (the surface of a table, a piece of newspaper, and part of a nutcracker) could be located. It would seem that these objects must be located in our space, but twisted from a horizontal to a vertical plane. Other items in the composition also

have a strange freedom to migrate in space. The numeral "3," for example, appears once in the mirror (reversed) and again between the rooster and the woman (on its back). These twisted spatial perspectives are evidence of Murin's dissatisfaction with the single, limited viewpoint of traditional realism. From a technical point of view, of course, the mirror must also be seen as a reference to the printing process, in which the printing plate, like a mirror, gives us an image in reverse. The printmaker needs a particularly flexible vision to conceive a work on the plate while visualizing what its final appearance will be. For Murin, who constantly reminds us of the reversals and transformations built into the printing process, artistic vision is clearly an active, creative, and playful process, never a simple registering of facts.[16]

Adoption of a traditional fool-the-eye technique need not mean that the artist has embraced a traditional naturalistic point of view. In *The Red Room*, 1968 (Pl. 13:10), for example, Igor Tiulpanov makes us aware of his artifice even as he creates a near-perfect illusion of folded pieces of paper, or objects, hanging on the wall.[17] The painting as a whole is constructed in such a way as to remind us that it is no more than a thin layer of pigment on a two-dimensional support. In the corners of the painting, for example, we find painted stretcher bars, which suggest that we are "really" looking at the back of the canvas. This reversal of front and back immediately makes the viewer aware of the material nature of the canvas support; the picture is *not* a window onto space, but a flat surface covered by a layer of paint. There are other reminders, too, of the thinness of the painted surface: for example, the way the leather of the chair in the foreground appears to be peeled back, revealing red floral upholstery underneath—just so, we imagine, the painted surface of Tiulpanov's picture might be peeled away in order to reveal something else underneath.

The Red Room is full of curious details: the flowers that appear to be sprouting from the floor, the tiny grotesque head with a protruding pin-filled tongue, the stretcher frame through which we see both the corner of the room and a surprising out-of-scale head. It is impossible to decide which objects are "real" and which are products of Tiulpanov's imagination. (One notably "surreal" touch is the severed arm with a metal "bone" projecting from it—presumably this is a prosthesis.) Many of the objects Tiulpanov depicts are deliberately confusing. The convoluted gray mass on the seat of the chair is organic in shape but metallic in texture; its folds seem almost ready to coalesce into something recognizable (an animal's face perhaps), but never do so. There is even something

Pl. 13:2
Oscar Rabin
*Ferris Wheel in the
Evening*, 1977
Oil on canvas
81 × 111 cm

Pl. 13:3
Boris Sveshnikov
(Untitled), n.d.
Oil on canvas
69 × 89 cm

Pl. 13:5
Viacheslav Kalinin
Self-Portrait, 1978
Oil on canvas
179.5 × 149 cm

Pl. 13:4 (*opposite*)
Mikhail Brussilovsky
Aggression, 1975
Oil on canvas
129.5 × 151.2 cm

284

Pl. 13:6
Eduard Zelenin
The Apple, 1973
Oil on fiberboard
78.5 × 48.3 cm

Pl. 13:7
Sergei Sherstiuk
The Sea, from the series
Couples , 1981
Oil on canvas
119 × 152 cm

Pl. 13:8
Georgii Kichigin
*Portrait of Sergei
Sherstiuk*, 1983
Oil on canvas
119 × 100 cm

Pl. 13:9
Igor Tiulpanov
The Mystery, 1975–76
Oil on canvas
40.2 × 201.2 cm

Pl. 13:10
Igor Tiulpanov
The Red Room, 1968
Oil on canvas
119.5 × 158.5 cm

Pl. 13:11
Alexander Petrov
Shoo!, 1985
Oil on canvas
150 × 148.5 cm

Pl. 13:12
Semyon Faibisovich
Boy, from the series
*Moscow Suburban
Electric Trains*, 1985
Oil on fiberboard
131 × 96 cm

Pl. 13:13
Semyon Faibisovich
Double Portrait of the
Artist at Work, 1987
Oil on canvas
150.4 × 75.6 cm

Pl. 13:14
Tatiana Nazarenko
Harvest Festival, 1985
Oil on canvas
170 × 120.3 cm

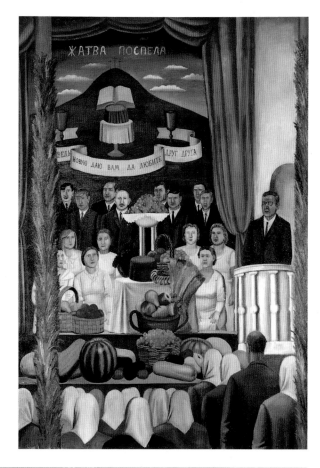

Pl. 13:15
Natalia Nesterova
Spaghetti, 1985
Oil on canvas
99.5 × 119.8 cm

Pl. 13:16
Nikita Meshkov
Marathon, 1983
Oil on canvas
198 × 149 cm

unsettling in the combination of textures it presents—a pitted metal object resting on a delicate lace-edged cloth.

In the hands of the Surrealists—René Magritte, for example—illusionistic painting became a vehicle for metaphysical speculation. If the images produced by the painter on canvas are only an illusion—no more than skin deep—are the retinal images that we rely on in everyday life any more trustworthy? Does what we see, or think we see, have any more claim to reality than the images that appear on the artist's canvas? Tiulpanov continues this tradition but with an aestheticizing twist of his own. His use of a self-consciously "beautiful" technique of painting and his many references to past art elevate painting itself to the status of an enduring value. Even though its images belong to a world of illusion, art has a beauty and dignity that mundane reality lacks.

In this canonization of art, Tiulpanov parts company with the Surrealists, who tended to deny a privileged status to the artwork. He is in tune, however, with the work of the *semidesiatniki*, a group of younger, officially accepted Soviet artists who came to the fore in the 1970s. The space that Tiulpanov represents in *The Red Room* is not, strictly speaking, his studio (according to the artist, it is the interior of his apartment). Still, *The Red Room* is clearly an artist's space and as such can be associated with the studio theme prevalent among the *semidesiatniki*. In the work of Tatiana Nazarenko (b. 1944), among others, the artist's studio is depicted as a sanctuary in which an intensely private and contemplative aesthetic experience can take place, away from the pressures of the material world.[18] Tiulpanov's red room, we might note, is located like saints' chambers in fifteenth-century paintings, high above ground level, away from worldly distractions; through its windows we see a landscape that seems to belong in an early Netherlandish painting.[19]

Most of the objects depicted belong to the past rather than the present (the ink well, the antique furniture, the old toys on the shelves); they evoke a vanished world in which art was more highly esteemed and utilitarian values had not yet emerged triumphant. In this respect, Tiulpanov's painting is a vote of no confidence in a present-day world from which the aesthetic, the metaphysical, the playful, and the excessive are excluded. Only a few of the items presented in his paintings could be called necessities of life; but, as the Bible tells us, man does not live by bread alone. This fact is highlighted when we actually see in *The Red Room* a partly eaten piece of coarse brown bread resting on top of a shiny gold box in the foreground. It is the only utilitarian object depicted.

In Tiulpanov's *The Mystery*, 1975–76 (Pl. 13:9), the painter's meticulous illusionistic effects take on an even more complex form. The expected separation of indoors and outdoors completely dissolves, so that it is difficult to say if the three figures in the painting are inside or outside. The painting seems to demand a symbolic reading: the interior and exterior spaces might, for example, be associated with the conscious and unconscious, and Tiulpanov supports the idea of unconscious content in this painting.[20] However, the artist has so thoroughly intermingled the interior and exterior spaces that we can no longer be certain the distinction holds.

There are religious images in the painting (a crucifix, a weeping angel), and Tiulpanov tells us that the painting has a religious theme, the weighing in the balance of good and evil. However, its most obvious message lies in a different area. A high proportion of the images allude to the senses. Sight is represented by the pair of glasses and the monocle; taste by the cup of coffee; smell by the flowers and the smoking pipe; and touch by the various textured surfaces. Only sound seems to be missing, until we imagine the voice of poet Konstantin Kuzminsky (the figure nearest the center). The overall effect is to produce a keen state of sensory awareness in the viewer (there is even erotic suggestiveness in some of the plant forms). This heightened sensory awareness might be seen as an antidote to the drabness and anaesthetic quality of Soviet daily life. Tiulpanov is no doubt aware of the symbolic language of the traditional still life, in which images of food, flowers, and so forth were meant to remind the viewer of the transience of worldly things. Indeed, transience is suggested in this painting by the worm-eaten apple at the far right (in fact, the picture's entire surface seems to be eaten away by a mysterious process of decay). In the end, however, the moralizing message is far less powerful than Tiulpanov's vivid and precise evocation of physical sensation.

Sensory experience is once again the subject in the work of Vladimir Yankilevsky (b. 1938). One series of his prints is actually entitled *Anatomy of the Senses*. In these prints and in his other series, *City—Masks* and *Mutants—Sodom and Gomorrah*, primal sensations reign supreme (Fig. 13:10). Mouths are open, tongues hang out, and noses are extended. At the same time, a peculiar confusion of "higher" and "lower" body parts occurs: we find noses replaced by penises (and vice versa), heads take the place of feet, and feet take the place of heads. Many of Yankilevsky's images have obvious sexual connotations, but a strange confusion prevails in matters of gender identity, since male and female body parts have been light-heartedly exchanged. Women wear male anatomy pulled

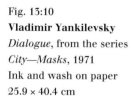

on over their torsos like bodysuits, while men don women's breasts and genitals; a woman in male disguise chases a man disguised as a woman; a man with superimposed female anatomy squeezes his own breasts. Gender roles are destabilized and a polymorphous sexuality prevails.

In some of these prints, male figures are represented simply as arms carrying briefcases, or to be more precise as arms and legs in one (we might call them "larms"). The "larms" engage in a variety of different activities: often they appear in ranks, as faceless slaves to some socially ordained activity, but they also appear trapped inside wheels and saluting their larger brethren. These larger "larms" appear to be embodiments of power, but even the smallest display a certain phallic assertiveness—debased, perhaps, but still their most obvious attribute.

In Yankilevsky's painting, *Pentaptych, No. 2: Adam and Eve*, 1980 (Fig. 13:11), male and female archetypes appear on a more elevated plane. This five-part work depicts male and female in both their temporal and their eternal forms. Two of the panels consist of mannequins standing in doorways; these represent "everyman" and "everywoman" in ordinary Soviet street clothes. The doorways are salvage from a Soviet apartment building, with mail-

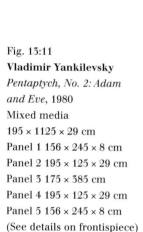

boxes, half-effaced notices, painted-over woodwork, and other hallmarks of authenticity. By contrast, the other panels depict a cosmic and eternal plane of existence: the panel at the far left contains a diagrammatic female hovering in the sky; at the far right is a similarly abstracted male.

The entire structure of *Adam and Eve* suggests a desire for synthesis. The two mannequins, for example, are half figures, so that male and female seem to need each other for completeness. The male and female "diagrams" at either end seem to have been torn out of some larger whole, and therefore are also incomplete. The center panel of the painting offers space in which a meeting might take place, but the union never occurs: just where we might expect a joining of the two extremes, there is empty space and a ragged hole cut away in the zone of the sky. According to Yankilevsky, the goal of his art is equilibrium, but he demands a special kind of equilibrium in which relationships are, as he puts it, "not absolute but ever changing."[21] The relationship between the sexes, eternal but constantly in flux, embodies just this sort of constantly changing and unstable equilibrium.

The appearance of Surrealist imagery in unofficial Soviet art of the 1970s was symptomatic of a breakdown of confidence in the prevailing codes of representation. However, the questioning of reality that occurred in the art of the 1970s frequently had the quality of a game, a cultivated and somewhat precious form of amusement. At the end of the 1970s, when Photorealism appeared and

Conceptual Art gained increasing prominence, the attack became more aggressive. Younger artists were quick to point out, for example, that even the most simple and apparently transparent recording of reality—the photograph—was in fact a cultural artifact, as much in need of decoding as a painting.

Even considered from a strictly technical point of view, the photograph is an imperfect document; accidents of framing, variations of focus, and other blind spots in a photograph often mean that we "see" less than we would like to see. Sergei Sherstiuk (b. 1951) (Pl. 13:8), one of the pioneers of Soviet Hyperrealism, has drawn attention to the ambiguities and difficulties inherent in the process of interpreting a photograph by enlarging his photographic source material and translating it into the medium of painting. In his *The Sea* (from the *Couples* series), 1981 (Pl. 13:7), for example, we must wonder if the man and woman have actually quarreled, or if their apparent disaffection is simply a trick of pose and camera angle. In a work of art, Sherstiuk tells us, "truth" will always remain outside our grasp; we know only fragments: "I think of myself as a man who is given a book printed on a Xerox machine. The book drops to the floor and I crawl along the floor assembling the book, page by page, not reading it. Only at times I read the top few lines of a page. It sounds like the truth. And that is the subject of my paintings."[22]

Various types of Hyperrealism and Photorealism began to emerge in the Soviet Union in the 1970s. Many of the practitioners of Photorealism were from the Baltic countries. However, Moscow artist Alexander Petrov was among the earliest advocates of a Hyperrealist (as opposed to a Photorealist) style. Petrov's elegantly crafted paintings utilize odd perspectives and startling details to draw attention to aspects of visual reality that would be missed by "normal" perception (Pl. 13:11).

Photorealists like Semyon Faibisovich (b. 1949) characteristically choose subjects that are prosaic in nature: Faibisovich depicts shoppers, riders on suburban electric trains, corpulent bathers on a beach. Compared with Sherstiuk's snapshot-like compositions, however, Faibisovich's photographs seem more deliberately composed, and he deals with a greater variety of human ages and conditions. There are aspects of Faibisovich's style that suggest traditional realism, but he parts company with Socialist Realism, and with Russian nineteenth-century Realism, by refusing to attach any moral judgments to his choice of subject matter. Art critic Matthew Cullerne Bown suggests that Faibisovich's use of photographic source material carries with it a certain moral ambiguity: "What, then, is the Soviet viewer, brought up to believe that art has a message, supposed to make of an image of men laughing in the queue for alcohol, or of old ladies sitting waiting for a train, or of a fat woman on a beach? Is it painted in criticism? Or in praise? Faibisovich, no less than an abstract painter, calls into question the tendentious nature of the 'social' role often played by painting in Russia."[23]

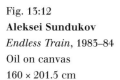

Fig. 13:12
Aleksei Sundukov
Endless Train, 1983–84
Oil on canvas
160 × 201.5 cm

This nonjudgmental attitude is not necessarily an abdication of responsibility, however; Faibisovich tells us that he wants to stimulate an intellectual effort on the part of the viewer: "I want, and will always want, my works to carry in themselves, among other things, energy that stimulates an intellectual effort in the viewer but does not suggest, as happens so often, a pretense to this effort. I do not want to make the viewer's life that much easier. I want him to receive satisfaction from trying."[24] Some of Faibisovich's images have an undeniable humanistic warmth (Pl. 13:12), but others are so complex that the viewer has difficulty in interpreting them. His *Double Portrait of the Artist at Work* (Pl. 13:13) presents us with a confusing number of reflecting surfaces. We see the artist with his camera reflected not once but twice; all the other reflected figures (travelers on the station platform) are in motion and visible only as a ghostly blur. Reality, as Faibisovich presents it, is complex, multilayered, and dynamic, and even the camera cannot fix it with absolute precision.

Photorealism was also responsible for introducing new subject matter into Soviet painting. By contrast with the "artiness" of work from the 1970s, Photorealist artists depicted an urban environment of city streets, shop windows, parking lots, and so forth. The cityscape represents, as Soviet critics like to say, a "second" nature, entirely artificial and manmade. This artificiality is

particularly evident in the paintings of Nikita Meshkov (b. 1954), such as *Marathon*, 1983 (Pl. 13:16), which superimposes the blurred silhouette of a running man on a window display of armed and hooded mannequins in an unidentified city, probably a Western European capital. The urban vistas of Georgii Kichigin (b. 1951), inspired by a visit to Finland, have a similarly apocalyptic character. However, even the tamer vistas of Faibisovich's cityscapes have a disorienting quality: familiar things become strange when they appear enlarged, or in fragments, or from unfamiliar angles.

In the 1980s, a reaction took place against the perceived elitism of the unofficial art produced in the 1970s. Photorealism was one symptom of this, but there were other indications of this feeling as well. The works of Natalia Nesterova (b. 1944), for example, are striking both for their calculated primitivism of style and for their down-to-earth subject matter (Pl. 13:15). Images of street life appeared around this time in the work of Tatiana Nazarenko as well (Pl. 13:14). By the middle of the 1980s, it was possible to speak of a new kind of social realism emerging in Soviet art, not Socialist Realism, with its enforced optimism and narrow range of themes, but an unvarnished look at shoppers standing in queues, passengers riding the metro, and so forth. The painting *Endless Train* 1983–84 (Fig. 13:12) by Aleksei Sundukov (b. 1952) is an outstanding example of this new Soviet realism.

With the advent of *perestroika*, artists of many different types have been brought into the public eye. Individuals as different as Yankilevsky, Sherstiuk, or Sundukov have been offered as representative of Soviet art in the 1980s. As Russian art ceases to be Soviet, however, there will certainly be changes. The dialogue with the official version of Soviet reality carried on for so long by unofficial artists is passing into history. Whether the art produced in the ter-ritories that formerly made up the Soviet Union will retain its special character or will be dissolved in the melting pot of the international art market remains to be seen. If a legacy does remain from the realist, Surrealist, and Photorealist art of the last twenty years, it may lie simply in the conviction that painting must challenge our identification of art with reality and open up a breach in the conventionally accepted forms and images we call "realism."

Notes

1. James H. Billington, *The Icon and the Axe* (New York: Vintage Books, 1970), p. 535. For the relevant portion of the Soviet Writers' Union text, see John E. Bowlt, ed., *Russian Art of the Avant-Garde: Theory and Criticism, 1902–1934* (New York: Viking Press, 1976), pp. 296–97.

2. Abram Tertz (Andrei Siniavsky), *On Socialist Realism*, introduced by Czeslaw Milosz and translated by George Dennis (New York: Vintage Books, 1960), pp. 218–19.

3. *Giper*, short for *Giperrealizm*, was the term commonly used by Soviet critics for the type of painting known in the West as Photorealism, Superrealism, or Hyperrealism.

4. For a brief essay on Sveshnikov and reproductions of some of his prison drawings, see Norton T. Dodge, ed., *Boris Sveshnikov: A Retrospective Exhibition*, exh. cat. (Jersey City, N.J.: C.A.S.E. Museum of Contemporary Art, 1991).

5. Igor Golomshtok and Alexander Glezer, *Unofficial Art from the Soviet Union* (London: Secker and Warburg, 1977), p. 94.

6. Ibid., p. 159.

7. Alexander Glezer, "Oleg Tselkov," *Iskusstvo* 8 (1990): 31. In the same issue of *Iskusstvo*, see also G. Anisimov, "Protiazhennye simvoly Olega Tselkova": 27–30.

8. Golomshtok and Glezer, *Unofficial Art from the Soviet Union*, p. 159.

9. Rukhin had died in a studio fire the year before; it was rumored, though never established, that the fire was set by the KGB.

10. For a discussion of Neizvestny's sculpture, see John Berger, *Art and Revolution: Ernst Neizvestny and the Role of the Artist in the USSR* (Harmondsworth, Eng.: Penguin Books, 1969), especially pp. 98–116.

11. Three of Magritte's favorite motifs (the tuba, the bird, and the flame) appear in Mishin's 1984 lithograph *Target*, but this print is not typical of Mishin's work. Traces of Magritte's imagery appear in the marginal scenes of Mikhail Brussilovsky's *Homo Sapiens*, 1974 (Pl. 6:8), where a solitary eyeball hovers in the sky and a group of figures have gray spheres instead of heads.

12. Out-of-scale apples appear in Zelenin's painting *The Apple* (1973) and in Viktor Pivovarov's drawings *N.O.01* (1974) and *The Fly on the Apple* (1972). These apples almost certainly relate to the apple in Magritte's well-known *Listening Chamber* (1953), but in Zelenin's case there is room for a traditional biblical reading as well.

13. Norma Roberts, ed., *The Quest for Self-Expression: Painting in Moscow and Leningrad, 1965–1980* (Columbus, Ohio: Columbus Museum of Art, 1990), p. 60.

14. Information about Surrealism was more readily available in the 1970s than it had been earlier because of the greater number of Western publications brought into the country by foreign visitors. Ironically, another source of knowledge was the defensive action taken by the Soviet authorities against Surrealism. Publication of books condemning Surrealism, for example A.K. Lebedev's *Iskusstvo v okovakh* (Moscow: Izdatel'stvo Akademii Khudozhestv SSSR, 1962) and I.S. Kulikova's *Siurrealizm v iskusstve* (Moscow: Nauka, 1970) were actually sought after for information about Surrealism and for reproductions of Surrealist works.

15. André Breton's 1928 essay "Surrealism and Painting" begins with a celebration of vision as the most vivid hallucinatory sense: Breton, *Surrealism and Painting*, trans. Simon Watson Taylor (New York: Icon Editions, 1965), pp. 1–2. For a fuller discussion of Surrealist imagery of the eye, see Jeanne Siegel, "The Image of the Eye in Surrealist Art and Its Psychoanalytic Sources," *Arts Magazine* 56 (Feb. 1982): 102–6, and 57 (Mar. 1982): 116–19.

16. For a further example of Murin's delight in the reversal of images that is native to the printmaking process, see her *Untitled* (1976), reproduced in Norton T. Dodge, ed., *New Art from the Soviet Union: The Known and the Unknown* (Washington, D.C.: Acropolis Books, 1977), p. 98.

17. Since emigrating to the United States, Tiulpanov has spelled his name *Tulipanov*; this spelling, although it violates accepted rules of transliteration, preserves the name's meaning (in Russian *tiulpan* means "tulip").

18. The *semidesiatniki* occupied a special place within the official art world; both the style and the subject matter of their work manifested a nostalgia for the past, and they avoided the traditional subject matter of Soviet art in favor of subjects that had an aesthetic or historical character. Artists' studios were frequently depicted in their work. See, for example, Tatiana Nazarenko's *Flowers in the Studio* (1973) and *In the Studio* (1973); S. G. Pustovoit's *In the Studio* (1974); and A. T. Akhaltsev's *In the Artist's Studio* (1973). Other examples of work by the *semidesiatniki* may be found in Anna Dekhtiar, *Molodye zhivopistsy 70–kh godov* (Moscow: Sovetskii Khudozhnik, 1979).

19. Tiulpanov's *The Red Room* also contains one detail—a blue tablecloth in which the folds remain marked—that clearly refers to the still lifes of Kuzma Petrov-Vodkin, for example his *Pink Still Life: Apple Branch* (1918). For Petrov-Vodkin, too, the studio represented a place for the contemplative experience of beauty, detached from the concerns of daily life.

20. In an interview with Norton Dodge, January 1977, the artist stated that *The Mystery* contains "material taken from beyond the boundaries of our consciousness." He also mentioned that the painting depicts a weighing in the balance of good and evil: "Which outweighs which? This is the mystery of the painting." The entire painting is tilted on a diagonal axis, emblematic of the action of the scales; but no scales are actually visible.

21. Vladimir Yankilevsky, "World through Man," in *Vladimir Yankilevsky* (New York: Eduard Nakhamkin Fine Arts, 1988).

22. *The Quest for Self-Expression*, p. 145.

23. Matthew Cullerne Bown, *Contemporary Russian Art* (New York: Philosophical Library, 1989), p. 61.

24. *The Quest for Self-Expression*, p. 80.

14 | "Discrete displacement"

Abstract and Kinetic art in the Dodge Collection

John E. Bowlt

Like the Russian Empire, the Union of Soviet Socialist Republics was a vast conglomerate of national, ethnic, and religious groups. In each case, the overlay of cultural superstructure on economic base (to paraphrase Karl Marx) was different and variously successful. The very distinct arts of Russia, the Ukraine, the Baltic states, Armenia, Georgia, and Belarus derive from diverse aesthetic and social impulses. The modern art of Estonia, Latvia, and Lithuania, for example, as represented by Ojārs Ābols, Raul Meel, Tõnis Vint, and Vladas Žilius, has much more in common with the local Art Deco of Sigismund Vidberg and Eduard Wiiralt than with any Russian borrowing. Similarly, the vivid canvases by Armenian and Georgian painters such as Henry Elibekian and Gia Edzgveradze reflect their own ancient legacy of decorative and monumental art rather than the very different Russian tradition. In other words, it would be misleading to regard these various schools as elements within a single organism, for each nation has endeavored—and continues to endeavor—to establish its own cultural identity. Without adequate knowledge of the linguistic, social, and cultural structures peculiar to these local entities, we should avoid uninformed commentary and description. Consequently, although the Dodge Collection contains key abstract works by artists from the non-Russian republics and references to them are important, my focus will be limited to the abstract and Kinetic art produced in Moscow and Leningrad.

The dissident, nonconformist, or unofficial tendencies in Soviet culture from the 1950s to the 1980s were never strictly about ideology. Even though much of that art and literature was generated by ideological imposition, the Soviet underground was, indeed, more an aesthetic or psychological gesture than a political and practical one. As one artist put it:

> The ways in which we resisted the machine that was bringing about a total neutrality were by no means proclamations, demonstrations or secret pacts, but rather apolitical art. It now seems strange that the opposition to the Great Power was jazz or the way we dressed.[1]

Of course, many would contend that an aesthetic response to a political issue is in itself a political statement, and that, as the painter Vladimir Serov affirmed in 1963, "abstract art is not form, but ideology."[2] But such rhetoric aside, it is clear that the radical artistic movements of the Khrushchev and Brezhnev eras were not intended to incapacitate the "total machine" (which at that time seemed impervious to real change), but to foster the enjoyment of individual expression. After all, the primary representatives of those dissident disciplines—jazzman Aleksei Zubov (currently a popular musician in Hollywood), poet Joseph Brodsky (recipient of the Nobel Prize for Literature in 1987), and sculptor Ernst Neizvestny (now fulfilling his ambitions in New York)—have gained their universal fame not as apologists for one political ideology or detractors of another, but as the distinguished practitioners of their particular métiers.

Since its inception after Stalin's death in 1953, dissident art in the Soviet Union has been constantly associated with the political mechanisms that both nurtured and opposed it. The Ministry of Culture of the U.S.S.R., the Union of Artists, and the Academy of Arts were, of course, the immediate extensions of the "total machine," and the doctrine that they supported, Socialist Realism, was an artistic system formulated by edict, decree, and statistical analysis in the same way as foreign policy and Five Year Plans. In other words, Socialist Realism was a political commodity and one more manifestation of that superabundance of ideology that Komar and Melamid parodied so successfully in their sardonic paintings, posters, and performances.

As a consequence, works of art that opposed the principles of Socialist Realism in the 1960s and 1970s have been read traditionally as political statements, even though their primary impetus may have been formal or aesthetic. In turn, this automatic association of radical art with radical politics has led to gross misrepresentations of Soviet underground culture, at least in the West. Interpreted as a gesture of political resistance, the Soviet nonconformist movement is often packaged and transmitted to the West in terms of political activism, much like the concurrent Vietnam antiwar protests in the United States, and the 1968 student protests in Italy and France. Some sense of this particular slant can be gleaned from the titles of a random selection of news articles on the subject: "The KGB Just Isn't Itself These Days," "Art and Politics and Money," "Smuggled Soviet Art Is a Witty Variation on Ideology," and so on.[3]

Among Western critics, a common complaint about the Soviet underground was that the art was too narrative and reportorial, placing too much value on the message and not enough on the medium. While there is some truth to this allegation, it is not the whole truth. Abstract art played an extremely important role in the nonconformist art of the 1950s to 1970s, and its laboratory of forms constitutes one of the clearest indications that dissident art was for the most part apolitical, even though it was anathema to the Soviet establishment.

In the Soviet context, the tension between abstraction and realism was particularly complex, partly because of the artificial prohibition against abstract art during the Stalin era and partly because of the weighty influence of nineteenth-century Realism. Many dissident artists continued to pay homage to historical realist styles, even while directing their attacks at the institution of Socialist Realism. Despite their refusal to "be in the vanguard of the fighters for a classless Socialist society,"[4] these artists often replaced the illusionism of Socialist Realist art with equally tendentious texts that assumed various religious, occult, sociological, or anecdotal forms. In this sense, artists as stylistically diverse as Aleksandr Kharitonov, Komar and Melamid, Aleksandr Kosolapov, Oscar Rabin, and Leonid Sokov shared the common denominator of narrativity. But this allegorical approach, while immediate, accessible, and "interesting," was not the only form of painting. So, perhaps the time has come to rectify the critical imbalance and to give greater attention to the "other" alternative, the abstract art of the dissident generation.

Any examination of abstract art within the dissident movement must begin with the question of sources: if these artists were nurtured on the principles of Socialist Realism and surrounded by the omnipresent Party propaganda, how did they learn about "bourgeois formalism" and abstract art? The answers to this question are complex, but at least two general responses can be delineated. First, there was a slow but sure rediscovery by dissident artists of the avant-garde of the 1910s and 1920s; and second, there were sporadic encounters by the Soviet artists with contemporary Western culture.

As with any artistic or political force, the Soviet nonconformist movement has its pioneers and disciples,

luminaries, and epigones. Without the iconoclastic statements of Mikhail Kulakov (b. 1933), Ernst Neizvestny (b. 1925), Vladimir Nemukhin (b. 1925) (Pl. 14:13), Oscar Rabin (b. 1928), Evgenii Rukhin (1943–1976), Ullo Sooster (1924–1970) (Pl. 14:1), and Oleg Tselkov (b. 1934) in the 1960s and early 1970s, the dissident movement would hardly have found the strength to grow further. The abrasive imagery of these artists and their brave polemics with the political status quo tested the weaknesses of the Soviet machine, establishing behavioral codes and strategies that helped subsequent generations face the KGB apparatus and threats of imprisonment, hospitalization, and banishment. No doubt these searing experiences prompted the marked Expressionist orientation of that first underground—the brooding urban ugliness of Rabin, the ruptured objects of Rukhin, and the gestural explosions of Yurii Dyshlenko (1936–1995) and Yakov Vinkovetsky (1938–1984).

In the 1950s, as the first wave of dissident artists and writers emerged, represented by Eli Beliutin (b. 1925), Ilya Glazunov (b. 1930), Neizvestny, Evgenii Yevtushenko, and Andrei Voznesensky, some of the old avant-garde artists were still alive. Most of the real pioneers, such as Pavel Filonov, Kazimir Malevich, and Vladimir Tatlin, had died. But there were still artists from that period who could remember and recount: Nikolai Akimov, Robert Falk, Artur Fonvizin, Pavel Kuznetsov, Vladimir Sterligov, Aleksandr Tyshler, and Lev Zhegin. These survivors played a major role in bridging the generation gap and, although their own art may not seem especially experimental, they were revered as apologists of artistic freedom and their paintings seen as symbols of aesthetic purity. They also formed a delicate link with the international heritage of Postimpressionism and Cubism that had long been concealed and maligned. For the younger artists and critics such as Boris Birger (b. 1923), Igor Golomshtok (b. 1929), Mikhail Odnoralov (b. 1944), Grigorii Perchenkov, Dmitri Sarabianov (b. 1923), Oleg Vassiliev (b. 1940), and Vladimir Veisberg (1924–1985), artists like Falk and Kuznetsov were an important source of alternative ideas.

A striking example of this organic connection with the radical past are the Rodchenko and Volkov families in Moscow, who pay homage to their senior members (i.e., Aleksandr Rodchenko and Aleksandr N. Volkov [1886–1956]) while investigating new visual resolutions. Aleksandr A. Volkov (b. 1937) and Valerii Volkov (b. 1928), for example, maintain the momentum of their father's impulse and consciously or unconsciously demonstrate a shared Oriental attachment to vivid color and solar light. Through his "impossible" collocations of red, yellow, orange, and black, Valerii Volkov produces vibrant surfaces that create a tension with the frame, demanding release (Pl. 14:2). Works such as *Kaleidoscope*, 1967 (Pl. 14:3) are less two-dimensional paintings than Kinetic machines about to take off and dance to some cosmic jazz. More contemplative in spirit is the painting of Aleksandr A. Volkov (Pl. 14:4). In works such as *White Composition*, 1968 (Pl. 14:6), he investigates the concepts of composition and decomposition, generating movement not so much by color contrast as by the dissonance of circles, squares, and trapezoids.

During the epoch of *zapasniki* and *spetskhrany*,[5] the average Soviet citizen was denied any possibility of seeing Dalí, Kandinsky, or other modernists, either at home or abroad, or of reading literature that discussed "modern art." That is also why the few collectors of the Russian avant-garde, such as George Costakis and Yakov Rubinshtein, were so important to the new generation. The collections displayed in their apartments provided artists with a first-hand knowledge of the works of Kandinsky, Malevich, Liubov Popova, Aleksandr Rodchenko, and others. Costakis even acquired works by artists of the new avant-garde, including Dmitrii Krasnopevtsev (1925–1995) and Dmitri Plavinsky (b. 1937). But the major collections of dissident art in the Soviet Union were assembled by other individuals, such as Alexander Glezer, Tatiana Kolodzei, Viacheslav Mikhailov, Evgenii Nutovich, and Leonid Talochkin.

A second way in which Soviet artists learned about abstract art was through encounters with contemporary Western culture. Nowadays it is hard to imagine the keen appetite for Pop Art, beatnik poetry, rock and roll, and jazz that young Soviets had in the 1960s, or the indignation that these artistic expressions elicited among their elders. It is also difficult to understand the severity of the sanctions—possession of an Elvis Presley record or of a Magritte reproduction could lead to interrogation and hard labor. Availability was also a problem, though there were "legal" channels of distribution, such as exhibitions of foreign art or official condemnations that included reproductions of the banned abstract art.[6] Of particular importance was the "Exhibition of American Painting and Sculpture" that the Archives of American Art organized in Moscow in 1959. This was the first public showing in the Soviet Union of works by Jackson Pollock, Willem de Kooning, Georgia O'Keeffe, and others. Artists who visited the exhibition, such as Neizvestny and Nemukhin, tell how it transformed their cultural lives, reinforcing their doubt about Socialist Realism and confirming their desire to establish alternative systems. Another key influence

was a U.S. State Department-sponsored exhibition of contemporary American prints by Jim Dine, Jasper Johns, Robert Rauschenberg, and others, which traveled to Moscow and Leningrad in 1963.

But perhaps the most curious manner by which dissident artists of the 1960s learned about abstract art was through descriptions and promotion of it in the scientific community. Specialists in the fields of cybernetic theory, higher mathematics, and atomic physics—the pride of Soviet scholarship—began to consider abstract art in the light of such concepts as aerodynamics or algebra. This rendered the art more palatable and "relevant." Individual scientists, such as Abram Chudnovsky, even began to collect avant-garde and dissident works. And, more importantly, several scientific centers either established studios where dissident artists could train (e.g., Viktor Umnov at the Moscow Energy Institute) or organized legal exhibitions of dissident art.[7] This tendency to link artistic deviation with scientific experiment continued throughout the 1970s and 1980s. As late as 1989, the Moscow House of Artists organized the exhibition "Scientific and Technological Progress and the Visual Arts," which included works by Francisco Infante (b. 1943) (Pl. 14:5), Viacheslav Koleichuk (b. 1941), Aleksandr Poteshkin (b. 1926), and Yurii Zlotnikov (b. 1930) (Pl. 14:7).

However complex these conditions, they informed and influenced much of the dissident output. Some of the interpretations that prospered in the dissident era were Abstract Expressionism (Beliutin and his students), Kinetic art (Nusberg and the Movement Group), environmental art (Infante [Fig. 14:1]), Action Painting (Kulakov), geometrism (Chernyshov [Pl. 14:11], Mikhail Roginsky, and Eduard Shteinberg [Pl. 14:10]), and lyrical abstraction (Henry Elinson, Lydia Masterkova, and Evgenii Mikhnov-Voitenko). This variety of abstract styles may seem surprising, especially given the tendency to overemphasize the narrative aspect of Soviet nonconformism. But a sober reappraisal of this period (as was undertaken by the exhibition "The Other Art" at the Tretyakov Gallery in Moscow in 1991) reveals the forceful presence of abstract and nonfigurative painting. True, leaders of the underground such as Eric Bulatov, Kalinin, and Rabin did interpret Soviet reality in a narrative and often tendentious fashion, questioning and inverting ideological messages. But many other important artists rejected this approach, and endeavored to reconnect with the Russian avant-garde (Fig. 14:2) and the New York School. Chernyshov (b. 1945), Roginsky (b. 1931), Oleg Yakovlev (b. 1948), and Zlotnikov, for example, were interested in the geometric systems of such masters as Lissitzky,

Fig. 14:1
Francisco Infante
Play of Gestures, 1977
Ferrotyped gelatin silver print
50.4 × 59.8 cm

Fig. 14:2 (*above right*)
Aleksandr Yulikov
In Celebration of Kazimir Malevich III, 1983
Aquatint
52.4 × 48 cm

Malevich, and Rodchenko, which they developed with particular grace and aplomb.

Aleksei Tiapushkin (1919–1988), who attained a remarkably mature colorism in the early 1960s, was perhaps the strongest abstract artist of the nonconformist movement. Like some of his colleagues, Tiapushkin saw Abstract Expressionism and Surrealism at the "Exhibition of American Painting and Sculpture" in 1959. Still, he could have had no sense of the stylistic diapason of the Russian avant-garde unless he had looked through Camilla Gray's richly illustrated monograph *The Great Experiment* (1962) or visited Costakis's incipient collection. In other words, the parallels between some of Tiapushkin's paintings, such as *Coloristic Experiment II*, 1963 (now owned by the artist's family), or *Painterly Experiment*, (1964; Nutovich Collection, Moscow), and the Suprematist compositions of Malevich and Olga Rozanova may be accidental rather than deliberate. There may be a gesture to Suprematism in the collocations of black, white, and red and reminiscences of Popova's architectonics in the strong impasto, but Tiapushkin introduces his own hieroglyphic complex which still emphasizes the surface treatment without surrendering to the narrative tradition. Tiapushkin's light harmonies of resonant colors, his measured fugues of squares and rectangles, belie the life of hardship and injustice that he endured.

Poteshkin, too, discovered the tranquility of color harmony, experimenting, as Mikhail Matiushin had done fifty years before, with the relationships of shape and ground on the emotional reception of color, and his numbered paintings, with their rectangular and triangular variations, might well serve as illustrations to Matiushin's variation conformity in color combinations.[8]

Golomshtok has maintained that there are two kinds of artistic innovation: those of form and those of the spirit.[9] Even though the Western observer may find the Russian insistence on the primacy of the spirit to be overwhelming, the intense aspiration toward spirituality has been a guiding force in twentieth-century Russian culture, from Kandinsky's *On the Spiritual in Art* to Vasilii Chekrygin's belief in the resurrection of souls.[10] Although it would be hazardous to link the "godseekers" of Russia's philosophical renaissance (Nikolai Berdiaev, Sergei Bulgakov, Vladimir Soloviev, et al.) with the artistic accomplishments of the Russian avant-garde, there can be no question that, in some contexts, the experimental art of Filonov, Kandinsky, Malevich, and their colleagues owed much of its energy to the theurgical explorations of the Silver Age. In rediscovering this lost heritage, many contemporary artists were also drawn to the spiritual quest of their forefathers and felt an immediate sympathy with Orthodoxy, Theosophy, Judaism, and the Oriental religions. As far as dissident painting was concerned, artists used these traditions either as a thematic source (depicting Russian churches, saints, Purim, etc.) or in more private, cryptic, and abstract ways.

Lydia Masterkova (b. 1929), who began to investigate abstract art in the late 1950s, seems to be following a spiritual path through the mystical cosmos that Malevich created with his Suprematist geometries. The apparent equilibrium of her restrained colors and forms and the pregnant silence of her compositions generate the same evocative force as prayers offered to a distant deity, unidentifiable yet omnipresent. Obviously, for Masterkova, as for Kandinsky and Malevich, nonfigurative painting is a vehicle of spiritual engagement with a higher harmony, a painted liturgy that invites the spectator to commune with her art in reverent solitude.

Other artists have paid homage to this "ecclesiastical" tradition as well. Valerii Yurlov (b. 1933), for example, studied the meaning and composition of Russian icons to produce his "meditational constructions" in 1957. He interpreted the abstract notions of harmony and balance as biblical counterpoints (Adam and Eve, good and evil, lightness and darkness), which he then elaborated into a visual concordance of paintings, drawings, and collages. Perhaps more than any other Russian abstract artist of the dissident generation, Yurlov was—and still is—also concerned with the tension between the pictographic surface and the edge of that surface. For Yurlov, work such as his *Counter-form* (Pl. 2:9) is a strictly limited entity that exists according to a code of formal shapes or signs, one that as in a Theosophical table of thought forms denotes states of mind such as "slowing of time" and "I do not exist." Reference to the evolution of this vocabulary helps to explain the direction of Yurlov's abstract enquiries, even as the message in individual pieces remains recondite.

Elena Keller (b. 1951), too, is intrigued by the tension between the word as label and the word as concept, an ambivalence summarized by her painting *Mystery of the Name* (1985–86). We sense this ultimate contradiction in all her work, whether it is abstract (as in *The Passage of Time* [1988]) or concrete (as in *Magadan*, 1985 [Pl. 14:12]). Her deduction seems to be that the only realism possible is an abstract one, because the very moment the word is conceived and recorded, it loses its organic connection to the thing it is supposed to represent. In other words, the meaning of a phenomenon such as Magadan can be rendered more precisely by a spontaneous deposition of paint or by a cryptic game of ellipse and hieroglyph than by a conventional language of narrative communication.

Mikhail Kulakov, on the other hand, broadened his sign language to include substantial references to Zen Buddhism, investigating and depicting concepts such as "cosmos" in 1959 and "embryo" in 1962. For Kulakov, as for Yakov Vinkovetsky (Pl. 14:8), abstract painting held an ecstatic, transcendental power, and both attempted to use it as an allegory of the ostensible disorder of the universe—controlled by its Creator in the same way that the painted composition is controlled by the artist.

To some extent, Lev Kropivnitsky (1922–1994) pursues the same avenue of enquiry in his occasional abstractions, visualizing invisible concepts such as "existence," "trajectory," and "fury" as manifestations of the supreme energy of the cosmos. A student of Chinese philosophy, Kropivnitsky retained and expressed a psychological distance and inner peace, establishing a defense system that not even long years of war, imprisonment, and persecution could weaken. Masterkova, Yurlov, Kulakov, Vinkovetsky, and Kropivnitsky teach us that beyond the brutal confrontation of tectonic shifts there exists a grandiose symmetry of silence and that the artist's primary mission, like the priest's, is to trace and transmit this ultimate truth.

Like the Symbolists of Russia's *fin de siècle*, many of these artists looked inward, seeking a private serenity through meditative philosophy. There is something of this Eastern acquiescence in the lyrical abstractions of Gennadii Zubkov (b. 1940) and his colleagues who, through the intervention of Vladimir Sterligov, a student of Malevich and Mikhail Matiushin, express a nirvanic translucency and harmony. Visually and philosophically, Zubkov draws on the traditions of the St. Petersburg avant-garde, establishing an organic link with Elena Guro, Nikolai Kulbin, and Matiushin. Like them, Zubkov and the *Sterligovtsy* sought to decipher the "hieroglyphs ... of the crystal"[11] and to experience the "merging of time and space."[12] This metaphysical dimension is, of course, a complex aspect of the Russian dissident movement, and it is often mentioned, but rarely explored.

Both Christianity and Judaism, as alternative faiths to Communism, played a major role in the Russian cultural revival that took place from the 1960s to the 1980s. Artists such as Kulakov, Vinkovetsky, Zubkov, Nikolai Vechtomov (b. 1923), Evgenii Mikhnov-Voitenko (1932–1988), Igor Zakharov-Ross (b. 1943), Eduard Shteinberg (b. 1937), and Evgenii Shvartsman (b. 1926) illustrated this quest for psychological peace in the face of physical disruption. The patterns of their abstract paintings, whether gestural (as in the case of Vechtomov) or pictographic (as with Shvartsman), can and should be read as extensions of this occult impulse. For example, both Kulakov and Vinkovetsky were deeply interested in the release of energy from matter and in the alignment of their pictorial statements with the idea of spiritual emancipation. Alternatively, artists such as Shvartsman and even Shteinberg seem to be presenting their painted geometries as blueprints for a new configuration—as molecular regroupings—that could impart a more efficient order to our tattered universe. Similarly, when Leonid Lamm (b. 1928) challenges the false sequences and equalities of the Positivist worldview with such acerbic irony, it seems that this dismissal is dictated by his search for the divine and irrational order. One suspects that even in the purest abstractions of the dissident movement, the shimmering surfaces of works by Mikhnov-Voitenko and Leonid Borisov (b. 1943) or the fission of forms in paintings by Bella Levikova (b. 1939) (Pl. 14:9) and Boris Zeldin (b. 1944), one might find something of this manifest mystery.

In this respect, Nemukhin's constant game of cards has particular significance, for it draws upon the leitmotif of gambling and divination central to Russian culture (Pl. 14:5). Pushkin's "Queen of Spades" and Dostoevsky's *The Gamblers* are obvious literary refractions of the theme. But the visual commentary on the topic is also manifold, from Alexei Venetsianov's *Fortune Telling by Cards* (1842; Russian Museum, St. Petersburg) to the ace of clubs in Malevich's *Aviator* (1914; Russian Museum, St. Petersburg), from Pavel Fedotov's *Gamblers* (1852; State Museum of Russian Art, Kiev) to Olga Rozanova's pictures of playing cards (*c.* 1915). As the nineteenth-century *lubok* called *The Demon of Card Playing* tells us, cardplaying is a satanic ploy that undermines social mores and unleashes sinister powers. In holding up his cards to the establishment, the sorcerer Nemukhin seems to be fully aware of these connotations. In other words, what might appear to be an abstract painting, dependent for its effect on a formal counterpoint of textures and rhythms, is, in fact, an intricate narrative charged with an ideological message.

The forceful presence in Leningrad of painters such as Zubkov, Borisov, and Mikhnov-Voitenko calls into question the conventional association of Moscow with spontaneous color and St. Petersburg with graphic line and architectural grace. Perhaps Moscow artists such as Vechtomov with his nervous pulsations would be unthinkable in the restrained milieu of St. Petersburg, while the fine etchings of William Brui (b. 1946) extend the elegant filigrees of those earlier St. Petersburg residents, Mstislav Dobuzhinsky (1875–1957) and Konstantin Somov (1869–1939). But the division is not altogether convincing, because these traditional artistic identifications are often contradicted by the productions of the artists themselves: Yurlov is a master of line and "rhythmical lattices"[13] and yet he is a confirmed Muscovite; Dyshlenko, on the other hand, is a passionate colorist and yet comes from St. Petersburg.

In any case, some of the dissident artists, notably Evgenii Rukhin, lived and worked in both capitals. This division of loyalties actually seemed to gratify rather than confuse their particular artistic demands. Rukhin's constant commute between Leningrad and Moscow was in fact symptomatic of his own hiatus and, ultimately, of the rootlessness (*bespochvennost*) of the dissident movement as a whole. Here was the caring family man who was subject to outbursts of violence, who wore long, unruly hair and an elegant suit as he oscillated between the two cities. His paintings, too, reflected this fracture and unease—the monochromatic surfaces punctured by a nail or hinge; Dadaist combinations of incompatible objects (pieces of newspaper, furniture, porcelain); eccentric adjustments of Western stimuli (Jasper Johns, Jim Dine) to Russian tradition (bronze icons, Malevich's Suprematism). With their savage gestures and rough surfaces, their cryptic symbols and textural metabolisms, Rukhin's paintings embodied the very spirit of dissension.

One of the most impressive abstract artists of the 1950s—yet one of the least familiar—is Vladimir Slepian, whose biography is as oblique as his paintings. Born in Vienna in 1930, Slepian studied art in Moscow and mechanics in Leningrad, before emigrating to Poland in 1958, and thence to France.[14] By the mid-1950s, Slepian was painting abstract, equilateral paintings which simultaneously call to mind Seurat and computer graphics. The two works dated 1957 and 1958 in the second volume of *Drugoe iskusstvo*, for example, could easily have been created in New York or Milan: spontaneous, gestural, and tactile, they combine the dynamism of Pollock and the eccentricity of Tancredi. In the absence of reliable information, it is hard to establish the exact derivation of Slepian's artistic style and philosophy, but the random curves and colored dots of *Science* (1958) seem to be moving across the screen of some magic oscillator, while *Composition* (1957) reminds us of some infernal game of tick-tack-toe. Slepian now lives in Paris, writing poetry under the pseudonym of Edik Pid, a chameleonic disguise that parallels the improvisational character and ephemerality of his paintings.

Sculptor Igor Shelkovsky (b. 1937), who also lives in Paris, has developed his own abstract system that, in its lightness and musicality, elicits associations with radio frequencies and luminescence. His constructions and reliefs resemble the holographic diagrams of marvelous beasts or prototypes of biomorphic species that have yet to evolve.

One of the most fervent apologists for abstract or near-abstract art during the 1950s and 1960s was Eli Beliutin, whose tempestuous insurgency and uncompromising behavior led to his expulsion from the Moscow Polygraphical Institute in 1959 "for propagating abstract art." Yet, in many ways, Beliutin is an organic extension of the very regime that punished him, for he was and is no less dogmatic in his artistic belief than the Socialist Realists were in theirs. He condemns the cultural establishment for bigotry and corruption in the same way that the Party accused the dissident movement of treachery and treason. Since 1946, Beliutin has headed a studio of committed students; this school, now tucked away in the woods of Abramtsevo, requires a dedicated, almost monastic commitment to abstraction. Beliutin is jealous of his artistic behests, is eager to explain them to the sincere observer, and, paradoxically, recognizes and ratifies the pedagogical methods of the Academy, even though his own artistic practice may seem antipodal.[15]

Beliutin's one-man exhibition in the United States in 1991 demonstrated the sheer force of his artistic talent.[16] Clearly, the work of Beliutin and his closest disciples, such as Petr Valius (b. 1958) and Boris Zhutovsky (b. 1932) (Pl. 14:14), owes something to the Action Painting of Pollock. But in their hands, the abstract paintings often carry thematic denotations, as in the case of Valius's *Motherland* (1966) or Zhutovsky's *In Memory of Ullo* [*Sooster*] (1970). But they also bring to mind the occasional gestural paintings of the Russian avant-garde, including Rodchenko's pencil drawings from 1921 and the series called *Negatives* (also 1921) by Lev Bruni, Beliutin's teacher in Moscow.

Beliutin's own paintings project the biological and geological structures that he has studied in an attempt to establish rational connections between the natural and the artistic worlds. The fact that Beliutin and his students work outdoors, hang their paintings from trees or place them on the grass, and create paintings and sculptures resembling organic forms emphasizes their desire to encode a "natural aesthetics," just as Pavel Mansurov was trying to do in Leningrad in the early 1920s. The disquieting feature of Beliutin's world, however, is the incongruity of his preference for concepts such as "genius," "masterpiece," and "painting" in a Postmodern world that appears to favor "uniformity," "seriality," and "alternative media."

By contrast, the activities of the Movement Group and its subsequent metamorphoses are more contemporary and more international. In theory and in practice, they are among the most exciting manifestations of the abstract tradition in Soviet culture.[17] Founded by the Napoleonic Lev Nusberg in Moscow in 1962, Movement has had a turbulent life checkered with personal antagonisms, jealousies, and internecine warfare. Even so, the group has produced paintings, constructions, machines, and installations that still engage us with their utopian orientation and sophisticated elegance. But the primary

artistic achievement of Movement was to transfer the Suprematist and Constructivist systems to a broader, synthetic environment in the form of functional design (e.g., urban designs celebrating the fiftieth anniversary of the October Revolution in 1966) and outdoor performance (e.g., the Galaxy Kinetic Complex of 1967). In this way, Movement operated on two social levels: as an "official" design team, receiving state commissions; and as a group of "unofficial" artists, provoking public anger for the "pornography" and "frivolity" of their Kinetic actions.

By the early 1970s, a division of loyalties and personal incompatabilities had undermined the solidarity of Movement, and the group's initial interests in Kinetic art were modified and expanded by members such as Infante and Koleichuk. Infante and his group ARGO began to give serious attention to the "geometric object introduced into the natural environment."[18] This is not the mechanical and calculated placement of a foreign body in virgin territory, but rather an action based on fortuity and instantaneity, what Infante calls a "discrete displacement."[19] For example, the artists place mirrors and other reflective surfaces in the natural landscape, using earth, water, snow, and foliage as partners in a formal dialogue (Fig. 14:3). In their lightness and ephemerality, these constructions evoke the sensation of organic continuity with the landscape, even though the deformed images of their reflections undermine it. Infante thus establishes a discourse between the natural landscape, the artist, and the spectator that raises issues about ambiguity, veracity, and artificiality. He then photographs each scenario, sometimes rearranging the sequence of frames into new series such

Fig. 14:3
Artifact made by Francisco Infante, Gorky Park, Moscow, April 1966
Standing by the tree are Nicoletta Misler and John E. Bowlt.
Photo by Francisco Infante, courtesy of the Collection of the Institute of Modern Russian Culture, Los Angeles

Fig. 14:5
Vitalii Rakhman
Chair-Lamp, 1976
Plexiglas and metal
104 × 56 × 48.5 cm

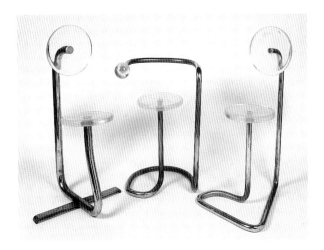

as the album *Prisutstvie* [Presence]. For Infante and his colleagues such as Nonna Goriunova (b. 1944), the artist is mediator between nature and the artifact, affirming at once that nature has no boundaries and that elemental, artificial forms in metal and plastic can also assume a natural character. This attitude was particularly evident in the snow performances that Infante and Goriunova undertook in the 1970s. In those actions, outlandish figures moved across snow or added silver foil to tree trunks and bushes. The very interplay of these conditions undermined the conventional notions of "symmetry" and "asymmetry," "here" and "there," and "start" and "finish."

The Kinetic artist Koleichuk remains closer to the original philosophy of the Movement Group in that he continues to explore the technological and mobile aspects of artistic production. For Koleichuk, the abstract concepts of reflectivity, transparency, negative space, energy, and temporal linearity are the only permanent attributes of the objective world and he symbolizes them in his schematic drawings and metal, wire, and plexiglas constructions. He invites the viewer not only to contemplate the artifact, but also to participate in a silent dialogue. However, his designs are among the least contrived expressions of the Russian abstract movement, untrammeled by recondite philosophy or moralistic message.

Like Koleichuk, both Aleksandr Brodsky (b. 1955) and Ilya Utkin (b. 1955) were trained as architects. They were leaders in the field of paper architecture, a movement that began with their surprising success in a competition sponsored by a Japanese architectural magazine in 1981. Their joint work illustrates how many creative professionals working in the confines of the Soviet system had to escape into a never-never land of fanciful design in order to exercise their creative capabilities (Fig. 14:4).

Industrial design in the Soviet Union was not as politically or stylistically fettered as painting. "Independent" exhibitions were organized by the designers' section of MOSKh in 1977 and 1978. These shows featured the work of many young creative designers who, like the paper architects, were not preoccupied with the realization of their projects. The chair-lamp prototypes of Vitalii Rakhman (b. 1945) are illustrative of this kind of imaginative design (Fig. 14:5). More sculptural than practical, these graceful tubular chairs have circular clear plastic seats and backs which glow from interior illumination. Four chairs that Leonid Yentus (b. 1945) designed in 1984–85 were only realized in 1988. One of these, known as "Chair with Russian Avant-Garde Design" (Pl. 14:15), was based on a prototype by Gerrit Rietveld but used Russian spades as distinctive features as well as Suprematist design elements. The *Green Chair*, with its fabric seaweed swatches, symbolized the Green movement. These exhibitions of young designers had a liberating effect on the nonconformist artists who saw them.

The new generation of artists that continues the struggle for self-expression in the Commonwealth of Independent States flourishes in an ambience quite different from that of the 1960s and 1970s. Artists such as Afrika (Sergei Bugaev), Igor Chachkin, Aleksandr Mareev, and

Fig. 14:4
**Aleksandr Brodsky
and Ilya Utkin**
(Untitled), 1988
Etching
73 × 59.2 cm

Konstantin Zvezdochetov emphasize irony, pollution, and indiscretion as their principal themes. They decorate the ailing body politic with gaudy colors, furious beasts, and salacious jokes. But the mystery is missing, and in their shrill and merciless messages the artists seem to create instant puzzles and rebuses as pale surrogates for style and idea. As Vadim Zakharov wrote recently:

> In the end . . . I would like to hide. Thrust myself in a corner, disappear behind a wall, where I can feel fine and be calm, where I will finally be able to die peacefully, after having misled everybody.[20]

Unlike their predecessors, these artists operate in a social vacuum where point and counterpoint, center and opposi-tion have merged. Heated debates on the spiritual in art and the meaning of God have been replaced by a rush to capitalize. Even the phrase "*A na Zapade . . .*" ("But in the West . . . ") has lost its resonance, for "there" has now become "here," just as the Western art market has replaced the Soviet Ministry of Culture. It is an uneasy way to enter the twenty-first century. Norton Dodge still acquires works of art, but his collection has suddenly become historical and museological, documenting an era and a country that exist no more. At the same time, the collection has already assumed its total meaning as a majestic tribute to one of the most dramatic and creative moments in the history of modern Russian culture.

Notes

1. L. Gurevich and E. Andreeva, *Leningradskii ander-graund. Nachalo. Nachalo* (Leningrad: Leningradskaia Gallereia, 1990), p. 8.

2. Vladimir Serov at the "Second Meeting of Representa-tives of the Party and Government with the Creative Intelligentsia," Reception Building, Moscow State University, January 1963. Quoted in the catalogue for "The Other Art" exhibition, *Drugoe iskusstvo: Moskva, 1956–76.* (Moscow: Moskovskaia Kollektsiia/SP Inter-buk, 1991), vol. 1, p. 115.

3. "The KGB Just Isn't Itself These Days," *The Econo-mist*, Sept. 21, 1974; Hilton Kramer, "Underground Soviet Art: A Publicized Pop Style," *New York Times*, Sept. 29, 1974; John Bowlt, "Art and Politics and Money: The Moscow Scene," *Art in America* (Mar.–Apr. 1975): 20–24; J. Leonard, "Smuggled Soviet Art Is a Witty Vari-ation on Ideology," *New York Times*, Feb. 19, 1976.

4. From Andrei Zhdanov's speech at the First Congress of Soviet Writers, Moscow, 1934. Translation in John Bowlt, ed., *Russian Art of the Avant-Garde: Theory and Criticism, 1902–1934* (London: Thames and Hudson, 1988), p. 294.

5. *Zapasnik* is a depository or storeroom. Until recently, many works of the Russian avant-garde languished in the *zapasniki* of the major Soviet museums. *Spetskhran* is a special depository in Soviet libraries where, until recently, "undesirable" publications were preserved with highly limited access.

6. See, for example, V. Kemenov: *Protiv abstraktsion-izma v sporakh o realizme* (Leningrad: Khudozhnik RSFSR, 1969), which reproduces numerous examples of abstract and "decadent" art; and N. Malakhov, *Sot-sialisticheskii realizm i modernizm* (Moscow: Iskusstvo, 1970), which includes a reproduction of a Malevich Suprematist painting on pages 192 and 193. As late as 1985, Valentina Kriuchkova maintained the same

arguments in her book *Antiiskusstvo. Teoriia i praktika avangardistskikh dvizhenii* (Moscow: Isobrazitel'noe Iskusstvo, 1985).

7. Among these exhibitions were the following: one-man shows of Mikhail Chernyshov (Moscow Insti-tute of Biophysics, 1965), Mikhail Grobman (Moscow Energy Institute, 1965), Mikhail Kulakov (Vavilov Insti-tute of Physical Problems, Moscow, 1967), Yulii Ved-ernikov (Kurchatov Institute of Atomic Energy, Moscow, 1965); and group shows of the Movement Group (Kurchatov Institute of Atomic Energy, 1966), Olga Potapova, Vasilii Sitnikov, and Valentina Kropivnitskaia, and others (Scientific-Research Insti-tute of Labor Hygiene and Profession Diseases, 1966), and Lev Kropivnitsky, Vladimir Nemukhin, Dmitri Plavinsky, Oscar Rabin, and Boris Sveshnikov (Institute of World Economics and International Relations, 1969). A number of dissident artists also trained as sci-entists: Evgenii Rukhin, Yakov Vinkovetsky, and the photographer Igor Palmin in Voronezh were all edu-cated as geologists.

8. Mikhail Matiushin, *Zakonomernost' izmeniaemosti tsvetovykh sochetanii. Spravochnik po tsvetu* (Moscow-Leningrad: Gosudarstvennoe Izdatelstvo Izo-brazitelnykh Iskusstv, 1932).

9. As reported in Alexander Glezer, *Russkie khudozh-niki na Zapade* (Paris: Tretiia Volna, 1986), p. 5.

10. Vasilii Kandinsky, *Über das Gesitige in der Kunst. Insbesondere in der Malerei* (Munich: Piper, 1912), and subsequent editions and translations. The painter Vasilii Chekrygin was much influenced by Nikolai Fedorov's philosophy of the common cause. See *Wassili Tschekrygin. Mystiker der Russischen Avantgarde*, exh. cat. (Cologne: Galerie Gmurzynska, 1992).

11. Nikolai Kulbin, "Free Art as the Basis of Life: Harmony and Dissonance (On Life, Death, etc.)"

(1908), translated in Bowlt, ed., *Russian Art of the Avant-Garde*, p. 15.

12. Mikhail Matiushin, "O knige Metzanzhe-Gleza 'Du Cubisme'," in *Soiuz molodezhi* 3 (1913), p. 25.

13. M. Bessonova, Introduction, *Valerii Yurlov*, exh. cat. (Moscow: Tretyakov Gallery, 1992), p. 6.

14. This information on Slepian is taken from Talochkin et al., eds., *Drugoe iskusstvo*, vol. 2, pp. 164–65.

15. Beliutin has published a number of essays dealing with the Academic teaching system. See, for example, Beliutin, *Nachal'nye svedeniia po zhivopisi* (Moscow: Iskusstvo, 1955); N. Moleva and E. Beliutin, *P.P. Chisti-akov, Teoretik i pedagog* (Moscow: Academy of Arts, 1953); and N. Moleva and E. Beliutin, *Russkaia khu-dozhestvennaia shkola vtoroi poloviny XIX-nachala XX veka* (Moscow: Iskusstvo, 1967). It is perhaps sympto-matic of his contrary nature that Beliutin refused to take part in the "Drugoe iskusstvo" [Other art] exhibi-tion in Moscow in 1991.

16. The exhibition "Censored in 1962, Celebrated in 1991: Eli Beliutin and the New Russian Avant-Garde" was shown at the Edith C. Blum Art Institute, Bard College, Annandale-on-Hudson, New York, May–Sep-tember 1991. There was no catalogue.

17. On the Movement Group, see *Lew Nussberg und die Gruppe Bewegung, Moskau 1962–1972*, exh. cat. (Bochum: Museum Bochum, 1978).

18. Infante, "Nature and Art," *The Structurist* 23–24 (1983–84): 95.

19. Infante, "On My Concept of the Artefact," in Elena Kornetchuk et al., *Francisco Infante*, exh. cat. (Sewickley, Penn.: International Images, Ltd., 1989), p. 18.

20. Vadim Zakharov, untitled statement, in *Contempo-rary Russian Artists/Artisti russi contemporanei*, exh. cat. (Prato: Museo d'Arte Contemporanea, 1990), p. 65.

15 | On some sources of Soviet Conceptualism

Margarita Tupitsyn

In searching for the roots of Soviet Conceptual Art, I was surprised to come across a promising lead in a definition put forward by one of the movement's Western practitioners. Curiously, this apparent common ground had developed not as a result of any similarities between conditions in the Soviet Union and the West, but precisely because of the immense differences. In 1970, Joseph Kosuth wrote: "Because of the implied duality of perception and conception in earlier art, a middleman (critic) appeared useful. . . . [Conceptual] art both annexes the functions of the critic and makes the middleman unnecessary."[1] In Moscow in the early 1970s, the interest in "art-as-idea" or "art-as-knowledge" emerged independently of Western art theory, but was also linked to the issue of the critical function of art. However, in Moscow, Conceptual Art was not based on a usurpation of the critic but on the prolonged absence of critics altogether.

In this regard, one could say that Ilya Kabakov's *Responses of the Experimental Group*, 1970–71 (Fig. 15:1), represents that moment when he became what Kosuth calls "a middleman." On one half of the large white panel, Kabakov (b. 1933) placed a hanger on a nail, another nail puncturing the lower surface, and a toy train. On the other half of the panel, Kabakov painted a text that comments on the work's content; the commentary is presented very much in the style of a conversation around the kitchen table. Kabakov has said of this and similar works: "The game consisted in showing on the same surface the picture itself and the thoughts of the viewers about it."[2] This intrusion of critical interpretation into the visual field was prompted by a desire to start the critical dialogue that had been lacking in the Soviet alternative art movement since its beginnings in the late 1950s.[3]

Despite this absence of critical debate, as Moscow critic Joseph Bakshtein points out, Conceptualism "expressed some very essential aspects of the entire artistic process in Russia." Bakshtein records Kabakov's remark that "[when] the word conceptualism descended to us . . . we revealed in ourselves what we had long possessed and utilized supremely."[4] Kabakov alludes to the fact that such important components of Conceptual Art as commentary,

interpretation, and self-interpretation had long been a part of alternative Russian art.

In addition to those aspects of Conceptual Art that were immediately recognized by Soviet artists, another, less familiar component was what Kabakov designates "the visualization of verbal concepts,"[5] or what another writer has called "the preference of the ideational over the visual" (Pls. 15:2–15:7).[6] Critic Victor Tupitsyn attributes the importance of this textual element to the "enormous empire of speech" in the Soviet Union. "Given such a situation," he continues, "the essence of the cure lies in fostering a culture of seeing, as has occurred in the West . . . making it possible for the visual to refer to the visual. I don't have much faith in nonliterary paradigms . . . when there is nothing but the pit bulls of speech at your back."[7]

The emergence of Soviet Conceptualism in the early 1970s can be linked to this sudden intrusion of speech into visual art and the wide variety of similar effects that it produced. Kabakov's *Responses of the Experimental Group* was complemented in 1972 by a series of "albums," in which the interpretational mechanisms were incorporated within the work itself. In the same year, the team of Vitaly Komar (b. 1943) and Alexander Melamid (b. 1945) declared, "We are not artists, we are conversationalists." Also in 1972, Eric Bulatov (b. 1933) began to execute a landscape with the word "Danger" painted in red over the image at each of its four edges (Pl. 15:1).[8] These gestures signaled a crucial shift in the history of Soviet alternative art. First, the use of text in the works of Kabakov, Bulatov, and Komar and Melamid stressed the "infection with speech practices" that pervaded the Soviet sociocultural atmosphere (Pls. 15:8–15:11, 15:15). Second, their use of generic language or other elements from "low" culture transformed the attitude of alternative practitioners toward the mass media, which was still regarded primarily as a vehicle for official propaganda. And, finally, as a result of these new attitudes toward text and Soviet mass culture, these artists redirected alternative art away from Western sources and closer to local ones.[9]

Significantly, similar attitudes had provided the main principles of the early twentieth-century Russian avant-

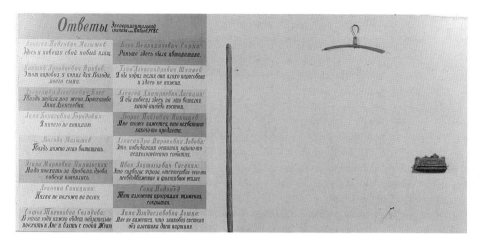

Fig. 15:1
Ilya Kabakov
*Responses of the Experimental
Group*, 1970–71
Mixed media on board
Courtesy of Feldman
Fine Arts

garde. In fact, despite their vastly different aesthetic and political contexts, there are important parallels between the historical avant-garde and Soviet Conceptual Art. Both demonstrated an orientation toward the visualization of verbal concepts and a willingness to appropriate aspects of popular culture. In 1908, the founders of the Russian avant-garde—the artists Mikhail Larionov, Natalia Goncharova, and Olga Rozanova—directed a large portion of their time to collaborations with poets Velimir Khlebnikov and Aleksandr Khruchenykh.[10] Although both poets and artists aimed at revolutionizing traditional aesthetics, it was precisely the inclination of these artists toward "the visualization of verbal concepts" that made the collaboration successful. In addition, both artists and poets borrowed from low culture, including folklore, popular icons, and *lubki* (popular woodcuts).[11]

After the Bolshevik Revolution, when formalism reached its peak, language continued to infiltrate abstract designs, particularly in the form of didactic political slogans.[12] After Lenin's death in 1924, when the use of such media as photomontage, posters, and photography began to reshape Soviet visual culture, political texts were incorporated as a crucial component of many artworks. Every image in a poster was accompanied by a slogan and every photograph or montage printed in a magazine was followed by an explanatory phrase or a short narrative.

By the end of the 1920s, nearly every major avant-garde artist, including Aleksandr Rodchenko, Gustav Klutsis (Klucis), Sergei Senkin, Varvara Stepanova, and Valentina Kulagina, was engrossed in work for the mass media. Forms of production generally associated with high art, such as painting and sculpture, were largely abandoned by these artists in favor of poster designs or work for popular magazines. Instead of scavenging forms from popular culture and transforming them into high art (as

was typical of early modern art in Russia and in the West), these Soviet avant-gardists became directly involved in making culture for the masses. It was not until the early 1930s, under Stalin, that mass-media images slipped from the guidance of artists and deteriorated into hollow vehicles of governmental propaganda.[13] By the beginning of World War II, communal consciousness and its close companion, communal speech, had begun to dominate Soviet society.

When alternative artists first emerged in the Soviet Union in the late 1950s, their primary goal was to create an aesthetic counter to the steady diet of Socialist Realism, mass culture, and stultifying verbal propaganda. They hoped to resurrect such disreputable concepts as pure form and abstract uses of color. This project, which Kabakov referred to as "visionary visuality," had achieved a certain degree of success in the Russian underground art world before it was undermined in the early 1970s by the Conceptualists. Kabakov, Bulatov, and Komar and Melamid declared that in the Soviet Union "speech is behind everything: I don't see, I speak."[14] As a consequence, these artists elected to stripmine precisely that culture which seemed most offensive, that is, the narrow version of Soviet communal speech and the cramped language of the state.

Thus, from radically different starting points, Soviet and Western Conceptualism once again arrived at comparable results: in this case, the completion or redefinition of the aims of the historical avant-garde. In the West, "conceptual art completed the break with traditional esthetics that the Dadaists, and notably Marcel Duchamp, initiated."[15] At the same time, in the Soviet Union, Conceptualists fulfilled the course of linguistic intrusion into visual art that had been laid down by the early avant-garde practitioners.

In one of his texts, Kabakov gives an account of the climate of the Moscow art community at the time he was making *Responses of the Experimental Group* and his first albums, united under the name *Ten Characters* (1973–75):

certain art circles in Moscow were particularly concerned with metaphysical and spiritual issues. Everywhere in studios and apartments, in the meeting places of the creative intelligentsia, people were talking about spiritual, higher problems, about the transcendental, about the experience of the absolute, and naturally also about the artistic means of expressing such emotions and experiences. Artists inclined toward the visionary created their own ontological worlds; others followed the technique prescribed by "outside" sources and from "above"; still others sought to represent the

Pl. 14:1
Ullo Sooster
(Untitled), 1963
Oil on illustration board
35 × 50.1 cm

Pl 14:3
Valerii Volkov
Kaleidoscope, 1967
Oil on canvas
135.5 × 136.3 cm

Pl. 14:4
Aleksandr A. Volkov
Three Red Squares, 1967
Oil on canvas
90 × 75 cm

Pl. 14:2
Valerii Volkov
*Composition for Antuanet
and Zherar*, 1968
Oil on canvas
88 × 109.4 cm

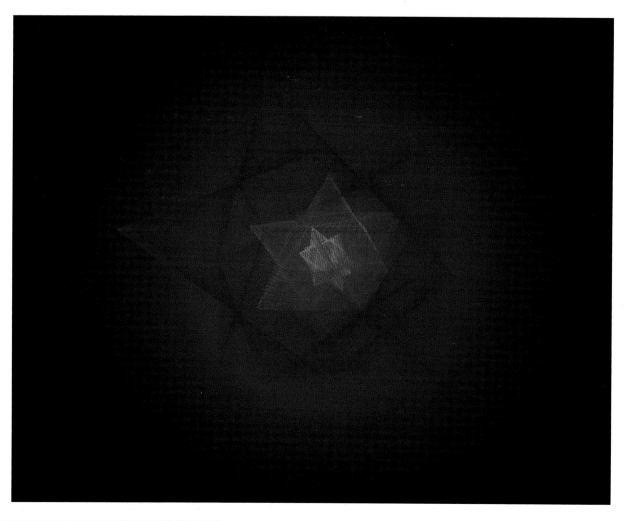

Pl. 14:5
Francisco Infante
Space—Movement—
Infinity (Project of Kinetic
Object), 1963
Pen and airbrush with
tempera on fiberboard
70.3 × 91 cm

Pl. 14:6
Aleksandr A. Volkov
White Composition, 1968
Mixed media on
fiberboard
61 × 82.7 cm

Pl. 14:7
Yurii Zlotnikov
No. 5 in the series
Seasons, 1986
Watercolor on paper
58 × 84 cm

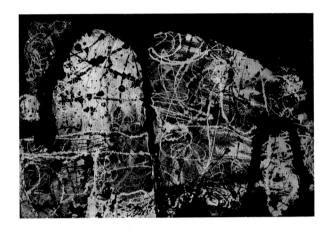

Pl. 14:8
Yakov Vinkovetsky
Nose of the Fox, 1962
Oil on fiberboard
80.6 × 119.7 cm

Pl. 14:9
Bella Levikova
(River Landscape), 1981
Oil on canvas
119.8 × 89.7 cm

Pl. 14:10
Eduard Shteinberg
Composition—Dec. 1976,
1976
Oil on canvas
115 × 69 cm

Pl. 14:11
Mikhail Chernyshov
(Untitled), 1980
Gouache on paper
51 × 67.1 cm

Pl. 14:12 (*right*)
Elena Keller
Magadan, 1985
Mixed media on canvas
97 × 138 cm

308

Pl. 14:14
Boris Zhutovsky
(Untitled), 1969
Mixed media
42.7 × 30.6 cm

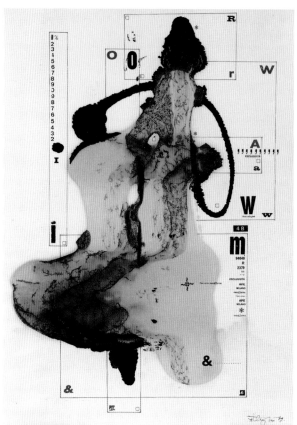

Pl. 15:1 (*opposite*)
Eric Bulatov
Danger, 1972–73
Oil on canvas
108.6 × 110 cm

Pl. 14:13
Vladimir Nemukhin
For Krasnopevtsev, 1983
Bronze
37 × 30.3 × 15.5 cm

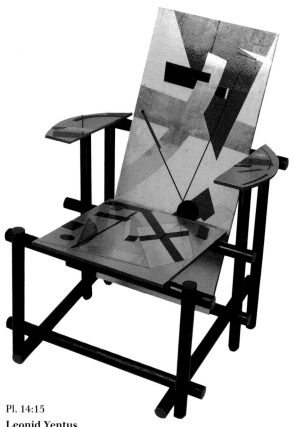

Pl. 14:15
Leonid Yentus
(Chair with Russian
Avant-Garde Design), 1988
Mixed media
100.6 × 69 × 75 cm

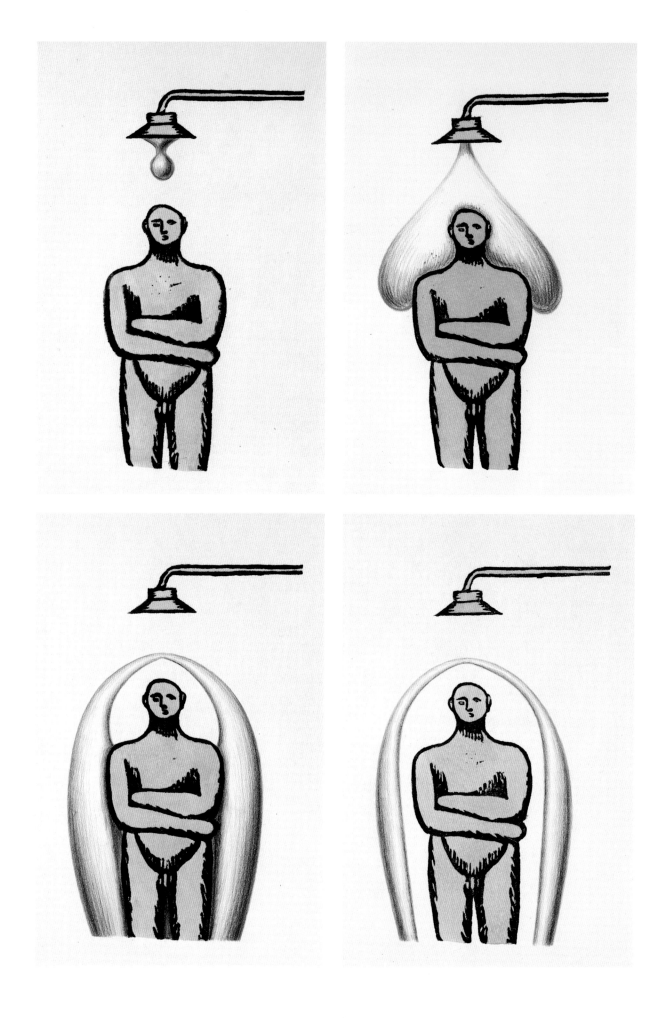

Pls. 15:2–15:7
Ilya Kabakov
(Shower—A Comedy),
1970s
Six from a series of
thirty-nine
Mixed media
22 × 16 cm (each)

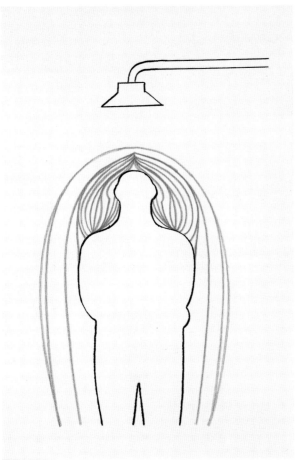

312

Pls. 15:8–15:11
Ilya Kabakov
Where Are They?, 1979
Four from a series of
twelve
Pen and ink and crayon
on paper
40.5 × 27 cm (each)

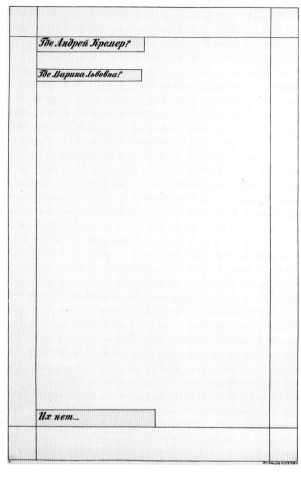

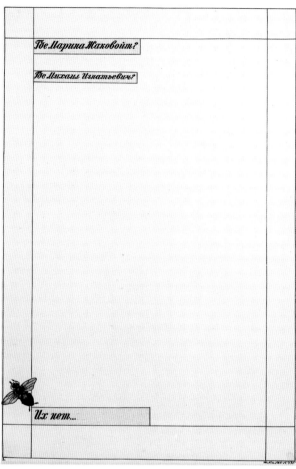

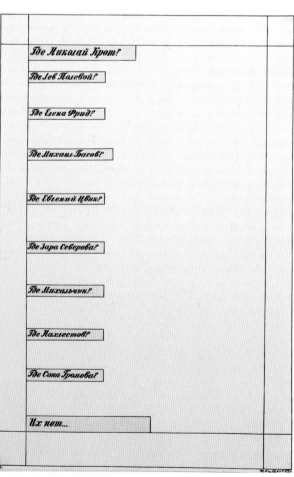

Pl. 15:12
Eric Bulatov
Two Landscapes on a Red Background, 1972–74
Oil on canvas
110 × 110.3 cm

Pls. 15:13 and 15:14
Vitaly Komar and
Alexander Melamid
Our Goal is Communism,
1972
We Were Born to Make
Our Dreams Come True,
1972
Tempera on cloth
39 × 195 cm (each)

Pl. 15:15
Eric Bulatov
Stop—Go, 1975
Oil on canvas
79.8 × 240.5 cm

Pl. 15:16
Mukhomor (Toadstool)
Group
(M.P.), 1982
Pen and ink on paper
61.6 × 86.6 cm

Pl. 15:17
**Lev Nusberg and the
Movement Group**
Performance, n.d.
Cibachrome photograph
27.6 × 34.5 cm

Pl. 15:18
**Mukhomor (Toadstool)
Group**
Spartak—Champion,
c. 1982
Watercolor, pastel,
gouache, and graphite on
paper
181 × 266.5 cm

Pl. 15:19
**The Peppers (Liudmila
Skripkina and Oleg
Petrenko)**
Sunna, n.d.
Mixed media on cloth
53 × 120.3 cm

Pl. 15:20
Sergei Anufriev
Unimaginable, from the
album *Podiaka*
Pen and ink on paper
28.5 × 21.8 cm

Pl. 15:21
Irina Nakhova
(Untitled), n.d.
Mixed media
36.1 × 48 cm

Pl. 15:22
Nikita Alekseev
Ironic Materialism, 1983
Pen and ink and collage
on paper
50.5 × 39.5 cm

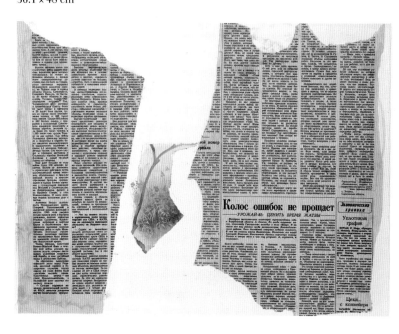

Pl. 15:23
Ivan Chuikov
All Power . . . [To the Soviets], 1985
Oil and collage on fiberboard
179 × 122.4 cm

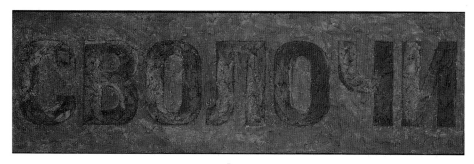

present conditions of the class struggle and of the anti-capitalist objectives which this entails.

These struggles which are developing in each country on the basis of national demands are being backed up, are joining together and are meeting on an international level, to present a front of solidarity against the almost identical attacks and retrograde measures which the employers and governments instigate in almost all the capitalist countries. **From this, new possibilities of international solidarity and cooperation are coming to the fore.**

The arms race, the serious nature of its social and economic consequences and the dangers it is bringing demands a renewal in the action of the workers and peoples. The fight for peace and for the mass movement which is its guarantee... of the warmongers. It urged the... Despite using... responsible for... has broad... of the... Trade... are...

УСКОРЕНИЕ

A wider... and decisive action... process of disarmament.

Since the 10th Congress, the struggle for real economic independence, against exploitation by the imperialist countries and the transnational corporations, and for economic sovereignty, has taken on new dimensions.

After the fall of the great colonial empires, through their national liberation struggles, a number of countries managed to pull free of colonialism and imperialist tutelage and chose a non-capitalist path of development. Many others, despite the struggles of their peoples, still remain in the vice-like grip of the major capitalist countries which are attempting to regain total domination. The food weapon and the economic weapon are being used as a means of enslavement. The majority of countries are staggering under the enormous weight of their foreign debt, which prevents independent development.

But the current trend is towards the development of a radical and broad movement to oppose this domination. There too this movement reaches the

21

Pl. 15:24
Sergei Volkov
Bastards, 1986–87
Oil on canvas
59.5 × 199 cm

Pl. 15:25
Dmitrii Prigov
(Acceleration), n.d.
Pen and ink on paper
20.5 × 14.5 cm

Pl. 15:26
Svetlana Kopystianskaia
(Landscape), 1984
Oil on canvas
69.5 × 89.5 cm

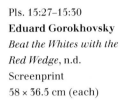

Pls. 15:27–15:30
Eduard Gorokhovsky
*Beat the Whites with the
Red Wedge*, n.d.
Screenprint
58 × 36.5 cm (each)

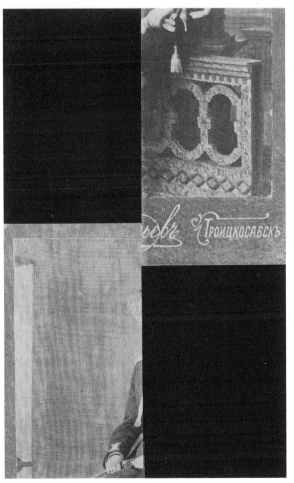

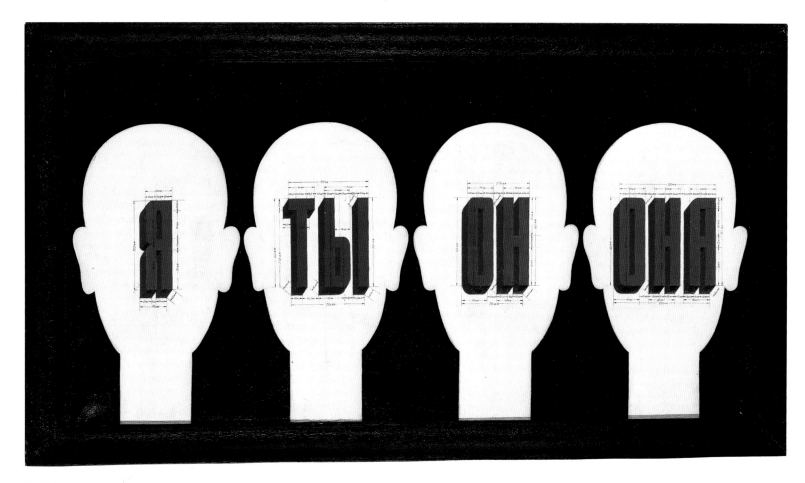

Pl. 17:1
Leonid Lamm
I, You, He, She, 1971
Oil on canvas
65 × 129 cm

plain reality around them in the light of these influences. The cycle of albums *Ten Characters* can be assigned to the third category.[16]

Kabakov's albums, like the paintings of his close friend Viktor Pivovarov (b. 1937), centered on images of fictional Russian citizens, lonely characters forced to undergo all the stages of Soviet upbringing and communal living in order to achieve the most desired "fourth level of loneliness." In his six paintings united under the title *Plan for the Everyday Objects of a Lonely Man*, 1975 (Pl. 4:22), Pivovarov describes this fourth level of "joyful and absolute" loneliness as "the attaining of a true freedom and the joining with the infinite." In their work, both Kabakov and Pivovarov combined verbal comments with the images of mundane Soviet reality, including views of the communal apartments and the private rooms of each tenant.[17] Despite drawing these pictures of "plain reality" and quoting from communal speech, Kabakov nevertheless continued to share the ontological stance of his colleagues by viewing the color white—as in white paint or white paper—as the signifier of the "metaphysical and spiritual." Kabakov suggested that a white piece of paper in his albums carries a double meaning: it is, simultaneously, simply nothing, a blank surface on which all sorts of things can be drawn, and infinite space, out of which radiant, benevolent light streams toward us.

The artist's fervent adherence to this second, metaphorical meaning of the white is apparent when he describes his series of "white" paintings called *Along the Edge* (1974). Kabakov writes:

> White . . . is understood as an uninterrupted and an even stream of emanation, the emanation of bright, almost blinding light which functions not as a flash but as a constant current of even energy. . . . In this case definite meaning and content are carried by the edges of such a "pseudo-painting." These edges become the contact points, the intersections between this "non-painting" and common objects of our reality. . . . The latter blur the edges of "such painting" creating a sort of "green halo" around the light discussed above.[18]

Thus, although Kabakov utilized common speech and mundane imagery in his work, he continued to associate himself with metaphysical issues by means of his own mystification of color. Later, he replaced many of his white surfaces with dirty green or brown ones (drawn from the color of communal interiors). In view of this change, his reference above to a "green halo" is significant. It is a sort of profane (ontic) aura which slowly advances toward the center of each white panel. Finally, in the green series

produced in the early 1980s, the "green halo" literally spreads across the painting's surface and fully obscures the "streaming light" of the white surfaces.[19]

In all his works, Kabakov insists on the contextual, rather than the formal, significance of color. Like the Sots artists who appropriated the red of Soviet propaganda, Kabakov forced the issue of the meaning of color in Soviet art. This topic has particular resonance in Soviet history, especially around the uses of red. In 1926, for example, Klutsis (Klucis) claimed that "color is to be studied as a tangible, industrial material and not as an aesthetic appendage." In the same year, critic Vladimir Friche claimed in his book *The Sociology of Art*:

> In some eras painters use primarily one color, in others—different ones. Often within the boundaries of one period various artists prefer different color combinations. Every era, every artist has his own favorite palette. This phenomenon is not accidental: different colors influence the psyche of individuals differently.[20]

At the time Friche made this statement, "collective-monumental" art was increasingly prevalent in the Soviet Union, and red began to dominate the palettes of designers preparing for demonstrations and public holidays. Soviet political leaders, who were indirectly influenced by the theories of such psychoideologists as Friche and Ivan Matsa, made no mistake in choosing the color red as the most effective tool for the manipulation of Soviet society. In their attitudes toward color, both Friche and Matsa demonstrated a shift away from the interests of, for example, Vasilii Kandinsky and Mikhail Matiushin, two modernist artists who developed concepts of color that were based on aesthetics rather than ideology. These psychoideologists specifically denied the modernist's formalist perception of color and sought to attribute to it a more strictly iconographic function. Friche and Matsa, therefore, initiated a tradition in Soviet art that has had a powerful presence in both official and alternative art.

At first a powerful propagandistic device, red lost its symbolic effectiveness over the years and became a fading reminder of long-lost utopian zeal. In the work of the Sots artists, red gained a new significance. They appropriated this stereotypical color as well as other formal aspects of official Socialist Realism and the Soviet mass media and re-presented them ironically in order to offer a revision or critique of their visual heritage.

Red intrudes into Bulatov's anxious representations of Soviet *byt* (everyday life) in the form of backgrounds, writing, grids, or horizon lines. In *Two Landscapes on a Red Background*, 1972–74 (Pl. 15:12), the artist superimposes two landscapes over a red banner. Here, Bulatov promotes a gesture of subtle warning, an index of ideological presence in an otherwise innocuous environment. In *Danger*, 1972–73 (Pl. 15:1), Bulatov depicts a country scene with a man and a woman sitting on a green lawn amid the trees, enjoying their leisure time. But the tranquility of this scene is abruptly interrupted by the bold warning "Danger" inscribed in red four times across the painting. The red in Bulatov's works signifies the presence of "dangerous objects" (agents of dystopia) in the pre-*glasnost* Soviet atmosphere. In such antiutopian paintings the "spaces of desire" so typical of Socialist Realism are recoded into alarming signals of what one may refer to as "minus dèsire."

Bulatov's *Danger* recalls Edouard Manet's *Le Déjeuner sur l'herbe* (1863) not only in its compositional similarity, but because both artists sought to subvert the official dogmas of art-making. At the same time, their different acts of nonconformity attest to the fundamental distinctions between representation in the West, based on "exclusive visuality," and representation in Russia, based on "the intrusion of speech."[21] Manet's work relied on visual devices to accomplish his revolutionary aims: he diverged from generally accepted academic rules regarding the appearance and positioning of figures, the degree of finish, and the use of perspective. But Bulatov broke with the official rules of representation exclusively through the use of verbal concepts. At first glance, *Danger* would not seem subversive to Soviet censors; the realist landscape is completely in line with state-approved production. But by inserting the word "Danger," Bulatov grafts onto the seemingly harmless landscape a verbal message that creates "spreading ripples of verbal responses and resonances formed around each and every ideological sign."[22]

Komar and Melamid's early Sots Art pieces were charged with a similar deconstructive power, in their case directed toward both the Soviet propaganda apparatus and alternative artists' claims on metaphysics and spirituality. If Kabakov appropriated the speech of the kitchens and other communal spaces, Komar and Melamid turned to the language of the state as it was manifested in political slogans. In the Soviet Union, the abundance of political slogans was a response to the Marxists' unfailing belief in the word as "the ideological sign par excellence."[23] Komar and Melamid's *Our Goal Is Communism*, 1972 (Pl. 15:13), and *We Were Born to Make Our Dreams Come True*, 1972 (Pl. 15:14), are simply examples of overcirculated political messages which the two artists wrote on red cloth banners and signed. In these works,

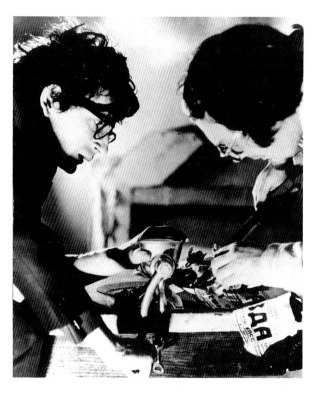

Fig. 15:2
Vitaly Komar and Alexander Melamid
The Essence of Truth
[Grinding *Pravda*], 1975
Gelatin silver print
48.7 × 39.8 cm

it is precisely the signature—the individual's usurpation of the collective—that constitutes the deconstructive gesture.

The relationship between the visual and the verbal takes a different tack in a number of other early works by Komar and Melamid. In those works, the artists try to turn political texts into purely visual forms by replacing the letters of various slogans by rows of blank white squares. In a similarly subversive vein, Komar and Melamid turned text into mute object in a performance that consisted of grinding the pages of *Pravda* into pulp (Fig. 15:2). This conversion of the textual into the visual resulted in a product, a sculpture shaped like a burger.

For Komar and Melamid, performance was an effective format for the presentation of their radical ideas. First, it allowed them to replace "the traditional object of art—that is to say that, in performance, artist and art object merge."[24] But, in addition, the dramatic nature of their actions was calculated to help publicize their ideas and to stir up the rather stale Moscow art community. In this regard, their lesser-known project *Paradise* (1973) is an important example of the transition from installation to performance. *Paradise* was inspired by the papier-mâché models of the heavens that the two artists had seen in the Buddhist temples of Soviet Central Asia. Their idea was to decorate a room in a friend's apartment with dozens of

Fig. 15:3
Francisco Infante and
Nonna Goriunova
Forest Ritual, 1968
Performance
Photo courtesy of Victor
and Margarita Tupitsyn

Fig. 15:4
The Red Star Group
Performance, 1975
Photo courtesy of Victor
and Margarita Tupitsyn

images, freely rendered and combined. The imagery of Komar and Melamid's "heavenly" environment displayed no purity—which, as the artists explain, should be credited to the "eclectic consciousness of atheists." For example, the main image—Christ's face—was painted in a variety of styles, then cut into four panels, and finally sewn back together and presented in the installation. Not too far away was Buddha, whose brutally rendered figure dangled in space. These sacred symbols of the traditional religions mingled with symbols from a newer system of belief: Soviet popular images and a bar loaded with bottles of vodka.

The performance aspect came about accidentally. During work on his "devilish" paradise, Komar dreamed

that he fell and fractured his hand. Several days later, while Melamid was standing on a stool installing objects for *Paradise*, he fell and broke his hand in exactly the same place as Komar in his dream. This incredible and dramatic merging of the conscious and subconscious, manifested through the bodies of Komar and Melamid, astounded even the most staunch atheists. The artists decided to commemorate the event by performing a ritual, which, in its closeness to the form and content of the dream, was Jungian rather than Freudian in nature. The event took place in "paradise" and was witnessed by a number of participants. The artists' mocking impersonation began with their announcing themselves as the "creators" and standing, with left hands bandaged, near Christ's face. The source of the injury, the stool, was installed between Komar and Melamid and served as an altar. The dream was retold through the metaphor of the Eucharist: in the performance, though, the bread was replaced by a chicken leg, and the wine by red paint. Each participant was "blessed" with a "holy" symbol depicting the evil stool which was stamped on his or her forehead. The ritual ended with the Russian way of feasting—by now familiar to Westerners—the imbibing of massive quantities of vodka.

This use of performance to simulate a religious ritual refers directly to the first such manifestations in the Soviet Union. In the late 1960s, Francisco Infante (b. 1943) and his wife Nonna Goriunova (b. 1944) staged a series of performances in a forest outside Moscow. In *Forest Ritual*, 1968 (Fig. 15:3), Goriunova appeared naked behind a wall of snow (erected beforehand by the two artists), while two candles positioned in front of the wall burned strategically placed holes in it. Goriunova's naked exposure was a bold challenge to the state's policy of sexual repression, rooted in the campaign against sexuality conducted by Andrei Zhdanov in the 1930s.

Also in the late 1960s, the performance group Movement (Dvizhenie), led by Lev Nusberg (b. 1937), staged semitheatrical re-creations of past times, including folk celebrations in medieval Suzdal and Dionysian rituals on the Crimea's picturesque seashore. Because Infante's and Nusberg's performances actively involved female artists (Movement included Galina Bitt, Natalia Prokuratova, Klavdia Nedelko, and Tatiana Bistrova), they helped these women to free themselves from the restraints and boredom of the Soviet *byt* and to participate in events far from the state's control and political inspiration (Pl. 15:17). By the mid-1970s, performance was gaining in influence and appeared to be a highly effective form of communication in a country with extreme sociocultural

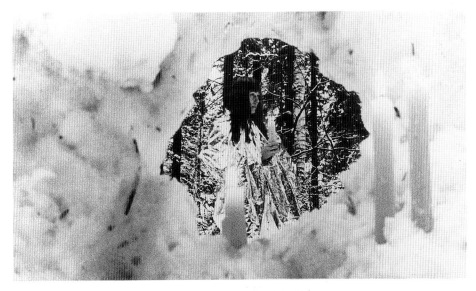

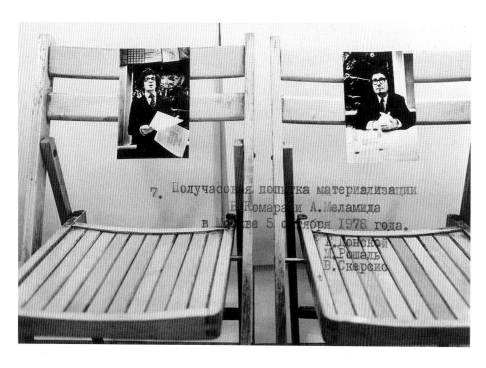

Fig. 15:5

The Nest (Mikhail Roshal, Gennadii Donskoi, and Viktor Skersis)

A Half an Hour's Attempt to Materialize Komar and Melamid, 1978
Performance
Photo courtesy of Victor and Margarita Tupitsyn

limitations (Fig. 15:4). Beyond the staging of these performances, the exchange of opinions among viewers and participants afterward constituted a sort of Russian version of the avant-garde salons held by Peggy Guggenheim and Gertrude Stein.

During a historical exhibition of alternative art at VDNKh (Exhibition of Economic Achievements) in 1975, the artists Mikhail Roshal (b. 1956), Gennadii Donskoi (b. 1956), and Viktor Skersis (b. 1956) united under the name Gnezdo (Nest), and staged their first performance on the exhibition premises. This was done by "hatching eggs" to suggest the irony of having a cultural event in a space dedicated to Soviet economic achievements. Other Gnezdo performances similarly dealt with significant international cultural and social events. For instance, *A Half an Hour's Attempt to Materialize Komar and Melamid* (Fig. 15:5) was performed on the day of the opening of Komar and Melamid's exhibition at the Ronald Feldman Gallery in New York in 1976. The three Gnezdo artists were separated from the audience by a plastic curtain and the brightly lit walls were covered with sheets of white paper. For half an hour, the performers sat facing two chairs on which portraits of Komar and Melamid were placed. Komar and Melamid did not materialize.

During *The Race to Jerusalem*, staged on September 29, 1978, an audience gathered in the center of Moscow to witness a "race" organized by Skersis, Roshal, and Donskoi. According to the artists, it was a rehearsal for the coming Moscow Olympic Games and was dedicated to the exhibition of battle paintings that had opened at the Manezh. Interestingly, the length of the "race" was 1.43 meters, the distance between Moscow and Jerusalem divided by the year in which the event took place. The winners of the "race" received prizes signed by the three artists. Despite its humor, the performance referred to a serious matter: emigration to Israel, and the direct or indirect involvement in it of many members of Moscow's intelligentsia. Gnezdo's other performances included the auction *Sell Our Souls*, organized in Moscow to coincide with Komar and Melamid's simultaneous performance of it in New York. Both groups auctioned various celebrities' souls that had been acquired by Komar and Melamid.[25] In the projects *Communication Tube* and *Let's Become One Meter Closer!*, Gnezdo dealt with the issues of global communication and collaboration between artists.[26] Both projects, utopian at the time of execution, have proved precursors of the possibilities opened to Soviet artists by *perestroika*.

Mikhail Chernyshov organized the Red Star performance group in 1975 to commemorate the thirtieth anniversary of the United Nations. His original plan was to celebrate the event by building a German airplane similar to one that was shot down by the Russians in 1941 and later displayed in front of the Bolshoi Theater. The airplane was intended to be semifunctional and could be operated (though only on the ground) by participants in the performance. Chernyshov's project was also a homage to Vladimir Tatlin's "flying machine," *Letatlin*, built by him during the early 1930s. *Letatlin* was created to be a "work of art in which a man could actually fly, using his legs as pumps, and the wings, perched on the wooden stays, as rotating ballast." Unfortunately, neither Tatlin nor Chernyshov was able to make his project a reality. Tatlin abandoned the idea after his glider was strongly criticized by the authorities; Chernyshov halted construction on the airplane when it became clear that they would be unable to finish it in time for the celebration.

As a result, Red Star decided on a different performance: the participants brought homemade flags (American, Soviet, British, and United Nations), painted signs (stars, circles, and swastikas) on a field covered with snow, and installed them in two rows. When the audience arrived, the signs were set on fire and some of them were partially burned. Chernyshov based his performance on the visual confrontation of familiar symbols and thus evoked various social and historical cataclysms and events, some of which were rather provocative (for example, the combining of a swastika with a Soviet star would have been considered a serious crime in the Soviet Union). But since the performance was staged away from Moscow and was attended only by "political allies," it ended peacefully.

It was the Collective Actions Group, however, that kept the Moscow art community under the spell of their "rituals" for a decade. Since the group's foundation in 1976, its members have involved Moscow poets, artists, and their friends in the performances, both as spectators and participants. The group originally included Nikita Alekseev, Nikolai Panitkov, Georgii Kizevalter (b. 1955), and Andrei Monastyrsky (b. 1949). They were later joined by Igor Makarevich (Fig. 4:5), Elena Elagina, and Sergei Romashko.[27] Monastyrsky considers the group's performances as part of what he calls the "ontology of surface (space)." He contrasts this notion with the "hermeneutic codes" of contemporary Western Conceptual Art, which for him evolve within a framework of the "ontology of action (time)." Unlike other Conceptual artists; however, Monastyrsky questions the act of making commodifiable objects in a country where the market for their consumption does not exist. Instead, the Collective Actions Group promoted the idea of action as a sufficient creative gesture. The group's "voyages into nothingness," or "empty actions," served as remedies to urban pressures and identified emptiness as the main characteristic of Soviet existence.

According to Monastyrsky, the group was initially influenced by the musical experiments of John Cage, especially by his concept of "sounding silence" as it is expressed in *4'33"*. The group's manifesto defines their general philosophy:

> Our activities are spiritual practice, but not art in any commercial sense. Each of our actions is a ritual with a purpose, namely, to create an atmosphere of unanimity among the participants. Unanimity is achieved with the aid of the archetypal primitive symbols of ritual. If it is indeed possible to consider our work as art, then only as a "tuning fork" for directing the consciousness outside the boundaries of intellect. All our performances take place in nature and can only be adequately appreciated aesthetically by direct participation.[28]

In each of the group's performances there are three categories of participants: author, coauthor, and performer; the third category subsumes the first two. The concept of each happening belongs to the author, and the coauthors must entirely accept that concept. *The Third Variant*, staged near Moscow in May 1978, clearly illustrates some

of the structural elements the group introduced in its performances. Twenty viewers were seated in a field close to a forest. From the right-hand side of the woods, a participant appeared, dressed in a violet costume. He walked through the field and lay down in a ditch. After three minutes of so-called "empty action," a second participant, in a similar costume, rose from a second ditch, thirty meters from the first. He had an orange balloon where his head should have been. He pierced it with a stick, and the explosion released a cloud of white dust. "Headless," he then lay back in the ditch. At the same time, the first performer, already back in street clothes, got up from his ditch and went into the woods. The "empty action" of the "headless" participant (lying in the ditch) lasted until the audience had left the field.

Figs. 15:6 and 15:7
Collective Actions Group
Balloon, 1977
Performance
Photos by Georgii Kizevalter, courtesy of Victor and Margarita Tupitsyn

The Third Variant demonstrated the group's attraction to existentialism, albeit with some Oriental accents adopted by avant-garde art. The performance symbolized a sort of transcendental "journey." It was based on such structural elements as "empty action," that is, the time extending beyond the demonstration itself, and "splitting," which is achieved by two participants playing the same role.

Two additional performances, titled *Lantern* and *Balloon* (Figs. 15:6, 15:7), make clear the group's interest in ritual. However, unlike Western ritualistic performances of the 1960s and 1970s, which, as a rule, were highly expressive and provocative, the rituals of the Collective Actions Group reflect a Zen-like attitude, downplaying action and stressing contemplation. No audience was even present for the staging of *Lantern* (November 15, 1977). At twilight, the four participants hung a lantern between two trees on a high hill. A piece of violet mica had been glued onto the lantern's glass and a red balloon was tied to the bottom of it. The tugging of the balloon kept the lantern swinging and rotating, producing flashes of violet light interspersed with pauses of darkness. The participants watched all this as they backed away from the lantern to a distance of two kilometers—to the point where they could no longer see the lantern. The culmination of the performance occurred when the lantern disappeared from the artists' view. As in *The Third Variant*, the action of the performers backing away from the light source in *Lantern* constituted a sort of transcendental "journey."

Some of the performances by the Collective Actions Group convey quite vividly the atmosphere of the pre-*perestroika* days: the artists' strong sense of isolation and their yearning to travel. These attitudes are best seen in *To Kizevalter*, staged in 1980. The idea originated when Kizevalter left Moscow for a long trip to Siberia as part of his postgraduate job. During his absence from the capital, the performances became a sort of link between the group's members. In the winter of 1980, Kizevalter received in Yakutia a package with a readymade banner and a letter. The letter asked him to take the banner to a field surrounded by a forest, and stipulated that it should be a desolate place. The slogan on the banner was covered with a black cloth. The instructions told Kizevalter to hang the banner between two trees and keep it covered at all costs. Then he was to take hold of the strings attached at each end and go into the field as far as the strings would allow. After proceeding about seventy meters from the banner, he was to face it and pull the strings to reveal the slogan. Clearly, from that distance he could not make out the writing. So, according to the instructions, the only

thing left to do was to take a picture of the panorama and to go on his way without, under any circumstances, going up to the banner to read the slogan. The bitter psychological struggle with oneself which appears to be inescapable in such a situation was recaptured by Monastyrsky:

> What's the meaning of all this? I've worked damn hard putting up this damn slogan and now they're asking me not to read it. Here I am, in Yakutia. I've been here for three years, like in jail, and now along comes a chance to have some fun, to get hold of some news. But they're asking me not to read it. What the hell's going on?[29]

Of course, Kizevalter could have decided that even if he did read the text, no one would find out about it in Moscow. Monastyrsky continues: "It's better not to read the slogan because whatever might be written on it will be garbage compared to the value of the decision not to read it and to overcome idle curiosity." Monastyrsky's point appears justified when we discover the content of the actual text written on the banner: "In winter, on the edge of a field, where he could not make out a thing, Kizevalter hung up a white, 10 × 1 meter sheet with an inscription in red letters." Although, according to Monastyrsky, the concept of the performance might thus have remained concealed in the descriptive text, we understand that no matter what Kizevalter may have done afterward, the basic goal of the action was achieved the moment the banner was put up. This basic action relates to the group's exploration of possible alternatives to the printed page as a medium for poetic language. Monastyrsky introduces the term "elementary poetry" to cover the series of projects he worked out, as well as some of the performances. He says:

> Why not introduce objects, events, attitudes, and so on, into the realm of poetry? After all, there are countless poetic forms that need not be connected verbally. In reality, this simply depends on us, that is, if we persist in telling everyone that photographs of a guy hanging up a slogan or the descriptive text of this event are poetry, well, sooner or later they will be poetry.[30]

The most successful manifestation of this concept was a performance with two slogans, each hung up in a forest and intended to be read by any passer-by. *Slogan 1977* was placed between two trees in a snow-covered forest on January 26, 1977. The following text was written across it: "I am not complaining about anything, and I like everything here, although I have never been here and know nothing about this place." *Slogan 1978* (Figs. 15:8–15:10), displayed on April 9, 1978, proclaimed: "Why did I lie to

Figs. 15:8–15:10
Collective Actions Group
Slogan, April 1978
Performance
Photos by Georgii Kizevalter,
courtesy of Victor and
Margarita Tupitsyn

myself that I had never been here and knew nothing about this place? Actually here is just like everywhere. Only one feels it more sharply and misunderstands it more deeply." Just as in *The Third Variant*, the time interval—in this case one year—was clearly meant to be interpreted as "empty action." All of the group's performances clearly indicate that the artists consider nature (forest and field) and the elements (snow and rain) to be important structural components of their actions. Weather conditions can also change the course of performances and thus become the group's "coauthor." Another reason for choosing to

perform in desolate places has to do with the group's idea of the "de-urbanization" of spectators. Since they come from Moscow by train and then walk to the site of the performance, often experiencing physical difficulties (deep snow or heavy rain), they are supposed to lose their urban orientation and be much better prepared for the action (all this is a part of the performance).

The avalanche of texts that accompanied each performance of Collective Actions (including the documentation of the participants' and viewers' impressions of the performances) once again exemplified the discomfort with pure visuality experienced by many Soviet Conceptual artists. And it is precisely this predominance of text that in the early 1980s began to elicit complaints from a younger generation of artists. In 1982, for example, fellow artist Sven Gundlakh (b. 1959) wrote:

> The performances [of the Collective Actions Group] had become overburdened by piles of documentation and abstruse texts. It was not clear what exactly constituted the product of creation: the action itself or its photographs and descriptions. The latter were lost in the thick files of the artists' remarks of a speculative nature.[31]

Another member of Gundlakh's generation, Konstantin Zvezdochetov (b. 1958), commented: "I never liked a concept, I always looked for a situation." Both statements signaled the beginning of a new era, which despite its seeming revolt against the previous generation of Conceptualists was deeply indebted to it. To different degrees, Kabakov, Monastyrsky, and the Sots artists provided a theoretical source for younger artists, making them less dependent on Western artistic models.

Fig. 15:11
**The Mukhomor (Toadstool)
Group**
First AptArt Exhibition,
Alekseev's apartment,
Moscow, 1982
Photo courtesy of Victor and
Margarita Tupitsyn

a Conceptual spectacle. The AptArt artists also gave the alternative movement a grittier edge by turning the chronic deficiencies of unofficial art, such as small canvases and poor materials, to their advantage. They stopped trying to solve the technical problems of painting (previously the main concern of Soviet modernists), and instead organized their art around deliberately shabby installations and cast-off materials. Rather than "attending (almost) exclusively to [an artwork's] *appearance*,"[33] the AptArt artists adopted a casual approach to artistic materials, incorporated mass-culture imagery into their work, saturated the visual elements with verbal ones, and subjected many sacrosanct political issues to parodic treatment.

Among the artists who belonged to the AptArt generation and continued to inseminate visual objects with elements of speech were Sergei Anufriev (b. 1964) (Fig. 15:12), Yurii Leiderman (Fig. 15:13), Nikita Alekseev, the Mukhomor (Toadstool) Group (Zvezdochetov, Gundlakh, Vladimir Mironenko, and Sergei Mironenko) (Pl. 15:18), Yurii Albert, and the Peppers (Liudmila Skripkina and Oleg Petrenko) (Pl. 15:19). While Kabakov, Bulatov, and

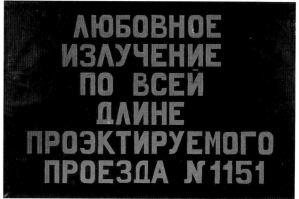

Today, when members of the former Soviet alternative art circles have the opportunity to exhibit freely both at home and abroad, it is important to remember that, until 1986, their main efforts revolved around the struggle for public exposure. Any considerations regarding the formal qualities or physical appearance of an artwork were predicated on the assumption that it would most likely never be shown publicly. So even the distinction between official and unofficial art was based less on stylistic or iconographic issues than on a more practical division between those who could show their art publicly (official) and those who could not (unofficial).

The so-called AptArt generation of the early 1980s effectively redefined the idea of the public exhibition in 1982, when they established an informal gallery in the apartment of the Conceptual artist Nikita Alekseev (b. 1953) (Fig. 15:11).[32] By organizing shows and performances there, they turned the twenty-year-old alternative tradition of showing art in apartments and artists' studios into

Komar and Melamid had attempted to crystallize the essence of the Soviet speech heritage in their work, the AptArt artists wanted to make this burdensome inheritance somewhat more eclectic and open-ended. In their work, the AptArt artists freely combined verbal cliché with pseudoscientific language drawn from outdated textbooks, and enhanced this mixture with words and phrases of a personalized and autonomous character. A good example of this approach is *Podiaka* (Pl. 15:20) by Anufriev. Here, the artist has taken elaborate preprinted certificates of merit for drawing, and has doodled over the original design and added comments that ridicule the purpose of this official document. Similarly, every work in Alekseev's series *Bananas*, 1983 (originally displayed outdoors on branches of the bushes) (Fig. 15:14), consists of an identically repeated sketch of the Mausoleum, with a different humorous phrase on each drawing. Invented expressions like "Ironic Materialism" (Pl. 15:22) or "Artistic Internationalism" target many of the pseudo-intellectual claims of official as well as unofficial culture.

The activities of the AptArt gallery were interrupted by the authorities in 1982, just five months after its establishment. Two further exhibitions, "AptArt in Plein Air" (May 1983) (Fig. 15:15) and "AptArt beyond the Fence" (September 1983), were organized in the countryside to escape the surveillance of the bureaucrats. When Mikhail Gorbachev assumed the Soviet leadership in 1985, the rigidity of the government's art-exhibition policies finally began to crumble. Already, by late 1986, the question for former AptArt artists was not where to exhibit, but rather where to produce large-scale works. Most ex-members of the AptArt community found work spaces in a group of abandoned Art Nouveau apartment buildings on Furmanny Pereulok (Furmanny Lane). These studios (which were closed down in late 1989 for reconstruction) functioned from early 1986 on as the key places to visit for Western

curators, collectors, and art dealers, who sought the newly profitable Soviet product. In the words of Zvezdochetov: "[If] AptArt was one type of socio-cultural psychopathology, [the *glasnost* period created] a different type."

At the dawn of *perestroika*, the work of Irina Nakhova (b. 1955) and Dmitrii Prigov (b. 1940), both veteran Conceptual artists, began to reflect the easing of official press restrictions. In 1985, Nakhova produced a series of collages that consisted of newspaper clippings which she made illegible by tracing over them with a labyrinth of intertwined abstract drawings, a kind of metaphor for the victory of aesthetics over the mass media (Pl. 15:21). Prigov likewise obliterated official newspaper and other propagandistic texts which he appropriated as the background for his own bold texts, often a single word painted over a cloud-like patch of color (Pl. 15:25). At about the same time, Moscow Conceptualist Ivan Chuikov, well-known for his fragmented paintings done on windows and other objects, began to make works incorporating fragments of famous Soviet slogans. His painting *All Power* (Pl. 15:23), for instance, includes a remnant of the heroic phrase "All Power to the Soviets." Chuikov's work marks one of the first signs of the erosion of the Soviet people's sixty-year-old faith in such exhortations.

Andrei Roiter (b. 1960), Sergei Volkov (b. 1956), and Svetlana Kopystianskaia (b. 1950) are primarily associated with the beginning of the *perestroika* era. Unlike Kabakov, who points to the power of "collective means of communication," often enjoying the process of narrating itself more than the meaning conveyed, Roiter and Volkov dismantle an overcrowded reservoir of verbal clichés and expose the harshness and absurdity of language by using concise and blunt expressions. Volkov's inscriptions like "Bastards" (Pl. 15:24) and "Idiots" simulate vulgar street language, turning his paintings into word-symbols of Soviet common speech. Roiter has also continued Komar

Fig. 15:16
Andrei Roiter
Radio Roiter (Input-Output),
1986–87
Oil on canvas
99.8 × 80.2 cm

and Melamid's experiment of conveying the repressive role of the speech-oriented practices in Soviet society, not through a direct appropriation of language but through visual means. Examples of this technique are his many canvases with cut-outs in the shape of old-fashioned radio speakers (Fig. 15:16), for most Soviet citizens the fount of a boundless stream of ideological "enunciation." Similarly, Roiter's canvases with punctured holes refer to the significance of the ellipses in ideological double-talk.

The intensity of Kopystianskaia's deconstructive practices vis-à-vis Soviet word-saturated culture is comparable to that of Kabakov. But if Kabakov does not differentiate between male and female speech, Kopystianskaia specifically targets the ways in which Russian literature is dominated by male creators. She adopts fragments of various literary texts and inscribes them on pieces of canvas or on landscape paintings, a favorite genre of the paternal traditionalism of Russian visual culture (Pl. 15:26). Some of these canvases she later crumples up, thereby achieving a distortion of the text as a symbol of the masculine power of speech.

Today, most of the Conceptual artists discussed in this essay are recognized as part of the so-called NOMA circle ("nomes" are the regions in Egypt where, according to legend, parts of Osiris's body were buried). As the symbolism of this word suggests, the intellectual and artistic practices of this milieu were of a highly secluded and esoteric nature. In Brezhnev's era, the perception of an artifact occurred on a verbal level and even Conceptual works initially identified with a text were subjected to the so-called communal speech *obsosy* (lickings). This situation created an excessive reliance on speech-oriented practices, which replaced most other functions associated with contemporary art in the West, including the viewing of exhibitions.

The new possibilities that *perestroika* provided to alternative artists led to the breakdown of all previous structures established within this Conceptual circle. First, Kabakov, who to a large degree fueled and shaped the activities of the NOMA artists by generating various dialogues with them and then circulating these and other texts, departed to work in the West. Second, the Collective Actions Group's *Journeys to the Countryside*, in which the NOMA artists participated and about which they constantly talked and wrote, became a nuisance in the busy climate of market-oriented values. Third, the *perestroika* epoch with its strong emphasis on exhibition activities weakened the power of text and speech in Soviet Conceptualism. As a result, the brooding of the NOMA circle within the space of communal speech (which in turn produced a condition of "back talk") gave way to a space in which the visual was no longer simply a byproduct of speech-oriented practices.

Notes

1. Joseph Kosuth, "Introductory Note by the American Editor," quoted in Ursula Meyer, *Conceptual Art* (New York: E.P. Dutton, 1972), p. viii.

2. Ilya Kabakov and Yuri Kuper, *52 Entretiens dans la cuisine communautaire* (Marseilles: Art Transit, Ateliers Municipaux d'Artistes, 1992), p. 16.

3. Beginning in the late 1950s, Soviet nonconformists functioned as both the creators and the beholders of their art. The function of the interpreter (critic) did not exist.

4. Joseph Bakshtein, "On Conceptual Art in Russia," in David Ross, ed., *Between Spring and Summer: Soviet Conceptual Art in the Era of Late Communism*, exh. cat. (Cambridge, Mass.: MIT Press, 1990), p. 73. Curiously, when Kabakov first came to New York in 1988 and was asked which artist he would like to meet, he named Kosuth.

5. Victor Tupitsyn, "From the Communal Kitchen: A Conversation with Ilya Kabakov," *Arts Magazine* (Oct. 1991): 53.

6. Meyer, *Conceptual Art*, p. xi.

7. Tupitsyn, "From the Communal Kitchen," p. 53. Tupitsyn initiated and developed in a number of articles the discourse of the relationship between communal speech and the visual in Soviet art, particularly within the framework of psychoanalytical theory. See also his "East-West Exchange: Ecstasy of (Mis)Communication," in Ross, ed., *Between Spring and Summer*, pp. 83–106; and "Goblinesque Art of Afrika: Late 1980s–Early 1990s B.C. (Before Coup)," in Louis Grachos, *Afrika*, exh. cat. (Los Angeles: University of Southern California, Fisher Gallery, 1992), pp. 31–44.

8. Although in most publications Bulatov's painting is called *Dangerous*, the title refers to a word that is used on road signs and hence should be *Danger*.

9. The appearance of Soviet alternative art became possible in the late 1950s precisely because Khrushchev's thaw brought a number of Western art exhibitions to Moscow.

10. On the history of collaboration between artists and poets, see my article "Collaborating on the Paradigm of the Future," *Art Journal* (Winter 1993). Such contemporary artists as Andrei Abramov were specifically influenced by the poetry of Velimir Khlebnikov. Abramov explains: "It was Khlebnikov who first interested me in the problem of working on the language of art itself. I work on the structure of language, searching for its sources (that is, the root words or basic elements in the plastic arts), its rules, and new expressive devices. I am particularly attracted by the mingling or, rather, the combination of the word and image as a new, complicated sign (or series of signs) that can be read in a different way" (Andrei Abramov, letter to Victor and Margarita Tupitsyn, 1980; my translation).

11. Although for Kabakov, Komar and Melamid, and Bulatov, popular culture was primarily associated with Soviet mass media, Leonid Sokov, another artist of the Sots Art movement, recognized and began to expose a crucial similarity between folkloristic and Soviet ideological patterns of mythmaking, as well as that powerful role which the process of mythologizing had played in the consciousness of contemporary or older generations of Russians. With the power of what may be called "mocking laughter" Sokov has conflated old myths with new and produced a new type of folklore which may be designated as "political *skazka*" (fairy tale).

12. One thinks, for example, of posters created by Kazimir Malevich and El Lissitzky in the early 1920s and of paintings by Ivan Puni, Natan Altman, and Sergei Senkin, in which purely abstract compositions were combined with political verbal messages.

13. At this point, official paintings themselves were structured as narratives or "painterly slogans."

14. Tupitsyn, "From the Communal Kitchen," p. 52. To this statement Kabakov adds: "I can paint a jackrabbit only because I have a story to tell about it" (p. 54).

15. Meyer, *Conceptual Art*, p. ix.

16. Ilya Kabakov, "Introduction to the Album *The Window*," *The Window* (Bern: Benteli Verlag, 1985), p. 20.

17. The album format was also extensively used by Eduard Gorokhovsky. His albums, however, have no verbal components and primarily utilize photographic images drawn from various archives found by the artist. Gorokhovsky's use of photography is among the earliest known manifestations of the interest in this medium among the pre-*perestroika* Soviet artists (Pls. 15:27–15:30).

18. Ilya Kabakov, unpublished essay, 1982.

19. For a further discussion of the meaning of green in Kabakov's work, as well as in the work of younger Conceptualists, see my catalogue for *The Green Show* (New York: Exit Art, 1990). Throughout the 1980s, Kabakov returns to white paintings and thus continues to explore the iconography of color in his works.

20. V. Friche, *Sotsiologiia iskusstva* (Moscow, 1926), p. 184.

21. This comparison between Manet's *Le Déjeuner sur l'herbe* and Bulatov's *Danger* was inspired by Igor Makarevich's painting *Danger* (1990). The latter is a hybrid of Bulatov's and Manet's paintings. For a discussion of all three paintings, see my "Playing the Games of Difference," in *Artistas Rusos Contemporaneos* (Santiago de Compostela: Auditorio de Galicia, Sala de Exposicions, 1991).

22. Valentin Voloshiniv, *Marxism and Philosophy of Language* (New York: Seminar Press, 1973), p. 9.

23. Ibid., p. 15.

24. Meyer, *Conceptual Art*, p. xiii. For a further discussion of Komar and Melamid's performances, see my "Komar and Melamid: The Red Guardians of Tradition," *High Performance* 28 (1984): 41–43, 95.

25. The results of the Moscow auction were very different from those in New York. For example, Norton Dodge's soul was highly valued in Moscow, whereas that of Andy Warhol barely found a buyer.

26. Both projects relate to Komar and Melamid's *Where Is the Line between Us?*, performed in 1976 in collaboration with Douglas Davis.

27. Makarevich is better known as a visual artist and in the Dodge Collection he is represented by two diverse types of work: a series of photographs documenting the theatrical transformations of his face, and Hyperrealist canvases. The latter depict gynecological instruments (found by the artist in the garbage), tombstone monuments with the artist's portrait, and scenes of funerals as they occur in provincial towns.

28. Andrei Monastyrsky, "Journeys to the Countryside," unpublished manuscript, 1980. Victor and Margarita Tupitsyn Archive; my translation.

29. Unpublished correspondence interview between Andrei Monastyrsky and Victor Tupitsyn, 1980. Victor and Margarita Tupitsyn Archive; translation by John Bowlt.

30. Ibid.

31. Sven Gundlakh, letter to Victor and Margarita Tupitsyn, 1982; my translation.

32. For an extensive discussion of the AptArt movement, see "Aptart: The Expansion of Postmodernism," in my *Margins of Soviet Art: Socialist Realism to the Present* (Milan: Giancarlo Politi Editore, 1989), pp. 99–114.

33. Meyer, *Conceptual Art*, p. viii.

16 | Nonconformist traditions and contemporary Russian art

A view from Moscow

Joseph Bakshtein

One way to trace the links between nonconformist Soviet art and contemporary art—as I intend to do—is by looking at the successful 1970s generation, of which I am a part. The key to understanding the psychological condition of those who matured in "Soviet times" is best expressed by the great nineteenth-century Russian poet Feodor Tiutchev, who wrote: "Blessed is one who visited this world in its fateful moments." Indeed, one may confidently say that the "Second Russian Revolution" was such a fateful moment, an event that changed the world—or, rather, returned the world to its traditional state, bringing back to Russia "traditional positive values."

The extent to which tradition became important to Russian culture in the late 1980s and the early 1990s exceeded the expectations of even Russian artists and writers. In just a few years, life in Russia has changed so much that we have found ourselves in an almost wholly different society, living a different life. For nonconformist artists of the 1970s generation, this is especially true; after having risked everything to challenge Soviet official culture, they now find themselves celebrated in the international art world. Strange to say, this sort of success is the most difficult thing for a nonconformist to handle.

In Soviet times, a nonconformist was quite obviously someone who opposed what were then traditional values: they were, after all, associated with the Soviet way of life, with the ideologized Soviet version of daily life. Hence, the nonconformist lived an unsettled life that did not include family ties or a permanent job. Someone who rejected the dominant system had to face the possibility that everything he had acquired could be lost, taken away, at any moment; that he, too, could be yanked out of his everyday environment and deported, or jailed, or put into a mental institution.

And now, all of a sudden—yes, it did happen very suddenly—the Soviet regime has gone. In 1986, when the scope of these changes could be seen but dimly, I wrote down a conversation with the artist Ilya Kabakov under the ironic title "Life in Paradise." In that conversation, Kabakov accurately pointed out that the metaphysical situation in which Russians had lived since 1917 was paradise. To all intents and purposes, Lenin had declared paradise among the first decrees of Soviet power. Before that, different cultures located paradise in different places and times: in heaven, in the past, in the future, or somewhere else (in the Bible, Eden was "in the East"). Never had man dared call the place where he lived paradise. And since paradise is, after all, a mythical concept, life in Communist Russia became, by its very nature, a double life. People were surrounded by seemingly ordinary things, but the meaning of those things had changed. As the great Soviet poet Vladimir Mayakovsky put it: "The streetcars were running, but now they were running under Socialism." It is this doubling and the understanding of its origins that provides the key to understanding the entire history of Russian art in this century, from Suprematism to Conceptualism.

This phenomenon can be given different names and interpretations, it can be projected onto a variety of philosophical or religious traditions, but we will always be speaking of a culture in which ideas are just as real as (or even more real than) so-called ordinary objects. Here, Marxism and Neoplatonism merge. One should add, of course, that the ideas in question are those of the dominant group, for which ideas are instruments of power.

The duality of a life in which the official perception of everyday reality is independent of the reality of the imagination leads to a situation where art plays a special role in society. In any culture, art is a special reality, but in the Soviet Union, art was doubly real precisely because it had no relation to reality. It was a higher reality. The heroes of Stalinist films were inhabitants of a Communist paradise. The goal of nonconformism in art was to challenge the status of official artistic reality, to question it, to treat it with irony. Yet that was the one unacceptable thing. All of Soviet society rested on orthodoxy, and nonconformism was its enemy. That is why even the conditional and partial legalization of nonconformism in the mid-1970s was the beginning of the end of the Soviet regime.

Who, then, is the nonconformist in the Communist paradise? How is he interpreted by Soviet consciousness, and how does he interpret it? Initially, in the first post-revolutionary years, the nonconformists were the "former people," i.e., the Russian bourgeoisie. Then, in the 1930s, they were the "enemies of the people," those who were hindering Stalin's efforts to reproduce an exact model of paradise; they were "fallen angels." In art, between 1917 and 1932, artists of the Russian avant-garde of the 1920s, as well as precursors of Socialist Realism, worked in different styles and were members of various groups vying for the right to represent the proletariat.

The first step in the codification of the Soviet mentality was Stalin's decision in 1932 to create a single artists' union. This act was also the first step toward institutionalizing nonconformist thinking, since any officially sanctioned view of art automatically categorized all artists whose styles differed from the accepted one as "alien elements," i.e., nonconformists. But before World War II this position was not a matter of free choice. Simply by belonging to a specific school, be it Suprematism, Cubism, or Futurism, an artist placed himself outside the boundaries of official art defined in 1932. The war on aesthetic dissent was then waged by the rules of martial law, and nonconformists—at that time, artists who could not adapt to the new circumstances—risked being eliminated, just as the entire Boichuk School of Ukrainian Art was physically eliminated in the 1930s. It was an important characteristic of early nonconformism that the artist's coming of age preceded the moment when he had to choose an aesthetic position. It is also important to note that, at that time, this aesthetic choice was tantamount to a political and ideological choice.

It was this inseparability of aesthetics and ideology that characterized the entire Soviet period in the history of the art of the Russian empire. Usually, this phenomenon is linked to the fact that a totalitarian state introduces a single system of interpreting any kind of expression, including artistic expression, and itself controls such interpretation. Thus, the institutionalized principle of the autonomy of art—fundamental to all modern European culture—is eliminated. Art becomes functional in relation to state ideology; art becomes a servant of this ideology. This theory is reminiscent of the medieval concept of viewing philosophy as a handmaiden of theology.

If Soviet art as a whole was a handmaiden of Communist ideology, visual art was its illustrator, the creator of Communist icons. The interest of Party leaders in the visual arts also had to do with the fact that it gave them an opportunity to familiarize themselves with the state of the arts in general. Unlike reading, watching films, or attending plays, visiting art exhibitions does not take much time. That is why it became a Soviet tradition for Communist

Party leaders to visit annual exhibitions of visual art. One such visit became a turning point in the history of Russian art, and created the second generation of nonconformists. I am referring to Nikita Khrushchev's 1962 visit to the exhibition commemorating the thirtieth anniversary of the Artists' Union, held in the Manezh, Moscow's main exhibition hall. An argument that erupted between Khrushchev and the artists at the exhibition signaled the end of the thaw.

Historically, Soviet nonconformism evolved as follows. In the 1930s, aesthetic differences were highly politicized but the ideology of Socialist Realism had not yet been systematically articulated. The speeches of Andrei Zhdanov, secretary of the Party's Central Committee and chief of Propaganda Administration, marked the first serious ideological campaign in the arts in the 1940s. The writers Anna Akhmatova and Mikhail Zoshchenko were officially named as nonconformists in the sweep that also targeted the followers of Postimpressionism, like artist Robert Falk (1886–1958).

Historians who study the emergence of Soviet culture and spend much time and energy studying ideological struggles usually pay little attention to the years of World War II (which is referred to in Russia as "the Great Patriotic War"). That is a big mistake. One could hardly overestimate the importance of this war as a factor in the construction of Soviet culture. What do I mean by this? The outstanding Russian historian Lev Gumilev once gave a lecture titled "Birthdate 1380." Who or what was born in that year, the year of the Kulikov battle in which the unified troops of Russian principalities triumphed over the Tartars? Gumilev argued that what was born on that battlefield was a new ethnos, the Russian people, synthesized from disjointed tribes by the tremendous energy necessary for victory. In the same way, we could say that in 1945 the Soviet people emerged as a "new historical community" (to quote Khrushchev), synthesized by the positive energy required for victory in the Great Patriotic War. The postwar generation was thus the first generation of genuinely Soviet people. What is more, the artists of that generation were the first to be able to reflect on their Soviet origins and, at the same time, on the totality of Soviet culture. But that, in reality, would be achieved only in the 1970s.

Meanwhile, after Stalin's death in 1953, during the era of the Khrushchev thaw, there was for the first time hope for change in the regime and for the "de-ideologization" of art. There was the first flowering of Soviet versions of Abstract Expressionism, such as the works of Yurii Zlotnikov (b. 1930), Vladimir Nemukhin (b. 1925), and Lydia

Masterkova (b. 1929). However, this period of mutual loyalty between the government and the intelligentsia ended quickly. In 1962, when Khrushchev made his visit to the Manezh exhibition, he argued openly with Neizvestny, Beliutin, Yurii Sobolev (b. 1928), Vladimir Yankilevsky (b. 1938), and Boris Zhutovsky (b. 1932). This public debate led to the persecution of nonconformists and, eventually, to the emergence of unofficial art. Such art could not have existed under Stalin, when an open disagreement with the Party's concept of art generally ended with the death of the artist. Under Khrushchev, poets and artists were no longer killed; they were merely deprived of work. This policy produced a sort of double existence: artists legally earned their livings through the applied arts (chiefly illustrating children's books) and pursued their "main" creative work after hours.

The second nonconformist period can be called "modernist." It included a belief in stoicism, the artist's outsider status, and isolationism. Stylistically, the nonconformist art of this period was dominated by borrowings from a great variety of styles and genres of Western art. Any deviation from realism and traditional figurative representation—even post-Cézannism—was considered an accomplishment. Elements of Cubism and Abstract Expressionism occurred in various combinations. Strangely enough, direct links to the Russian avant-garde of the 1920s were rare; among the few artists who maintained this tradition were Gennadii Zubkov (b. 1940), Gleb Bogomolov (b. 1933), and Vadim Filimonov (b. 1947). Only a few artists—among them Aleksandr Arefiev (b. 1931), Vladimir Piatnitsky (1938–1978), Vladimir Yakovlev (b. 1934), and Anatolii Zverev (1931–1986)—were able to rise above this eclecticism and imitation.

There are two main reasons why this second nonconformist period might be regarded as modernist. First, the principal artistic characteristics of this group were negative ones. That is, what mattered most were not the positive characteristics of new ideas and techniques, but rather the establishment of their own differences from the official realism. As a result, political and aesthetic positions converged, taking each other into account. And the explicit expression of one's nonaesthetic position by aesthetic means is one of the chief attributes of the modernist sensibility. This is true even if the aesthetic methods in question cannot lay claim to originality.

Second, the nonconformist aesthetic of that period was rooted in the notion of self-expression. For the artist, this meant defending the independence of art from the political system, and promoting a view of art as the fixed embodiment of the artist's inner reality. The outside world belonged to the state, which at that time was evolving from a totalitarian into an authoritarian one and was leaving loopholes for private life.

Here, it would be appropriate to consider the extent to which nonconformist art is a specifically Russian phenomenon. Indeed, it was only in Russia that alternative art developed in such a sophisticated form, although related alternative art phenomena were also observed in the Baltic states (where unofficial artists were never persecuted as systematically as in Russia) and in Eastern Europe, as well as in the Ukraine and other republics of the Soviet Union. However, as a specific aesthetic phenomenon, nonconformism existed only in Russia. Moreover, it was nonconformist art that brought Russia back to the international art scene. Why did this happen? I believe there are three basic reasons: 1) the specificity of the Russian relationship between the intelligentsia and the state; 2) the specificity of Russian Socialism; and 3) the imperial structure of the Soviet Union and the entire Eastern Bloc, along with the dominant status of Russians in that empire.

Throughout recorded Russian history, the Russian state never had an intellectual dimension. As a result, the Russian intellectual was always in absolute opposition to the state. He could not have a dialogue with the state and he was not part of the same "hermeneutic community" as representatives of the power structure. Beginning in the time of Pushkin, whatever contacts took place between artists and the regime involved only agents of the secret police. Hence, the Russian intellectual was by definition a nonconformist. The monopolization of Russian culture created a situation in which the goal of the intellectual's public existence was "to tell the truth, and die," since the state left no room for autonomous action. In the private sphere, the intellectual's existence was reduced to the sort of "endless talk" very accurately described in the classical Russian novel and even included in the visual arts by Moscow Conceptualists.

Russian Socialism only exacerbated and sharpened the conflict between the intellectual and the state, since it created the precedent of absolute totalitarianism. As a result, nonconformism under the Soviet regime acquired new traits and qualities. When the division between official and unofficial culture took place after Khrushchev's thaw, the functions of culture were divided among them in a most interesting way. Official Soviet culture, backed by the power of government structures and infrastructures, possessed all the functions of the culture of any developed society—except one. It lacked the capacity for self-description. Therefore, the function of describing official Soviet culture was assumed by the unofficial artists. The nonconformists possessed the reflective qualities that are absolutely vital to the development of culture and the establishment of an adequate dialogue between the individual and culture, between the state and the intellectual. In this sense, the entire process of *perestroika* in the Soviet Union was an attempt by the official culture to master the reflective functions, and at the same time to eliminate the very division of culture into official and unofficial. Just how difficult this process was can be seen from the fact that, for the sake of self-reflection, the entire Soviet state had to be sacrificed: its ideological structures proved incapable of radical self-comprehension, and Gorbachev, the last ideologue, lost his post. Like political nonconformism, aesthetic nonconformism outlived itself: only after the 1991 coup, when Russia gained its independence, did aesthetic nonconformism finally lose its meaning.

But the Soviet empire made a significant contribution to the emergence of Russian nonconformism. First, the imperial status and function of the Russian language (including the language of Russian graphic art in its Soviet version) served to suppress the diverse languages of all ethnic, political, and cultural minorities. This suppression naturally provoked a response, which included an aesthetic response. But the mission of the Russian nonconformists did not cancel their sense of belonging to imperial Russian culture or their concern for its fate.

In the countries of the Eastern Bloc, on the other hand, the relationship of local intellectuals to "Big Brother" in Moscow was mediated and often softened by their relationship to local Communists, with whom they shared membership of a suppressed culture. Russian artists had no such mediation, nor did they have any sense of membership in a common culture, since that common culture was the dominant culture that nonconformists were committed to opposing. That is why their relationships with the authorities were completely antagonistic. But this antagonism also generated a tremendous energy that gave birth to an entirely original artistic tradition, which took shape in the 1970s. The creation of this nonconformist tradition was impelled by the fact that an outsider in the Soviet empire stood alone against a tremendous state machine, a great Leviathan that threatened to engulf him. To preserve one's identity in this situation, one had to create a separate value system, including a system of aesthetic values.

This brings us to what might be called the third wave of nonconformism, the 1970s generation—what I have called the first "Soviet generation." This generation included Ilya Kabakov (b. 1933), Eric Bulatov (b. 1933), Vitaly Komar (b. 1943) and Alexander Melamid (b. 1945), Ivan Chuikov (b. 1935), Aleksandr Kosolapov (b. 1943), Valerii Gerlovin (b. 1945) and Rimma Gerlovina (b. 1951), and others united by the Moscow Conceptual movement. We refer to them as the "Soviet generation" because they were the first generation of intellectuals who had ambivalent—or, at least, not totally negative—feelings toward the Soviet regime. To them, Stalin was not only a tyrant but an object of childhood memories: it was this partial identification with Soviet culture that allowed them to reflect upon it. And Sots Art as a style was, historically, the first autonomous language to describe Soviet culture.

The event that provided an identity for the third generation of nonconformists was, of course, the famous "Bulldozer Exhibition" of September 15, 1974. After that event, unofficial art was officially acknowledged and nonconformists were given the opportunity to unite into an organization of their own. If the events at the Manezh forced nonconformism to go underground, the events of 1974 allowed it to come out. The conflict over the "Bulldozer Exhibition" ended in the artists' victory over the Soviet regime, and showed that the state was no longer an ideological monolith.

Unlike the modernists of the 1960s, the Moscow Conceptualists did not employ vague stylistic allusions. Instead, they comprehended Soviet culture as their unique context, creating a visual language that, on the one hand, could be interpreted in the terms of the international art scene and, on the other hand, could introduce to that scene a previously quite unknown thematic source: the clichés of Soviet mass media, stories from the life of communal apartments, and so on. Of course, Russian Conceptualism was a much broader phenomenon than Western Conceptual Art. In Moscow, Conceptualism was used as a label for the general concept of "modern art" or, more narrowly, as a synonym for Postmodernism.

But what constitutes the peculiarity of the third wave of nonconformism is the fact that these artists had a conscious view of art. In other words, they developed a meta-aesthetic position that helped remove the issue of the political engagement of nonconformist art. Since aesthetic means were always used in a methodologically correct way, the political effect of a work (which was certainly there) was seen against the backdrop of the aesthetic effect. Unlike the aestheticism of the second wave of nonconformism, which did not turn to topical political material, Conceptualism was able to depoliticize its view of the world through "controlled politicization." The pathos of avant-gardism (i.e., an active polemic with society) was balanced by an almost Kantian "aesthetic disinterestedness." In Russian art, such a degree of neutrality had rarely been found since the *Peredvizhniki* (Itinerants) of the nineteenth century.

While Conceptualism represented the avant-garde in relation to official art, it remained unwittingly loyal to the precepts of Western modern art. In their almost entire cultural isolation in the 1970s and 1980s, the adepts of Moscow Conceptualism were able to reproduce the basic aesthetic principles of art of the modernist and Postmodern periods. In this regard, they differed from the artists of the 1960s, who identified with certain trends in commercial art (and were, therefore, largely misunderstood when they emigrated to the West). At the same time, the success of artists such as Komar and Melamid served only to confirm the accuracy of their absentee hypotheses about the aesthetic norms of modern art. Sots Art proved as comprehensible in New York as it was in Moscow.

This sense of absentee membership of an international art community engendered an entire Conceptual philosophy in Moscow in the 1970s and 1980s. Andrei Monastyrsky, one of the leading theorists of Moscow Conceptualism, put it in this way: "We regarded ourselves as part of a regional (Russian) section of a certain central geographic club located somewhere in the West; we regarded ourselves, in a way, as Livingstones in Africa. We did not identify with the aborigines but only observed, described, and sent out findings to the Central Club."

This moving identification with an imaginary West also had a defensive function. Since the Conceptualists—or, as they were also called, the MANI circle (Moscow Archive of New Art) or, later, NOMA (a term of the Medical Hermeneutics group, which represented the youngest generation of this circle of artists)—were outsiders in Soviet society, confirmation of the aesthetic significance of this movement was achieved through the creation of an imaginary world of "Western culture." The paradox is that, in the long term, this romanticism proved the most practical position. Loyalty to one's own principles is sooner or later appreciated for its true worth.

Another aspect of the historical significance of this generation of nonconformists was their creation of an intellectual tradition that was all their own. Like everything else about the movement, this enterprise was not without paradox. In their ironic interpretation of Soviet life as paradise, the Moscow Conceptualists proceeded from the assumption that the real paradise was in the West, while their life as social outsiders was gloomy and hopeless. When they did find themselves in the West (as émigrés or, after *perestroika*, as participants in international art exhibitions), they realized that life there was not exactly like heaven either. Rather, life is a reality with strictly defined spaces where the functions of the imagination can be performed.

The drama of the nonconformist's life, then, is the realization that, if one were to speak of paradise in Russia, it would exist not "now" but "then." In the Soviet period, the nonconformist's outsider status, his unlimited free time, and his lack of social responsibilities meant endless free play for his imagination. And, for the artist, that is paradise. But the horror is that one cannot go back to that Russia, for it is no more. Russia is on her way to capitalism, and the easy, pleasant, free atmosphere of the exhibitions of the 1970s and 1980s has vanished forever. Today, artists at exhibitions in Moscow act no differently from artists in SoHo—that is, they are business-like and cautious. That is why the nonconformist today is like a character from *Paradise Lost*.

But the drama of nonconformism did not become a drama for the country. Nonconformists are "out"; conformists are "in." A young artist in Russia today cannot find anything to be against. He is "for" the government, "for" reform, "for" the West, but also "for" the East. Finally, he is "for" the nonconformists of the 1970s. This position fits easily into the Postmodernist game of playing with signs; that is why fashionable Russian artists are either Postconceptualists or Neoconceptualists.

What, then, is the essence of neoconformism in Russia? As we have seen, what has happened in Russia is not a revolution but a restoration. That is why all the processes, contradictory though they may be, boil down to the restoration of all the elements of a civilized society, which Russia never really was—not even before 1917. Among these elements of civilization requiring rehabilitation are the institutions that comprise the infrastructure of visual art: galleries, museums, art schools, journals, collections, fairs, auctions, etc. As a result, the energies of artists, critics, curators, and gallery owners are directed more toward building new institutions than toward encouraging the creation of new artworks. Russians must also overcome their dependence on the Western art scene and move beyond the Soviet habit of thinking in economic analogies. Too many Russian artists think that, as the poet and artist Dmitrii Prigov put it, "if the world's biggest stock exchange is in New York, the world's greatest artist has to be in New York as well."

Any hope for surviving this return to the international art scene is bound up with a new historical sense that has two principal features. One is the understanding of the extent to which Russian art has become an inalienable component of world art. It is no longer simply a matter of the individual merit of Malevich, Kandinsky, Tatlin, Rodchenko, and other artists of the Russian avant-garde. Rather, it is the recognition that in order to understand these artists, one must understand Russian culture in general. The point is given further support by the emphasis placed on context by Postmodern theorists. This view confers an additional relevance upon those who are contextually closer to the subject of interpretation. One might put it this way: it does not hurt to have famous relatives.

The second dimension of this new historical sensibility is the transition from a polarized view of the world (built on "us versus them" dichotomies) to a more open one. This perspective provides the recognition that any historical analogue to one's own situation can be considered historically pertinent, since it is not necessary to prejudge it morally. With this observation, the Russian turned from black and white to color.

Finally, to conclude the story of the misfortunes of nonconformism in the midst of its success, here is a specific historical analogy. The nonconformism of the 1970s became famous for its incredible creative energy. One of the sources of that energy was opposition to a totalitarian state, when each individual nonconformist went one-on-one with the state. Only someone with a great reserve of vitality could survive. In art, this was expressed in the desire to shock society with every work. This wish largely came true. Neoconformism, on the other hand, has no desire to shake anyone up. In a way, it repeats the sentiments of that turn-of-the-century Russian reformer, the tsarist prime minister Petr Stolypin, who said to the radicals of the time: "You want great turbulence; we want a great Russia." Participation in the creation of a new great Russia is a noble task for neoconformism. What kind of art will emerge in the light of that greatness is another question.

17 | The view from the United States

Matthew Baigell

For the last few years, I have accompanied my wife, Renee, to her interviews with artists whose works are in the Dodge Collection. These meetings have taken place in Moscow, St. Petersburg, and New York City. Visits to the artists' studios and apartments have been rich in ambience and have provided me with an introduction to a great variety of artworks. But since the interviews take place in Russian, a language I do not speak, I really enter into the conversations only later when I read Renee's translations.

After often intense discussion of the works of particular artists and after studying many catalogues and articles about art before and after *perestroika*, I have acquired a sense of the history and nature of nonconformist art. What follows are some observations on the phenomenon, with the caveat that, as a visitor to the world of Soviet art, my remarks are inevitably incomplete.

In my opinion, it has not been emphasized nearly enough that the history of nonconformist art is one of the great heroic stories of the last half of this century. It is the story of several generations of artists who learned their skills in the rigorous state-supported system of training but who insisted on the kind of interior freedom that was anathema to the authorities. Some artists were jailed, some were placed in life-threatening situations, and almost all were harassed. They certainly suffered economic and psychological deprivation in ways Westerners can barely understand, but their desire to create from a sense of inner necessity and honesty prompted their refusal to accept the authority of the state in matters of art.

Their story is not a monolithic one, though, and the degree of terror each artist experienced varied from the mild to the truly horrifying—nothing in the experience of Western artists is in any way comparable. Generally speaking, the earlier nonconformists seem to have suffered a greater degree of opposition than the more recent ones. For example, Boris Sveshnikov (b. 1928) was eighteen years old when he was sent to a concentration camp for eight years. Although he remains traumatized by his experiences to this day, he still did not make works completely acceptable to the art authorities after his return to

his home in Moscow (Fig. 13:1; Pl. 13:3). Eli Beliutin (b. 1925), a painter and a teacher comparable in significance to such American artists as Robert Henri and Hans Hofmann for bringing out what was individual and unique in his students, lost his teaching position after participating in the infamous Manezh exhibition in Moscow in 1962 (Pl. 4:1). Leonid Lamm (b. 1928) was jailed from 1973 to 1976 after applying to emigrate from the Soviet Union, and on at least one occasion was the victim of temporary drug-induced psychosis. Yet, on his return to Moscow, he painted works that were also unacceptable (Figs. 2:1, 2:5; Pls. 3:7, 17:1).

Ivan Chuikov (b. 1935), like many others, was questioned, intimidated, and threatened by the KGB on more than one occasion (Pl. 15:23). Yurii Dyshlenko (1936–1995), when he arrived by car to hang his paintings at an officially sanctioned nonconformist exhibition in Leningrad in 1974, told his friend to drive off with the paintings still in the trunk if he had not returned from the exhibition hall within five minutes. He did not know if this was a ruse to get all the artists inside in order to arrest them. And Konstantin Zvezdochetov (b. 1958) was drafted into the army and sent to a post in eastern Siberia that was, to all intents and purposes, the end of the world.[1] The message here is that both the act of creation and the public exhibition of certain artworks were probable causes for arrest and detention.

Yet some artists, when asked if they thought of themselves as heroic, denied any interest in the concept, associating it rather with Stakhanovite tractor drivers from the Stalinist era.[2] Nor did they think of themselves as the kind of heroic artists Westerners have long since mythologized into attics and garrets, starving for their art and dying of tuberculosis. But I feel that there has been too little hero-ization of the nonconformists; far more than any School of Paris modernists, they fulfill the long-celebrated role of the suffering, misunderstood avant-garde artist. As critic Donald Kuspit has observed, the avant-garde artist has been perceived as a heroic resister of bourgeois civilization, a risk-taker, "a kind of Promethean adventurer." This has led to a fetishization of the modern artist because "he

[was] able to be himself in a way that is impossible for other people." The avant-garde artist has been imagined as a person who confronts officialdom and who is subversive through "his perceptual and personal authenticity [and who] transmutes the lives of others, giving them a liberation they were too sunk in suffering to know they needed."[3]

I would not argue for the fetishization of nonconformist artists (the excessive popular adulation of Vincent van Gogh has forever spoiled that notion for me). Rather, I would simply say that we should recognize the role the nonconformists played in maintaining whatever sanity, whatever mental health existed within the decadence and moral rot of the Soviet system. One might argue that the increasing weakness of the system allowed artists to flourish because during the 1930s and 1940s they would have been summarily imprisoned or killed. Nevertheless, they did flourish within a system of what Robert Jay Lifton has called "ideological totalism."

Lifton defines one aspect of this system as "the principle of doctrine over person." This occurs when a conflict exists between what one feels oneself experiencing and what the doctrine says one should experience. Another aspect, the "dispensing of experience," occurs when one who is placed in the category "of not having the right to exist can experience psychologically a tremendous fear of inner extinction or collapse."[4] Several artists who were interviewed gave personal accounts of just such experiences; that which Lifton described in theoretical terms was for most nonconformists their lived reality.

Igor Makarevich (b. 1943) described the situation succinctly. He said that the double life he and others had to live in order to survive "bred in us a duplicitous way of thinking. We lived a double life intellectually. There is something wrong with that, something negative in our upbringing and development, a whole generation of people formed in a double manner." Everyone had to "mask who he really was." To resist the authorities was to become isolated: "If he did not comply officially, he stopped existing. He was blotted out, erased." Excluded from the Artists' Union, and therefore unable to purchase supplies, an artist "ceased to exist as a material person."

The achievements of the nonconformist artists are all the more astonishing when we realize that some of them did not live lives as societal outlaws devoted totally to their art, but functioned as illustrators, decorators, and laborers during normal working hours and as artists only in their spare time. They lived both within and outside of the Soviet system, leading, in effect, parallel lives, with no easy commerce between the two.

When did nonconformists realize their nonconformity? Vitaly Komar (b. 1943) said only half-jokingly that in the Soviet Union everybody was born a nonconformist. You were labeled as one only when you came out of the closet. Most Soviet artists found like-minded friends in art school. Some of the more rambunctious ones, over the decades, were dismissed for not painting proper subjects. But most, as Sholom Shvarts has indicated, led "acceptable" lives on the surface while "behind the scenes, between friends, we were looking for new ways to express new ideas, and new solutions."[5]

Hard decisions had to be made upon graduation from art school. To paint acceptable subject matter in acceptable styles meant capitulation to the system. Refusing to do so meant that an artistic career was an impossibility. Thus, many entered less politically charged fields such as illustration and theatrical design. The making of art became an escape into sanity, into self-awareness, and self-understanding, an act of defiance against the government, an act of honesty in the face of the falsely optimistic subject matter required of official artists. As Makarevich has said, "any attempt at serious analysis [of society] was suspect."

Artists, then, went underground. Those who came of age in the 1950s and 1960s tried to distinguish themselves as much as possible from official art. Even today, they insist that they were not dissident artists, which implies political dissent. Rather, they argue that they wanted to use art for more private purposes than conforming to the dictates of the authorities. But the very desire to distance oneself from Socialist Realism and all that it represented was clearly a political act, if not a directly adversarial one. What else is one to make of the definition of art of Eric Bulatov (b. 1933) in the face of the steady barrage of Soviet propaganda concerning collective cooperation? Art is, he said, "a rebellion of man against the everyday reality of life.... A picture interests me as some kind of system, not hermetically sealed, but opening into the space of my everyday existence."[6] In other words, art was a vehicle to deconstruct the Soviet construction of reality (Pls. 15:1, 15:12, 15:15).

Artists of Bulatov's generation were particularly aware of the subversive quality of their art, of the inevitable discrepancies between public utterance and inner need. Gleb Bogomolov (b. 1933) stated that he "hated Socialist Realism, its lying and superficiality. [Art] was my personal rebellion. I had to understand the world and making paintings was a way of consolidating that understanding" (Pl. 5:10).[7] Vladimir Yankilevsky (b. 1938) summed up the situation succinctly when he said: "Nurtured only by simple straightforward acts, man loses his imagination—that is, he loses his inner freedom. He lives according to stereotypical social behavior. He is less and less an individual as he becomes integrated into a gigantic theater of marionettes that are manipulated by the legislators of fashion, sowing their seeds of banality, vulgarity, and depersonalization" (Fig. 13:11).[8]

Younger artists, responding to modifications in official policies in the 1970s and 1980s, revealed different concerns. As the need for self-assertion became less important, they could either indulge their aesthetic interests to a greater extent, or, building on the brave example of their predecessors, allow their art to become more confrontational. Olga Bulgakova (b. 1951) appeared less concerned with using art to reflect the position of an artist in society when she said: "the most important theme for me is the interrelationship of creative work and life" (Pl. 2:11).[9] Igor Kopystiansky (b. 1954) asserted: "I create new contexts and play with art, which for me is a game of the spirit and intellect on the highest level" (Fig. 6:5; Pl. 6:1).[10] The more confrontational Vitaly Komar (b. 1943), who developed Sots Art with Alexander Melamid (b. 1945) in the early 1970s, compared American overproduction of consumer goods with Soviet Russia's overproduction of ideology, and concluded that Sots Art "puts our mass poster art into a frame for examination."[11]

Artists who were born in the 1960s and came to maturity at a time when Western images and ideas were more available often sound positively Postmodern in their manipulation of those ideas and images. The attitudes of two young artists will suffice to make this point. First, there is Andrei Yakhnin (b. 1966), who objectifies himself by photographing, drawing, and videotaping himself (Fig. 4:10) in order to provide a distance from himself. Yakhnin says that through such actions the artist "removes himself from all responsibility not only for the pictures, but also for the actions and the further life of his hero, who is himself."[12] In the second case, we have Afrika (Sergei Bugaev) (b. 1966), who recently asserted that he would spy for the KGB if asked: "Perhaps now such work might appeal to me because of my interest in theoretical aspects of how the ideological system functions and how it controls. I could learn better being on the inside."

Clearly, these new kinds of attitudes—morally, politically, and aesthetically neutral at best—mark both the end of nonconformist art and the merging of contemporary art in the former Soviet Union with Western neo-avant-gardism. Yakhnin's point of view, if it is a generally held one, suggests that his generation has institutionalized the old Western avant-garde and the premises on

which it was based. His point of view suggests a recycling of old patterns within the art world rather than an ongoing exploration of new ideas, thoughts, and feelings beyond that sphere. Afrika seems concerned only with manipulation, unlike earlier nonconformists who refused offers to collaborate with the KGB.

One might argue that many, perhaps all, nonconformist artists based their art on Western avant-garde styles. For this reason, they could be regarded as little more than belated followers, working in styles already a generation or two old, filtered down from the cosmopolitan centers of Moscow, Paris, and New York City. I would argue the opposite, if for no other reason than that we would have to assign a similar position to all but a small handful of form-givers such as, say, Picasso, Kandinsky, and Matisse. Much more importantly, we need to assess the damage inflicted upon modern Russian art by the Stalinist disavowal of earlier Western as well as Russian avant-garde art. And finally, we need to realize that nonconformists tried to restore an organic continuity, to reestablish and to maintain a dialogue with those earlier styles, despite minimal availability of visual and written information.

In interview after interview, artists said that the first modern Western works they saw were those exhibited in the late 1950s during the thaw.[13] Others said that when they worked in various museums they discovered and surreptitiously studied paintings locked in vaults. Western art magazines, although rare, were available, and articles were translated by those who could read French or English. The artist Valerii Lukka (b. 1945) was not really far off the mark when he said: "our present [art] is not determined by the past. . . . We have neither memory nor history" (Fig. 5:14).[14]

But the saddest comment concerning the nonconformist desire to connect with anything other than Socialist Realism was offered by Vladimir Nemukhin (b. 1925). After first seeing modern Western art, he and his fellow nonconformists began, he said, "to recognize in foreign artists their own selves and their own strivings."[15] In effect, they had to apprentice themselves to avant-garde artists, perhaps like the Americans who, on visiting Paris around 1910, had to digest Picasso and Matisse. Or perhaps some nonconformists followed the pattern of Arshile Gorky, who painted in the manner of several masters—Cézanne, Picasso, Miró—before developing a style of his own. Regardless, the nonconformists needed and wanted to learn the vocabulary prior to expressing "their own strivings."

Just as Picasso and Matisse hold a special place for Western artists, Malevich is a sort of model figure for

Russian artists. He, as well as other early Russian avant-gardists, had to be confronted in one way or another so that the nonconformists could move on. From this point of view, it is therefore totally beside the point to call the works of Eduard Shteinberg (b. 1937), as one Western critic has done, "beautiful but essentially lifeless academic variations on constructivist themes."[16] First, I would agree completely that Shteinberg's paintings are beautiful (Pl. 14:10). In my opinion, his handling of the tonal relationships of creams and tan-browns is among the most subtle created since the late work of Georges Braque in the 1940s. But beyond that, I would disagree with the statement that he makes lifeless academic variations. Had he grown up in the West, where the history of Suprematism and Constructivism was known and where examples could be seen in museums, a case against him might possibly be made, but Shteinberg grew up in the Soviet Union and did not discover Malevich until the early 1960s, when he saw a few in the George Costakis Collection.[17] Western models of criticism simply do not apply here.

There are other factors reaching beyond the stylistic

Fig. 17:1
Leonid Lamm
Sphere, 1965
Oil on fiberboard
107 × 54 cm

that need to be considered in any assessment of non-conformist art. For Shteinberg, an artist like Malevich has served purposes other than merely as a model to develop an abstract look or a manner. Shteinberg, an artist of mystical tendencies, found in Malevich's *Black Square* (1915) both a portent of doom for Russia—"a child doomed to solitude"—and a path to truth and transcendence. Of this and other similar works, Shteinberg has said: "By allowing the spectator to retain his freedom, the language of geometry forces the artist to renounce his Ego. Attempts to make him an ideologue, or utilitarian, constitute a violence against his person."

Neither appropriating Malevich's style nor making mere variations on it, Shteinberg used the work of his mentor to ameliorate his situation in the Soviet Union. "It seems to me," he said, "that the human mind will always return to such a language in moments of mystical suffering at the tragedy of God's abandonment." So Malevich provided Shteinberg with a way to turn inward, to find and to explore his own spiritual and religious feelings through his art.[18] Whatever else might be said about Shteinberg and Malevich, it is also clear that the Soviet system forced Shteinberg to rediscover the past in order to find himself as an artist and to find his own sense of personhood. The situation provided him with an enemy against which self-discovery became possible. As cited earlier, Bulatov said: "Art is a rebellion of man against the everyday reality of life. . . . A picture [is] some kind of system . . . opening into the space of my everyday existence."

Leonid Lamm also reveals religious feelings in his abstract paintings (Fig. 17:1) and has also confronted Malevich, but his responses are entirely different from Shteinberg's. He has rejected Malevich's insistence on a "two-dimensional world which he [Malevich] wanted to impose as a creator of Space, as a 'Chairman of Space,' the title he used in referring to himself. But the world of [the] real Creator is infinity. The world of Malevich is two-dimensional, but the world of Nature is three-dimensional. . . . We witness here the idea of unfreedom as a foundation of Malevich's world."[19]

Where Shteinberg found Malevich's flatness a door through which to pass to his own inner world, Lamm found Malevich's flatness an act of violence. It is interesting to note that Lamm, who was imprisoned for three years during the 1970s, agrees with Kuspit, who argues that Malevich's sense of abstraction is "an authoritarian revelation of a doctrinaire self that crushes every other self." Malevich's paintings of squares and crosses are, for Kuspit, "forms to swear on, not a geometry to play with. . . . You either stand on their side—the side of abstraction—or on the side of nature—the enemy's side."[20]

I mention all of this because there must be dozens upon dozens more collaborations and confrontations among and between the nonconformists and earlier Russian (and Western) avant-gardists waiting to be discovered and analyzed. The point is not to determine whose work is superior, but to understand the nature of nonconformist art before *perestroika*. One more example: we know that Barnett Newman's stripe paintings and some of Lamm's abstract works are based on precise kabalistic sources concerning the idea of creation.[21] Yet Newman's work is totally flat, while Lamm's paintings are quite three-dimensional. What prompted such opposite stylistic interpretations? As the art of the nonconformists becomes better known and understood, many more questions such as this will have to be framed and answered.

Given the extraordinary difficulties that these artists had to tolerate, it is remarkable that there is a relative lack of what Robert Motherwell termed, when considering Max Ernst's work, "a sense of a vicious past . . . , a black mass, a bloody nun, an invader from the east." According to Motherwell, who made this statement in 1948, such images do not arouse deep feelings in most Americans (in the 1990s, read "white Americans"). But it would seem that such images or ideas did not arouse the nonconformists either.[22] True, Sveshnikov, confined to concentration camps for eight years, has said that everything he paints is about death, and Yankilevsky, projecting his frustrations and grievances through his art, has said that "for me the ideal in art is the ability to scream silently, and not merely to imitate a scream" (his ink sketches, particularly, invoke a world of grotesque, deformed, and mutant creatures). However, only a few artists allude in writing to the dark underside of Soviet life, the kind that projects a bleak vision of both the present and the future different from and foreign to American sensibilities, but akin to what can easily be found in Central and Eastern European literature. Certainly, there must be other writings, and it is essential that they surface because, even as the nonconformists join the international mainstream, they still come from a different place and that difference must be recognized and noted.

One example is Lamm's *Sots-Geo Manifesto-Manifestation of the Procrustean Bed*, written in 1987–88; another is Ilya Kabakov's article titled "On Emptiness." Both were published in 1990. Lamm's manifesto, filled with mordant irony (perhaps the only way he was able to deal with his experiences in and out of Soviet camps), concerns the brutal standardization of individuals on a Procrustean bed

as a way of ensuring their equality and "freedom."[23] Kabakov, in his article, tries to describe the idea of emptiness not as a space or a place, but as a state of mind and of being. He claims that people (meaning, I believe, the Soviet people) live in a state of emptiness and interact only with acquaintances or people they can trust, but with no one else. Emptiness, as Kabakov describes it, is not a space waiting to be filled, but an active volume "opposed to genuine existence, genuine life, serving as the absolute antipode to any living existence."[24]

Kabakov suggests four ways to deal with such emptiness: ignore it or accept it as natural; try to change it; search for a higher truth in a mystical or religious way; or describe it as it is.[25] In his installations, he has opted for descriptions of Soviet existence. These works, profoundly moving as statements about Soviet life and also stylistically exacting for their extraordinary balance between description or accretion of detail and suggestion, employ the kinds of "degenerate" ideas, forms, and materials the Soviet authorities would have termed unacceptable in order to show how degenerate Soviet life was. He has used a previously condemned format to condemn the Soviet Union, and, as such, his installations are among the most confrontational and political works created by a nonconformist artist. Since Kabakov calls himself a Soviet rather than a Russian man, meaning that he is a product of the Soviet system, these works, as well as his earlier artist's books, are, in effect, a view from within that state of emptiness of which he has written so touchingly.

As the various kinds of works by nonconformist artists become better known through exhibitions such as this one, I believe it will become clear that these artists are among—or simply are—the best trained and most technically secure artists anywhere in the world. Singling out one or another does a disservice to the rest, whether the artist works in an abstract or representational manner, whether the particular style is hard-edged or soft-focused, Photorealist or Expressionist, magic realist or free-form, whether the medium is painting, sculpture, or some type of installation art. However, I do want to mention Yankilevsky, whose technical facility and imaginative resources in a variety of media—ink drawings, paintings, collage, relief sculpture—are among the most astonishing of all.

I must also admit that saying this adds its small measure to the loss of unity and common purpose most nonconformists shared before *perestroika* in general, and before the Sotheby's auction in particular, which occurred in Moscow in 1988. At that event, the Western market economy imposed itself in a way that could no longer be ignored, despite earlier sales to Western buyers. Currency values were assigned to the works of many artists, thus exploding forever the sense of equality and solidarity among the nonconformists. Furthermore, after *perestroika*, artists could travel abroad easily, some becoming virtual gypsies, commuting between major art centers in the West and their home cities in the former Soviet Union.

It is small wonder, then, that Chuikov, a wonderful Conceptualist, is to this day nostalgic for the pre-*perestroika* period, despite the hardships and authoritarian impositions. His nostalgia must be qualified, however, by saying that it is for the camaraderie rather than the loss of individuality brought about by the sudden overwhelming availability of Western art. Virtually all nonconformists I have met insist that *perestroika* has not changed their styles or thematic interests, an assertion easily demonstrated by studying works done before and after 1987.

Some artists joined émigré communities upon leaving the Soviet Union, their work still individual and personal in style but easily absorbed within the transatlantic mainstream, even if it might contain Russian subject matter. (I am using Russian as a generic term here for "formerly Soviet.") In the United States, these artists have become the latest group to join the several generations of hyphenated American artists—Jewish-American, Italian-American, Mexican-American, Chinese-American, Japanese-American, African-American—whose works can easily move back and forth between the mainstream and the recognizably ethnic or national, whatever the particular style or subject matter.

Given the internationalization of the art world in the last decades, the former nonconformists, compared to artists of earlier generations, seem less in conflict in that inner dialogue between where they came from and where they are. Their artistic strength comes as much, if not more, from themselves and the history of modern art than it does from a mystic sense of, and the traditions of, a homeland. Some, of course, might be homesick and, especially in the case of Sots artists, they might use Soviet subject matter. But there seems to be little or nothing that can be called essentially or intrinsically Russian (however that might be defined) about their work—at least to my way of seeing. There are exceptions, of course, such as the late Aleksandr Kharitonov (1931–1993), whose wife called him the personification of the Russian spirit.

Whether the nonconformists will ever become domesticated in a Western country or remain forever internationalists is yet to be determined, and is perhaps not even a relevant concern. Most of the nonconformist artists I have met insist that they are simply artists, with no qualifying adjectives concerning location. Suffice it to say that as a group they have rejoined the history of modern art, at tremendous cost for some, which would indicate that the gravitational pull of modernism itself was far stronger than any sense of nationalism or even the Soviet system. Now this is a topic worth pursuing.

Notes

1. Andrew Solomon, *The Irony Tower* (New York: Alfred Knopf, 1991), pp. 117–22. Unless otherwise noted, information about the artists comes from Renee Baigell's interviews.
2. The term Stakhanovite was derived from the name of Aleksei Stakhanov (1906–1977) who, according to legend, cut 102 tons of coal between August 30 and 31, 1935. This being fourteen times the norm for the time period, his name became a byword for exceeding expectations. Workers from that day forward who produced much more than the norm were referred to as Stakhanovites. Stakhanovite brigades were even formed as means for increasing productivity.
3. Donald Kuspit, *The Cult of the Avant-Garde Artist* (New York: Cambridge University Press, 1993), pp. 1–2.
4. Kuspit uses these passages in his epigraph to *The Cult of the Avant-Garde Artist*. For the entire essay from which it is drawn, see Robert Jay Lifton, "Cults: Religious Totalism and Civil Liberties," in his *The Future of Immortality and Other Essays for a Nuclear Age* (New York: Basic Books, 1987), pp. 209–19.
5. Selma Holo, ed., *Keepers of the Flame: Unofficial Artists in Leningrad*, exh. cat. (Los Angeles: University of Southern California, Fisher Gallery, 1990), p. 76.
6. Norma Roberts, ed., *The Quest for Self-Expression: Painting in Moscow and Leningrad, 1965–1990* (Columbus, Ohio: Columbus Museum of Art, 1990), p. 72.
7. Holo, ed., *Keepers of the Flame*, p. 46

8. Roberts, ed., *The Quest for Self-Expression*, p. 168.
9. Ibid., p. 74.
10. Ibid., p. 108.
11. Hedrick Smith, "Young Soviet Painters Score Socialist Art," *New York Times*, Mar. 19, 1974, p. 30.
12. Roberts, ed., *The Quest for Self-Expression*, p. 166.
13. For lists of exhibitions and general chronology, see, most recently, Elena Kornetchuk, "Soviet Art and the State," in Roberts, ed., *The Quest for Self-Expression*, pp. 21–47.
14. Ibid., p. 110.
15. Igor Golomshtok, "Unofficial Art in the Soviet Union," in Golomshtok and Alexander Glezer, *Soviet Art in Exile* (New York: Random House, 1977), p. 89.

16. David Ross, "Provisional Reading: Notes for an Exhibition," in Ross, ed., *Between Spring and Summer: Soviet Conceptual Art in the Era of Late Communism* (Cambridge, Mass.: MIT Press, 1990), p. 23.

17. Eduard Shteinberg, *An Attempt at a Monograph* (La Chaux-de-Fonds, Switzerland: Editions d'en Haut and Moscow: Art MIF, 1992), p. 12.

18. Ibid., pp. 67–68.

19. Leonid Lamm, "Supersignal," unpublished manuscript, 1992.

20. Kuspit, *The Cult of the Avant-Garde*, pp. 50, 51.

21. Thomas Hess, *Barnett Newman*, exh. cat. (New York: Museum of Modern Art, 1971), pp. 52–61; and Lamm, "Supersignal."

22. Motherwell, "Prefatory Note to *Max Ernst: Beyond Painting and Other Writings by the Artist and His Friends*" (1948), in Stephanie Terenzio, ed., *The Collected Writings of Robert Motherwell* (New York: Oxford University Press, 1992), p. 48.

23. Lamm, *Sots-Geo Manifesto-Manifestation of the Procrustean Bed* (New York: Eduard Nakhamkin Fine Arts, 1990).

24. Ilya Kabakov, "On Emptiness," in Ross, ed., *Between Spring and Summer*, pp. 53–54.

25. Ibid., p. 59.

Select bibliography

Abashidze, I., et al., eds. *Dekada gruzinskogo iskusstva i literatury v Moskve: Sbornik materialov*. Tbilisi: Zarya Vostoka, 1958. In Russian.

Afanasiiev, Vasyl'. *Stanovlennia sotsiialistychnoho realizmu v ukrainskomu obrazotvorchomu mystetstvi*. Kiev: Mystetstvo, 1967. In Ukrainian.

Afrika. Los Angeles: University of Southern California, Fisher Gallery, 1991.

Anatoli Belkin. New York: Eduard Nakhamkin Fine Arts, 1989.

Andrej Monastyrskij. Berlin: Kunst-Werke, 1994. In German.

Anisimov, G. "Protiazhennye simvoly Olega Tselkova." *Iskusstvo* 8 (1990): 27–30. In Russian.

Apinis, Jēkabs, et al. *Latvijas telotajas maksla pieci gadi 1934–1939*. Riga: Latvijas rakstu un makslas kameras izdevums, 1939. In Latvian.

Arbeiten auf Papier von Gia Edzgveradze. Dortmund: Das grafische Kabinett Galerie Utermann, 1989. In German.

"Art de Georgie—URSS." In *La Puissance de l'Art*. Montreux, Switzerland, 1990. In French.

Artaud, E., and M. Chassat. *Perestroikart*. Paris: Cercle d'Art, 1990. In French.

Bankovskis, Peteris. "Zhivopis' na puti k novomu bytiiu." *Iskusstvo* 7 (1990): 1–6. In Russian.

Basin, A., ed. *Gazanevskaia kul'tura o sebe*. Leningrad and Jerusalem: Abudalo, 1974–89. In Russian.

Basmadjian, Garig. *Armenian Colors: 12 Contemporary Artists from Soviet Armenia*. New York: AGBU Gallery, 1978.

Berger, John. *Art and Revolution: Ernst Neizvestny and the Role of the Artist in the USSR*. Harmondsworth, Eng.: Penguin Books, 1969.

Beridze, V.V., and N. Ezerskaia. *Iskusstvo sovetskoi Gruzii, 1921–1970. Zhivopis', grafika, skul'ptura*. Moscow: Izdatel'stvo Sovetskii Khudozhnik, 1989. In Russian.

——, D.Sh. Lebanidze, and M.Zh. Medzmariahvili. *David Kakabadze: Put' khudozhnika, khudozhnik i vremia*. Moscow: Sovetskii Khudozhnik, 1989. In Russian.

Bernard, Hélian. *Volodymyr Makarenko*. Lyons: L'Association Champs des Arts, 1985. In French.

Besancon, A. "Soviet Painting: Tradition and Experiment." *Survey: A Journal of Soviet and East European Studies* (Jan. 1963): 82–89.

Bilzens, Indulis, et al., eds. *Valdis Abolins, Miss Vietnam mit rohem Hering im Mund: Fluxus, Realismus und die Riga–Konnekschen*. West Berlin: Elefanten Press, 1988. In German.

Bird, Alan. *A History of Russian Painting*. Oxford: Phaidon Press, 1987.

Bojko, Szymon, et al. *Russian Samizdat Art*. New York: Willis Locker and Owens, 1986.

Borgs, Janis. "Aktuella knoststromnigar i Baltikum." *Artes: Tidskrift for Litteratur, Kohst och Musik* 3 (1981). In Swedish.

Bowlt, John E. *Russian Art, 1875–1975: A Collection of Essays*. New York: MSS Information Corporation, 1976.

——. "Soviet Art in the 1970's." *Flash Art* 139 (1974).

——. "The Art of Change." *Journal of Russian Studies* (1975).

——. "Art and Politics and Money: The Moscow Scene." *Art in America* 63 (Mar.–Apr. 1975): 20–21.

——. "The Soviet Art World: Compromise and Confusion." *Art News* 74 no. 10 (Dec. 1975): 30–34.

——. "Soviet Unofficial Art: Ethics or Esthetics?" *Cornell Review* 3 (1978).

——. "Henry Ellinson." In *Henry Ellinson*. New York: Eduard Nakhamkin Fine Arts, 1980.

——. "Letter from Moscow." *Apollo* (Oct. 1988): 269–70.

——. "How 'Glasnost' Is It?" *Art News* 87 no. 9 (Nov. 1988): 216.

——. "Introduction." *Evgenii Rukhin.* Washington, D.C.: Fonda del Sol, 1989.

——. "From Avant-Garde to Avant-Garde." In *Moscow Treasures.* Washington, D.C.: Smithsonian Institution, 1990, pp. 208–36.

Bown, Matthew Cullerne. *Contemporary Russian Art.* London: Phaidon Press, and New York: Philosophical Library, 1989.

——. *Art under Stalin.* New York: Holmes and Meier, 1991.

Boyars, Yury. "Nationality and Minority Policies in Latvia." *Baltic Observer*, Sept. 24–30, 1992, p. 11.

Brumfield, William C., and Milos M. Velimirovic, eds. *Christianity and the Arts in Russia.* Cambridge, Eng.: Cambridge University Press, 1991.

Calneck, Anthony, ed. *The Great Utopia.* New York: Solomon R. Guggenheim Museum, 1992.

Carlisle, Olga. "Moscow 1960: Young Artists and Their World." *Art News* (Sept. 1960): 26.

Chornovil, Viacheslav. *Lykho z rozumu.* Paris: First Ukrainian Printers in France, 1967. In Ukrainian.

——. *The Chornovil Papers.* New York: McGraw Hill, 1968.

Clemens, Walter C., Jr. *Baltic Independence and Russian Empire.* New York, 1991.

"Contemporary Russian Art Photography." Edited by Diane Neumaier. *Art Journal* 53 (Summer 1994).

Contemporary Soviet Painters from Riga, Latvia. New York: Eduard Nakhamkin Fine Arts, 1989.

Contemporary Ukrainian Art. London: Red Square Gallery, 1990.

Crispolti, Enrico. *Mikhail Koulakov: Un itinerario segnico spiritualistico dal Surrealismo astratto all'oggettualita spaziale.* Milan: Nuove Edizioni Gabriele Mazzotta, 1988. In Italian.

Dekhtiar, Anna. *Molodye zhivopistsy 70–kh godov.* Moscow: Sovetskii Khudozhnik, 1979. In Russian.

Dodge, Norton T. "Two Worlds of Soviet Art." In *Non-conformists: Contemporary Commentary from the Soviet Union.* College Park: University of Maryland, 1980. (Catalogue for an exhibition at the Art Gallery, University of Maryland.)

——. "Preface." *Artists of Odessa.* New York: Cultural Center for Soviet Refugees, 1987.

——. "Preface." *Eric Bulatov—Oleg Vassilyev.* New York: Phyllis Kind Gallery, 1991.

——, ed. *New Art from the Soviet Union: Selected Works on Paper.* Mechanicsville, Md.: Cremona Foundation, 1976. (Catalogue for an exhibition at AAASS Convention in St. Louis.)

——, ed. and contributor. *Ely Bielutin and Sophie Schiller.* Mechanicsville, Md.: Cremona Foundation, 1977. (Catalogue for an exhibition at St. Mary's College of Maryland Gallery.)

——, ed. and contributor. *Two Artists in Two Worlds: William Brui and Boris Zeldin.* Mechanicsville, Md.: Cremona Foundation, 1979. (Catalogue for an exhibition at St. Mary's College of Maryland Gallery.)

——, ed. *New Art from the Soviet Union: An Exhibition of Soviet Non-Conformist Art from the 1960's and 1970's.* Mechanicsville, Md.: Cremona Foundation, 1979. (Catalogue for an exhibition at St. Mary's College of Maryland Gallery.)

——, ed. *New Art from the Soviet Union: An Exhibition of Soviet Non-Conformist Art from the 1960's and 1970's.* Carlisle, Penn.: Dickinson College, 1980. (Catalogue for an exhibition at the Dickinson College Gallery.)

——, ed. *Russian New Wave.* Mechanicsville, Md.: Cremona Foundation, 1981. (Catalogue for an exhibition at the Contemporary Russian Art Center of America, New York.)

——, ed. *Vagrich Bakhchanyan: Top Secret—Art Catalogue # 25-Tank.* New York: Contemporary Russian Art Center of America, 1981.

———, ed. *Vagrich Bakhchanyan: Mr. Mental.* Mechan-icsville, Md: Cremona Foundation, 1981.

———, ed. *Vagrich Bakhchanyan: Diary 1/1/80–12/31/80.* Mechanicsville, Md.: Cremona Foundation, 1981.

———, ed. *Henry Khudyakov: Visionary Wearables.* New York, NY: Contemporary Russian Art Center of America, 1982.

———, ed. *Lydia Masterkova: Striving Upward to the Real.* New York, NY: Contemporary Russian Art Center of America, 1983.

———, ed. *Apt Art: Moscow Vanguard in the 80s.* Introduc-tion by Victor and Margarita Tupitsyn. Mechanicsville, Md.: Cremona Foundation, 1985. (Catalogue for an exhi-bition at the Contemporary Russian Art Center of America, New York, and at the Washington Project for the Arts, Washington, D.C.)

———, ed. *Leonid Lamm: Recollections from the Twilight Zone, 1973–1985.* Mechanicsville, Md.: Cremona Founda-tion, 1985. (Catalogue for an exhibition at the Firebird Gallery, Alexandria, Va.)

———, ed. *Eduard Gorokhovsky.* Jersey City, N.J.: C.A.S.E. Museum of Contemporary Russian Art, 1989.

———, ed. *The Journey of Alexandr Zhdanov.* Mechan-icsville, Md.: Cremona Foundation, 1989. (Catalogue for an exhibition at the Von Brahler Gallery, Alexandria, Va.)

———, ed. *Dmitri Krasnopevtsev: A Retrospective Exhibition.* Jersey City, N.J.: C.A.S.E. Museum of Contemporary Russian Art, 1990.

———, ed. *Alexander Shnurov: Twelve Year Perspective, 1978–1989.* Jersey City, N.J.: C.A.S.E. Museum of Contem-porary Russian Art, 1990.

———, ed. *Sergei Sherstiuk: Soviet Post Socialist Realism.* Jersey City, N.J.: C.A.S.E. Museum of Contemporary Russian Art, 1990.

———, ed. *Boris Sveshnikov: A Retrospective Exhibition.* Jersey City, N.J.: C.A.S.E. Museum of Contemporary Russian Art, 1991.

———, ed. *Alexander Kharitonov.* Jersey City, N.J.: C.A.S.E. Museum of Contemporary Russian Art, 1991.

———, ed. *Baltic Art during the Brezhnev Era: Noncon-formist Art in Estonia, Latvia and Lithuania.* Mechan-icsville, Md.: Cremona Foundation, 1992. (Catalogue for an exhibition at the John B. Aird Gallery, Toronto.)

———, ed. and introduction. *Leningrad—St. Petersburg Non-conformist Art.* Mechanicsville, Md.: Cremona Founda-tion, 1992. (Catalogue for an exhibition at the Maryland Communications Center Gallery, Baltimore.)

———, and Alison Hilton. *New Art from the Soviet Union: The Known and the Unknown.* Washington, D.C.: Acropolis Books, 1977. (Catalogue for an exhibition at the Arts Club, Washington, D.C., and Herbert F. Johnson Museum of Art, Cornell University, Ithaca, N.Y.)

———, and Alexander Glezer, eds. *Evgeny Mikhnov-Voitenko: Abstract Visions.* Jersey City, N.J.: C.A.S.E. Museum of Contemporary Russian Art, 1988.

Douglas, Charlotte, and Margarita Tupitsyn. *Gennady Zubkov and the Leningrad "Sterligov" Group: Evidence of Things Not Seen.* New York: Contemporary Russian Art Center of America, 1983.

Dzhanberidze, Nodar. *Quest and Tradition.* Tbilisi, 1989.

Edzgveradze, Gia. *Back to the Truth.* Leipzig: Michael Beck, 1993.

———. "Das Weisse Manifest." In *Gia Edzgveradze: Olbilder und Papierarbeiten.* Munich: Galerie Thomas, 1991. In German.

Egeland, Erik. *Ernst Neizvestny: Life and Work.* Oakville, Ont., and New York: Mosaic Press, 1984.

Eight Artists from Moscow. Grenoble: Musée de Grenoble, 1974.

Elii Bieliutin. Moscow: Assotsiatsiia "Mir kultury," 1990. In Russian.

Erik Boulatov. Paris: Editions Centre Georges Pompidou, 1988. In French.

Erik Bulatov. London: Parkett/ICA, 1989.

Eugene Rukhin: A Contemporary Russian Artist. Raleigh: North Carolina Museum of Art, 1975.

Evgenii Rukhin. Los Angeles: Gallery 1912, 1989.

Exposition Internationale Art Graphique du Livre et d'Illustration. Brno, 1966.

Ezerskaia, N. "Vsegda v poiske." *Iskusstvo* 6 (1965): 34–36. In Russian.

Fields, Marc. "Komar and Melamid and the Luxury of Style." *Artforum* 16 (Apr. 1982): 58–63.

Furmanny Zautek [Furmanny Lane]. Warsaw: Fundacja Polskiej Sztuki Nowoczesnej, 1989. In Polish, with English translation.

Gambrell, Jamey. "Komar and Melamid: From behind the Ironical Curtain." *Artforum* (Apr. 1982).

——. "Notes on the Underground." *Art in America* 76 (Nov. 1988): 126–36.

——. "Perestroika Shock." *Art in America* 77 (Feb. 1989): 124–34.

Gardner, Paul. "Art and Politics in Russia." *Art News* 73 (Dec. 1974): 44–46.

Gela Zautashvili: Zhivopis', kollazhi 1988–1989 gg. Moscow: VTPO Tsentr Khudozhestvennoi Kul'tury, 1990. In Russian.

Georges Mgaloblishvili. Paris: Galerie Jaquester, 1991. In French.

Georgia on My Mind. Kassel: Museum Fridericianum, 1989.

Georgian Paintings of the Eighteenth Century to the Twentieth Century from the Art Collections of Soviet Museums. Leningrad: Aurora Art Publishers, 1977.

Gia Edzgveradze. Stockholm: Boibrino Gallery, 1991.

Gia Edzgveradze—Sweet Rice: Bilder und Zeichungen. Munich: Galerie Thomas, 1989. In German.

Glezer, Alexander. *Chelovek s dvoinym dnom*. Montgeron: 1979. In Russian.

——. *Russkie Khudozhniki na Zapade*. Paris: Tretiia Volna, 1986. In Russian.

——. *Contemporary Russian Art*. Paris, New York, and Moscow: The Third Wave Publishers, 1993.

——. "Oleg Tselkov." *Iskusstvo* 8 (1990): 31. In Russian.

Golomshtok, Igor. *Totalitarian Art*. New York: Icon Editions, 1990.

——, and Alexander Glezer. *Soviet Art in Exile*. New York: Random House, 1977. Also published as *Unofficial Art from the Soviet Union*. London: Secker and Warburg, 1977.

Gookin, Kirby. "Ilya Kabakov." *Artforum* 27 (Sept. 1988): 135–36.

Grishin, S. *Vadim Sidur: A Study in Modern Soviet Sculpture*. Adelaide, 1972.

Grosvalds, Jazeps. "L'Art letton (Les Jeunes)." *Revue Baltique* 8 (1919): 25–28. In French.

Groys, Boris. "Ilya Kabakov." *A-Ya* 2 (1980): 17–22.

Gundlakh, Sven. "APT ART—Kartinki s vystavki." *A-Ya* 5 (1983).

Hagop Hagopian. Introduction by Sofia Yerlashova. Moscow: Sovetskii Khudozhnik, 1983. In Russian.

Harten, J. *Sowjetische Kunst um 1990*. Cologne: DuMont, 1991. In German.

Heartney, Eleanor. "Sots Art." *Art News* 83 (Mar. 1984): 212.

——. "Ilya Kabakov at Ronald Feldman Fine Arts." *Art in America* 76 (Sept. 1988): 179.

Henrik Igitian. Armenska Paleta. Bratislava: Tartan, 1986. In Czech.

Hiatt, Fred. "Russian Intelligentsia Adrift." *International Herald Tribune*, July 20, 1992.

Holo, Selma, ed. *Keepers of the Flame: Unofficial Artists in Leningrad*. Los Angeles: University of Southern California, Fisher Gallery, 1990.

Horbachov, Dmytro. "Kozak-Paryzhanyn." *Vsesvit* 6 (1992): 193. In Ukrainian.

Ilya Kabakov. Bern: Kunsthalle, 1985.

Indiana, Gary. "Komar and Melamid Confidential." *Art in America* 73 (June 1985): 94–101.

James, C.V. *Soviet Socialist Realism: Origins and Theory*. London: Macmillan Publishers, 1973.

Johnson, Priscilla, and L. Labedz, eds. *Khrushchev and the Arts: The Politics of Soviet Culture*. Cambridge, Mass.: MIT Press, 1965.

Jóvenes Artistas de Leningrado. Mexico City: Galeria Fernando Gamboa, Museo de Arte Moderno, 1991. In Spanish.

Jurkus, Paulius. "Art in Independent Lithuania and after World War II." In *Encyclopedia Lithuanica*, vol. 1. Boston: J. Kapočlaus Publishing House, 1970.

Kabakov, Ilya, and Yuri Kuper. *52 Entretiens dans la cuisine communautaire*. Marseilles: Art Transit, Ateliers Municipaux d'Artistes, 1992.

Kalnacs, Janis. "Nomals latviesu grafikis" [A forsaken Latvian graphic artist]. *Literatura un maksla* 15/2513 (Apr. 16, 1993): 4. In Latvian.

Kartna, A. *Soviet Estonian Art*. Tallinn, 1967.

Khantadze-Andronikashvili, P. "Gagimardzhis! Pobedy tebe!" *Iskusstvo* 4 (1990). In Russian.

Khudozhesvennaia Galereia. "Moskovskaia Kollektsiia." In *Drugoe iskusstvo: Moskva 1956–76*. Moscow: Moskovskaia Kollekstiia/SP Interbuk, 1991. In Russian.

Kliueva, T.Yu., ed. *Vladimir Kandelaki*. Moscow: Sovetskii Khudozhnik, 1992. In Russian.

Konstante, Ilze. *Leo Maurins*. Riga: Liesma, 1992. In Latvian.

Konstants, Zigurds. *Auskelis Bauskenieks*. Riga: Liesma, 1990. In Latvian.

——. *Janis Pauluks*. Riga: Liesma, 1992. In Latvian.

——. *Maija Tabaka*. Riga: Liesma, 1992. In Latvian.

Kornetchuk, Elena. *Andrei Gennadiev: Contemporary Leningrad Artist*. Sewickley, Penn.: International Images, Ltd., 1986.

——. *Dzemma Skulme and Juris Dmiters: Contemporary Latvian Artists*. Pittsburgh: International Images, Ltd., 1986.

——. *The Supernatural World of Juri Arrack*. Sewickley, Penn.: International Images, Ltd., 1987.

——. *Malle Leis: A Contemporary Estonian Artist*. Pittsburgh: International Images, Ltd., 1989.

——. *Alexander Sitnikov: A Contemporary Moscow Artist*. Pittsburgh: International Images, Ltd., 1990.

——. *Anatoli Kaplan: A Contemporary Leningrad Artist*. Pittsburgh: International Images, Ltd., 1990.

——, et al. *Francisco Infante: A Contemporary Moscow Artist*. Sewickley, Penn.: International Images, Ltd., 1989.

——. "The Politics of Soviet Art." *Bulletin of the Atomic Scientists* (Oct. 1977): 33–37.

——. "Contemporary Russian Printmaking: An Overview." *Graphics Magazine* 3 no. 5 (Oct.–Nov. 1979): 58–63.

——. "Contemporary Soviet Prints: A National Diversity." *Print News* 2 no. 5 (Oct.–Nov. 1980): 3–8.

——. "Malle Leis: Flowers and Rainbows." *Journal of the Print World* 7 no. 2 (Spring 1984): 16.

——. "Andrei Gennadiev: Innovations/Imagination." *Journal of the Print World* 8 no. 4 (Fall 1985): 17.

——. "The Watercolors of Dzemma Skulme." *Journal of the Print World* 9 no. 2 (Spring 1986): 14.

——. "Lithographs and Etchings: Yuri Liushkin." *Journal of the Print World* 9 no. 1 (Winter 1986): 15.

——. "Observations on Contemporary Soviet Art." In *Artwork of the Soviet Union—Guernsey's*. Auction catalogue. New York: Guernsey's, Oct. 22–23, 1988.

——. "Rukhin: Reflections and Recollections." In *Evgenii Rukhin*. Los Angeles: Gallery 1912, 1989.

Kostina, Olga. "Memorial Pobedy v Tbilisi." *Dekorativnoe iskusstvo SSSR* 5 (1988): 6. In Russian.

Kotchar. Exhibition catalogue. Paris: Galerie Basmadjian, 1989.

Krivulin, Victor. "Yurii Dyshlenko." *A-Ya* 5 (1982). In Russian.

Kunz, Martin, ed. *De la Revolution à la Perestroika: Art soviétique de la Collection Ludwig*. Saint-Etienne: Musée de l'Art Moderne, 1989–90. In French.

Lamm, Leonid. *Sots-Geo Manifesto-Manifestation of the Procrustean Bed*. New York: Eduard Nakhamkin Fine Arts, 1990.

Larsen, Niels Peter Juel. "Im Schatten des Gulag." *Zeit Magazin*, Mar. 27, 1992. In German.

Lebedev, A.K. *Iskusstvo v okovakh*. Moscow: Izdatel'stvo Akademii Khudozhestv SSSR, 1962. In Russian.

The Leningrad Show: The Fellowship for Experimental Art. Point Reyes Station, CA: Gallery Route One, 1988.

Levkova-Lamm, Inessa. *Back to Square One*. Translated by William Spiegelberger. New York: Berman-E.N. Gallery, 1991.

Lidia Masterkova: Adieu à la Russie. Paris: Galerie Dina Vierny, 1977. In French.

Lytle, Richard. *Contemporary Art from Ukraine: An American Perspective*. New Haven: Yale University School of Art, 1992.

Malakhov, Nikolai. *Sotsialisticheskii realizm i modernizm*. Moscow: Iskusstvo, 1970. In Russian.

Miller, J. "Russians Use Bulldozers to Halt Art Show." *Daily Telegraph*, Sept. 16, 1974.

Minas Avetissian. Introduction by Henrik Igitian. Leningrad: Aurora Art Publishers, 1975.

Misiano, Victor. "Back in the USSR." *Contemporanea* 1 (May–June 1988): 96–107.

Modern Art Museum of Fort Worth. *10 + 10: Contemporary Soviet and American Painters*. New York: Harry N. Abrams, and Leningrad: Aurora Art Publishers, 1989–90.

Mudrak, Myroslava M. *The New Generation and Artistic Modernism in the Ukraine*. Ann Arbor, Mich.: UMI Research Press, 1986.

——. *Contemporary Art from the Ukraine: An Exhibition of Paintings, Drawings, Sculpture*. Exhibition catalogue. Munich, London, New York, and Paris: 1979.

——. "The Odessa Group of Contemporary Artists in Ukraine." In *Art in Eastern Europe in the Twentieth Century*. Berlin: Verlag Arno Spitz Gmbh: 1991.

——. "What Does the World Know about Us?" *Obrazotvorche mystetstvo* 2 (Mar.–Apr. 1992): 15–16.

Myth and Abstraction: Actual Art from Estonia. Karlsruhe: Badischer Kunstverein, 1992.

Nagys, Henrikas. "Foreword." *Second Lithuanian International Art Exhibition*. Toronto: O'Keefe Centre for the Performing Arts, 1963.

Naishul, Viktor. "Pamyatnik v Gurdzhaani." *Dekorativnoe iskusstvo SSSR* 5 (1988): 7. In Russian.

Nalbandian, Dmitri. "Falshivye tsennosti abstraktsionizma." *Ogonyok* 32 (Aug. 1975). In Russian.

Nefedova, Inara. *Džemma Skulme*. Riga: Liesma, 1981. In Latvian.

Nodieve, Aija. *Latviesujaunaka gleznieciba* [The new Latvian painting]. Riga: Liesma, 1981. In Latvian.

Nussberg, 1961–1979. Wiesbaden: Galerie Karin Fesel, 1979. In German.

Oleg Vassilyev and Eric Bulatov. New York: Phyllis Kind Gallery, 1991.

Olshevski, V. "Dorogaia tsena chechivichnoi pokhlebki." *Sovetskaia kul'tura*, June 14, 1966. In Russian.

Parming, Tõnu, and Elmar Jarvesoo, eds. *A Case Study of a Soviet Republic: The Estonian SSR*. Boulder, Colo.: Westview Press, 1978.

Peschler, Eric A. *Ateliers de Moscou: Dessins contemporains*. Paris: Navarra-Galerie de France, 1989. In French.

——. *Kunstler in Moskau: Die neue Avantgarde*. Schaffhausen: Edition Stemmle Verlag Photographie AG, 1988. In German.

Pohribny, Arsen, Peter Spielman, and Helmut Lumbro, eds. *Progressive Stromungen in Moskau 1957–1970*. Bochum: Museum Bochum, 1974. In German.

Rabin, Oscar. *L'Artiste et les bulldozers: Être peintre en URSS*. Paris: Editions Robert Laffont, 1981. In French.

Reuschemeyer, Marilyn, Igor Golomshtok, and Janet Kennedy. *Soviet Emigré Artists: Life and Work in the USSR and the United States*. Armonk, N.Y.: M.E. Sharpe, 1985.

Reuter, Jule. *Gegen Kunst in Leningrad*. Munich: Klinkhardt and Biermann, 1990. In German.

Roberts, Norma, ed. *The Quest for Self-Expression: Painting in Moscow and Leningrad, 1965–1990*. Columbus, Ohio: Columbus Museum of Art, 1990.

Rosenfeld, Alla, and Jeffrey Wechsler. *Struggle for the Spirit: Religious Expression in Soviet Nonconformist Art*. New Brunswick, N.J.: Jane Voorhees Zimmerli Art Museum, 1993.

Ross, David, ed. *Between Spring and Summer: Soviet Conceptual Art in the Era of Late Communism*. Cambridge, Mass.: MIT Press, 1990.

Rothamel, Jork. "The Dimension of Conservatism. Aspects of St. Petersburg Art Today." In *Contemporary St. Petersburg Art*. Auction catalogue. St. Petersburg, 1992.

Rozwadowska-Janowska, Nina, and Piotr Nowicki, eds. *No!—and the Conformists: Faces of Soviet Art of the 50s to 80s*. Warsaw: Fundacja Polskiej Sztuki Nowoczesnej, 1994.

Rudolfs Pinnis: Gleznieciba [Rūdolfs Pinnis: Painting]. Riga: Liesma, 1990. In Latvian.

Rukhin. Jersey City, N.J.: Museum of Contemporary Russian Art in Exile, 1989.

Russian Avant-Garde and Soviet Contemporary Art. Auction catalogue. Moscow: Sotheby's, 1988.

Ryklin, Mikhail. "Medical Hermeneutics." *Flash Art* (Russian edition) 1 (1989): 115–16.

Sarje, Kimmo, ed. *Erosion: Soviet Conceptual Art and Photography of the 1980's*. Helsinki: Amos Andersen Museum, 1990.

Schnitgerhans, Holger. "Kaufen Sie Gia Edzgveradze." *Manager Magazin* (Nov. 1990): 430. In German.

Schwarz, S. "Russia's Underground Art Market." *Artforum* 10 (June 1972): 54–55.

Shteinberg, Eduard. *An Attempt at a Monograph*. La Chaux-de-Fonds, Switzerland: Editions d'en Haut and Moscow: Art MIF, 1992.

Sjelochka, Paul, and Igor Mead. *Unofficial Art in the Soviet Union*. Berkeley and Los Angeles: University of California Press, 1967.

Smith, Hedrick. "Young Soviet Painters Score Socialist Art." *New York Times*, Mar. 19, 1974, p. 30.

Solomon, Andrew. *The Irony Tower*. New York: Alfred Knopf, 1991.

——. "Igor Kopystiansky." In *Novostroika (New Structures): Culture in the Soviet Union Today* (ICA Documents 8). London: Institute of Contemporary Arts, 1989.

Soviet Contemporary Art: The Property of the Kniga Collection, Paris. Auction catalogue. New York: Habsburg-Feldman, 1990.

Soviet Socialist Realist Painting. Oxford: The Museum of Modern Art, 1992.

Stevens, Mark. "Artnost: What Happened to Moscow 'Unofficial' Artists When Sotheby's Came to Town." *Vanity Fair* (Nov. 1988).

Stevens, Nina. "Outsider Art inside Russia." *Art in America* (Sept.–Oct. 1968).

Sullivant, Robert. *Soviet Politics and the Ukraine, 1917–1957.* New York: Columbia University Press, 1962.

A Survey of Russian Painting from the Fifteenth Century to the Present. Preface by George Riabov. New York: Gallery of Modern Art, 1967.

Svede, Mark Allen. "What Next? New Art in Latvia." *Dialogue: Arts in the Midwest* (Jan.–Feb. 1992).

———. "The Bluff and Bluster of Russian Neorealism." *Dialogue: Arts in the Midwest* (May–June 1993).

———. "Not Quiet on the Eastern Front: Challenging the Monolithic Presentation of European Art in American Museums." *Midwest Museums Association Annual* (1994).

Tertz, Abram [pseud. Andrei Siniavsky]. *On Socialist Realism.* Translated by George Dennis. New York: Vintage Books, 1960.

Transit: Russian Artists between the East and West. Hempstead, N.Y.: Fine Arts Museum of Long Island, 1989.

Le Troisième Etage. Paris: Coopération Arménie, 1989. In French.

Tupitsyn, Margarita. *Russian New Wave.* Edited by Norton T. Dodge. Mechanicsville, Md.: Cremona Foundation, 1981.

———. *Sots Art.* New York: New Museum of Contemporary Art, 1986.

———. *Margins of Soviet Art: Socialist Realism to the Present.* Milan: Giancarlo Politi Editore, 1989.

———. *The Green Show.* New York: Exit Art, 1990.

———. "Komar and Melamid: The Red Guardians of Tradition." *High Performance* 28 (1984).

———. "Leonid Sokov." *Flash Art* 123 (Summer 1985).

———. "Ilya Kabakov." *Flash Art* 126 (Feb.–Mar. 1986): 67–69.

———. "Alexander Kosolapov." *Flash Art* 126 (Feb.–Mar. 1986).

———. "From Sots-Art to Sov-Art: A Story of the Moscow Avantguard." *Flash Art* 137 (Nov.–Dec. 1987): 75–80.

———. "The Studios on Furmanny Lane in Moscow." *Flash Art* 142 (Oct. 1988): 103, 123–25.

———. "Timur and Africa." *Flash Art* 151 (Mar.–Apr. 1989): 122–25.

———. "Sots Art: Round Dance or Ritual." *Social Text* 22 (Spring 1989): 148–53.

———. "Veil on Photo: Metamorphoses in Supplementarity in Soviet Art." *Arts Magazine* 64 (Nov. 1989): 79–84.

———. "Unveiling Feminism: Women's Art in the Soviet Union." *Arts Magazine* 64 (Dec. 1990): 63–67.

———. "Andrei Monastyrsky and Conrad Atkinson." *Contemporanea* 24 (Jan. 1991): 106.

———. "Against the Camera, for the Photographic Archive." *Art Journal* 53 (Summer 1994): 58–62.

———. "Shaping Soviet Art." *Art in America* 82 (Sept. 1994): 41–45.

———, and Margaret Bridget Betz. *Lydia Masterkova: Striving Upward to the Real.* New York: Contemporary Russian Art Center of America, 1983.

———, and Martha Rosler. *After Perestroika: Kitchenmaids or Stateswomen.* New York: Independent Curators, Inc., 1993.

———, and Victor Tupitsyn. "Six Months in Moscow." *Flash Art* 137 (Oct. 1989): 115–17.

Tupitsyn, Victor. *Eric Bulatov.* New York: Phyllis Kind Gallery, 1994.

———. "Ideology Mon Amour." *Flash Art* 137 (Nov.–Dec. 1987): 84–85.

———. "Ilya Kabakov." *Flash Art* 151 (Mar.–Apr. 1990): 146–47.

——. "From the Communal Kitchen: A Conversation with Ilya Kabakov." *Arts Magazine* (Oct. 1991): 48–55.

——. "L'Arte russa in esilio dall'essere al non essere." *D'Ars* 141 (Fall 1993): 42–45. In Italian.

——. "Neo-Faktografie." *Neue Bildende Kunst* (June 1994): 30–43. In German.

——. "The Sun without a Muzzle." *Art Journal* 53 (Summer 1994): 80–84.

Valeska, Adolfas. *Lithuanian Art in Exile*. Munich: T.J. Bizgirda, 1948.

Vladimir Jankilevskij, 1958–1988. Bochum: Museum Bochum, 1988. In German.

Vladimir Nemukhin. Jersey City, N.J.: C.A.S.E. Museum of Contemporary Russian Art in Exile, 1986.

Von Tavel, Hans Christoph, and Markus Landert. *Ich lebe-ich sehe: Kunstler der achtziger Jahre in Moskau*. Bern: Kunstmuseum Bern, 1988. In German.

Weiss, Evelyn, ed. *Sowjetkunst Heute*. Cologne: Museum Ludwig, 1988. In German.

Werth, Alexander. *Russia under Khrushchev*. New York: Hill and Wang, 1962.

Die Wiege der Meschheit: Luka Lasareishvili. Frankfurt: Freiss Lebenstudien-Gesellschaft Melchiorgrund, 1991. In German.

Williams, Robert. *Russian Art and American Money*. Cambridge, Mass.: Harvard University Press, 1980.

Wollen, Peter. *Komar and Melamid*. Edinburgh: Fruitmarket Gallery, 1985.

Yankilevsky, Vladimir. "World through Man." In *Vladimir Yankilevsky*. New York: Eduard Nakhamkin Fine Arts, 1988.

Yastrebova, N. *Sovetskoe iskusstvo 60–80 gg*. Moscow: Nauka, 1988. In Russian.

Yuri Bourdjelian. Paris: Galerie Garig Basmadjian, 1987. In French.

Zeberins, Indrikis. *Kas velas ar lmani krampjos vilkties*. Riga: Maksla, 1992. In Latvian.

Zvontsov, V. "Esli tebe Khudozhnik imia." *Leningradskaia Pravda*, Oct. 16, 1975. In Russian.

Zwanzig Jahre unabhangige Kunst aus der Sowjetunion. Bochum: Museum Bochum, 1979. In German.

Notes on contributors

Alfonsas Andriuškevičius
Chairman, Department of Art Theory, Academy of Arts and Sciences, Vilnius, Lithuania

Matthew Baigell
Professor of Art History, Rutgers, The State University of New Jersey, New Brunswick, New Jersey

Joseph Bakshtein
Director, Institute of Contemporary Art, Moscow (ICM)

Vartoug Basmadjian
Director, Galerie G. Basmadjian, Paris, France

Olga Berendsen
Professor Emeritus, Department of Art History, Rutgers, The State University of New Jersey, New Brunswick, New Jersey

John E. Bowlt
Professor of Slavic Languages and Literatures, University of Southern California, Los Angeles, California, and Director, The Institute of Modern Russian Culture at Blue Lagoon, University Park, Los Angeles, California

Phillip Dennis Cate
Director, Jane Voorhees Zimmerli Art Museum, Rutgers, The State University of New Jersey, New Brunswick, New Jersey

Norton T. Dodge
Professor Emeritus, Department of Economics, St. Mary's College of Maryland

Alison Hilton
Associate Professor of Art History, Georgetown University, Washington, D.C.

Janet Kennedy
Associate Professor of Art History, Henry Radford Hope School of Fine Arts, Indiana University, Bloomington, Indiana

Elena Kornetchuk
President and Director, International Images, Ltd., Sewickley, Pennsylvania

Myroslava M. Mudrak
Associate Professor of Art History, Ohio State University, Columbus, Ohio

Alla Rosenfeld
Curator of Russian and Soviet Art, Jane Voorhees Zimmerli Art Museum, Rutgers, The State University of New Jersey, New Brunswick, New Jersey

Michael Scammell
Professor of Writing and Translation, School of the Arts, Columbia University, New York, New York

Mark Allen Svede
Independent scholar and curator of modern and contemporary Latvian art

Margarita Tupitsyn
Independent scholar and curator of Russian art

Victor Tupitsyn
Critic and theorist of Russian culture

Acknowledgments

Special Credits
Project Organizer: Alla Rosenfeld
Assistants to Project Organizer: Marianne Ficarra and
Sabina Potaczek
Project Consultant: Margarita Tupitsyn
Manuscript Editor: Brian Wallis
Editorial Consultant: Anne Schneider

Zimmerli Museum Staff
Administrative
Phillip Dennis Cate, Director
Ruth Berson, Associate Director
Jeffrey Wechsler, Assistant Director for Curatorial Affairs
Donna DeBlasis, CFRE, Director of Development
Marguerite M. Santos, Business Manager
Judy Santiago, Secretary
Hilary Brown, Development Assistant
Ulla-Britt Faiella, Receptionist
Nina Danielson, Receptionist

Curatorial
Trudy V. Hansen, Director, Morse Research Center and
Curator of Prints and Drawings
Katherine Tako-Girard, Curator of Education and
Publicity Coordinator
Pamela Phillips, Publicity Assistant
Alla Rosenfeld, Curator of Russian and Soviet Art
Marianne Ficarra, Assistant Curator of Soviet
Nonconformist Art and Public Relations Officer for
Soviet Nonconformist Art
Sabina Potaczek, Research Assistant for Soviet
Nonconformist Art
Roberto Delgado, Preparator
Elaine Beca, Wordprocessing and Desktop Publishing
Coordinator
John Campbell, Computer Graphics Specialist
Gail Aaron, Curatorial Assistant
Patricia Cudd, Curatorial Assistant
Caroline Goeser, Assistant Curator
Yuko Higa, Assistant Director, International Center for
Japonisme

Registrarial
Barbara Trelstad, Registrar
Caroline Lair Jordan, Assistant Registrar 1 and Off-Site
Storage Supervisor

Leslie Kriff, Assistant Registrar 2
Leonard Iannaccone, Registrarial Intern for Soviet
Nonconformist Art

Publications
Anne Schneider, Publications Coordinator

Exhibit Installation/Security
Edward Schwab, Director of Museum Installation/
Physical Plant
John Nasto, Workshop Manager
Eleuterio Peralta, Senior Guard
Michael Hall, Installation Preparator

Friends of the Zimmerli
Marilyn Hayden, Coordinator
Lynn Biderman, Museum Store Manager
Ruth Rockoff, President

Zimmerli Museum Board of Overseers
Norma Bartman
Diane Burke
Norton Dodge
Richard Drill
Alvin Glasgold
Thomas Gorrie
Carleton Holstrom (Chairman)
Harold Kaplan
Deborah Lynch
Allan Maitlin
Bruce Newman
Kenji Otsubo
Frank Pallone, Jr.
Robert S. Peckar
Joseph Potenza
Edward Quinn
George Riabov
Mindy Tublitz
Ralph Voorhees
Scott Voorhees
Ex Officio
Phillip Dennis Cate
Bruce Newman
Ruth Rockoff
Honorary Member
Mrs. David A. Morse

Index